BUSINESS & MANAGEMENT

Paul Hoang

First published in 2007 by IBID Press, Victoria.

Reprinted 2008, 2009, 2010.

Published by IBID Press, Victoria.

Library Catalogue:

Hoang, P.

1. Business & Management.

2. International Baccalaureate. Series Title: International Baccalaureate in Detail.

ISBN-13: 978-1-876659-63-9

ISBN-10: 1-876659-63-7

Acknowledgements

While every care has been taken to trace and acknowledge copyright, the publishers tender their apologies for any accidental infringement where copyright has proved untraceable. They would be pleased to come to a suitable arrangement with the rightful owner in each case.

The publisher and author would like to thank the following individuals and organizations for their kind permission to reproduce personal and copyright material:

Pages: 26 Reload Juice outlet: Reload Juice and Salad Bar; 29 EXP The Chinese Experience: Keith and Tonina Hoang; 43 Adidas logo: Adidas Group; 68 Vodafone logo: Vodafone; 69 Skoda logo: Skoda Auto; 103 Shell logo: Royal Dutch Shell; 121 A.S. Watson Group logo: A.S. Watson Group; 122 HBOS logo: Halifax Bank of Scotland; 141 Kodak logo: Eastman Kodak Company; 143 English Schools Foundation logo: English Schools Foundation; 157 Carlsberg Group logo: Carlsberg Group; 219 Ferrari: © AllSportAuto.com Sébastien Morliere; 275 Richer Sounds logo: Julian Richer; 301 The Body Shop logo: The Body Shop International plc; 314 Deutsche Telekom logo: Deutsche Telekom AG; 448 Wallington High School for Girls emblem: Wallington High School for Girls; 486 Pink Ladies logo: Pink Ladies Car Hire; 511 Virgin Atlantic photo: Virgin Group Ltd; 514 Johnson & Johnson logo: Johnson & Johnson; 517 FCUK, Festival Walk branch, Hong Kong: French Connection Group plc; 521 Ford Focus: Ford Motor Company; 535 Sony PlayStation 3: © Sony Computer Entertainment Inc.; 562 Yoda postage stamp: © 2007 USPS. All Rights Reserved.; 568 Lamborghini (Salon Auto plaisir 2007): © AllSportAuto.com Sébastien Morliere; 570 Kim Do Yi logo: Kim Do Yi Ltd.; 578 Costco logo: Costco Wholesale Corporation; 584 Carrefour logo: Group Carrefour; 599 HMV logo: ® Trade Mark of HMV Group plc through HMV (IP) Limited; 649 A380 Airbus: © AIRBUS – Central Entity; 667 BSI Kitemark: ® British Standards Institution; 690 Tetra Pak: Stellan Stebe; 696 Oasis photo: Oasis Hong Kong Airlines.

Cover design by Adcore.

Published by IBID Press, 36 Quail Crescent, Melton 3337, Victoria, Australia.

Printed in Australia by Trojan Press.

DEDICATION

Dedicated to Kin, Jake and Luke, for always.

I have written this book for three main reasons:

1. Frustration of not having a dedicated textbook for the past six years of teaching the Business & Management course.
2. Encouragement from my delightful students at Sha Tin College who have urged me to put my notes and case studies into a book. To them, no resource beats the satisfaction of having a physical book that they can delve into at any time.
3. My passion for teaching and learning this wonderfully challenging and most practical subject.

Some people have said to me, 'What about the money?' Unit 2.5 in this book explains that some people are not motivated simply by money. If I did this for money then I might as well have spent the time doing private tuition over the past 18 months. That way, not only would I have pleased the tax man, but I would also have been able to spend a lot more of my weekends and evenings with my dear family. For this reason, I dedicate this book to them.

I would also like to thank Roz and Richard Paisey, Ian and Pauline Ashworth, Margo Goodchild and Lisa Hoang. You have all shaped me in more ways than you will ever know. I am forever grateful for all the things that you have done for me and the family.

Finally, to my publishers and editor at IBID Press: Rory McAuliffe who believed in me and gave me the opportunity to undertake this project; Fabio Cirrito for your guidance and trust in my approach; and Marcia Bascombe for your endless hours of proofreading and editing. I could not have completed this project without your ongoing advice and support. It has been a pleasure to have worked with you.

Thank you all so very much.

Paul Hoang

HOW TO USE THIS BOOK

At a glance

- This book follows the format of the IB Business & Management syllabus (first examination in 2009). It is a dedicated text for both the Standard Level (SL) and Higher Level (HL) courses.
- Units that only apply to HL students are clearly labelled. These specific Units are: 1.8 (Change and the Management of Change), 2.6 (Organizational and Corporate Culture), 2.7 (Employer-Employee Relations), 2.8 (Crisis Management and Contingency Planning), 3.4 (Budgeting), 5.6 (Innovation) and 5.8 (Project Management).
- In addition, most Units have 'HL Extension' content, as per the IB B&M syllabus. Again, these are clearly marked in the text. Refer to your syllabus guide for more information.
- Questions appear in all Units. In the main text, case studies based mainly on real-life businesses are used. There are over 215 case studies with examination-style questions in the textbook. Businesses from around the world have been used in these case studies. This signifies the international nature of Business & Management.
- Examination tips appear from time to time in the text. These tips mainly stem from common student blunders in the examination.
- The book is not intended to be read chronologically; the format simply matches the sequence of Topics in the IB B&M syllabus guide. Different teachers teach different aspects of the course in different orders. Your teachers will be able to guide you on which Units to refer to during your studies.
- All currencies are expressed as American dollars (USD). Where case studies refer to other currencies, these have also been converted into the USD equivalent for ease of comparison.

Features of each Unit

- The contents and introduction sections at the beginning of each Unit shows the concepts, theories and issues to be covered within each Unit.
- Case study questions appear throughout each Unit. These are mainly based on past examination-style questions. The vast majority of businesses mentioned in this book are real.
- Each Unit ends with a section on linkages with Unit 6 Business Strategy. These sections aim to conclude the contents covered in each Unit, bringing in points for evaluation. There are also references to other Units, which highlights the interrelated nature of the subject. I have deliberately not noted these sections as 'Higher Level' only, since I believe Standard Level students would benefit immensely from reading these sections. Indeed, to gain Level 7 in the examination, irrespective of whether a candidate is following the SL or HL course, students must show evidence of critical thinking and evaluation in their arguments.
- Review questions test your understanding of the contents covered in each Unit. The questions follow the chronological order of the text, making it easier for students to follow.
- Key terms covered in the Unit are summarized and defined at the end of each Unit. The key terms appear in alphabetical order to make searching easier. There are over 500 definitions in the textbook.

Paul Hoang
Head of Business Education
IB B&M Diploma Examiner
Sha Tin College
Hong Kong

CONTENTS

UNIT 3 ACCOUNTS AND FINANCE 333

EXAM TECHNIQUE

'**Proper preparation prevents poor performance**' – the 5 P's of effective exam preparation

COMMAND WORDS

It is crucial that command words are read properly in the examinations. Each command word in a question indicates to students the skill level that is being tested (see below). Hence, if asked to **calculate** the break-even point for a business, there is no need to **define** or to **explain** the concept of break-even.

Command word	Skill level	Command word	Skill level
Classify	1	Analyse	3
Complete	1	Apply	3
Define	1	Examine	3
Describe	1	Interpret	3
Identify	1		
Outline	1	Advise	4
		Discuss	4
Calculate	2	Evaluate	4
Comment	2	Justify	4
Compare	2	Recommend	4
Construct	2	To what extent	4
Contrast	2		
Distinguish	2		
Explain	2		
Prepare	2		

Refer to the syllabus guide (pages 74–76) for an explanation and example of each of these command words.

TACKLING THE EXAM PAPERS

Due to the intertwining topics in Business & Management, pre-issued case studies are useful in promoting a holistic approach to the study of the subject. Paper 1 assesses all six Topics (five for SL students) of the Business & Management syllabus and also carries the largest component weighting in the examination (for HL students). It is based on a pre-issued case study about a hypothetical business. The Paper 1 examination consists of the following structure:

- **Section A** (HL and SL) – Answer any **two** out of three structured questions. (30 marks)
- **Section B** (HL and SL) – Answer the **one** compulsory, evaluative structured question. (20 marks)
- **Section C** (HL only) – Answer the **one** compulsory strategic decision-making question using extension material. (30 marks)

Paper 1 Examination

Level	Total Marks	Weighting (%)	Timing (hours)
SL	**50**	**35**	**1¼**
HL	**80**	**40**	**2¼**

Paper 1 is 'difficult' in that it seeks extensive **analytical** and **critical thinking** skills. The pre-issued case study paper will assess a student's skills of problem identification, data handling and analysis, critical thinking, judgemental ability, logical reasoning and justified decision-making.

The guidelines in this section should enable students to be better prepared to tackle the Paper 1 questions in the exam. It is by no means an exhaustive set of guidelines and alternative or additional approaches can be used. The Teachers' Guidance materials are invaluable to this purpose.

What to do when you get the case study

1. Make a copy of the case study – one as an original reference and one to write notes on.
2. Read through the case study carefully to get an overall feeling and idea about the business, the people involved and the problems the business faces. Do this twice!
3. Make sure that you understand all the issues arising from the case study. Use a dictionary to look up key terms or words that you do not understand.
4. Use one copy of the case study to highlight all possible key terms. Make sure that you can define each and every one of these terms in the context of the case study. Definition questions will appear in the examination. Key theories, decisions, constraints, opportunities or problems can be written in the margins for future reference.
5. Attempt the Paper 1 Preparation Activities below.
6. Try answering some of the Practise Questions from past exam papers (in the context of the latest case study).

Whilst tackling the pre-issued case study, it is important to remember:

- Avoid copying large chunks of the case study, even if these are in quotation marks, since this wastes time and does not really reveal a candidate's level of understanding.
- Information and quantitative data presented in the case study should be used to support written answers.
- Refer to the mark allocations for each question when writing your answers.

Paper 1 Preparation Activities

In preparing for the Paper 1 examination, students may want to tackle the following (generic) tasks. It is important to write your answers in the context of the actual case study.

- Identify and define all the **key terms** in the case study. There are usually well over one hundred key terms in a pre-issued case study and any of these can be asked in the actual exam!
- Produce a **time line** of events. Read the case to produce a chronological list of events and the people involved.
- Produce, as far as possible, an **organizational chart** for the organization. Alternatively, you could produce a **personnel profile** of all people mentioned in the case study.
- Carry out a full **ratio analysis**. Figures may be given, or ratios can be worked out from the final accounts, usually attached in the appendices of the pre-issued case study.

- Produce a **stakeholder map** (see Unit 1.4).
- List all the **problems** faced by the business. One method could be to place these problems under the headings of either: Finance, Personnel, Marketing or Production. Alternatively, the problems could be split as internal and external constraints or problems.
- Conduct a fully applied (and therefore functional) **SWOT analysis** of the business.
- Conduct an overall **PEST analysis** for the business by examining the opportunities and threats outlined in the case study.

When tackling examination questions, consider the following points:

- Use relevant examples from the study to support your answers. There is no need to reference the line number as examiners will be fully familiar with the case study.
- Analogies can be used to help clarify your arguments. Business & Management is an integrated subject, so examples from other (relevant) case studies that you have studied can be used to help illustrate your answer.
- Finally, read through (or try to mark) your own answers when you have finished. Alternatively, use peer marking so that you can receive and give feedback to fellow students.

Paper 2 Examination

The Paper 2 examination consists of the following structure:

- **Section A** (HL and SL) – Answer any **one** out of two questions based on a quantitative aspect. (25 marks for HL, 20 marks for SL)
- **Section B** (HL and SL) – Answer **two** out of three structured questions. (50 marks for HL, 40 marks for SL)

Level	Total Marks	Weighting (%)	Timing (hours)
SL	**60**	**40**	**1¾**
HL	**75**	**35**	**2¼**

The following example is based on Section B of the Paper 2 examination. For ease of illustration, it looks mainly at one Topic in the syllabus, although students are reminded that Business & Management is an interrelated subject, so in the real exam there are likely to be questions based on other aspects of the course. Again, use past examination papers for practise.

Human Resource Management

Wilkinson Hill is a private selective secondary school. There are 1,200 students aged between 11 and 18 years and a total of 100 teaching and 80 support staff. The school achieves outstanding examination results and was described in a recent inspection as "an exemplar school that offers a wide and challenging curriculum for all students".

This year, a total of 11 members of staff have resigned for a number of reasons (such as external promotion or taking a break from the teaching profession). One of the positions to be filled is for the Head of Economics and Politics Department. The current post holder, Andy Smith, is retiring, having been at Wilkinson Hill for over 10 years.

Andy believes in centralized decision-making and fails to believe in the talents of his staff. The senior management team (SMT) know this as Andy has said to the Head that none of the other three members of the department is ready to be Head of Department (even though they have over 20 years of teaching experience between them), so he has suggested that the school recruits externally.

Andy's leadership style has caused much conflict within his own department and with the SMT. He is known to be outspoken and an extrovert. Even members of staff outside his Department have complained to the SMT about his poor interpersonal skills. The Departmental staff members are dedicated to the school, mainly because of the excellent standards at the school, so they tend to put up with the management style adopted by their line manager.

SMT are, nevertheless, sad to see Andy go. He has worked very hard during his time at Wilkinson Hill and results in the Department are above those of the national average for both Economics and Politics. In fact, during the past two years, the Department has managed to get the best results at IB level in the whole school.

a Given the information above, produce a suitable *person specification* for the purpose of recruiting a new Head of Department. *[5 marks]*

b In the context of the case study, explain how the *culture* of an organization affects *both* recruitment and training. *[6 marks]*

c Examine how the new Head of Department might be expected to deal with any *conflict* within the Department. *[6 marks]*

d Discuss the factors that contribute to *effective leadership*. *[8 marks]*

Final message from the author

Dear students,

I hope that you will find this book interesting and useful in preparing you for learning Business & Management. I hope you enjoy reading the text as much as I did writing it.

Best wishes for your examinations.

Paul Hoang

paulhoang88@hotmail.com

Business Organization and Environment

Unit 1

UNIT

Nature of Business Activity

UNIT 1.1

Business, that's easily defined; it's other people's money.

Alexandre Dumas (1802–1870), French author

Key topics

- What is a business?
- Inputs, outputs and processes of a business
- Factors of production
- Business functional departments: production, marketing, finance and human resource management
- Business activity in different sectors: primary, secondary and tertiary

Higher Level extension

- Changes in economic structure and their impact on business activity

INTRODUCTION

A **business** is a decision-making organization involved in the process of using inputs to produce goods and/or to provide services (see Figure 1.1a). *Inputs* are the resources, such as labour and raw materials, which a business uses in the production process. This process produces *outputs*, which are also known as products.

A **product** can refer to both goods and services. **Goods** are physical products, such as cars, computers, books and food. **Services** are intangible products such as a haircut, a bus ride or a visit to the cinema. Businesses may also provide goods and services to other businesses, such as freight transportation and distribution.

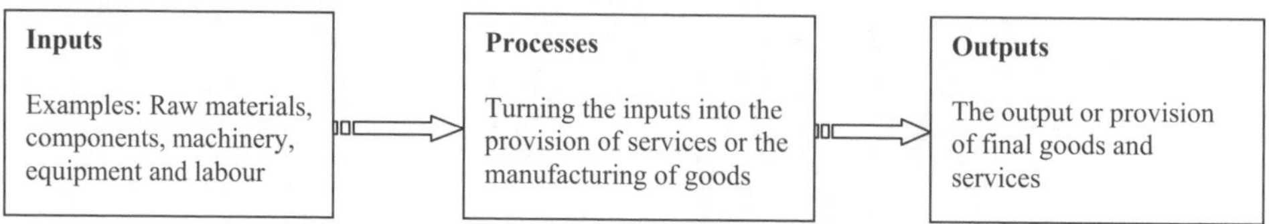

Figure 1.1a Inputs, processes and outputs

This Unit looks at the nature of business activity, i.e. what businesses are, what they do and why they do it. Many of the concepts discussed here are developed further in the rest of the textbook.

WHAT IS A BUSINESS?

Businesses and their purpose

Put simply, a business is an organization that is involved in the production of goods and/or the provision of services. Management guru Peter Drucker famously put forward the premise that the only purpose of a business is to create customers. Businesses exist to satisfy the *needs* and *wants* of people, organizations and governments.

- **Needs** are the basic necessities that a person *must* have in order to survive, e.g. food, water, warmth, shelter and clothing.
- **Wants** are the desires that people have, i.e. things that they would *like* to have, such as a larger home, a new mobile phone or a foreign holiday. Wants are said to be infinite since people always want more than they need.

As a business gets larger, it becomes more important to have clearly defined functions (or processes), such as human resource management, production, marketing and finance. These functions are likely to be carried out by specialist departments.

Businesses are also affected by external factors, those which are beyond its control (see Unit 1.5). For example, businesses need to take account of social changes, technological developments, the level of economic activity, environmental issues, and government legislation and policies. In addition, they may be affected, from time to time, from external shocks, such as an oil crisis, a health scare, natural disasters or the outbreak of a war. The Chinese proverb "It is easy to open a business but much more difficult to keep it open" highlights the conditions in which businesses operate.

The marketplace

A **market** is simply a place or process whereby buyers (customers) and sellers (businesses) meet to trade. This usually refers to a physical outlet, such as a shop, restaurant or cinema. However, a market can also exist in a non-physical form, such as e-commerce (trading on the internet, which is covered in Unit 4.8) or using the telephone to buy shares or motor insurance.

Customers are the people or organizations that buy a product whereas **consumers** are the ones that actually use the product. These may be the same entity, e.g. someone who buys and eats a burger meal. However, they are not necessarily the same, such as parents (customers) paying for their children's (consumers) birthday presents.

Exam Tip!

The words 'consumer' and 'customer' are often used interchangeably by candidates, although they have different meanings. Make sure that you are able to distinguish between the two concepts and to use them in the right context.

Types of products

All businesses produce goods and/or services.

Consumer goods are products that are sold to the general public, rather than to other businesses. These can be further split into either *consumer durable goods* (products that last a long time and can be used repeatedly, such as electronic gadgets, clothes and home furniture), or *non-durable goods* (those that need to be consumed very shortly after their purchase as they do not last, such as fresh food and newspapers).

Capital goods, or **producer goods**, are products purchased by other businesses. Examples include computers, machinery, specialist equipment and tools. These products are then used to produce other goods or services.

Services are intangible products provided by businesses. The service is not tangible, but the results are. Examples include the services provided by doctors (health care), bus and rail companies (transportation), restaurants (food), gyms and sports centres (recreation), solicitors (legal advice), and teachers (education).

Adding value

All businesses must add value in the production process. **Value added** is the difference between the value of inputs (i.e. the costs of production) and the value of outputs (i.e. the goods and services that are sold to customers). Value added allows a business to sell its products for more than its production costs, thereby earning the business a **profit**. For example, suppose that the input costs (such as labour, power and components) for producing a car totalled $6,000. If customers are willing to pay a price of $18,000 for the car, then the value added is $12,000. This surplus will contribute towards the firm's overall profits. The concept of value added also applies to the service sector. In using the services of a plumber, accountant, martial arts instructor or private dance tutor, customers are paying for the skills, expertise and experience that they do not personally have.

Customers are willing to pay prices in excess of the costs of producing goods and services due to several reasons. For example, value added can come in the form of:

- Speed and/or quality of service
- Prestige associated with the purchase
- Feel-good factor
- Perceived value for money
- Quality of the finished product

- Brand image and/or brand loyalty
- Taste or design
- Inability to obtain such products cheaper elsewhere.

Question 1.1.1

Explain how the following products have value added. *[6 marks]*

a A 100-page fashion magazine.

b A photo of a famous celebrity with a signed autograph.

c A state-of-the-art laptop computer.

Opportunity cost and business activity

Businesses have to make decisions that affect their daily operations and their long-term prospects. **Opportunity cost** is defined as the best alternative that is forgone when making a decision. Due to limited resources, such as time and money, businesses are confronted with choices. Opportunity cost differs from accounting costs in that accounting costs do not look at the cost (or value) of foregone choices. For example, if a student decided to go into higher education, the accounting cost would include the tuition fees and other costs associated with studying at university. However, opportunity cost also considers the foregone income that could have been earned had the person chosen to work (the best alternative choice) instead of studying. Of course, the student would hope that by studying for a degree that he or she would earn a higher salary in the future to offset both the accounting and opportunity costs associated with studying.

The study of Business and Management assumes that people are **rational decision-makers**, i.e. they choose the option that gives them the most benefit. For example, the marketing department of a business will need to decide on the various ways in which to spend its allocated budget. It should choose the option(s) that will generate the highest valued benefits to the business. Hence, the concept of opportunity cost is useful when assessing the true costs and benefits of competing choices. Box 1.1a outlines some ways in which the concept of opportunity cost has been used in the real business world.

Box 1.1a Examples of opportunity cost in business

- Mirrors have long been used in places with lifts (elevators), such as in hotels and department stores. Customers do not necessarily notice the waiting and transit time as they stare at themselves in the mirror, and hence refrain from being annoyed at the business.
- Music and entertainment is a major feature at many theme parks. The Disneyland operators try to distract time-conscious customers by providing music, live entertainment and large movie screens to distract customers whilst they wait in line for thrill rides and other attractions. This all helps to provide a better overall experience for their customers.
- Whilst waiting at the checkouts at any supermarket, you may notice the 'bins' next to the counter. These are a last minute attempt by the supermarkets to lure customers to buy miscellaneous items (hence the term 'bins') such as confectionery and batteries. The other purpose is, again, to distract people waiting in the queue.

(cont.)

- Airlines companies often overbook the number of seats on a flight. This is because, statistically, flights are rarely booked at full capacity. However, as a result of the policy, sometimes airlines face the problem of overbooking and will need to 'bump off' passengers, i.e. to offer them compensation for having to wait for the next available flight. Passengers for whom time is not important can purchase a stand-by ticket which is cheaper but may be somewhat inconvenient.
- Women's clothes retailing is a massive business. However, women are often accompanied by their husbands and boyfriends who tend to have less patience in a shopping mall – look out for this trend next time you are out shopping! Marketers have noticed this fact and have responded. Many retail outlets now provide newspapers and male-orientated publications (such as motor vehicle or male fashion magazines) so that the female partner can shop in peace! The retail outlets, of course, hope that this strategy will then allow the customers to spend much longer in their shops, thereby increasing the chance of more sales.

Question 1.1.2

Business opening hours

It wasn't until the mid 1990s that supermarkets went against government advice and began to trade on Sundays. Supermarkets in the UK realized the **opportunity cost** of being closed on Sundays. They were fined for such actions, as licensing to trade on Sundays had not been enacted, but the fines were so insignificant compared to the revenues that they were earning by opening on Sundays that the supermarkets continued with this practice. McDonald's Corporation have followed by opening some 24-hours stores around the world. Some banks in Hong Kong have opened on Sundays since 2006.

a Define the term **opportunity cost**. *[2 marks]*

b Use the case study to examine the reasons why opportunity cost is an important concept in business decision-making. *[6 marks]*

The role of profit in business activity

Profit refers to the positive difference between a firm's *total revenues* and its *total costs* (see Unit 5.2), per period of time. Revenues are the inflows of money, usually from the sale of products. Costs are the outflows of money, to finance production activities. By contrast, if business costs are greater than revenues, the organization makes a **loss**. Most businesses will aim to provide goods and services (to satisfy their customers' needs and wants) at a profit. This will ensure that they earn a return on their investment.

The role of profit is important for a business. The functions of profit include:

- Profit acts as an *incentive to produce*. The profit motive is probably the key driving force for most businesses to provide goods and services.
- It acts as the *reward for risk takers* engaged in business activity.
- It *encourages invention and innovation*. Coming up with new technological ideas and processes that cut costs of production will result in higher profits for the owners of a business.
- Profit acts as an *indicator of growth* (or decline). Hence, it signals to the owners and investors of a business to switch from low profitability to high-profitability business activities.
- It is a *source of finance* and used to fund the internal growth of a business (see Unit 1.7).

All businesses must make profits in order to survive in the long run. Even for *non-profit organizations* (see Unit 1.2) it is important to make a **surplus** (revenues exceeding costs). The difference between profit and surplus is that any surplus generated is all ploughed back into the business, rather than having some of it being distributed to its owners (as in the case of profits).

FACTORS OF PRODUCTION

To produce a good or to provide a service, resources must be used. These resources are called **factors of production** or **factor inputs**. Books, for example, are produced by using resources such as paper, ink and equipment for printing and binding. Human resources (such as the author, editor and agents or distributors) are also needed in addition to the other factor inputs. To produce any good or service, there are four vital factors of production that are required: land, labour, capital and enterprise.

- **Land**. Land refers to all natural resources found on the planet that are available for production. Examples include wood, water, fish, crude oil, minerals, metal ores and physical land itself. Some countries have an abundance of raw materials and therefore they specialize in the extraction and production of these natural resources. For example, many Middle Eastern countries such as Iraq and Saudi Arabia are well endowed in oil supply. Land resources can be categorized as being either renewable resources or non-renewable resources. **Renewable resources** are those that replenish themselves, such as fish stocks, trees and water. **Non-renewable resources** are those that cannot be replaced once consumed, such as minerals and fossil fuels.
- **Labour**. Labour means the physical and mental effort of people used in the production of a good or service. For example, workers are needed to operate machines and to sell products to customers. However, the quantity of people available to work is not always as desirable as the quality of work that is delivered. Some people are better educated and trained and have more experience than others.
- **Capital**. Capital refers to all non-natural (manufactured) resources that are used in the creation and production of other products. Examples include money, buildings, equipment, tools, machinery and vehicles. When firms increase their spending on capital stock, this is called investment. Investment increases the productive capacity of the economy and is crucial for the growth of an economy (see Unit 1.5). Government also contribute to **investment** expenditure. For example, they might build new schools, hospitals, museums, libraries and universities. They might also spend money to expand road and motorway (highway) networks.
- **Enterprise**. Enterprise, also known as **entrepreneurship**, refers to the management, organization and planning of the other three factors of production. Entrepreneurs have the skills needed to oversee the whole production process, whilst having the ability and willingness to take potentially high risks. Successful entrepreneurs tend to be creative, innovative and passionate. Although entrepreneurs are essentially people, they are categorized separately from labour because the success or failure of a business rests on the abilities of the entrepreneur. Famous examples of entrepreneurs include Sir Richard Branson (Virgin Group) and Anita Roddick (The Body Shop) who both built business empires from scratch.

Different products will require varying amounts of factor inputs. In *labour-intensive* industries, such as teaching or consultancy, labour is used in proportionally larger quantities than other factors of production. In *capital-intensive* industries, such as car manufacturing, capital is used more than any other factor input. Nevertheless, all products need a combination of all four factor inputs (see Table 1.1a).

Table 1.1a Examples of factors inputs used in teaching and car manufacturing

	Teaching	Car manufacturing
Land	Wood (for producing writing paper, books and furniture) and physical land (for the building)	Natural resource for producing plastics, rubber, glass and steel
Labour	Teacher, teaching assistant, technicians, cleaners and support staff	Assembly line workers, engineers, designers, quality controllers and distributors/agents
Capital	Equipment such as tables, chairs, whiteboard, stationery and textbooks	Manufacturing plant, machinery, technology and stock of components (e.g. tyres and windscreens)
Enterprise	Heads of Department / Management team	Production managers and Chief Executive

The four factors of production have a financial return for their part in the production process:

- The reward for the use of land is known as **rent**. Land owners earn rental income for letting out their property.
- The return for the use of capital is called **interest**. Capital that is hired out to others earns interest.
- The remuneration for labour is **wages** or **salaries** in return for their physical and mental efforts into the production process.
- Entrepreneurs receive **profit** (if there is any) for their responsibilities and risk-taking in the production process.

The four returns for the factor inputs are collectively known as **income** (see Figure 1.1b). Hence, the more factor inputs a person or business has, the higher their income tends to be.

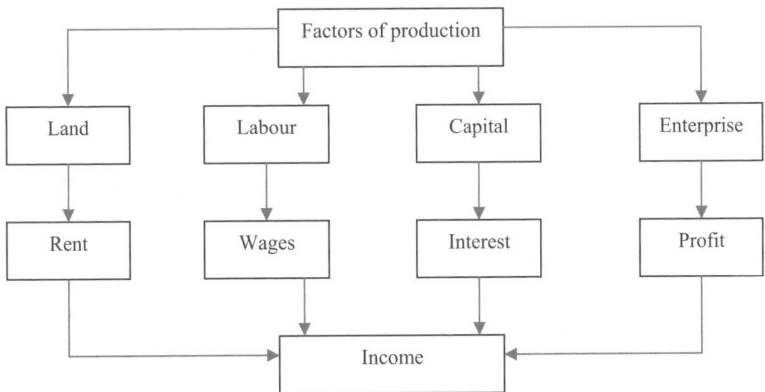

Figure 1.1b Factors of production and their returns

SPECIALIZATION

Specialization means that a business concentrates on the production of a particular good or service or a small range of similar products. For example, an Italian restaurant specializes in the provision of food such as pastas and pizzas. In the production of a particular product, there can be further specialization of a particular activity—there are likely to be different specialists, such as chefs, waiting staff, cleaners and drivers (for home deliveries). Specialization will tend to increase the level of employee efficiency because they become more proficient in their specialized operation. For instance, it is unreasonable to assume that a chef could efficiently take customers' orders and do home deliveries.

Specialization occurs at different levels:

- *Individual* – People specialize in a profession, for example, lawyers, teachers, farmers, doctors, engineers and taxi drivers.
- *Departmental* – Departments within an organization specialize in various functions. These are typically the marketing, personnel, finance and production activities of a business.
- *Corporate* – Most firms specialize in the provision of a limited range of products. For example, Dell manufacture computer hardware, Hilton specializes in the provision of hotel services and Sony produce electronic goods.
- *Regional* – Certain regions within a country also specialize. For example, the City of London and Wall Street, New York both specialize in financial services. Murano, Italy is well known for its glass making; Cheddar, UK is famous for its cheese; and Champagne, France is famous for its champagne.
- *National* – Countries also specialize, some more than others. Japan and Germany are renowned for their manufacturing, whilst France and America have thriving agricultural industries. French wines, German cars, Japanese electronics, Brazilian coffee, South African gold, Scottish whiskey and Belgian chocolates are all examples.

Division of labour is the term is used to refer to the specialization of people, rather than organizations. It involves defining different aspects of a job or task and assigning different people to each particular part of the work. Instead of one person doing all the tasks, through division of labour the final level of production should be much higher and more efficient.

Advantages of specialization

- *Increased productivity* – Output increases because the business uses specialized machinery and/or staff are more proficient at what they do.
- *Increased efficiency* – There is better use of scarce resources with specialization. Less time and resources are wasted simply because employees are more competent. Average costs of production are likely to fall as a result.
- *Standardization* – Specialization results in product specifications being consistently met. Specialized machinery, for instance, will mean that output is of the same standard and quality.
- *Higher profit margins* – Customers may be prepared to pay a higher price for specialist goods and services. Highly specialized professionals are therefore able to make a relatively large amount of profit, e.g. suppliers of custom-made cars, divorce lawyers, cosmetic surgeons, architects, interior designers and professional footballers.

Disadvantages of specialization

- *Boredom* – People are likely to become fed up with doing the same repetitive tasks. This can negatively affect the level of staff productivity and motivation.
- *Inflexibility* – Employees who (over) specialize will be less flexible as they lack the skills and opportunities to adapt to different roles and responsibilities. Workers who overspecialize may find it very difficult to switch to alternative occupations if there is an adverse change in demand for their products or services.
- *A lack of autonomy* – Specialization results in interdependence in the production process. A breakdown or delay in one part of the process will cause problems for the entire business.
- *Capital costs* – The purchase and maintenance of specialist machinery and equipment may be extremely expensive. This will therefore exhaust much of a firm's finances.

BUSINESS FUNCTIONS

A business must carry out several vital functions if it is to operate effectively. These functions are carried out by functional areas or departments that must work together to achieve the objectives of the organization. The four functional areas of a business organization are production, marketing, finance and human resources.

Production (Operations)

The Production department is responsible for the process of converting raw materials into finished goods, ready for delivery to customers. The term also applies to the process of providing services to customers. Examples of production include the extraction of crude oil, the construction of roads and provision of financial services.

Functions of the production department will be coordinated and monitored by the production manager. These tasks may include:

- Determining how the good will be manufactured or how the service will be delivered
- Deciding on the resources needed for production, e.g. technical and specialist equipment
- Planning the timescale of production, e.g. when production should occur and how long the process will take
- Stock management and control
- Performing quality control and inspections
- Arranging for delivery of finished stocks to customers
- Meeting production targets and deadlines
- Carrying out research and development (R&D) into new products and work processes.

The operations manager has a vital role in ensuring that production plans are carefully planned out to ensure that there is efficient production. Poor planning and control may lead to a delay or halt in the production process and this could cost the business a lot of money. Operations management is covered in Units 5.1–5.8.

Marketing

The marketing department is responsible for identifying and satisfying consumer wants and needs. They are ultimately in charge of ensuring that the firm's products sell. This is done through a series of activities such as market research, test marketing, packaging and advertising. Functions of the marketing department can be summed up as the four P's of marketing:

- **Product** – ensuring that goods or services meet the customer's requirements, such as a product's various sizes, colours, packaging and core functions. Other activities related to the product include market research, branding and product development (see Unit 4.3).
- **Price** – using various pricing methods to sell the products of a business. There are numerous pricing strategies (see Unit 4.4) that can be used depending on factors such as the level of demand, the number of substitute products and the costs of producing the good or service.
- **Promotion** – making sure that customers know about the firm's products (see Unit 4.5). This is often done through the mass media, such as on television or in newspapers. Alternatively, cheaper methods of informing and persuading customers about a product include the use of sales promotions, special discounts and free samples.
- **Place** – ensuring that goods and services are available in convenient places for consumers to buy. Marketing managers must ensure that they select appropriate ways to distribute products to the marketplace (see Unit 4.6).

Finance

The finance department is in charge of managing the organization's money. The finance manager must ensure that accurate recording and reporting of financial documentation takes place. This is to comply with legal requirements (such as to prevent deliberate understating of profit figures in order to avoid corporation taxes) and to inform those interested in the financial position of the business. Finance is covered in Units 3.1–3.6.

Human resources (Personnel)

The human resources department is responsible for managing the personnel of the organization. In managing people, the HR department is likely to deal with the following issues: workforce planning, recruitment, training, appraisal, pay and benefits, equal opportunities, health and safety matters, and fostering working relations. Human Resource Management is covered in Units 2.1–2.8.

A large business organization is able to allocate resources to each function and so the functions would be easily identified. In a small business, owned by just one person, each function would need to be carried out by the same person. In practice, these four functional areas of a business are highly interrelated. The production department, for example, relies on the talents of effective marketing staff to sell their products. Equally, marketers can only do their jobs if they have a decent product to sell and the relevant financial resources to do so.

Question **1.1.3**

The business of education

Education is a big business. Schools can earn revenue from numerous sources, such as tuition fees (for fee-paying schools), grants from the government and fund-raising events. They might also hire out their facilities. They use revenues to finance their costs, such as wages to the teaching staff. Parents have to pay for a host of items such as uniforms, books, sports equipment and food.

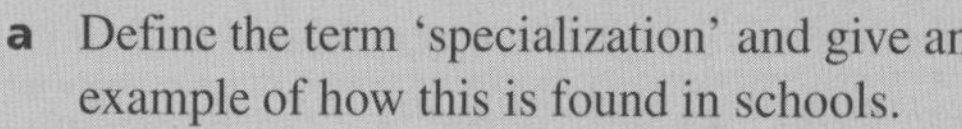

a Define the term 'specialization' and give an example of how this is found in schools. *[2 marks]*

b Examine how business functions operate in an organization such as schools. *[6 marks]*

BUSINESS SECTORS

Businesses can be classified according to the stage of production that they are engaged in. There are three main sectors of business activity.

Primary sector

Businesses operating in the primary sector are involved with the extraction, harvesting and conversion of land (i.e. natural resources) as a factor of production. These resources are then used in the secondary sector. Examples of business activities in the primary sector include: agriculture, fishing, mining, forestry and oil extraction.

Employment and output in the primary sector tends to dominate in *less economically developed countries*, such as in many African countries. Farming, for example, accounts for a large percentage of employment in these countries. However, in *more economically developed countries*, businesses operating in the primary industry are more developed through the use of mechanization and automation such as tractors, combine harvesters and automatic watering systems.

As economies develop, there is less reliance on the primary sector in terms of employment and national output. Part of the reason for this trend is that there is little value added in primary production. Less economically developed countries, for example, can only sell tea leaves and coffee beans at relatively low prices.

Secondary sector

Businesses that operate in the secondary sector are involved in using raw materials and other resources for the manufacturing or construction of finished and useable products. An example would be an aircraft manufacturer using steel, rubber and plastics to produce aeroplanes. Other examples of businesses in this sector include: construction firms, pharmaceutical companies, clothes manufacturers, publishing firms, electronics manufacturers and energy production companies. The output is then sold to customers, be they other business, foreign buyers or domestic customers.

Developing countries tend to have a dominant secondary sector that accounts for a relatively large percentage of the country's national output. Economists argue that the secondary sector of the economy is the wealth creating sector because manufactured goods can be exported worldwide to earn income for the country. Value is added to the natural and raw resources during the production process. The mass production and export of motor vehicles and consumer electronic products, for example, have helped nations such as South Korea to develop. Nevertheless, as an economy develops, there is a tendency for the manufacturing sector to decline in importance in terms of employment and output in the economy.

Tertiary sector

Businesses and people that work in the tertiary sector provide services to their private and corporate customers. An example would be a worker in a bookstore selling a book to a customer; no book is actually produced in this sector but the worker provides a service to the customer who purchases the book. Hence, the tertiary sector is also known as the **service sector**. Examples of industries in the tertiary sector include: retailing, education, travel and tourism, entertainment, insurance, transport, banking, finance, healthcare and catering.

Note that goods can be transformed in the process of providing a service. This happens in a restaurant when the chef prepares a meal with fresh ingredients. The focus is, nevertheless, on the people who are providing the service – the chef and the waiting staff who serve the diners.

In more economically developed countries (MEDCs), such as Canada and Italy, the tertiary sector tends to be the most substantial sector in terms of both employment and as a percentage of **Gross Domestic Product** (the value of the country's output each year). The decline in the manufacturing sector in these nations also helps to explain a MEDC's increasing reliance on the service sector.

The three sectors of production are linked through the **chain of production**. This tracks the stages of an item's production, from the extraction of raw materials used to produce the product all the way through to it being delivered to the consumer. For instance, the construction of a house may require the following process in the chain of production:

- *Primary* – Timber workers, miners and farmers extract materials such as wood, stones, sand and metal ores.
- *Secondary* – Engineers and builders use machinery and equipment to turn the raw materials into usable items, such as doors, bricks, windows and so forth.

- *Tertiary* – Sales agents, financiers and solicitors are needed to supply the finished product to the consumer. For most products, distribution and transportation will also play a vital role in this sector.
- The final stage in the chain of production is the product actually getting to the consumer.

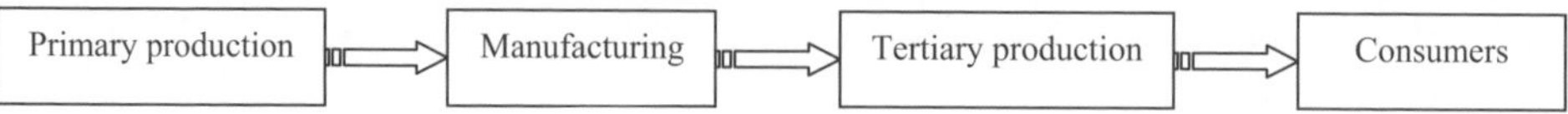

Figure 1.1c The chain of production

All three production sectors are said to be *interdependent*. This is because each sector relies on the other two to remain in existence. For example, raw materials such as crude oil would not be extracted if there were no need for oil refinery. At the same time, there would not be any need for oil refiners if there were no customers of the oil, such as motorists and airline companies in the tertiary sector. Likewise, businesses in the secondary sector rely on their suppliers for stocks to ensure that their production targets are met. Businesses are also interdependent as they all need energy, manufactured producer goods and financial services.

HIGHER LEVEL

HIGHER LEVEL EXTENSION: CHANGES IN ECONOMIC STRUCTURE

Structural change refers to a shift in the relative share of national output and employment that is attributed to each business sector. Structural change can be observed in an economy over time. Typically, countries develop by moving the majority of national output being contributed by the primary sector (such as agriculture, fishing and mining) to manufacturing and then eventually to the tertiary sector. Economists argue that primary sector production yields low value added, so in order to develop there must be a shift of business activity to manufacturing and service sectors which both have higher value added.

When a country moves away from primary production towards manufacturing as its principal sector for national output and employment, then it is said to have experienced **industrialization**. However, some developed countries are still able to exploit their natural advantage and specialization in the supply of agricultural and primary products. For example, even though only 2% of the French population work in the primary sector, the country has benefited immensely from its export of agricultural products all around the world.

Similarly, countries that are able to exploit the tertiary sector as the key contributor to national output and employment are said to be **developed countries**. Businesses such as Lenovo see themselves as operating in the service sector, despite also producing computer hardware. Lenovo realize that there is more value added in the tertiary sector. Rather than receiving one-off payments from selling manufactured equipment, it can receive a flow of money from offering after-sales services such as maintenance and support services. Hence, the tertiary activities generate more profit for the business than the manufacturing activities.

The shift towards the tertiary sector being the predominant sector in developed countries has occurred due to changes in factors such as:

- Higher household incomes – As a nation develops, consumers demand more services simply because they can afford to. The demand for services is positively correlated to changes in income levels, such as eating out at restaurants, visits to the hairdresser or financial planning.
- More leisure time – One feature of higher standards of living is the increase in leisure time. As nations develop, people tend to have more time for recreational purposes, such as participating in sports, visiting the theatre or cinema, going on holiday and so forth. This trend has provided many opportunities for the service sector.

- Larger focus on customer relations management – Businesses have realized that good customer service before, during and after the sale of an item can be an important source of competitive advantage.
- Increasing reliance on support services – Businesses need ever more sophisticated support services. For example, advances in *e-commerce* (see Unit 4.8) have meant a need for after-sales services such as technical support. Firms are increasingly relying on the services of other businesses, such as subcontractors, advertising agencies, market research analysts and management consultants. As businesses grow internationally, they will also rely more heavily on the services of financial lenders, accountants and lawyers.

HIGHER LEVEL

Question 1.1.4

Production sectors

Study the data below and then answer the questions that follow. **A**, **B** and **C** represent three countries: Belgium, Czech Republic and Indonesia (although not in that order).

Table 1.1b Structure of Employment (%)

	A	B	C
Agriculture	43	2	4
Industry	13	25	40
Services	44	73	56

a Identify the countries **A**, **B** and **C**. *[3 marks]*

b Use the data in Table 1.1b to justify your answer to Question **4a**. *[7 marks]*

NATURE OF BUSINESS ACTIVITY AND BUSINESS STRATEGY

Business activity is the process of turning factor inputs (land, labour, capital and enterprise) into outputs of goods and services in order to meet the needs and wants of different customers. The rest of this textbook will explore ways in which businesses strive to add value in the production and provision of goods and services. For example, the functional areas of a business (such as marketing, human resource management, finance, and operations management) are all instrumental in determining the nature of business activity.

Essentially, the purpose of business is to satisfy the needs and desires of customers whilst also fulfilling the organization's own objectives (see Unit 1.3), such as profit maximization. In the long run, all businesses must generate a profit or surplus in order to survive. However, the complexities of business organizations mean that the chances of a new business succeeding are often very low.

Opportunity cost is at the heart of business decision-making, whether there is a conscious or subconscious awareness of the concept. Due to scarce resources, including time and finance, competing decisions need to be made and any decision that involves a choice between options will incur an opportunity cost. Managers will take opportunity cost into consideration when looking at areas such as Investment Appraisal (see Unit 3.2), Product Life Cycles (see Unit 4.3) and the Working Capital Cycle (see Unit 3.3), to name but a few.

External forces (see Unit 1.5) will also affect the nature of business activity. Changes in economic structures over time, for example, will present both opportunities and threats to organizations and will therefore influence the activities undertaken by businesses.

REVIEW QUESTIONS 1.1

1 What is a 'business'?

2 What are the purposes of business activity?

3 Distinguish between 'customers' and 'consumers' of a business.

4 What are the four factors of production and their respective rewards for being used in the production process?

5 Outline three advantages and three disadvantages of specialization.

6 What are the four functional areas of a business?

7 Describe the three business sectors of the economy.

8 What is meant by the 'chain of production'?

Higher Level extension

9 How has the structure of business sectors changed over time?

10 Outline the implications of such changes on business activity.

Businesses are organizations that are involved in the production of goods and/or the provision of services.

Capital refers to all non-natural resources used in the production process. Probably the best example of capital is money, but the term also includes resources such as machinery, tools, equipment and factories.

Division of labour refers to the specialization of workers in the provision of goods and/or services by breaking a job down into particular roles or components that are repeated by the same workers.

Entrepreneurs are people who manage, organize and plan the other three factors of production. They are risk takers who exploit business opportunities in return for profits.

Factors of production are the inputs (or resources) necessary for the production process: land, labour, capital and enterprise (also known as entrepreneurship).

Functional areas is the term used to refer to the different sections of a business. These are usually named as the marketing, production, finance and human resources departments.

Industrialization is the process experienced by a country that moves away from primary production towards manufacturing as its principal sector for national output and employment.

Labour refers to physical and mental human effort used in the production process.

Land means natural resources that can be found on the planet. This includes renewable and non-renewable natural resources such as water, fish, wood and physical land itself.

Opportunity cost refers to cost measured in terms of the next best alternative that is foregone when a choice is being made, e.g. money today can be either spent for immediate benefit or saved for the future.

Primary sector refers to businesses involved in the cultivation or extraction of natural resources, such as farming, mining, quarrying, fishing, oil exploration and forestry.

Private sector is the part of the economy under the control of private individuals and businesses, rather than the government. Examples might include sole traders, partnerships and companies.

Public sector is the part of the economy under the control of the government. Examples might include state health and education services, the emergency services (police, fire service and ambulance) and national defence.

Secondary sector refers to the section of the economy where business activity is concerned with the construction and manufacturing of physical products. Automation and mechanization in modern societies has seen this sector decline in terms of employment.

Structural change refers to a shift in the relative share of national output and employment that is attributed to each business sector, i.e. primary, secondary and tertiary sectors.

Tertiary sector refers to the section of the economy where business activity is concerned with the provision of services to customers. In modern societies, it is the largest sector in terms of employment and output.

Value added is the difference between a product's price and the total cost of the inputs that went into making it. It is the extra worth created in the production process.

Types of Organization

UNIT 1.2

To open a business is very easy;
to keep it open is very difficult.

Chinese proverb

Key topics

- Private and public sector organizations
- Starting a business: the reasons, the process and the problems
- Profit-based organizations: sole traders, partnerships and companies (corporations)
- Non-government organizations and non-profit organizations

Higher Level extension

- Relationship between organizations in the private and public sector
- Public-private enterprises/partnerships

INTRODUCTION

This Unit looks at the various types of business organizations. Some businesses operate in the **public sector** (owned and controlled by the government) whilst others operate in the **private sector** (run and owned by private individuals and businesses). Within these two sectors of the economy, there are further classifications of business organizations.

Business organizations also differ in terms of ownership and control (you do not have to control or run a business simply because you own it), how they raise finance, and how the profits of the organization are distributed. These issues will all be examined within this Unit.

PRIVATE SECTOR AND PUBLIC SECTOR ORGANIZATIONS

Businesses that operate in the **private sector** are *not* owned by the government. Instead, they are businesses that are owned and controlled by private individuals and organizations. Business organizations in the private sector differ in their size, ranging from those owned and run by just one person to multinational companies that operate throughout the world. The main aim of most, although not all, private sector businesses is to make **profit**. In simple terms, profit is the positive difference between a firm's **costs** of production (such as the payment of wages and purchase of components) and its **revenues** (the money earned from selling its products). There are three main types of profit-based businesses in the private sector: Sole Traders, Partnerships and Companies (also known as Corporations). These are examined later in this Unit.

Organizations that operate in the **public sector** are under the ownership and control of the government. Traditionally, public sector organizations are run to provide essential goods and services that would be inefficiently provided or underprovided by the private sector, even if this means the government does not make any profit in doing so.

Organizations that are wholly owned by the government are called **public corporations**, such as the UK's BBC (British Broadcasting Corporation), Hong Kong's KCRC (Kowloon Canton Railway Corporation), China's Nanjing Automobile, and America's United States Postal Service. Through government intervention (see Unit 1.5) and public sector ownership, the government is able to affect the level of economic activity in the best interest of the general public. There are several reasons why some organizations belong in the public sector:

- To ensure that everyone has access to basic services such as education, health care, public parks and public libraries
- To avoid wasteful competition since the government is able to achieve huge *economies of scale* (cost savings from operating on a large magnitude) in the provision of certain services, such as postal services or national defence
- To protect citizens and businesses through institutions such as the Police or the courts that govern the law and order system
- To reduce unemployment, e.g. governments tend to be a large employer of teachers, doctors and nurses.

Public sector ownership of resources is much less common today due to the benefits of private sector ownership. Therefore, many public corporations and assets have been **privatized** (sold-off or transferred to the private sector). Box 1.2a outlines some of the benefits of privatization.

Regulatory bodies have been set up by the government to monitor the conduct and performance of privatized companies. These organizations will usually have some influence over the level of customer service and the pricing policy of the privatized firm, in order to safeguard the interest of the general public. Regulatory bodies can also be used for controlling business activity in the public sector. For instance, the Office for Standards in Education (Ofsted) regulates standards in teaching and learning for state and private schools that follow the British education system.

Box 1.2a Benefits of privatization

- Efficiency gains – Inefficient public sector monopolies are exposed to competitive markets when privatized. This should force them to improve their efficiency and customers should therefore benefit from improved quality.
- Lower costs of production – In an attempt to earn profits, coupled with pressure from competitors, privatized companies will aim to reduce their costs. Customers should therefore benefit from more competitive prices.
- Increased choice – Introducing competition to former public sector monopolists gives customers more choice.
- Incentives to innovate – Competition encourages firms to be more dynamic and innovative (coming up with new ideas to stay competitive and to continuously improve).
- Less financial burden – The government can save money by not having to fund public corporations and their activities. This, therefore, leads to less financial burden on taxpayers.
- Source of government revenue – Privatization has raised huge amounts of money for governments that have sold off their businesses to private investors (although these are one-off gains only).

STARTING A BUSINESS

Starting a new business is a risky project as the owner or investors are taking a step into the unknown. Most new businesses fail, mainly due to mismanagement of the business. For example, the owners may have underestimated the challenges faced when setting up a business. The level of demand may be insufficient for the business to recoup its start-up costs (see Box 1.2b), let alone to earn its owners any profit. Nevertheless, the pursuit of profit is a key incentive for people to take risks in setting up a business.

Box 1.2b Examples of set-up (start-up) costs of a business

- Premises – e.g. purchase costs, mortgage deposit payment or rental deposit costs
- Buildings – e.g. alterations, fixtures and fittings and insurance costs
- Capital equipment – e.g. furniture, telephones, computers, machinery, tools, motor vehicles and stationery
- Legal and professional fees – e.g. licences, permits and copyright permission
- Marketing costs – e.g. market research, advertising and promotional campaigns

The **entrepreneur** is the person who takes risks to manage, plan and organize the other three factors of production in order to provide goods and services. Entrepreneurs will need to go through a *decision-making process* (see Unit 1.6) to decide where the firm wants to be, how it is going to get there, and how success will be monitored. To start a business and run it successfully, the entrepreneur will need to take account of the issues outlined in Figure 1.2a.

Figure 1.2a Factors to consider when setting up a business

- A **business idea** that will sell in the marketplace is needed. This might be done by setting up a business that is not currently available, by identifying and filling a *niche* (unfilled gap) in a market or by providing products that have a *unique selling point*. Amazon.com (online book retailing), Dell (custom-made personal computers) and Dyson (bagless vacuum cleaners) are examples of successful businesses that have exploited innovative business ideas. Of course, it is possible to enter existing markets and compete in saturated markets although the chances of great success may be much lower.
- **Finance** is needed to fund all forms of business activity, such as production and marketing of the firm's products. However, finance is usually the key barrier to setting up a new business since most entrepreneurs need to borrow money to fund their start-ups. Record keeping of financial accounts (see Unit 3.5) also needs to be considered. Many businesses will hire accountants to help them do this.
- **Human resources** are needed at all stages of business activity, from the design and development of a good or service to delivering the product to the consumer. Entrepreneurs will have to consider the need for hiring, training, retaining and motivating their staff.
- **Entrepreneurial skills** (industrial and personal skills) are required to successfully plan, organize and manage the business. Effective leadership and negotiation skills are required to deal with different *stakeholder groups* (see Unit 1.4) such as employees, suppliers and the government. Entrepreneurs must also have self-confidence and a passion for what they do.
- **Fixed assets**, such as premises and capital equipment, are needed. The location decision (see Unit 5.5) is also a crucial but problematic one; choose a popular location and the chances of attracting customers are greater, but so are the costs of land and property.
- **Suppliers** are needed to provide a business with its raw materials, finished stock of products and support services. Contact with suppliers will therefore need to be made. Negotiations over issues such as price and delivery times also need to be undertaken.
- **Customers** must be attracted because without them the business will fail. Obtaining customers means the business must undertake marketing research and produce products that are desirable, available at the right prices and sold in the right places. The size of the market will also determine the amount of sales. Publishers, for example, are generally not interested in authors whose work only caters for a very small market.

- **Marketing** is essential, irrespective of how good a business idea might be. Many investors turned down Anita Roddick's idea of The Body Shop and J.K. Rowling's Harry Potter books. Marketing is needed to convince lenders and buyers that the product is a winner.
- **Legalities** (legal issues) also need to be considered. For example, business laws relating to consumer rights, copyright and patent laws and employment legislation must all be adhered to. Infringement of legal issues may present huge problems for a business, such as a restaurant breaking food hygiene laws, and may even cause it to cease trading.

The above considerations are usually set out in an official **business plan** (see Unit 1.6). This document sets out what a business proposes to do, how it plans to achieve this, the cost implications and the expected financial returns. Potential investors and financial lenders will scrutinise the contents of a business plan before parting with their money.

REASONS FOR SETTING UP A BUSINESS

There are many different reasons why people decide to set up a business. These reasons can be remembered by the mnemonic GET CASH:

Growth. Some assets, such as property and land, tend to increase in value over time. This is called *capital growth*. Entrepreneurs such as Donald Trump who own their own businesses benefit personally when there is an appreciation in the value of their assets. Quite often, the capital growth of a business is worth more than the value of the owners' salaries.

Earnings. There is a Chinese saying: "You can never get rich earning money from working for someone else." What this means is that the potential returns for setting up your own business may far outweigh the costs, even though the risks are high. It is common that self-employed people earn salaries far in excess of earnings from any other occupation that they might pursue.

Transference and inheritance. In many cultures and societies it is normal to pass on assets, including businesses, to the next generation. Many self-employed people view their business as something that they can pass on (transference) to their children (inheritance). This helps to give them a sense of security that may not be possible if they chose to work for someone else.

Challenge. Some people may see setting up and running a business as a challenge. It is this challenge that drives them to perform and what gives them personal satisfaction. Being successful in business boosts self-esteem and self-achievement. This is perhaps one reason why billionaires such as Warren Buffet and Li Ka-Shing continue to work despite being past the official retirement age. Research has also shown that small businesses can be highly successful in 'niche' and unexplored markets if such challenges are pursued.

Autonomy. Working for someone else means exactly that. Employees have to follow the instructions and rules set by the organization that they work for. Employers have the largest say in the conditions of employment, working hours, benefits and holiday entitlement. Conversely, being the employer means that there is autonomy (independence, freedom of choice and flexibility) in how things operate within the organization.

Security. On a similar note, there is usually more job security for someone who is their own boss. By contrast, employees can be dismissed, made redundant, or even replaced by technology. In addition, although the risks are great, being self-employed makes it potentially easier to accumulate personal wealth to provide higher funds for (early) retirement.

Hobbies. Some people may set up a business to sell a new invention or to turn their hobbies and personal interests into a business. Successful entrepreneurs have a passion for what they do and this is made easier if the nature of the work is directly related to their interests. Examples are top selling author, J.K. Rowling and Jamie Oliver, the celebrity chef who has set up several of his own restaurants.

IDENTIFYING MARKET OPPORTUNITIES

The term 'market opportunities' refers to the identification of new or unsatisfied consumer needs. Being able to identify and exploit market opportunities allows entrepreneurs to have a better chance of survival and success. Market opportunities can come about in several ways, including:

- Identifying a gap in the market. Small firms and new businesses tend to thrive in **niche markets**. A niche refers to a small or unfilled segment of a market. Large organizations are often put off from entering niche markets because they feel that the market is too small and hence profits are very limited. This allows opportunities for smaller businesses to cater for these markets. Niche markets do not necessarily stay small however; indeed personal computers, flat-screen televisions and mobile phones all started as small niche markets. Unit 1.7 examines other reasons why small firms can survive in a highly competitive business environment.
- Innovative ideas and creations. Entrepreneurs may come up with new products and/or processes to meet consumer needs. Apple's iPod, Google's search engine and eBay's auctioning business are some examples. The key benefit of this approach to identifying market opportunities is that the owners have good market and product knowledge. They may use their innovation as a form of product differentiation and market this as their *unique selling point*. New product designs and processes can be legally protected via copyright and patent legislation. Legal protection will help to prevent others from replicating the firm's ideas or supplying exactly the same product.
- Developing the entrepreneur's personal qualities and skills. Entrepreneurs such as real estate mogul Donald Trump and Russian oil tycoon Roman Abramovich have built their businesses largely on their personal interests. Donald Trump is a big golf enthusiast so in addition to his huge real estate business, he owns several golf courses around the world. Roman Abramovich's passion for European football led him to buy Chelsea Football Club. Although the Club was making huge losses at the time, Abramovich's riches significantly improved the fortunes (and trophies) of the organization.

Market research (see Unit 4.2) is imperative if business start-ups are to have a decent chance of survival. Many people go into business thinking that they know what is best, or that things will simply fall into place. The reality is that a significant number of new businesses fail (see 'Possible problems faced by start-ups' below). The benefits of conducting thorough market research will allow owners to better understand the nature of the industry and their customers' needs and wants. In turn, this should improve the business's chances of success.

POSSIBLE PROBLEMS FACED BY START-UPS

Results from around the globe consistently show that around 40% of new businesses fail to survive their first year. A new business is likely to face a host of problems which must be dealt with immediately to prevent these from escalating and threatening the firm's survival. The problems faced by business start-ups are likely to include:

- **Lack of finance capital**. All businesses need finance for the purchase or rental of *fixed capital*, such as premises, buildings, machinery and equipment. However, most owners of new or small businesses do not have the credentials or experience to secure external funding without major difficulties. Even if entrepreneurs are able to borrow money, the funds may be insufficient or the relatively high interest repayments may seriously affect the cash flow position of the firm. As a result, business owners often have to remortgage their own homes to raise the finance needed. This option offers the lender more *collateral* (borrowers have some form of security in case they fail to repay the loan).

- **Cash flow problems**. Financing *working capital* (the money available for the daily running of a business) is also a major problem for many new businesses. For instance, a business may have a lot of stock that cannot be easily turned into cash, such as raw materials or semi-finished output. Customers may also demand a lengthy *credit period* (buy now pay later schemes) ranging from 30–90 days. This means that the business will not receive the cash payment until the credit period is over. However, even during times of poor cash flow, businesses need cash to pay for their ongoing costs such as wages, purchase of stock from suppliers, rent, utility bills, taxes and interest payments on bank loans. **Budgetary problems** (failure to control costs of production) are another cause of cash flow problems. For example, many new businesses often forget about making provisions for tax payments to the government. Research has shown that poor cash flow management, i.e. a lack of working capital, is the largest cause of business failure. Hence it is common for new businesses to produce a cash flow forecast (see Unit 3.3) in their business plan to identify likely periods of poor cash flow so that provisions can be taken to cover any shortfalls.
- **Marketing problems**. Marketing problems arise when businesses fail to meet customer needs, thereby resulting in poor sales. Supplying the right products to the right market is especially crucial for new businesses. However, small and new businesses may lack the know-how to do this. Research has shown that the key to small business success is to identify a *niche* (or gap) in the market and then fill it. For example, Amazon.com and Lastminute.com identified the huge opportunities of using the internet as a channel of distribution for books and holidays respectively. European companies such as easyJet and Ryanair identified early on the niche for no-frills airline travel. All of these firms have successfully grown to operate on an international scale.
- **Unestablished customer base**. A large problem facing new businesses is attracting customers, i.e. building a customer base. The problem is intensified when there are several well established businesses which already operate in the market. Customer loyalty is built over a long period of time. This may require marketing and other strategies, which not only cost large amounts of money but also requires marketing know-how.
- **People management problems**. New businesses may lack the experience in hiring the correct staff with appropriate skills for all the necessary roles to be fulfilled. This can lead to poor levels of customer service and a need to retrain staff or to rehire people, all of which can be very expensive to a business. Furthermore, new businesses may not know the ideal *organizational structure* (see Unit 2.2) that best suits their needs.
- **Legalities**. Paperwork and legal requirements of setting up a new business can be tedious, confusing, time consuming and expensive. In order to avoid business failure, it is necessary for businesses to comply with all necessary legislation (such as company registration procedures, insurance cover for staff and buildings, consumer protection laws and copyright rules). Any oversight could result in the business having to pay out large sums of money for compensation or penalty fees. This would obviously damage the already vulnerable cash flow position of new firms.
- **Production problems**. It is relatively difficult for new businesses to forecast levels of demand and therefore they are more likely to either over produce or under produce. Overproduction tends to lead to stockpiling, wastage and increased costs. On the other hand, underproduction leads to dissatisfied customers and a loss of potential sales.
- **High costs of production**. New businesses are likely to experience high production costs because of the huge amount of money needed for purchasing assets needed for production (such as machinery, equipment and stocks). In addition, they will have to pay for other *start-up costs* (see Unit 5.2) such as rent, advertising and insurance. Smaller businesses will also be at a cost disadvantage as they cannot benefit from *economies of scale* (see Unit 1.7). Economies of scale allow a business to benefit from lower average costs of production due to

larger scale operations, such as being able to get bulk purchase discounts from their suppliers or being able to borrow money at a lower interest rate because of their large size.

- **Poor location**. Businesses face a dilemma in the location decision: busy areas will offer the highest potential number of customers, but the premises in these areas will also cost the most. Fixed costs, such as rent or mortgage repayments, form a huge percentage of business costs. An aim for any new firm is to break-even as soon as possible, by keeping fixed costs down. This is one reason why many entrepreneurs set up small businesses that operate initially from their own homes (which also has some tax advantages, thereby further helping to keep costs down). Of course, this option is not ideal for all businesses such as restaurants where location plays a key factor in business survival.
- **External influences**. All businesses, irrespective of size or how long they have been in business, are prone to exogenous shocks that create a difficult trading environment, such as an oil crisis or economic recession (see Unit 1.5). However, more established firms tend to be better resourced to handle these external influences. Hence, new businesses are more vulnerable to external shocks so the potential for business failure is greater.

In conclusion, people set up their own business to satisfy their personal desires, such as to be their own boss, to fulfil a personal vision or business opportunity, to have the opportunity to achieve success or simply to live a more extravagant lifestyle (if and when the business is a 'success'). However, a significant number of new businesses fail to survive. There are three interrelated reasons for this: management incompetence, a lack of cash in the business and poor cost control.

Question 1.2.1

Reload

Reload Juice and Salad Bar (or Reload for short) is a small New Zealand fast-food chain founded in 2003. It focuses on providing healthier fast foods than those found in the larger, more established outlets such as Subway and Delifrance. In 2007, the organization announced its expansion plans into Europe by setting up a first store in Glasgow, Scotland.

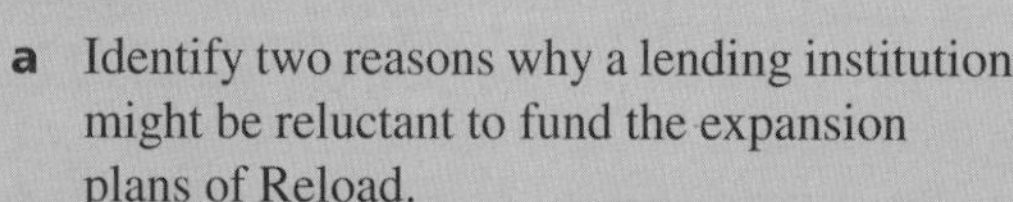

a Identify two reasons why a lending institution might be reluctant to fund the expansion plans of Reload. *[2 marks]*

b Explain two problems that Reload might have in building a customer base in new overseas markets such as Scotland. *[4 marks]*

PROFIT-BASED ORGANIZATIONS

Most businesses that operate in the private sector aim to make profit. After all, the only way for a business to survive in the long term is for it to be profitable. The three main types of businesses that aim to make profit are sole traders, partnerships and companies.

Sole traders

A **sole trader** (also known as a **sole proprietor**) is an individual who is the owner of his or her own business. The owner also runs and controls the business and is the sole person held responsible for its success or failure. Sole proprietorships are the most common type of business ownership. Examples include self-employed painters and decorators, plumbers, mechanics, restaurateurs and freelance photographers.

Sole traders may work alone or they may employ other people to help run the business. Sole proprietorships are usually small family-run businesses that can be set up with relatively little capital. Start-up capital for a sole trader is usually obtained from personal savings and borrowing.

One important legal point about sole traders is that the business is **unincorporated**. This means that the *owner* is legally the same as the *business* – he or she is treated as a single legal entity. If the business fails or is sued, then creditors and prosecutors can take the owner to court. Since there is no legal difference between the business and the owner, the sole trader could end up losing his or her personal possessions if the firm collapses. This is because the sole trader is personally responsible for all the debts of the business.

Many of today's well-known companies started off as sole traders. For example, Chanel (The House of Chanel) was started by Coco Chanel back in 1910 and now has a huge global presence. Marks & Spencer was set up in 1904 by two partners, Michael Marks and Thomas Spencer (who originally operated as sole traders). Tesco, the UK's largest retailer, was set up in 1919 as a sole proprietorship by Jack Cohen.

Advantages of the sole trader

- **Few legal formalities** exist, meaning that sole proprietorships are quite easy to set up. In addition, start-up costs are usually much lower in comparison to setting up other forms of business.
- The sole trader is the only owner and therefore receives all of the **profits** made by the business. This gives the sole trader an incentive to work hard to become successful.
- **Being your own boss** can also bring about its advantages. These include not having to take orders from any one else, flexibility in working practices such as being able to dictate your own working hours, and higher self-esteem from being successful. Decision making is also quicker as there is no need to discuss or consult issues with others.
- Sole traders can provide **personalized service** to their customers. Larger businesses may not have the time to get to know their customers and often their services become very impersonal. A sole trader is likely to get to know their customers on a more personal level and this can lead to better working relationships.
- Unlike some other forms of business ownership, sole traders enjoy **privacy** as they do not have to make their financial records available to the public or other interested parties. This allows the owner to enjoy confidentiality and also to cut down on the costs of having to prepare detailed accounting records. There is no formal system of accounting expected from sole traders although their accounts can be scrutinized by the Inland Revenue (tax authorities).

Disadvantages of the sole trader

- A sole trader has **unlimited liability**. This means that there is no limit to the amount of debt that a sole trader is legally responsible to pay if the business fails. As the sole trader is unincorporated, any loss made by the business must be paid back even if that requires using the personal assets of the owner. Hence, sole traders risk losing personal possessions such as their jewellery, car or home if the business falls into debt.
- **Limited sources of finance.** It may be difficult to raise finance to establish the business. Sole traders may find it difficult to secure any funds beyond their personal savings. Trying to expand the business will also be difficult due to the lack of sources of finance (see Unit 3.1) available to sole traders.

- **High risks.** Statistically, sole proprietorships have the largest risk of business failure. Even the successful ones usually face intense competition due to the vast number of sole traders that exist. In addition, the presence of larger and more established businesses often poses a huge threat to the survival of smaller businesses.
- **Workload and stress.** The success of a sole proprietorship largely depends upon the abilities and commitment of the owner. Sole traders more often than not have to do their own accounts, marketing, human resource management and operations management. The sole trader is unlikely to be equally effective in all these different roles. Having to do all these tasks adds to the workload and stress for a sole trader. After all, there is a limit to how much any one person can do.
- **Lack of continuity.** The running of a business may be jeopardized if the owner is not present. For example, if the owner decides to go on holiday, or becomes ill, or dies then the business may have problems in continuing.
- **Higher costs of production.** A sole trader is not able to exploit the benefits of large scale production (see Unit 1.7). Subsequently, their prices may be less competitive compared to those of larger competitors.

Question 1.2.2

Exquisite Flowers

Natalie Tran is a self-employed florist who operates from her home in Kuala Lumpur, Malaysia. She is married with three school-aged children. Her husband's work commitments mean that he only comes home at the weekends. Natalie arranges and delivers flowers to hospitals and schools in central Kuala Lumpur. From time to time she also receives large orders for weddings.

a Analyse the costs and benefits to Natalie in operating as a sole trader. *[6 marks]*

b Examine whether sole traders, like florists, benefit from a high degree of specialization. *[6 marks]*

Partnerships

A **partnership** is a profit-seeking business that is owned by two or more persons. For most ordinary partnerships, the maximum number of partners allowed by law is twenty (although this may vary from one country to another). The few exceptions to this rule include professions such as solicitors and accountants where the issuing of shares is prohibited.

Similar to sole proprietorships, partnerships are financed mainly from the personal funds of each partner. However, unlike the sole trader, partners can pool their funds together to raise more finance. Partnerships can also raise money from partners who do not actively take part in the running of the business but have a financial stake in the firm. These investors are known as **silent partners**, or **sleeping partners**, and they are eligible for a share of the organization's profits. At least one partner must have unlimited liability, as partnerships are unincorporated businesses, but typically every partner has a share of the liability.

Although it is not a legal requirement, it is advisable for partnerships to formulate a legal agreement between each of the partners. Without a contract, profits or losses must be shared equally amongst the partners and each partner has the same rights in the running of the business. If a legal contract is drawn up, known as a **Deed of Partnership**, or **Partnership Deed**, then it is likely to include:

- The amount of finance contributed by each partner
- The roles, obligations and responsibilities of each partner
- How profits or losses will be shared among the partners
- Conditions for introducing new partners
- Clauses for the withdrawal of a partner from the business, and
- Procedures for ending the partnership.

Advantages of partnerships

- Partnerships have more **financial strength** than sole proprietorships as there are more people who can invest in the business, yet they are still fairly easy to set up.
- Unlike the sole trader, partners can benefit from **division of labour** and **specialization**. In a law firm, for example, there could be partners who specialize in corporate law, divorce law and criminal law. Hence the firm's client base is likely to be much larger as a result of the range of different skills offered by the business.
- As in the case of sole proprietorships, partnerships do not have to publicize their financial records. Therefore they can enjoy a fair degree of financial privacy.

Disadvantages of partnerships

- Partners still have unlimited liability, except for the rare case of *limited partners* who have been elected to have limited liability. Legally, partnerships are responsible for their debts 'wholly or severally' meaning the debts can be repaid by either one partner (wholly) or shared among the partners (severally). This can often cause major disputes as to which partner's personal assets should be used to repay debts. Hence it is usually a good idea to have an agreement set out clearly in a partnership deed.
- In comparison to sole traders, decision making in partnerships is likely to take longer as there are more owners involved. Disagreements and conflict are also more likely to occur.
- A lack of continuity may still exist if a partner dies or decides to leave the firm. This is because the original partnership deed may become invalid and so the partnership has to be set up again. It is possible to accommodate changes in a partnership deed, although this is a difficult task for which lawyers will spend much time (and money) on drafting the contract.
- There must be a huge amount of mutual trust within a partnership. Each partner is legally and financially answerable to all the other partners. A mistake made by one partner may harm the business and reduce the profits for all other partners.
- Many partnerships may still face difficulties in raising capital. It is probable that they will need to seek bank loans and other forms of borrowing.

Question 1.2.3

EXP: The Chinese Experience

EXP is a small Chinese restaurant with take-away service located in Brockley, London (UK). It was established in early 2006 by partners Keith and Tonina Hoang. They had been in business before, having set up another successful take-away **franchise**, The Wok Express, in nearby towns.

EXP is run as an **ordinary partnership** with Keith and Tonina each having 50% of the stake in the business. EXP relies heavily on local customers who have a choice from neighbouring competitors, such as pizza outlets and Indian restaurants. They have a workforce of 12 people, from chefs to delivery staff.

Their popularity has grown with a budding and loyal customer base. Keith and Tonina even had to decide to discontinue with the distribution of take-away menus in the local area as business was already steady and EXP was working at near capacity. Keith and Tonina thought it best to maintain the quality of their food and the punctuality of their home deliveries in order to maintain the image that they have established in the local area. This does not mean, of course, that they wouldn't like more customers if opportunities allowed!

- **a** Define the terms **franchise** and **ordinary partnership**. *[4 marks]*
- **b** Outline the advantages and disadvantages of running the restaurant as a partnership. *[6 marks]*
- **c** EXP is a small business. Explain the potential problems that this might create, compared to larger restaurants. *[4 marks]*
- **d** Examine the benefits to the owners of EXP of remaining small as a business. *[6 marks]*

Companies (Corporations)

Companies are essentially businesses that are owned by their shareholders. Shareholders are individuals or other businesses that have invested their money to provide capital for a company. Companies are sometimes called **joint-stock companies** because the shares (or 'stock' as they are sometimes known) of the business are jointly held by numerous people or institutions. In North America the more common term for 'company' is **corporation**.

Companies are **incorporated** businesses. This means that there is a legal difference between the owners of the company (the shareholders) and the business itself. The company, being treated as a separate entity, has its own legal rights and duties. For example, directors can sign legal contracts for and on behalf of the company, rather than use their own names. Another example would be that the company, rather than the owners, would take those who infringe copyright laws to court.

Since they are incorporated, companies benefit from having **limited liability**. Shareholders do not have to bear the responsibility of a company's debts and will not stand to lose personal belongings if the company goes into arrears. The maximum a shareholder can lose is the value of their investment in the business, and hence there is a limit to how much they can lose. This is to safeguard investors in the stock market – imagine an ordinary individual having to share the debts of a large multinational company that she or he had invested in!

Setting up a limited company can be very complicated and expensive. For example, there are rules and regulations that must be obeyed in order for shares to be sold on the stock exchange.

One reason for such legislation is to protect investors who buy shares in businesses that they do not run or control. A **board of directors** is elected by shareholders to run the company on their behalf. They are elected because of their skills and expertise and because shareholders do not necessarily want to get involved in the day-to-day running of the business. The directors are held responsible for the daily running of the business and held accountable to their shareholders. Each share held equals one vote, so obviously the more shares held by an investor the more voting power they have. In reality, individual shareholders tend to have very little say as it is the large institutional investors and directors who hold the majority of the shares.

The term '**limited companies**' is sometimes used to clarify the fact that all companies have limited liability. There are two types of limited companies – private limited companies and public limited companies.

A **Private Limited Company** is a company that cannot raise share capital from the general public. Instead, shares are sold to private family members and friends. The company will usually have the word 'Limited' or the letters 'Ltd.' after its name. However, this practice varies from one country to another, such as in Australia and Hong Kong where 'Ltd.' is also used by public limited companies. Shares in a private company cannot be traded without the prior agreement from the Board of Directors. One reason for this, unlike with public limited companies, is so that the Directors can maintain overall control of the business. For this reason, many private companies are run as family businesses. One advantage of a private company is that the owners have greater control of the business, as their shares cannot be traded on the open stock exchange. It is also usually cheaper to set up a private limited company than a public limited company. In the UK, for example, private limited companies can be set up by issuing just two £1 ($2) shares. However, private companies do not tend to be able to raise as much finance as public limited companies.

By contrast, a **Public Limited Company** is able to advertise and sell its shares to the general public via the stock exchange. It must carry the letters 'PLC' after its name. One disadvantage of allowing the general public to buy shares in the public company is that there is *dilution of control.* This means that by issuing more shares, the company has more owners (and voters), thereby weakening its ability to control the business. Moreover, public companies are exposed to *takeover bids* from other investors that seek to purchase a majority stake in the company (see Unit 1.7). Table 1.2a gives some well-known examples of private and public limited companies.

Table 1.2a Examples of private and public limited companies

Private Limited Companies	Public Limited Companies
Chanel – fashion and cosmetics (France)	China Mobile – mobile phone services (China)
Ernst & Young – accounting (USA)	Coca-Cola Company – soft drinks (USA)
IKEA – home furnishing (Sweden)	HSBC – banking (UK and Hong Kong)
Lego – toys (Denmark)	Michelin - tyre manufacturer (France)
Mars Limited – confectionery (USA)	Microsoft Corporation – computer software (USA)
PriceWaterhouseCoopers – accounting (USA)	Nike, Inc. – sportswear and sports equipment (USA)
Rolex - prestigious wristwatches (Switzerland)	Porsche – automobiles (Germany)
Tutor2u Limited – online education (UK)	Samsung – electronics (South Korea)
Virgin Group – global conglomerate (UK)	Vodafone – telecommunications (UK)

Exam Tip!
Students often use the words 'business' and 'company' interchangeably. Whilst this can be true, it is important to remember that companies are owned by shareholders and so there can only be two types of companies – private limited and public limited companies. 'Business' will cover other forms of ownership, such as sole traders and partnerships. In summary then, all companies are businesses but not all businesses are companies.

Two documents must be produced by both private and public limited companies and submitted to the appropriate authorities before they can commence trading:

- The **Memorandum of Association** includes the fundamental details of the company, such as its name, its main purpose, its registered address, and the original amount of share capital invested. This is a relatively brief document.
- The **Articles of Association**, the longer of the two documents, stipulates the internal regulations and procedures of the company. Details will include issues such as the rights, roles and power of the board of directors and shareholders. Administrative issues are also covered in this document, such as the conduct of the Annual General Meeting (AGM) and the procedures for the appointment of directors. There is also likely to be a section on how profits will be distributed.

Once the authorities are satisfied with the submitted documents and an application fee has been paid, a **Certificate of Incorporation** is issued to the firm. This licence recognizes the business as a separate legal unit from its owners and allows the business to start trading as a limited company.

Flotation occurs when a business first sells all or part of its business to external investors (shareholders). Floating a company allows it to be listed on a stock exchange and this helps to generate additional sources of finance. For example, the Industrial and Commercial Bank of China (ICBC) raised approximately $22 billion from its flotation, or **initial public offering** (IPO) in 2006, setting a new world record along the way.

There are three reasons why investors tend to buy shares in a limited company, although only the first two apply to most shareholders:

1. **Dividends.** Companies listed on a stock exchange usually pay dividends to their shareholders biannually. The dividends represent a share of the profits that are distributed to its owners. The declared dividend is paid on each share that a shareholder owns, so the more shares held the higher the total payment.
2. **Capital growth.** Stock brokers and investment bankers argue that over the medium to long term, shares outperform the return from savings in a bank account. Over time, the value (or market price) of shares may increase and the shareholder can then sell the shares at a higher price, thereby making a financial gain. This gain is known as *capital growth* or a *capital gain*. However, this is not true for all companies, and due to the volatility of stock markets, share prices can indeed fall sharply without warning.
3. **Voting power.** Shareholders who hold enough shares in a limited company can become a major influence in the management and operation of the company. This reason is generally held by people who are risk takers and possess high entrepreneurial spirit, such as the senior directors of a company.

The largest shareholders of companies tend to be institutional and commercial investors. This means companies have shares in other companies. For example, Cathay Pacific Airways is the largest stakeholder of Dragonair; Prudential (insurance company) is the majority stakeholder of Egg, the world's largest pure online bank; Renault owns a majority stake in Nissan; and Porsche own a significant percentage of shares in Volkswagen.

Nevertheless, shareholders often face potentially serious risks, despite their liability being limited. Companies that are not so successful will tend to distribute very little, if any, dividends. Their share prices are also likely to fall as a result, leading to negative capital growth. Shareholders also place their trust in the directors and management to run the business on their behalf, although the interest of managers and shareholders may conflict (see Unit 1.4). For example, managers and directors may push for better pay and conditions but this is likely to reduce the funds available to pay dividends to the company's shareholders. Although statistically low, there is also the chance that if the company fails and declares itself bankrupt, then shareholders will lose the money invested in the business.

All companies must hold an **Annual General Meeting** (AGM) to allow the owners to have a say (or vote) in the running of the business. There are three main processes at a typical AGM:

- Shareholders vote on *resolutions* (promises or declarations) and the re-election (or sometimes election) of the Board of Directors.
- Shareholders ask questions to the chief executive officer, directors and the chairperson about various aspects of the company.
- Shareholders approve the previous year's financial accounts.

Limited companies must produce an Annual Report and Final Accounts (see Unit 3.5). The annual report includes details such as the reporting of profits (or losses), the assets of the business and where cash has been spent during the last twelve months. These accounts are scrutinized by an external **auditor** (usually chartered accountants) before they are distributed to shareholders. This can prove to be a very expensive exercise, especially for larger companies. More recently, companies are placing their annual reports on their company websites.

Advantages of companies

- Companies can raise large amounts of capital by selling shares. Public limited companies can often raise vast sums of money for financing their investment projects. The money raised through selling shares becomes **permanent capital**, meaning that it does not have to be repaid, unlike loans. Shareholders can buy and sell shares on the second-hand market via the stock exchange; but the initial money raised from selling the shares remains with the company. Interest does not have to be paid; instead, shareholders are paid a **dividend** (but only if the company makes a profit).
- As companies have limited liability, it is easier for them to attract both private and commercial investors. The lower the risk to investors, the more likely they are to invest their money.
- Unlike sole proprietorships and partnerships, companies benefit from **continuity**. Since there is a legal difference between the business and its owners (a concept known as the **divorce of ownership and control**), should anything happen to one owner, the business does not need to cease trading but can continue as a separate entity from that owner.
- Directors of a company generally own a large amount of shares in the business. Although this may give them significant voting power, it also means they have an incentive to perform well in order to achieve capital growth (higher share prices) and dividends from the shares.
- Due to their larger scale business, companies can benefit from **economies of scale** (see Unit 1.7). For example, it is usually cheaper for a company to borrow money than it is for sole proprietorships or partnerships. This is because commercial lenders see limited companies as less of a financial risk; most banks would probably not hesitate to lend large multinational companies such as Nike and McDonald's money to finance their expansion plans.

Furthermore, if a competitive rate of interest was not offered, these companies may turn to a rival of the lender for financing.

- In addition, limited companies can hire specialist directors and managers to run the firm as there is no need for the owners to be directly involved in the daily running of the business. They are also more likely to employ specialist staff such as marketers, lawyers and accountants. This can increase the productivity of the overall business due to the advantages of division of labour and specialization (see Unit 1.1).

Disadvantages of companies

- Financial information must be provided to all shareholders. Only a summarized set of accounts is required, although this can still prove to be a time consuming and expensive exercise – auditors have to be paid and Annual Reports have to be published and distributed. Privacy no longer exists, in comparison to that enjoyed by sole traders and partners.
- There is far more bureaucracy involved in the setting up and running of a limited company, such as the need to produce a memorandum and articles of association. For example, in the Republic of Ireland, a minimum of €38,000 ($51,600) must be issued as share capital, with at least 25% being paid into the company account for business use. Lawyers must be hired to ensure that all documentation is legally accurate. Advertising and promotion of the company's share flotation also adds to the costs. Hosting the Annual General Meeting can be a huge and expensive task.
- For shareholders, dividends are only paid out if the business makes a profit. Even if profit is made, the Board of Directors may decide to retain a large proportion of the profits for financing investment projects; this then leaves less profit that can be distributed as dividends to shareholders.
- Quite often, very large organizations suffer from communication problems (see Unit 2.3). As the firm becomes larger, services and relationships may become more impersonal to both customers and employees.

Question 1.2.4

Mars Incorporated

Mars is a global manufacturer of confectionery operating in over 65 countries and with annual sales in excess of $18 billion. Perhaps more surprisingly, and unusual for a business of this size, Mars is entirely owned by the Mars family making it one of the largest family-owned businesses in the world.

It all started with Frank Mars back in 1911 when he and his wife Ethel started making and selling a variety of butter-cream candies in their home in Washington, USA. In 1920, Frank and his son Forrest produced the Milky Way bar – known in Europe and other parts of the world as the Mars bar. It was an immediate success. Today, the portfolio of Mars brands includes Snickers, M&M's and Twix. Having diversified into pet foods, its brands also include Pedigree, Whiskas, Cesar and Sheba. Mars brands are recognized, used and trusted on every continent and in almost every country.

Source: adapted from Mars website (www.mars.com)

a Define the meaning of 'private limited company' in the context of the case study. *[2 marks]*

b Discuss the costs and benefits to the Mars family of keeping their business as a private limited company rather than as a public limited company. *[8 marks]*

NON-PROFIT AND NON-GOVERNMENTAL ORGANIZATIONS

Non-profit organizations (NPOs)

A **non-profit organization**, also known as a **not-for-profit organization**, is an establishment that is run in a professional and business-like manner but without profit being the major objective. Instead, such organizations aim to provide a service (such as leisure and tourism) or to promote special causes. Examples include public libraries, state schools, museums, government hospitals and social services.

The term 'non-profit organization' does not mean that the firm doesn't make a surplus. Profit is the reward that is distributed to its owners or investors in return for risking their money and resources in the business. By contrast, NPOs return this 'profit' (or surplus) back into the business for the benefits of its members. For example, many private fee paying schools are NPOs because any surplus that they make is reinvested into the schools to enhance their facilities.

Non-governmental organizations (NGOs)

As the name suggests, a **non-governmental organization** (NGO) operates in the **private sector,** i.e. it is not owned or controlled by the government. However, NGOs differ from other private sector businesses, such as sole traders and limited companies, in that they are a type of *not-for-profit organization* so do not aim primarily to make a profit. Instead, such organizations are set up and run for the benefit of others in society, although they are typically independent of the government. Hence, NGOs are also known as **Private Voluntary Organizations** (PVOs). Examples include Friends of the Earth (environmental protection), Amnesty International (human rights) and Unicef (children's welfare).

There are two types of NGOs. **Operational NGOs** are established from a given objective or purpose. These organizations, such as Oxfam and Unicef, tend to be involved in relief-based and community projects. **Advocacy NGOs**, such as Greenpeace and Amnesty International, take a more aggressive approach to promote or defend a cause. They strive to raise awareness through direct action, such as lobbying, public relations and mass demonstrations. The greatest strength of NGOs is that they are run and supported by highly committed people.

QUANGOs (Quasi-autonomous non-governmental organizations) are semi-NGOs. They are funded by the government but are run by people independent of the government, i.e. they are semi-independent organizations that support certain interests of the national government. Examples might include National Tourist Boards and Environmental Agencies. *Lay people* (those who work on an ad hoc basis and may not be paid) are appointed by Quangos for their specific expertise in managing particular government initiatives.

Charities

A charity is a type of registered *non-profit organization* with the key function of collecting donations from individuals and organizations in order to support a cause that is beneficial to society. Since they do not 'sell' anything to customers, charities must use refined marketing strategies to catch the attention of donors. Such strategies might include the use of celebrity endorsements, holding special charity events or promoting their cause in a wide range of media. A more recent strategy has been to develop online donations via the websites of charities.

Some charities are very large organizations, such as Oxfam and World Wildlife Fund. They are run by a group of managers and trustees, similar to a limited company's board of directors. Depending on the organization itself, some managers and employees of charities will be paid for their services, whilst others operate on a voluntary basis. The USA has the largest number of registered charities, standing at well over one million organizations.

One important point to note is that although charities are not profit-seeking organizations, this does not mean that they do not strive to make a surplus. The surplus is not classed as 'profit' because it does not get distributed to the workers or owners of the organization.

Advantages of charities

- They provide financial support for the welfare of society, whether domestically (such as Age Concern) or internationally (such as Friends of the Earth). Many charities help to raise funds for medical research, such as cancer research, and other worthy causes including the protection of children and the prevention of cruelty to animals.
- As non-profit organizations, charities are usually exempt from paying income tax or corporation tax.
- Donors, be they private individuals or organizations may get income tax allowances on the funds that have been donated to charity. This can raise the incentive for donors to give money to charities.
- Charities can also register to be limited companies so as to protect the interest of employees and management who have limited liability.

Disadvantages of charities

- The lack of a profit motive may cause major problems, such as staff demotivation. Most volunteers cannot continue to offer their services for extended periods of time. Even salaried workers are likely to be paid far less than what they could earn in other occupations.
- Trustees, who are at the top of the charity's organization chart, are not allowed to receive any financial benefits. Again, this may cause motivational problems.
- Charities must go through the process of being registered before they can commence their activities. In Australia, for example, charities are registered with the Taxation Office (www.ato.gov.au/nonprofit). UK charities must register with the Charity Commission (www.charity-commission.gov.uk). These governing bodies also place restrictions on what charities can and cannot do.
- Financial activities and records must be recorded and reported to a governing body set up by the government. This is to protect the interest of donors and to prevent misuse of charitable donations (known as **charity fraud**).
- Limited liability charities protect the owners and workers. However, this also means that those who run the charity are not held liable for any debts of the organization. This may lead to inefficiencies or a degree of charity fraud.
- Charities survive solely on one source of finance – donations. With the huge number of competitors and limited finance from donors, charities have to constantly compete for donations. Since there is a positive, albeit weak, correlation between the levels of income and donations, charities tend to be the first to lose out when there is a recession (when national income falls) in the economy.

Pressure groups

Pressure groups are non-profit organizations established by their members to address a special interest of the group. They may, for example, campaign against environmental neglect, smoking in public areas or testing substances on animals. Examples include trade unions, animal rights activist groups and environmental protection groups.

Pressure groups aim to win public and media support from their actions. They also try to influence government legislation, such as the introduction of national minimum wage laws to support low income earners. One advantage of pressure groups, from society's point of view, is that they force businesses and the government to take account of the true costs of business activity (such as pollution and environmental damage). Pressure groups are covered in more detail in Unit 1.4.

HIGHER LEVEL EXTENSION: RELATIONSHIP BETWEEN ORGANIZATIONS IN THE PRIVATE AND PUBLIC SECTORS

Traditionally, the public sector tends to provide services to the general public rather than selling products for a profit. Governments can choose from three options in the provision of essential services:

- Supply the services themselves, e.g. emergency services and the legal system
- Allow private firms to tender (bid) to provide these services, e.g. refuse collection and street cleaning
- Form a public–private sector partnership to supply these services

There are clearly some goods that should be provided only by the private sector. These **private goods** (such as mobile phones, cars, cinemas and hair salons) are *excludable*, i.e. those who cannot afford to pay simply go without. Therefore, most goods and services are private goods. However, there are certain goods and services that may be under-provided if there is no government intervention. Political interference will take place in order to provide two kinds of products that are unlikely to be sufficiently provided by the private sector: public goods and merit goods. The funding for the provision of public goods and merit goods comes from central government taxation.

Public goods are products that are enjoyed by the general public but are unlikely to be provided without government intervention. Box 1.2c shows the key characteristics of public goods. Examples of public goods include National Defence, public roads, lighthouses and street lighting. Public goods are not necessarily produced in the public sector, but are funded by the government to benefit its people.

Box 1.2c The three key characteristics of public goods

Non-rivalry – The consumption of a public good by one person does not reduce the benefits available to other individuals. This contrasts with a private good where the purchase and use of a product diminishes the amount that is available for others.

Non-excludability – People cannot be excluded from the benefits of consumption, even if they do not pay. This feature means that private sector firms are unlikely to want to supply such products. By contrast, a person who cannot pay for a private good is simply denied the benefits of its consumption.

Non-rejectable – Households can choose to reject the consumption of private goods simply by not purchasing them. By contrast, once provided, people cannot simply reject the provision of public goods since they are provided for everyone.

Merit goods are products that yield higher *social benefits* of consumption than *private benefits* to an individual. They are therefore the goods and services that people feel should be provided in greater quantities. Examples include education, training, public libraries and health care. Private firms (such as private fee-paying schools or hospitals) can provide these goods and services, but not enough consumers will use these (due to a lack of ability to pay) unless there is government support to provide merit goods to everyone in society. Hence, both private and public sector organizations provide merit goods. Rather than being direct rivals however, their services are complementary to the benefit of society as a whole.

HIGHER LEVEL

HIGHER LEVEL EXTENSION: PUBLIC–PRIVATE ENTERPRISES

Public–private enterprises take place when governments create partnerships with the private sector in the provision of certain services. Hence, they are sometimes referred to as **public–private partnerships** (PPP). The Japanese refer to such businesses as operating in the Daisan sector (or the third sector), since they refer to hybrid organizations of both the private and public sector. In some countries, for example, the private sector has taken over the running of public sector hospitals and schools, without the services being actually privatized.

It is argued that a public–private sector partnership can benefit from the dynamics and efficiency of the private sector alongside the benefits of public sector funding and support. Private sector firms are hired for their expertise for projects that are funded by both private investors and the government. Examples of such projects include the Sydney Harbour Tunnel, London's Olympic Stadium, New York's Central Park, the World Health Organization (WHO) and Hong Kong Disneyland (see Question 1.2.5).

Question 1.2.5

Hong Kong Disneyland

Hong Kong Disneyland (HKDL) is a theme park with two on-site hotels owned jointly by the Hong Kong government (the majority shareholder) and the Walt Disney Company. The project was announced in November 1999 with media reports suggesting that up to 36,000 jobs would be created. The Park finally opened on 12th September 2005. The government estimated that the first phase of the theme park would generate HK$148 billion ($19 billion) in net benefits to the economy over a 40-year period.

a Examine two benefits of the HKDL public–private enterprise to Hong Kong. *[6 marks]*

b To what extent should a government use tax revenues to fund public–private enterprises? *[8 marks]*

TYPES OF ORGANIZATION AND BUSINESS STRATEGY

There are various factors that affect the choice of business organization. These factors include:

- **Amount of finance**. Sole traders need less capital than a public limited company to set up. A change in the legal status of a firm will usually require more finance.
- **Size**. The larger the business operation, the more likely it is to be a limited company rather than a sole trader or partnership. Sole traders, for instance, find it unnecessary or unaffordable to hire lots of workers.
- **Limited liability**. The desire to have limited liability, in order to protect the personal possessions of the owners, may also affect the choice of legal status of a business.
- **Degree of ownership of control**. Owners who wish to retain control and ownership of a business may prefer to stay as a sole trader, a partnership or as a private limited company.
- **Type of business activity**. The nature and scale of business activity can also influence the legal status of a firm. Mass market manufacturers, such as personal computers or motor vehicles, are likely to rely heavily on external sources of finance and hence they are likely to be formed as public limited companies.

Whatever their legal structure, most new businesses fail. It is important then for managers to learn from the mistakes of others. For example, evidence shows that one of the main causes of business failure is poor cash-flow management. Hence, entrepreneurs must ensure that they have plans for surviving during periods of negative cash flow (see Unit 3.3). By looking into the causes of business failure, managers can try to devise strategies to avoid or deal with any contingencies. Nevertheless, external factors (those beyond the control of the entrepreneur) will mean that even the best of business plans can fail to become a profitable venture. For instance, thorough market research may suggest that a business is feasible, but sudden changes in market conditions (such as a recession or change in fashion) can harm the business. Despite this, careful planning can help to maximize the chances of success.

REVIEW QUESTIONS 1.2

1 Outline the reasons why people set up their own business. (*Hint*: think of the mnemonic GET CASH.)

2 Why is the concept of 'limited liability' important for investors?

3 Compare and contrast the benefits of running a business as a partnership with those of a sole trader.

4 What is the difference between a 'public corporation' and a 'public (limited) company'?

5 What are 'non-profit organizations' and 'non-governmental organizations'?

Higher Level extension

6 Differentiate between 'public goods' and 'merit goods'.

7 What is a 'public–private enterprise'?

8 What is the 'Daisan' sector?

9 Outline the benefits of public–private enterprises and partnerships to society.

Articles of Association is the name given to the document that sets out the internal organization and rules of a limited company. Details may include the powers of each director and voting rules. It is one of the compulsory documents needed to set up a company.

Certificate of Incorporation is the name of the document issued to a limited company to show that it has been legally formed and is therefore a separate legal entity from its owners (who have limited liability). Possession of this certificate then allows the company to start trading.

Charities are not-for-profit organizations that are established to support good causes, from society's point of view. Examples include the prevention of cruelty to animals, the preservation of the natural environment or providing assistance to the elderly.

Company refers to a business that is owned by shareholders. It has been issued a certificate of incorporation, giving it a separate legal identity from its owners.

Deed of Partnership is the legal contract signed by the owners of a partnership. The formal document will include the fundamental issues of the business, such as the name and responsibilities of each partner and their share of any profits or losses.

Incorporation means that there is a legal difference between the owners of a company and the business itself. This ensures that the owners are safeguarded against any losses made by the company as the owners are protected by limited liability.

Limited liability is a restriction on the amount of money that can be lost from the owners of a business if it goes into bankruptcy. The owners will lose no more than the amount of capital that they put into the business.

Memorandum of Association is the name of one of the legal documents required to create an incorporated company. The Memorandum will include the basic information of the organization such as: the name and address of the company, its objectives and details of its share capital.

Non-governmental organization (NGO) refers to any private sector organization that does not primarily aim to make a profit. Instead, they operate for the benefit of others in society. Examples include World Wildlife Fund and Friends of the Earth.

Partnerships are a form of private sector business owned by 2–20 people (known as partners). They share the responsibilities and burdens of running and owning the business.

Private Limited Company is a business organization owned by shareholders with limited liability but whose shares cannot be bought by or sold to the general public.

Public Limited Company is an incorporated business organisation that allows the general public to buy and sell shares in the company via a stock exchange.

Stock exchange is the market place for trading stocks and shares of public limited companies. Examples include the London Stock Exchange (LSE) and the New York Stock Exchange (NYSE).

Silent partner, or **sleeping partner**, refers to an investor of a partnership who is not directly involved in the daily running of the business.

Sole trader refers to a self-employed person. He or she runs the business on their own and has sole responsibility for its success (profits) or failure (unlimited liability).

Unlimited liability is a feature of sole traders and ordinary partners who are legally liable for all monies owed to their creditors, even if this means that they have to sell their personal possessions to pay for this.

Value added is the difference between a product's price and the total cost of the inputs that went into making it. It is the extra worth created in the production process.

Organizational Objectives

UNIT 1.3

To accomplish great things, we must not only act, but also dream, not only plan, but also believe.

Anatole France (1844–1924), Nobel Prize for Literature

Key topics

- The importance of organizational objectives
- Mission and vision statements
- Organizational aims, strategic objectives and tactical objectives
- Ethical objectives
- Corporate social responsibility (CSR)
- Social and environmental audits

Higher Level extension

- Changes in corporate objectives and strategy over time
- Changes in society's expectations of business behaviour

INTRODUCTION

Decision-making is the core role of management. In going through the decision-making process, businesses ask themselves four key questions:

1 Where are we now?
2 Where do we want to be?
3 How do we get there?
4 How do we know we are there?

This Unit focuses on the second question, i.e. the aims and objectives of business organizations. Organizational objectives serve to guide a business and give it a sense of direction, rather like a road map helps to direct a driver. Organizational objectives have three key functions:

- *To control* – Objectives can help to control a firm's plans (such as a department setting consistent targets with the rest of the organization), i.e. they set the boundaries for business activity.
- *To motivate* – Objectives can help to inspire managers and employees to reach a common goal.
- *To direct* – Objectives provide an agreed and clear focus (or sense of direction) for all individuals and departments of an organization.

In reality, an organization's objectives will be formed by the various stakeholders of a business (see Unit 1.4). If the organization is a sole trader, then the owner will set the objectives. If the business is a large public company, then other stakeholder groups (such as the directors, employees or the shareholders) will have some influence regarding the setting of the organization's objectives. In addition, public sector and private sector businesses (see Unit 1.2) are likely to have rather different objectives.

THE IMPORTANCE OF OBJECTIVES

Target setting is vital in all businesses. Without having clear aims and objectives, organizations have no sense of direction or purpose. It is rather like getting into a car and not knowing where you are driving to! Organizational aims and objectives are set for several crucial reasons:

- They serve to give businesses a sense of direction, purpose and unity. This can help to unify and motivate management and workers.
- They form the foundation for business decision-making. Organizations can then create strategies to achieve these goals.
- They can help to encourage *strategic thinking*, i.e. planning for the long term.
- They provide the basis for measuring and controlling the performance of the workforce, the management and the business as a whole.

There are many groups that are interested in and affected by, financially or otherwise, the performance and activities of a business. These **stakeholder groups** may have different objectives and expectations of the business. For example, shareholders are interested in the profitability of businesses whereas the local community may be more concerned with the social responsibilities of businesses.

Business objectives can be set at different levels:

- *Corporate objectives* deal with the whole organization's goals, such as business survival, growth or profit maximization.
- *Departmental objectives* are specific objectives for the various sections of a business. Departmental targets need to be consistent with the overall corporate objectives.
- *Individual objectives* are targets that are set for and/or by individual employees. They are often used as part of a *performance appraisal* (see Unit 2.1) where the productivity of a worker is measured by the extent to which his/her individual targets have been met.

MISSION STATEMENTS AND VISION STATEMENTS

Having **vision** means to have an image of an ideal situation in the future. A **vision statement** therefore outlines a business's aspirations (where it wants to be) in the distant future. For example, "To be the leading sports brand in the world" is the vision of Adidas, the German sportswear and sports equipment giant. Vision statements also tend to relate to the attainment of success, i.e. visualization of what success would look like. Martin Luther King Junior's famous "I have a dream" speech shows how having a clear vision can bring about dramatic change.

Having a **mission** means to have a clear purpose. It explains in general terms what the business is trying to achieve and outlines the organization's values. A **mission statement** tends to be a simple declaration that broadly states the underlying purpose of an organization's existence. For example, a school may set its mission as 'provision of achievement for all students'. Hence, a mission statement outlines how a vision statement will be achieved. A company's mission statement is usually found in its annual report and its home page on the internet. Unlike business objectives, the mission statement does not have a distinct time frame and tends to be qualitative rather than quantitative statements. A well-produced mission statement is clearly defined and realistically achievable. In addition, the mission statement should serve to unify all people and corporate cultures within the workforce in their attempt to achieve the organization's vision. Managers need to ensure that decisions are consistent with the organization's mission statement.

Although vision and mission statements are quite often confused, they do serve complementary purposes. There are, however, several important differences:

- Vision statements are focused on the very long term, whereas mission statements can focus on the medium or long term.
- Subsequently, mission statements are updated more frequently than vision statements.
- Vision statements do not have to have actual targets that must be realized (this is the purpose of setting mission statements). Instead, vision statements allow people to see what *could* be.
- The mission statement tends to outline or highlight the values of the business, i.e. its beliefs and guiding principles. This sets the tone for how managers and employees behave on a day-to-day basis.

Despite the advantages and purposes of having a vision and mission statement, there are a few limitations. Critics argue that vision and mission statements are no more than a public relations stunt. After all, the ultimate purpose of most business, they argue, is to maximize profits. In addition, devising vision and mission statements can be very time consuming; it is very difficult to draft a statement that caters for all the dynamics of a business. Finally, even the best thought out statements may not be supported by all the employees, especially if there are staff on part-time or temporary contracts. If this is the case, it can be a lengthy process in converting people's beliefs and behaviour.

Question 1.3.1

Vision and mission statements

"To be the most successful premium manufacturer in the industry" – BMW

"The company exists to benefit and refresh everyone it touches" – Coca-Cola

"To organize the world's information and make it universally accessible and useful" – Google

"We work to help people and businesses throughout the world realize their full potential" – Microsoft Corporation

"Connecting people has always been, and continues to be, our reason for business" – Nokia

"We believe in making a difference: value for money, quality, innovation, fun and a sense of competitive challenge" – Virgin Group

Source: company websites

a What is a **mission statement**? *[2 marks]*

b Using the above examples, analyse the role of vision and mission statements in a business organization. *[6 marks]*

AIMS AND OBJECTIVES

Aims are the general long-term goals of an organization. They are broadly expressed as vague and unquantifiable statements, such as 'to provide high quality education to the local community' or 'to promote social and environmental integrity'. Aims serve to give a purpose to the general direction of an organization and are often expressed in a *mission statement* (see 'Mission statements and vision statements' on page 43). Long-term aims are usually set by senior directors (or equivalent) of a business.

Objectives are the short term and more specific goals of an organization, based on its aims. They are more likely to be quantifiable or measurable. For example, a school may set the objective 'to achieve a 95% pass rate at IB examination level' or 'to encourage the use of ICT facilities in the classroom to enhance teaching and learning'. Setting objectives (which must be consistent with the firm's mission statement) may be delegated to senior or middle management.

Exam Tip!
Students often misuse the terms 'aims' and 'objectives' opting to use the words interchangeably. This reveals a lack of understanding and application of these concepts. Remember, the main difference between aims and objectives is the time scale; with a longer time frame for corporate aims. Another difference between the two concepts is that objectives tend to be more specific whereas aims may be quite vague.

SHORT-TERM VERSUS LONG-TERM OBJECTIVES

Strategy is the term used to refer to any plan or scheme to achieve the long-term aims of a business. Strategy is used for trying to achieve *strategic objectives*. **Tactics** are short-term ways that firms can use to achieve their aims and objectives, i.e. they are used to achieve an organization's *tactical objectives* (see next subsection). Both strategy and tactics serve matching purposes, i.e. they deal with the third question in the decision-making process (*how* do we get to where we want to be?).

Once a business has decided on its short- and long-term objectives, it will then decide on the most suitable methods to use in order to achieve these objectives. There are several levels of strategy that a business can adopt:

- *Operational strategies* are the day-to-day methods used to improve the efficiency of an organization. These are aimed at trying to achieve the tactical objectives of a business. For example, a restaurant may investigate how to reduce customer waiting time without compromising the quality of its service.
- *Generic strategies* are those that affect the business as a whole. Michael Porter's generic strategies (see Unit 1.7) looks at ways in which a business can gain a competitive advantage in order to meet its short-term or medium-term goals.
- *Corporate strategies* are aimed at the long-term objectives of a business, i.e. they are used to achieve the strategic objectives of an organization. For example, a firm may aim for market dominance, which might be achieved through a programme of mergers and takeovers of rivals in the industry.

TACTICAL (OPERATIONAL) OBJECTIVES

Tactical objectives (also known as **operational objectives** or **secondary objectives**), are short-term objectives that affect a segment of the organization, such as a department. They refer to specific goals that guide the daily functioning of certain operations that are in line with the primary objectives of the business. Departments will tend to set their own short-term departmental objectives, such as the sales department planning to raise sales by $20,000 within the next year or the personnel department planning to keep staff turnover below 10%. Short-term objectives tend to refer to targets set for the next 6–12 months.

A tactical objective for many businesses is **survival** (although this could be interpreted as a strategic goal by other businesses). New and unestablished businesses are likely to encounter a number of problems (see Unit 1.2) such as limited recognition by customers and/or intense competition from existing firms. Hence survival becomes a key priority. Survival can also be important for more established organizations. For example, an economic *recession* (see Unit 1.5) is likely to make trading very difficult as both consumer spending and confidence levels will be low. This can quite easily threaten the survival of a business, especially if the recession is prolonged. Another potential threat to business survival is a sudden takeover bid from a rival company. If the business becomes the target of a takeover (see Unit 1.7), then the survival of the firm, as it currently exists, could easily become the number one objective of the business.

A second tactical objective might be **sales revenue maximization**. New businesses will strive to maximize their sales in order to establish themselves in the marketplace. Sales people and agents, such as those selling insurance or property, will favour this objective since their earnings are linked to the level of sales. However, sales revenue is not profit (the latter is the money remaining after all costs of production have been paid). In the long run, a business that has high sales but little or no profit will struggle to survive.

STRATEGIC OBJECTIVES

Strategic objectives, or **primary objectives**, refer to the longer term aims of a business organization, e.g. targets for the next few years. Typical strategic objectives are outlined below (but note that these may vary from one business to another, based on their own financial circumstances and priorities).

Profit maximization

Traditionally, the number one strategic objective of most private sector businesses is to maximize profits. In its simplest form, profit is the positive difference between a firm's *total revenues* and its *total costs* (see Unit 5.2). Hence, profits are maximized when the positive difference between revenues (the money from sales) and costs of production is at its highest level.

Profit acts as the incentive for entrepreneurs to take risks in setting up and running a business. For limited companies, a proportion of the profits (known as the **dividends**) is distributed to its shareholders. Without profit, the owners and investors of a business will find it difficult to justify its existence.

Some businesses may have short-term profit maximization goals, such as a private tuition college or a beach resort hotel, because there are peak periods and quiet periods in the year. This means that such firms will strive to maximize their profits during busy periods in order to survive during the off-peak periods. Other firms will plan to achieve profit maximization over the longer term by developing corporate strategies to achieve the organization's aims. A share of the profits will be ploughed back into the business for financing its expansion plans, such as new product development (see Unit 4.3). Long-term goals of profit maximization tend to have greater benefits for the owners, employees, suppliers and customers.

In reality it is very difficult and time consuming to determine the exact level of output that will maximize profits. Even if it were possible, firms may choose not to produce or operate at this level, simply because it would put a huge strain on the firm's resources. Owners of the business may be content with the current level of profits and to increase this further may require them to work longer hours, employ more staff and take on greater financial risks.

Growth

Many businesses plan for growth as a key strategic objective. Growth is usually measured by an increase in *sales* (total revenues earned from business activity) or by *market share* (the percentage of the industry's sales made by the business). It has become increasingly accepted that growth is essential for business survival. With the exposure of businesses to mergers and takeovers (see Unit 1.7) a failure to grow may result in a loss in competitiveness. The benefits of growth include:

- **Economies of scale.** Larger firms are able to enjoy lower average costs of production, such as being able to borrow money from banks at a lower cost. Having lower unit costs helps a firm to improve its price competitiveness.
- **Market power**. By being larger, the business is able to enjoy more monopoly power such as being able to charge higher prices.
- **Reduced risks.** Growth through diversification can help to reduce the risks of doing business. Diversification means that the business caters for different markets, so if one product or market is unsuccessful the firm has a range of others to turn to.

Image and reputation

Businesses may aim to enhance their image and reputation. A bad image, perhaps portrayed by the media, can turn customers against a firm's products and services. Box 4.2d shows some examples of famous blunders that have hindered the image of certain businesses. Increasingly, businesses are delivering better levels of customer service, such as better on-site facilities, after-sales care and trained customer relations staff.

The presence of rivals in a market means that in order to remain competitive, a business needs to increasingly consider the needs of their customers. In addition, employees are likely to be motivated and proud of their business if it has a positive corporate image and reputation. This can also help to attract high calibre staff to apply for jobs in the business. Finally, suppliers prefer to do business with firms that are reputable and reliable.

Market standing

Market standing is interlinked with the corporate image and reputation of a business. **Market standing** refers to the extent to which a firm has presence in the marketplace. To have high market standing, people need to feel that the business offers something extra special. For example, Microsoft has high market standing for being number one in the computer software industry, with its innovative products. Wal-Mart, the biggest employer in the USA, has high market standing for being the world's largest retailer. With improved products and higher demand for their products, Japanese motor manufacturers have enjoyed increasing market standing in Europe and the USA. Toyota recently enjoyed higher market standing by taking over General Motors as the world's largest car producer. Apple has high market standing due to its innovate products and designs. The Body Shop has high market standing for being a forerunner as a socially responsible business.

Exam Tip!

Students should ensure that they understand the link between aims, objectives and corporate strategy:

- Aims state what an organization wants, e.g. to become the number one supplier of a product.
- Objectives state what an organization needs to achieve in order to get what they want, e.g. increased market share.
- Strategies are the actions that facilitate an organization to meet its objectives, e.g. expanding into overseas markets.

In practice, businesses will have a combination of the aforementioned strategic objectives. Furthermore, objectives will change from time to time, such as survival being a key objective when a firm is threatened by a takeover bid or during an economic slump. Whether a business operates in the private or public sector also affects the combination of objectives it sets.

Question 1.3.2

Lenovo

Lenovo, the Chinese multinational technology firm, bought out the personal computers division of IBM in 2005. The aim was to establish itself outside of the Asian market by owning IBM's globally recognized brands such as ThinkPad laptops. The company is committed to four key values:

- Customer service
- Innovative and entrepreneurial spirit
- Accuracy and truth-seeking
- Trustworthiness and integrity.

Recently, Lenovo has also tried to increase its market dominance by sponsoring key sporting events. Examples include its sponsorship deals with the Williams Formula One (Grand Prix) racing team and the National Basketball Association (NBA) signed in 2007, and being a key official sponsor of the 2008 Beijing Olympic Games.

Source: www.lenovo.com

a Explain why is it important for Lenovo to specify its organizational objectives. *[4 marks]*

b Examine the reasons why Lenovo might not be able to meet its objectives. *[6 marks]*

ETHICAL OBJECTIVES

Ethics are the moral principles that guide decision-making and strategy. **Morals** are concerned with what is considered to be right or wrong, from society's point of view. Business ethics are therefore the actions of people and organizations that are considered to be morally correct. An ethical business is likely to be responsible for its treatment towards its workers, customers, shareholders and the natural environment. Socially responsible actions, such as treating and paying employees fairly, would be considered as being ethical. Other examples of ethical objectives might include:

- Reducing pollution by using more environmentally friendly production processes
- Increased recycling of waste materials
- Disposal of waste in an environmentally friendly manner
- Offering staff sufficient rest breaks during their work shift
- Fairer conditions of trade with less economically developed countries.

Pressures to act ethically may come from within the business. Employees, for instance, may push their employer to introduce better opportunities for training, development and promotion. Ethics may be also be imposed upon a business by external factors and organizations. Customers, for instance, do not want to be associated with any business that earns profit through illegal, immoral or irresponsible actions. McDonald's Corporation, faced with the negative messages presented by best-sellers such as *Fast Food Nation* and movies such as *Super Size Me*, responded to public demand for improved options at the fast-food chain. Since 2003, McDonald's have broadened its range of products to include salads and other healthier alternatives.

Examples of unethical business behaviour include:

- **Financial dishonesty.** This means that a business mismanages its finances, such as deliberate misrepresentation of its financial accounts (which is illegal). There may also be moral issues, such as extravagant business expenses reimbursed to the directors of a company.
- **Environmental neglect.** Business activity is often associated with harmful consequences on the natural environment, such as pollution and depletion of non-renewable resources.
- **Exploitation of the workforce.** Employers may mistreat staff, such as through deliberate neglect of employee welfare issues. For example, in 2006, Indian Airlines was heavily criticized for grounding female flight attendants for being 'too fat' to travel. They were told to lose weight or risk losing their jobs. On a larger scale, many multinationals have been criticized for the poor pay and working conditions offered to staff in less economically developed countries.
- **Exploitation of suppliers.** Large businesses are able to take advantage of suppliers, forcing them to cut prices. This is a controversial issue especially when prices are not necessarily passed on to consumers or when the business exploits suppliers in developing countries.
- **Exploitation of consumers.** Firms may knowingly sell products that harm the welfare of people or society, such as tobacco, alcohol, gambling services and petrol. Large firms with few if any competitors may charge excessive prices. These examples are considered by most people to be controversial if not unethical.

In order to achieve their ethical objectives, an increasing number of businesses have adopted an **ethical code of practice** and publish this as part of their mission statement or in their annual report. The code refers to the documented beliefs and philosophies of a business. For example, the document is likely to include guidelines and expectations on employee behaviour, such as having personal integrity and consideration for others.

Box 1.3a A moral dilemma

A student sees a teacher drop her wallet in the corridor, but the teacher doesn't realize she's done so. There are no other people around. What should the student do?

The answer will depend upon the values or moral principles that the student feels are important. In turn, these could be determined by a number of factors, such as:

- Integrity – how honest the student is
- Sympathy – whether there are any feelings for the teacher losing her wallet
- Empathy – if the student has ever lost his/her own valuables and understands how the teacher feels
- Loyalty – whether the student knows the teacher – could be the student's form tutor or someone who they admire
- Unease – whether the student has any concerns or feelings of guilt
- Justice – whether the student thinks the teacher is rather careless and should learn the hard way!

Advantages of ethical behaviour

Businesses that adopt an ethical stance can gain from numerous advantages, which include:

- **Improved corporate image.** Acting in an ethical way, such as treating employees fairly or by being environmentally friendly, can help to enhance the image and reputation of a business. McDonald's, for example, claim to be the world's first company to voluntarily phase out the use of chlorofluorocarbons (CFCs) in the production of foam packaging back in 1991, thereby helping to reduce the harmful effects on the ozone layer. This move may therefore give McDonald's a better corporate image amongst the general public. Perhaps more importantly, the media will report on unethical business behaviour and this could seriously damage the image and reputation of an organization.
- **Increased customer loyalty.** Customers are more likely to be loyal to a business that does not act immorally. The Body Shop, for example, has built its large multinational customer base on its ethical policy of not testing any of its products on animals.
- **Cost cutting.** It may be possible to reduce certain costs of production through ethical behaviour. For example, by being more conscious of the environment, many businesses are reducing the amount of (excess) packaging used for their products. Recycling of waste materials is another possible source of cost savings. In addition, businesses may benefit from *lower litigation costs* (costs associated with legal action taken against a business). Firms that are unethical and socially responsible may be taken to court for their actions.
- **Improved staff motivation.** Ethical and moral behaviour can be a driving force for improved employee motivation, productivity and loyalty. People are more likely to be proud of the business they work for if it acts ethically (or if it does not act unethically or illegally). Furthermore, *labour turnover* will probably be lower (i.e. people are less likely to leave a firm) if the firm is socially responsible, such as being fair in the treatment of its workers.
- **Improved staff morale.** A firm with an ethical stance is more likely to be able to recruit and retain high quality staff who are actually motivated to work for such a business.

There are many ways in which a business may try to meet its social responsibilities:

- **Providing accurate information and labelling.** This can help consumers to make better informed decisions. For example, food manufacturers might provide truthful nutritional information.
- **Active community work.** This includes voluntary and charity work, helping to give something back to society. Sponsoring and participating in local community events are further examples.
- **Having consideration for the environment.** Firms may, for example, seek to use more recycled materials in the production process, recycle a greater proportion of their waste materials and aim to reduce any pollution caused by their activities.
- **Adhering to fair employment practices.** Firms can fulfil their social responsibility to their workforce by providing decent working conditions and training opportunities. Conversely, some multinational firms have been criticized for ignoring their social responsibilities when hiring under-aged workers, i.e. the exploitation of child labour.

An ethical code of practice is important because people need to know what is considered acceptable or not acceptable within an organization. These values may differ from one individual to another and from one business to another. Hence, a code of ethics can provide a framework for consistency and uniformity.

Limitations of ethical behaviour

However, there are potential drawbacks and problems for a business adopting an ethical approach. These disadvantages may include:

- **Compliance costs.** This refers to the potentially high costs of acting ethically. For example, organic agricultural products are far more expensive to harvest than genetically modified crops because of the additional time and money needed to produce organic food. Using recycled materials can actually be more costly than simply replacing them.
- **Lower profits.** If the compliance costs cannot be passed onto the consumer in the form of higher prices, then it is likely that profitability will fall. An **ethical dilemma** for a business exists when ethical decision-making involves adopting a less profitable course of action.
- **Stakeholder conflict.** It is not necessarily the case that all stakeholders are keen on the business adopting an ethical approach, especially if this conflicts with other organizational objectives such as profit maximization. Speculative shareholders and financial investors, for instance, are more likely to be concerned with the short-term profits of a firm rather than its long-term ethical stance. Hence, managers may be pressured into pursuing goals other than ethical ones.

Ethical behaviour is, however, rather subjective. Views about what is considered right or wrong will depend on the beliefs and principles held by individuals (see Box 1.3a on page 49). For example, some firms do not mind that their staff spend time checking their personal emails. Others frown upon such practice as the worker is using the employer's time and resources for their individual benefit. Legislation can help to provide some guidelines about what is socially accepted. For example, the use of direct marketing techniques aimed at children is banned in many countries. Health and Safety at Work legislation (such as the provision of regular rest breaks and a safe working environment) helps to prevent exploitation of employees in the workplace. Anti-discrimination laws also prohibit various forms of prejudice in the workplace, such as a person's race, gender, religion or age.

Question 1.3.3

McDonald's versus Burger King

Ronald McDonald House Charities (RMHC) is a non-profit organization, created by McDonald's. The mission of the charitable organization is to "directly improve the health and well-being of children". Operating in around 50 countries, RMHC has raised more than $430 million around the world to help seriously ill children and their families.

Source: www.rmhc.org

Burger King, the world's second largest fast-food chain and the largest rival of McDonald's, announced it would use supplies of humanely sourced meat and eggs from 2007. Burger King gives priority and better deals to suppliers that provide cage-free chickens and free-range pigs. Animal rights groups commended the company's decision, hoping that other retailers and suppliers would follow the move.

a Define the meaning of **ethical business behaviour** in the context of the case study. *[2 marks]*

b Discuss with reference to the case study whether acting ethically can provide McDonald's and Burger King with commercial and competitive advantages. *[8 marks]*

CORPORATE SOCIAL RESPONSIBILITY (CSR)

Socially responsible firms are businesses that act morally towards their stakeholders (see Unit 1.4), such as their employees and the local community. These responsibilities are known as **corporate social responsibilities** (CSR). For example, one of the daily roles of staff at McDonald's is to go on litter patrol, whereby staff regularly collect rubbish (including trash that has not been generated by McDonald's) in the vicinity of their restaurants.

For a very long time, businesses have realized that reputation (how others view the organization) can give them an important competitive edge. According to *Fortune* magazine, the top 500 American businesses donate more than 2% of their post-tax profits to charity. This may be due to their desire to act in a socially responsible way, or it may be due to the fear of a negative corporate image due to non-compliance. Being socially responsible can help to improve the reputation of a business, but compliance costs are likely to result in higher costs for the firm. Employees must also be convinced that CSR is in their interest in order for them to help the organization to meet its ethical objectives. Moreover, it can be difficult to measure or monitor the extent to which a business is behaving ethically or morally.

There are different views and attitudes towards the role of businesses in delivering social responsibility:

- **Free-market (or non-compliance) CSR attitude.** Many economists believe that the role of businesses is to generate profits for their owners. They argue that governments, rather than businesses, are responsible for sorting out any social problems. They believe that in pursuing the profit motive, businesses will become more efficient and prosperous, thereby helping society indirectly (such as through job creation and payment of corporation tax).
- **Altruistic CSR attitude.** This view takes the opposite argument to that of free-market economists. Altruism refers to acting in a humanitarian and unselfish manner. These businesses do what they can to improve the society, regardless of whether their actions help to increase their profits. For example, such firms may willingly donate money to charity or invest in local community projects. It can be difficult to determine in reality whether businesses help society due to altruism or because they believe that such action would (selfishly) help to improve their corporate image.

- **Strategic CSR attitude.** Those that adopt this view argue that businesses ought to be socially responsible only if such actions help the business to become more profitable. Such firms see CSR as a method of long-term growth.

CSR is further complicated when dealing with businesses that operate in different countries. What is considered acceptable in one country may be totally undesirable in others. For example, Greece and Japan are huge consumers of tobacco and therefore cigarette advertising is less stringent than in other countries such as the UK or Singapore. Australia and Canada place environmental concern as a key indicator of CSR, whereas India and China do not regard environmental protection so highly.

Question 1.3.4

Wal-Mart

Wal-Mart has, on numerous occasions, been forced to pay millions of dollars to the American government for violating air and water pollution legislation. This obviously harmed the image of the global retailer, with the media alleging that up to 8% of customers had stopped shopping at Wal-Mart as a result of its neglect of the environment. Wal-Mart has also been taken to court for forcing employees to work without proper rest breaks.

a State two possible barriers to ethical and socially responsible business behaviour. *[2 marks]*

b Discuss whether it is morally correct for businesses to put profits before the environment or the welfare of their employees. *[8 marks]*

Finally, some analysts argue that it should not be the role of a manager to decide what is right or wrong. This is simply because managers do not use their own money when making what they personally regard as being socially responsible decisions. Instead, they are employed to run a business on behalf of the owners who seek profit, rather than having their money being spent on socially responsible actions such as donating their money to charity. Managers need to be cautious of what is considered right or wrong as much of CSR is highly subjective in nature. Nevertheless, the potential benefits to a firm that acts in a socially responsible way suggests that managers have a role in promoting and encouraging CSR in the workplace (see Box 1.3b).

Box 1.3b Encouraging corporate social responsibility

- The media – for example, encouragement from the media
- Government assistance – for example, subsidizing the purchase of energy-efficient equipment and machinery
- Government legislation – for example, pollution penalties
- Ethical codes of practice – provide guidelines and parameters for the workforce
- Competitors' actions – pressure from rivals to adopt CSR policies
- Training – for example, updating employee skills in delivering CSR such as good customer care.

The extent to which a firm will act in a socially responsible manner depends on several factors:

- The level and power of various stakeholder groups (see Unit 1.4), such as pressure groups and employees
- Corporate culture and attitudes towards CSR
- Consumer awareness of, and concerns for, CSR issues
- Exposure and pressure from the media
- Short-term versus long-term perspectives
- The financial and human resources of the business
- Compliance costs.

Exam Tip!
Worked example

Question: Justify any three strategies of a profit-seeking company that chooses to adopt corporate social responsibility. *[9 marks]*

Answer: Possible CSR strategies may include a review of:

- HRM strategies, e.g. fair employment practices, health and safety policies and bonuses paid to executives
- Marketing strategies, e.g. misleading and offensive advertising techniques
- Finance strategies, e.g. accuracy and integrity of recording and reporting of financial accounts
- Natural environment policies, e.g. the impact of business activity on the environment or the testing of products on animals
- External business environment, e.g. issues concerning consumer rights and responsibilities towards the local community.

Ultimately, acting in accordance with CSR will need to be financially beneficial in the long term in order to convince the board of directors to adopt any proposed change.

SOCIAL AUDITING

The main reason why most businesses engage in CSR is to enhance their corporate image and reputation. Social auditing is a way to ensure that socially responsible objectives are being implemented. A **social audit** is an independent assessment of how a firm's actions affect society. The audit is likely to include a review of a firm's environmental impact (such as pollution and waste levels), staff management (such as workforce health and safety) and contributions to society (such as involvement in local community projects). An independent review of a firm's activities that examines only the impacts on the environment is known as an **environmental audit**. The majority of large multinational companies use social and environmental audits. Many firms use social audits as a way to reassure their stakeholders that they are doing the 'right' thing.

A key part of social auditing is for the firm to devise policies to deal with its impacts on society, i.e. to devise CSR policies. These policies may include:

- using renewable and sustainable resources
- using reputable and socially responsible suppliers
- systems that cater for the well-being of employees
- establishment of an ethical code of conduct, e.g. integrity of marketing practices
- methods to monitor management and employee commitment to CSR policies.

Firms employ an independent agency to assess the extent to which a business has followed the above policies and the impact it has made on society. The auditors, who charge a fee for the service, will provide written feedback on the effectiveness of the firm in meeting its CSR. They would also identify areas that are in need of attention and make several recommendations for development.

However, there are potential limitations in using social audits. First, the business must have sufficient financial and other resources to satisfy any recommendations made in the audit. This will allow the organization to quickly resolve any problems. Second, the contents of the audit may not be very positive and this can publicize the weaknesses of the business. Subsequently, if the social audit is less than complimentary, then it may harm the image and reputation of the business.

Question 1.3.5

MySpace

MySpace is a highly popular internet-based social network for sharing photos, blogs and digital media. Users can leave messages for anyone and everyone to see. Despite being founded only in 2003, it has grown to become one of the most visited websites in cyberspace.

Despite its popularity, MySpace has been condemned for its lack of social responsibility. Critics have claimed that MySpace is a forum for sending spam (unsolicited and time wasting messages). Security and privacy matters are also an issue. For example, celebrity Paris Hilton had her personal email posted on MySpace and was inundated with messages from fans. In April 2007, gatecrashers wrecked a house in County Durham, UK after having seen an invitation to a party held there. Child safety and legal obligations (such as copyright laws) have also caused problems for MySpace.

a Define **social auditing** in the context of MySpace and outline the details that might appear in a social audit. *[5 marks]*

b To what extent should firms such as MySpace pay attention to their social responsibilities? *[7 marks]*

HIGHER LEVEL

HIGHER LEVEL EXTENSION: CHANGES IN CORPORATE OBJECTIVES AND STRATEGY OVER TIME

There are many factors that affect the aims and objectives of an organization. Some of the **internal** factors include:

- *Corporate culture* (see Unit 2.6) – This refers to the accepted norms and customs of a business and its workforce. Businesses with a flexible and adaptable workforce are more likely to have varying objectives over time.
- *Type and size of organization* (see Unit 1.2) – Any change in the legal structure of a business is likely to cause a change in the organization's objectives. A sole trader that expands into a partnership will need to consider the objectives of other owners of the new business. If there is a separation of ownership and control, such as in public limited companies, then there may be a conflict of interest. For instance, managerial objectives (such as higher bonuses) may clash with the objectives of the owners (such as higher profits).
- *Age of the business* – Newly established firms (see Unit 1.2) will tend to place break-even and survival as their key objectives. More established businesses may strive for market leadership or corporate growth as their key objectives.

- *Finance* – The amount of finance will determine the scale of a firm's objectives. For example, if the objective is to expand into overseas markets then the firm is likely to need a huge sum of money.
- *Risk profile of key stakeholders* – If managers and owners, for example, have a relatively high willingness and ability to take risks, then more ambitious objectives are likely to be sought after.
- *Private versus public sector organizations* – Whether a firm is in the public or private sector will affect its objectives. Traditionally, public sector corporations do not aim to profit maximize but to provide a service to the general public.

External factors that affect the objectives of a business include:

- *State of the economy* (see Unit 1.5) – Whether the economy is in a boom or a slump will also change corporate objectives. Booms (times when national income and employment are rising) provide many opportunities for businesses, whereas slumps (when unemployment is high and confidence levels are dampened) provide many threats.
- *Government constraints* (see Unit 1.5) – Some government rules and regulations can limit what a business might strive to achieve. For example, environmental protection laws may limit the extent to which a firm can profit maximize due to the potentially higher costs of being environmentally friendly.
- *Presence and power of pressure groups* (see Unit 1.4) – Pressure groups may force a business to review its approach to ethics through their lobbying. Pressure groups may harm a firm's image if it is not adopting a socially responsible approach to conducting business.

A change in any of the above factors is therefore likely to change the significance of an organization's objectives over time. For instance, if a public sector organization is *privatized* (sold to the public sector), then the business may change its aim from providing an affordable service to one of profit maximization. Therefore, **corporate strategy** (the tools used to achieve a firm's aims and objectives) will subsequently change. A change in the direction of a business will automatically require a change in corporate strategy in order to achieve its revised targets. Changes in society's expectations of businesses (see next section) will also directly affect their corporate strategy. Finally, an obvious reason why objectives change over time is that the business has already achieved its original targets and needs to set new ones for the future.

HIGHER LEVEL EXTENSION: CHANGES IN SOCIETY'S EXPECTATIONS OF BUSINESS BEHAVIOUR

Attitudes towards CSR may change over time. What was once considered acceptable by society, such as smacking or caning disruptive students in school, may no longer be the case. Environmental protection was not a major issue prior to the 1980s. Many countries do not think it is necessary to impose a national minimum wage, whilst other nations feel that this would help to stop some businesses from paying ridiculously low wages to their employees. The advertising of tobacco products is considered unethical and socially immoral in some parts of the world (advertising of tobacco products is banned in certain countries), but this is not the case in many other countries. The point again is that CSR is a rather subjective issue – what is considered 'right' or 'wrong' is largely based on public opinion, which has a tendency to change over time.

Changes in societal norms mean that businesses need to review their objectives from time to time. For instance, corporate objectives and strategies have changed in recent times due to a more positive attitude towards the hiring and promotion of female staff. Through education, there has also been a greater tolerance and acceptance of multiculturalism and this has directly affected employment practices (see Unit 2.1). Media exposure in many countries has meant that large firms are expected to donate part of their profits to charity.

In addition, pressure group action, such as the prevention of cruelty to animals, has also affected organizational objectives. Customers are more careful about spending their money on products from socially irresponsible firms. Investors are more wary of placing their money with unethical firms, such as those that employ child labour.

Through pressure group action and educational awareness, an increasing number of businesses are actively trying to do their part for the environment. Global warming and environmental damage are huge concerns of governments and citizens around the world, so businesses are changing their objectives to reflect their part in the preservation of the planet. Firms that continue to pollute and damage the environment are likely to earn themselves a poor corporate image with long-term consequences.

Hence, society's changing views of what is considered socially moral will directly affect a firm's view of its own social responsibilities. Its views are also likely to change over time to be in line with societal norms.

ORGANIZATIONAL OBJECTIVES AND BUSINESS STRATEGY

Vision and mission statements serve to provide a clear focus and a shared sense of purpose within an organization. Management experts such as Peter Drucker and Tom Peters argue that a clear vision is essential for high business performance. Successful businesses have a clear vision of their aspirations and a mission that outlines their ultimate purpose. The use of organizational aims and objectives are the starting point to achieving the vision and mission of a business. Strategies can then be devised in order to achieve these targets. In turn, the **performance** of a business can be judged by the extent to which it achieves its objectives.

Businesses need to be able to assess the effectiveness of their aims and objectives. One popular way to do this was put forward by Drucker, who suggested that organizational objectives should ideally be **SMART**:

- Specific – Objectives need to be precise and succinct rather than vague.
- Measurable – Objectives should be quantifiable, e.g. to increase market share, raise sales revenue or reduce staff absenteeism by a certain amount.
- Agreed – Objectives must be accepted and understood by everyone in the organization.
- Realistic – Firms should ensure that they are not attempting too much given their limited resources, e.g. it is not rational for a new business to strive to become the market leader within the first twelve months.
- Time constrained – There should be a time frame within which objectives should be achieved.

Hence, an objective such as 'to achieve 20% sales growth within the next three years' might be classed as being a SMART objective for a growing multinational company.

In addition to setting SMART objectives, targets should also relate directly to the mission statement of the business. This ensures that all departments or decision-makers setting objectives do so in a consistent and unified way. Objectives also need to be clearly communicated to all employees and other key stakeholders.

Ethical business behaviour has become a major focus for many businesses. With increased educational awareness of ethical issues, it is increasingly important for organizations to adopt a socially responsible attitude to the way they conduct business. Firms such as The Body Shop have been able to use this to their advantage by marketing their ethical code of practice as a *unique selling point.* A reputation for CSR that exceeds societal norms and expectations can provide a business with competitive advantages over its rivals: an enhanced corporate image, motivational effects on the workforce, attracting high-calibre staff to join the organization and attracting investment in the business. Nevertheless, if the costs of complying with ethical and socially responsible behaviour are too great, most businesses would refrain from implementing a thorough CSR policy. For example, a profit-seeking business is likely to close down any unprofitable divisions of its business even if this will result in job losses and negative effects on the local community.

Furthermore, in the pursuit of organizational objectives, managers must be aware of potentially conflicting objectives. For example, employees may demand better pay and working conditions which may subsequently reduce profits, at least in the short term.

Organizational objectives are also likely to change over time. In periods of difficult trading times, such as during a business start-up or during an economic downturn, the main organizational objective is survival. Struggling firms are not likely to worry too much about public opinion caused by job losses. Conversely, during favourable trading periods, businesses have to decide on whether to expand for future growth or to reap the benefits of higher profits. Alternatively, such firms may aim to pursue a high degree of market standing. Ultimately, there is no single organizational objective that is suitable for all businesses to follow. However, having clearly defined and realistic objectives and sufficient resources to implement appropriate strategies can make success more likely to happen.

REVIEW QUESTIONS 1.3

1 Why are objectives important to business organizations?

2 What is the purpose of a mission statement?

3 How do mission statements and vision statements differ from one another?

4 Differentiate between 'strategic objectives' and 'tactical objectives'.

5 How might objectives of organizations in the public sector differ from those in the private sector?

6 When might survival be an important organizational objective?

7 What internal and external factors affect changes in organizational objectives?

8 Why might a business consider the objectives of the local community in which it operates?

9 What is 'social auditing' and why might a business choose to carry out a social audit despite the costs of doing so?

10 What does it mean to set SMART objectives?

Higher Level extension

11 Why do objectives have changing significance in different situations?

12 Outline two recent changes in society's expectations of business behaviour.

Aims are the long-term goals of a business, often expressed in the firm's mission statement. They are a general statement of a firm's purpose or intentions and tend to be qualitative in nature.

Corporate social responsibility (CSR) refers to the consideration of ethical and environmental issues relating to business activity. A business that adopts CSR will act morally towards its various stakeholder groups.

Ethics are the moral values that determine and affect business behaviour and decision-making, such as taking actions that are in the best interest of the world's scarce resources.

Mission statement refers to the declaration of an organization's overall purpose. It forms the foundation for setting the objectives of a business.

Objectives are the relatively shorter term targets of an organization. They tend to be expressed as SMART objectives.

SMART objectives mean that well-set objectives ought to be specific, measurable, agreed, realistic and timed.

Social audit refers to an independent assessment of how an organization's actions affect society. The audit is likely to include a review of the firm's environmental impact, staff management and contributions to society.

Social responsibility refers to a business being conscientiously concerned about the well-being of the general public as a whole. Hence socially responsible organizations are likely to act in an ethical manner and consider the needs of all their stakeholders.

Strategy refers to the various methods that businesses can use in an attempt to achieve their mission or vision. Strategies then form the long-term plans for the whole organization.

Tactics refer to the short-term methods that firms can use to achieve their objectives.

Vision statement refers to an organization's long-term aspirations, i.e. where it ultimately wants to be.

Stakeholders

UNIT 1.4

Just because we aren't all the same doesn't mean we have nothing in common.

Kirk Kerekes, American entrepreneur

Key topics

- Internal stakeholders: employees, shareholders, managers and directors
- External stakeholders: suppliers, customers, special interest groups, competitors and the government
- Conflict between stakeholders

Higher Level extension

- Resolving stakeholder conflict

INTRODUCTION

A **stakeholder** refers to any person or organization that has a direct interest in and is affected by the performance of a business. The main stakeholders include the owners of a business (shareholders), managers, employees, customers, suppliers, investors, competitors, the local community and the government (see Figure 1.4a).

Some stakeholders, such as pressure groups, do not have formal authority in the operations of the business. However, management theorists such as Charles Handy argue that it is in the best interest of an organization to listen to the needs of all stakeholders. This Unit looks at the role of different stakeholder groups and why businesses pay attention to their differing needs.

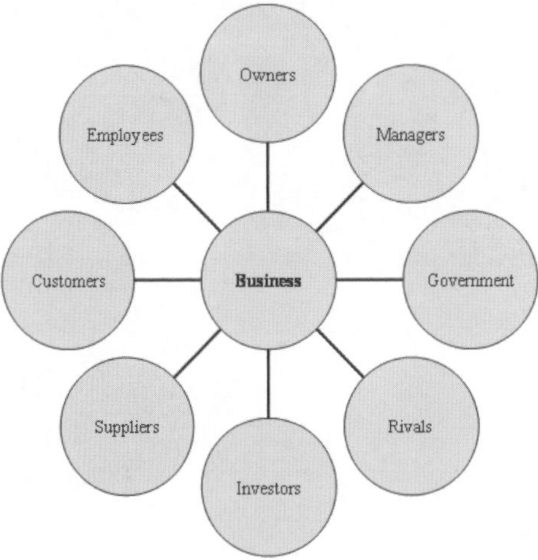

Figure 1.4a Stakeholders of an organization

Stakeholders can be further categorized as internal or external. **Internal stakeholders** of a business are members of the organization. They consist of the employees, shareholders (who own the business), managers and directors of the organization. **External stakeholders** do not form part of the business (such as customers, suppliers and the government), but have a direct interest or involvement in the actions of the organization.

INTERNAL STAKEHOLDERS

Employees

The staff of a business will have a stake (an interest) in the organization they work for. Employees are likely to strive to improve:

- Pay (wages and salaries) and other financial benefits
- Working conditions, such as hours of work and the working environment
- Job security
- Training and career progression opportunities.

These can only be offered to employees if the business is performing well. Many theorists, such as Charles Handy and Chris Argyris, argue that employees are an organization's best assets. It is the staff who produce goods and services for sale; it is the staff who communicate with a business's customers. Consequently, employers have in recent times encouraged their workers to be more involved in decision-making. As American comedian, Fred Allen (1894–1956) once said, "Treat employees like partners, and they act as partners."

Sir Richard Branson would agree with Handy and Argyris. Branson famously declared that he puts his people first, customers second and shareholders third. He claims that by doing this, customers and shareholders both benefit. After all, demotivated staff are unlikely to produce good quality products or deliver good customer service. Worse, disgruntled staff may even take industrial action (see Unit 2.7). For example, Hyundai, South Korea's largest car maker, reported a 47% drop in net profits in 2006 largely because of a labour strike which cut production by 141,882 vehicles (more than its annual domestic sales of Hyundai cars). A motivated workforce is more dynamic and loyal. Hence, it is important for managers to meet, as far as possible, the needs of their employees and to ensure that they are motivated.

Shareholders (Stockholders)

Shareholders are the owners of private and public limited companies. They invest their money in a company by purchasing shares as they expect the company to generate a healthy return on their investment. They are a powerful stakeholder group as they have voting rights and a 'say' in how the business is managed. Since shareholders are the owners of a company, they are entitled to a share of its profits. Shareholders have two main objectives:

- To maximize share **dividend** payments (a proportion of the company's net profits paid to shareholders)
- To achieve a rise in the value of the share price, known as **capital gains**.

For owners of other private businesses, such as sole traders and partnerships, **profit** is a key aim. How profits are distributed depends on the type of business organization (see Unit 1.2). For example, sole traders can choose to keep all of the profits made whereas a limited company will need to decide how much of the profit is to be distributed to shareholders in the form of dividends.

Question 1.4.1

L'Oreal and The Body Shop

Shareholders of L'Oreal, the French cosmetics and beauty giant, voted in favour of a takeover bid for The Body Shop. In March 2006, The Body Shop was sold for a staggering £652 million ($1.2 billion). Six months later, L'Oreal announced plans to expand The Body Shop's 2,000 stores to 5,000 outlets. The expansion was targeted mainly at new markets such as China, India, Brazil, Argentina and Chile.

Critics of the takeover argued that L'Oreal would harm the ethical image of The Body Shop. L'Oreal, however, claimed that they share The Body Shop's ethical stance against animal testing. Instead, the company tests products on artificially produced human skin and volunteers from its workforce. The Body Shop was also criticized for selling the company because Nestlé (a **stakeholder** which owns a significant proportion of the shares in L'Oreal) had gained a poor reputation due to its unethical marketing of baby powdered-milk in developing countries.

a Use the case study to distinguish between **shareholders** and **stakeholders**. *[3 marks]*

b Examine how different stakeholder groups are affected by the developments at L'Oreal. *[6 marks]*

Managers and directors

Managers are the people who plan, organize and control the daily running of the business. Directors are senior executives who have been elected by the company's shareholders to oversee business operations. If the business is a sole proprietorship, then the senior manager is also the owner, whereas in a limited company the senior staff and directors are elected to run the company on behalf of their owners.

Senior managers and directors might aim to maximize their own benefits, such as their annual bonuses and other perks. Hence, they are likely to aim for profit maximization. This would also please their shareholders, thereby safeguarding the jobs of top executives who are held accountable to the owners of the business. However, senior staff are also likely to look at the long-term health of their organizations. They may aim to retain profits for further investment in their business. Indeed, growth is a major organizational objective that many businesses pursue.

EXTERNAL STAKEHOLDERS

Suppliers

Suppliers provide a business with stocks of raw materials, component parts, finished goods and other resources needed for production. Suppliers can also provide business services, such as maintenance and technical support. Suppliers may demand or aim for regular contracts with clients at good prices and request that customers pay their outstanding bills on time.

Businesses will wish to establish a good working relationship with their suppliers in order to receive quality raw materials and stocks on time and at a good price. For example, airline companies rely very heavily on their catering suppliers since flights may need to be cancelled if there is a dispute between the airline and the caterers. Having a good relationship will also allow the business to place and receive orders at short notice. In addition, suppliers may offer preferential credit terms, which allows a business to buy today but pay at a much later date.

Customers

Customer relations management (CRM) is very important in the retailing sector. SavaCentre, a division of Sainsbury's supermarkets, operate hypermarkets in the UK. All employees enter the stores by passing a huge poster that reminds them of two rules:

1 The customer is always right.

2 If the customer is ever wrong, read rule 1.

The purpose is clearly to highlight to SavaCentre staff that their customers are a key stakeholder group. This idea was adapted from Marshall Field (1834–1906), the founder of Marshall Field and Company (a chain of American department stores) who said, "Right or wrong, the customer is always right."

Ultimately, it is the customer who determines the financial performance of a business. A business will not survive without customers as they are the ones who provide a business with most of its revenues. Sam Walton (1918–1992), founder of the world's largest retailer Wal-Mart believed that the customer was boss. This is because customers can simply choose to spend their money elsewhere thereby threatening the survival of a business.

Hence, it is vital that businesses pay attention to the needs of their customers. Customers may demand more choice of better quality products at competitive prices. They also demand a pleasant and efficient purchasing experience.

Businesses use *market research* (see Unit 4.2) to find out what the customer wants and then try to meet these demands. Many businesses, such as fast-food restaurants and hotels, have 'suggestion schemes' and 'customer satisfaction surveys' for both internal and external customers. These are completed by customers and then read by staff in the customer relations department. Complaints can be followed up and any comments or suggestions can be considered by management. Businesses will aim to keep the customer loyal to their organization and to become *repeat-purchasers*, who may even promote the business to their friends via word of mouth.

Special interest groups

A **special interest group** (SIG) is an organization that advocates certain issues, such as the prevention of cruelty to animals, protection of the environment or prevention of smoking in public areas. They consist of members who are passionate about influencing changes in government policy and legislation for a specific cause. In essence, they serve to protect the specialist needs and concerns (interests) of their members or followers. Examples include trade unions, pressure groups, industry trade groups and the local community. The existence of such groups allows an exchange of information and ideas between individual members with a shared interest.

Trade unions, or **labour unions** (see Unit 2.7), aim to uphold and enhance the conditions of work for their members. They may seek or campaign for:

- Wages and salaries to rise in line with inflation, because inflation erodes the value of money and increases the cost of living.
- The introduction of a minimum wage to improve the earnings of those on relatively low incomes.
- Better working conditions, including the provision of regular breaks or improving the physical working environment in the workplace.

Pressure groups are another example of SIGs. Pressure groups consist of individuals with a common interest who seek to place demands on organizations to act in a particular way or to influence a change in their behaviour. Examples include organizations set up to protect the environment and groups campaigning against smoking, deforestation and the harmful treatment of animals.

Pressure groups often try to achieve their objectives by aiming to influence government policy, such as lobbying for a change in legislation. Some pressure groups, such as Friends of the Earth and Greenpeace, do this by acting on an international level and getting the support of the general public who are more aware and concerned about damage to the environment.

Pressure groups, especially international ones, have increasingly influenced the decisions and actions of businesses. Growing public awareness and support of the objectives of pressure groups has strengthened their influence on business behaviour. Box 1.4a shows the various actions that pressure groups can take to make sure that businesses take notice of their views.

Industry trade groups are a third example of SIGs. These are organizations that specialize in public relations with the aim of promoting a particular industry, through education and advertising. An industry trade group is funded by the businesses that operate in that specific industry. The advertising and promotion carried out by industry trade groups differ from those produced by individual firms in that the former carries out promotion to support the interests of the whole industry, rather than those of individual companies or brands. Anti-piracy advertising would be an example of a PR campaign by an industry trade group. Movie and music companies fund the advertising and educational campaign to reduce the number of people involved in illegal downloading of music and movies from the internet. Alternatively, industry trade groups may promote the products of the industry, such as a farmers' association collaborating to promote the benefits of eating fruits and vegetables.

Box 1.4a Actions taken by pressure groups

Boycotting is the recommendation to refuse to buy the products from a certain business. This might be done by creating adverse publicity for the business.

Lobbying means using the strength of a pressure group to discuss and influence key issues (with employers, legal representatives and the government) in favour of its cause. Gaining public support can also help to influence governments to introduce legislation against socially undesirable business activities.

Public relations (PR) means getting positive publicity about a specific opinion or cause, e.g. charities have often used famous celebrities in support of their mission. PR is very important since it helps to raise public awareness and support.

Direct action means the pressure group itself takes action to express their views. Examples include staging mass protests and taking legal action against firms who may have acted illegally.

Question 1.4.2

Canadian Association of Petroleum Producers

The Canadian Association of Petroleum Producers (CAPP) consists of businesses that carry out oil explorations and develop and produce Canada's petroleum resources. CAPP is a **special interest group** that represents 150 member companies which collectively account for more than 95% of Canada's output of natural gas, crude oil, oil sands and elemental sulphur. With active participation from its members, CAPP also strives to achieve consensus on industry codes of practice and guidelines that meet or exceed government standards.

Source: www.capp.ca

a Describe why CAPP might be classed as a **special interest group**. *[2 marks]*

b Explain the benefits of being a member of an industry trade group such as CAPP. *[4 marks]*

A final example of SIGs is the **local community**, which will place demands on the businesses that operate in their community. These may include:

- Job creation and opportunities to provide extra income and spending in the local community
- The need to be considerate of the local environment, i.e. organizations must be socially responsible for their activities
- A wide choice in the provision of products and at competitive prices
- Sponsorship of local and fund-raising events.

The above considerations are paramount to the local community's acceptance of businesses setting up in the area. Local residents do not simply welcome businesses which offer job opportunities. Many popular holiday destinations, for instance, have been negatively damaged by the influx of tourists. Traffic congestion and damage to beaches and the countryside will harm local residents. As a result, there will undoubtedly be complaints and protests from members of the community if any business activity causes major traffic congestion, pollution or damage to the natural environment, irrespective of any jobs that the firm may create. At the same time, the local community can provide opportunities for a business because much of the labour force and customers are likely to come from the local area.

Special interest groups are more likely to succeed in achieving their aims and objectives if certain interrelated factors are accomplished:

- *Funding.* SIGs tend to be stronger if they have a greater amount and variety of financial resources. Trade unions can only carry out their roles if there is a sufficient number of employees who pay their union membership fees. Some organizations, such as Greenpeace, have the funding to operate on a global scale, thereby broadening their influence.
- *Public opinion.* If the general public sympathise and support the cause of an SIG, then it is more likely to succeed in influencing the actions of businesses. Campaigns such as anti-smoking or anti-littering have led to public and government support in many countries. Littering carries a very heavy financial and imprisonment penalty in Singapore, for instance. Animal protection groups, such as the World Wildlife Fund, can use social marketing techniques (see Unit 4.1) to gain positive press coverage. By contrast, SIGs that are seen as more aggressive in their approach may be less successful.
- *Number of members.* The larger the number of active participants in an SIG, the more influence it is likely to have. The largest labour unions have the most profound influence on business and government activity. Such trade unions have managed to secure minimum wage legislation in many countries throughout the world.
- *Commitment of members.* A united group of members who truly believe in the cause of the SIG will strengthen its ability to influence business behaviour. For example, labour unions may collapse because a significant number of their members may not agree to strike action (see Unit 2.7).

Whether a business should devote time and resources to the demands of an SIG depends on a number of factors:

- Effectiveness of the SIG in making its voice heard (see above factors). The stronger the SIG, the greater its influence will be and the more pressure a business will face if it chooses to ignore the views of the SIG.
- Market power of the business. If the business has some monopoly power (i.e. there are very few alternative products on the market), then it may not need to react to the demands of the SIG.
- Costs of complying with the demands of the SIG. For example, can the business afford to give its workers the pay increment demanded by the labour union? Can the business afford to introduce more environmentally friendly production technologies? Are economic conditions right to lower corporation tax and interest rates to meet the demands of industry trade groups?
- Views of directors, senior managers and shareholders. If the owners and directors of the business feel that non-compliance would damage the image or performance of the business, then it is more likely to pay attention to SIGs.
- Aims and objectives of the business. For instance, businesses that are committed to social and ethical responsibility will have a code of conduct and be more sensitive to the views of workers, customers and the local community.

Competitors

Competitors are the rival businesses of an organization. For example, the main rivals of Cathay Pacific Airways include Japan Airlines, Singapore Airlines, Qantas and Air China. Competitors will be interested in the activities of a business for several reasons, including:

- To avoid anti-competitive practices of rival firms. Larger firms may wish to exploit their monopoly power, although this may be restricted by government intervention.
- As a stimulus to innovation and product development. Firms may benefit from some competition as rivalry can lead to more ideas being generated. A monopolist may not have the incentive to create new products or to be innovative, due to the lack of competition.

Exam Tip!
Worked example

Question: Examine how poor performance of a school or college will affect any TWO of its stakeholder groups. *[6 marks]*

Answer: Explanation of two relevant stakeholder groups and how they are affected, such as:

- Employees – Morale of teaching and non-teaching staff is likely to fall and there may also be negative effects on pay, job security, productivity and labour turnover.
- Customers – The parents (and the students) may become dissatisfied with reduced quality of teaching and learning and perhaps look at alternative schools for their children.
- Local community – Schools play an important role in influencing the reputation of the local area and house prices, both of which are likely to fall in this case.
- Competitors – Other schools in the local area are likely to benefit from their rival suffering from poor performance.
- Government – There may be some government intervention and funding implications due to the poor performance of the school. In very extreme cases of poor performance, the government may even close down the school.

Therefore, the poor performance of the school will normally have negative impacts on its stakeholders, at least in the short run. Rival schools and colleges are perhaps the only exception to this.

Government

The government is an important external stakeholder that is likely to have a large influence on business behaviour. The government will be interested in business activity for several reasons, including assurances that:

- Unfair business practices are avoided.
- Health and safety standards at work are met.
- The correct amount of corporation tax is paid from business profits.
- Payment of *business rates* are adhered to (these are taxes paid for the provision of local business services such as maintaining the local road network).
- Consumer protection laws are observed and followed.
- Employment legislation is being upheld by the organization.

Governments may also have a financial stake in a business organization (see Unit 1.2). For example, the largest shareholder of Hong Kong Disneyland is the Hong Kong government. They invested a huge amount of money into the development of the theme park in an attempt to boost tourism in Hong Kong. Hence, it will have a vested interest in the performance of the organization.

Ultimately, the government aims to ensure that businesses act in the public's interest. On the one hand, the government can stimulate business activity. This might be done by lowering interest rates or taxes to create employment and investment opportunities. Organizations can also benefit from having a good reputation or relationship with the government. For example, the government may offer incentives to multinationals to locate in their country. Such incentives include offering cheap or free rent, lower tax rates and loans with minimal interest charges. The government may also introduce initiatives which benefit organizations, such as job creation schemes and investment in road building and communication networks. On the other hand, government intervention can constrain businesses. For instance, Microsoft Corporation was broken up into two smaller companies due to numerous law suits against the monopolist for malpractice and unfair competition.

STAKEHOLDER CONFLICT

Since different stakeholder groups have varying interests in an organization, it is likely that conflict will arise. Businesses will need to take decisions that will address the interests of some stakeholder groups but at the expense of not being able to meet the needs of other groups. Margaret Thatcher, a former UK Prime Minister, once said that standing in the middle of a road would get you get hit by traffic coming from both sides. What she suggested by this was that she had to take decisions which pleased certain members of the public but that she could not please all the people all the time. This is the same for businesses.

Conflict arises because the business cannot necessarily meet the needs of all its stakeholders simultaneously. For example, if the owners want more profit, then this may come about by cutting staff benefits. This will obviously upset the employees. Suppliers would like their customers to pay the full price in one transaction, in order to gain more revenue in the shortest possible time, but business customers will expect to receive discounted prices for regular custom and for buying in large quantities. Paying their suppliers on time will also improve the supplier's cash flow position but could harm that of the business. This can cause conflict between the business and its suppliers.

A major cause of potential stakeholder conflict is the pay and remuneration of the directors of a company. Shareholders and employees may argue that top management are 'overpaid' and that there should be a fairer distribution to shareholders (in the form of dividends) and staff (in the form of better wages and salaries). Advocates of large salaries and benefits packages for senior executives would argue however that the remuneration needs to be adequate to compensate for the higher risks involved in decision-making. They argue that this could ultimately lead to more profits for the business, and hence lead to higher dividends and wages in the future.

Another source of potential conflict is that some stakeholders have more than one interest in an organization. For example, managers are employees of a company, and some employees may also be shareholders of a company. A customer is also likely to be a member of the local community. Based on the differing objectives of these stakeholder groups, some degree of conflict is likely to occur.

Modern management thinking suggests that stakeholder conflict is a short term, albeit potentially ever present, phenomenon. For example, meeting the needs of both employees and managers can lead to a highly motivated and productive workforce with low rates of absenteeism and staff turnover. This in turn can lead to improved customer relations, corporate image, market share and profits. Shareholders will also be pleased as a result of this. Greater output may also lead to higher levels of employment in the local community. Hence, it is argued that meeting the needs of all stakeholder groups can be achieved, although this may only occur in the medium to long term.

Exam Tip!

Favourite examination questions ask students about:

- The difference between internal and external stakeholders
- The difference between stakeholders and shareholders
- The different aims of stakeholder groups and how they conflict with each other.

Question 1.4.3

Vodafone

Mobile phone giant Vodafone has been criticized by major investors after its poor stock market performance. Whilst highly successful in European markets, Vodafone's business in Japan and America were below par. Shareholders and investors placed heavy pressure on Vodafone to sell its stake in Verizon Wireless, an American mobile phone operator.

Vodafone's misfortunes baffle some people since its sales revenue and customer numbers have risen (reported as being in excess of 200 million customers worldwide at the beginning of 2007). However, Vodafone also holds the record for the largest loss in British corporate history – a staggering sum of £15 billion ($30 billion) for 2005–06.

a Use the case study to outline two reasons why Vodafone's shareholders might be concerned about its performance. *[4 marks]*

b To what extent should a business like Vodafone listen to the views of its stakeholders. *[6 marks]*

HIGHER LEVEL

HIGHER LEVEL EXTENSION: RESOLVING STAKEHOLDER CONFLICT

Conflict refers to situations where people do not see eye to eye due to differences in their opinions. Conflict exists in every organization. From time to time, employees will disagree with management decisions; customers will be disgruntled; suppliers will fail to deliver the right goods on time; shareholders will be unhappy with the performance of the business, and so forth.

Nevertheless, for any business to progress there must be some form of resolution to the conflict. The outcome of any negotiation will depend largely on the **relative bargaining power** of the different stakeholders. For example, large multinationals such as Honda or Ford will have better bargaining power with their suppliers than mechanics operating as sole traders trying to negotiate prices for motor vehicle parts.

It is highly unlikely that a business can fulfil the aims of all its stakeholders at the same time; yet it is undesirable to aim to maximize the needs of just one stakeholder group. If a particular stakeholder group is not catered for, then it is likely that they will cause disruptions and problems for the business. Most businesses will aim for a 'best fit' compromise so that stakeholder groups are all reasonably pleased with the conduct of the business.

In their book *Exploring Corporate Strategy*, Gerry Johnson and Kevan Scholes argue that not all stakeholders groups are equal. Their **stakeholder mapping** model can be used to assess the relative *interest* of stakeholders in a business and their relative *power* (or influence) on business behaviour. A business would place stakeholder groups into the grid, as shown in Figure 1.4b, based on their relative level of power and interest in the organization.

Level of power \ Level of interest	Low	High
Low	A	B
High	C	D

Figure 1.4b Stakeholder mapping

Stakeholder mapping allows managers to assess how to deal with conflicting stakeholder objectives. Whilst it is extremely difficult to please all stakeholders at the same time, managers can use this mapping tool to prioritise their actions. Using this model, it is unlikely that stakeholders in quadrant A will receive much attention from the decision-makers. Conversely, stakeholders in quadrant D will receive the most attention as they are what Johnson and Scholes called the *key players* of an organization. They suggest that stakeholders in quadrant B need to be kept informed and those in quadrant C must be kept satisfied, perhaps by consulting these stakeholder groups on key decisions.

One of the limitations of this approach is that the model is static. The relative power and level of interest of stakeholders is likely to change with time. For instance, environmental pressure groups have gained much support in recent times whereas the power and image of many trade unions have deteriorated.

Another way to deal with stakeholder conflict is to use **public relations** (PR), perhaps by employing a good public relations firm. PR specialists will have the expertise to handle negative publicity. They will publicize the good work that the business is doing to repair or promote good public relations. Communications are also very important in encouraging good PR. Firms can reduce the chances of conflict occurring by fully involving their stakeholders, such as employees and the local community, and by keeping them up to date and informed about decisions made by the business.

Question 1.4.4

Skoda Auto

Skoda Auto is one of the oldest automobile manufacturers in the world, having been founded in 1895. In early 2007, workers at the Czech company, which became part of Volkswagen in 1991, went on strike over concerns regarding pay and benefits. It was reported that industrial action would cost Skoda, the country's largest exporter, 60 million crowns ($2.9 million) per day in lost output. Economists warned that there could be repercussions on the economy should wage negotiations lead to inflationary pressures.

a Identify two internal stakeholder groups suggested in the above case study. *[2 marks]*

b Explain one conflict that exists between the different stakeholders in the case study. *[3 marks]*

c Discuss how the conflict outlined in your answer above could be minimized. *[7 marks]*

STAKEHOLDERS AND BUSINESS STRATEGY

Different stakeholders have varying degrees of interest in the activities of an organization. In deciding how to deal with conflicting stakeholder needs, leaders will need to look at three key issues:

- The type of business organization in question. A partnership may aim for profit as a priority whereas a charitable organization is likely to have different aims. Hence, the partners may see the owners as the key stakeholder whereas the local community may be the most important group for the charitable organization. A limited company will be accountable to its shareholders, so will have to give them priority as a stakeholder group.
- The aims and objectives of the business. If a business has expansion plans, for instance, then the proportion of profits allocated to its owners will be less than otherwise. Instead, the views of managers and directors will be given a higher priority in such situations.
- The source and degree of power of each stakeholder group. Customers will have more power if the business is selling a product in a mass market where there are plenty of substitute products to choose from. Access to the media can also give power to pressure groups.

Many leading theorists believe that the *stakeholder concept* holds priority over the *shareholder concept*. This means that to be successful, a company will need to be aware of the needs and objectives of their stakeholders even though the business ultimately belongs to its owners (the shareholders). For example, in ever competitive markets, businesses have to increasingly listen to the opinions of their customers. Bill Gates, founder of Microsoft, has built his fortune by meeting the needs of customers all around the world. He said that dissatisfied customers are the best source of learning for any business.

By contrast, Milligan and Smith argue that employees are the key stakeholder group. They state in their book *Uncommon Practice* (2002) that although customers are vital to any business, it is the interest of employees that need to be considered first. They argue that businesses need to hire the right people and devote time and money to train and develop them. In turn, employees will automatically deliver a first-rate service to their customers.

Other external stakeholders, such as pressure groups, have become increasingly effective in influencing business activity. Due to public awareness of the detrimental effects of globalization (such as exploitation of child labour or the damaging effects of global warming), businesses are finding it ever more difficult to simply ignore the views of their external stakeholders.

Johnson and Scholes have shown that different stakeholder groups have varying degrees of influence on business activity. Organizations will, whether deliberate or otherwise, behave differently in response to the varying demands of their unequal stakeholder groups. The relative importance of each stakeholder group to an organization will largely determine how it responds to their needs. After all, meeting the needs of one stakeholder group may conflict with those of other groups.

Finally, if the demands of stakeholders are ridiculous or the messages being spread by special interest groups are misleading, then the business will take counter measures to correct this problem. The business will defend its position by issuing statements to correct any rumours or false messages being communicated, use counter publicity campaigns, or take legal action against parties that makes false allegations about the business.

REVIEW QUESTIONS 1.4

1 Using examples, explain the difference between 'internal' and 'external' stakeholders.

2 What is the difference between 'stakeholders' and 'shareholders'?

3 Distinguish between a 'director' and a 'shareholder' of a company.

4 What are the four main types of special interest groups (SIGs)?

5 Differentiate between 'lobbying' and 'boycotting'.

6 How might pressure groups affect the success of a business?

7 Outline four sources of conflict in a business.

Higher Level extension

8 How might businesses resolve conflict in the workplace?

9 Explain how the use of Johnson and Scholes's stakeholder mapping tool can be used to aid management decision-making.

Conflict refers to situations where people have disagreements on certain matters due to differences in their opinions. Conflict can often lead to arguments and tension between various stakeholder groups.

Directors are the senior members of staff who have been elected by shareholders of a company to run the business on their behalf.

External stakeholders of a business do not form part of the organization but have a direct interest or involvement in the actions of the organization. Examples include customers, suppliers and the government.

Internal stakeholders of a business are members of the organization, i.e. the employees, shareholders (who own the business), managers and directors of the business.

Managers are the people responsible for the day to day running of a business or a department within a business. They are accountable to Directors and responsible for their staff teams.

Pressure groups are a type of special interest group which consists of individuals with a common concern who seek to place demands on organizations to act in a particular way or to influence a change in their behaviour. Examples include Greenpeace and People for the Ethical Treatment of Animals (PETA).

Shareholders, also known as stockholders, are the people who own shares in a private or public limited company, i.e. they are the part-owners of a company.

Special interest group (SIG) refers to the organization of people who have a common interest, such as the protection of the global environment, and collectively act to achieve that interest by swaying public opinion and support, lobbying government policy and influencing business behaviour.

Stakeholder mapping is an analytical tool developed by Johnson and Scholes which places different stakeholder groups into quadrants depending on their relative levels of power and interest in an organization.

Stakeholders are individuals or organizations that have a direct interest (known as a stake) in the activities and performance of a business. Examples of stakeholder groups include shareholders, employees, trade unions, customers, financial investors, suppliers, managers and the government.

External Environment

UNIT 1.5

The reasonable man adapts himself to the world; the unreasonable one persists in trying to adapt the world to himself.

George Bernard Shaw (1856–1950), Irish author

Key topics

- PEST analysis and the external business environment
- External opportunities and threats: social, technological, economic, environmental, political, legal and ethical
- Relationship between PEST and SWOT analysis as decision-making tools

INTRODUCTION

In the pursuit of achieving their aims and objectives, businesses face challenges from both within and outside of their organizations. Internal and external opportunities and threats will affect a firm's performance. Understanding these factors can facilitate effective decision-making.

Internal factors are the constraints and opportunities (facing a business in the attempt to achieve its aims and objectives) within a firm's own control. These limitations tend to be dominated by the rules, policies and culture of the business. Examples of internal constraints include:

- **Finance** – Most firms lack sufficient sources of finance. Not all firms, for example, can afford to use television advertising. Nevertheless, firms can either seek additional sources of finance (see Unit 3.1) or to use alternative ways to achieve their objectives.
- **People** – Poor working relations can really harm a firm's ability to achieve its objectives. Poor communication systems will also hinder the performance of a business. Motivational strategies (see Unit 2.5) can go some way towards resolving conflict in the workplace.
- **Marketing** – Firms may not have as attractive marketing campaigns as their rivals, such as inferior products, packaging, customer service and promotions.
- **Production** – A firm's operations such as its production techniques or stock control systems may be improved to enhance its overall efficiency and competitiveness. However, the firm may lack the resources or expertise to achieve this.

The focus of this Unit is, however, on the external business environment in which an organization operates. **External factors** are those issues which either restrict or aid the performance of a business but are beyond its control. These factors tend to be classed under the concept of a PEST framework.

PEST ANALYSIS

This section looks at PEST analysis in more detail. The external environment is a complicated topic for many students, so it is advisable to revisit this section towards the end of the course and when preparing for the Paper 1 (pre-released) Case Study.

PEST is an acronym for the Political, Economic, Social and Technological opportunities and threats of the external environment within which businesses operate. These factors, unlike internal factors, affect all businesses in the economy and are beyond the control of any individual organization. It is mainly used at the start of a strategy review process, such as assessing the feasibility of an overseas investment project. The issues that arise from a PEST analysis might include:

- **Political** – Government legislation (such as employment law, consumer protection rights, copyright and trademark regulations) define the boundaries within which businesses can operate. Government intervention such as taxation and interest rate policies also affect the political and economic stability of a country.
- **Economic** – The state of the economy in which businesses operate is determined by four key variables: inflation, unemployment, economic growth and international trade (export earnings less import expenditure of a country). In addition, consumer and business confidence levels also affect the level of economic activity. The actions and activities of rival firms can also constrain the performance of a particular business.

- **Social** – Social, cultural and demographic changes (see Unit 4.2) can also present opportunities and threats to a business. For example, with a more liberal and modern attitude towards women in society, firms have benefited from having a more flexible labour force. Multiculturalism has also led to a boom in the trade of *cultural exports* (see Unit 4.7), whereas pressure for firms to be more environmentally friendly has led to a change in business behaviour.
- **Technological** – Advances in technology and work processes (such as the microchip revolution or the introduction of just-in-time stock control systems) have improved the efficiency of businesses. At the same time, the high cost of staying up to date with technological progress can hinder the performance of businesses. Airbus faced lengthy delays in the production of the A380, the world's largest commercial aircraft. As a result, it had to make huge, yet undisclosed, sums of compensation to its customers such as Emirates Airlines and Singapore Airlines.

External factors that can harm a business (such as an economic recession, oil crisis or high inflation) are seen as **threats**. Hence PEST is an appropriate acronym to use. However, external factors (such as lower taxes and interest rates) can also present **opportunities**. In this case, the concept is called by its more optimistic name **STEP analysis**. Variations of PEST include PESTLE analysis (where the last two letters stand for the external **L**egal and **E**nvironmental opportunities and threats) and STEEPLE analysis (where the third E stands for **E**thical opportunities and threats).

> **Note:** Candidates will not be tested on country-specific laws, regulations or economic policies. (© IBO 2007)

There are three general steps needed to carry out a PEST analysis:

1. **Brainstorm** external factors likely to affect the business, under each of the PEST headings.
2. **Discuss** these factors to decide which ones are most likely to have a significant impact on the business and hence its strategy. This step may involve devoting time and resources to research these factors and to gather relevant information in order to scientifically weigh the importance of the different factors.
3. **Summarize** the information in a PEST analysis template to further the development of business strategy.

A simplistic worked example of how a PEST analysis can be used is shown in Box 1.5a. It looks at some of the opportunities and threats of foreign businesses moving into India.

The importance of each opportunity and threat identified in a PEST analysis can be weighted in a scientific manner. This is useful when trying to weigh up the advantages and disadvantages of a decision. If the overall opportunities of a decision outweigh the threats, then a business is likely to pursue that option. However, in reality, some factors in the external business environment are subject to rapid and unforeseeable change. An exogenous shock, such as a war or an oil crisis, can reduce the chances of success, despite what the PEST analysis initially revealed.

Nevertheless, one key advantage in using a PEST analysis is that it is quite simple to use. The analysis helps managers to be thorough and logical in their analysis of the external opportunities and threats faced by the business. It is also a useful brainstorming and discussion tool. PEST analysis promotes proactive and forward-looking thinking rather than static thinking based on gut feelings. Hence, it is more likely that a business will be better prepared to deal with external shocks and to devise more appropriate organizational strategies.

Box 1.5a PEST analysis of multinationals operating in India

Political

- Political and economic reforms to encourage better trade relations with other nations
- Less stringent legislation than in developed nations, thereby placing fewer constraints on business activity
- Still regarded as less politically stable compared to many other countries
- Less protection for patents and copyrights discourages technology transfer to India

Economic

- Huge growth potential in financial and stock markets
- Significant economic growth, suggesting improving disposable incomes (spending power) in India
- Improved infrastructure and market opportunities, especially in cities such as Mumbai and Delhi
- Relatively low costs of production (average wage rates are still very low)
- Infrastructure and economic stability are less attractive than in other countries such as China
- Vast majority of the Indian population is still very poor

Social

- Potential market of over 1.1 billion people (the second largest population in the world and expected to overtake China as the most populated nation by 2050)
- Well-educated workforce with English proficiency
- Large yet increasing discrepancies in income and wealth distribution (which might cause social unrest)
- Language barriers in rural cities and/or a clash of cultures

Technological

- Growing number of technologically aware population (huge opportunities for firms providing technological products such as mobile phones, personal computers and internet services)
- Technologies easily copied due to a lack of appropriate legislation.

Typically, a PEST analysis will be presented in a tabular template with four quadrants, one for each of the four PEST headings.

SOCIAL AND CULTURAL OPPORTUNITIES AND THREATS

Social and cultural factors can directly affect the activities of a business. The attitude of society towards a wide range of different issues (such as business ethics, social welfare, women, religion or animals) will affect what goods and services are provided in the economy. For example, the growing knowledge and support for environmental protection has altered business behaviour in an immense way. More businesses are now reporting on non-financial aspects of their activities such as recycling and waste management.

Demographic changes in society also present opportunities and threats to businesses. Demographic changes in developed nations, such as a more educated and flexible workforce (see Unit 2.1) alongside an ageing population, have affected recruitment practices, marketing strategies and the products provided by businesses. The changing attitudes towards the role of women have had profound impacts on businesses. Women in modern societies are opting to have children at a later age as they give their careers priority. Businesses are increasingly more receptive to the recruitment and promotion of female staff.

The increased awareness and acceptance of **multiculturalism** in modern societies has also led to many business opportunities. The most consumed take-out food in the UK is not fish and chips or the American burger but the Indian curry. The largest non-Asian importer of Malaysian laksa (spicy noodle soup) is Finland. The growth in sales of such *cultural exports*, the rise in global businesses that think locally and the phenomenon of *globalization* have undoubtedly brought about opportunities for many businesses and industries.

Question 1.5.1

Comment on how the demographic changes below may present both opportunities and threats to a business: *[12 marks]*

a Growing number of self-employed people.

b Increasing number of single parent families.

c Parents choosing to have fewer children and at a later stage in their lives.

d More people graduating with university degrees.

TECHNOLOGICAL OPPORTUNITIES AND THREATS

The technological environment presents constant threats and opportunities for businesses. For a very long time now, technology has affected all aspects of business functions. For instance, the internet has directly affected Human Resource Management (in the recruitment process), Marketing (such as e-commerce), Finance (annual reports are now 'published' online) and Operations Management (such as access to benchmarking data).

The internet presents an array of opportunities for businesses:

- Speed of access to information. Businesses and customers can gain instant access to the most up to date information from any part of the world. Most large companies have a dedicated website and there is a huge range of news and media websites that can provide invaluable information to users in a cost-effective way.
- Reducing language and cultural barriers. Information in emails and web pages can be easily translated into different languages by using dedicated software. This can help to reduce the costs of trading overseas or running multinational corporations.
- Reduced costs of production. Firms that have an online presence (see Unit 4.8) can benefit immensely from e-commerce. Trading can take place from any part of the world at any time without the need for having a physical outlet for customers to visit. Subsequently, staffing costs can also be reduced.

The internet does, however, also present potential threats for businesses:

- Price transparency. Businesses are exposed to the forces of competition brought by the internet. Customers can easily compare the prices of different businesses without leaving their home or office.
- Online crime. Hackers have cost online businesses a huge amount of money. Online banking and credit card fraud are quite commonplace. This threat has also prevented or slowed the growth in the number of customers making regular online purchases.

- Higher costs of production. In addition to the costs of online crime, businesses also face maintenance costs and training costs to ensure that employees are competent and confident in the use of internet technology.

Apart from the internet, other examples of opportunities that technology brings to businesses include:

- New working practices. For example, many more people are working from home (see Unit 2.1) by using information and communication technology. Global businesses are also increasingly using video conferencing to cut the costs of face-to-face meetings and international recruitment. Marketing activities have also been affected, such as e-commerce and advertising on the internet.
- Increased productivity and efficiency gains. Robots and machines are much faster yet more accurate than humans, especially in the mass production of products over a long time period. Unlike humans, machinery can be made to work very long hours without the need for breaks, financial rewards, motivation or maternity leave! Firms are also more likely to achieve *zero defects* (no wastage) due to the use of technology. Automated stock control systems can even automatically re-order stocks. Technological progress has also enhanced business communications (see Unit 2.3). Hence, despite the large initial costs of automation and technology, in the long run *capital intensive* industries can benefit from cost savings in the form of *technological economies of scale* (see Unit 1.7).
- Quicker product development time. For example, the use of CAD/CAM technology has allowed businesses to produce prototypes quickly and cost-efficiently. This helps to accelerate the design, manufacturing and launch of new products. The use of CAD/CAM has, for instance, led to the mass production of products such as home furniture at a relatively low cost to producers.
- New products and new markets. Technology is a source of innovation and brings about new products in the market. Examples of technological gadgets in consumer markets have included wireless internet broadband services, digital mobile camera phones and high-definition plasma televisions. Apple's highly successful range of iPod MP3 players has made Steve Jobs (co-founder of the company) one of the richest men in the world. Marketing managers have used the idea of technology that improves our living standards as a means of selling such products.
- The creation of jobs. Advances in technology also bring about an increased need for maintenance and technical support. Examples include computer programmers, hardware and software technicians, graphic designers and ICT teachers.

The technological environment also presents certain threats to businesses, such as:

- Technology is not always reliable or secure. Computer failure or hacked files can present serious problems for businesses.
- It can be costly. Furthermore, equipment and software may become obsolete quickly and hence need upgrading or replacement.
- Shorter product life cycles (see Unit 4.3). Fierce competition in the consumer electronics industry means that there are continuous improvements in products such as mobile phones, personal computers and home entertainment systems. This means businesses need to devote more resources to new product development.
- Automation has led to job losses in primary and secondary sector industries, such as commercial farming, oil extraction and car manufacturing. Businesses will therefore need to carefully manage the process of making staff redundant.

When adopting or implementing technology in the workplace, managers need to consider several factors:

- Costs – such as the cost of purchase, installation, maintenance, replacement and insurance of new technologies.
- Benefits – such as the expected gains in efficiency (as measured by productivity, flexibility and communications) and profits.
- Human relations – such as the impact of technology on resistance to change, staff morale and workforce planning. Technological advancements in the workplace have also meant more flexible working patterns, thereby threatening any sense of job security.
- Recruitment and training – such as the costs of training, the number of people who need training and where to find the time to train people. Recruiting computer-literate people also becomes necessary.

Question **1.5.2**

Nintendo and Apple

Nintendo's Wii games console and Apple's iPod are huge hits with customers. Nintendo's latest console appeals to new market segments such as women and the elderly. Demand is high in Asia, Europe and the USA (where it outsells its nearest rival by a ratio of 2 to 1). In April 2007, Apple announced the sale of its 100 millionth iPod, making it the most successful music player in history.

- Explain how the technological environment can present opportunities for hi-tech firms such as Nintendo and Apple. *[4 marks]*

ECONOMIC OPPORTUNITIES AND THREATS

The economic environment refers to the large-scale economic factors affecting the economy as a whole, such as government policies, the attitudes and actions of foreign countries and the levels of business and consumer confidence in the economy.

Governments tend to have four key macroeconomic objectives that they strive to achieve: controlled inflation, economic growth, reduced unemployment and an acceptable international trade balance. Government macroeconomic policies are used to achieve these four fundamental goals and they will have either a direct or indirect effect on business activities.

Controlled rate of inflation

Inflation can be defined as the continual rise in the general level of prices in the economy. Most governments of wealthy nations regard low and sustainable inflation as an absolute priority for economic prosperity. They see the control of inflation as a prerequisite to achieving its other three macroeconomics objectives in the long run. There are two main causes of inflation:

- **Demand Pull inflation** is caused by excessive aggregate demand in the economy. Any factor that causes a rise in consumption, investment, government spending or international trade earnings will lead to an increase in the economy's aggregate demand. For example, if consumer and business confidence levels are very high this will encourage people and firms to spend more money and at a faster rate, thereby fuelling inflation.
- **Cost Push inflation** is caused by higher costs of production leading to a rise in prices so that firms can maintain their profit margins. Examples include increased wages caused by trade union action, soaring raw material prices caused by an oil crisis or higher rents demanded by landlords.

Inflation can make business planning and decision-making more complicated. Contracts of employment, for example, may need to build in pay structures that take account of the changing costs of living caused by changes in the general price level. Raw material costs, catalogue prices and menus are also affected by inflation. Essentially, inflation that is not sustainable is a threat to businesses due to the uncertainty that is caused.

Inflation also has an effect on the international competitiveness of a country. A nation that has a higher inflation rate than its rivals will tend to be less price-competitive when trading overseas. This will, other things being constant, lead to a fall in export earnings, lower national output and perhaps higher unemployment.

In general, inflation can be controlled by limiting demand-pull and cost-push factors. For example, the domestic government might raise taxes to control the amount of consumption in the economy. Equally, it could subsidise production of local businesses to reduce their costs of production, thereby combating cost-push factors. Alternatively, the government could pursue *supply-side policies* that improve the **productive capacity** of the economy, such as investment in education, health care and training. These programmes will help to increase the quality and productivity of the economy's resources over time.

Question 1.5.3

Zimbabwe's inflation problems

Zimbabwe has been suffering the impacts of hyper inflation for a number of years, with rates reaching 231,000,000% in July 2008. This meant that prices of goods and services in the country were more than doubling each week! In June 2006, the country's Reserve Bank had to issue a new bank denomination – the 100,000 Zimbabwean dollar note (less than $1 at the time). By mid 2008, the government launched a Z$500,000,000 (Z$500m) bank note. The government estimates that 10.5 million Zimbabweans (around 80% of the population) live below the poverty line. Economists argue that the problem will continue to be a major problem unless the government deals with the root causes of inflation.

a Outline three factors that could be causing inflation in Zimbabwe. *[3 marks]*

b Evaluate the impact of uncontrollable inflation on the Zimbabwean economy. *[7 marks]*

A high level of employment / reducing the rate of unemployment

The rate of unemployment measures the proportion of a country's workforce not in employment. The unemployment rate at any point in time is caused by the interaction of the levels of aggregate demand and aggregate supply in the economy. If aggregate demand is high, then there will be a higher level of derived demand for labour and hence there will be low unemployment. If aggregate supply is high, then that generally means more national output is being produced, and again there will tend to be a higher level of employment as a result.

Governments aim to deal with the problems of unemployment as there are both economic and **social costs** of high unemployment. The costs to society include the effects on the unemployed themselves, such as stress, depression and low self-esteem. Unemployment also affects the network of family and friends, with negative effects such as arguments, separation and divorce. A final social cost is the negative impact of unemployment on the local community, such as poverty and increased levels of crime. The **economic costs** of unemployment refer to the **opportunity costs** of unemployment, i.e. what else could have been produced if unemployment was not such a problem. The economic costs of high unemployment might include the increased burden for taxpayers and increased government spending on unemployment benefits. High unemployment will therefore lead to a loss of international competitiveness due to lower levels of national output in the long run.

In order to reduce the level of unemployment, governments will look at the type of unemployment in question (see Box 1.5b) and its causes. In general, governments can use a combination of demand and supply side policies to tackle the problems of unemployment. **Demand-side policies** are those that directly target increasing the level of aggregate demand in the economy. For example, the government may use **expansionary fiscal policy** to reduce unemployment. This entails reducing taxes and/or increasing government spending. This should, in theory, help to expand the level of spending in the economy. It may also use **expansionary monetary policy** to boost aggregate demand. This entails reducing the level of interest rates in the economy to encourage consumer and business borrowing and spending. A third demand-side policy is for the government to use **protectionist measures** to protect domestic businesses (and jobs) from international competition. This might involve placing tariffs (a tax on foreign goods) to give domestic producers a price advantage. Box 1.5d on page 85 outlines the main methods of protectionism.

Supply-side policies can also be used to tackle unemployment. These policies aim to increase the level of aggregate supply (or output) in the economy. Lowering the level of corporation tax or interest rates should stimulate business activity and investments. Government spending on education and training should help to make the future generation of workers more skilled and flexible (labour mobility). Supply-side policies tend to have more permanent effects on the economy than demand-side policies but the goals take longer to accomplish.

Box 1.5b Types of unemployment

Frictional unemployment happens when people are changing jobs as there is usually a time lag between leaving a job and finding or starting another. As it is temporary unemployment, there is relatively little social hardship. Frictional unemployment, sometimes called **transitional unemployment**, is always present in the economy.

Seasonal unemployment is unemployment caused by seasonal changes in demand for a product. During the pre-Christmas trading period, many temporary staff are employed in the retail industry but when the season is over these people become unemployed. Likewise, beach resorts tend to suffer from a lack of tourists during the winter months. Perhaps the most seasonally unemployed person is Santa Claus!

Technological unemployment results in people losing their jobs due to the introduction of labour-saving (capital-intensive) technologies, which can cause mass scale unemployment.

Regional unemployment refers to the different unemployment rates that exist in different areas of a country. Busy urban business districts tend to have higher levels of employment than remote rural areas. This reflects the preferences of businesses to locate in different locations (see Unit 5.5), depending on the nature of the business and the size of its market.

Structural unemployment occurs when the demand for products produced in a particular industry continually declines. The industry therefore suffers from structural and long-term changes. For example, foreign competition has led to the decline in the UK automobile, shipping, textiles, coal and steel industries. The structurally unemployed tend to suffer from occupational and geographical immobility (see Unit 2.1).

Cyclical unemployment is the most severe type of unemployment as it tends to affect each and every industry in the economy. It is caused by a lack of aggregate demand in the economy, i.e. when the economy suffers from an economic recession. Cyclical unemployment, also known as **demand deficient unemployment**, is often associated with a decline in both domestic economic growth and world trade.

Economic growth

Economic growth refers to an increase in a country's economic activity over time. This is measured by the change in total output of the economy per year, known as the **Gross Domestic Product** (GDP). Higher rates of economic growth suggest that the average person is earning more income and therefore the economy is more prosperous.

Figure 1.5a illustrates how economic activity fluctuates over time. These changes represent changes in economic growth and the pattern is known as the **trade cycle**, or the **business cycle**. There are several key phases in the trade cycle.

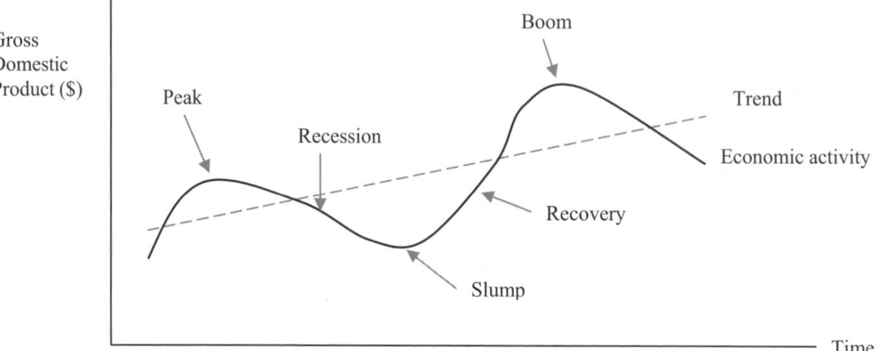

Figure 1.5a The trade cycle

- During the **peak** or **boom** of a trade cycle, economic activity is at its highest level. Consumer expenditure, investment and export earnings will be high. Unemployment will be low whilst consumer and business confidence levels will be high. People are likely to be receiving pay rises as businesses make higher levels of profit. Businesses will tend to have very good cash flow during this period.
- A **recession** occurs when there has been a dip in the level of economic activity for two consecutive quarters (half a year). Features of a recession include declining aggregate demand, lower investment expenditure, falling export sales and rising unemployment. Businesses most likely to be affected during a recession are those that sell a small range of products and those that sell products that are sensitive to changes in incomes (e.g. houses, cars, jewellery and overseas holidays). Box 1.5c outlines ways that businesses can deal with the problems of a recession.
- A **slump** or **trough** refers to the bottom of a recession and the last stage of decline in the trade cycle. There will be a high level of unemployment alongside very low levels of consumer spending, investment and export earnings. Businesses will suffer from poor cash flow and many will have already closed down due to poor *liquidity* (insufficient money to run the business on a daily basis). Consumers have little confidence in the economy and workers suffer from a lack of job security, thereby limiting their overall spending.
- **Recovery** or **expansion** occurs when the level of GDP starts to rise again, after the economy has experienced a slump. Since national income begins to increase again, consumption, investment, exports and employment will all gradually rise.

Box 1.5c Coping with a recession

Cost reduction methods, such as efforts to cut lighting and energy bills, finding alternative suppliers who can offer better prices, or relocating to cheaper premises should help to improve cash flow. If there is an absolute need, firms may need to make some staff redundant to reduce the size of the workforce.

Price reductions may help to sustain or increase sales. People become more aware of prices during a recession, so lower prices will be very welcome by the general public.

Non-pricing strategies (such as repackaging, special offers or outstanding after-sales care) can help to sustain or revitalise the volume of sales.

Branding can have a considerable impact on sales and reduce the degree of *price* and *income elasticity of demand* (see Unit 4.4). Customers who are loyal to a brand, despite changes in price or their income, can help to maintain sales during unfavourable trading times for the economy. Similarly, if the price elasticity of demand for exports is high, then these will do well when prices fall due to a weaker exchange rate.

Outsourcing production overseas where costs of production are lower can help a business to gain a competitive price advantage and to increase its profits, thereby reducing the impact of any recession in the domestic market.

Improved *efficiency* in the production process (better use of existing resources) can contribute to economic growth. Economists also attribute economic growth to both enhanced *quantity* and *quality* of factors of production. Growth via improved *quality* of factors of production normally requires an **investment** in key resources of the economy:

- **Capital goods**. The greater the level of investment, the higher economic growth tends to be. Spending on developing an economy's infrastructure will aid economic activity and help to attract more business investments in the future.
- **Education and training**. A better educated and trained workforce becomes a more productive and internationally competitive labour force.
- **Health technology**. Advances in health care helps to ensure workers are healthy and therefore more productive. It can also prevent workers having to take time off work or retire early due to illness.

Growth via an increase in the *quantity* of resources can occur in numerous ways. Discovering new sources of raw materials, for instance, will increase the productive capacity of an economy. Changes in the labour force can be caused by a number of factors:

- *Changes in demography.* A fall in the birth rate in developed economies has led to an ageing population and a smaller workforce. If people choose to start work later (due to higher education commitments) and retire earlier (due to rising incomes), this will also reduce the size of the workforce. Conversely, a baby boom will lead to a larger workforce in a couple of decades time.
- *Changes in participation rates.* The participation rate measures the number of people who are self-employed or employed as a percentage of the total labour force. A higher participation rate can be caused by government incentives (such as lower rates of income tax or reduced welfare payments). An increase in the number of women returning to or starting work has also led to higher participation rates in many regions of the world.
- *Changes in net migration.* This refers to the difference between *immigration* (the number of people entering a country for work purposes) and *emigration* (those leaving a country). If the net migration figure is positive, then the size of the workforce will increase, thereby helping to raise the productive capacity of the economy.

Poorer countries and regions of the world have found it difficult to grow. **Barriers to economic growth** exist and these could be a restraining force for many businesses that wish to expand overseas. A country will find economic growth is more difficult to achieve if:

- There is a lack of infrastructure (communications and transport networks). Countries without basic electricity, road networks, schools, hospitals, housing, factories and offices will find it difficult to prosper.
- It lacks the technical knowledge and a skilled labour force. These are essential resources for generating economic activity and growth.
- There is rapid population growth. Countries with a high net birth rate will tend to find that there are too many mouths to feed. Around half of India's population are children and this has, to some extent, hindered its economic development.
- It suffers from high foreign debt repayments. Highly indebted poor countries are obliged to repay their huge interest-bearing loans, leaving very little money for domestic investment and growth.

An improvement in the balance of payments

The balance of payments is a record of a country's money inflows and outflows, per time period. it is made up of two components: the **current account** (export earnings and import expenditure) and the **capital account** (flows of money for government reserves, foreign currencies or investment reasons). The Current Account is further split into two parts: the 'visible' trade balance (international trade in tangible goods such as oil, steel and cars) and the 'invisible' trade balance (foreign trade in intangible services, such as banking, distribution and insurance).

In the long term, governments strive to avoid a deficit on the Current Account. Just as an individual cannot spend more than she or he earns in the long term, the same applies to countries. Governments may attempt to correct a deficit on the Current Account by encouraging higher Capital Account inflows and/or by a devaluing its exchange rate.

The **exchange rate** measures the value of one currency in terms of foreign currencies. A higher exchange rate (known as an **appreciation** of the currency) means that export prices will be relatively higher, thereby reducing the exporter's price competitiveness. Hence, the government's attempt to devalue the exchange rate should give domestic firms a relative price advantage. On the other hand, a lower exchange rate (known as a **depreciation** of the currency) also means that domestic firms that import raw materials and components will suffer from having to pay relatively higher prices, thereby raising their production costs. Hence, government attempts to change the exchange rate, in order to correct an imbalance on the Balance of Payments, are likely to have a direct effect on businesses.

Continual and large fluctuations in the foreign exchange rate can create difficulties for businesses. Business planning and forecasting becomes very complex and perhaps impractical. For example, businesses may not be able to accurately forecast export earnings or costs of imported materials due to exchange rate volatility. International trade deals may be postponed until the business can benefit from more favourable movements in the exchange rate (although there is no guarantee that this will ever happen).

Governments may set up international trade barriers to correct any disparity in its balance of payments or simply to protect their domestic industries. **Protectionism** refers to any policy used by a government to safeguard domestic businesses from foreign competitors. Protectionist measures therefore present a threat, or barrier to trade, for foreign businesses trying to establish themselves in overseas markets. Common methods of protectionism are outlined in Box 1.5d.

Box 1.5d Examples of protectionism

Tariffs, also known as **customs duties**, are a form of tax placed on imported products, thereby raising their price. They can be *ad valorem* (e.g. 12% tax) or *specific* (e.g. $5 per unit). This helps to give the domestic firms a slight price advantage.

Quotas are quantitative limits preventing too many foreign products entering a country. Hong Kong, India, China and the UK, for instance, place quotas on the number of American Hollywood movies that can be released in their countries (in order to protect their respective film industries).

Subsidies are payments made by a government to domestic firms as a form of financial aid. This helps to reduce the costs of production of domestic firms, thereby giving them a competitive advantage over foreign rivals.

Embargos are physical bans on international trade with a certain country. Such restrictions are usually due to political conflict, strategic reasons or severe health and safety concerns.

Technical and safety standards refer to the imposition of strict technical or health and safety standards being placed on the import of foreign products. The administration and compliance costs involved in meeting these standards will tend to raise production costs (and hence prices) for foreign producers.

Question 1.5.4

K&Q Jeans

K&Q sell jeans in the UK. They buy their jeans from an American supplier and import 10,000 pairs of jeans for a cost of $30 each, per month. K&Q then sell these to their customers at a price of £30 each.

a Use the various exchange rates to complete the table below for K&Q. *[5 marks]*

Exchange Rate	Purchase cost ($)	Purchase cost (£)	Sales revenue (£)	Profit or Loss (£)
£1 = $1.00				
£1 = $2.00				
£1 = $1.50				
£1 = $2.50				
£1 = $0.75				

b Comment on the relationship between changes in the exchange rate and the level of profits. *[2 marks]*

c By engaging in international trade, explain two other costs that K&Q might incur. *[4 marks]*

d Examine how a high exchange rate can be both an opportunity and a threat to a business such as K&Q. *[6 marks]*

ENVIRONMENTAL OPPORTUNITIES AND THREATS

Citizens, organizations and governments are increasingly aware and concerned about the negative impacts of business activity on the global environment. Without government intervention, private sector businesses are unlikely to consider the **external costs** of production. External costs, also known as **negative externalities**, are costs incurred by a third party in a business transaction, i.e. costs borne by society or the environment rather than by the buyer or seller. Examples of such costs include passive smoking, air and noise pollution, packaging waste and global warming. Global warming and climate change have also been blamed for the increase in natural disasters such as tsunamis and hurricanes.

Public concerns and changes in social attitudes about the environment have meant that businesses are increasingly reviewing their operations. Firms that do not respect the environment face ruining their reputation and long-term profitability. As with so many decisions in business, such firms must calculate the relative costs and benefits of their activities. If compliance costs are too high, then firms may simply choose not to become more environmentally friendly. The extent to which businesses will consider environmental issues depends on their aims and objectives, the attitudes of workers and management, the likely impact on their profits and the resources (financial, human and capital) at their disposal.

Changes in the weather and the seasons can also present opportunities and threats. Torrential rain or flooding, for example, will affect a large number of businesses, such as theme parks and car wash firms. The Indian Ocean tsunami (SE Asia, 2004) and Hurricane Katrina (USA, 2005) caused havoc to businesses. However, some businesses may be able to exploit changes in the season, such as tour operators focusing on ski holidays in winter and beach resorts in the summer.

Finally, health scares and epidemics will also present threats to businesses. The SARS (2003) and bird flu (2006) outbreaks in SE Asia caused turmoil in the region, with many businesses collapsing due to a loss of consumer and business confidence. Mad cow disease (late 1990s) and foot and mouth disease (2001) had similar effects in many European countries.

POLITICAL OPPORTUNITIES AND THREATS

A government is said to adopt a *laissez-faire* approach to managing the economy if it does not intervene significantly in business activity. The argument for such an approach is that leaving businesses to their own devices should stimulate healthy competition and efficiency. The belief is that state intervention through the application of legislation and government policies can present barriers to business growth. Moreover, a laissez-faire business environment is more likely to attract *foreign direct investment* because it is easier to conduct business in such countries. In reality, most governments adopt an *interventionist* approach to managing the economy. They use legislation and apply government policies to control business behaviour and to influence the level of economic activity.

Government intervention takes place for several reasons and these can present either opportunities or threats to businesses in the economy. Government policies can be broken down into two main categories: fiscal policy and monetary policy.

Fiscal policy

Fiscal policy refers to the use of government **taxation** and government **expenditure** policies to influence the economy. Taxation, examples of which are summarized in Box 1.5e, can be classified in two broad ways:

- **Direct and Indirect.** *Direct taxation* is tax that is paid straight from the income, wealth or profit of an individual or a business. Examples include income, inheritance and corporation taxes. *Indirect taxation* refers to tax paid on the trade in goods and services. Examples include sales taxes and excise duties.
- **Progressive, Regressive and Proportional.** A *progressive* tax (such as income tax or stamp duty) is one where the proportion of tax paid increases as the income, wealth or profit of the taxpayer rises. This is seen as being fair since taxpayers are charged on their ability to pay. A *regressive tax* is one where the proportion of tax paid actually falls as the income of the taxpayer rises. A wealthy person pays the same absolute amount of airport tax to that of a less wealthy traveller, for example, but the tax represents a much smaller percentage of the wealthier person's income. A *proportional tax* (such as government sales taxes) is one where the percentage of tax paid remains the same, irrespective of income, wealth or profit levels.

The government will spend the tax revenue that it raises, in addition to other sources of government finance, on a number of areas including: social security, transport and infrastructure, health care, education and training, national defence, and law and order. An increase in government expenditure can help to stimulate economic activity in the economy.

Fiscal policy can take two forms: deflationary fiscal policy or expansionary fiscal policy. **Deflationary fiscal policy** is used when the economy is experiencing high rates of economic growth and inflation, so needs to be slowed down, i.e. via a combination of higher taxes and reduced government expenditure policies. By contrast, **expansionary fiscal policy** is used to boost the economy, perhaps to get it out of a recession. This is done by a combination of tax cuts and increased levels of public sector spending.

Box 1.5e Common examples of taxes

Income tax is a levy on personal incomes from wages, rent, interest and dividends. It is the most important source of tax revenue for most governments. Income tax tends to be progressive in nature since rising rates of incomes attract higher rates of tax

Corporation tax is a levy on the profits of businesses. Small businesses tend to be charged a lower percentage tax on their profits than large multinationals.

Sales taxes are taxes on an individual's expenditure. Examples include Value Added Tax (charged in most European countries) and the Government Sales Tax (used in the Americas).

Capital gains tax is a tax on the surplus (known as 'capital gains') made from investments in shares and other assets, such as property.

Inheritance tax is a tax on the value of assets (such as cash, property or stocks and shares) passed onto another party following the death of an individual.

Excise duties are taxes are levied on *demerit goods* such as alcohol, tobacco, petrol and gambling.

Customs duties are taxes on foreign imports. The taxes not only help to raise government revenue but also give domestic suppliers a relative price advantage.

Stamp duty is a tax paid when commercial or residential property is bought. It tends to be progressive, so the higher the property value, the greater the tax rate tends to be.

Monetary policy

Monetary policy is designed to control the amount of spending and investment in an economy by altering interest rates to affect the money supply and exchange rates. Interest rates refer to the price of money, both in terms of the price of borrowing money and the return for saving money in a bank account. If the economy was believed to be *overheating* (growing too much and too fast) thereby causing inflation to be too high, then the government is likely to increase interest rates.

Increasing interest rates makes borrowing less attractive because households and businesses face higher costs of interest repayments on their loans. In addition, people and businesses with existing credit card bills, loans and mortgages face escalating interest repayments when interest rates are hiked. Higher interest rates will automatically reduce people's **discretionary income** (disposable income after all interest-bearing loans have been paid for). Hence, consumers may need to cut back on their spending elsewhere. The same will apply to businesses with outstanding loans. Overall, an increase in interest rates is likely to reduce consumption and investment expenditure in the economy, therefore being a threat to businesses, even though this may help to control inflation.

Businesses are charged varying levels of interest rates for four main reasons:

- **Risk**. The greater the risk of a business *defaulting* on a loan (failing to repay the borrowed money), the higher the interest rate tends to be. Large multinational businesses offer less risk so are able to borrow more money at a relatively lower rate of interest.
- **Time**. The longer the period of a loan, the higher the real interest rate tends to be. Higher interest rates are charged to compensate lenders for the opportunity cost of money being lent out for long periods of time.
- **Administration costs**. The higher the administration costs involved in lending money to a business, the higher the interest rate tends to be. For example, lending a total of $100 million to 100 different customers is far more administratively costly than lending the same amount to a single customer.
- **Expectations**. If the government expects the economy to do well (with higher levels of spending, investment and export earnings) then it is likely to announce an interest rate hike to dampen the effects on inflation in the economy.

Interest rates also have a direct impact on the exchange rate. There is a positive correlation between a country's interest rate and its exchange rate. An increase in interest rates in a country tends to stimulate demand for its currency since foreign investors are attracted by better returns on their saving. If Germany and Australia have relatively higher interest rates than Japan or Taiwan, then that would mean funds move abroad from the Asian banks, thereby increasing the demand for Euros and the Australian dollar. This would, all other things being equal, subsequently increase the price (or exchange rate) of these currencies. A rise in the exchange rate, caused by increasing interest rates, raises the price of exports relative to imports, and therefore tends to reduce the demand for exports. Hence, higher exchange rates tend to be damaging for domestic businesses in the long run.

Some economists argue that government intervention to control business activity, such as through the use of fiscal and monetary policies, may be counterproductive. This is because rules and legislation may restrict business activity and discourage foreign investment in the economy. Furthermore, higher taxes or interest rates create disincentive effects, such as limiting profit maximization, Research and Development and innovation. Furthermore, many rules and regulations increase the administration burden and costs on businesses, such as having to comply with health and safety laws.

Exam Tip!
Students often comment on higher interest rates creating incentives for people to save more money. The truth is that governments in developed nations will only tend to change interest rates by 0.25% at a time; hardly an incentive to spend less in order to save more. *Some* people may save more (probably those without commitments to mortgages, credits cards and loans), but this is highly unlikely for the majority of households and businesses who do have outstanding loans. Higher interest rates have a much larger impact on reducing the spending ability and confidence levels of individuals because of a fall in their discretionary income.

LEGAL OPPORTUNITIES AND THREATS

The government imposes rules, regulations and laws to ensure that the general public is protected from the negative aspects of business activity. Government intervention also takes place to protect the interests of businesses. Common legislation affecting businesses include:

- **Consumer protection legislation**. Laws exist that make it illegal for a business to provide false or misleading descriptions of their products and services (see Question 1.5.5). Products must meet certain quality standards and be fit for their purpose. Businesses are held liable for any damage or injury caused to the customer by their defective products.
- **Employee protection legislation**. Laws have been passed to protect the interest and safety of workers (see Unit 2.1). For instance, anti-discrimination legislation helps to ensure that businesses act in a fair manner towards their employees, irrespective of their age, gender, religion or ethnicity.
- **Competition legislation**. Government laws ensure that anti-competitive practices are stopped in order to protect customers and smaller firms from businesses with monopoly power (see Unit 4.4). The government will step in and fine any business it deems to be acting against the public interest, such as large firms engaging in price fixing, charging unjustifiably high prices, or significantly restricting consumer choice. Although competition legislation can restrict the activities of businesses, some laws can present opportunities. Copyright, trademark and patent legislation, for instance, gives businesses legal protection against others replicating their works or inventions. Hence, the existence of these laws can stimulate innovation (see Unit 5.6), which can give a business a competitive advantage over its rivals.
- **Social and environmental protection legislation**. Laws exist to prevent or reduce the consumption of demerit goods. The social costs (to the whole community) of consuming such products outweigh the private costs of consumption (incurred by the consumer). Examples of demerit goods include tobacco, petrol, alcohol and illegal drugs. It is argued that without government legislation, the consumption of demerit goods would be much higher and therefore the costs to society would be much greater (e.g. passive smoking, pollution and crime).

Question 1.5.5

Amoy Food

Amoy Food, one of Hong Kong's oldest food brands, was charged for false advertising in 2006. The firm had claimed in its advertisements and packaging that its sauce products were free of monosodium glutamate (MSG). The Food and Environmental Hygiene Department found traces of MSG, an artificial flavour enhancer, in the company's oyster and soy sauce products. Hong Kong laws impose a maximum penalty of $50,000 and six months in jail for anyone convicted of issuing false labelling and advertisements for food and drugs. According to its website, Amoy has been the best-selling soy sauce in Hong Kong and Britain since 1994 and 1998 respectively.

- Examine how Amoy Food may have acted unlawfully *and* unethically. *[6 marks]*

ETHICAL OPPORTUNITIES AND THREATS

Business ethics are the moral principles that are, or should be, considered in business decision-making, i.e. what is good or bad and what is right or wrong. Most people believe that ethical firms are socially responsible towards their stakeholders (see Unit 1.4), especially their customers, employees and the local community. Such firms would aim to protect the natural environment by using resources efficiently and minimizing waste. They would not employ workers below the legal minimum age or allow their employees to operate in poor working conditions. They would not use misleading advertising and marketing messages or deal with corrupt businesses, sponsors and governments.

Although there are **compliance costs** (see Unit 1.3) in acting ethically, firms that are socially responsible can benefit in several ways:

- They attract and retain good quality workers. Google, for example, have a very loyal and dedicated workforce because the company provides all its workers with free buffet meals, gym access and a host of other on-site benefits.
- They attract new consumers and retain existing customers. More and more customers are concerned about environmental protection. As a result, they are likely to lose interest in businesses that do not consider the impact of their operations on society and the environment.
- It generates good publicity and public relations. Organizations such as The Body Shop and Friends of The Earth have used their ethical stance to propel their business and cause.

Traditionally, businesses only report figures for their financial performance. However, firms are increasingly prepared to have external **social audits** conducted. These are reports on the ethical and social stance of a business, examined and reported by an external agency. The social audit will report both external matters (such as the level of pollution caused by a firm or its involvement in community projects) and internal issues (such as the efficiency of its waste management processes or its ability to provide workers with a safe working environment).

Choosing to be ethical and socially responsible may bring its benefits, but there are also costs involved in such decisions. A business may not always be able to pursue the cheapest or the most profitable option due to compliance costs of being ethical and socially responsible. For instance, firms may not choose to use the cheapest supplier if they are seen by customers and other stakeholders as being unethical businesses.

THE DIFFERENCES AND RELATIONSHIP BETWEEN PEST AND SWOT

SWOT analysis (see Unit 1.6) is a frequently used decision-making tool. SWOT is an acronym for the strengths, weaknesses, opportunities and threats of a business proposition. The main differences between a SWOT and a PEST analysis are:

- A PEST analysis tends to be broader, examining all factors in the external business environment. SWOT analysis can have a much narrower focus, such as the assessment of a business proposition.
- PEST analysis is useful for producing a SWOT (and not the other way round). A thorough PEST analysis helps to identify the *opportunities* and *threats* within a SWOT analysis.
- PEST analysis tends to be more useful and relevant when dealing with larger or more complex issues.
- A PEST analysis does not directly consider the internal factors (strengths and weaknesses) of the issue being considered.

There are similarities between a PEST and SWOT since similar factors appear in both analyses.

EXTERNAL ENVIRONMENT AND BUSINESS STRATEGY

PEST Analysis gives managers an overview of the external business environment, the factors that might affect business activity and the issues that should be addressed in any business strategy. It is a useful and straight-forward framework that aids decision-making. It can be used to analyse decisions such as:

- the potential costs and benefits of a joint venture, merger or acquisition (see Unit 1.7)
- marketing planning, such as the opportunities and threats of using international marketing (see Unit 4.7)
- business propositions, such as whether to set up operations overseas
- investment opportunities, such as deciding on the location of business (see Unit 5.5).

Governments will use a range of policies to achieve their macroeconomic objectives. Some of these will present threats, whilst others will be opportunities for businesses. Social, cultural, technological and environmental factors will also affect business activity. Different businesses are affected by different external factors and to varying degrees. This will largely depend on factors such as:

- The size of the business. Smaller and newer firms tend to be less able to deal with external shocks to the business environment.
- The ability of management. Experienced and skilled managers will be able to predict, and successfully react to changes in the external business environment.
- The *price elasticity of demand* (see Unit 4.4) for the products sold by the business. Products with price inelastic demand have very few substitutes. This means that the level of demand for such products will not be significantly affected by external factors such as fluctuations in the exchange rate. *Brand loyalty* (see Unit 4.3) can also make the demand price inelastic.
- The degree of diversification. Firms that have a diversified product portfolio and have operations overseas are more able to handle any changes in the external business environment. By contrast, firms that specialize in one or two products in a specific market are more vulnerable to external factors.
- The level of a firm's *gearing*. Gearing measures the extent to which a firm relies on external borrowing. Those that are highly geared are more defenceless if interest rates were to rise.

External factors will also affect the international competitiveness of a business. International competitiveness refers to a firm's ability to compete against overseas competitors. This will be based on internal factors such as price, brand awareness and loyalty, product design and quality. External factors such as the exchange rate against foreign currencies will also directly affect a firm's international competitiveness. Management guru Michael Porter suggests that businesses need to find their source of competitive advantage. This can be through low prices (such as Ryan Air or Ikea) or through outstanding quality (such as BMW or Gucci). This will then allow the business to devise appropriate marketing strategies in order to maintain or improve its competitiveness.

In conclusion, PEST analysis is a useful management tool for assessing how various external factors affect business activity. Careful planning through the use of a PEST framework can help businesses to identify the opportunities and threats present in the external environment. Planning can then better prepare organizations to deal with the dynamic nature of business.

REVIEW QUESTIONS 1.5

1. What does the acronym STEEPLE analysis stand for?
2. Outline the purpose of a PEST analysis.
3. What are the three general steps needed to carry out a PEST analysis?
4. Explain how each of the PEST components can represent either opportunities or threats for a business.
5. What are the four key macroeconomic objectives of most governments?
6. What is meant by the 'trade cycle'?
7. State three ways in which a business may be able to cope with a recession.
8. Using examples, distinguish between 'economic' and 'political' opportunities and threats.
9. Distinguish between 'fiscal policy' and 'monetary policy'.
10. How does the legal system present both opportunities and threats for businesses?

Balance of Payments is an annual record of a country's export earnings and its import expenditure. A surplus exists if the value of exports exceeds that of imports (vice versa for a deficit on the balance of payments).

Deregulation refers to the removal of government rules and regulations which constrain an industry, thereby enhancing its efficiency. Deregulation should also encourage more competition within an industry.

Direct tax is a levy that is paid from the income of individuals or businesses, such as personal income tax and corporation tax.

Economic growth measures the change in the Gross Domestic Product of a nation over time. Growth is said to occur if there is an increase in GDP for two consecutive quarters.

Ethics are the moral values and judgements (what is right and just) that society believes organizations should consider in their decision-making.

Exchange rate refers to the value of a country's currency in terms of another currency.

External shocks, also known as **exogenous shocks**, are unforeseeable and unexpected changes in the external business environment that tend to affect all businesses in the economy, such as natural disasters or wars.

Fiscal policy refers to government policies that deal with taxation and government expenditure in order to affect the level of economic activity.

Gross Domestic Product is the total value of a nation's annual output. It is used as an indicator of the level of economic activity in a country.

Indirect tax is a levy placed on the purchase of goods and services, such as sales taxes and excise duties.

Inflation occurs when the general price level in an economy continuously rises. It is calculated by measuring changes in the cost of a representative basket of goods and services purchased by the average household over a period of time.

Interest rate is a measure of the price of money. It can be expressed in terms of the amount charged for money that is borrowed or how much is offered on money that is saved.

Monetary policy refers to government policies concerned with changing interest rates in order to control the money supply, and the exchange rate.

PEST analysis is a framework used to analyse the opportunities and threats of the political, economic, social and technological environments on business activity. It is one of many tools that can be used in the decision-making process.

Protectionism refers to any measure taken by a government to safeguard its businesses from foreign competitors. This presents a threat or barrier to trade for businesses trying to operate in overseas markets.

Tariffs are a method of protectionism whereby the domestic government taxes foreign imports, thereby giving domestic producers a relative price advantage.

Trade cycle, also known as the **business cycle**, refers to the fluctuation in the level of economic activity over time. Economies tend to move through the cycle of booms, recessions, slumps, recovery and growth.

Unemployment refers to the number of people in the workforce who are willing and able to work but cannot find employment.

Organizational Planning Tools

UNIT 1.6

The rich man plans for tomorrow,
the poor man for today.

Chinese proverb

Key topics

- Business plans
- SWOT analysis
- Decision-making framework

Higher Level extension

- Scientific versus Intuitive decision-making processes
- Decision-making frameworks: Decision trees and Fishbone/Ishikawa/ Cause-and-Effect models
- Internal and external constraints on decision-making

INTRODUCTION

At the heart of business and management is decision-making. Managers are involved in making decisions every day. Decision-making involves managers having to make a choice between competing alternatives. If they make the right decisions, the business will thrive. If the wrong decisions are made, this can be very costly to the business. There are three levels of decision-making in an organization:

- **Operational decisions** refer to the routine and day-to-day decisions, such as those handled by junior management, e.g. deciding when a worker should go for their break and how to deal with customer enquiries or complaints.
- **Tactical decisions** refer regular and short-term decisions that are normally handled by middle management, e.g. decisions about pricing strategies or recruitment and selection of staff.
- **Strategic decisions** refer to high-level and long-term decisions that set the overall direction for a business. Such decisions are dealt with by senior management since they carry more risk, e.g. which products to be developed, which new markets to enter, the location (or relocation) of the business, and the review of salaries and benefits paid to all staff.

Therefore, what makes one management job different from another is the amount of decision-making that is involved and the scale of importance of these decisions. There is an element of risk associated with almost every business decision. For example, when a firm recruits new workers there is always the risk of selecting the 'wrong' candidates. It is the role of skilled managers to ensure that business decision-making carries as much quantifiable risk as possible. This will help to ensure that decisions are made in a rational way. This Unit examines various planning tools that aid business decision-making.

BUSINESS PLANS

In simple terms, a business plan is a report detailing how a new business sets out to achieve its aims and objectives. The business plan is a useful planning tool as it requires the owner to plan marketing, financial and human resources of the business. However, the main aim of producing a business plan from the entrepreneur's point of view is to gain financial backing from lenders such as banks and venture capitalists (see Unit 3.1). It can also be used by other stakeholders such as shareholders to assess the potential gains from their investment in the business.

Financiers will want to see a business plan because it shows that the entrepreneur has comprehensively researched the business opportunity and has given reasons to support the venture. This will help financial lenders to make a more objective judgement regarding the firm's likely success rate and hence its ability to repay any loans. Financiers will look very carefully at how the forecast cash will flow into and out of the business in its early stages. This is because managing *working capital* (see Unit 3.3) in a new business can be an extremely difficult task. There is a huge risk that the market may not be as large as predicted and that customers may not respond to the price or product as hoped. Start-up costs are likely to be high, so overestimating cash inflows or underestimating cash outflows could lead to major liquidity problems.

Investors will assess both risks and opportunities that may be reflected in a business plan before making any judgement. They will also look for potential problems with the business venture, even if these are not outlined in the business plan.

Once an entrepreneur has come up with a business opportunity, the business plan can be produced. Although there is no universally accepted format for writing business plans, the contents of a typical business plan will include the following information:

- **The business**
  - Name and address of the proposed business
  - The type of business organization, such as sole proprietorship or partnership
  - A statement of quantifiable aims and objectives of the proposed business
  - Cost of premises and other start-up costs
  - Details of the owner(s) and their past business experience
- **The product**
  - Details of the good(s) and/or service(s) being offered
  - The forecast level of demand (both present and future demand) with any supporting evidence showing why customers will pay for this product
  - How and where production will take place, such as the equipment that is needed
  - Details of the suppliers of resources such as raw materials or stocks
  - Costs of production, i.e. the running costs of operating the business
  - Pricing strategies to be used
- **The market**
  - The size of the market as determined by the potential number of customers for the product, for example, IB Business & Management is a small market compared to IB Economics or IB Biology
  - The nature of the market such as the customer profile and market segmentation (see Unit 4.2)
  - The recent growth rate of the market and the expected growth rates in the foreseeable future
  - An outline of both direct and indirect competitors, including their market share, strengths and weaknesses
- **The finance**
  - Proposed sources of finance (see Unit 3.1) to show how the business will be funded
  - Break-even analysis (see Unit 5.3) to project the firm's break-even level of sales
  - Steps to be taken to deal with cash flow problems
  - Security (financial guarantee) that can be offered to lenders in case the borrower defaults on the loan, i.e. fails to repay the loan
  - A cash flow forecast showing the projected earnings from sales and the expected monthly cash payments for the ongoing costs of the business
  - A projected profit and loss account showing the estimated profit (or loss) at the end of the first year
  - A projected balance sheet for the end of the first year showing the firm's *assets* (value of items it owns) and *liabilities* (value of its legal debts)
  - Forecast rate of return for investors of the business venture
- **The personnel**
  - The number and positions of the workers likely to be employed
  - Organizational chart (see Unit 2.2) showing the internal structure of human resources
  - Details of payment systems such as wage rates, salaries and remuneration packages (see Unit 2.5)

- **The marketing**
  - Details of the promotional mix that will be used to reach customers and make sales
  - The distribution plan, detailing where the products will be sold
  - Evidence of whether any market research, such as test marketing, has been carried out
  - Any unique selling point that the business can use to differentiate itself from its competitors.

In addition, business plans may have a section devoted to a **SWOT analysis** (see next subsection). Business plans may also contain a **contingency plan** outlining what the entrepreneur plans to do in case the business does not go as well as planned. Finally, any appropriate reference material (such as statistics, charts and other supporting evidence) should appear in an **appendix** at the back of the business plan.

Since bank managers are busy people, it is generally recommended to produce a business plan of no more than 5–6 pages long. If this is not possible, such as in the case of an international joint venture, then an executive summary (see Unit 2.3) is written and then placed at the beginning of the business plan. This summarizes the information given in the main report of the business plan with key points highlighted including the conclusions. The **executive summary** can be read within a few minutes to get an idea or an overview of the business plan, and the bank manager can then decide whether or not to read the whole document.

Note: Higher Level students must be able to analyse and interpret business plans.
(© IBO 2007)

SWOT ANALYSIS

SWOT analysis is a simple yet extremely useful decision-making tool. SWOT is an acronym for Strengths, Weaknesses, Opportunities and Threats. It can be used to assess the current and future situation of a product, brand, company, proposal or decision. A SWOT analysis considers both internal factors (the strengths and weaknesses) and external factors (the opportunities and threats) that are relevant to the issue or problem under investigation. A SWOT template is shown in Table 1.6a.

- **Strengths** are the internal factors that are positive compared to competitors. For example, the business may have a strong brand, a good corporate image or highly skilled workers. These advantages help the business to better achieve its organizational objectives. Hence, the strengths of a business need to be developed and protected.
- **Weaknesses** are the internal factors that are negative when compared to competitors, i.e. they are sources of competitive disadvantages. These factors are therefore likely to prevent or delay the business from achieving its organizational objectives. Hence, weaknesses need to be reduced or removed in order to be in a position to compete with rivals.
- **Opportunities** are the external possibilities and prospects for future development. For example, India and China present many opportunities for European and American businesses, such as a huge customer base and the relatively lower labour costs. Changes in the external business environment can create favourable conditions for a business. Hence, a SWOT analysis should help a business to formulate its corporate strategy.
- **Threats** are the external factors that hinder the prospects for an organization, i.e. they cause problems for the business. For example, in 2003, SARS (severe acute respiratory syndrome) meant that tourists stayed away from South East Asia. Airlines suffered hugely as did travel agents and hotels. In May 2003, the *South China Morning Post* reported that Ocean Park (one of Hong Kong's most visited sites) was losing HK$15 million ($2 million) a month due to the SARS outbreak.

Exam Tip!
When carrying out a SWOT analysis, remember that strengths and weaknesses are the *internal* factors that an organization *currently* faces. Opportunities and threats are the external factors that the organization is *likely* to face in the near future.

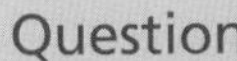

Question **1.6.1**

Kidzplay Bouncy Castles

Kidzplay Bouncy Castles is an independent business that caters for children's parties and events in the south-east region of the UK.

Explain whether the following scenarios represent a strength, weakness, opportunity or threat to the firm:

a Limited competition in a niche market.

b Limited business on its newly launched website (www.kidzplaycastles.com).

c Struggling to recruit suitable staff.

d Weak demand in the winter months.

e Highly profitable earnings attracting competitors. *[10 marks]*

SWOT analysis can be an extremely useful tool for investigating all sorts of business situations. It can be used to provide a good framework for:

- *Evaluating business proposals or ideas*, e.g. expanding the product range
- *Assessing opportunities* for the development and survival of the organization
- *Strategic planning*, e.g. the decision to diversify or expand overseas to capture a wider customer base
- *Competitor analysis*, e.g. the threats posed by a rival, the strengths of a competitor, or the position of a product or brand in relation to its rivals
- *Reviewing strategy*, e.g. the position or direction of a business
- *Risk assessment*, e.g. the probable effects of investing in a certain project.

Exam Tip!
When using a SWOT analysis in the exam, do *not* present the SWOT in tabular form. Using such a format can encourage candidates to try and squeeze their answers to fit inside the table (drawn by the student). Examiners tend to prefer written explanations and justifications. Instead, it is reasonable to write in bullet point format under each SWOT heading so long as the examiner can understand the reasoning behind the student's arguments.

Table 1.6a SWOT analysis template (an example)*

Strengths	Weaknesses
• Unique selling point • Brand recognition and loyalty • Experience, knowledge, expertise and skills • Market share • Corporate image and reputation • Accreditation, endorsement or official support • Core competencies (e.g. product quality and reliability) • Geographical location • Value for money (price in relation to quality)	• Limited sources of revenue • Escalating costs of production • Higher prices than competitors • Demotivated and/or unproductive workforce • Limited sources of finance • Lack of spare capacity • Restricted product range
Opportunities	**Threats**
• Economic development and trade liberalization • Weakening exchange rate • Upswing in the business cycle • Technological developments • New markets and locations • Mergers and acquisitions of rival firms	• New entrants in the marketplace • Outbreak of infectious diseases • Pressure group action, e.g. protests • Social, environmental and legal constraints • Media coverage and publicity • Unfavourable changes in seasons and weather • Changes in fashion and tastes • Price and non-price competition from rivals

* Note: What might be strengths for one firm, such as its reputation and expertise, might actually be weaknesses for another business. Equally, some threats, such as a change in weather, might also be considered as opportunities for some businesses.

Advantages of SWOT

- Completing a SWOT analysis can be quite simple and quick.
- It can be used for a wide range of decisions, such as how to react to the threat of a competitor entering the market.
- SWOT analysis helps to determine the organization's position in the marketplace and therefore aids the formulation of corporate strategy for its long-term survival.
- The SWOT framework encourages foresight and proactive thinking, rather than relying on emotional or intuitive feelings.
- It can help to reduce the risks of decision-making by demanding objective and logical thinking.

Limitations of SWOT

- Critics of SWOT analysis argue that it is too simplistic and does not demand detailed analysis.
- The model is static whereas the business environment is under constant change, so the shelf life of a SWOT analysis is rather limited.
- SWOT analysis is only useful if decision-makers are open about the weaknesses and willing to act upon them. This will involve devoting time, people and money to tackling weaknesses and threats.
- SWOT analysis is not typically used in isolation. Businesses are usually able to make better decisions if they have more information available; thus the use of other strategic tools such as PEST analysis (see Unit 1.5) should also be used.

Nevertheless, a properly produced SWOT can be a powerful management tool to aid decision-making.

Exam Tip!
A typical exam question will require students to analyse the position of a business by using a SWOT framework. Be sure therefore to learn how to use a SWOT properly. Remember that the strengths and weaknesses refer to the current internal position of the firm. The opportunities and threats should stem from a PEST analysis.

DECISION-MAKING FRAMEWORKS

The core of Business and Management lies in decision-making. All businesses, irrespective of their legal status or size, have to make decisions on a daily basis. Businesses have to make decisions in order to achieve their organizational objectives. Typically, a business will have to decide:

- What production should take place, e.g. which goods or services to produce or supply?
- How production should take place, e.g. what combination of capital and labour should be used?
- For whom production should take place, e.g. only for those with high disposable incomes?

A **decision-making framework** is a systematic process of dealing with business problems, concerns or issues in order to make the best decision. In a simple decision-making model, the following seven steps take place:

1. Identify the business problem, concern or issue (linked to the objectives of the organization).
2. Gather sufficient data and information in order to make rational decisions.
3. Analyse data and information to produce a list possible options.
4. Assess the consequences (in terms of costs and benefits) of each option.
5. Select the most favourable option, in terms of the costs and benefits and what is realistically achievable.
6. Communicate this decision to the staff since the proposal is very likely to affect them.
7. Review and evaluate the outcome, i.e. did it help to achieve the organization's objectives and what lessons were learnt?

The above process can be remembered by the acronym 'IDEAL' which stands for:

Identify the problem, concern or issue.

Define (or describe) the problem.

Explore possible solutions and their effects on the organization.

Action to tackle the problem.

Look back to review the progress and level of success in dealing with the problem.

There are many models or frameworks that a business can use to limit the risks involved in decision-making. Commonly used decision-making frameworks include:

- **Cost-benefit analysis (CBA).** This model examines the financial costs and benefits of a decision. It is used when both costs and benefits can be quantifiable. It is a rather simple but effective process whereby if the financial benefits (of a decision) outweigh the financial costs, then the decision or proposal can go ahead. *Break-even analysis* (see Unit 5.3) and *investment appraisal* (see Unit 3.2) are two examples of CBA tools. However, CBA methods ignore the non-financial aspects of decision-making, such as their implications on the workforce and whether the decision is ethical.

- **Six Thinking Hats**. This model was devised by psychologist Edward De Bono who argued that it is important to look at decisions from (six) different perspectives. This would allow managers to make better decisions by forcing them to move away from their normal way of thinking. His model uses six different coloured hats, each representing a different way of thinking: *white hat* (factual information), *red hat* (thinking based on emotions and feelings), *black hat* (consideration of only the bad points of a decision), *yellow hat* (all the benefits of a decision), *green hat* (creative solutions to a problem) and *blue hat* (neutral thinking, i.e. someone who chairs the meetings of decision-makers and ensures that each 'hat' is represented). De Bono's model has been used by a large number of companies, including Coca-Cola and Ericsson. His model helps managers to better understand the complexities of different decisions and to 'think outside the box'.
- **Force Field analysis**. This model was devised by Professor Kurt Lewin as a technique for examining the forces for and against a decision. *Driving forces* refer to the advantages of implementing a decision whereas *restraining forces* are the limitations or disadvantages of the decision. These forces affecting change are then weighted according to the level of importance of each one as valued by the decision-makers. By carrying out force field analysis, Lewin suggested that decision-makers can plan to strengthen the driving forces and reduce the impact of the restraining forces. Unit 1.8 (Change Management) covers this theory in more detail.
- **Pareto analysis**. Vilfredo Pareto, an Italian economist, found that approximately 80% of a country's wealth was owned by just 20% of the population. This finding became known as the **Pareto principle** (or the *80/20 principle*), i.e. 20% of the work can generate 80% of the output. Pareto analysis is a technique that identifies the decisions that will provide the greatest benefits or the most important problems that needs to be solved. A score or weighting is applied to each decision or problem faced by the business. The problem or decision with the highest score is the first decision to undertake because this will generate the greatest benefits if solved. The decisions with the lowest scores may be ignored since attempts to solve these issues may cost the business more than they are worth in terms of time, energy and money.
- **The 5 Why's**. This decision-making and problem-solving technique was devised by Japanese industrialist Sakichi Toyoda (1867–1930). It is a simple process of asking, five times, why an issue or concern has happened in order to get to the root cause(s) of the problem. Toyoda argued that failure to determine the source of a problem will result in a firm having the same problems time after time. To illustrate the model, suppose the issue is that a student continually forgets to hand in homework on time. *Why?* He doesn't note it in his diary. *Why?* He isn't organized to remember. *Why?* He suffers from a lack of sleep. *Why?* He sleeps late. *Why?* He spends too much time surfing the internet and chatting on the phone with his friends at night. The solution is then clearly identified: be organized by sleeping earlier, spending less time on the internet and chatting less on the phone! Note that the actual numbers of Why's does not matter so long as the root cause is discovered.

There are many other decision-making tools that are covered in the rest of this book, such as SWOT analysis (covered earlier in this Unit), Stakeholder mapping (see Unit 1.4), PEST analysis (see Unit 1.5), the Ansoff matrix (see Unit 1.7), Ratio analysis (see Unit 3.6), Five Forces analysis (see Unit 4.2) and Break-even analysis (see Unit 5.3).

Question 1.6.2

Royal Dutch Shell

Royal Dutch Shell (or Shell for short) is Europe's largest energy and oil company that was formed by the merger of Holland's Royal Dutch and Britain's Shell in 1907. The BBC reported in early 2007 that the Anglo–Dutch company earns £1.5 million ($3 million) per hour! This staggering figure obviously draws the attention of Shell's **internal stakeholders**. However, being a global energy and oil company also means that Shell's activities are carefully scrutinized by environmental and human rights groups, such as Greenpeace and Witness.

a Use an example to describe what is meant by **internal stakeholders**. *[3 marks]*

b To what extent should a global company such as Shell allow environmental and human rights groups to exert influence on their decision-making? *[7 marks]*

HIGHER LEVEL EXTENSION: SCIENTIFIC VERSUS INTUITIVE DECISION-MAKING PROCESSES

All the decision-making frameworks covered in the above section are examples of **scientific decision-making**. This means that decisions are made objectively on the basis of following a formal and prescribed procedure. Decisions are based on quantifiable facts and evidence rather than being based on subjective opinions, past experiences, feelings or intuition.

One benefit of scientific decision-making is that decisions are made rationally and logically. This means that decisions are simpler to justify, since they are based on factual evidence, and easier to communicate to the workforce. It also reduces the risks involved in taking a decision.

By contrast, **intuitive decision-making** is based on a person's beliefs, perceptions, instincts and gut feelings. Entrepreneurs are risk takers and they often have to make decisions that are based on their intuition. This might be due to a lack of time to collect data and evidence, or due to the information not being available. Highly experienced managers will certainly use this approach more since decision-making is quicker and less expensive than using scientific decision-making frameworks. However, the risks are therefore likely to be higher.

Intuitive decision-making gets around the problems and disadvantages of scientific decision-making. Decision-makers that use this approach will consider issues that are not necessarily quantifiable, such as the impact of decisions on employees and the local community. They will also consider ethical issues such as whether the decision is morally correct or socially responsible.

In reality, most decisions are based on a combination of both scientific and intuitive aspects. The business environment is dynamic in nature and successful decisions taken in the past may not prove so triumphant in the current or future climate. The choice of decision-making depends on numerous factors, both scientific and intuitive. For example, highly successful senior managers may make lots of intuitive decisions based on their acquired knowledge and past experiences. Less experienced managers, however, may feel that they need evidence to support their decision-making. The scale of the decision (strategic, tactical or operational) is another factor. For instance, simple and routine decisions may not require any detailed analysis so using scientific models would be unnecessarily costly and time consuming.

HIGHER LEVEL

HIGHER LEVEL EXTENSION: DECISION TREES

A decision tree is a quantitative decision-making tool. It is a diagrammatic representation of the different options that are available to a business in the decision-making process, showing their probable outcomes. The tool allows managers to calculate the expected value of each decision in order to identify the best option to follow.

For example, consider the following options available to Mr. Trump who is deciding whether or not to sell his apartment in New York. If he sells this year, he would get $500,000. However, waiting until next year when the housing market is expected to pick up increases the chances of him selling the property at a higher price. The factors for Mr. Trump to consider include the following information:

- He could sell the property at the current market price of $500,000. This option would incur costs of $8,000 for estate agency and solicitors' fees, i.e. this option yields a return of $492,000.
- He could postpone the sale until next year with a 70% chance of receiving a higher price for the apartment. The estimated value of Mr. Trump's property is $550,000 if he sells it next year. Selling costs would also rise to $10,000, i.e. the return would be valued at $540,000.
- However, market reports suggest that within the next twelve months there is a 10% chance of the housing market declining and a 20% chance of house prices remaining stable. If prices drop, Mr. Trump's apartment is estimated to be worth $450,000 after all associated selling costs.

Mr. Trump can now use this information to calculate the expected value of each decision. This is done by multiplying the values of each outcome by its probability and then adding up the results. A decision tree is the diagrammatic version of this process (see Figure 1.6a).

Rules used to construct and interpret decision trees

- The diagram is constructed from left to right.
- **Decision nodes** or decision points are shown as squares. These are used when there is a decision to be made, such as whether to launch a new product, to invest in new machinery or to move into overseas markets. In the above example, Mr. Trump has two options, one of which has a definite outcome (selling today). Note that the business has at least some control over decision nodes.
- **Chance nodes** are shown as circles. These are used to show the different possible outcomes of a decision. Typical outcomes include criteria such as 'failure or success' and 'improvements or deteriorations'. For Mr. Trump, by opting to sell his apartment next year (i.e. chance node B), there are three possible outcomes, none of which will definitely happen. Businesses do not have direct control over chance nodes.
- For each chance node, there will be two or more routes (outcomes). These show the **probability** of the different outcomes for each chance node. The probabilities for each chance node must add up to 1.
- The actual values of each outcome are stated at the end of each **branch**. It is important to remember that the costs of each option must be deducted prior to writing down this figure.
- Each unwanted branch of the decision tree is cut-off (rejected) by drawing in two parallel lines. This will then leave one best option to follow.

The expected values in Figure 1.6a (those appearing to the right of the decision tree) are calculated as follows:

- The decision to sell the property today would generate a known value of \$492,000, i.e. \$500,000 less the associated selling costs of \$8,000.
- For chance node B, the decision to postpone the sale has a 70% chance of earning a sale price of \$550,000. After associated selling costs, the value would be \$540,000 and therefore the expected value is \$378,000 (\$540,000 × 0.7).
- There is a 20% chance that property prices will remain unchanged in the next year. Hence, the expected outcome here is \$98,400 (\$492,000 × 0.2).
- Finally, there is a 10% chance that property prices will fall within the next year. Therefore, the expected value in this case is \$45,000 (\$450,000 × 0.1).
- Therefore, the total expected value of chance node B is \$521,400.

The above analysis then suggests that Mr. Trump should delay the sale of his property since the total *expected value* of doing so is higher (\$521,400 compared to \$492,000). The expected value refers to the average outcome if the decision was made many times over and is calculated by multiplying the actual value of a decision by its probability of occurring.

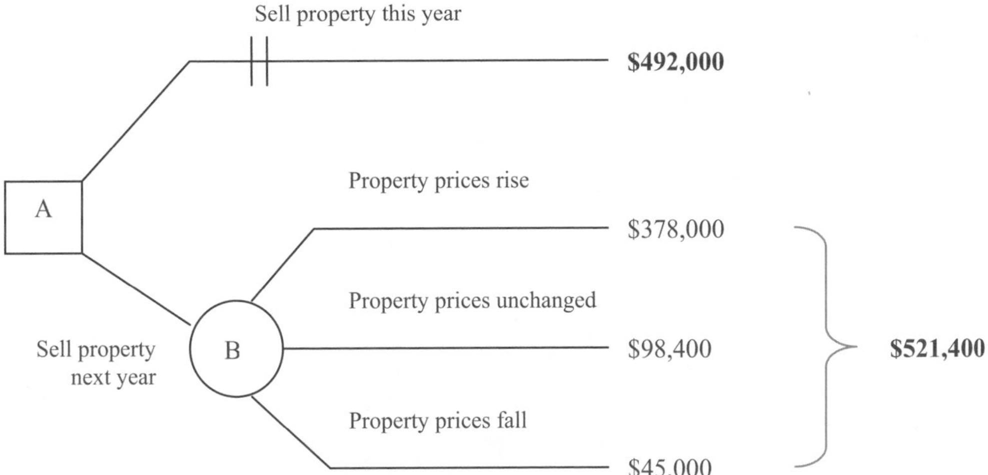

Figure 1.6a Decision tree for Mr. Trump

Advantages of decision trees

- They allow managers to set out problems in a clear and logical manner.
- All potential options can be seen at the same time, thereby speeding up the decision-making process.
- They consider the risks involved in decision-making, such as the likelihood of negative outcomes.
- They aid better decision-making since the likely costs of decisions are considered and shown on a decision tree.
- They are a visual stimulus and are, therefore, a tangible insight to a problem, rather than having to rely on people's thoughts or imagination of the problem.

HIGHER LEVEL

HIGHER LEVEL

Disadvantages of decision trees

- The probabilities given in any decision tree are only estimates and subject to forecasting error.
- Decision trees are based on quantitative data only, so qualitative issues that affect a decision (such as the effects on staff morale or the compatibility of a decision with the firm's ethical stance) are totally ignored.
- The task of assigning probabilities is rather subjective so results can be deliberately biased in order to justify the preference of management.
- Any delays incurred whilst making a certain assessment of an option may void the data by the time the decision is actually made. Time lags are often inevitable in the real business world.
- The technique does not necessarily reduce the amount of risk involved in decision-making.

Question 1.6.3

Peckham Traders Ltd.

The management at Peckham Traders Ltd. is considering a move into overseas markets and a decision must be made between two locations: Kazakhstan or South Korea. Finance is limited so only one location can be chosen. Market research results are shown in the table below. All financial figures are in $ for ease of comparison.

	Probability	Costs/Revenues ($)
Kazakhstan		
Cost		250,000
High return	0.60	400,000
Low return	0.40	250,000
South Korea		
Cost		175,000
High return	0.75	300,000
Low return	0.25	180,000

a Explain how the above scenario is an example of opportunity cost. *[2 marks]*

b Construct a decision tree to show which of the two options is best on financial grounds. *[6 marks]*

c Evaluate the value of decision trees as a decision-making tool for Peckham Traders Ltd. *[8 marks]*

HIGHER LEVEL EXTENSION: ISHIKAWA'S FISHBONE MODEL

Japanese quality guru, Professor Kaoru Ishikawa (1915–1989) came up with the **Fishbone model** of decision-making, also known as the **cause-and-effect diagram**. The fishbone model is a graphical representation of the most likely causes and effects of an important decision. Ishikawa is also credited as the person who coined the term *quality circles* (see Unit 5.4) in 1962.

The fishbone model is a management tool used to identify the root causes of a problem or issue. It is useful when dealing with a problem that has several elements or root causes. The diagram shows the problem or issue of concern on the right-hand side. The 4 M's (management, manpower, machines and materials) are used to identify different categories of causes. These form the four 'bones' in the model (see Figure 1.6b).

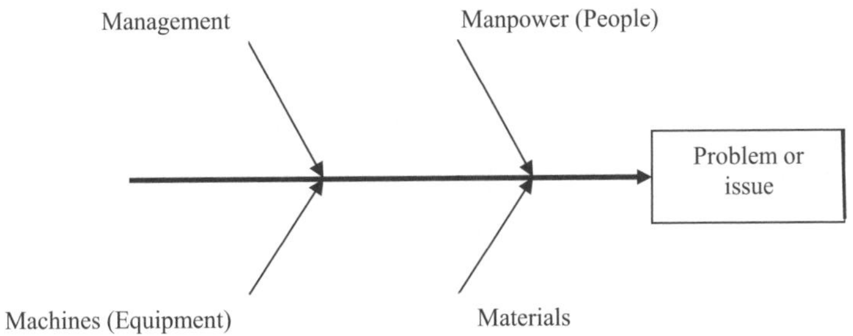

Figure 1.6b Example 1 of fishbone diagram

The following causes may be found from using the fishbone model:

- Management, e.g. unsuitable management style used and/or miscommunication with workforce
- Manpower, e.g. demotivated employees, unskilled workers, lack of training and insufficient staffing
- Machinery, e.g. technological failures, faulty equipment and/or use of obsolete machinery
- Materials, e.g. substandard (poor quality) materials and/or delayed deliveries.

Note that the 4 M's do not have to be the nodes used in the model. In fact, the nodes can refer to any group or category that is related to the problem. For example, *paraphernalia* (*equipment*), *policies*, *procedures*, and *people* are the 'bones' often used for problems related to administrative and service-related problems (see Figure 1.6c). Essentially, the categories used are flexible and should meet the needs of the decision-makers.

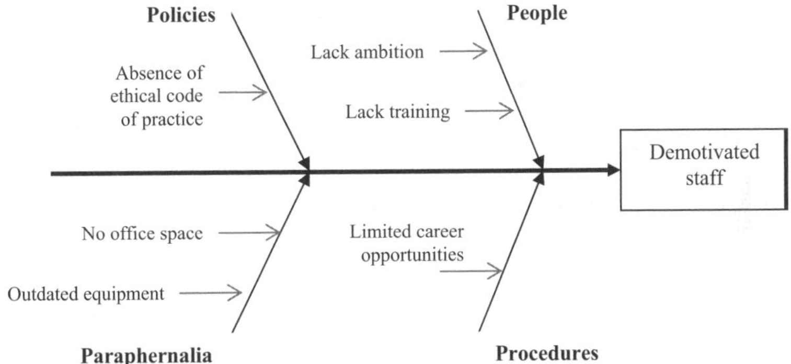

Figure 1.6c Example 2 of fishbone diagram

When the entire fishbone diagram is completed, discussion takes place to decide on the most likely root causes of the problem being looked at. The ultimate purpose of using the Fishbone diagram is to find the key source(s) of the problem so that they can then be targeted for improvement. In the above example, this means that there needs to be a review of management styles which are clearly having a negative impact on staff morale and productivity levels. The human aspects of the problem, such as adequate provision of training, must undoubtedly be addressed.

To successfully construct a fishbone diagram, the following steps must be observed:

1. The problem or issue must be clearly stated and agreed upon before further discussions begin.
2. Contributors must be concise and to the point. Causes rather than symptoms must be identified.

3 For each 'bone', brainstorm the possible causes and place these onto the node.

4 For each branch on the diagram, try to identify the root cause.

5 Consider either combining rather empty branches or scrapping them altogether.

6 Likewise, consider separating overcrowded nodes.

7 Consider which root cause(s) that may warrant further investigation by circling these on the diagram.

8 Discuss how each circled item affects the problem or issue being investigated.

9 Once the root causes have been established, the fishbone exercise is complete and decision-makers move onto devising appropriate strategies to deal with the sources of the problem.

A key strength of the Ishikawa model is that it is easy to use and understand. The model allows decision-makers to brainstorm ideas in a systematic, holistic and logical way. The exercise facilitates an understanding and visual diagnosis of the problem or issue of concern. Today, computer software programmes based on Ishikawa's ideas can be used to aid decision-making.

However, the model tends to be rather too simplistic for some real world problems. In practice, the fishbone model is often used in conjunction with other decision-making frameworks, such as the 5 Why's model, to establish the root cause(s) of a problem.

HIGHER LEVEL

HIGHER LEVEL EXTENSION: INTERNAL AND EXTERNAL CONSTRAINTS

This section looks at the internal and external constraints on business decision-making. **Internal constraints** are the factors that hinder decision-making but are within the control of the business. As stated in the previous Unit, these internal constraints tend to be dominated by the rules, policies and culture of the business. The use of a SWOT analysis can help a business to identify potential internal constraints. For example, the workforce may lack the necessary skills, ambition and motivation for a business to implement a decision. Using a cause-and-effect framework can also help the business to deal with internal constraints.

External constraints are those barriers that hinder decision-making but are uncontrollable by the business. They refer to the factors in the external business environment, i.e. the PEST factors (see Unit 1.5). Political, economic, social and technological issues are beyond the control of any single organization.

In reality, factors affecting decision-making will include consideration of internal and external constraints and opportunities. The use of decision-making frameworks, such as SWOT and cause-and-effect diagrams, can help to reduce the risks involved in making certain choices by identifying the potential constraints that need to be dealt with.

Question 1.6.4

Examine the internal and external constraints for any **one** of the following business decisions: *[8 marks]*

- **a** Cadbury Schweppes announce that they are to demerge.
- **b** Singapore Airlines plans to move its call centre to India.
- **c** Disney is set to open a new theme park in Shanghai.
- **d** Virgin Atlantic unveils plans to start daily flights to Nairobi, Kenya.

Note: You may want to refer to the content in Unit 1.5 before attempting this question.

ORGANIZATIONAL PLANNING TOOLS AND BUSINESS STRATEGY

The business environment is said to be dynamic in nature, i.e. it is exposed to constant change and nothing remains unchanged for very long. It is the responsibility of the management team to forecast and detect change and to take appropriate decisions.

Managers are highly likely to face constraints on business planning and decision-making. These limitations include:

- The availability of finance. All decisions require some form of funding. Whilst certain options may seem favourable, they may not be financially feasible.
- Organizational culture. The traditions and norms of an organization can create barriers to planning and decision-making. A 'that's not the way things are done around here' attitude can prevent certain paths from being pursued. By contrast, cultures that are adaptive to change and have flexible company policies are more receptive to change.
- The dynamics of the workforce. A highly skilled workforce is able to adopt a wider range of options. Decision-making is therefore less onerous if managers can rely on staff to implement decisions.
- External constraints. Businesses may be constrained in their decision-making by government rules and regulations. The reaction and behaviour of rival firms in the industry may also create some problems for business decision-making. The state of the economy may also mean that the timing of introducing certain changes may be inappropriate (such as implementing expansion plans during a recession).

Nevertheless, the use of organizational planning tools (such as business plans, SWOT analysis, decision trees and the fishbone model), can help managers to make more rational decisions. Indeed, several of the planning tools covered in this Unit are revisited in other areas of the textbook. The quality of decision-making will affect the long-term prospects of an organization. Hence, the use of appropriate planning tools can help businesses to make better and more informed decisions.

REVIEW QUESTIONS 1.6

1. Explain the meaning of 'operational', 'tactical' and 'strategic' decision-making.
2. What is a 'business plan'?
3. Outline the components found in a typical business plan.
4. What is a 'SWOT analysis'?
5. Outline three advantages and two disadvantages of using a SWOT analysis.
6. What are 'decision-making frameworks' and why do businesses use them?
7. The five steps taken in a decision-making framework can be remembered by the mnemonic IDEAL. What does IDEAL stand for?
8. What is the Pareto principle?
9. What is the 5 Why's model?

Higher Level extension

10. Distinguish between 'intuitive' and 'scientific' decision-making.
11. What is a 'decision tree' and why do businesses use them?
12. What is meant by a 'cause-and-effect' diagram?
13. Use examples to differentiate between internal and external constraints on decision-making.

Business plan is the name given to a report detailing how a business sets out to achieve its aims and objectives. It requires managers to plan their marketing, financial and human resources.

Decision-making is the process of choosing between the alternative options available to a business.

Decision-making framework is the phrase used to describe a systematic process of dealing with business problems, concerns or issues in order to make the best decision.

Decision trees are a type of quantitative decision-making tool that allows firms to calculate the probable values of different options if they are pursued. They can therefore help to minimize the risks involved in decision-making.

Fishbone diagram is a decision-making framework based on identifying the root causes of a problem or issue. It is also known as the **cause-and-effect model** or the **Ishikawa model**, named after its creator.

Intuitive decision-making refers to decision-making that is based on gut feelings, hunch and/or instinct rather than relying on quantitative factors which may be quite time consuming.

Planning tools are the various methods that businesses use to aid their decision-making. Examples of planning tools include Business Plans, SWOT analysis, the 5 Why's model and Decision Trees.

Scientific decision-making refers to decision-making that is based on a systematic and logical framework. The purpose is to remove, as far as possible, subjectivity and emotions from decision-making.

Strategy refers to any medium to long-term plan of how a business intends to achieve its goals.

SWOT analysis is a popular analytical tool used to assess the internal strengths and weaknesses and the external opportunities and threats of an organization or a decision.

Growth and Evolution

UNIT 1.7

Be not afraid of going slowly;
be afraid only of standing still.

Chinese proverb

Key topics

- Economies and diseconomies of scale
- The relative merits of small and large businesses
- Internal growth strategies
- External growth strategies: joint ventures, strategic alliances, mergers and takeovers
- Franchising as a growth strategy
- The Ansoff matrix

Higher Level extension

- Porter's generic strategies

INTRODUCTION

This Unit looks at the driving and restraining forces for growth and evolution of different businesses. Growth is a continual aim of established businesses. Growth of a business refers to the expansion in size of its operations and this can be measured in several ways, including:

- The value of the firm's **sales turnover** (also known as sales revenue)
- The firm's **market share**, i.e. the sales revenue of the business as a percentage of the industry's sales
- The value of the firm's **capital employed** (see Unit 3.5)
- The number of **employees** hired by the business.

There are several reasons why businesses seek to grow. These reasons include:

- To reap the benefits of larger scale production. this is known as *economies of scale* (see below).
- To gain a larger **market share** in order to gain better market standing (see unit 4.1) and market power. This may allow the business to charge higher prices to its customers yet gain more profit at the same time.
- As a means of **survival** against rivals in the industry. Competitors are likely to aim for growth, so businesses may need to run faster to stay still, i.e. aim to grow in order to compete with their growing competitors.
- To **spread risks** by diversifying into new markets and industries. This helps to spread the risk of only focusing on a specific market. If there are detrimental changes in a particular market, then having operations in other different markets may help to safeguard the survival of the business.

Ultimately, the reasons for seeking growth are be summarized as the desire for businesses, especially those in the private sector, to gain more **profit** in the long run. However growth is neither easy nor cheap to achieve. It requires access to more financial and non-financial resources (such as human resources). Furthermore, some firms can actually *overtrade* (expand too quickly by taking on more orders than they can handle) or expand in the wrong direction (perhaps by entering markets where they lack any local expertise). Such firms are therefore exposed to even greater risks of failure.

ECONOMIES AND DISECONOMIES OF SCALE

One major reason why businesses aim to grow is so that they can benefit from economies of scale. **Economies of scale** refer to the lower average costs of production as a firm operates on a larger scale due to an improvement in productive efficiency. For instance, the Airbus 380 super jumbo is reported to have 35% more seats than the Boeing 747 jumbo jet but burns 17% less fuel per seat. Hence, the average cost of fuel for Airbus is lower. Economies of scale, sometimes referred to as **increasing returns to scale**, can help businesses to gain a competitive cost advantage over smaller rivals because lower average costs can mean a combination of lower prices being charged to customers and a higher profit margin being made on each unit sold.

Economies of scale fall into two main categories. Those that are within the organization's control and occur within the firm are known as **internal economies of scale**. Those that occur within the industry that the business operates and are largely beyond the control of the business are known as **external economies of scale**.

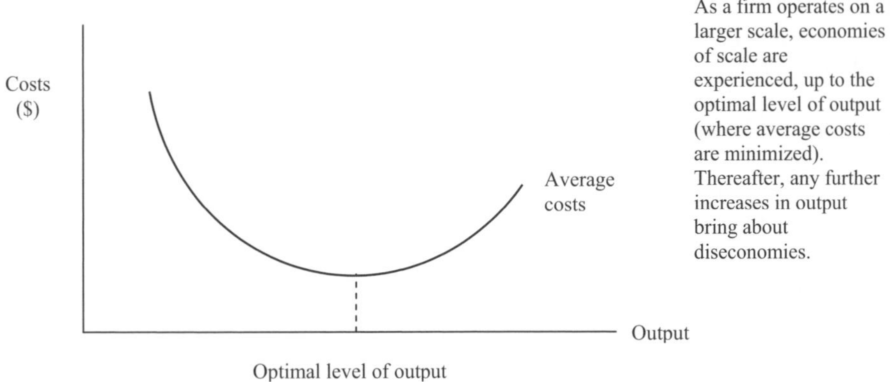

Figure 1.7a Economies and diseconomies of scale

Internal economies of scale

By producing on a larger scale, a business may be able to reduce its average costs of production due to any combination of the internal economies of scale outlined below. The relative importance of each depends on the type and size of business under consideration.

- **Technical economies.** Large firms can use sophisticated machinery in an intensive way to mass produce their products. For example, due to the huge scale of production, the Phillips factory in Shenzhen, China produces complete hi-fi systems within a few seconds! The high fixed costs of their equipment and machinery are spread over the huge scale of output, thereby reducing the **average costs** of production for Phillips. Due to the large **market demand** that exists for Phillips' products, they also benefit from having a large and efficient distribution and transportation arrangement. Small businesses do not find it feasible (because of the excess supply produced) or cost-efficient to buy and use such technology.
- **Financial economies.** Large firms can borrow massive sums of money at lower rates of interest than smaller rivals. This is because larger firms are seen as less risky to financial lenders. In addition, a large and established business looking to borrow money will probably choose a lender that can offer the most attractive rate of interest, i.e. there is rivalry amongst the financial institutions to lend to large businesses. By contrast, smaller firms often struggle to raise external finance and have to pay higher rates of interest on overdrafts and loans (see Unit 3.1).
- **Managerial economies.** A sole trader (see Unit 1.2) often has to fulfil the functions of marketer, accountant and production manager. Of course, people cannot be equally good at everything so specialization tends to lead to higher productivity. Large firms split up management roles by employing specialist managers. This may cost more money overall but the resulting increased productivity means that average costs of production still fall. Increasing specialization can also create benefits of **synergy** for the business. Synergy is typically defined as the whole being greater than the sum of the parts, or 1+1 = 3. This means that through growth, such as takeovers or organic growth, a business can avoid duplication of effort in planning, communication, marketing, distribution and production processes. This will therefore help to reduce its unit costs of production.
- **Specialization economies.** This is similar to managerial economies of scale but results from division of labour of the workforce, rather than the management. Motor vehicle manufacturers that use *mass production* benefit from having specialist labour such as designers, production staff, engineers and marketers. These specialists are responsible for one part of the production process and their expertise means that there is a boost to the firm's productivity.

- **Marketing economies.** Large firms can benefit from lower average costs by *selling* in bulk. Large businesses will benefit from reduced time and transactions costs, such as administration and the cost of invoicing customers, associated with selling in bulk. For instance, a small retail outlet might sell 1,000 cans of Coke in a month to hundreds of different customers. This will cost a lot more money than Coca-Cola who can sell 1,000 cans in one transaction to just one customer (such as a supermarket that stocks Coke's products). Another example of marketing economies is that large businesses that can exploit **global marketing economies**. Global firms such as McDonald's and Nike can spread the high cost of advertising across the world. McDonald's and Nike market their products to a world audience using the same marketing campaign (language translation tends to be a relatively small cost within a marketing budget).
- **Monopsony economies.** These savings can be enjoyed by large firms that have strong buying power (known as monopsonists). Monopsonists negotiate with their suppliers for huge discounts on their large bulk purchases. According to Eric Schlosser, author of *Fast Food Nation*, McDonald's is the world's single largest purchaser of beef, pork and potatoes. This gives McDonald's huge buying power and the ability to demand low prices from its suppliers. Large supermarket chains such as Carrefour and Tesco, for example, have huge buying power over their suppliers of fruit, vegetables, wines and meat products. Similarly, IKEA, the world's largest home furniture retailer, contract out the manufacturing of most of their products to the most cost-efficient suppliers.
- **Commercial economies.** These are similar to monopsony economies in that firms can lower their average costs by buying resources in bulk. However, even relatively small firms can exploit commercial economies as they gain a discount for bulk purchases. Of course, the larger the order the greater the bulk discount might be, so this is an advantage to being big in business. Commercial economies of scale are also known as ***purchasing economies*** or ***buying economies***.
- **Risk-bearing economies.** These economies of scale can be enjoyed by *conglomerates* (firms that have a diversified portfolio of products in different markets), such as the Virgin Group. Conglomerates can spread their fixed costs, such as advertising or research and development, across their wide range of operations. Unfavourable trading conditions for certain products, services or even industries can be offset by more favourable conditions in other sectors of the business. For example, Daewoo Corporation – the South Korean conglomerate – failed to establish ground in the global motor vehicle industry, but its huge presence in the steel and electronics industries makes it one of South Korea's most powerful corporations. Cheung Kong Group, Hong Kong's largest company, has an incredibly diverse range of operations, including: supermarkets, mobile telecommunications, electronics, food and drink, internet and broadband television services, media, hotels and property development. It is also the world's largest port operator and health and beauty retailer. In 2003, the infectious SARS outbreak affected the whole of the South East Asian region, but for conglomerates such as Daewoo Corporation and Cheung Kong Group, the loss in one area of their business does not jeopardise their overall business.

Exam Tip!

Many students define economies of scale as 'the benefits of buying in bulk'. However, even *small* businesses can buy in bulk; the term refers to the cost-reducing benefits enjoyed by firms engaged in *large* scale operations. Financial, technological and managerial economies of scale are probably far more important in reducing the average cost of production for most businesses than their ability to buy in bulk.

External economies of scale

External economies of scale are those that arise from *outside* the firm due to its favourable location or growth in the industry. Examples of factors that may create external economies of scale include:

- **Technological progress** which increases the productivity of trading within the industry. The internet, for example, has granted huge cost savings to many businesses engaged in e-commerce (see Unit 4.8).
- **Improved transportation and communication networks** help to ensure that deliveries arrive on time. In addition, employees who are late to work due to poor transportation links cost the business money. Customers also want convenience and will prefer to visit retail outlets that are easily accessible. Ultimately, congestion increases the costs of production and reduces revenue for the business. The widespread adoption and use of a common language can also help to reduce costs in an industry. Although the European Union's use of a single currency (see Unit 1.9) has resulted in huge cost savings for businesses trading in euros, the lack of a common language still acts, to some extent, as a hindrance to international trade.
- More and **better trained labour** in an industry exists, perhaps through government supported training programmes or reputable education and training facilities in a certain area. This provides local businesses with a suitable pool of educated and trained labour, thereby helping to cut their recruitment costs without compromising productivity levels.
- **Regional specialization** means that an area or country may have a highly regarded and trustworthy reputation for producing a particular good or service. For example, Murano, in Venice, Italy, is famous throughout the world for its glass products such as vases, jewellery and chandeliers. This allows the industry to benefit from having specialist and efficient labour, subcontractors and suppliers. In addition, the highly regarded reputation allows firms in the Murano glass industry to charge a premium price for their products. Good location decisions can also mean a ready supply of local back-up firms and suppliers who compete by offering businesses the best service at the most competitive prices. This should help to reduce average costs of production for the industry.

Internal diseconomies of scale

Contrary to the belief of many people, businesses can become too large. There comes a 'tipping point' when economies of scale can no longer be exploited. **Diseconomies of scale**, sometimes called **decreasing returns to scale**, are the result of higher unit costs as a firm continues to increase the size of its operations, i.e. the organization becomes outsized and inefficient and average costs therefore begin to rise. Internal diseconomies of scale usually arise due to managerial problems. Examples of internal diseconomies include:

- As a firm becomes larger, managers may **lack control and coordination** as the span of control (see Unit 2.2) is likely to increase and cause problems for management. These difficulties, such as the additional time needed to communicate effectively with a larger number of staff, ultimately slow down decision-making. Coordination and control could also be a problem for a business with operations in many different locations throughout the world. Furthermore, workers in larger organizations may feel a sense of alienation and this is likely to harm staff morale (see Unit 2.5). These issues will add to total costs without any corresponding increase in productivity of the workforce. Hence unit costs will begin to rise.
- There are likely to be **poorer working relationships** in an oversized business. With a larger workforce, senior management are more likely to become detached with those lower down in the hierarchy, thereby making them feel alienated or out of touch. This can negatively affect communication flows and the morale of staff (see Unit 2.5), thereby reducing their productivity and leading to higher unit costs.

- Outsized organizations are more likely to suffer from the disadvantages of specialization and division of labour. Workers become bored of undertaking repetitive tasks. With a larger workforce, there may also be scope for **slack** (inefficiency and procrastination) amongst the workforce. This leads to lower productive efficiency and hence an increase in the average cost of production.
- The amount of **bureaucracy** (administration, paperwork and company policies) is also likely to increase. This makes decision-making time consuming and adds to the costs of the business, but is unlikely to contribute to any extra output of goods and services to the customer. Bureaucracy can also make communication more difficult, thereby worsening working relationships. Hence, unit costs are likely to rise.
- **Complacency** with being a large and dominant player or even the market leader in the industry can also cause many problems. Essentially, complacency is most likely to reduce productivity and raise unit costs at the same time.

The potential for large firms in experiencing diseconomies of scale, although quite rare in the real business world, means that some businesses prefer to grow via **franchising** (covered later in this Unit). Multinationals such as McDonald's have used this strategy to expand their business and to raise brand awareness, without having to face the higher unit costs of being too large.

External diseconomies of scale

External diseconomies refer to an increase in the average costs of production as a firm grows due to factors beyond its control. They occur when problems affect the whole industry perhaps because there are too many firms in the market. Unit costs of production increase for all businesses in the industry. Examples include:

- Too many businesses locating in a certain area will result in land becoming more scarce thereby *increasing market rents*. This will add to the fixed costs of all businesses in the area, but without any corresponding increase in output. Hence, unit costs will begin to rise. The high demand for businesses to locate in busy city districts such as Manhattan (New York), Causeway Bay (Hong Kong) and The City (London) has resulted in a sustained and continuous rise in the rental value of land in these areas.
- *Traffic congestion* will result from too many businesses being located in an area. Deliveries are likely to be delayed due to the overcrowding. This will increase transportation costs for businesses, thereby contributing to the increase in unit costs of production.
- The supply of local labour may also increase due to the opportunities being offered by the many rivals located in the same area. Since workers have a choice over the large number of employers in the local, businesses may have to offer *higher wages* and financial rewards in order to attract new workers. This will increase costs, but not necessarily increase output and therefore raises the average costs of production.

Dealing with diseconomies of scale

Since diseconomies of scale result in higher unit costs of production, firms will need to take appropriate action in order to protect their competitiveness. Firms have two main options in dealing with diseconomies – to reduce their level of output (firms may simply have grown too fast and expansion plans need to be reviewed) or to introduce measures to remove productive inefficiencies. The methods used will depend on the cause of the diseconomy. For example, if workers are slacking then **outsourcing** (see Unit 5.7) or **performance-related payment systems** (see Unit 2.5) may be introduced. **Motivational strategies** such as training, development, empowerment and teamworking (see Unit 2.5) may be introduced to avoid staff feelings of neglect and alienation.

SMALL VERSUS LARGE ORGANIZATIONS

This section looks at the relative merits of small versus large organizations. All businesses have an appropriate scale of operation. For instance, the market for mobile phones is enormous whereas that for IB Business and Management textbooks is rather small. The size of a market can be measured in several ways:

- Market share – a firm's sales as a percentage of the industry's total sales revenue
- Total revenue – the annual sales of a business
- Size of workforce – the total number of employees hired by the business
- Profit – the value of a firm's annual profits
- Capital employed – the amount of capital invested in the business
- Market value – can be measured by either the *balance sheet valuation* (see Unit 3.5) or the *stock market valuation* of a business.

An increase in the value of any of the above figures for a firm would suggest that it is getting larger. Essentially, the size of a business is measured in relative terms, i.e. its size in comparison to that of other firms.

In addition to economies of scale, large organizations may also benefit from **economies of scope**. This occurs when it becomes cheaper to produce a range of related products (economies of scale refers to cost savings from producing the same product on a larger scale). For example, cost savings may come about by the firm sharing management and staff in the production of several products. Facilities and other resources can also be shared, thereby helping to cut average costs. Economies of scope give businesses the foundation to diversify into other activities. Jeff Bezos started online retailer Amazon.com by selling only books. Scope economies have meant that he has diversified into selling a much larger range of products such as DVDs, CDs, toys and electronic gadgets. Similarly, publishers benefit from huge cost savings by providing a range of genre rather than specializing in one type of book or magazine.

Apart from economies of scale and scope, other benefits of being large include:

- **Brand recognition** allows businesses to market their products to a wider audience. Familiarity with a brand will tend to boosts its sale. Some firms are large and established enough to have global brand recognition.
- Larger firms tend to be more trusted due to their **image** and record of reliability.
- Added **convenience** is offered to customers of larger businesses. Larger firms have the resources to provide a wider range of facilities to enhance the shopping experience, such as longer opening hours and the ability to offer interest-free credit instalments.
- Larger firms are able to offer customers larger **discounts** through their ability to enjoy economies of scale. This leads to more customers and improved **customer loyalty**.
- **More choice** is available from larger businesses. For example, Amazon.com sells a huge range of books, music and DVDs compared to a small local book or music retailer.

A final point to note is that *barriers to entry* prevent many firms from becoming, or wishing to become, large businesses. The pharmaceutical and car manufacturing industries are examples of businesses that have high entry costs. In addition, well-established market leaders such as Johnson & Johnson and Toyota would have a major cost advantage over smaller and less established rivals. Only large firms have the financial resources needed for the research and development needed to maintain their competitive position.

Despite the benefits of large scale operations, such as economies of scale and increased market power, small businesses can still thrive. Small organizations can survive and flourish due to several reasons:

- **Cost control**. Large scale operations may mean that a business encounters diseconomies of scale. Owners of small businesses may not want to expand since they could face higher unit costs due to control, coordination and communication problems as their organizations grow. Furthermore, expansion may require extra borrowing or a dilution of ownership and control; things which may not be desirable.
- **Financial risk**. Since the costs of running a large global business are huge (such as the costs of research and development, marketing or recruitment and training), the financial risks are also high. General Motors and Ford, both global giants in the car manufacturing industry, have both experienced massive losses in recent times (Ford reported losses of $5.8 billion in November 2006). By contrast, owners of small businesses can better manage and control their organizations and retain all decision-making power.
- **Government aid**. Financial support in the form of grants and subsidies may be offered to small businesses to help them start up. Funds for training may also be available for small businesses that provide employment opportunities in the local community.
- **Local monopoly power**. Small businesses may enjoy being the only firm in a particular location. Examples might include a local restaurant, a franchised petroleum retailer and a small convenience store located in a remote town. Large businesses may be reluctant to locate in remote areas (see Unit 5.5) and this provides an opportunity for a smaller firm to establish itself in the area.
- **Personalized services**. Smaller firms are more likely to have the time to devote to customers. For example, supermarkets rely on a high number of customers being served in minimal time. High staff turnover is also a feature of most large supermarket chains. By contrast, workers at a small local convenience store are not as pressured due to a lower number of customers and may therefore get to know their customers better. The lack of alternative job opportunities in the local area also means staff turnover is likely to be lower.
- **Flexibility**. Small businesses tend to be more flexible and adaptive to change. If a sole trader runs a beauty salon that is rather unsuccessful, then he or she might change the business to something completely different, such as a small restaurant or children's toy shop. Large businesses have heavy financial commitments and conflicting stakeholder objectives (see Unit 1.4) which combine to reduce its ability to change.
- **Small market size**. Some businesses, such as a local hair salon or private tuition firm, are unlikely to attract the attention of large firms because of the very limited size of the market. Large corporations may not find it financially worthwhile to compete with these small local firms, thereby allowing them to thrive.

The **optimum size**, or best size, for a business will depend on its internal structure, its costs and the size of the market (the latter of which is beyond the control of the firm). The most appropriate size for a business also depends on its aims and objectives. For example, both Mars Limited and IKEA are privately owned companies (see Unit 1.2) because the owners want the business to remain in the control of the founding families rather than external owners (shareholders and directors). In financial terms, firms minimize their costs when they operate at the lowest point of their long run average cost curve (see Figure 1.7a). If a firm operates beyond its optimum size (i.e. the firm is too large) then diseconomies of scale will be experienced, thereby raising unit costs and reducing profits.

In reality, a firm may not operate at its financially optimum level because of a lack of resources or demand. A firm cannot expand if it is unable to secure appropriate and sufficient sources of finance. Furthermore, it cannot expand output if it lacks the productive capacity (see Unit 5.7) to do so. It will also not seek to expand if there is insufficient demand, even if producing more units means lower average costs of production.

Question 1.7.1

Small versus large

Businesses come in all shapes and sizes. For example:

- A vast number of sole traders only supply a limited number of products.
- Airbus and Boeing manufacture aircraft for airline companies only.
- Ferrari and Rolex supply luxury goods to a small consumer market.
- Ford, General Motors and Toyota mass produce their cars.
- Burger King, KFC and McDonald's have outlets throughout the world.
- Nokia, Motorola, Samsung and Sony–Ericsson collectively produce billions of mobile phones.
- Microsoft supplies computer software for over 95% of the personal computers on the planet.

Some of these businesses prefer to stay small. Airbus and Ferrari, for example, deliberately limit growth in their operations. Others, such as McDonald's and Toyota, continually strive for expansion.

a Explain the circumstances when economies of scale might not actually benefit customers. *[4 marks]*

b Explain why economies of scale might be inappropriate, undesirable or inaccessible for certain businesses. *[4 marks]*

c If economies of scale are so important, examine the reasons why so many small firms continue to survive and thrive. *[5 marks]*

d To what extent do large businesses operate in the best interest of the general public? *[7 marks]*

INTERNAL (ORGANIC) GROWTH

There are two methods of business growth and these are known as organic growth and external growth. **Organic growth** occurs when a business grows internally, using its own resources to increase the scale of its operations and sales revenue. Internal growth is typically financed through the profits of the business.

External growth refers to business growth through mergers and acquisitions (M&A). This type of growth is also known as **amalgamation** or **inorganic growth** and is considered in more depth in the next section.

A business can grow organically, or internally, in several ways such as:

- Changing **price**. More customers tend to buy a product at lower prices. However, whether a firm should reduce or raise prices depends on the **price elasticity of demand** (see Unit 4.4) for a firm's product. If there are only a few substitutes for a firm's products, then the business will earn more sales revenue by raising prices. The opposite is true for products in highly competitive markets where a price reduction should generate proportionately more sales revenue.

- **Advertising** and **promoting**. People are more likely to buy a product if they are informed, reminded or persuaded about the benefits of a product. The Coca-Cola Company spends US$2 billion each year on promoting and advertising its products, which is one contributing factor to it being the world's most valuable brand.
- Producing improved or better **products**. Through methods such as market research, innovation and new product design, businesses can produce products that are more appealing to the market, thereby raising their level of sales. Most new products on the market fail, so it is quite common for firms to improve on the design or features of an existing product.
- Selling in different locations (**placement**). If a product is widely available, customers are more likely to make a purchase. One of the world's most expensive cars, with a starting price of approximately $1 million, is the Maybach. Wealthy customers who want to purchase one of these hand-made executive cars can go to one of 25 locations situated around the world. Apart from the high price, the number of outlets also limits the potential number of Maybach customers. Coca-Cola, on the other hand, is widely available throughout the world in different places, such as supermarkets, restaurants, cinemas, airlines and vending machines. This therefore increases the potential for more customers and more sales.
- Offering customers preferential **credit** payment terms. Customers are more likely to make a purchase if they are offered the ability to 'buy now and pay later'. Allowing customers to pay in regular instalments perhaps over 12 or 24 months for the purchase of expensive products, such as motor vehicles or large-screen plasma televisions, will attract more customers to the market. However, firms must be careful about offering too much credit as this will affect their cash flow position (see Unit 3.3).
- Increasing **capital expenditure** (investment). This can be in the form of expanding the business in new locations or the introduction of new production processes and technologies to improve productive efficiency. However, this risk may not pay off and therefore careful planning, such as *investment appraisal* (see Unit 3.2), is required.
- Improving **training and development**. People (employees) are often said to be a firm's most important asset. Training and development (T&D) is very important for people working in sales as customers are unlikely to make purchases from sales people with little or no sales knowledge. T&D not only helps to make staff more confident and competent in their jobs, but it can also help to motivate the workforce as they feel more valued by the employer. This can help to improve the level of customer service, thereby contributing to better customer loyalty and higher sales.

Benefits of organic growth

- Better control and coordination. It is often easier to grow internally than to rely on external sources. In addition, growth through organic methods means the firm maintains control, whereas growth through external methods can lead to a loss of control and ownership of the business.
- Relatively inexpensive. The main source of organic growth comes from retained profits. There might also be a need to raise interest-bearing capital, but there is less risk with organic growth as the amount of capital involved is relatively lower than that needed for external growth. The relatively high cost of external growth means that for many firms organic growth is the only suitable method of business expansion.
- Maintains corporate culture. One problem facing mergers and acquisitions occurs when two firms with potentially very difficult cultures join to form a new company. By contrast, internal growth means that there are no problems related with culture clash (see Unit 2.6).

Question 1.7.2

A.S. Watson Group

A.S. Watson Group

With a history dating back to 1828, the A.S. Watson Group has evolved into an international retail and manufacturing business with operations in 36 markets worldwide. The A.S. Watson Group employs over 98,000 staff and its portfolio encompasses some of Asia's best-known brands and retail chains. These include Watson's personal stores, Park 'n' Shop supermarkets, Fortress electrical appliance stores, Watson's Wine Cellar and Nuance–Watson airport duty free shops. A.S. Watson is also a major producer and distributor of water products and beverages in the region. Growing the business remains a long-term strategy at A.S. Watson.

Source: Adapted from A.S. Watson Group website (www.aswatson.com)

a Outline the type of business organization that A.S. Watson might be classified as operating. *[2 marks]*

b Explain how A.S. Watson benefits from synergy by its growth and evolution strategies. *[3 marks]*

c Despite its enormous size and global presence, examine why A.S. Watson still aims to grow larger as part of its long-term strategy? *[6 marks]*

Limitations of organic growth

- Diseconomies of scale. Higher unit costs of production can arise from both internal and external growth. Internally, hierarchical structures (see Unit 2.2) may increase, thereby causing communication problems and slower decision-making as a firm grows.
- Overtrading. This term is used to describe a business that is growing beyond its means. A firm, for example, may take on too many orders and is unable to control its costs or manage its human resources as a result.
- A need to restructure. When a firm grows in size, there is a need to change its management and personnel structure. A sole trader, for example, may be able to control and coordinate the business very easily but if it eventually grows into a large multinational company, then the organizational structure has to be changed. Restructuring requires time, effort and money. It will also entail some training, retraining and updating of skills. Communications (see Unit 2.3) will also have to be handled with more care due to the larger number of people in the organization.
- Dilution of control and ownership. If a firm grows by changing its legal status, for example from a partnership to a public limited company, then the original owners (the partners) will have to share decision-making with the new owners (the shareholders). With more owners, the decision-making process is prolonged and there is more likely to be conflict of interests between the different shareholders. Specialist managers will also be hired as a firm and its workforce expands. This requires delegation of decision-making powers to these managers, thereby reducing control of the original owners.

Question 1.7.3

Halifax Bank of Scotland

The Halifax Bank of Scotland banking group (HBOS) has built a reputation of **organic growth**. The global banking giant reported a 27% increase in international profits in 2006, extended by a further 19% in 2007. HBOS is the UK's largest lender of mortgages with an approximate **market share** of 21%. Plans were unveiled to open another 100 branches in the UK by 2011 in order to gain greater market share. Its medium- to long-term strategy is to focus on organic growth in Australia, Ireland and the UK.

a Define **organic growth** and **market share**. *[4 marks]*

b Outline two methods that HBOS may have used to achieve organic growth. *[4 marks]*

c To what extent is organic growth desirable for a business such as HBOS? *[7 marks]*

EXTERNAL GROWTH

External growth, often referred to as **inorganic growth**, occurs through dealings with outside organizations. Such growth usually comes in the form of alliances or mergers with other firms or through the acquisition (takeover) of other businesses. Mergers and acquisitions are collectively known as the **amalgamation** or **integration** of firms.

The general benefits of external growth include:

- It tends to be a much faster way to grow and evolve. For example, if a chain of supermarkets merges or buys up another chain, then this is much quicker than having to buy or rent new land to open more outlets.
- It is a quick way to reduce competition in a market. By taking over a rival, for example, a firm is able to eliminate a competitor. It should also allow the new larger firm to have greater market power. However, such strategies may be prohibited by the government because the lack of competition may not be in the best interest of the general public.
- External growth can bring about greater market share (see Unit 4.2) with its associated benefits.
- Working with other businesses means a sharing of good practice and ideas. External growth can therefore generate new skills, experiences and customers.
- External growth can help a firm to evolve, thereby spreading risks across several distinct markets. Hence, such firms can benefit from risk-bearing economies of scale.

The main disadvantage of external growth is the cost. The cost of external growth tends to be relatively higher than that of internal growth. Takeover bids can be especially expensive. Disney's takeover of Pixar (see Question 1.7.5 on page 128) cost $7.4 billion – that's over 50% more than Coca-Cola's annual profits! Other advantages and disadvantages of the different methods of external growth are covered below.

Joint ventures

A **joint venture** occurs when two or more businesses decide to split the costs, risks, control and rewards of a business project. In doing so, the parties involved in the joint venture agree to set up a new legal entity. For example, Coca-Cola has a joint venture with San Miguel with shared ownership of Coca-Cola's bottling plant in the Philippines. BMW has a joint venture with China's Brilliance Automobiles in sharing paint facilities. Typically, a joint venture between two firms will involve a 50:50 split of costs, responsibilities and profits (or losses).

Probably the most famous example of a joint venture is that of Sony Ericsson, the joint venture between Japan's Sony and Sweden's Ericsson. Sony Ericsson was established in 2001 to compete in the mobile communications industry. Their joint venture established a new company in its own right and Sony Ericsson has been very successful in reducing the market share of more established mobile manufacturers, namely Nokia, Motorola and Samsung.

Businesses may opt for joint ventures as a method of growth since they allow organizations to enjoy some of the benefits of mergers or acquisitions, such as higher sales and market share, but without having to lose their corporate identity. Other advantages of joint ventures as a means of growth include:

- **Synergy**. The pooling of experiences, talents and resources of the firms in collaboration should create synergy. A joint venture between a bank and a supermarket (very common in the UK) means that both parties can specialize in their area of expertise and gain access to new technologies and customers in order to achieve larger profits for both organizations.
- **Spreading of costs and risks**. Financial costs, risks and losses are shared in a joint venture. This helps to reduce the financial burden and risk on any single organization. Joint ventures can also allow firms to diversify their products, further helping to spread risks.
- **Entry to foreign markets**. Joint ventures have been used by companies to enter foreign countries by forming an agreement with overseas firms. National laws may make joint ventures the only option for businesses wishing to enter foreign markets. For example, many foreign firms managed to enter China prior to its joining of the World Trade Organization (WTO) by forming joint ventures with local Chinese businesses.
- **Relatively cheap** as a method of external growth. Takeovers and acquisitions can be very expensive. There are lengthy legal procedures and administrative costs involved with mergers and takeovers. The cost of a hostile takeover bid is often unknown. It is also relatively easier to pull out of a joint venture if necessary.
- **Competitive advantages**. Competition may be reduced by forming a joint venture. Companies cooperating in a joint venture are highly unlikely to compete with each other directly, yet their pooled resources make them a stronger force against their rivals. Their collective size may also mean that further economies of scale and economies of scope can be enjoyed.
- **Exploitation of local knowledge**. Firms that expand via international joint ventures can take advantage of each other's local knowledge and reputation. This may not be the case with mergers or acquisitions which are exposed to potential problems of overseas expansion (such as differences in business etiquette, cultural values, language, traditions, and marketing issues).
- **High success rate**. Whilst mergers and takeovers are often unfriendly and hostile, joint ventures tend to be friendly and receptive. The parties pool their funds and resources and share responsibility for their mutual benefit. Such a positive attitude is more likely to lead to the success of a joint venture. By contrast, mergers and acquisitions quite often fail due to management conflict.

Joint ventures and strategic alliances (see 'Strategic alliances' on page 124) share similar potential drawbacks. Partners in the joint venture tend to rely heavily on the resources and goodwill of their counterparts. In addition, there is likely to be a dilution of the brands, yet firms spend huge amounts of money in trying to develop their own brands (see Unit 4.3). Finally, when firms work together on a project, there is likely to be some sort of organizational culture clash between the businesses and this can lead to problems for the joint venture.

Question 1.7.4

Sony Ericsson

Sony–Ericsson is a **joint venture** between Sony and Ericsson, established in 2001. Within the first 5 years of operation, the company had sold close to 75 million phones, thereby becoming the world's fourth largest mobile phone manufacturer. Strong demand for mobile phones with built-in camera and music functions has helped Sony Ericsson to report record sales and **profits**, which doubled in 2007.

a Define the terms **joint venture** and **profits** as stated in the case study above. *[4 marks]*

b Explain the reasons why a merger between the two companies may not be appropriate. *[4 marks]*

c Examine the benefits of the joint venture to Sony and Ericsson. *[7 marks]*

Strategic alliances

A strategic alliance is similar to a joint venture in that two or more businesses seek to form a mutually beneficial affiliation by cooperating in a business venture. The firms in the strategic alliance also share the costs of product development, operations and marketing. However, unlike joint ventures, forming a strategic alliance means that the affiliated businesses remain *independent* organizations.

Strategic alliances can come in all shapes and sizes. For example, Ocean Park (Hong Kong's only theme park before the arrival of Disneyland) announced a strategic alliance with Japan's 7-Eleven in 2001. Through this strategic alliance, Ocean Park admission tickets are available for sale at all 7-Eleven stores in Hong Kong. A much larger scale example is the 'Star Alliance', set up in 1997, between many airline carriers such as Air Canada, Singapore Airlines and South African Airways. They share the costs and benefits of airline operations.

Typically, there are four key stages to the formation of a strategic alliance:

1. *Feasibility study* – investigating and establishing the rationale, objectives and feasibility of an alliance.
2. *Partnership assessment* – analysing the potential of different partners, such as what they have to offer to the alliance in terms of both human and financial resources.
3. *Contract negotiation* – negotiating to determine each member's contributions and rewards and the formulation of a mutually acceptable contract.
4. *Implementation* – initiating operations with commitment to the contract from all parties.

The main purposes of strategic alliances are to gain synergy from the different strengths of the members of the alliance and the pooling of their resources. For example, the partners can benefit from each other's expertise and financial support. A strategic alliance might also be more likely to gain creditability and brand awareness than separate companies trying to compete with one another. Two airlines both with half-empty aircraft could directly compete or they could collaborate by using a single full aeroplane to cut staff and fuel costs for mutual benefits. Another benefit for firms is that by working together on a larger scale, they can all gain from economies of scale such as purchasing and marketing economies. Customers are also likely to benefit from the added value services under a strategic alliance, such as the convenience of access to wider channels of distribution (see Unit 4.6).

Mergers and takeovers (or mergers and acquisitions)

The phrase 'mergers and takeovers' refers to the amalgamation or integration of two or more businesses to form one single company. The new firm will usually benefit from economies of scale and have a larger share of the market(s) that it operates in.

A **merger** takes place when two firms actually agree to form a new company, such as the merger between the UK's British Petroleum and USA's oil company Amoco in 1998 to form 'BP Amoco', which has since been renamed and shortened to 'BP'. Other examples of large mergers include Daimler Benz and Chrysler (1998), Hewlett–Packard and Compaq (2001), and Nokia and Siemens (2006).

A **takeover** occurs when a company buys a *controlling interest* in another company, i.e. by buying enough shares in the target business to hold a majority stake. In order to entice shareholders of the target company to sell their shares, the price offered by the buying company is likely to be well above stock market value of the shares. Takeovers, also known as **acquisitions** because of its aggressive nature of growth, have been used as a method of business growth for a long time. Heineken, the Dutch beer company, was established in 1864 by Gerard Adriaan Heineken and came to dominate the Dutch brewing industry by taking over many of its competitors. In 2006, internet giant Google acquired YouTube for $1.65 billion (not bad for a business that was only 10 months old at that time!). Box 1.7a outlines reasons why a certain business may become a takeover target.

Box 1.7a Reasons why some businesses become takeover targets

- They have growth potential but lack sufficient funds for internal growth.
- They are seen as a rival that has growth potential.
- They have a widely recognized brand or corporate name but are facing a financial crisis.
- They are vulnerable (an easy target for a takeover) as they have experienced a drop in profits and share prices have fallen as a result.
- The purchaser is sought as a white knight (see below) by the target company.

The purchasing company in a hostile takeover bid is referred to as the **black knight**. Strategically, the target company may seek an alternative to the black knight by amalgamating with a preferred company (known as the **white knight**). The white knight is more likely to be a friendly bidder and partner for the company. It is ultimately up to the shareholders of the target company to approve a merger by either selling or holding onto their share holdings. If the purchaser offers a good enough price for the shares of the target company, then shareholders are likely to sell their shares to the buyer.

There are four types of integration that can occur in a merger or acquisition:

1 **Vertical integration** takes place between businesses that are at different stages of production (primary, secondary or tertiary industries). Vertical integration can be further classed as either forward or backward integration. *Forward vertical integration* implies merging of businesses that head towards the end stage of production (towards the consumer). An example would be a coffee manufacturer that takes over a chain of cafés. This should help to reduce the final price of the product, possibly giving the business a competitive advantage. *Backward vertical integration* means a merger or acquisition of businesses towards an earlier stage of production. For example, a coffee manufacturer merges with its supplier of coffee beans. This strategy will help the manufacturer to secure lower costs of raw materials.

2 **Horizontal integration** occurs when there is an amalgamation of firms that operate in the same industry. This is the most common type of integration. An example is Time Inc. and Warner Communications, both in the media industry, merging to form Time Warner. Horizontal mergers and acquisitions do not represent growth in the industry but a larger market share for the amalgamated business, i.e. there is a larger *concentration ratio* in the industry. The benefit of horizontal integration is that with a larger market share the business is likely to benefit from greater market power (dominance).

3 **Lateral integration** refers to amalgamation between firms that have similar operations but do not directly compete with each other. For example, Ford Motor Company (considered a mass market brand) bought up Jaguar Cars (considered as a luxury brand) in 1990. Another example is Cadbury–Schweppes, formed by two businesses in 1969 that operated in completely different industries (confectionery and soft drinks respectively).

4 **Conglomerate mergers and takeovers** refer to the amalgamation of two businesses that are in completely distinct markets. This is a form of **diversification** strategy (see 'The Ansoff matrix' on page 131). Conglomerates are formed to enter new markets and to spread risks. Berkshire Hathaway, for example, owns businesses in a vast range of industries, including: insurance, property, clothing, flight services, home furnishing, news media, confectionery, beverages, meat products and carpet manufacturing! Successful conglomerates can benefit from economies of scale, the spreading of risks, having access to new and diverse markets, and global recognition.

Mergers and takeovers can benefit from several interrelated advantages:

- **Greater market share**. The integrated firm is likely to benefit from having greater market power and a larger customer base. For example, Diageo (the world's largest beers, wines and spirits company) was formed by the merger of drinks companies Guinness and Grand Metropolitan in 1997.
- **Economies of scale**. Larger scale operations help to lower the unit cost of production, therefore increasing the chances of earning higher profits.
- **Synergy** (1 + 1 = 3). The new combined firm has access to each other's resources, such as new technologies, control of distribution channels, management know-how and human resources. Hence they are able to better use their combined resources to boost the productivity and profits of the new firm.
- **Survival**. Amalgamation is a fast method of growth to protect the survival of a business. The merged firm is in a much stronger position to compete with rivals in the market. Amalgamation is a *defensive strategy*, whereby the merged firm responds to the growth of their rivals which could otherwise threaten their competitive position.
- **Diversification**. Some mergers or acquisitions allow businesses to diversify their product mix. This allows them to benefit from a larger customer base and reduced risks.

Mergers and takeovers can also suffer from some disadvantages:

- **Loss of control**. The original owners or management group will lose some degree of control as the new team of Board of Directors will need to be restructured.
- **Culture clash**. People and processes will need to adapt to the desired corporate culture of the new merged organization. This may entail changes to the firm's core values and mission statement. There are also likely to be difficulties for employees trying to adapt to new management styles and new methods of working.
- **Conflict**. Despite mergers being relatively friendly in comparison to takeovers, there are still potential disagreements and arguments between the two businesses which can either delay or end the merger. Takeovers tend to be quite hostile, so conflict is inevitable. Furthermore, there is often conflict regarding the purchase price or the conditions attached to a merger or takeover.

- **Redundancies**. Due to cost savings brought about by the synergy created in a merger or acquisition, there is no need to have two separate boards of directors (for example, the new business will not need two marketing or finance directors). Jobs may be duplicated and this means there is excess supply of labour. As a result, staff redundancies are likely to take place (see Unit 2.1). Managing this process of making staff unemployed is very stressful and potentially expensive. Even if redundancies do not take place, there will be other aspects of people management to deal with, such as people's anxieties of the unknown, changes to work practices, organizational restructuring and possibly changes to pay structures.
- **Diseconomies of scale**. Large scale operations do not always work. The larger firm may suffer from increased bureaucracy and slower channels of communication, leading to less effective decision-making and production.
- **Regulatory problems**. Governments may be concerned about the merger or acquisition of firms because they might create a monopoly. Hence the proposed takeover of Manchester United Football Club by Sky Television (the monopolist supplier of satellite television in the UK) was blocked by the British government who argued that the company would charge extortionate prices for watching football matches of the world's most valuable sports club (at that time). Alternatively, the government may require the amalgamated company to sell or split some of its operations. For example, Vodafone had to sell off Orange when it took over Mannesmann as the government believed that Vodafone would have too much market power if it also owned Orange (which has since been rebranded as '3').

Mergers and takeovers are very common in today's fast-paced business environment. Businesses are finding that they have to 'run faster to stay still' in increasingly competitive markets, i.e. they have to grow in order to maintain their market share and competitiveness. Amalgamation is a strategy to enable firms to remain or enhance their competitiveness. In addition, the boom in the number of people and organizations that are actively involved in stock markets has made mergers much more attractive. *Deregulation* has also enabled mergers to take place more efficiently. Finally, the phenomenon of *globalization* (see Unit 1.9) has also fuelled the interest in international mergers.

The degree of success of mergers and takeovers depends on several factors. First, the level of planning involved is crucial. A clear rationale of the benefits of the merger or takeover must be communicated to key stakeholder groups to win their support. Success also depends on the aptitudes of senior management of the two businesses involved. Conflict and disagreements can easily lead to the demise of any proposed integration. Managers will need to exert their negotiation skills and be able to handle the added pressures and responsibilities that they will face. Finally, regulatory problems may also present a barrier to success. The government may step in to prevent mergers or acquisitions taking place in order to prevent the business from having too much monopoly power.

Due to diseconomies of scale, not all mergers and acquisitions are successful. In these cases, a **demerger** might take place. This happens when a company sells off a significant part of its business. In 2007, for example, IBM sold a large proportion of its investment in China's largest computer manufacturer Lenovo (IBM's parent company). In the same year, Cadbury's Schweppes also announced that they were planning to demerge, and global car manufacturer Daimler Chrysler was also looking to split. A company might choose to demerge or break up in order to:

- Offload unprofitable sections of the business
- Avoid rising unit costs and inefficiency by being too large (diseconomies of scale)
- Raise cash to sustain operations of existing parts of the business
- Help management have a clearer focus by concentrating their efforts on a smaller range of operations.

Question 1.7.5

Disney's takeover of Pixar

In 2006, The Walt Disney Company agreed to a $7.4 billion deal to take ownership of Pixar Animation Studios, the firm responsible for movies such as *Toy Story*, *Finding Nemo*, *Cars* and *The Incredibles*. Disney's decision came at a time when its distribution deal with Pixar was about to expire. The company said that high demand for Pixar's movie merchandise (such as Buzz Lightyear toys and DVD movie sales) had earned Disney over $3.2 billion. The real value to Disney, however, is the synergy that would be created from the integration of the two firms.

a Explain two benefits to Disney in acquiring Pixar. *[4 marks]*

b Examine two potential problems for businesses during a takeover. *[6 marks]*

c Discuss the benefits for a business, such as Disney, in acquiring other firms. *[7 marks]*

Management buy-out is a defensive strategy that many businesses use when faced with a hostile takeover. A MBO involves the management team of the target business buying shares in the company to become the owners, or part-owners, of the business thereby preventing it from being taken over. The management team will probably use their own money to fund the purchase, although borrowing from banks is also likely. Alternatively, the management team can seek financial assistance from investment experts known as *venture capitalists* (see Unit 3.1). Of course, managers would only do this if they felt that the long-term prospects of owning the company outweighed the benefits of the hostile takeover. MBOs also mean that the workforce do not face the threat of job losses which could be the case with a takeover.

Another alternative to a complete takeover of a target business is to buy just one of the brands from the firm. This strategy is known as **brand acquisition**. For example, BMW bought the Rolls-Royce brand in 2003 to enhance its product portfolio. Firms may decide to sell one of their brands if they are facing a *liquidity problem* (see Unit 3.3), i.e. they are so short of cash that it jeopardizes the survival of the firm. They may also sell a brand because they wish to demerge or feel that the brand no longer suits their corporate image.

Exam Tip!
Higher Level extension
It should go without saying that evaluation is a key skill that is tested in the exams. In this case, students should be able to evaluate the use of different growth strategies as a means of business growth. A strategy that is suitable for one business is unlikely to be appropriate for other businesses. It is also important to put answers in the context of the business and to consider short-term and long-term factors in the evaluation.

FRANCHISES

A **franchise** is a form of business ownership whereby a person or business buys a license to trade using another firm's name, logo, brands and trademarks. In return for this benefit, the purchaser of a franchise (known as the **franchisee**) pays a license fee to the parent company of the business (known as the **franchisor**). In return, the franchisee pays a **royalty payment** (similar to commission which is paid according to the amount sold by the franchisee). McDonald's, Pizza Hut, Subway and The Body Shop all use franchises as a means of growth.

The **benefits of franchising as a method of growth for the franchisor** include:

- The parent company can experience rapid growth without having to risk huge amounts of money as the franchisee pays for the outlet itself. Hence, franchising can be less risky than organic growth.
- Franchising allows a business to have a national or international presence without the relatively higher costs of organic growth or mergers and acquisitions because the franchisee helps to finance the expansion.
- Through growth and expansion of operations, the franchisor can benefit from economies of scale.
- The franchise can benefit from growth without having to worry about running costs such as staff wages, purchase of stocks and staff recruitment.
- Franchisors receive a royalty payment from the franchisee, usually set as a percentage of any profits made by the franchisee. In addition they may also charge a membership fee to their franchisees.
- Franchisees have more incentives to do well than salaried managers of a business, thereby increasing the chances of success for the franchisor.
- Local franchisees will have greater awareness of local market conditions and cultural differences.

Franchising has the following **advantages for the franchisee**:

- There is relatively low risk since the franchisor has a tried and tested formula so the chances of business success are high.
- There are lower start-up costs (such as market research and product development) because the business idea has already been developed by the franchisor.
- It is in the best interest of the franchisor to ensure that the franchise succeeds. This means that they will provide added-services to the franchisees, such as advice on financial management and providing training for staff.
- The franchisee is likely to benefit from large scale advertising used by the well-known parent company. Therefore the franchisee receives 'free' advertising and promotion, thereby helping to reduce their costs.

However, there are several potential **pitfalls of franchising to the franchisor**:

- It may prove difficult to control the activities of franchisees and to get them to meet the quality standards set by the business.
- Franchisors take a huge risk when allowing other people or businesses to use their names. Franchisees that do not follow set procedures or do not meet expectations may end up harming the reputation of the whole company.
- Although franchising is faster than organic growth, it is not as quick a method of growth as mergers or acquisitions.

The **disadvantages to franchisees** include:

- The money needed to buy a franchise can be very expensive. There is no guarantee that this money will ever be recouped.
- Franchisees have to pay a significant percentage of their revenues to the franchisor, thereby leaving them with less profit than would otherwise be the case.
- There is less flexibility for franchisees to use their own initiative or to try out new ideas because they are constrained from doing so by the franchisor. For instance, the owner would be told what prices to set and what promotional campaigns to use.

Question 1.7.6

Pizza Hut

Pizza Hut, founded in 1958, is the world's largest chain of pizza restaurants. Within a year, the American company opened its first Pizza Hut franchise. Today, its operations span the globe with restaurants in over 100 countries. The company also plans to continue opening new stores in existing and new locations. Pizza Hut's home page even has a section titled 'Become a Franchisee' with all the necessary information that interested parties can consult before submitting their applications.

Source: www.pizzahut.com

a Explain the reasons for Pizza Hut's decision to use franchising as its main form of growth. *[4 marks]*

b Examine the potential problems of Pizza Hut's growth strategy. *[6 marks]*

HIGHER LEVEL

HIGHER LEVEL EXTENSION: PORTER'S GENERIC STRATEGIES

Dr. Michael Porter's **generic strategies** outline the ways that any business can gain a competitive advantage. If a profitable product or idea can be copied easily, then other firms will take advantage of this by entering the market. Rivals may also offer an improved product or offer the product at more competitive prices. Hence the original firm does not retain its competitive advantage and this will mean that its profits will fall. Porter argued that every successful business must have a competitive advantage to prevent profits being eroded by rivals entering the market. He suggested that there are three general or broad strategies that firms can use to sustain a competitive advantage:

1. **Cost leadership** means to become the lowest cost supplier of a product within the market. For example, Malaysia's Air Asia is the largest low-cost airline carrier in South East Asia. Aldi is Germany's largest chain of discount supermarkets. McDonald's and Ikea have also used this strategy. Although these firms charge low prices in their respective industries, they are highly profitable and market leaders. They do not compete with firms that offer higher-quality products since this would require price hikes. The only way to directly compete with these firms is by using penetration or predatory pricing strategies (see Unit 4.4) which may be prohibited by certain governments.
2. **Differentiation** happens when a firm makes its mass-market products distinct from those of its competitors. This could be done through various methods such as packaging or branding (see Unit 4.3) to make the product seem unique. The focus here is on the *quality* rather than the cost of a product. Successful differentiation will allow a business to charge a *premium price* (a price higher than the industry average), thereby earning a higher profit margin for the firm. Coca-Cola, BMW, Nike and Apple's iPod use this strategy to maintain their competitive advantage. A key drawback of this method is that it may be expensive, such as the amount of money needed to successfully develop and promote a product.
3. **Focus** occurs when a firm targets a niche or single segment of the market. In the case of Gucci, Rolex and Chanel, focus can be a highly profitable strategy due to the high prices that can be charged and the lack of competition. However, focus can also be used by low-cost businesses that cater for a certain market segment, such as discount bric-a-brac stores. The drawback of focus as a strategy is that the market size is very limited.

Porter suggests that it is not possible in the long term to adopt a mixture of these strategies. For example, it is not feasible to maintain high quality by using a cost leadership strategy, i.e. firms cannot expect to be highly profitable *and* to have an image of outstanding quality by charging low prices. Hence, Porter's ideas help managers to concentrate on a specific strategy that best serves their organizations.

Question 1.7.7

Which generic strategy?

a Identify which of Porter's generic strategies are used by the following businesses and explain your answer:

i Harrods (a single department store in central London catering for the rich and famous).

ii KFC (a market leader in fast-food with a globally recognized brand). *[6 marks]*

b To what extent does Porter's theory apply to global conglomerates? *[7 marks]*

THE ANSOFF MATRIX

The Ansoff matrix (1957) is an analytical tool that helps managers to devise their product and market growth strategies. It is named after its creator, Professor Igor Ansoff (1918–2002). It shows the various strategies that businesses can take depending on whether it wants to market new or existing products in either new or existing markets (see Figure 1.7b). The four growth strategies (or growth options) in the Ansoff matrix are explained below.

Markets	Products: Existing	Products: New
Existing	Market penetration	Product development
New	Market development	Diversification

Figure 1.7b The Ansoff matrix: product and market growth strategies

Market penetration

This is a low-risk growth strategy for businesses that choose to focus on selling existing products in existing markets, i.e. to increase their market share of current products. This might be achieved by improving a firm's marketing mix, such as using better advertising to enhance the desirability of the product or by offering more competitive prices. In addition to trying to attract new customers, firms may also attempt to entice existing customers to make more frequent purchases, perhaps by offering membership loyalty schemes. Brands might also be repositioned (see Unit 4.2) to achieve market penetration.

One advantage of using market penetration as a growth strategy is that the business is focusing on markets and products that it is familiar with. Market research expenditure (see Unit 4.2) can therefore be minimized. This is also the safest of the four growth strategies in the Ansoff matrix.

A limitation of this strategy is that competitors, especially stronger rivals, will react to firms trying to take away their customers and market share. This may lead to aggressive techniques, such as price wars, to the detriment of business profits (at least in the short run).

Product development

This is a medium-risk growth strategy that involves businesses aiming to sell new products in existing markets. Apple's launch of the iPhone is an example of a firm introducing a new product to the mobile phone industry. McDonald's is frequently adding new products to its menus. Car manufacturers introduce new models and occasionally limited editions of their vehicles. It is likely that this strategy relies heavily on *product extension* strategies and *new product development* (see Unit 4.3) that appeal to the existing market.

Product development is suitable for products that have reached the saturation or decline stage of their product life cycle (see Unit 4.3) in order to prolong their life, and hence their ability to earn revenues for the business. The strategy is also a reason for acquiring another company. Ford's acquisition of Jaguar in 1989, for example, meant that the company could cater for a different type of customer, but without the costs of having to start a new company from scratch along with all its associated risks. Finally, this strategy is also useful for businesses that use *brand extension* strategies. A well established firm, such as Sony or Nike, can use its brand to introduce new products to the market. There are lower risks when launching a new product under a well-known brand name.

Market development

Market development is the medium-risk growth strategy that relates to businesses selling existing products in new markets, i.e. an established product is marketed to a new market segment. This might be done by using new distribution channels to sell the product in a different location or overseas, although this could be quite risky if the business is unfamiliar with local market conditions and cultures. Alternatively, the product could be tweaked by using more attractive or appealing packaging to suit the new audience. Prices could also be changed to attract different market segments.

One advantage of this growth method is that it is not high risk since the business will be familiar with the product that is being marketed. For example, Nokia and Motorola use market development to sell their mobile phones which have a short product life cycle in developed nations (because customers frequently upgrade their phones). Their phones, which are mass produced, are then sold in developing countries such as India, Indonesia, Russia and South America. However, the success of a product in one market segment does not necessarily guarantee its success in other market segments.

Diversification

Diversification refers to the high risk growth strategy that involves a business marketing new products in new markets. The Virgin Group is an example of a diversified business with its various strategic business units such as Virgin Atlantic, Virgin Blue, Virgin Mobile, Virgin Trains and Virgin Cola.

In addition to being able to gain market share in established markets, a key driving force for diversification is that the business can spread its risks. This means that if one part of the business is underperforming then other more successful sections of the organization may be able to compensate for this, thereby helping the overall establishment to survive. It is also suitable for firms that have reached saturation in their markets and are seeking new opportunities for growth.

One way to diversify is to become a **holding company**. This is a business that owns a controlling interest in other diverse companies, i.e. it owns enough shares to be able to take control and management of other businesses. Holding companies, also known as **parent companies**, can benefit from having a presence in a range of products and markets in different regions of the world. An example is Time Warner, the parent company of **subsidiaries** (firms owned by a holding company) such as Warner Brothers, CNN, HBO, AOL and *Fortune* magazine.

Another similar method is to establish **strategic business units (SBU)**. These are similar to subsidiaries in that they have a separate vision and mission statement and are independently run from their parent company. However, SBUs do not have to be a whole company but can include different product lines or individual brands. For example, the major Japanese mass-market car manufacturers (Toyota, Nissan and Honda) all have SBUs that cater for higher income customers (Lexus, Infiniti and Acura, respectively).

However, this growth strategy remains the riskiest of the four options in the Ansoff matrix since the business is not on familiar territory when launching new products in markets it has little if any experience. New distribution channels will also need to be established and this could be time consuming and costly for the firm. All these distractions can lead to an organization losing focus of its core business with serious consequences.

In conclusion, the Ansoff matrix provides four growth options for businesses. It highlights risk implications of each growth strategy. Critics argue that it is rather simplistic and that it needs to be used alongside other decision-making tools, such as Porter's generic strategies.

Note: Higher Level students should be able to evaluate internal and external growth strategies as methods of business expansion. (© IBO, 2007)

Question 1.7.8

Use the Ansoff matrix to explain the growth strategies in the following cases:

a Cadbury's, the chocolate manufacturer, launches new products under the names of Crème Eggs, Flake, Crunchie and Heroes. *[3 marks]*

b Nissan, a mass-market car manufacturer, launches a new line of upmarket cars under the name of Infiniti to cater for wealthier customers. *[3 marks]*

GROWTH AND EVOLUTION AND BUSINESS STRATEGY

This Unit has looked at the two main forms of business growth and evolution – internal growth and external growth. Internal growth or organic growth allows owners to maintain their level of control although usually requires financing through the use of retained profits and bank loans. Hence, this usually proves to be a slower, albeit safer, growth method. Alternatively, managers may use external growth methods such as mergers and acquisitions (collectively known as growth through amalgamation). Regardless of the method of growth, businesses will seek to grow as a strategy for survival in today's increasingly competitive business environment.

A key reason for pursuing growth is to reap the benefits of economies of scale. Economies of scale not only give a firm cost-saving benefits as it grows in size, but can also act as a **barrier to entry** into a market. For example, it would be very difficult and costly for a new business to compete with large pharmaceutical companies such as Pfizer or multinational oil companies such as Shell. This is largely due to the economies of scale that these firms enjoy because of their huge scale operations. In addition, there would need to be a vast amount of money invested in research and development in order to enter such markets.

This Unit has also looked at the various strategies that businesses often try to use to achieve growth. These include:

- Offering products that have a **unique selling point (USP) is important**. This is the technique that makes one product stand out from other products that are available on the market.
- Being the first product in a market, known as having a **first-mover advantage**, is another growth strategy. It allows a business to establish a good reputation and a loyal customer base before other firms have a chance to launch their products.
- Being a **market leader** means that customers are more willing to pay a higher price. Customers also become less sensitive to price changes in the future. Porter's cost leadership or product differentiation strategies might also be used to pursue market leadership.
- **Branding** can be vital to a firm's competitive advantage. A well-established and recognized brand is an opportunity for business growth.
- **Diversification**, whereby a business produces new products in new markets, is a potentially high-risk strategy. However, it helps a business to spread its risks and to gain revenue from an untapped market (as it is new to the industry).

The Ansoff matrix provides four strategic opportunities for enlarging a business. However, an option that is right for one business does not necessarily mean that it is suitable for another. For example, firms that have a high risk profile are more likely to opt for diversification whereas businesses that prefer to use brand extension strategies may opt for product development as a strategy.

Porter's generic strategies also help businesses to determine their growth strategy. Porter suggested that any mass market business can choose from cost leadership or product leadership (via differentiation). The third option he suggested was for businesses to focus on niche markets. Any of these strategies can help a business to gain a competitive advantage to maintain market share and profits.

Franchising is a popular strategy of growing nationally and internationally. Its high success rate relies on the know-how, brand recognition and trust of a parent organization coupled with the incentives and enthusiasm of the franchisee to make the franchise a success. For example, Burger King, the world's second largest fast-food chain, has more than 11,000 outlets, with around 90% of them being franchises.

Although many businesses may seek growth and evolution, there are plenty of constraints. An understanding of the restraints can help managers to deal with the problems. For example, a key barrier to a firm's growth is the amount of finance needed for expansion. Firms can work round this problem by trying to seek alternative sources of finance such as the flotation of shares or by issuing debentures (see Unit 3.1). If the size of a market is the limiting factor then businesses might seek growth by expanding overseas or by diversifying its product portfolio.

Successful businesses may achieve rapid growth, but there are also potential dangers of being too large in an industry. For example, firms may experience diseconomies of scale or encounter overtrading. Expanding businesses tend to use money borrowed from banks to fund their growth. However, this means that these firms are more vulnerable during unfavourable trading periods as they will still need to repay their debts. Hence a sensible and affordable level of **gearing** (or long-term borrowing) is important.

In fact, businesses that become too large will often choose to **downsize**, also known as **rationalization**. Factories, stores or outlets will be closed down or sold off and staff redundancies (see Unit 2.1) will take place to cut costs. For example, in order to cut production costs, Airbus announced in 2007 that there would be 10,000 job losses across Europe by 2011. Rationalization will also allow the business to focus on its core products rather than struggle to handle a diverse product portfolio.

REVIEW QUESTIONS 1.7

1 Outline four ways in which the size of a market can be measured.

2 Why do businesses seek to grow in size?

3 Using examples, explain the meaning of 'economies of scale'.

4 Distinguish between 'internal' and 'external' economies of scale.

5 What is meant by the 'optimal size' of a business?

6 Distinguish between 'internal' and 'external' growth.

7 Distinguish between 'joint ventures' and 'strategic alliances'.

8 What are the benefits of mergers and takeovers as a form of external growth?

9 What are the advantages and disadvantages of franchising as a method of growth?

10 Explain the quadrants of the Ansoff matrix.

Higher Level extension

11 What are Porter's generic growth strategies?

Ansoff matrix is an analytical tool that helps managers to devise their product and market growth strategies, depending on whether they want to market new or existing products in either new or existing markets.

Backward vertical integration is a form of amalgamation that takes place when a business acquires or merges with a firm operating in an earlier stage of the chain of production, e.g. a car manufacturer buying out a supplier of tyres or other components.

Conglomerates are businesses that provide a diversified range of products and operate in an array of different industries. Conglomerates are likely to have resulted from external growth strategies.

Diseconomies of scale are the cost disadvantages of growth. Unit costs are likely to eventually rise as a firm grows in size due to internal factors (such as a lack of control, coordination and communication) and external factors (such as saturated markets which create a need for cost cutting).

Diversification is a growth strategy of large businesses by spreading risks over a variety of products and markets. Conglomerates, for example, provide a whole range of goods and services to clients all around the globe.

Economies of scale refer to the lower average costs of production as a firm operates on a larger scale. Benefits include easier and cheaper access to finance, marketing economies, division of labour and technological economies.

External diseconomies of scale refer to an increase in the average costs of production as a firm grows due to factors beyond its control. This is often caused by problems associated with too many firms being in the industry.

External growth occurs when a business grows by collaborating with, buying up or merging with another firm. It is a more expensive but quicker method of growth than organic growth. External growth is also known as **inorganic growth** or **amalgamation**.

Forward vertical integration is a growth strategy that occurs with the acquisition or merger of a firm operating at a later stage in the chain of production, e.g. a book publishing company merging with a book retailer.

Franchise refers to an agreement between a franchisor selling its rights to other businesses (franchisees) to allow them to sell products under its name. In return, the franchisee pays a fee and a royalty (percentage of the profits) to the franchisor.

Horizontal integration is an external growth strategy that occurs when a business acquires or merges with a firm operating in the same stage of the chain of production, e.g. two commercial banks decide to merge.

Joint venture refers to a strategy that combines the contributions and responsibilities of two different organizations to a shared project by forming a separate enterprise. Unlike a merger or takeover, both businesses in a joint venture retain their original identity.

Organic growth occurs when a business grows internally, using its own resources to increase the scale of its operations and sales revenue. Also known as **internal growth**, it occurs through a firm's efforts to sell more of its own products by using its own resources.

Porter's generic strategies outline the ways that any business can gain a competitive advantage, i.e. cost leadership, focus or differentiation.

Management buy-out (MBO) occurs when the managers of a company purchase all the shares in the business, thereby becoming the firm's legal owners.

Merger refers to the method of external growth whereby two (or more) firms agree to form a new organization, losing their original identities.

Takeover, also known as **acquisition**, is a form of external growth whereby one business buys up another. This is done by purchasing a controlling interest in that company, often against the wishes to their directors.

Change and the Management of Change

UNIT 1.8

You must be the change you wish to see in the world.

Mahatma Gandhi (1869–1948), political and spiritual leader of India

Key topics

Higher Level only

- The dynamic nature of change in businesses
- Factors causing change and resistance to change
- Driving and restraining forces of change
- Managing the change process
- Models and frameworks of change management

INTRODUCTION

Businesses are dynamic in nature and are always subject to the forces of change. Globalization and e-commerce, for example, have meant that multinationals have had to adapt in order to survive. One of the most difficult tasks for any manager is to manage the change process. **Change management** refers to processes and techniques used to plan, implement and evaluate changes in business operations in order to achieve a required objective.

Change may include new product development, a change in organizational structure, new policies, new targets, mergers and acquisitions, disposals, crisis management, relocations, pay deals and so forth. Change moves a business away from its equilibrium so any change needs to be explained to staff. Trying to force change may cause problems; people can be resistant to change and be uncooperative if change is simply made compulsory. The key is to win support from the staff. Yet, it is important to remember that without change there is always the danger of complacency and there can be no progress without change.

Motor vehicle manufacturers, for example, have been forced into being conscious of environmental challenges. This has led them to exploring a range of alternative and sustainable technologies. Toyota's Earth Charter, for instance, was set up back in 1992. It launched the Toyota Prius, the world's first mass produced gas–electric hybrid, in Japan back in 1997. This Unit looks at the dynamic nature of change and the management of change in business organizations.

FACTORS CAUSING CHANGE

There are six main factors that will influence change:

1 **Customers** demand better quality products at competitive prices. This obviously presents challenges for any business. Customers may also change their habits and tastes, such as the desire to purchase more environmentally friendly products. Businesses will need to adapt to these ever-changing expectations and preferences of the customer.

2 **Competitors** will try to provide better services and products, perhaps through new product development and other marketing strategies. Hence, to stay competitive and maintain market share, the business will need to change its practices. Apple's iPod, for example, led Sony to remarket their Walkman brand for MP3 players. Growth of rival firms through mergers and acquisitions will also present potential threats to a business.

3 **Management** will need to stay abreast of market trends to ensure that the business remains competitive. They must ask, for example, whether better customer service can be achieved and how it might be achieved due to higher levels of customer expectations.

4 **Technological progress** such as the microchip revolution, communications technology, the internet and e-commerce (see Unit 4.8) have forced firms to change the way they conduct their business. Amazon.com and eBay have revolutionized the way products are sold today. Most multinationals have their own dedicated website and more and more businesses are offering payments to be made online.

5 **Government** changes in legislation, such as employment laws, can have a profound impact on businesses. In Hong Kong, for example, there is no anti-ageism legislation. Hence, airlines such as British Airways and Cathay Pacific still insist that their air staff retire at 45 years of age (20 years earlier than their counterparts in the European Union!). Of course, any change in such legislation will mean that the airlines have to reconsider their workforce planning. Partygaming, the world's largest online gaming business, was badly affected by new

legislation in the USA in late 2006 when the government made online gaming illegal. Partygaming said that the new law fundamentally changed its business as it suspended all its dealings in the USA.

6 **External factors** including changes in fashion, the state of the economy (such as a recession) and globalization will create change in an organization. Some external factors may disrupt businesses so much that there is a need for Crisis Management (see Unit 2.8), such as an oil crisis or terrorist attacks.

In today's business environment, it is the organizations that can adapt to these forces of change that will survive and remain in business. Planet Hollywood, a restaurant chain set up by several Hollywood celebrities, failed due to their inflexibility to meet changing consumer demands. They failed to listen to the views of their customers, who basically demanded better value for money, and as a result went out of business.

Question 1.8.1

Headline news

"Companies report 10% growth in sales for holiday trading season"

"**Interest rates** forecast to rise again"

"Further job losses expected to slow the economy"

"**Takeover bid** expected to benefit shareholders"

a Define the terms in bold in the text above. *[4 marks]*

b Use the above examples to examine why businesses are said to be 'dynamic' in nature. *[6 marks]*

RESISTANCE TO CHANGE

One of the major barriers to effective change management is the resistance to change from the workforce. According to Professor John Paul Kotter (1979), there are four main reasons why people tend to be resistant to change:

1 **Self-interest** takes priority over corporate objectives. People may be more interested in the implications of change for themselves rather than the benefits that change might bring for the organization. Hence, they may feel that any change involves extra effort.

2 **Misunderstandings** occur because the *purpose* of change has not been communicated properly. Staff often feel that change is not necessary as things are going well, so as the saying goes "If it isn't broken, don't fix it." In addition, uncertainties will arise due to the anxieties of the unknown and of the future.

3 **Different assessments of the situation** occur when management and staff disagree on the advantages and disadvantages of change. Managers may feel that a restructuring of the workforce is necessary, for example, but workers may think otherwise as they are the experts in the roles that they fulfil and may not see the need for such change.

4 **Low tolerance of change** because people prefer familiarity rather than disruptions and uncertainties. A lack of security is sensed when people are put out of their 'norms'. There may also be an element of fear of being made redundant. For example, new production techniques may mean that less people are required within the organization. Staff may also fear failure in adapting to the change. They may, for instance, have the fear of not being able to work within an automated environment.

HIGHER LEVEL

There is also the possibility of **ambivalence** which could underestimate the actual resistance to change. This means the internal conflict surrounding change where some people do not necessarily voice their concerns. When people are in a group situation, for example, they may conform to the majority view, but would prefer to act differently themselves. Others may feel that if they resist change then they are overlooked in future for any promotional opportunities within the organization.

Kotter proposed the **Six Change Approaches** model to deal with resistance to change (see Figure 1.8a):

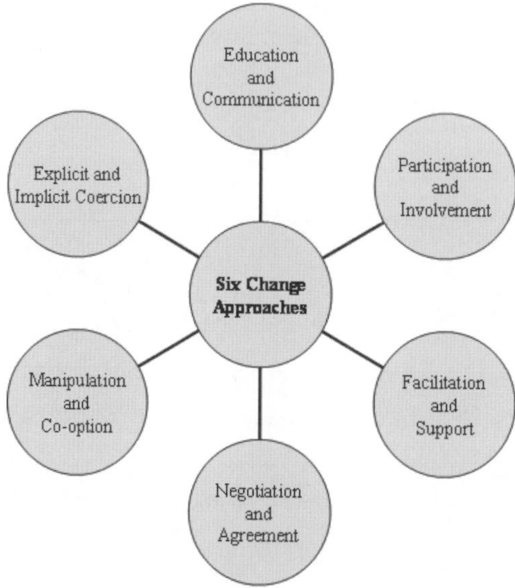

Figure 1.8a Kotter's Six Change Approaches model

1 **Education and Communication**. This approach aims to inform and educate staff (and other stakeholders) about the change beforehand. Early communication and clarification can help stakeholders to see the rationale for change and establish a degree of trust. Perhaps more importantly, this approach reduces unsupported and incorrect rumours about the effects of change in the business.

2 **Participation and Involvement**. This approach links with several motivational theorists such as Mayo and Herzberg (see Unit 2.5) who argue that employee involvement in decision-making can motivate and improve morale amongst the workforce. Kotter argued that by involving employees in the change process, perhaps through a series of consultation sessions, they are then more likely to accept change instead of resisting it. However, this approach is likely to be quite time consuming.

3 **Facilitation and Support**. This approach is rather paternalistic in style as managers become supportive of staff during difficult times, thereby averting potential resistance to change. Managerial support can be in numerous forms, such as counselling employees to deal with their fears and apprehensions or the retraining of staff to enable them to accommodate the new changes.

4 **Negotiation and Agreement**. This is the 'carrot' approach to dealing with resistance to change whereby managers use incentives to remove or limit any resistance to change. This can be done for example by inviting employees to accept amendments in their employment contracts to accommodate the new changes. Alternatively, employees who are resisting

change may be offered early retirement or redundancy incentives to leave the organization. In other circumstance, managers may be willing to compromise in order to provide an incentive for staff to settle for the change.

5 **Manipulation and Co-option**. This approach involves bringing a representative of those resisting change into the change process. The purpose, in theory, is to give them representation but in fact the underlying reason for this is to convert the representative's thinking so that the advantages of change can be communicated to those resisting change. Quite often, these representatives, such as trade union leaders, are given a symbolic role but the reality is that their view will not affect the desire of management to push for the change. This approach is, of course, seen as unethical and may backfire if those resisting change discover what the management are really trying to do.

6 **Explicit and Implicit Coercion**. This is the 'stick' approach to dealing with resistance to change and is often used as a last resort strategy. Managers can use coercion (bullying tactics) to force staff into accepting change, by threatening disciplinary action, dismissals, job losses, redeployment (transferring employees to other jobs), or not promoting employees. Due to employment legislation (see Unit 2.1) which exists to protect employee rights, much of this coercion may be carried out implicitly by managers.

Question 1.8.2

Kodak

For generations photography was synonymous with Kodak. Founded in 1888, Kodak was one of the best-known brands of the 20th century.

However, with the rapid rise in demand for digital cameras, the market for camera film (Kodak's main product) declined rapidly. From 2000, Kodak had started to lag behind the change of times, and responded by expanding its global workforce and raising production levels of the old format. By 2006, it was selling an obsolete product and its survival depended on restructuring and transforming itself into a key player in the digital market.

a Explain why it is vital that businesses are aware of the forces of change if they are to remain competitive. *[4 marks]*

b Examine the strategies available to Kodak in re-establishing itself as a market leader. *[6 marks]*

PLANNING CHANGE

American novelist, Ellen Glasgow (1873–1945) once said, "All change is not growth, as all movement is not forward." In other words, change should only be pursued if there is a clear set of goals. Figure 1.8b shows the two types of forces of change. **Driving forces** push for change whereas **restraining forces** act against a proposal for change. The relative strength of the forces will determine whether the change takes place. It is due to all these conflicting forces that change must be managed within organizations if they are to move forward and remain competitive.

HIGHER LEVEL

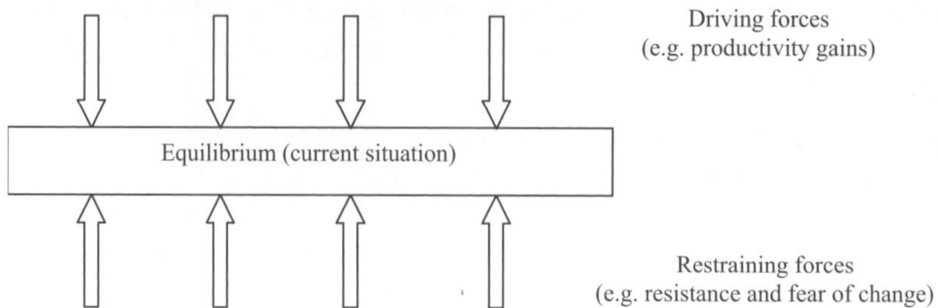

Figure 1.8b Forces of change

Before instigating any organizational change, managers must ask themselves:

- Why is change needed?
- What do we hope to achieve with such change?
- Who is affected by this change and how are they likely to react to the change?
- How will we know that the change has been successfully achieved?

These aspects operate in a cycle as businesses constantly face change.

One method to aid managers facing change is **Force Field analysis**. It is a framework for helping managers to understand the pressures for and against any change situation. By identifying these forces, managers are able to assess the effects that the forces may have and to decide on a course of action. By carrying out force field analysis, managers can then plan to strengthen the forces supporting a decision of change, and reduce the impacts of opposition to it.

LEWIN'S FORCE FIELD ANALYSIS

Force field analysis was first developed by Kurt Lewin in 1951. He argued that successful businesses tend to be constantly adapting and changing. Businesses that do not succeed are fixed in outdated practices and are unable to see any way forward.

There are four stages in carrying out a force field analysis:

1. List the encouraging forces for change and the burdening forces against change.
2. Allocate a weight to each of these forces, from 1 (weak) to 5 (strong).
3. Draw a diagram (see Figure 1.8c, for example) showing the forces for and against change.
4. Show the relative effect of each force by a number next to it.

HIGHER LEVEL

For example, you are a managing director deciding whether to automate production to increase your firm's productivity. Your force field analysis might look similar to the one in Figure 1.8c:

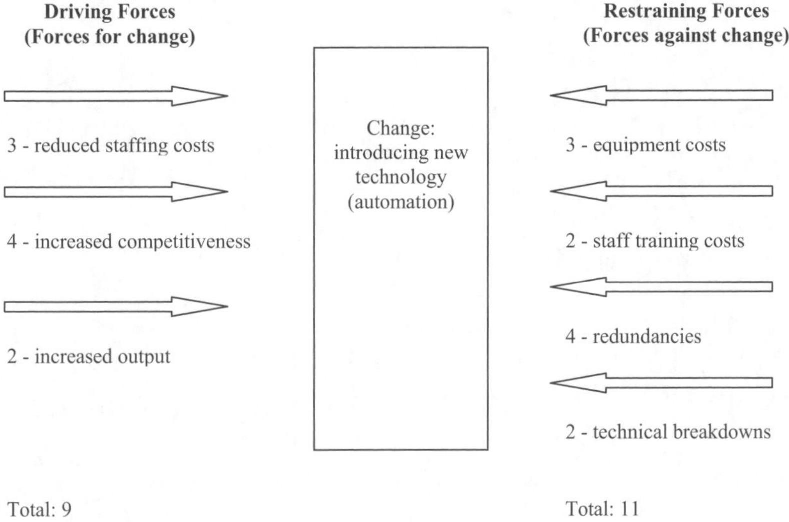

Figure 1.8c Example of a force field analysis

From studying Figure 1.8c, you may think managers would be reluctant to opt for automation. However, if a manager has already decided on this option, force field analysis can help to work out *how* to improve a project's chances of success. Managers can investigate how the driving forces can be strengthened and how the restraining forces can be reduced or eliminated. Lewin argued that these forces should be investigated if there is to be improvement in an organization.

This model does not solve the problems of change management, but it helps managers to assess the forces more clearly. Lewin argued that improvements in business organizations are not the result of one-off changes but that a small adjustment to the forces can result in many small changes and improvements.

Nevertheless, the main disadvantages in using force field analysis are:

- Weightings attached to the forces may be subjective rather than referring to facts or evidence.
- Not all relevant forces may be considered, perhaps to deliberately over-emphasize the need for change.

Effectively, Lewin's force field analysis is a useful technique of weighing advantages and disadvantages to help decide whether any proposed change is worth implementing. If a change is desired, then managers can analyse the forces and influence the factors when making that change.

HIGHER LEVEL

Question 1.8.3

The English Schools Foundation (ESF)

In late 2005, the new Chief Executive of the English Schools Foundation (ESF) in Hong Kong decided to implement a package to reduce teaching staff salaries and remuneration. Heather Du Quesnay came under pressure from the government to reduce pay to staff in its 19 schools. Ms. Du Quesnay's initial proposals included:

- A 5% cut in basic pay as a contingency against the potential loss of the government subsidy (which accounted for approximately 28% of the ESF's annual budget at the time)
- A 5% cut in gratuity (end-of-contract bonus) to bring the ESF into line with other international schools
- A 50% cut in responsibility allowances to reduce the overall salary bill
- Introduce performance-related pay for all teachers.

Despite the favourable economic climate at the time (economic growth and consumer confidence levels were at an all time high since the 1997 handover of Hong Kong), Ms. Du Quesnay argued that ESF teachers' salaries had to be cut by 10% overall. Not surprisingly, her proposals were not met with enthusiasm and a pay dispute ensued.

Sources: Association of Professional Teachers of the English Schools Foundation and www.esf.edu.hk

a Produce a force field analysis for the English Schools Foundation. *[4 marks]*

b Using the above analysis, recommend a course of action to manage the change process. *[6 marks]*

CHANGE MANAGEMENT MODELS AND FRAMEWORKS

Essentially, there are four steps to any change management model:

1. Identify the proposed change and the rationale for change.
2. Brainstorm the driving forces and the restraining forces of the change.
3. Develop and communicate an understanding of these issues to key stakeholders.
4. Implement actions to take advantage of the driving forces and to overcome the restraining forces.

It is important to produce action plans (step 4) that are based on the findings (steps 2 and 3). By involving stakeholders in the change process, it is more likely that management will win their support, thereby facilitating the planned change.

The key points of Kotter's model, explained above, are: communication, education, clear goals and rationale, compromise, consultation, training, and incentives. If these do not tempt employees to accept change, then the sixth and final approach of using threats can be used. Many managers argue that if too many compromises are made, then this can negatively affect the success of the change outcome.

Implementing and controlling change often proves to be difficult largely because of the resistance to change but also because of management attitudes and approaches to change. In addition to Lewin's force field analysis and Kotter's Six Change Approaches model, managers can use a range of other change management models such as the Iceberg model, Change Phases, Change Masters, Storey's Change model and Stakeholder analysis.

Iceberg model

Wilfried Kruger's Iceberg model of change argues that there are two levels of change but that managers often only concentrate their efforts on the top level of the iceberg:

- Top level: Cost, Quality and Time
- Bottom level: People: Attitudes, beliefs, perceptions, acceptance and behaviour of stakeholders (which can be negative or positive).

Change cannot work without the commitment of the workforce, especially in the modern business environment where teamwork is so important. People present the largest barrier to change and hence managers that ignore the bottom of the iceberg (the larger section in terms of breadth and impact) fail to implement change successfully. Kruger suggests that there are several groups of people who may hinder or enhance the change process:

- **Opponents** have a negative attitude towards change as they do not generally see any personal benefit from the change.
- **Promoters** have a positive attitude towards change. They therefore support the change as they feel that they will personally benefit from it.
- **Hidden opponents** have an overall negative attitude towards change but seem to accept change in a superficial way, perhaps to avoid conflict or getting into trouble. They do not, however, express their discontent in public.
- **Potential promoters** generally have a positive attitude towards change, but they are not yet fully convinced about the particular change in question.

Kruger suggests that these four groups of people need to be dealt with in a different manner; perhaps by using incentives or coercion for the opponents and consultation with the hidden opponents. Kruger argues that managers, whatever their stance towards people, have a permanent and challenging role in dealing with change.

Change Phases model

Professor J.P. Kotter's Change Phases model (1990) suggests that there are eight reasons why change management might fail. His reasons are because managers:

- Allow too much complexity
- Fail to win support from staff
- Do not have a clear vision
- Fail to communicate a vision to stakeholders
- Allow obstructions to the vision
- Do not focus on small continuous changes (to win support)
- Declare success too soon
- Ignore corporate culture when implementing change.

By identifying the source of the problems, Kotter's model allows managers to have a clearer idea about how to manage, in phases, any change process.

Change management should involve thoughtful planning and insightful implementation. Change must be specific, measurable, achievable, realistic, and set within a time frame (SMART). To ensure that staff are not alienated, there should be a **consultation process** as they are affected by the changes. If managers force change on staff, then problems normally arise. Kotter argues that involvement of staff breeds commitment to change.

Change masters

Rosabeth Moss Kanter argues that successful managers must be able to react quickly to changes in the external environment. She termed such people '**change masters**'. In today's business environment where the pace of change is rapid yet unpredictable, this is a growing skill that managers need to possess. Change masters will push to the limit what can be done with existing resources and come up with new ideas to improve the business.

To control any change effectively, managers need certain qualities or skills:

- A vision is needed to see how a change will benefit the organization and to provide a clear statement about the purpose to staff.
- Communications skills are required to communicate their vision to show stakeholders *why* the change is good for the organization. Notices or emails dictating a change, for example, are usually weak at conveying reasons for change.
- Trust building must be embedded to ensure that staff assist in the implementation of change.
- Tolerance will mean managing in a way that people can cope effectively with change.
- Change cannot happen through just one person; rather it is through collaboration and team effort. Hence, managers should encourage team spirit by getting staff actively involved in the change process.
- Listening and inquiry skills are also important; perhaps to listen to complaints or suggestions during the consultation period and then to act accordingly.
- Change cannot happen without the financial resources to be able to implement the change successfully. Hence budgetary and financial controls are further skills of change masters.

Kanter argues that change masters stick with their vision, even in the face of opposition, because they believe their vision will ultimately benefit the organization. Persistence and perseverance are therefore important characteristics of effective managers. The internet, for example, took many years to develop but it was through commitment and determination that it really took off.

Ultimately, it is vital that managers openly communicate with and involve their staff throughout the change process. A Bulgarian proverb "Gentle words open iron gates" charmingly illustrates this argument. It is essential that staff understand the need for change in an organization. How managers do this largely depends on their management style. If managers are adamant about implementing change, coercion may be used to force the change through. Nevertheless, managers need to be aware that people do not like change being forced upon them without any consultation. This is rather like the famous children's tale of the North Wind and the Sun (see Box 1.8a).

Box 1.8a Children's tales and change management: The North Wind and the Sun

The North Wind and the Sun argued which force was the stronger. To resolve the conflict they agreed to see which one could get a passer-by to take off his coat. The North Wind blew hard to force the jacket off the passer-by. However, the more it blew, the more the man had to hold tight onto his coat to keep warm. The Sun decided to take a different approach and used its rays of light to gently warm the man, who eventually took off his jacket to stay cool.

Storey's Change model

Research by Professor John Storey (1987), a leading writer on human resource management and the management of change, put forward four approaches to managing the change process in an organization:

1. **Total imposed package**. This approach entails delivering a package of change to employees as an executive decision by management without any process of negotiation or consultation. The management team decide on the changes they feel is necessary and then basically impose this on the staff. The advantage of this approach is that change takes place rapidly based on the vision of management. However, one limitation of this approach is the need for a compliance culture where staff are willing to be directed in such a way; otherwise, there could be considerable resistance to change from the staff.
2. **Imposed piecemeal initiative**. The piecemeal (gradual) approach is not as extreme as the total imposed package but change is still imposed on the employees; only in stages rather than all in one go. This approach has the benefit of allowing workers more time to adapt to change. Examples of such an approach include offering financial and non-financial incentives for the successful implementation of change. The approach may also involve the use of *quality circles* (see Unit 5.4) to aid the required changes.
3. **Negotiated total packages**. This approach is the opposite of method 1, as the aim is to seek a package of change via negotiations with the staff. The benefits of this approach are that employees are more likely to push for change and resistance to change is minimized. However, the approach also limits the amount of change that is likely to take place, especially as there is a natural tendency within a workforce to resist change. Hence, this approach may not be suitable if management have a clear vision of the changes they wish to implement, since any negotiations may lead to a changed vision.
4. **Negotiated piecemeal packages**. This approach sees a gradual implementation of change through a series of negotiations with the workforce. An example of this approach would be setting incentives such as productivity deals between trade union members and their employers, i.e. the unions may negotiate to receive higher remuneration packages in return for reaching higher output targets set by the firm.

Stakeholder analysis

This model is a slight modification to the concept of **stakeholder mapping** (see Unit 1.4) and can be useful when considering how to deal with change. In particular, it is used to identify which stakeholders need to be involved in the change process by looking at their *level of influence* and their *reaction to change*.

By using the stakeholder map in Figure 1.8d, managers are able to see the scale of the impact of the change on each stakeholder group. For example, stakeholders who have a high degree of influence and are committed to the change need to be communicated with in a different manner from stakeholders that have a low amount of influence and who don't really care or mind about the change (on the fence). The stakeholder analysis model highlights that appropriate communication and involvement of different stakeholder groups is a vital part of effective change management.

Whichever model of change management is used, the success of managers in the process is judged in terms of the future performance of the organization. The worked example below outlines how to tackle a typical exam question based on change management. Reference to, and application of, any of the above theories of change management would warrant high marks being awarded.

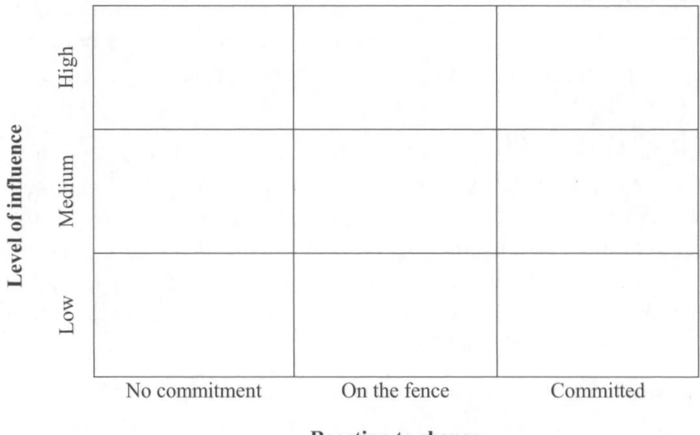

Figure 1.8d Stakeholder analysis

Exam Tip!
Worked example

Question: Recommend how a business proposing to relocate its operations overseas should manage the change process to reduce potential conflict. *[8 marks]*

Start by defining the term 'change management'. Relevant issues that managers need to consider include:

- Careful planning of the proposed change and how to communicate this vision with staff
- Explanation of the rationale for change to key stakeholders, i.e. why there is a need for change
- Communicating the key benefits of the proposed change, with supporting evidence of these arguments, in order to win staff support and to create a common vision
- Consultation with employees, managers, directors and other stakeholders
- Negotiation with key stakeholders to ensure that those most affected by the change are given a say and are treated as fairly as possible
- Handling fear of the unknown in a sensitive but realistic manner.

An organization that already has a positive attitude towards change (i.e. there is a change culture within the business) will be more receptive to the proposal and is more likely to embrace the change. Ultimately, strong leadership will instil a positive change culture and it will allow management to deal effectively with any resistance to change.

Question 1.8.4

Drinks and child obesity

The Union of European Beverages Associations announced in 2006 that its members (such as Coca-Cola and Schweppes) would limit advertising aimed at children. The initiative is aimed at tackling the rising problem of child obesity. Another driving force behind the change comes from shifting consumer attitudes towards healthier diets and lifestyles. The group pledged to make available a wider range of sugar-free and low-calorie drinks.

- **a** Explain why a 'vision' is important when introducing change. *[3 marks]*
- **b** Comment on how the changes in the case study might affect the sales and marketing practices of drinks and beverage firms such as Coca-Cola? *[4 marks]*
- **c** Examine two constraints to effective change management in the context of the case study. *[6 marks]*

CHANGE MANAGEMENT AND BUSINESS STRATEGY

Change management is a business strategy that is vital in today's fast-paced global environment. However, in the pursuit of change with the purpose of improving and remaining competitive, managers often face resistance to change from their staff. Resistance to change is a sign of discontent and/or uncertainty from the workforce. Management can use these restraining forces as a guide to find the root cause of the resistance to change. It is not until the root of the problem is established that managers can then devise strategies to handle the forces against change. Simply imposing change will result in opposition to the change process.

It is also important for managers to remember that one change often leads to other changes, i.e. change is compound. For example, the marketing mix of a business may need to change following a change in the pricing policy of a competitor.

Managing change that has been planned, such as an expansion strategy, tends to be a lot easier than managing unplanned and unexpected changes. Perhaps the most difficult change situation to deal with is a crisis. Such change is likely to force a business to handle the situation in order to retain any competitive advantage.

One final point to note is that change management cannot be studied in isolation. For example, due to the *globalization* of markets (see Unit 1.9) and the developments in *e-commerce* (see Unit 4.8), businesses may have to increasingly focus on the quality of their products and services. One way to do this is to focus on developing a *Total Quality Management* approach (see Unit 5.4) whereby quality is the responsibility of every employee at every stage of the production process. Indeed, firms with a TQM culture tend to be more receptive of change and this can help the organization to better pursue their corporate objectives. Another example of the integrated nature of business and management is that *market research* (see Unit 4.2) may be necessary to establish changes in consumer habits and tastes in order to develop appropriate global marketing strategies to deal with these changes.

In conclusion, as change is inevitable and if change is to be successful, then the change process has to be managed with care. This may ultimately mean a change in corporate culture so careful change management will be required. There is no doubt that managing change is difficult. Nevertheless, as with so many aspects of management and leadership, it is important to lead by example if change is to be managed successfully. Management must be committed to the change otherwise they are unlikely to win the support of the workforce. Despite the potential resistance, effective implementation of change can help managers improve their organization's success and future. George Bernard Shaw (1856–1950), an Irish author, put this nicely when he said, "The only man I know who behaves sensibly is my tailor; he takes my measurements anew each time he sees me. The rest go on with their old measurements and expect me to fit them." Managers need to remember that in a constantly changing business environment, organizations need to adapt in order to keep up to date and to remain competitive. After all, there cannot be progress without change.

REVIEW QUESTIONS 1.8

1. What is meant by 'change management'?
2. List four factors that cause change within a business organization.
3. List four reasons for resistance to change within an organization.
4. Distinguish between 'driving' and 'restraining' forces.
5. What are the advantages of Lewin's force field analysis in assessing the management of change?
6. What are the limitations of Lewin's force field analysis?
7. Outline the management of change theories of Kruger, Kotter, Kanter and Storey.
8. What is 'stakeholder analysis' and when might it be useful to management?

Change management is the management process of planning, forecasting, controlling and steering change within an organization. Change management considers the human and financial resources and their implications that are involved in any change process.

Change masters are skilled managers in the art of change management. They are able to deal with change by adapting and reacting quickly to different scenarios.

Driving forces are the forces (or reasons) acting for change. These usually refer to benefits to the organization, such as reduced costs or improved productivity following the implementation of change.

Force field analysis is Kurt Lewin's model of change management that deals with the forces for and against change.

Resistance to change refers to the pressures from staff against change being introduced, i.e. a reluctance to change, due to factors such as unfamiliarity or a lack of understanding of the benefits of the change.

Restraining forces are the causes of resistance to change, i.e. the forces that act against any proposal for change.

Globalization

UNIT 1.9

In business, the competition will bite you if you keep running. If you stand still, they will swallow you.

William Knudsen (1879–1948), former president of General Motors

Key topics

- Globalization: the causes and impacts
- Reasons for the growth of multinational companies
- The role and impact of multinationals in the global business environment
- Regional trading blocs

INTRODUCTION

Economists have, for a very long time, put forward arguments for free international trade. It was not until after World War II that international trade and cooperation really took off. **Globalization** is the integration of the world's economies in terms of economics, sociology and politics. For businesses, this means an attempt by firms to efficiently produce and sell the same products or services simultaneously in different countries. The outcome of globalization is that markets, cultures and tastes have converged at an accelerating pace (see Box 1.9a).

Some businesses simply export their products, largely to benefit from a larger customer base and to reap the cost savings from larger scale operations (economies of scale). For example, Heineken, the Dutch brewery, exports its beer to 170 different countries. Other companies, such as McDonald's and Pizza Hut, have 'gone global' by establishing overseas franchises. Alternatively, other companies such as Honda and Toyota have gone global by setting up manufacturing facilities and plants in overseas countries.

Box 1.9a Some indicators of globalization

- Higher value of world trade over time
- Higher levels of foreign direct investment (FDI), e.g. Japanese car manufacturers setting up production facilities in the USA and Europe
- Multinational corporations (MNC) accounting for a higher share of world Gross Domestic Product (GDP)
- Greater cultural awareness and exchange, such as the export of cultural foods
- Spreading of multiculturalism, such as Hollywood and Bollywood movies
- Higher spending on international travel and tourism
- Information and communication technology spreading throughout the world, such as increased usage of the internet.

This Unit looks at the phenomenon of globalization which has been intensified by the growing presence of multinational corporations and the power of regional trading blocs (both of which are covered later in this Unit).

GLOBALIZATION

Globalization can be defined as the growing integration and interdependence of the world's economies. It has led national economies to integrate towards a single global economy, where consumers have ever-increasingly similar habits and tastes. With globalization, economic and political decisions taken in one region of the world are likely to affect those in other parts of the world too. Box 1.9b lists the ten most globalized countries in the world.

Multinationals such as McDonald's and Coca-Cola design and market their products to a world audience. Consumers around the world easily recognize and have similar tastes for their products. In the case of McDonald's, even the production processes are the same throughout the world; burgers and fries are cooked in exactly the same way irrespective of where the McDonald's restaurant is located in the world. The Coca-Cola brand is the most recognized brand in the world. Thus, such firms are able to exploit global marketing and production economies of scale (see Unit 1.7).

Box 1.9b Top 10 most globalized countries in the world

KOF is a Swiss organization that carries out world rankings of the most-globalized countries as measured by economic, social and political indicators of globalization. The KOF Index of Globalization covers 123 countries around the world. The 2007 report of the top 10 most globalized nations shows some significant changes to the 2006 report.

Rank	2008	2007	2006
1	Belgium	Belgium	USA
2	Austria	Austria	Sweden
3	Sweden	Sweden	Canada
4	Switzerland	United Kingdom	United Kingdom
5	Denmark	Netherlands	Luxembourg
6	Netherlands	France	Austria
7	United Kingdom	Canada	France
8	Czech Republic	Switzerland	Australia
9	France	Finland	Switzerland
10	Finland	Czech Republic	Hong Kong

Source: KOF Index of Globalization http://www.globalization-index.org/

Factors contributing to the growth in globalization

- The **liberalization of international trade** (i.e. the removal of global trade barriers) has encouraged more trade in exports and imports. Trade protection methods, such as tariffs and quotas, have been reduced through the cooperation of member states of the World Trade Organization, China and Eastern European countries have opened themselves to international trade. The European Union has introduced a single currency and continues to enlarge. Subsequently, multinational companies have been more able to set up overseas trading facilities and outlets.
- **Technological progress** has reduced the cost of information interchange. The internet has revolutionized the way in which many businesses and consumers purchase products. Businesses are now able to sell their products to a world wide market if they have an *online presence* (see Unit 4.8). Theodore Levitt (1983), a contributor to the *Harvard Business Review*, wrote about advances in communications and technology leading to the globalization of markets. He claimed that advances in technology would lead to a convergence of consumer habits and tastes all across the world. Other technological developments that have encouraged globalization include the widespread applications of mobile telephones, satellite communications, global media networks such as the BBC and CNN, and video-conferencing. Technological advancements have also reduced barriers to international trade as costs of production are decreased.
- The **deregulation** of business activity has meant that the costs of transportation and distribution have fallen. For example, with the opening up of competition of previously state-owned monopolies in the transport market, businesses are now able to distribute their products worldwide at a lower cost than before. Former communist countries, such as China and the Eastern European countries, have removed trade restrictions placed on foreign businesses operating in their countries. This has encouraged the growth of multinational corporations to enjoy more of a global presence.

- The growth in **cultural awareness and recognition** has meant that consumers around the world have increasingly similar tastes. Hollywood movies, for instance, have had a huge impact on the rest of the world. Consumers are also more willing to buy foreign products and this has led to a huge increase in the market for **cultural exports** (see Unit 4.7).
- **Language** has been another factor that has stimulated the growth in globalization. English is the official business language in many parts of the world, including the second most populated country in the world, India. The *South China Morning Post* (15th Jan 2005) reported that public sector organizations and NGOs are seeking to enhance their use of English due to the forces of globalization. In much of Asia, English speakers are the ones targeted for fast-track promotion and bonuses. In South Korea, more than 60% of kindergartens now offer English courses. The use of a common language can help an organization benefit from economies of scale. For example, there is no need to produce different promotional advertisements, instruction manuals or information on packaging in so many different languages.

Question 1.9.1

McDonald's

In 2000, McDonald's (the world's largest fast food chain) reported global **sales** in excess of $20 billion for the first time in its history. Revenue was boosted by strong sales in the USA, Japan, Russia and Europe. Another contributing factor was McDonald's revamp of its **global business** by adding salads and other healthy options to its traditional menu of burgers and French fries. The company communicated this change by publicizing nutritional facts of its products.

Critics have argued that McDonald's food and drinks remain unhealthy and high in calories. Their marketing strategies aimed at children, such as their trademark Happy Meals, have been attacked due to soaring obesity levels amongst children.

a Define the terms in bold in the case study above. *[4 marks]*

b Examine two reasons for the growth in McDonald's global sales. *[6 marks]*

c Outline one possible problem created by the critics of McDonald's for the business. *[2 marks]*

d Discuss the extent to which the fast food industry is a globalized industry. *[8 marks]*

The effects of globalization on business activity

Globalization has not taken place without its critics, however. Pressure groups and the media have provided another perspective on the effects of globalization. For instance, in his book *Fast Food Nation* Eric Schlosser discusses how globalization of the fast food industry has led to increased obesity in China and Japan. The documentary movie *Super Size Me* and the film adaptation of Schlosser's book have also highlighted some of the drawbacks from the spread of American fast food throughout the world.

The forces of globalization provide both opportunities and threats for businesses:

- Globalization considerably increases the level of **competition**, such as Vodafone (UK) competing with mobile operator '3', owned by Hutchison Telecom (Hong Kong) in the mobile telephone market. The internet has also reduced costs for many industries, thereby reducing barriers to entry and opening up competition. For example, Lastminute.com has proved highly successful in many countries in taking on the more established and traditional travel agents.

- Meeting **customer expectations and needs** becomes increasingly more demanding. Businesses must now meet the ever-greater customer demands for quality, customer service, price and after-sales care. With the competition that globalization brings, businesses must meet the demands of their customers in order to have any competitive advantage.
- Businesses that are able to build a global presence are likely to enjoy the benefits of **economies of scale**. For example, a global business can take advantage of global marketing economies and risk bearing economies of scale (see Unit 1.7). Asia's richest man, Li Ka-Shing, has a reported wealth of over $22 billion and it is believed that his wealth has been accumulated through the sheer diversity of his businesses in property, food, telecommunications, consumer electronics, utilities and ports.
- Multinationals have greater **choice of location** of their production facilities. Apple, like many other global businesses, has chosen to locate in China due to the relatively low costs of labour and rent. Apple's iPod media players are 'Created in California and assembled in China'. The choice of location can therefore help to reduce the firm's costs of production.
- **Mergers, acquisitions and joint ventures** allow businesses to grow at a faster pace than if they were to grow organically (see Unit 1.7). With globalization, businesses have more choice in their expansion plans. For example, BMW's sales in 2005 soared by 37% following its joint venture with Brilliance China Automotive which gave the German company access to the lucrative Chinese market.
- Multinational corporations and e-commerce businesses in particular will benefit from the **increased customer base** that globalization allows. With China and India both embracing changes in the global business environment, there are vast opportunities for businesses that deal with the two most populated countries in the world (combined to account for around 35% of the world's population).

Despite the forces of change brought by globalization, countries still have their national identities through language, culture and other unique characteristics. Businesses are likely to need to adapt their products and services to meet the varying needs of their international clients (also see Unit 4.7).

Question 1.9.2

Bollywood brings business to the UK

The Yorkshire Tourist Board in the UK announced that the International Indian Film Academy (the Bollywood Oscars) held in the summer of 2007 generated more than £20 million ($40 million) worth of media coverage. With an estimated 500 million viewers worldwide, there were huge economic opportunities for businesses in Yorkshire. It also gave the town the chance to market its tourism and **local culture** to an international audience. Bollywood, India's version of Hollywood, has spread across the world as people get to know one another better. This has been possible as globalization and the media makes information access much faster.

a Using an example, explain what is meant by **local culture**. *[3 marks]*

b Examine the view that knowledge and awareness of local cultures are important aspects of successful global businesses. *[7 marks]*

MULTINATIONAL CORPORATIONS

A **multinational corporation (MNC)** is a business organization that operates in two or more countries. The terms MNC and **transnational corporation** are often used interchangeably, although some commentators say that a MNC has its Head Office based in the home country whereas a transnational corporation has regional head offices rather than a single international base. Examples of large MNCs include: Coca-Cola, Dell, Exxon, General Motors, HSBC, Microsoft, Nike, Nokia, Samsung and Wal-Mart, which all excel within their industries in sales, profits, assets and market value. The rise of MNCs and the ever growing importance of international trade have intensified globalization.

Why become a multinational?

Businesses may strive to become multinationals for several reasons, and these have had differing effects on the global business environment:

- Businesses can increase their sales turnover by expanding internationally to widen their **customer base**. For example, many businesses (such as HSBC, KFC, McDonald's, Starbucks, Lamborghini, Volkswagen, Wal-Mart and Cathay Pacific Airways) have expanded into China to benefit from the huge customer base. Furthermore, international brand recognition can be brought about by the global marketing strategies used by MNCs.
- By catering for a larger customer base, production levels must increase so MNCs may well benefit from economies of scale. Furthermore, by expanding overseas, there are external economies of scale to be exploited. MNCs may want to locate overseas to benefit from the host country's infrastructure, such as their road, telecommunication and port networks. The host country may also offer better quantity and quality of land in terms of the amount of space and/or the cost of land. There may also be financial incentives from the host country's government which helps to reduce costs of production whilst allowing the business to expand.
- By producing within a particular country, a firm can usually avoid any **protectionist policies**, such as tariffs, quotas or unfair trade practices (see Box 1.9c) that a country may impose. This is why many Japanese motor vehicle manufacturers, including Toyota, Nissan and Honda, have set up factories in the European Union and North America.
- In addition, many firms have expanded overseas in order to benefit from **cheaper production costs**, especially inexpensive labour. For example, the relatively high cost of labour in Germany, partly due to the imposition of minimum wage legislation, has meant that businesses such as Adidas and BMW have production facilities in overseas regions with cheap labour.
- Multinational corporations are also able to **spread risks**. Unfavourable market situations in one country or region suffering from a recession, for example, may not damage the overall business if it can spread risks internationally. Natural disasters (such as tsunamis), terrorist acts (such as the September 11 attacks) and diseases (such as bird flu and mad cow disease) have affected different areas of the world. Over-specialization in any one of these regions could have led to a serious dent in profits for such businesses.
- The **globalization of markets** has meant the world is a smaller place (in terms of time, distance and conditions of international trade). Improved information and communications technology (ICT) and high-speed travel mean that multinationals can trade even more efficiently. Multinationals have had a huge impact on converging lifestyles and tastes throughout the world economy – American fast food restaurants, Brazilian coffee, German sports cars and Japanese electronic gadgets to name but a few. Businesses that have an international approach, such as Dell computers and eBay, are therefore able to reap the benefits of globalization. A business that is able to expand overseas before its rivals may also give the business a *first-mover advantage* as it establishes itself and builds up a loyal customer base.

Box 1.9c Artificial trade barriers

Tariffs are a tax on imported products. This adds to the price of foreign products, thereby making them less price competitive. MNCs can overcome this problem by establishing production facilities in the tariff-imposing nation.

Quotas are quantity limits on the sale of foreign imports. This results in a lower supply of imported products and hence forces up their prices. Again, this reduces the price competitiveness of foreign products.

Unfair trade practices are acts that unfairly, although not illegally, discriminate against foreign firms since they do not apply to domestic firms. Examples include strict administrative procedures and strict safety standards, which have the effects of raising the cost and limiting the availability of imports.

Question 1.9.3

Carlsberg Group

In 2006, Carlsberg reported an 8% increase in its annual profits, driven by strong growth in sales in Russian and Eastern European countries. The Danish beer firm acknowledged that it needs to rely on new markets, such as Eastern Europe and Asia, for sales and profits growth. Carlsberg's long-established market presence in Western Europe gives it a competitive advantage, but in a stagnant market.

a Identify the evidence that suggests Carlsberg is a multinational business. *[2 marks]*

b Explain two reasons for Carlsberg choosing to expand in overseas markets. *[4 marks]*

c Outline the factors that may have led to the globalization of the beer market. *[4 marks]*

d Examine the possible threats to Carlsberg in operating in overseas markets. *[6 marks]*

Potential problems of expansion overseas

Despite the benefits of expanding overseas, there are certain problems that MNCs may encounter:

- A lack of local knowledge and experience may create problems for firms operating in new markets (see Unit 4.7). For example, marketing may be problematic due to a lack of brand recognition in overseas markets.
- Storage, transportation and distribution costs will increase and this may create problems for firms that are unable to control their costs.
- External factors (those beyond the control of a business) have a greater weighting in decision-making. These may create problems or limitations for the MNC, such as legal restrictions, language barriers and cultural differences.
- Political and economic conditions in foreign countries may also limit the extent to which MNCs can prosper in overseas markets. For example, aerospace giant Rolls-Royce pulled out of Sudan in 2007 due to concerns over the country's violence and conflict surrounding humanitarian issues.
- Infrastructure, such as road and communications networks, may be less developed in overseas markets, thereby limiting the efficiency of the operations of a multinational corporation.

MULTINATIONALS AND THEIR EFFECT ON HOST COUNTRIES

A **host country** is any nation that allows a multinational corporation (MNC) to set up in its country. In addition to the effects MNCs have on the global business environment, they have impacts on host countries, some of which are beneficial whilst some are detrimental.

One benefit of MNCs to the host country is their ability to **create jobs**. Volkswagen's manufacturing plant in Kaluga, Russia created over 3,500 jobs with an initial investment of US$400 million. This not only reduces the burden of the host country's government, but can also increase the national income of these countries, thereby improving their standard of living. Although some MNCs have been criticized for paying 'low' wages to staff in poorer countries, MNCs tend to offer better pay than local firms in these countries. Nike's plant in Indonesia, for example, means that their factory workers are paid relatively well. The multinational company also benefits Indonesia's *balance of payments* (an annual record of a country's trade with other nations) through the export earnings of Nike's products that are manufactured in Indonesia.

Multinationals that operate in less affluent countries can also help to boost their *Gross Domestic Product* (the value of a country's annual output) by creating consumption expenditure (since more people are in paid employment) and by boosting export earnings for the host country. Coca-Cola, for example, recently opened a bottling plant in Afghanistan. Hungary's largest exporter is the German car manufacturer Audi which has its Audi TT sports car produced in western Hungary.

Multinationals have also introduced new skills and technology in production processes. This concept is known as **technology transfer**. Japanese firms, for example, have introduced the concepts of *quality circles* and *kaizen* (see Unit 5.4) to western economies. With new ideas in management thinking and technology transfer, the efficiency of production in the host country is raised.

Multinationals can also create more **competition** in the host country. Ford, Hyundai, BMW, Renault and Volkswagen all produce motor vehicles in Russia. A growing number of other foreign car makers are also lining up to establish manufacturing plants in Russia. This should lead to more efficiency with firms competing on price and non-price factors to attract customers. It can be argued that without the threat from MNCs, domestic and existing foreign businesses do not necessarily have the incentive to be innovative or to respond to market forces.

On the other hand, multinationals have often been criticized for their treatment of those in poorer nations. Anti-globalization groups and environmentalists are concerned about the **social responsibility** of MNCs in their attempt to expand and exploit the planet's scarce resources. Furthermore, due to the market power of large MNCs, there are some concerns about the ability of host nation governments to control their actions. Wal-Mart, for example, has sales revenues in excess of the Gross Domestic Product (GDP) of Indonesia, the fourth most populated country on the planet. This is not to say that all MNCs act in a socially undesirable manner. There are many opportunities to be exploited and MNCs can provide facilities that national governments may not be able to. For example, the Ronald McDonald House is a highly successful charity set up by McDonald's to provide housing for underprivileged children in several different countries.

Whilst MNCs can create employment, they are also capable of causing **unemployment** in the host country. Multinationals often pose a threat to domestic businesses. Competition can be good if it causes local firms to improve their efficiency, but it can also be a setback if it means that domestic businesses are unable to compete and end up making people redundant or even having to close down their business. Hollywood movies, for example, are a large threat to the Asian movie industries. To safeguard domestic market share, governments often step in to protect domestic industries and jobs from foreign competition. This is why countries like China and India limit the number of Hollywood movies that are released each month in their respective countries.

Due to the fierce competition that may be present, domestic businesses may also be forced into reducing prices to remain competitive. Capital-intensive industries, such as car manufacturing, pose a further threat as domestic firms may need to invest more money to maintain market share. However, this may not be an affordable option for many businesses and they therefore become prone to **takeover bids** or collapse outright.

Question 1.9.4

Motorola

Motorola unveiled its plan to invest a further $60 million in Singapore between 2006 and 2008, and hire 200 local workers. Motorola already has four factories in Asia (Singapore, Malaysia and two in China). The American company employs more than 20,000 people in Asia. Both Motorola and its larger rival Nokia are expanding in the region since restrictions on telecommunications have been relaxed. The huge rise in average incomes has also stimulated demand for mobile phones.

a Explain how globalization might affect the location of businesses such as Motorola. *[4 marks]*

b Examine the benefits to Motorola in having production facilities overseas. *[6 marks]*

REGIONAL TRADING BLOCS

This section looks at some of the major trading blocs in the world and their major implications for businesses. Regional trading blocs (RTB) are also known as **regional economic blocs**.

Members of an RTB strive to eliminate trade barriers on the movement of goods, services, labour and capital. It is argued that member countries can enjoy mutual benefits from being engaged in free international trade. There are differing levels of 'free' trade within trading blocs:

- **Closer Economic Partnership Agreement (CEPA)** is a free trade agreement, under World Trade Organization (WTO) (see Box 1.9d) rules, between two or more countries. CEPA gives preferential access to markets for businesses within the member countries.
- **Free Trade Area (FTA)**, such as the North American Free Trade Agreement, where member states agree to trade freely with each another, but have separate trade barriers with non-member countries.
- **Common Market** (also known a **Customs Union**) refers to a RTB where there is free trade *and* free movement of labour and capital between member countries. However, all commodities imported from outside the union have the *same* trade restrictions placed upon them (known as a **common external tariff**). In addition, there are common safety standards and other regulations imposed on non-member countries.

A regional trading bloc will impose **physical barriers** to international trade. The imposition of **tariffs** increases the price of exports, thereby reducing the competitiveness of the product. Marketers are then faced with the problem of selling their higher priced products in overseas markets. **Quotas** are limits on the *volume* or *value* of foreign goods and services. The limited supply has two effects: first, it reduces the amount available for sale in foreign markets and second it tends to raise prices due to the limited supply. Again, the imposition of quotas by a RTB means that marketers have a problem when competing in foreign markets. The main regional trading blocs around the world are examined in the following pages.

Box 1.9d The World Trade Organization (WTO)

The WTO is an international organization that consists of 150 member countries which agree to work on reducing and eliminating barriers to international trade. As advocates of free and fair trade, member states resolve trade disputes through the WTO. It was set up in 1995 in Geneva, Switzerland to replace its predecessor, the General Agreement on Tariffs and Trade (GATT).

Source: www.wto.int

The European Union (EU)

This is probably the best known regional trading bloc (see Box 1.9e). The EU is an example of a Customs Union, where member states charge a *common external tariff* to non-member countries. For example, all EU states impose a 40% tariff on imported apples (mainly to protect EU apple producers).

The EU is a major market for the exports of a member nation to other member countries. One major advantage for businesses operating in the EU is the potential to exploit economies of scale. Businesses in the UK, for example, operate in a country where there are approximately 60 million people compared to the much larger community of over 500 million people in the EU. Membership of the trading bloc increases the customer base for businesses operating throughout Europe. Despite this, changes in economic activity and/or economic policy in member countries will affect the economic performance of those member states. For example, changes in interest rates set by the European Central Bank will affect most businesses throughout the EU, but especially those that use the single currency (the euro).

Box 1.9e The 27 member countries of the EU

- Belgium, (West) Germany, France, Italy, Luxembourg and the Netherlands were the original members when they signed the Treaty of Rome in 1957.
- In 1973, the UK, Ireland and Denmark joined.
- In 1981, Greece joined.
- Spain and Portugal joined in 1986. The imposition of a common external tariff was finally completed in 1986.
- In 1995 Finland, Austria and Sweden joined the Union.
- Ten other member states joined on 1st May 2004: Cyprus, Czech Republic, Estonia, Hungary, Latvia, Lithuania, Malta, Poland, Slovakia and Slovenia.
- Bulgaria and Romania joined in January 2007.

The European Free Trade Association (EFTA)

The EFTA was established in May 1960. Its members are Iceland, Norway, Switzerland, and Liechtenstein (from 1991). There are no import restrictions between these members. In 1972, the European Community (the predecessor of the European Union) signed agreements with EFTA members, setting up a free-trade area of over 300 million consumers. A further treaty signed in October 1991 provided for the creation of a European Economic Area (EEA) in 1994, allowing EFTA members freer trade with the EU states. This allowed EFTA members to benefit from freer trade with the EU members for those countries that were not eligible or did not want to join the European Union. Of the original EFTA members, Britain and Denmark left in 1972 to join the European Community (now the European Union), as did Portugal in 1985. In 1995, Austria, Finland, and Sweden also left to join the EU.

The North American Free Trade Agreement (NAFTA)

The origins of NAFTA lay in a mutual free trade agreement between the USA and Canada, effective from 1989. NAFTA was set up in August 1992 between the USA, Canada, and Mexico, with the aim to promote trade and investment between the members. It became effective from January 1994. NAFTA is the first trade deal of its kind to link two highly industrialized countries to a developing one. It consists of a free market of over 430 million people, with a total GDP in excess of $13 trillion (over 30% of the world's GDP). Tariffs were to be progressively eliminated (over a 10–15 year period) and investment into Mexico by Canada and the USA progressively increased. NAFTA members have more multinationals and a higher GDP per capita than any other trading bloc.

The Association of South East Asian Nations (ASEAN)

The ASEAN was established on 8th August 1967 in Bangkok, Thailand. With a population of well over 550 million people, ASEAN makes up one of the largest regional trading blocs in the world (see Box 1.9f). ASEAN has also established close links with the European Union. For example, the EU is ASEAN's second largest export market (exceeding €62 billion) and the third largest trading partner after the United States and Japan. Likewise, annual EU exports to ASEAN exceed €30 billion. Nevertheless, there are large economic and social disparities between the ASEAN countries, such as issues with regards to democracy and human rights. This makes conducting business in these countries less predictable.

Box 1.9f ASEAN member states

- The five original member nations were: Indonesia (home to the ASEAN Headquarters), Malaysia, Philippines, Singapore, and Thailand.
- In Jan 1984, Brunei was admitted as the sixth member.
- Vietnam also joined in July 1995.
- Lao People's Democratic Republic (Laos) and Myanmar (Burma) became members in July 1997.
- Finally, Cambodia joined in April 1999.

Closer Economic Partnership Agreement (CEPA)

A Closer Economic Partnership Arrangement (CEPA) is an economic agreement between two countries. In essence, CEPA is a WTO-compliant free trade agreement. For instance, the governments of Hong Kong and China signed a CEPA deal which came into full effect on 1 January 2004. Strategically, this CEPA was a new step in cross-border trade and investment between the two countries and reinforced Hong Kong's role as a bridge between China and the rest of the world. The purpose of signing the CEPA is to strengthen their trade and investment cooperation. This can be achieved by:

- Steadily reducing or eliminating tariffs and non-tariff barriers on the trade in all goods and services between the two nations
- Promoting trade and investment facilitation.

Other CEPA deals include Mexico's trade agreements with the EU and New Zealand. These agreements will enable Mexico's businesses to compete on equal terms with their rivals in these countries. Furthermore, New Zealand's CEPA with Hong Kong could mean that its companies would use Hong Kong as a springboard into mainland China and other markets in the Pacific Rim.

Whenever countries form or join a regional trading bloc, there are likely to be both winners and losers. **Trade creation** takes place when a country switches from buying commodities from a high cost country to buying them from a lower cost country, following the formation of a RTB.

This should happen within a free trade area. For example, UK customers can buy French cars without tariffs, rather than buying tariff-imposed Japanese cars. **Trade diversion** results in losers in a trading bloc when a country switches from buying commodities from a low-cost country to buying them from a higher cost country. For example, UK businesses used to purchase much of their foodstuff from cheaper suppliers in Australia and New Zealand, but due to EU obligations they now buy most of this from higher-priced European trading partners.

Nevertheless, RTBs and globalization aim to improve the overall efficiency of world economies. As China and HK increase their economic cooperation, for example, China uses its strong manufacturing sector to pull in foreign direct investment (China attracted a record $60.6 billion in actual FDI in 2006), whilst HK exploits its expertise in service industries to support China's manufacturing growth.

GLOBALIZATION AND BUSINESS STRATEGY

The phenomenon of globalization has meant that ever-increasing numbers of managers are thinking about their global strategy rather than focusing on national markets. Globalization brings with it fantastic opportunities for businesses, such as: more customers, larger choice of suppliers, greater economies of scale and additional choice in the location of production facilities. Japanese management guru, Kenichi Ohmae put forward the claim that businesses that do not have a global presence in the three largest trading blocs (in Europe, the United States and the Pacific Rim) are at a competitive disadvantage.

There is no doubt that regional trading blocs have accelerated the pace of globalization. Businesses operating in a regional trading bloc have great opportunities to be exploited. There is scope for expansion with relatively lower costs. For example, joint ventures between EU and Chinese companies have become quite common, such as Peugeot Citroen of France and Dongfeng (China's third largest car manufacturer). Strategically, businesses can benefit from locating in a RTB which brings about a wider customer base, without the business having to face international trade barriers such as quotas, tariffs and administrative obstructions. Overall, trading blocs promote freer international trade and specialization, which ultimately allows businesses to become better off. Even so, businesses operating in trading blocs may still need to deal with some degree of protectionist measures and other external influences such as fluctuating exchange rates.

Finally, it is important to remember that a 'global' strategy may need to be tweaked to cater for the local (overseas) market. Roland Robertson called this strategy **glocalization**. Robertson recognized that cultures often clash and that a place may be better understood by recognizing both the local culture and the global forces of change. HSBC's slogan "The world's local bank" and Sony's slogan "Global localization" highlight both their approach and commitment to glocalization. These businesses recognize that a global strategy alone may not work and that local knowledge can enhance the strategy of a global business. Pizza Hut is another example; they produce identical pizzas throughout the world but also have pizzas which cater for the tastes of the locals. From a marketing perspective, businesses have to take into account different cultures and the ethical and moral viewpoints of customers in overseas markets. After all, different cultures do exist and it is therefore not always possible to communicate to all cultures in an identical way.

REVIEW QUESTIONS 1.9

1 What is meant by 'globalization'?

2 State five indicators of globalization.

3 Outline four factors that have led to globalization in the world economy.

4 Explain how some businesses benefit from globalization, whilst others are constrained by it.

5 What is a 'multinational corporation'?

6 What are the reasons for a business wanting to become a multinational?

7 What are the advantages and limitations to a host country of multinationals?

8 What is a 'regional trading bloc'?

9 How might a business benefit from being located in a regional trading bloc?

10 Distinguish between 'trade diversion' and 'trade creation'.

Common market refers to a customs union, such as the European Union, that allows the free movement of factors of production (land, labour, capital and enterprise) between member countries.

Customs union refers to a group of member countries that trade freely with each other but impose a *common external tariff* (CET) on imports from non-member states. This means that all members must enforce the same (common) trade barriers to non-member countries.

Free trade occurs when countries trade without any international *trade barriers* such as tariffs, quotas and bureaucratic procedures.

Globalization is the integration of economic, social, technical and cultural issues of the world's economies. This has taken place largely due to the expansion of multinational corporations and governments advocating freer international trade.

Multinational corporations (MNC) are companies that operate production or service facilities outside their home country.

Regional trading bloc refers to a group of countries that agree to freer international trade with each other, through the removal of trade barriers. Examples of trading blocs include the European Union (EU) and the North American Free Trade Agreement (NAFTA).

Protectionist measures are the policies used by a government to guard the interest of its domestic industries from foreign competition. Examples of protectionist policies include the use of import taxes and imposing higher safety standards on foreign products.

HUMAN RESOURCES

UNIT 2

UNIT

Human Resource Planning

UNIT 2.1

A thousand workers, a thousand plans.

Chinese proverb

Key topics

- Supply of human resources and demographic changes
- Domestic and international labour mobility
- Workforce planning
- Recruitment, appraisal, training and dismissal
- Changes in work patterns and practices: homeworking, teleworking and portfolio work

Higher Level extension

- Employment rights and legislation
- Handy's shamrock organization

Note: Higher Level students will need to be able to analyse reasons for changes in work patterns and practices and the consequences for employers and employees. (© IBO 2007)

INTRODUCTION

Labour is one of the four factors of production. Many theorists argue that people are a firm's most valuable resource. Employing the right people will help a business to achieve its aims and objectives. To do this, a firm needs to use **human resource planning**, sometimes referred to as **workforce planning**. This is the management process of anticipating an organization's current and future staffing needs. It includes the number of employees required and the type of worker sought, such as graduates or ICT-literate workers. Anticipating the human resource needs of a firm can be carried out by looking at:

- Historical data and trends. Data on trends, such as the rate of change in the size of the workforce over the past few years or the shift to part-time and flexible working hours, can assist management in planning.
- Sales and income levels. Employers will require more workers if the level of customer demand is increasing. Higher levels of income and spending in the economy will lead to more jobs being created.
- Labour turnover rates. This measures the number of employees who leave a firm as a percentage of its workforce, per year. The higher the staff turnover rate, the more workers a firm will need to recruit.
- Demographic changes. Government data regarding changes in the demographics of the workforce, such as the changes in the number of female workers in the economy or the number of graduates, can help managers to forecast human resource needs.
- Technological changes. Advances in technology, such as e-commerce, can bring both opportunities and threats. There are employment opportunities for people to work from home, for example. However, firms that are capital intensive may not require as many workers in the future.

Despite attempts at effective workforce planning, there are external influences that will affect the accuracy of the forecasts. This is because businesses are constantly exposed to the forces of change (see Unit 1.8), such as an economic recession which will reduce the demand for human resources. Changes in employment patterns are also considered later in this Unit.

Exam Tip!

The term 'labour force' or 'workforce' can mean one of two things, so it is important to put the term in the correct context. 'Workforce' can refer to the nation's labour force, i.e. all those people who are available for work (the employed, the self-employed and the unemployed). The same term can also refer to all people employed in a particular firm, i.e. the workforce within a business.

Human resource management (HRM) refers to the management function of using and developing people within a business in order to meet the objectives of the organization. This will entail interrelated roles, which are covered later in this Unit, such as:

- Workforce planning (also known as human resource planning)
- Recruitment, selection and induction of new employees
- Training and development of staff
- Performance management and performance appraisals
- Promotion and relocation of staff
- Reviewing remuneration packages
- Disciplinary and grievance procedures
- Looking after the welfare of employees.

People are important to an organization as they **add value** to its output. This can be achieved by increasing productivity (output per worker), improving quality, coming up with new ideas and providing better customer service to enhance the overall purchasing experience of customers.

SUPPLY OF HUMAN RESOURCES AND DEMOGRAPHIC CHANGES

The supply of human resources within a country is affected by demographic changes of the labour force. Demography is the statistical study of population characteristics. Demographic changes can be caused by adjustments in various factors, as outlined below. Businesses will need to understand these changes in demographics so that they can respond appropriately.

- The **net birth rate**. This is calculated as the difference between the number of births and the number of deaths per period of time. Countries with a high net birth rate will, in the long term, have a larger supply of human resources.
- The **net migration rate**. This measures the difference between the number of people entering a country (immigrants) and the number of people leaving a country (emigrants). If the net migration figure is positive, then the supply of human resources will increase.
- The **retirement age**. This is the legal age when people can stop work and claim money from their pension. If the retirement age is raised, then this will automatically increase the number of people in the labour force, i.e. those of legal working age. In many countries, the retirement age is 65 for men and 60 for women. Many western economies, faced with increasing numbers of elderly people, have considered increasing the retirement age. In other countries, such as Hong Kong, there is no statutory retirement age and this serves to increase the supply of human resources.
- The **flexibility of the workforce**. Businesses or countries that have multiskilled people tend to have more flexible workers. Businesses that employ a large proportion of part-time workers, such as fast-food restaurants and supermarkets, are also able to take advantage of workforce flexibility as the supply of labour can be quickly changed according to the needs of the organization. This is a reason for the growth in the number of teleworkers (covered later in this Unit).
- The level of **unemployment** in the economy. A high rate of unemployment means a high potential supply of labour in the economy. This will increase the choice for a business seeking to employ workers. Note that unemployment is an economic factor, rather than a demographic change, but it has a direct influence on the supply of human resources.
- **Women** returning to work. A more positive attitude towards female workers in terms of employment practices, will boost the supply of human resources. There has also been an increase in the number of people taking up **part-time jobs**, especially women. This gives businesses and staff greater flexibility in determining working hours.
- The **mobility of labour**. This refers to the extent to which labour can move to different locations (known as *geographical mobility*) and their flexibility in changing to different jobs (known as *occupational mobility*). The more mobile that workers are (both geographically and occupationally) the higher the supply of labour tends to be. Box 2.1a outlines the factors that can affect the level of labour mobility.

Box 2.1a Labour mobility

Labour can be *geographically mobile*, especially within a country, but there are some limitations:

- Family and friends – Friend and family ties tend to be the key constraint for most people's geographical mobility.
- Relocation costs – Moving expenses include selling or remortgaging property and consideration of different house prices.
- Language and cultural differences – These will tend to limit international mobility.
- Fear of the unknown – People may resist change since they prefer 'home comforts' (familiarity).

The limitations on *occupational mobility* include:

- The acquired attributes of a worker – The higher the level of education, qualifications, skills, experience and training possessed, the greater the occupational mobility tends to be.
- Age – Younger people tend to be more occupationally mobile as they tend to change careers. More mature workers may feel that they are 'too old' to retrain or may have heavier financial commitments so are less willing to take risks in changing careers.
- Specialization – Whilst being multiskilled and multitalented can increase occupational mobility, some workers are immobile because they are over-specialized in their area of expertise. Hence, these people will find it difficult to seek employment opportunities in other industries.
- Discrimination – If employers are biased against people's age, gender, religion or race then this will hinder the occupational mobility of workers.

In addition, the supply of human resources to a particular business will also depend on:

- The **internal workforce**. This refers to employees who already work for the organization. If the internal workforce are highly flexible and can adapt to change, then it may not be so necessary to hire workers externally. Thus the skills, expertise and experience of the existing workforce also form part of the supply of human resources to a business, both now and in the future.
- The **competition**. Existing and potential workers will consider the overall package of financial and non-financial factors offered by a business in relation to those provided by rival employers. A less favourable package being offered to employees may mean less supply of human resources to the firm.
- The **cost of living** in a particular area. Although more people tend to live in cities, the higher cost of housing and other expenses may deter others from locating in these areas, thereby reducing the potential supply of labour to a business.
- The **cost and availability of transportation**. Businesses located in areas with good transportation systems will tend to attract a larger supply of workers. Those living or working in remote areas may need to rely on private transport which could be costly, both in terms of finance and time. This could therefore reduce the potential supply of human resources to businesses located in rural areas.
- The rate of **unemployment** in the local area. The higher the rate of regional unemployment, the higher the available supply of human resources will be. This will allow a business to hire workers at a relatively low wage rate.

At times, there may be surplus human resources. During off-peak seasons, for example, many temporary or part-time workers are not required. This increases the available labour supply. If there is an excess supply of workers, then businesses have two choices – to make some of the workers *redundant* (their services are no longer required so their job disappears) or to *redeploy* (relocate) workers to other departments or parts of the organization that may be in need of extra staffing.

One distinct demographic change in modern societies is the increasing longevity of the population which has led to an **ageing population**. An ageing population occurs when the average age of the population increases. The effects of this include:

- *Increased dependent population.* The dependent population consists of those who are below the national working age (such as those in compulsory education), those out of work and people above the retirement age. They are supported by the working population who are taxpayers. With an ageing population, less people will be working in proportion to those who have retired, thereby adding to the pressure placed on taxpayers to contribute towards government expenditure.
- *Reduced labour mobility.* Young people tend to be more geographically mobile. They have fewer reservations about moving to different places, including overseas locations. They are also more likely to switch between different occupations. Labour immobility reduces the flexibility of a country's workforce, thereby making it less internationally competitive.
- *Changes in consumption patterns.* Different age groups have different spending patterns. Children, for example, may spend much of their money (or that of their parents!) on toys and schooling. Elderly people are likely to spend a larger proportion of their money on holidays and products related to health care. Hence, an ageing population can create opportunities for firms to cater for more mature age groups.
- *Change in employment patterns.* With more and more people going to university, the average age of people entering the workforce has also risen. Coupled with an ageing population, this means that firms are more likely to retain staff beyond their retirement age due to labour supply shortages. Some firms may also consider international relocation decisions (causing unemployment if the business moves overseas) if domestic labour supply is insufficient or not suitable.

Question 2.1.1

300 million Americans

In October 2006, the population of the USA reached a new milestone figure of 300 million, making it the third most populous nation on the globe. The last milestone of 200 million people was recorded in November 1967. The USA is the only industrialized country with significant population growth – a net increase of one person every 11 seconds. However, many people question America's ability to sustain its population growth, given that it is the largest consumer of the planet's scarce resources. Concerns mount as forecasts show that the population will reach 400 million by 2050.

- Outline two constraints and two opportunities from a business perspective that are provided by the demographic changes in the USA. *[4 marks]*

WORKFORCE PLANNING

Workforce planning, also known as **human resource planning**, is the process of anticipating the current and future demand for workers in an organization. This will require businesses to be prepared for supply changes in the labour market.

Workforce planning can be short term or long term. Short-term planning deals with the existing and upcoming demands of an organization, such as employing workers to cover for staff who are about to retire, go on maternity leave or depart to work for another firm. Long-term planning looks at the human resource needs of the business in the future. For example, Disney recruited and trained employees up to two years before the Hong Kong Disneyland and Shanghai Disneyland theme parks were opened.

Planning the human resource needs of an organization requires consideration of the firm's level of demand for labour. The greater the demand for labour, the higher the number of vacancies (unfilled positions or jobs) tends to be. The level of demand will depend on several factors, such as:

- **Historical data** (time series data) of changes in staffing allows a business to identify trends. For example, if workers stay at a firm for an average of 5 years, this trend might be expected to continue. Hence, time series data can help managers to plan changes to a firm's workforce. *Labour turnover* rates will inform a business of the number of people (as a proportion of the workforce) that leave the firm each year. If trends can be identified, this allows a business to better plan its recruitment needs as it can anticipate the likely number of new recruits that are required. However, past data is not always indicative of what will actually happen in the future.
- **Flexibility and workload** of employees will provide information on whether to either raise or reduce the demand for human resources. A highly flexible workforce may be able to cope if there is a sudden change to staffing. In a firm where people are over-specialized and where workload is soaring, it may be necessary to employ more workers. The skills and expertise of existing workers may mean that they can be reassigned to different jobs, as and when necessary, thereby reducing the need to recruit new staff. A restructuring of human resources, such as management opting for a smaller hierarchical structure (see Unit 2.2), will also affect the demand for labour.
- **Capital intensity** measures the amount of capital usage in comparison to other factors of production. An automated business, such as computer manufacturing, may be able to raise productivity without the need to hire more workers. A change to automation will result in a business requiring less labour. By contrast, low capital intensity (or high labour intensity) results in a need to hire more workers if output is to be raised. For example, if waiting lists for a national health service are to be reduced, it is likely to require recruiting more doctors and nurses.
- **Work study** is a scientific management tool devised by F.W. Taylor aimed at measuring the best way to complete certain processes. Work study, also known as **time and motion study**, will look at the best number of people needed to complete a task efficiently rather than to overestimate or underestimate the actual number of workers needed in the future.
- **Derived demand** for labour means that the level of demand for labour, like all other resources, depends on the demand for the product that labour is required to produce. So, for example, there is no need for a school to hire German language teachers if students do not opt for this subject. Likewise, if the demand for personal computers or mobile phones increases, then the demand for people who work in manufacturing these products will also increase. Those working in related services, such as maintenance and sales, will also see an increase in their demand from employers.

The demand for labour may also decline due to **natural wastage**. This occurs when a person leaves a job (rather than being dismissed) but their position is no longer available, i.e. the job is not replaced. This often happens when firms undergo restructuring. Natural wastage can happen when people either resign from their jobs (perhaps to raise young children or simply due to better opportunities with another employer) or when people retire from work. Dismissals and redundancies do not count as natural wastage.

Workforce planning uses up time and money, but it can help to save time and money in the long term. For example, a recent report in the *South China Morning Post* revealed that poor recruitment practices in Hong Kong cost businesses HK$39 billion (over $5 billion) per year, which is equivalent to 3% of Hong Kong's Gross Domestic Product (value of a country's annual output). The same report showed that managers in Hong Kong spent a fifth of their time correcting the mistakes made by their staff.

Before a business recruits new workers, managers usually carry out a **job analysis**. This involves scrutinizing the different components of a job, such as the routine tasks and responsibilities of the post holder, in order to determine what the job entails. The study may also want to verify:

- Skills and training required to do the job
- Qualifications and personal qualities needed to carry out the job
- Rewards needed to recruit and retain the post holder.

The job analysis will help to create two important documents needed for the recruitment and selection of staff. These documents, the *job description* and the *person specification*, are explained in the next section.

Question 2.1.2

Trump International Golf Links

When American tycoon Donald Trump announced a £1 billion ($2 billion) golf development at Balmedie, near Aberdeen, Scotland, the local community were understandably excited about the prospects of the 6,000 jobs that would be created. Trump's plans included two championship golf courses, a five-star hotel and hundreds of holiday homes. Trump, who has popularized the phrase 'You're fired!' on reality television programme *The Apprentice*, said that **labour turnover** is not a problem at the Trump Organization.

a Explain two reasons why a business may need to hire new workers. *[4 marks]*

b Define the meaning of **labour turnover**. *[2 marks]*

c Comment on the importance of understanding labour turnover in business organizations. *[4 marks]*

Some organizations will tend to have higher rates of staff turnover than others. Firms that hire many part-time temporary staff, such as McDonald's and Burger King, are likely to accept higher rates of labour turnover, mainly due to the nature of the job (such as the relatively low wages paid to unskilled workers). The main reasons why people leave their jobs can be summed up by author M.J. Yate who used the acronym **CLAMPS** to describe the six acceptable reasons for why people leave their jobs: Challenge, Location, Advancement, Money, Pride (or Prestige) and (Job) Security.

Firms with high staff retention tend to offer training for both personal and professional development. This helps to boost staff morale as they view their employers valuing the contributions and development of its people. Staff with career development needs are also catered for through being able to attend professional training and development courses.

RECRUITMENT AND SELECTION

The recruitment and selection of employees is vital to the running of any business. Labour is one of the four factors of production (see Unit 1.1) necessary for the provision of any good or service. Hiring the right people helps to ensure that the businesses can function effectively. Since the recruitment and selection process for a business is likely to be quite time consuming and rather expensive, it is crucial that managers ensure the procedures are as effective as possible.

The recruitment and selection process starts when a vacancy becomes available within the organization. The position may become available perhaps due to expansion of the business or simply to replace staff who have decided to leave the organization. People may leave a job for all sorts of reasons, such as wishing to spend more time with their children to being fired for misconduct. Box 2.1b shows the main steps in the recruitment process for a typical business.

Box 2.1b Summary of the recruitment process

1. Perform a job analysis to determine the firm's need to hire new employees.
2. Write a job description and person specification.
3. Advertise the vacant post.
4. Screen applications and short-list suitable candidates.
5. Interview the short-listed candidates.
6. Test the aptitude of the candidate (this step does not apply to all jobs).
7. Check the candidate's references.
8. Offer the job to best candidate.
9. Sign the contract of employment.
10. Carry out induction of the new recruit.

Once the initial job analysis has been performed, the human resources manager will produce a **job advertisement** to get as many suitable people as possible to apply for the vacant post. There are usually two documents that are produced before writing a job advertisement: the job description and the person specification. Both these documents are important in objectively assessing the suitability of applicants.

A **job description** is a document that outlines the details of a particular job. It will include the job title, the roles and duties to be undertaken by the post holder and their responsibilities. A good job description will provide information about the job in relation to other jobs within the organization. Good job descriptions also have an element of flexibility in order to exploit the skills of workers; a rigid job description will limit the potential of workers who will not be able to try anything new. This is especially important because businesses constantly experience organizational change (see Unit 1.8). A typical statement in a job description that allows flexibility is 'and any other reasonable job assigned by the employer'. This document refers specifically to what the job entails rather than the type of person required for the job.

A **person specification** is a business document that gives the profile of the ideal candidate. Details will include the type and level of qualifications, skills and experience sought by the employer. It will also list the personal attributes that the successful applicant should possess, such as the ability to lead a team or to think in a logical and critical manner. Box 2.1c shows a list of common attributes sought by employers. For some jobs, such as fashion models or sports personalities, the person specification may even state physical attributes of the ideal candidate.

Box 2.1c Employment skills sought by employers

- Analytical and evaluative
- Communication
- Decision-making
- Information technology
- Information seeking
- Interpersonal
- Numeracy
- Planning
- Problem solving
- Time management

Both the job description and person specification are also used as a basis for gauging training needs and for conducting job appraisals.

Once the job description and person specification have been finalized, it is time to advertise the job. A job advertisement will also usually include other important information such as the hours of work, the rate of pay and fringe benefits. It is also important to state a contact name and address for the business and to set a deadline date for receiving applications. It is usual to advertise the job both internally (within the organization) and externally. A good job advertisement will ultimately attract only suitable applicants who have the potential to work at the firm. Therefore, human resource managers should consider the 5 **'TRAPS'** in designing effective job advertisement:

- Truthful – The advertisement does not make exaggerated or false claims about the job, the pay or the organization. Exaggeration and dishonesty might attract more applicants in the short term, but it is obviously unethical and can create more problems for the business in the long term.
- Relevant – Job advertisements need to be to the point in order to attract people's attention and interest.
- Accurate – The job description and person specification are precise so that the number of unsuitable people applying for the job is minimized.
- Positive – This helps to encourage people to apply for a job with the organization.
- Short – Given that advertising space is expensive, only appropriate and necessary information need to go in a job advertisement.

Question 2.1.3

Fonthill Primary School

Fonthill Primary School is seeking to hire an Educational Assistant ($15 per hour) to work for up to 17 hours a week in the Learning Support Department. The successful candidate will be required to facilitate specially designed educational activities working in collaboration with a classroom teacher and the Head of Department. Applicants should demonstrate patience, initiative and preferably have previous experience working with children who present specific learning difficulties. This position involves working specifically with a single child on a one-to-one basis. Closing date: Friday, 20 April.

a Examine whether the above would make an effective job advertisement. *[6 marks]*

b Explain why it is important for a business to produce well-defined job descriptions. *[4 marks]*

The application process

Applicants for a job will usually apply for a vacancy using a combination of three methods:

- **Application form**. This is a standardized form produced by the business for selecting appropriate applicants for a job. The business can tailor questions to meet its specific needs. Application forms also make applicants answer the same questions in a consistent format, allowing the employer to compare like-with-like (unlike a curriculum vitae).
- **Curriculum vitae**. This is a personal statement outlining an applicant's education, employment history, skills and professional qualifications. The curriculum vitae (CV), also known as a **résumé**, allows the employer to see what the candidate has achieved and to judge whether the experiences meet the requirements of the job.
- **Covering letter**. This is an introductory letter written by the applicant which states the purpose of the letter (i.e. which position is being applied for) and why the applicant should be considered for the job. The covering letter, also known as a **letter of application**, allows the HR Manager to scan through potential applications, without having to first read all the CVs or application forms (many of which will be inappropriate). Hence the covering letter must attract the attention of the recruiter.

Businesses have traditionally sent out application forms to prospective applicants. It is more common today for candidates to send in their CV or to apply using an online application form. These methods speed up the recruitment process and help to cut printing and mailing costs for the business.

The selection process

Once the completed application forms or CVs have been returned to the business, then the HR Manager will sieve through these to identify candidates who are suitable for the job (a process known as **short-listing** candidates). The short-listing process will involve comparing the application form and the CV of a candidate against the job description and person specification. This should help to identify the most suitable applicants to invite for a job interview. There are three main methods that can be used to select the best candidate for a job. These methods are: interviews, testing and references.

Interviews

An interview is a two-way process of dialogue between the interviewer (representing the employer) and the interviewee (the candidate applying for a job). The purpose is to help a business to make more informed choices when choosing the best candidate for a job. It is the most common method of selection. However, to get the most out of the interview process, all other prerequisites (such as job analysis) must have been carried out effectively.

Interviews are important as they provide a chance for an employer to meet with the applicant face to face (whether in person or via video-conferencing). The interview will allow the employer to get a better idea about what the applicants are like, whether they are suitable for the job(s) being offered and whether they will fit into the organization. At the same time, interviews allow the applicants to obtain more information about the job and the business and to assess whether they would be happy to work at the organization.

Interviews need to be well planned and conducted professionally. For example, interviewers must organize an appropriate venue where there will be no disruptions; appropriate questions need to be prepared to avoid negative discrimination; the job description and person specification must be readily available for the interviewing panel; and the interviewers should have studied the candidate's CV and references in order to get to know the applicant before the interview commences. Successful interviews also require managers to have good interview skills.

Interviews can take various forms. A *video-conferencing interview* takes place using ICT technology to save on the costs of people having to physically meet. Video-conferencing interviews are increasingly being used to recruit people from overseas to fill middle and senior management posts. *Face-to-face interviews* are usually carried out at the business, allowing the manager to meet and chat with the applicants. These interviews can range from having just one interviewer to several people interviewing the candidate at the same time (known as a *panel interview*). A business may also choose to use various stages of interviews to complement the selection process. This is more likely for senior positions in a firm where a series of interviews, each with a different focus, are conducted.

One drawback of the interview process is that it is very time consuming. Each interview can last over an hour and some jobs may require candidates to have further interviews with other key personnel. Another limitation of interviews is that a person's actual ability is not tested. Interviews can be unreliable in selecting the best candidate for a job because applicants can lie, twist the truth or simply perform well during the interview. However, the selected candidate may not have the ability to perform as expected.

To objectively select the best candidate, interviewers often use a predetermined checklist to assess the interviewees. Having such a checklist helps interviewers to make more logical decisions by weighing up the strengths and weaknesses of all candidates in the same way. Two frequently used models are the outlined in Table 2.1a. Professor Alec Rodger's seven-point plan (1952) and John Munro–Fraser's five-fold grading system (1971) are still widely used today. Variations of the Rodger and Munro–Fraser models are also frequently used by businesses when preparing a person specification.

Research has shown that the most effective interviews tend to follow a structured approach, with the same questions being asked to different candidates. These interviews do have some form of flexibility, such as asking further questions based on what the respondent says in the interview. However, if the same core questions are asked of all candidates, interviewer bias tends to be reduced in the selection process.

Table 2.1a Models of interview selection criteria

Alec Rodger's seven-point plan	Munro–Fraser's five-fold grading system
Physical make-up, e.g. appearance and speech	Impact on others, e.g. mannerisms and physical make-up
Attainments, e.g. educational and training	Qualifications, e.g. acquired knowledge, experience and training
General intelligence, e.g. reasoning and accuracy	Innate (natural) abilities, e.g. special aptitudes and ability to comprehend
Specialized aptitudes, i.e. speciality skills	Motivation, e.g. determination and success rate
Interests, e.g. team sports and intellectual hobbies	Emotional adjustment, e.g. ability to handle stress and to get on with people
Disposition, e.g. outlook, temperament and reliability	
Circumstances, e.g. ability to work unsocial hours	

The objective of the interview process is to establish the best match between the applicants and the vacant job. This is done by asking a series of questions (see Box 2.1d) that link to the job description and the person specification. There are two categories of interview questions:

- **Behaviour-based questions** are used to assess an applicant's behavioural pattern and initiative. Such questions typically start off as 'Explain an example of when you …' or 'Tell me about …'.

- **Situation-based questions** are used to assess an applicant's judgemental ability. The interview will start with a scenario (a hypothetical situation) and ask the interviewee for his or her response. An example would be a question similar to, "If one of your team members was constantly late for work, what would you do?" The idea behind such questions is to evaluate the critical thinking ability of the applicant who should consider the various options that exist in each given scenario. In the above example, the applicant might consider the reasons why the team member is consistently late for work, such as whether there are personal issues at home. Additional information is needed before an objective judgement can be made about how to deal with the situation.

Box 2.1d Ten common interview questions

1. Why do you want this job?
2. What do you know about this organization?
3. What makes you think that you will fit into this organization?
4. What are your key interests and how might these help you in this job?
5. What are your key strengths?
6. What are your main weaknesses and what have you done about them?
7. Who was the most difficult person you had to work with and how did you manage this?
8. Which leader/person do you admire most? Why?
9. Describe your key responsibilities in your last job.
10. Why did you leave your last job?

The ultimate purpose of any job interview is to select and appoint the best person for the position. Candidates can improve their chances of success at interview by reflecting on common sense protocol (see Box 2.1e).

However, as mentioned earlier, interviews have their limitations. For example, some applicants might perform very well at an interview but are not so competent in actually doing the job. They may even lack the desired qualities or skills needed for the job, which may not have been picked up in the interview. Hence, other forms of selection, such as testing, may also be used to aid management decisions about selecting the best employees. This will also help to prevent the high costs involved by hiring the wrong person.

Box 2.1e Do's and Don'ts for interviewees

Do's

- Prepare – Research the organization and its industry; plan on how to get to the venue (on time!); reread your CV and letter of application; prepare questions to be asked at the interview.
- Dress appropriately – First impressions count and can have a long lasting impact on the interviewers.
- Practise interview skills – It helps to answer questions more confidently.

Don'ts

- Be late – This will give a very bad first impression and managers don't like waiting!
- Be critical – Criticizing others (current or previous employers or employees) will not impress the interviewing panel.

Testing

Due to the limitations of using interviews for selection, **testing** is often also used. Although selection testing is time consuming, it increases the chances of hiring the best candidate for a job, thereby reducing the costs incurred if the wrong applicant is recruited. The four main types of testing used in recruitment are:

- **Psychometric tests** are an assessment of an applicant's personality. The tests will help to gauge the attitude of potential recruits and to assess their level of motivation. Since it is important to recruit people who will fit into the culture of an organization, many large companies use some sort of psychometric testing in their recruitment programme, especially for more senior positions.
- **Aptitude tests** assess the ability and skills of potential employees. Applicants for a secretarial job, for example, may be tested on the speed and accuracy of their typing. Problem solving and reasoning skills are also often tested.
- **Intelligence tests** assess the mental ability of an applicant, such as their skills of numeracy, literacy and general knowledge.
- **Trade tests** are used to examine a candidate's specific skills. Trade tests are useful when standards or skills cannot be judged from an interview or from a candidate's application form. For example, voice tests are used when recruiting television newsreaders and radio presenters.

References

References are written statements about an applicant from an independent source, such as a previous employer. *Referees*, the people who write references, may be asked to confirm the strengths and weaknesses of an applicant. They serve as a final security check to ensure the information given by candidates in their application form, CV and interview are accurate and truthful. Employers can then determine the suitability of the applicant for the advertised position.

The contract of employment

Once a suitable applicant has been selected, it is common in most countries that the new employee is entitled by law to receive either a contract of employment or a written statement of the terms and conditions of their employment. Box 2.1f outlines the information contained in a typical contract of employment.

Box 2.1f Contents of an employment contract

1. Job title
2. Job role and job specification
3. Date the job starts (and ends, if the agreement is a finite contract)
4. Hours and days of work
5. Rate(s) and method of pay
6. Holiday and sick pay entitlements
7. Pension scheme arrangements
8. Outline of disciplinary procedures
9. Period of notice that must be given when employment is terminated (by either party)
10. Names and signatures of both parties (employee and employer)

Induction

For most newly appointed staff it is common to receive induction training to help them settle into their new role. This can also apply to staff who have been internally recruited, perhaps due to a promotion or due to restructuring within the organization. Although the internally appointed person may still need some induction for their new post, the duration and breadth of the training will be less since s/he is already familiar with the policies, practices and culture of the business.

Note: Higher Level candidates must be able to examine how recruitment enables a firm to achieve workforce planning targets. (© IBO 2007)

INTERNAL AND EXTERNAL RECRUITMENT

Internal recruitment

Internal recruitment involves hiring people who already work for the firm to fill a vacant position. This often happens when a business restructures its organization of human resources (see Unit 2.2) or when internal candidates apply for a promotional post within the firm. Internal posts are usually advertised on staff notice boards, in newsletters or via staff emails.

Advantages of internal recruitment include:

- *Cost effective.* It is usually cheaper and quicker to recruit from within an organization. Suitable candidates may be readily available and the internal job advertisement will help to minimize recruitment costs.
- *Less down-time.* Internal people are already familiar with how the business operates and its culture. They are therefore usually more able to adapt and settle into the new position than those who are new to the organization. The amount of resources devoted to induction and training will also be reduced. Hence the internal recruit can take up his or her new role with minimal down-time (time used to get familiar with the operations of a business rather than time actually spent on getting work done).
- *Less risk.* Employing a new worker from outside the organization could be risky in that their actual abilities and skills may not have been truly tested in the recruitment process. By contrast, management will be familiar with the strengths and weaknesses of their internal staff and so recruiting internally may ensure that the vacancy is filled by a highly suitable candidate.
- *Motivational.* Internal recruitment, especially for promotional posts, can act as a form of motivation in the workplace. By providing internal people with opportunities for promotion suggests to staff that management value their employees. Hence, internal promotion can create employee loyalty and commitment to the firm.

Disadvantages of internal recruitment include:

- *Fewer applicants.* Internal advertisements limit the number of potential applicants for a job. External candidates could be of better quality but they have been overlooked.
- *Time consuming.* Redeploying, relocating or promoting an internal candidate will usually lead to another unfilled vacancy in the organization. This position may be subsequently advertised internally or externally. Therefore the process could potentially be more time consuming than if external recruitment had been used from the outset.
- *'Dead wood'.* Without external recruitment, it could be difficult to get new ideas introduced from outside the organization. Businesses do not benefit from having stale and outdated working practices (known as dead wood) because staff have been at the organization for too long. Quite often, management will discover that internal staff lack the necessary skills to take up an internal position and they have to result to using external recruitment.

- *Internal politics.* There could be resentment and conflict amongst fellow workers who were unsuccessful for the internal position. This can create a very uncomfortable working environment for the people involved. In addition, if no internal candidates are suitable, then the business will still have to use external recruitment.

External recruitment

External recruitment is the process of hiring employees from outside the business. There are various methods of external recruitment, including:

- *Newspaper advertising* is very common as it has a wide audience. However, targeting the right people can be difficult and the advertising costs are high.
- *Specialist trade publications* can be used to better target the right audience. For instance, management jobs in the supermarket industry are advertised in T*he Grocer* and teaching jobs around the world are published in the weekly *Times Educational Supplement.*
- *Internet advertising* is growing in popularity as more and more businesses use websites to advertise their jobs. They may use specialist recruitment websites (such as www.stepstone.com) or their own corporate website to advertise vacancies. Internet advertising can have a global reach yet it only incurs relatively low costs.
- *Commercial employment agencies* advertise and interview suitable applicants for a job. They make recommendations for selection to the hiring firm. Using agencies costs money (as they charge a fee for their services) but saves a huge amount of time for the employer who may prefer to rely on the recruitment expertise of the agency.
- *Job centres* are non-profit organizations funded by the government to help people find employment. Businesses can advertise their posts at job centres free of charge. However, job centres tend to be used for advertising relatively low paid jobs so this method may not be suitable for some businesses.
- *Headhunting* refers to the poaching of a person from his or her current employer. The person is sought for their experience and expertise. In order to entice them to leave their current job, the hiring company will try to offer a contract, including a pay deal, that is simply too good to resist.
- *University visits* involve businesses going to various universities to advertise their jobs. These jobs tend to be junior managerial posts. Visiting universities means that there is a large pool of potentially suitable and talented people to choose from.
- *Direct contacts* are personal recommendations made by a current employee who has contacts with people who possess the necessary skills and qualities to fill a vacancy. As is so often the case in the business world, sometimes it really is *who* you know rather than *what* you know that matters.

Advantages of external recruitment include:

- *New blood.* People hired from outside the organization can bring in new ideas. They can contribute to the sharing of good practices and give the business some insight to how a rival firm may have done things.
- *Wider range of experiences.* Similarly, external recruits may have gained experiences and skills suitable for the business but not possessed by any of the internal candidates.
- *Larger pool of applicants.* Businesses will have a wider range and larger number of people applying for the job. This increases the chances of finding and selecting the most ideal candidate for the job.

Disadvantages of external recruitment include:

- *Time consuming.* Although internal recruitment can also be time consuming, external recruitment tends to take even longer to complete. External advertising, screening of all the applications, short-listing suitable candidates, interviewing and taking up references all take up valuable management time. Employers may also be obliged by law to consider anti-discrimination laws when advertising jobs and interviewing applicants. This further lengthens the process.
- *Expensive.* External recruitment can be an extremely expensive process. Advertisements in newspapers, for example, can be highly expensive. Businesses may also need to reimburse short-listed candidates for their travel expenses. There is also the opportunity cost of management time involved in recruitment and selection.
- *Greater degree of uncertainty.* When hiring external recruits, managers take a risk in that they do not really know the candidates or their ability to do the job effectively.

APPRAISALS

An appraisal is the formal assessment of an employee's performance in fulfilling his or her job based on the tasks and responsibilities set out in their job description. It is common for appraisals to be carried out on an annual basis by someone senior to the person being appraised.

The main reasons for appraisals are to:

- Assess and record an employee's performance in line with their job description and targets
- Identify appropriate training and development needs of the appraisee
- Aid professional development, and help employees to plan their careers
- Identify barriers that may hinder the performance of an employee
- Set new targets and goals
- Assist staff in reflecting on their performance at work
- Provide an opportunity to praise staff on their good performance
- Aid management in assessing the suitability of individuals for a pay rise or promotion.

Appraisals form part of what is known as **performance management**. This is a continuous process involving the planning, reviewing and coaching of employees in order to enhance their performance at work. Managers will use a range of data, information and interviews to assess each employee. Typical interview questions in an appraisal meeting include those in Box 2.1g.

Appraisals can also be used as part of **job evaluation** to work out levels of pay. This can be done by looking at the different tasks, skills, responsibility, qualifications and effort that a job entails. The appraisal process can then allow a business to objectively reward more demanding jobs at higher rates of pay.

Box 2.1g Typical questions asked in appraisal meetings

- What has gone well for you this year? What has not gone so well for you?
- What are your key strengths and weaknesses?
- What can be done to help improve your overall performance?
- Where do you see yourself in five years' time?
- What ideas do you have to help you improve or develop as a team member?

Advantages of appraisals include:

- They are used to set targets in order to make changes that should lead to progress.
- They allow managers to objectively praise staff on their strengths and their contributions to the organization.
- Managers can use appraisals to provide constructive criticism to employees, thereby allowing staff to focus on improving their areas of weakness.
- Appraisals are a useful method of getting feedback from staff.

Disadvantages of appraisals include:

- Appraisals are time consuming and can be a costly exercise.
- Formal appraisals tend to take place annually, so the regular monitoring of targets can prove difficult.
- It can be a daunting experience for both the employee and the appraiser, especially with *upwards appraisals* (where a worker appraises his or her line manager).
- By their very nature, appraisals can be very subjective as personal feelings and relationships at work can interfere with the process.
- Staff may get offended by comments from the appraiser, such as the employee's areas of weakness.
- Many appraisers lack the experience and confidence to carry out appraisals and this therefore diminishes the credibility of the process and the results.
- Where appraisals are linked to pay, it can create unnecessary anxiety and stress to the appraisee.
- There must be a confidential feedback session (which again lengthens the exercise) and follow-up action which can be funded and monitored; otherwise the process will be pointless.

Some businesses will aggregate the findings of all appraisals in order to identify common areas of strengths and weaknesses. This can help such firms to identify areas in need of improvement and the training and development needs of the workforce.

Methods of appraisal

There are many ways to carry out an appraisal. These are some of the more well-known methods.

- **Upwards appraisal** refers to an employee appraising someone more senior in the organization, i.e. appraisals carried out by a subordinate. Although growing in popularity, this is not a common appraisal method due to its subjective nature especially as the exercise can be somewhat intimidating for both parties. The appraisee may also lack the experience to conduct an appraisal. Furthermore, many subordinates are often unwilling to criticize their line managers for fear of being reprimanded at a later date.
- **Essay appraisal** involves the appraiser preparing a written statement about the appraisee, describing specific strengths and weaknesses in terms of job performance. It is also common for the appraiser to suggest strategies for dealing with any shortcomings. The appraisee will usually get to review the statement and any necessary corrections are made before a final copy of the statement is produced; a copy of which is kept by the employer and another copy given to the employee. The key advantage of the essay appraisal is that it is very flexible. It allows the appraiser to inspect any relevant issue regarding job performance. This compares to other methods that are rigid and compare worker traits to predetermined scales or criteria. However, essay methods can be very time consuming to conduct and administer. Appraisers need to be appropriately trained and have excellent written communications skills. Since the method is very open-ended, the written statement might lack a sufficient structure to allow managers to compare results of different individual employees.

- **360 degree appraisal** involves the appraiser collecting the opinions about the appraisee from the people who work with the appraisee. Thus, constructive feedback and opinions are sought from peers, subordinates, line managers or other parties (such as suppliers or customers) who have direct contact with the appraisee. Opinions and comments are usually obtained by the use of questionnaires. The questions are mainly focused on the core competencies of the appraisee. This method of appraisal is a popular method of appraising management with the aim of providing useful and practical feedback to improve managerial effectiveness. However, 360 degree appraisals rely heavily on opinions rather than factual evidence. Hence, this method of appraisal is not suitable for all businesses and it is important for managers to consider group norms and corporate culture before embarking with 360 degree appraisals.
- **Rating system** is a highly structured appraisal method that examines the different components of a job and then rates each specific part of the job on a scale, such as from 'poor performance' to 'outstanding performance'. Almost any aspect of an employee's job performance can be scaled, including traits such as communication skills, punctuality, competence, technical knowledge and initiative. Rating systems get around the problems of more flexible appraisal methods such as the essay appraisal. The use of rating scales means that appraisals are conducted in a structured and standardized manner, thereby making appraisals relatively easier to conduct and to compare the results with those of other employees. The method also allows for the equal treatment of employees in the appraisal process. A potential drawback of rating systems is that some traits chosen for assessment may not be directly or as relevant to the jobs of all employees. The use of initiative, for example, would be more relevant to the appraisal of managers than the appraisal of machine operators. The latter are likely to score low on their use of initiative, but not necessarily because they lack initiative but because their jobs do not give as many opportunities for them to display this trait. Another problem is that the perceived meaning of the scales can vary from one appraiser to another. What one person interprets as 'above average performance' may not be perceived in the same way by another person. With an odd number scale system (3, 5 or 7 options), it is common for appraisers to 'play safe' by opting for the middle of the scale (placing someone 'below average' may spark conflict and require further justification). This act in itself is subjective and the results become less meaningful.
- **Management by Objectives (MBO)** involves assessing the extent to which an employee has met his or her objectives, as set and agreed by the employee and the appraiser. An objective for a sales manager, for example, might be to increase sales by an agreed amount within a given time frame. If the objective is met, then this indicates satisfactory job performance. Exceeding the objective may be seen as good or excellent job performance. The MBO method therefore assesses people according to actual outcomes rather than basing results on the opinions or inferences of an appraiser. MBO methods also provide clarity about what is to be assessed to both appraiser and appraisee. However, appraisers must be careful when setting objectives since unrealistic targets may simply be too difficult to achieve. If the objectives are far too unrealistic and unachievable in the first place, this would lead to the conclusion that the employee is incompetent or substandard – even if in reality this is not the case.
- **Peer appraisal** involves using employees on the same level in the organization's hierarchy as the appraiser and the appraisee, for example, using the marketing manager to appraise the finance manager of a firm. Peer appraisal is often used by retail businesses with different outlets, such as branch managers assessing other branch managers. An advantage of using this method is that both the assessor and appraisee are familiar with the requirements of the job. Job performance should therefore be relatively easy to assess. A disadvantage of peer assessment is that appraisers are often too reluctant to criticize (identify weaknesses of) their peers or team members. This then defeats one of the purposes of carrying out an appraisal.

- **Self-appraisal** involves employees appraising themselves based on predetermined criteria. Appraisees are expected to be honest about their strengths and his weaknesses. They also need to set realistic targets for improvement.

Whichever method of appraisal is used by a business, a performance appraisal usually includes the following steps:

- Staff *records and reports* are used to assess the performance of an employee over the past year.
- A formal and structured *appraisal meeting* (or interview) is conducted to allow the appraisee to reflect on their performance. Feedback is important and an action plan for the future may be formulated by both parties.
- The appraiser completes a *written report* on the assessment of the appraisal. There is usually a rating system used to judge the performance of the appraisee, perhaps ranging from 'Outstanding' to 'Unsatisfactory'.
- Both appraiser and appraisee *sign* the final written report.
- At times, there may also be a *countersignature* from a more senior manager, such as the supervisor of the appraiser to ensure that the appraiser has carried out the assessment in an honest and objective way.

If an appraisee has an overall rating that is below 'Moderate', the following actions can be taken:

- Issue an advisory letter to the appraisee (this is similar to a warning letter being issued).
- Counselling the appraisee and giving advice of their shortcomings (in their job performance), i.e. discussion of strategies for improvement.
- There may also be dialogue concerning the consequences if there is no improvement in job performance.
- Closely monitor the performance of the appraisee, perhaps by calling for quarterly reports or updates.
- In the case of no improvement being made within an agreed time period, action will be taken to dismiss the employee.

Note: Higher Level candidates must be able to examine how appraisal enables a firm to achieve workforce planning targets. (© IBO 2007)

TRAINING

Training can be defined as the process of providing opportunities for workers to acquire employment-related skills and knowledge. The amount and nature of training required for a job will vary from one job to another. Some jobs require constant training or updating of skills and qualifications (such as those in the ICT or medical professions). Other jobs will only require basic training to be carried out (such as unskilled machine operators in a factory).

The general **objectives** of training and development (T&D) include:

- Help staff adapt to change (technological, organizational, social and legal changes)
- Develop a multiskilled and productive workforce
- Improve the quality of work (including customer service) by the employees
- Enhance the efficiency and effectiveness of staff
- Facilitate career and personal development of each staff member.

The general **benefits** of training and development include:

- A better skilled and more flexible workforce leads to (higher) targets being met. Quality is also likely to increase as a result of the enhanced skills.
- Higher levels of competence leads to less *wastage* and *reworking* (having to do things again due to errors the first time round). Hence, greater efficiency and better productivity help to reduce operating costs.
- Morale improves as workers progress within the organization. This may help to reduce absenteeism and to reduce staff turnover, as staff feel valued by their employers who have invested in them. Workers also have higher chances of securing promotion as they become more skilled.
- By having a good reputation for training and developing staff, businesses may find it easier to attract good quality recruits.
- Better levels of customer service may be achieved as staff become more confident and competent in their roles.
- T&D can also help employees to adjust better to change. By updating their skills and being multiskilled, workers are better able to cope with organizational change.

Training and development programmes are a key strategy in helping organizations to achieve a flexible workforce. The term **workforce flexibility** refers to the ability of workers to multitask (carry out a range of different tasks or jobs) and to adapt to changes in the business. For example, many businesses have benefited enormously from hiring part-time workers as it means they can open for longer periods. Flexibility allows a business to be more efficient and can help to cut costs (part-time workers, for instance, cost less to hire).

Ultimately, the above benefits mean that the workforce becomes more flexible and productive. If the outcome of training results in net benefits, then the training can be judged to be financially successful and justified because the business makes more profit.

The largest drawback or limitation of providing training opportunities is the financial cost involved. This does not only include the costs of training courses, but also the loss of output whilst workers are being trained. In addition, effective training takes time to plan and this often consumes much of management's valuable time. Furthermore, there is no guarantee that training will help to solve business problems.

Question 2.1.4

Northern Ireland's hotel industry

In a recent report on the recruitment situation in Northern Ireland's hotel industry, it was found that workers suffered from low wages (earning not much more than the national minimum wage), very limited career and promotion prospects and a lack of training and professional development. Professor Tom Baum and Frances Devine's report also showed that most hoteliers felt training to be a burden rather than a benefit, and so should be kept at a minimum.

a Explain why low wages and few opportunities for promotion may create problems for businesses, such as those in the hotel industry. *[4 marks]*

b To what extent do you agree with the commonly held view of Northern Ireland's hotel businesses that training is a burden and so should be minimized? *[6 marks]*

Induction training

Induction training is training aimed at introducing new employees to the organization. Such a training programme may require a new recruit to:

- Meet key personnel, such as the employee's line manager and departmental team members
- Tour the premises including the recruit's main work space or area
- Learn about their new job role and other relevant duties and procedures
- Look at company policies and practices, such as the health and safety policy and fire evacuation procedure of the firm.

Quite often, a **mentor** is introduced to the new recruit. This is a person to whom the new recruit can turn to for general advice. Having a mentor may help new recruits to settle in quicker. Induction can also help to avoid costly mistakes made by the new employee who is not aware of the procedures or code of behaviour required to carry out their duties.

Advantages of successful induction training include:

- Good working habits and expectations are established from the start.
- New recruits are helped to understand the corporate culture of the organization.
- The new recruit settles in quicker and can contribute to the organization sooner.
- Morale is boosted as new recruits feel welcome and are confident and competent in what they do at work.

Disadvantages of induction training include:

- Planning and preparing an induction programme can be time consuming.
- Key personnel need to be 'freed' from their other duties because they are involved in the induction programme.
- 'Information overload' can be counter-productive as the new staff have to absorb so much fresh information.

On-the-job training

On-the-job training refers to training carried out whilst at the workplace. For example, the training can be delivered by a head of department or other specialists. The trainees learn from the skilled colleague delivering the training at the place of work. For example, junior managers may shadow (observe and learn from) more senior managers as part of their training. Essentially, this type of training involves 'learning by doing'. As Confucius once said, "I hear and I forget. I see and I remember. I do and I understand."

Advantages of on-the-job training include:

- It can be relatively cheap as the firm uses in-house specialists to give the training.
- The training is relevant as it is targeted at issues directly related to the firm's needs.
- There are fewer disruptions to daily operations as the trainee is still 'at work' rather than being overseas to attend a training course, for example.
- It can help to establish relationships at work as team working is involved.
- The location is convenient for the employees and employers, rather than them going off-site.

Disadvantages of on-the-job training include:

- Trainees may pick up bad working habits of the trainer.
- Internal trainers may lack the most up-to-date training experience and skills.
- Trainers will not be able to conduct their own work whilst giving the training.

Off-the-job training

Off-the-job training refers to training carried out off-site, such as at a tertiary college or hotel conference room. First Aid training, for example, may require specialist trainers and equipment that is not available in the business. This category includes day-release for training and evening classes. It is common that key personnel (e.g. middle managers) are chosen to attend these courses and are then expected to **cascade** (pass on) the knowledge that they have acquired to the rest of their team members.

Advantages of off-the-job training include:

- Experts used to provide the training.
- A wider range of training can be provided, such as training in ICT, foreign languages and first aid.
- There are no distractions from colleagues and other staff as training is conducted off-site.
- Networking can take place, whereby employees get to meet other people who can form the basis of business contacts

Disadvantages of off-the-job training include:

- Hiring the specialist trainers and the venue can be very expensive. Staff may also have to be reimbursed for transportation and accommodation costs for residential training courses.
- There is a potential loss of output whilst the employee attends the training course.
- It is debatable whether all the skills and knowledge learnt are relevant and therefore transferable to the firm.
- Finding the time to cascade the information from the training course can be a difficult task in itself.
- As with on-the-job training, employees who receive training and gain new skills and qualifications may decide to leave as they are better qualified for other jobs.

Whilst *training* tends to be specific to the tasks and responsibilities of a certain job, *development* focuses on enhancing the personal skills of a person. The argument is that developing these personal skills helps the employee to be more effective and flexible in their jobs. Examples of personal skills development include: assertiveness, counselling, time management, stress management, first aid and foreign language courses. It is clear that employees wishing to attend such courses must be able to justify how their personal development helps to improve the performance of a business.

It is common for those who attend a training course to give the employer some kind of feedback, such as the suitability of the course content and to what extent they feel that the training will help to improve their work performance. The most common method of giving feedback on a training course is to get the trainees to complete a questionnaire. This can also help businesses to determine whether the training could be extended to others in the organization, based on the cost effectiveness of such training.

> **Note:** Higher Level candidates must be able to examine how training enables a firm to achieve workforce planning targets. (© IBO 2007)

DISMISSAL AND REDUNDANCY

Whilst the HRM department has the crucial role of attracting and recruiting workers, it also has to ensure that the termination of employment contracts is carried out as efficiently as possible. Employment contracts can be terminated in one of four situations: dismissal, redundancy, retirement (when workers, due to their age, withdraw from the workforce) and resignations (when the employee chooses to leave their job).

Dismissal means the termination of a worker's employment due to incompetence (unsatisfactory performance) or a breach of contract. In everyday language, this is when a person is 'sacked' or 'fired'. When dismissing a worker, managers have to present a good case for the release of an employee and be seen to act in a fair manner in dealing with the case. Dismissal is usually seen as being fair in the following situations:

- **Incompetence** – The employee may lack ability, qualifications or effectiveness required to carry out the job.
- **Misconduct** – The employee may exhibit unacceptable behaviour, such as being constantly late for work, harassing other employees or frequently underperforming in the job. Employees will get a series of warnings for misconduct before they are dismissed.
- **Gross misconduct** – The employee may commit major misdemeanours (bad behaviour), such as theft, fraud, endangering others or turning up to work drunk. Gross misconduct can lead to instant dismissal without any warning.
- **Legal requirements** – If an employee does not have the necessary skills or requirements for their job, then the employer can legally dismiss the worker. For example, a worker may have been dishonest about his or her qualifications at the time of being offered the job which the employer later finds out not to be the case.

However, not all cases of dismissal are justified. **Unfair dismissal** occurs when an employee is dismissed without a valid reason. For example, the employee may have been wrongly accused on misconduct such as theft. In the event of unfair dismissal, the employee has the legal right to take their case to a hearing, such as in court. If the employee can prove his or her innocence, then the court can demand **reinstatement** of the employee (they get their job back) and/or financial compensation from the employer for the loss of earnings and the mental stress caused.

The two main causes of unfair dismissal are **discrimination** and **constructive dismissal**. For instance, an employer might discriminate against a worker's age, race, gender or religion and dismisses the person for this reason. In countries with equal opportunities legislation, women cannot be dismissed because they are pregnant. This act would be seen as unfair dismissal. Constructive dismissal occurs when a worker is forced into resigning from their position because the employer has made it very difficult or uncomfortable for the worker to continue in the job. The employer might have, for example, changed the terms and conditions of the worker without any consultation, such as a change in responsibilities or hours of work. In all cases of unfair dismissal, the employee has the legal right to sue the business for damages.

Redundancy occurs when the employer can no longer afford to employ the worker or when the job ceases to exist. For example, many retail workers are hired temporarily during the busy trading period prior to Christmas but are thereafter laid-off (made redundant). Redundancies are often referred to as **retrenchments** or **lay-offs**.

When a business has to lay off workers, there are two main methods it can choose from:

- **Voluntary redundancy** takes place when the employer asks for volunteers to be laid off. The workers that choose to give up their jobs are offered a *redundancy package*, such as several months of pay. The amount of redundancy pay offered to volunteers depends on their level of pay and benefits and the length of time that they have worked for the organization. Voluntary redundancy is the least likely method to cause conflict and hardship to the workforce.
- **Compulsory redundancy** (or involuntary redundancy) takes place when the employer has to choose which workers to make redundant. There are two ways they can choose from: the **LIFO** method (last in, first out) is most commonly used where the most recent recruit is the first to be made redundant or the **retention by merit** method where the least productive workers are made redundant first. The LIFO method has the advantage of being seen as fairer, although highly effective workers may be lost this way. Retention by merit can be highly subjective (a worker might be laid off because the manager doesn't like her rather than

because of her ability to carry out her job) but can be beneficial to the business if unproductive and inefficient workers are removed from the organization.

For larger businesses, rather than opting for redundancies a business might try to **redeploy** its staff. This means transferring the staff member from the department or branch that no longer requires his or her services to another department or branch where a vacancy exists. This ideal situation would mean that the worker is not made redundant. In reality, redeployment is not usually an option for most businesses. Furthermore, redeployment can cause anxiety and demotivate workers who are transferred to an unknown environment.

Note: Higher Level candidates must be able to examine how dismissals and redundancies enable a firm to achieve workforce planning targets. (© IBO 2007)

Question **2.1.5**

Ford's redundancy deals

In December 2006, Ford Motor Company announced that is was to halve its hourly-paid staff by making 38,000 workers redundant. The motor giant stated that these workers had either accepted early retirement deals or redundancy packages, but would save the company around $5 billion a year. Ford has been struggling with fierce competition from foreign rivals such as Toyota. Lower demand for Ford cars and overproduction were cited as the key reasons for the retrenchments.

a Distinguish between 'redundancy' and 'dismissal'. *[4 marks]*

b Analyse how retrenchment might enable Ford to better achieve its workforce planning targets. *[6 marks]*

HIGHER LEVEL

HIGHER LEVEL EXTENSION: EMPLOYMENT RIGHTS

In November 2000, Coca-Cola was made to pay out $192.5 million (worth around 300,000,000 cans of Coke) in lawsuit allegations that they treated black workers unfairly. Businesses can get into all sorts of trouble if they do not comply with employment legislation. Some laws constrain business activities whilst others can enhance the performance of a business. Although countries vary in their use of employment legislation, the laws typically found in most developed countries are outlined below.

Anti-discrimination legislation

These laws make it illegal to discriminate (show prejudice) against individuals because of their gender, race (ethnicity), religion, disability, marital status or age. The social argument for such laws is that it provides *equal opportunities* to everyone in society. The economic argument behind such laws is that it is inefficient to decline a person a job or career opportunity simply because of these factors, especially if s/he is clearly the best person for the job. *Sex discrimination* laws make it illegal to discriminate workers on the grounds of their gender or marital status for recruitment, training or promotion. In 2001, Wal-Mart (the world's largest retailer and the largest employer in the USA) were alleged by 1.6 million female workers in a court case of favouring men over women in pay and promotion. Since 2005, Wal-Mart has publicly released data on its employment of women and minority groups. *Racial discrimination* laws mean that it is illegal to discriminate employees because of their nationality, ethnic background or the colour of their skin. *Disability discrimination* makes it unlawful for employers to mistreat a person because of his or her disability. As with all legislation, there are some exceptions to the laws where *positive discrimination* can lawful. For instance, it is possible for modelling agencies to recruit only female models, for Chinese restaurants to employ only Chinese people, or for an all-girls school to recruit a female teacher of PE (physical education).

Equal pay legislation

Equal pay legislation makes it illegal to pay people differently if they are doing the same work or jobs deemed to be of equal value. It is possible, however, to offer greater rewards for those with higher qualifications and greater experience. Geographical considerations are also a possible exemption to equal pay legislation; it is more expensive to work/live in central business districts such as London, New York, Paris or Tokyo and so employers in these areas compensate workers with relatively higher pay.

Health and Safety at Work

Health and Safety at Work Acts (HASAWA) cover the provision of safe and adequate working conditions. A business will, for example, need to offer a secure and hygienic working environment for its workers. Adequate facilities, such as lighting and washrooms, are also required. Training must be provided so that workers know how to operate equipment and machinery in a safe manner. Implementing HASAWA can prove to be expensive. For instance, training costs can be high. Maintaining health and safety standards also costs money. However, in the long run, a business should be able to benefit from having lower absenteeism and fewer compensation claims caused by injuries at work. Businesses may also benefit from a better corporate image, thereby reducing staff turnover. Furthermore, maintaining health and safety standards is a necessary *hygiene factor*, according to Professor Herzberg, that is necessary to prevent a demotivated workforce (see Unit 2.5).

Statutory benefits

Statutory benefits are the legal benefits that every business in a country is obliged to offer its workers. Typical statutory benefits are shown in Box 2.1h. These benefits will clearly add to the costs of a firm so in order to protect it, employees must first qualify for certain statutory benefits, such as maternity leave or holiday pay. This is usually based on a qualifying period linked to the length of time that the worker has been employed for by the business. Some businesses may choose to offer more than the statutory benefits, such as extended paid maternity and paternity leave. However, all businesses must offer the statutory benefits as a minimum benefits package.

National Minimum Wage (NMW)

The imposition of a NMW means that all businesses operating within the governing nation must pay no less than this rate of pay. The main reason for the use of a NMW is that the government believes there are benefits to raising the income of the poorest paid workers in the country. The NMW is usually expressed as an hourly rate and must be paid to all workers, irrespective of the work they do or the experience they hold. However, it is possible to have different rates of the NMW for different age categories (as is the case in the European Union where younger workers are paid less per hour than those aged 22 and older). For example, the UK's NMW in October 2007 was £5.52 (around $11) per hour, having increased by over 53% since its introduction in April 1999. The NMW can therefore present a threat to businesses as their costs are increased.

Just as there are laws to protect employees from mistreatment at work, there are expectations governing employees in their conduct at work. Some of these expectations, which may or may not be stipulated in an employment contract, include the need for employees to:

- Be willing and able to carry out the roles and tasks as set out in their job description and employment contract
- Comply with reasonable (and lawful) orders given by the management team
- Act in a professional, honest and fair manner at all times
- Take care not to damage property of the business, such as machinery and equipment
- Avoid misconduct, such as theft of business property, discrimination against fellow employees, deliberate misuse of corporate finance, accepting bribes, drunkenness in the workplace or violent behaviour.

If an employee is unable to fulfil these responsibilities, then it is lawful for the employer to begin dismissal procedures against the worker.

Box 2.1h Statutory Employment Benefits

- *Statutory Sick Pay* – Payment made to workers who are unable to work due to general illness. Firms may request a doctor's certificate as proof of the employee's sickness before wages or salaries are paid.
- *Statutory Maternity Pay* (SMP) – Payment made to female workers who are expecting a baby. They are entitled to paid leave for a period of time after the baby is born and are guaranteed their job on the same terms and conditions as before on their return.
- *Statutory Paternity Pay* (SPP) – Payment made to male workers whose partner or spouse is expecting a baby. The period of time tends to be shorter for males than for expectant mothers. In many countries, both SMP and SPP laws extend to the adoption of a child and not just for natural births.
- *Statutory Holiday Pay* – Payment made to staff during statutory holidays such as Christmas and New Year. Staff who work during statutory holidays are usually offered an overtime rate (premium wage rate). Employees are also entitled to a period of paid holiday leave, which is usually dependent on their length of service.
- *Retirement Pension Scheme* – Contribution paid by employers towards the retirement fund of the worker. This is called a 'superannuation fund' in some countries.

Question 2.1.6

Wal-Mart

Global retailer Wal-Mart was charged with breaking local labour laws in late 2006. Wal-Mart had been found guilty of exploiting employees in Pennsylvania, USA by forcing them to work during their rest breaks without pay. The courts demanded Wal-Mart pay $78 million in damages. The following year, approximately 1.6 million female workers also filed for **discrimination** charges, claiming that Wal-Mart denied them promotion due to their gender. They also claimed that Wal-Mart paid male counterparts higher wages.

a Outline the meaning of **discrimination** in the context of the case study. *[2 marks]*

b Justify why employers such as Wal-Mart need to be aware of employment legislation. *[8 marks]*

CHANGING EMPLOYMENT PATTERNS AND PRACTICES

In modern societies, there have been a number of observable changes in employment patterns and work practices, such as the increase in the number of people working from home. Some of the main trends are examined below, with a look at the consequences of theses changes for both employers and employees.

> **Note:** Higher Level students must be able to analyse the reasons for changes in work patterns and practices, and their implications for both employees and employers.
> (© IBO 2007)

Employment sector

There are three employment sectors in an economy – primary, secondary and tertiary (see Unit 1.1). Generally, as a country develops, the proportion of workers employed in the primary industry will fall, with a shift to secondary industries and finally the tertiary sector. In developed economies, the tertiary sector accounts for the largest proportion of employment. For example, less than 2% of people in the USA, UK and France (some of the most developed economies in the world) work in agriculture, whereas over 75% of the working population are employed in the services sector.

Ageing population

The net birth rate in many developed societies has been falling. This means that the size of the future workforce will also fall. Yet people are living longer, so the average age of workers will tend to rise. Hence the shortage in labour supply will affect workforce planning, recruitment and training. Firms will be more willing to appoint and retain older employees. They will also be more flexible in keeping staff beyond retirement age. Women and part-time employees, who help provide more flexibility, will also be sought after. Training opportunities will be provided for existing staff to enhance their performance and to offer them the prospect of internal promotion, i.e. using training as a means of retaining staff.

Flexible work structures

Handy's theory of the *shamrock organization* (see below) suggests that businesses will increasingly use fewer core staff in order to improve their flexibility. For example, firms are increasingly using consultants and outsourcing projects. Reducing the number of the core staff and employing more part-time workers and peripheral workers will also help a business to reduce its labour costs. Greater flexibility may also mean that a larger number of people work from home. Flexible working patterns will have many consequences for workforce planning, recruitment and training, including:

- *Organizational restructuring* – There is less likely to be a traditional organizational structure as the firm employs various combinations of core, part-time and peripheral staff.
- *Flexi-time* – Staff such as consultants, contractors and part-time employees are more likely to be allowed to work hours that suit their individual needs. Businesses will also offer flexible working hours to cater for people who have to balance work with other priorities such as childcare or higher education.
- *Changing recruitment practices* – Firms shift to hiring more flexible workers (in terms of location, working hours and skills). Hence they are likely to employ more part-time, temporary and peripheral staff.
- *Retention of core staff* – Key employees of an organization will need to be recruited for their outstanding skills and experience. In addition, these people will need to be retained, perhaps by offering first-rate financial rewards.
- *Training* – Firms will be less likely to invest in training, except for their core staff. However, there will be pressures for staff to be constantly updating their skills. Firms may pay for this (for core staff at least) or people may have to update employment skills at their own expense (such as enrolling for online training courses). Traditional induction training may not be necessary or may be reduced in content and time.

Likewise, workers will have to be more flexible. There is no such thing as a 'job for life' and people have to be prepared to move between occupations and perhaps industries to maintain employment. However, a multiskilled and flexible worker will be highly attractive to potential employers. Examples of flexible working practices include teleworking, homeworking, portfolio working, part-time employment and flexitime.

Teleworking

Teleworking refers to working away from the employers or customers by using electronic forms of communication, such as a telephone, fax and email. It has become increasingly popular in the USA, Canada, Sweden, Finland and the UK. The trend has been partly due to the commuting problems in central business districts but mainly due to the technological advances in ICT.

Examples of businesses that operate teleworking include insurance firms, banks, technical support for computer manufacturers, market research firms and airlines. These businesses establish a 'call centre' where a dedicated team of workers deal with customer enquiries and complaints on the telephone. This frees up management time at individual branches as they do not have to deal with so many telephone calls from customers. Another type of teleworkers is the *mobile teleworkers*, such as sales people who spend most of their time travelling and visiting clients.

Home working is a category of teleworking which refers to people actually working from their own home. The International Telework Association and Council (ITAC) estimated that approximately 20% of the American workforce worked from home (during business hours) at least one day per month in 2004, rising to around 33% (over 40 million people) by 2010. With advances in wireless broadband technology, which allows employees to operate in almost any location, the actual number of teleworkers may well be much higher.

There are advantages of teleworking and homeworking to a business and its employees. These advantages include:

- Geographical distance is no longer a problem with teleworking; customers can save time and money in travelling to and from retail outlets. Instead, they pick up the phone and speak to a customer service advisor on the other end of the telephone.
- Businesses do not need to locate call centres in busy city offices, for which expensive rent is charged, as customers do not need to 'visit' the call centres. The ITAC claims that improved productivity and cost savings from teleworking saves American companies an average of $5,000 per employee per year.
- Absenteeism is not such an issue for teleworkers and homeworkers; research has shown reduced absenteeism rates compared to office-based workers. Pacific Bell, an American telecommunications company, reported absenteeism being 25% lower than that of its company-based workers.
- Employees do not need to travel to and from work; employees can save time and money in travelling. They may also benefit from not having to suffer from the stress of commuting.
- Employees can enjoy autonomy in decision-making as working practices tend to be less formal than in a traditional office setting. They also have more choice in how they organize their work.
- Workers can benefit from additional income tax allowances for using their personal property for conducting business activity.
- For many people, childcare is another consideration of working from home. The BBC has reported that the average cost of childcare for a two year old was £7,300 ($14,500) per year. For parents with young children, childcare represents an opportunity cost to working. Home working can help to reduce this financial burden.

In addition, entry costs used to be a major expense (such as the price of a mobile phone, a personal computer, printer and broadband internet connection). With huge reductions in these costs, brought about by increased competition and technological progress, more people can afford to work from home. Furthermore, teleworking helps many businesses to get around the problem of being somewhat constrained by laws governing the maximum hours of work in a given time period. For example, the EU's Working Time Directive states that all workers must not be required to work more than 48 hours in a week, with a minimum rest period of at least 11 hours each day. Having a more flexible workforce can help a business to work around this directive.

Home working makes work more independent for both employees and employers, although it relies heavily on good communication and use of ICT. In addition, employees are likely to face more distractions whilst working at home. This is even more difficult for those with young families who have the dual roles of child care and work. However, home workers are more likely to get bored from working in isolation every day rather than benefiting from the social interaction that they might enjoy whilst being at work with others. This idea is known as **social isolation**. Furthermore, teleworkers tend to suffer from a lack of training opportunities and career development.

Table 2.1b Advantages and disadvantages of teleworking and homeworking for employees and employers

	Employees	Employers
Advantages	• Job creation opportunities, especially for those living in remote areas • Suitable for people who have to care for family members • Flexible working hours • Benefits of not having to travel to work, e.g. costs, time and stress	• Reduced office overheads as less prime office space is needed • Flexible and extended working hours made available to customers • Flexible working practices to cater for peak and off-peak trading periods • Continuity of service from those with young children or other dependents
Disadvantages	• Heavy reliance on use of ICT communication and equipment • Teleworking is not always possible, e.g. lack of space at home or lack of confidentiality of data being held at home • Teleworkers, partly due to the nature of the job, often exceed legal limits on working hours • Suffer from social isolation • There is often less job security and less trade union representation for teleworkers	• Set up costs (the amount of equipment required and the size of the investment) can be very high • Requires tight control in recruitment as not everyone has the right profile, e.g. independent, experienced, and self-motivated • Management and control are made more difficult as staff are off-site • Technological breakdowns can cause major disruptions to the business

Portfolio working

A **portfolio worker** is a person employed in a number of different jobs, carried out simultaneously, usually on a part-time or temporary basis. For example, the portfolio worker might be working on a project for one business, whilst conducting research for another and providing consultancy services for yet another organization. The worker will charge a fee for the work carried out. The term was coined by Charles Handy in his book *The Age of Unreason* (1990).

Portfolio working increases the flexibility and mobility of an organization's human resources. One advantage for the portfolio worker is that the variety of experiences may contribute to a more fulfilling career. The key drawback for portfolio workers is the lack of job security. Ad hoc employment opportunities mean that the portfolio worker may have no contracts at a particular point in time whilst being very busy at other times. For instance, professional home improvement specialists (such as plumbers, electricians and landscape gardeners) tend to have many projects going on at the same time in the summer months, but are less busy during the winter months.

William Bridges wrote about similar trends in his book *Job Shift* (1994). He used the term **dejobbing** to explain the increasing number of workers becoming independent workers rather than the conventional meaning of being an employee. Couriers, for example, are often classed as self-employed although they work directly for various companies and are held accountable for their own costs.

Part-time employment

In developed economies, an increasing number of people are working **part-time**. This is partly due to the greater number of females and students who choose to work part-time and the benefits of labour flexibility for the employer.

A key advantage to a business in hiring more part-time staff is that they are cheaper to employ. Part-timers are generally entitled to lower remuneration (pay and benefits) compared to their full-time counterparts. In addition, they are easier to replace if there is a need. There is also a large pool of workers that can work part-time, so again this keeps wages relatively low and gives the employer plenty of choice in who to recruit (e.g. working mothers or full-time college and university students who want to limit their hours of work). Hence, part-timers are said to be easy to 'hire and fire'. Perhaps more importantly though, is that part-time employment gives a business more flexibility, i.e. it is easier to adjust labour hours to accommodate fluctuations in demand. Hours can be reduced during off-peak periods and raised again during busier times.

However, part-time employment suffers from two main disadvantages. First, part-time employees feel less valued and therefore are less loyal to a business. This can negatively affect the organization's level of motivation, productivity and labour turnover. Second, a lot of time and resources are consumed in the hiring, induction and training of new part-time staff. Since part-timers do not tend to stay at the firm for very long, this ongoing process of recruiting and training part-timers uses up a lot of valuable management time. It may be more cost effective for some firms to hire full-time workers from the outset.

Flexitime

The traditional working hours in western economies was a 9 a.m. start and a 5 p.m. finish. This rigid system no longer applies to the vast majority of businesses. One alternative is to have **shift work** with different groups of people working at different time allocations, such as one team of workers on a 9 a.m. to 5 p.m. shift and another team on an 11 a.m. to 7 p.m. shift. A second alternative is to employ staff under a system of **flexitime**. This system requires employees to work a core period of the day when they are expected to be at work (say between 9 a.m. and 2 p.m.), but the rest of the time is 'flexitime'. This means that staff determine where they will work, subject to them getting their work completed by set deadlines. For example, a worker who is required to work a 40-hour week might be able to work 10-hour shifts from Monday to Thursday and have Friday as a day off.

Flexitime is increasingly popular in the UK and USA, where over 25% of women are employed on a flexitime basis. Legislation in the UK, introduced in 2003, has made flexitime more accessible to parents of young and/or disabled children. Since April 2007, the law extended to give carers of adults the right to request flexitime from their employers.

Both shift work and flexitime can help to extend normal working hours of a business (thereby generating more sales or getting more work done). They also help to reduce the need for paying staff to work overtime. Offering flexitime can also improve a firm's image as it is seen to be providing equal opportunities to staff who are unable to work standard hours due to their other important commitments. Flexitime can also be beneficial to employees as it gives them a greater degree of freedom to balance their work and personal life.

Finally, flexible work structures such as portfolio working and teleworking have meant that the average number of hours worked is increasing. This has happened despite employment legislation in some countries, such as within the EU, where there is a maximum working week (48 hours). This trend is not necessarily a bad thing for firms since they can potentially earn more money for each extra hour that they stay open for trading (see Question 2.1.7).

Question 2.1.7

McDonald's

McDonald's is the most globalized fast-food restaurant in the world. Part of its successful growth strategy has been the ability to adopt **flexible work structures**. The company uses the catchphrase 'Your money, Your hours, Your way' as part of its recruitment plan. Most of the workers at McDonald's are part-timers – mainly of students and women. In Australia, McDonald's actively encourages students to apply for jobs by using slogans such as 'Learn While You Earn' and 'Work with mates, buy what you want'. Their careers web page (www.mcdonalds.co.au/careers) even has sections titled 'Send Site to Friend' and 'Info for your parents'. Having a flexible workforce has enabled the fast-food giants to open some of their stores on a 24-hour basis.

- **a** Describe the meaning of **flexible work structures**. *[2 marks]*
- **b** Analyse the costs and benefits of flexible work structures to employers, such as McDonald's, and their employees. *[6 marks]*
- **c** Discuss the likely consequences of flexible working patterns on a firm's workforce planning, recruitment and training. *[9 marks]*

HIGHER LEVEL EXTENSION: HANDY'S SHAMROCK ORGANIZATION

Charles Handy, co-founder of the London Business School in 1967, believes that people are the most important resource within any organization. His ideas differed remarkably from those of F.W. Taylor (see Unit 2.5) who believed in tall hierarchical structures with close supervision of workers. By contrast, Handy recommended that businesses ought to place greater emphasis on meeting the needs of workers, which could be done by methods such as *job enrichment* (giving workers more interesting and challenging tasks) and flexible working practices. Handy believes that by doing this, businesses help to improve the well-being and morale of their workers. For example, students in part-time employment and mothers with young children would have more choice over the time that they work.

Handy also emphasized the dynamic nature of change within organizations and the external business environment. He did not believe in 'jobs for life' but instead that short-term jobs or contracts were more appropriate. The trend in the number of businesses that subcontract or contract out business activities supports Handy's beliefs. Indeed, it is often more efficient to use an outside firm to complete specific jobs as they have the necessary labour, know-how and experience. He argued that non-essential work (i.e. jobs that can be done by others) should be contracted out to specialist people who should be able to do the work more productively and cost efficiently.

Due to these changes, Handy came up with the concept of the **shamrock organization**. This model gets its name from the shamrock plant (a three-leaved clover, as shown). Handy argued that within a shamrock organization there should be three groups of staff:

- **Core staff** (the first leaf) consists of full-time professional workers (such as managers and technicians) who handle the daily operations of the business. They are crucial to the organization's operations, survival and growth. The core group of workers is becoming an increasingly smaller group with developments in e-commerce (see Unit 4.8) and teleworking. This has led to downsizing and restructuring of the workforce in many businesses.

HIGHER LEVEL

- **Peripheral workers** (the second leaf) of workers are what Handy called the **contingent workforce** (also referred to as the **insourced workers**), consisting of part-time, temporary and portfolio workers who are employed as and when they are required. They tend to be paid by the hour or day for short periods of employment, so this helps to reduce labour costs for the firm. The peripheral group of workers forms the flexible workforce for an organization and constitutes a greater proportion of the workforce for large companies. For example, supermarkets such as Wal-Mart, Tesco and Carrefour employ more part-time staff than full-time workers.
- **Outsourced workers** (the third leaf) consists of individuals or businesses that are not employed by the organization but are paid to complete particular and specialized tasks, such as advertising campaigns or skills training. Freelance workers, subcontractors, agencies and the self-employed are examples of outsourced workers; they are hired by an organization for their skills and paid by results. For instance, most large firms use marketing agencies to design appropriate promotional campaigns for their business clients. This group of outsourced workers is also known as the **contractual fringe**.

The three components of the shamrock have their own advantages and limitations for an organization. The core workers, vital to the organization, must be well paid and remunerated. They are likely to also enjoy some degree of job security, be well motivated and highly productive. The insourced workers will suffer from a lack of job security thereby negatively affecting their levels of morale. However, they present flexibility for an organization and are easier to 'hire and fire'. For the insourced workers, they are able to develop two or more careers simultaneously (portfolio working). The costs and benefits to a firm choosing to use outsourcing are covered in Unit 5.7.

Although Handy introduced the idea of the shamrock in the early 1990s, time has shown that organizations are indeed restructuring to become more flexible, reducing their core staff and using more peripheral workers. The trend in modern businesses that increasingly use more part-time workers and teleworkers supports Handy's foresight.

HUMAN RESOURCE PLANNING AND BUSINESS STRATEGY

Human resources are an essential part of any business. Labour represents one of the four factors of production. If managers do not make the most of their human resources (such as poor recruitment, motivation and retention of workers), then they will face a number of consequences (which can be remembered as the 5 R's):

- *Recruitment* – higher recruitment, induction and training costs
- *Resources* – increasing amount of resources and management time spent on dealing with personnel problems, rather than achieving organizational objectives
- *Reservations* – lower morale and higher levels of uncertainty suffered by existing staff who experience constant change in staffing
- *Returns* – lower levels of labour productivity, competitiveness and profits
- *Reputation* – poorer corporate image, since the business cannot retain its staff.

Managers are increasingly keen to establish the reasons for staff leaving their firm. **Exit interviews** are used for this purpose. These are interviews carried out with staff who have resigned from the organization. The main purpose of conducting exit interviews is to understand the true reasons behind staff choosing to leave the business. For example, employers might think that the remuneration package offered is competitive, although this may not necessarily be the view of the majority of the employees. There may also be certain aspects of the job, management or organization that the firm is not fully aware of. Data and information from exit interviews can then be used by personnel managers to improve training and development to improve staff retention.

Whilst there are costs associated with improving staff retention, most analysts believe that the long-term benefits are far greater. Theorists and entrepreneurs such as Charles Handy, Richard Branson and Donald Trump argue that human resources should be viewed as an investment and that training and development are an essential part of successful human resource planning. An organization's training strategy must first identify the training needs of its employees and then devise an action plan to show how the training will aid the workforce in achieving its organizational objectives. Once the training programme is implemented, managers must monitor its progress and evaluate the effectiveness of the training.

It is also important for managers to acknowledge the need for ongoing training (continuous professional development), whichever method(s) of training is offered by the firm. Symptoms of poor training or a lack of training include: higher staff absenteeism, low morale, higher staff turnover, poorer quality output, greater waste and more mistakes being made. Hence, provision and funding of adequate training is vital for the long-term success of the firm. However, not all training programmes are effective so managers need to devise criteria to evaluate the training that they provide, such as whether the training has led to improvements in the quality of services being provided. Ultimately, human resources can be an important source of competitive advantage for a business if they are used and developed properly.

A successful training and development plan should:

- Show commitment to the training and development needs of all staff
- Link training and development needs to departmental and organizational objectives
- Help to promote a culture of continuous learning and development
- Assess the operational requirements of the organization against the skills of the staff
- Provide equal opportunities for all staff yet be cost effective.

In addition, all businesses face the same problems when offering professional training for their staff. First, there needs to be equal opportunities of access to training and development – not always feasible in large organizations due to the time and financial commitment to continually train every employee. Second, employees who become more skilled and qualified may develop an expectation of higher remuneration in recognition of their enhanced value to the organization. Third, workers who have been trained and developed by the firm may actually choose to leave for promotional posts in other organizations. Hence, these problems may justify limiting the amount of money devoted to training and development and instead using externally recruited staff. Nevertheless, providing training can be a motivator which ultimately benefits both employees and employers.

Another key strategic role in HR planning is the use of appraisals. The main purpose of appraisals is not to blame or to reward, but to develop people in the organization. Hence, in some organizations, appraisals are termed **personal development plans**. Planning and conducting appraisals is often one of the most difficult tasks for a manager, especially when they have to appraise underperforming or uncooperative members of staff. Trainers and appraisers often consider the acronym KASH (Knowledge, Attitude, Skills, and Habits) when evaluating the different areas of success of an appraisee. Both *knowledge* and *skills* can be trained and developed, whereas attitudes and habits can only be influenced, at best. Attitudes and habits are determined by external factors such as personality and emotions so are largely beyond the control of a business. Hence, in conducting appraisals, it is important that the appraiser is appropriately chosen. This is why line managers tend to appraise their staff rather than using other managers who know little about the appraisee. The choice of appraisal method is also important and must be appropriate to the needs of the organization and appraisee. In this way, both parties are more comfortable with the arrangements and the employee is more likely to take the process seriously and positively. As a result, employees are more willing to act on the changes recommended in their appraisal feedback.

There is consensus that most businesses spend a significant amount of money on their workforce. This includes the costs of recruitment, training and development, appraisals, salaries, bonuses and fringe benefits. It is important then that managers can measure the effectiveness of this investment in the workforce. **Personnel effectiveness** refers to the measures that can be used to indicate the level of success of human resource planning and management (see Box 2.1i). There are four main measures of personnel effectiveness:

1 **Labour turnover** measures the percentage of the workforce that leave the firm in a given time period, usually one year. A low labour turnover rate suggests that managers have recruited the right people for the job and that the existing employees are motivated at work. By contrast, a high labour turnover rate suggests that staff are incompetent or they lack job satisfaction. This could be because the correct people have not been recruited or sufficiently trained or perhaps because of better employment conditions and remuneration packages offered by other employers. A high labour turnover rate will clearly add to the costs of recruiting and training new staff.

2 **Absenteeism** measures the percentage of the workforce not present at work within a particular time period. A low rate of absenteeism (or high presenteeism) suggests that staff are motivated to work. High absenteeism however suggests that staff are deliberately avoiding coming into work, perhaps due to poor staff morale or poor management techniques being used in the workplace. High absenteeism will mean that productivity suffers at the same time as costs rising (those absent may qualify for statutory sick pay and other employees may have to be brought in to cover for the absent staff).

3 **Labour productivity** is a measure of the efficiency of the workforce by assessing the level of output of the staff. The most common measure is to measure the **output per worker**. Many people argue that labour productivity is the key indicator of effective human resource planning. This is because labour productivity directly affects the firm's average cost of production since higher productivity means that more output is generated with the same amount (and cost) of factor inputs. Hence, higher labour productivity leads to improved competitiveness, sales and profits for the business.

4 **Waste levels** refer to the amount of waste products (lost, damaged or poor quality output) as a proportion of the firm's total output. The higher the level of wastage, the more reworking (reproducing the work) that has to be done. In addition, the waste has to be discarded due to its substandard quality, meaning that the firm incurs higher costs. High levels of waste may be caused by poorly trained staff who suffer from a lack of motivation and job satisfaction. Wastage can also be caused by a firm using outdated capital equipment and production techniques. Whatever the reasons, it is the role of the manager to investigate the causes of high wastage and to deal with the problem. It is crucial that this is done swiftly in order to prevent problems escalating, such as higher levels of customer complaints and an organizational reputation of providing poor quality products.

Box 2.1i Formulae for calculating personnel effectiveness (per time period)

- Labour Turnover = (Number of staff leavers ÷ Total number of staff) ×100
- Absenteeism = (Number of absent staff ÷ Total number of staff) × 100
- Productivity = Total output ÷ Number of workers
- Wastage = (Waste ÷ Total output) × 100

All figures should relate to a specified time period, e.g. per month or per year.

REVIEW QUESTIONS 2.1

1 What is meant by 'workforce planning' and what is involved in the process?
2 Outline four factors that affect the supply of human resources in a country.
3 Why do businesses need to recruit people?
4 What is a 'job analysis' and why is it important?
5 What is the purpose of producing a job description and person specification?
6 Identify five factors that might appear in a typical job advertisement.
7 Differentiate between 'internal recruitment' and 'external recruitment'.
8 Why do businesses spend so much money on training and developing their staff?
9 State three reasons why internal recruitment might be preferred to external recruitment.
10 Distinguish between 'training' and 'development'.
11 What is the difference between 'off-the-job training' and 'on-the-job training'?
12 Explain the difference between 'redeployment' and 'retirement' of staff.
13 Under what circumstances would dismissal be classified as 'fair' rather than 'unfair'?
14 Differentiate between 'teleworking', 'portfolio working' and 'flexitime'.
15 How might homeworking affect labour productivity?

Higher Level extension

16 Explain three categories of employment legislation that organizations are likely to observe.
17 What are the three components of Handy's shamrock organization?
18 The consequences of poor human resource planning can be remembered by the 5 R's. What are they?
19 What are the four measures of the effectiveness of a firm's human resource planning?

Appraisal refers to the formal process of evaluating the contributions and performance of an employee, usually conducted through observations and an interview with the appraisee's line manager.

Cascading is the vertical transfer of information in a hierarchy, via meetings between staff at different levels of the hierarchy.

Contract of employment refers to the legal agreement between an employer and employee, detailing the terms and conditions of employment (such as the job title, pay and responsibilities of the post holder).

Employment legislation refers to the set of laws that govern employment practices, such as anti-discriminatory behaviour when recruiting, selecting, training and promoting workers.

External recruitment involves recruiting staff from outside the organization to fill vacant posts. This can be done in various ways, such as by headhunting a suitable person or advertising the post on the firm's own website.

Flexible work patterns means the trend in using less core staff and more peripheral workers (such as part-time staff and consultants) and subcontractors. Such structures improve the flexibility of the workforce.

Human resource management refers to the role of managers in developing the organization's people (or human resources). This will include tasks such as the recruitment, selection, dismissal and training and development of employees.

Human resource planning, or **workforce planning**, is the management process of forecasting an organization's current and future staffing needs.

Internal recruitment refers to the practice of hiring people who already work for the firm to fill a position, rather than recruiting someone new to the organization.

Job description is a document that outlines the nature of a job, i.e. the roles, tasks and responsibilities involved in a particular job. It is used for the recruitment and performance appraisal of employees.

Labour productivity measures the output per worker. The level of labour productivity is an indicator of the current level of skills and motivation of the workforce.

Labour turnover measures the number of workers who leave a firm as a percentage of the workforce, per year. It is often used to gauge the level of motivation in an organization.

Person specification is a business document that gives the profile of the ideal candidate for a job, such as their skills, qualifications, experience and other attributes.

Portfolio working means to simultaneously carry out a number of different jobs, often for various employers, usually on a part-time or temporary basis. Examples include freelance editors and management consultants.

Recruitment refers to the process of hiring suitable workers. This will entail a thorough *job analysis* in order to ensure that the best candidate is hired.

Shamrock organization refers to Charles Handy's idea that organizations are increasingly made up of core (vital) staff who are supported by insourced part-time workers and consultants and by outsourced staff and contractors.

Short-listing refers to the process of sifting through applications to identify candidates who are suitable for the job. It is the stage that precedes the interview in the recruitment process.

Teleworking is a method of workforce planning whereby employees work in a location away from the employer's workplace, such as those working from home or at a call centre.

Organizational Structure

UNIT 2.2

The best executive is the one who has sense enough to pick good men to do what he wants done, and self-restraint enough to keep from meddling with them while they do it.

Theodore Roosevelt (1858–1919), 26th president of the USA

Key topics

- The formal organization: job roles
- The formal organization: organizational charts
- Delegation and span of control
- Delayering
- Levels of hierarchy
- Chain of command

Higher Level extension

- Delegation and accountability
- Bureaucracy
- Centralization and decentralization
- Matrix Structure / Project teams
- Flexible organizational structures: theories of Mintzberg and Peters
- Role and importance of the informal organization
- Outsourcing, offshoring and the migration of human resources

INTRODUCTION

This Unit looks at the various ways that businesses organize their human resources. In a small business, such as a sole proprietorship, there may be an informal organizational structure; the owner or boss has a range of job roles including being a marketing, operations and finance director. They also carry out more mundane tasks such as being a sales person and a stock controller. The sole trader changes roles depending on the demands of the job at a particular point in time.

However, in most businesses there is a need for a more formal and organized structure. This can help a business to function more efficiently as it can determine:

- **accountability** – shows who is held responsible (or answerable) for what job, such as the marketing staff being held accountable to the marketing director for their performance
- **responsibility** – shows who is in charge of whom, such as the Operations Manager being in charge of all production workers.

Figure 2.2a shows a typical structure for a secondary (high) school. The Head Teacher is at the top of the organizational structure and is ultimately responsible for all the staff in the school. Managers are responsible for their own teams, such as the Head of Modern Foreign Languages who is in charge of the language teachers. S/he is accountable to the Deputy Headteacher in charge of the school curriculum. Likewise, the Head of PSE (Personal and Social Education) is accountable to the Heads of Year and responsible for working with the form tutors.

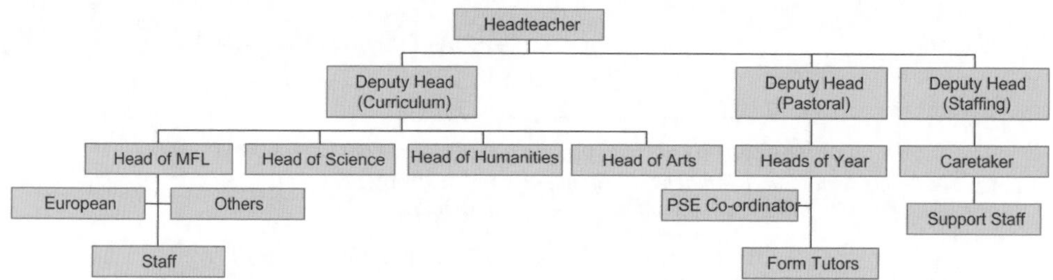

Figure 2.2a Example of an organizational chart for a secondary school

THE FORMAL ORGANIZATION: JOB ROLES

As a business becomes larger and more complex, the organization has to become more structured in order for tasks and roles to be fulfilled in a manageable and coherent way. A formal organizational structure can help an employee or manager to address the following queries in a easy and quick manner:

- The overall structure of the business, such as its size, levels of hierarchy and functional areas (specialist areas)
- Who their supervisor or line manager is so that there is some form of accountability
- Which people have authority and the extent of the responsibility they have for others
- Determine how different areas of the business link to one another
- Verify their own position in the overall organization
- Identify the various channels of communication in an organization.

Although businesses differ in their design of a formal structure, the typical configuration consists of different levels of directors, management and workers (as shown in Figure 2.2b).

Figure 2.2b Human resources in an organization

The CEO / Chairperson

At the top of an organization is the chief executive officer (CEO), also known as the managing director (MD). The CEO represents the head of the Board of Directors (BOD). The CEO may appoint a chairperson who chairs the BOD meetings. Although it is quite common for a CEO to also be the chairperson, this is not a necessary requirement. The CEO and Board of Directors are ultimately responsible for running the business and are accountable to the shareholders of the company. Shareholders collectively approve the appointment of the Board of Directors at the Annual General Meeting of the organization.

The main roles of the Managing Director or CEO are to:

- Act as a figurehead or ambassador for the organization
- Lead the team of directors
- Represent the desires, ideas and beliefs of the BOD
- Formulate organizational objectives and policies with the BOD
- Communicate with the directors regarding any problems, concerns and decisions that they need to be aware of
- Devise and implement corporate strategy.

The Board of Directors (BOD)

The directors (sometimes called executives) are responsible for the overall running of the business. In a large firm, there is likely to be a director responsible for each key functional area of the business, e.g. Marketing Director, Finance Director, Human Resources Director and Operations Director. There are two main types of directors:

- **Executive directors** work full-time at the organization and make decisions about the daily running of the business.
- **Non-executive directors** do not work full-time at the organization but are consultants used for their particular area of expertise. They advise the Board of Directors on corporate strategy.

Duties of the board of directors are broad and varied, but will typically include:

- Target setting
- Devising long-term plans
- Establishing organizational policies and codes of practice
- Monitoring and controlling of the organization's activities

- Overseeing staffing issues, such as the recruitment, promotion, performance management and dismissal of workers
- Advising and supporting the managing director.

Management

Management tend to be responsible for a team of people and/or certain tasks. Managers are decision-makers who are responsible for the day-to-day implementation of the organization's policy. They assist and are accountable to the Board of Directors. It is the duty of a manager to take on tasks and responsibilities as delegated to them by the directors. For example, Heads of Department are in charge of a team that work in one section of the organization. The functions of managers are covered in Unit 2.4.

Supervisors and team leaders

Supervisors and team leaders are junior managers so will carry out some, but not all, of the duties of a middle or senior manager. They are more likely to be involved in making operational decisions (those based on daily routine) for the organization. They will have direct contact with the workforce, for whom they are responsible.

Other employees (Operatives)

There will be a host of other employees that exist in a large organization. They form the majority of an organization's workforce. Consider the example of a school. Typically, the employees near or at the bottom of its organizational structure may include:

- The majority of teaching staff, i.e. those who are not in a management position
- Office staff, e.g. secretary and administration staff
- Technicians
- Caterers for the canteen
- Caretaker, cleaners and janitors
- Security staff.

Some of these staff, for example the teachers, will have greater levels of skill and responsibilities. Nevertheless, operatives tend to:

- Work to achieve the targets set by their team leader or department manager
- Work as a member of a team or department
- Make routine decisions concerning their job role only
- Provide support and assistance to other people in the organization.

THE FORMAL ORGANIZATION: ORGANIZATIONAL CHARTS

An **organizational chart** is a diagrammatic representation of a firm's formal organizational structure, such as that in Figure 2.2c. Formal groups are set up by the business to carry out specific functions, such as a department of finance specialists or a team of marketers. Most formal groups are permanent although businesses can set up temporary groups to investigate a particular issue or problem. An organizational chart shows four important features of a business:

1. The different *functional departments* within a business. Figure 2.2c shows that there are four different functional departments – Marketing, Production, Finance and Human Resources. Each of these areas is headed by a Director.
2. The *chain of command*. This shows the various positions of authority in the organization. In particular, it shows which people have direct (vertical) line authority over others. For example, the Production Director has line authority over all employees in the Production

Department, i.e. the Operations Manager, the Security Director, the Quality Controller, Production operatives and the Security staff.

3 The *span of control*. This measures the number of staff that are directly accountable to a single (horizontal) line manager. For example, the CEO has a span of control of four people (the Directors). Each Director has a span of control of one (their deputy manager) except the Production Director who has a span of control of two (the Security Director and the Operations Manager).

4 The official *channels of communication*. This refers to the route that messages are communicated within the organization. For example, communications that concern only the security team would go through the CEO, Production Director, Security Director and the security staff. There is no need to communicate this message to other departmental managers or workers.

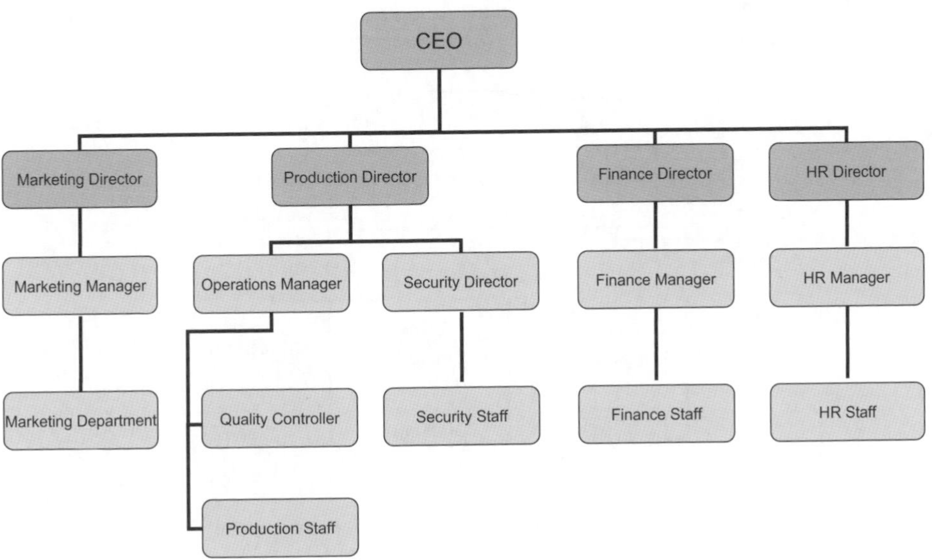

Figure 2.2c Example of an organizational chart

In addition, the organizational chart in Figure 2.2c also shows that there are five levels in the organizational hierarchy. The CEO is at the top level whereas production operatives are on the bottom (fifth) level. The horizontal levels in an organizational chart give an indication of an employee's rank within the firm (although this varies from one organization to the next).

Organizations are traditionally structured according to their functions, as in the above example. However, other possibilities include:

- **Organization by product**. Large businesses will usually have a broad range of products that cater for various types of customers. Hence, they may choose to structure themselves according to the various types of product. Ford uses this structure for its various strategic business units such as Mazda and Volvo. However, within each strategic business unit, the business is still likely to be organized by functional departments.
- **Organization by process**. This is an adaptation of organization by function whereby the structure is based on the different processes carried out in the business. It is suitable where there are clearly different stages in the production process (see Unit 5.1) of a product. For example, a publishing firm might be organized into departments based on their part in the production process as follows: the Editorial Department (who also sort out page design and

layout), the Print Department, the Sales and Marketing Department and the Dispatch Department.

- **Organization by geography.** Multinational corporations often choose to organize themselves by geographical region or area. This method allows the business to be more aware and responsive to local cultural differences and consumer needs. In addition, such structures allow empowered regional managers to have better overall control over staffing and training.

Figure 2.2d shows organization by functional, geographical and product departmentalization.

- *Functional* – There are three Vice Presidents of the organization, one in charge of each functional area (Marketing, Production and Finance).
- *Geography* – Plant managers are located in Taiwan, Singapore and Vietnam. They are accountable to the Vice President in charge of Production. A similar structure would exist in these locations for the Marketing and Finance Departments.
- *Product* – Each functional area of the organization is based on either consumer products or industrial products.

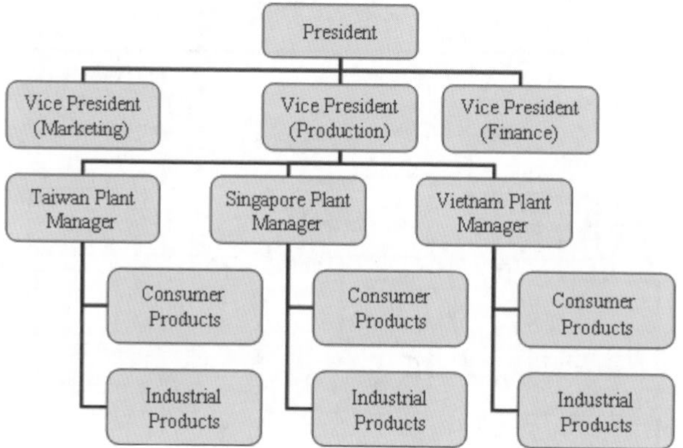

Figure 2.2d Multiforms of organizational structure

Question 2.2.1

a Describe what is meant by 'span of control' and 'levels of hierarchy'. *[4 marks]*

b With reference to Figure 2.2d, identify who the plant managers are accountable to and responsible for. *[2 marks]*

c Explain how an organizational chart might be used in a firm's induction programme. *[4 marks]*

DELEGATION AND SPAN OF CONTROL

Delegation

As a business grows, managers will need to relinquish some of their roles and responsibilities because they will not be able to effectively control all aspects of the business. This passing on of control and authority to others is known as **delegation**. It involves the line manager entrusting and empowering their staff to complete a task or project but holding them *accountable* for their actions. The *responsibility* still remains with the line manager although the actual work is done by the authorized person.

Many people argue that the art of effective delegation is one of the most important skills of managers. They cannot and should not, given time and other constraints, deal with every single matter themselves. Effective delegation has major benefits for both managers and employees:

- The manager saves time by not having to tackle every single task, so can focus more on the strategic issues facing the organization.
- Delegation can motivate and develop employees who feel that they are trusted and that their talents have been recognized.

On the other hand, poor delegation can lead to confusion and a feeling of inadequacy. This will lead to demotivated staff, resulting in a failure to achieve the task set. Managers often use the SMARTER acronym as a quick checklist for ensuring that delegation is properly assigned. The tool is adapted from Peter Drucker's SMART Objectives (see Unit 1.3). For it to be effective, delegated tasks must be:

- ***S*pecific** – Tasks must be clearly defined so that subordinates can carry them out.
- **Measurable** – Results must be quantifiable in order to assess the extent to which subordinates have achieved the delegated task.
- **Agreed** – Both managers and subordinates must agree to the delegated task in order to avoid any potential conflict. They should also agree on the amount of power and freedom that goes with the assigned work.
- **Realistic** – Delegated tasks must be reasonably achievable, otherwise workers will not be dedicated to completing them. This will depend on the subordinate's own ability to accomplish the delegated work and formal empowerment of the worker to carry out the task.
- **Time-bound** – A time frame must be set so that tasks are completed in an orderly manner.
- **Ethical** – Tasks must be delegated fairly to prevent dissatisfaction and resentment. Delegating only dull and unchallenging tasks will only serve to demoralise and demotivate staff.
- **Recorded** – Tasks should be documented in order to provide guidance and to aid recognition of them being accomplished. In this way, staff can be credited for their achievements.

Note that it is not necessary to financially reward people when tasks are delegated to them. Delegation is a form of empowerment and can in itself act as a non-financial motivator (see Unit 2.5).

Span of control

Span of control refers to the number of subordinates that are controlled by a manager, i.e. the number of people who are directly accountable to a manager. Hence, the higher up a person is in a hierarchy, the wider their span of control tends to be. Although the CEO of a company is directly responsible for the Board of Directors, he or she is also indirectly in charge of all workers in the organization. Hence, the CEO's direct span of control is narrow, but the indirect span of control is very wide.

A *wide span of control* occurs when a manager has many people under his/her control (see Figure 2.2e). One advantage of such an arrangement is that fewer layers in the hierarchy of the organization are needed. This will mean that costs are kept under control as there are less managerial positions in the firm. In addition, the flatter organizational structure will mean that communications between different levels of the hierarchy should be more effective (in terms of speed and accuracy).

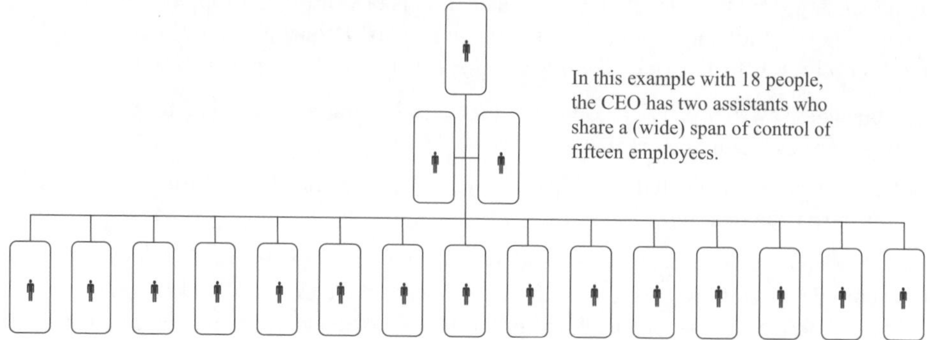

Figure 2.2e Wide span of control

By contrast, a *narrow span of control* means that there are fewer subordinates who are accountable to a manager (see Figure 2.2f). The advantages of having a narrower span of control are that it is easier to communicate with and control the team of subordinates. Smaller teams may also be more productive since there is likely to be more team spirit and cohesiveness. Larger teams tend to suffer from communication problems which may cause tension and conflict. However, due to more levels of management in the structure, this system tends to be more costly.

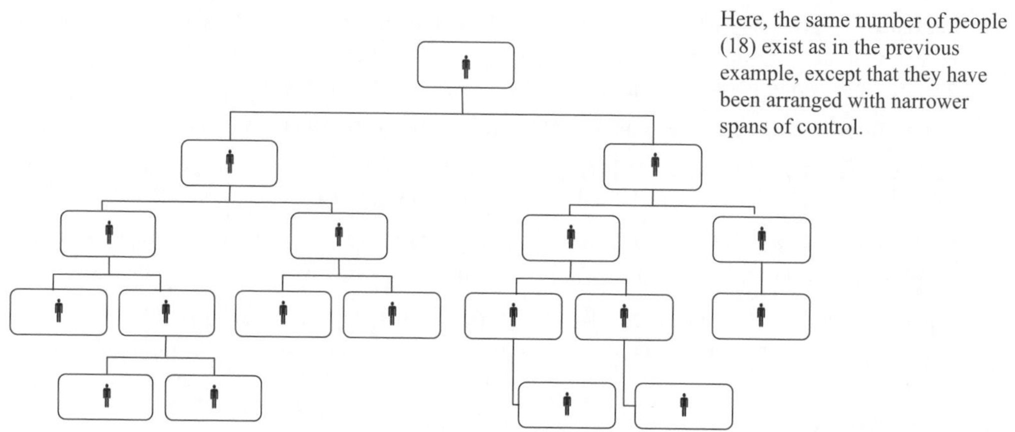

Figure 2.2f Narrow span of control

There is an inverse relationship between the span of control and the number of layers within an organization. Organizations with narrow spans of control result in tall hierarchical structures whereas ones with wider spans of control create flatter structures with fewer layers in the organization.

Advantages of wider spans of control (flatter structures) include:

- Delegation becomes a relatively important part of managing the organization. Hence, there are opportunities for subordinates to take on extra responsibilities and to develop their professional careers.
- Communication should be improved overall since there are fewer layers in the hierarchy.
- It is cheaper to operate a wider span of control because there are fewer levels of management. Many of these managerial functions are either eliminated or delegated. By contrast, taller structures will require far more managers to be employed.
- There is a smaller psychological distance between those at the top and those at the bottom of the organization. This can help to eliminate a 'them and us' culture where workers feel alienated from senior management.

Advantages of narrower spans of control (taller structures) include:

- There is quicker communication between smaller teams. Feedback from subordinates should also be more effective. There are clearer lines of communication between the different layers of management. By contrast, a wide span of control means the manager can communicate with many more people.
- Smaller teams are also easier to control and manage.
- Greater specialization and division of labour can help to increase efficiency and productivity. Managers therefore do not have to spend so much time on monitoring their (relatively small) teams.
- There are greater opportunities for more people to earn promotion since more levels exist in the hierarchy. This can help to motivate employees to work harder.

So what is the ideal span of control for an organization? Managers have been asking this question for decades. The question stems from the works of management theorist Henri Fayol (1841–1922). It was V.A. Graicunas (1898–1947), a Lithuanian management consultant, who first used empirical evidence to address the question of the optimal span of control. Graicunas suggested that the maximum number of subordinates should be four (in most cases) or five. He argued that the span of control should be limited because “one of the surest sources of delay and confusion is to allow any superior to be directly responsible for the control of too many subordinates”.

However, as the business environment continues to evolve, many businesses have opted for wider spans of control. There is no consensus on the optimal span of control. In essence, the decision is judgemental. The degree of control granted to a manager will depend on several factors, which collectively should help to determine the optimal span of control for an organization. These factors include:

- Experience, competence and traits of the manager – Clearly, the more skilled and experienced the manager, the higher the chances are that they will have a wider span of control. By contrast, junior managers will only have a narrow span of control.
- The nature of management styles – Narrower spans of control may be required where management feel a need to tightly control their subordinates. By contrast, democratic managers (see Unit 2.4) tend to delegate and empower their subordinates, thereby reducing the need for a narrow span of control. Such managers prefer the term ‘span of support’ to span of control.
- The skills and dynamics of subordinates – Highly skilled workers are more likely to work in smaller teams with their line manager having a relatively narrower span of control, especially when dealing with key decision-making. However, small teams may also operate when unskilled and/or lazy workers exist in the workplace and need to be monitored to prevent them from slacking off. Highly skilled staff may also operate independently for much of their work, in which case the span of control can then be quite wide.
- The nature of the work – Complex and important tasks will tend to require a narrower span of control. Communication will be more important so it is probably more effective to have smaller teams where both accountability and responsibility can be clearly identified. By contrast, products that can be mass-produced easily or tasks that require highly skilled people mean that less supervision is needed. Hence, the span of control can be widened in such cases.
- The type of production system used – For example, in *flow production* (see Unit 5.1), a manager’s span of control can be very wide since workers have relatively simple tasks that can be completed with minimal supervision.

Question 2.2.2

a Construct two organizational charts based on the following information:

i A partnership with two partners, each with a 50% stake in the business, who have direct control over five employees.

ii A private company with three people on the board of directors, three department managers, each with a team of three people. *[7 marks]*

Use your organizational charts from Question **2a** to answer the remaining questions.

b Contrast the two charts by referring to the span of control and the chain of command. *[4 marks]*

c Explain two consequences to a business that chooses to adopt a wider span of control. *[4 marks]*

LEVELS OF HIERARCHY

The hierarchy in a business refers to the organizational structure based on a ranking system. Those at the top of the hierarchy include the CEO, chairperson and the board of directors. At the other extreme, the most unskilled employees in the organization appear at the bottom of the hierarchy. Levels in an organizational hierarchy are best shown in an organizational chart. Each level in the hierarchy refers to a different rank with its associated degree of authority and responsibility. Figure 2.2g shows an organization with five levels in its hierarchical structure.

The person directly above an employee on the next hierarchical level is known as the **line manager**. For example, in Figure 2.2g, those on level 5 of the chart report directly to their line manager on level 4. A line manager is responsible for the day to day management of the people (known as *subordinates*) who are directly on the next level down the hierarchy.

There are two main advantages of using hierarchical structures. First, they show clear lines of communication within the organization. This can then improve coordination and productivity of the workforce. Second, hierarchical structures establish departments or teams. This can create a sense of belonging in the workplace and act as a form of motivation (see Unit 2.5).

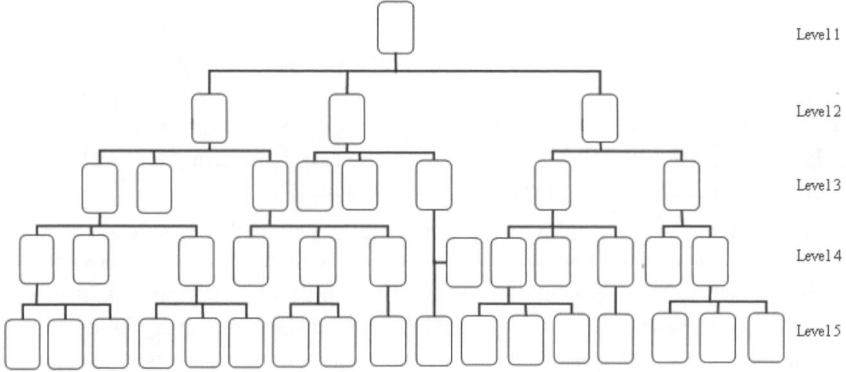

Figure 2.2g Hierarchical structures

However, hierarchical structures also have their limitations. Departmentalization can lead to workers being isolated to their official teams (see below for benefits of informal structures). In addition, hierarchical structures tend to be rather inflexible. This might prove problematic when there are changes in the external business environment that require structural changes in the organization.

Flat and tall organizations

Hierarchical structures can be described as being either flat or tall. Tall structures have many layers in the organizational hierarchy. Therefore, it is likely that each manager will tend to have a narrower span of control. By contrast, in flat structures there are fewer levels in the hierarchy (see Figure 2.2h). Thus, each manager will tend to have a wider span of control.

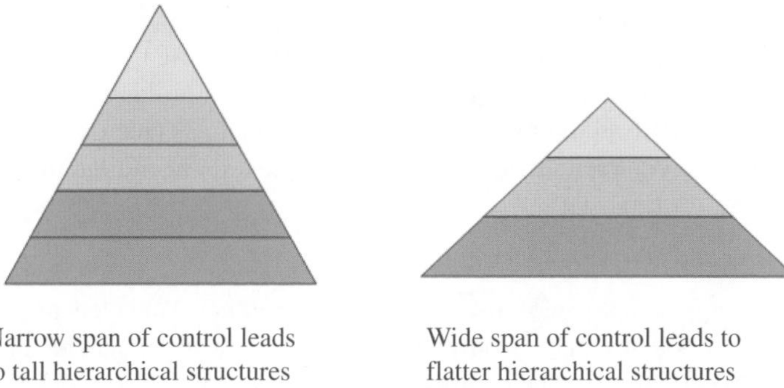

Figure 2.2h The inverse relationship between span of control and hierarchical structures

Question 2.2.3

Departments or Faculties?

Many secondary (high) schools are organized by functional departments. For example, Humanities subjects such as Economics, Business & Management, Geography, History, Religious Education and Psychology may be organized as completely separate departments. The organizational structure for schools that departmentalize the above subjects is shown below. However, in other schools, these subjects are grouped together as a Faculty whereby the individual subjects are coordinated by Head of Subjects who are held accountable to the Head of Faculty.

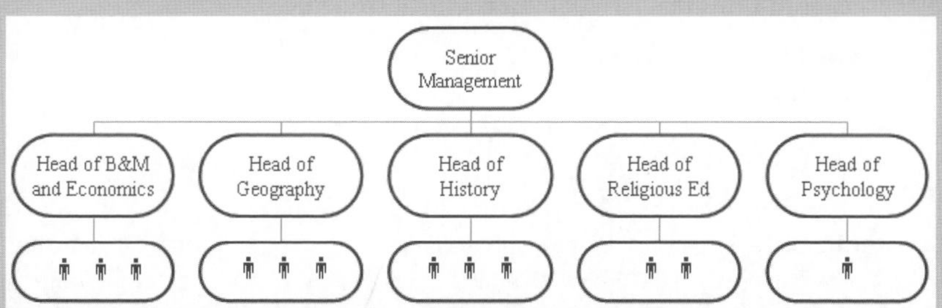

a Explain how the above organization chart would be affected if the separate departments were to be managed and led by a Head of Faculty. *[3 marks]*

b Discuss whether it is better for schools to be organized as departments or as faculties. *[7 marks]*

Delayering

Many large businesses have opted to delayer their organizations. Delayering is the process of removing one or more levels in the hierarchy in order to flatten out the organizational structure. This will therefore reduce the number of layers of management and widen the span of control.

There are three main purposes to delayering:

- Reduce costs by removing levels of management
- Improve the speed of communication flows by having flatter hierarchical structures
- Encourage delegation since wider spans of control should provide opportunities for employees to take on more responsibilities.

Delayering is often associated with **downsizing**. This happens when the size of the core workforce is reduced. This can further reduce a firm's costs because there are fewer core staff who are remunerated on full benefits (such as statutory sick pay, holiday pay and contributory pensions). Downsizing can lead to more flexible working practices (see Unit 2.1) as businesses hire more peripheral and contractual workers. These people are not entitled to the same remuneration as core full-time staff.

However, delayering and downsizing have their drawbacks:

- They create anxiety and a sense of insecurity among workers. Managers and workers will be worried about their position in the restructured firm. Some workers will be made redundant as the firm downsizes. Others will be demoted if the firm delayers. These issues will therefore affect the level of employee motivation and productivity.
- Delayering can overstretch employees as their workload increases. This can have a counter-productive effect on the quality of work and/or the employee's ability to meet deadlines.
- Flexible working practices will require workers to regularly upgrade their skills and hence there are cost implications to consider.
- Decision-making may take longer since managers are dealing with larger teams. By contrast, tall hierarchical structures mean that managers with a narrower span of control enjoy speedier communication and decision-making within their teams.

Chain of command

The chain of command refers to the formal line of authority through which orders are passed down in an organization. It can be seen through a firm's organizational chart. Businesses that have flat hierarchical structures have a short chain of command. By contrast, communication is passed through many stages in firms that have tall hierarchical structures.

Question 2.2.4

Restructuring at Havant College

In May 2007, over 50 teachers at a Sixth Form College in Hampshire, UK went on strike over staff restructuring plans set out by management. The College argued that restructuring at Havant College was necessary to cut costs and to generate funds to invest in equipment and staff training. The restructured organization would generate minimal redundancies and some **middle managers** would be demoted to classroom teachers in order to cut staffing costs. Teachers were angry as the restructuring meant that some teachers would get a pay cut of up to £7,000 ($14,000) per year.

a Describe what is meant by **middle managers** in the context of Havant College. *[2 marks]*

b With reference to relevant Business and Management theory, to what extent do you think the decision to restructure the College was a good decision? *[8 marks]*

HIGHER LEVEL EXTENSION: DELEGATION AND ACCOUNTABILITY

Recall that **delegation** refers to the process of passing on authority and responsibility from a line manager to a subordinate. As an organization grows, it is inevitable that managers must relinquish some of their authority and control by empowering and entrusting employees to carry out the delegated tasks. However, the line manager still retains overall responsibility for the tasks. In other words, whilst authority can be delegated to someone else, responsibility ultimately remains with the line manager.

Accountability is the term used to describe the extent to which a person is held responsible for the success or failure of a task. Having a clear organizational structure allows workers to see who is held accountable for which functions and which teams. Accountability allows senior managers to have better control over the running of their organizations. Those who achieve or exceed their targets are recognized for their accomplishments. However, those who fail to meet deadlines or targets can be clearly identified and held accountable for their mistakes. For example, in Question 2.2.4 on page 214, the Heads of Department are held accountable for the examination results in their department. These middle managers may delegate tasks to their team of teachers, but the Heads of Department still hold overall responsibility for the degree of success of their teams.

Note: Higher Level candidates must be able to explain the effects of organizational structures on employee motivation, communication and performance. (© IBO 2007)

HIGHER LEVEL EXTENSION: BUREAUCRACY

Bureaucracy refers to the execution of tasks that are governed by official administrative and formal rules of an organization. Bureaucratic organizations are characterized by prescribed rules and responsibilities, standardized procedures, and formal hierarchical structures. Bureaucracy is often associated with the concept of **red tape** (excessive administration, paperwork and formalities in the workplace). For example, within an organization this might include:

- Frequent requirement to fill out unnecessary paperwork
- Staff working in several departments and therefore reporting to more than one manager
- Too many 'working parties' being set up to investigate issues of concern to the organization
- Long official chains of command
- Management with duplicate roles and responsibilities.

Karl Marx (1818–1883), a philosopher and political economist, argued that bureaucracy has a cost to organizations and society. However, as a socialist, he believed that the cost could be justified if bureaucracy is enforced properly in order to bring about social order. Max Weber (1864–1920), a German economist and socialist, built on the work of Marx. Like Marx, he believed that bureaucracy was the ideal organizational form. He argued that bureaucracy can be synonymous with efficiency because it is simply division of labour being applied to the administrative tasks within an organization. This is one reason why many private sector firms have dedicated administrative departments. He suggested that a bureaucratic organization is governed by several principles, which include:

- Continuity – Tasks and activities are conducted on a continuous basis. This means that the establishment must follow official rules and regulations rather than taking high risks that could jeopardise its survival and continuity.
- Rules and regulations – Business activity is conducted in accordance with the official policies of the organization, such as clear lines of authority, responsibility and accountability.

HIGHER LEVEL

HIGHER LEVEL

- Hierarchical structures – Authority and responsibilities form part of a formal hierarchical structure with line managers carrying out their tasks in an impersonal way.
- Accountability – Business activity is conducted in a formal way with written documentation being used as evidence of compliance with the organization's policies. Formality therefore makes every worker accountable for his/her performance.

However, there are drawbacks with bureaucracy. The core problem with bureaucracy can be summarized by Parkinson's Law (1955) which states that "Work expands so as to fill the time available for its completion". Today, most experts feel that red tape and bureaucracy hinder and/or prevent creativity, risk taking and decision-making. They argue that, at best, bureaucracy and red tape simply slow down decision-making. Bureaucratic organizations tend to be highly inflexible since decision-making becomes slow and perhaps overly cautious.

HIGHER LEVEL EXTENSION: CENTRALIZATION AND DECENTRALIZATION

Decision-making power can be either kept in the hands of a few people or it may be spread out among the workforce. The extent to which authority is concentrated or diluted within an organization will depend on the characteristics and skills of managers and workers, such as the degree of trust and the corporate culture.

Centralized structures

In a centralized structure, the vast majority of decision-making is performed by a very small number of people. These decision-makers, usually the senior management team, simply hold onto decision-making authority and responsibility. As shown in Figure 2.2i, decisions are made through the person(s) in the centre, without any form of communication between other members of the organization. This model was favoured by management practitioners and theorists such as Henri Fayol, Frederick Taylor and Henry Ford.

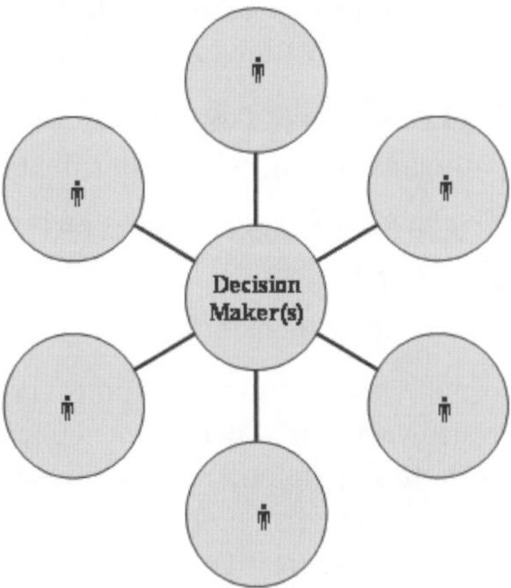

Figure 2.2i The centralized structure

The **advantages** of centralized structures include:

- Rapid decision-making – There is no need to consult employees on decisions and therefore quick decision-making can take place.
- Better control – Centralized structures allow managers to have a better overview and tighter control of what is happening in their organizations. This is particularly important in large organizations where communications can break down due to a lack of overall control and

authority. The centralized control also means that tasks are less likely to be repeated by different people or departments in the organization.

- Better sense of direction – Decisions are made by the senior management team, i.e. the people who are most qualified to lead the business in a certain direction. In addition, since there are fewer decision-makers, consistency in approach across the whole business is more likely to be achieved.

The **disadvantages** of centralized structures include:

- Possible delays in some decision-making – Since a centralized group make all the decisions, it is likely that many decisions will eventually be delayed. This is simply due to the sheer amount of decisions that they need to make.
- Increased pressure and stress for senior management – Decision-makers may face huge pressures by not being able to efficiently delegate tasks to middle managers (even senior managers have a limit to the workload that they can handle).
- Inflexibility – The organization becomes rather bureaucratic and inflexible since workers have very limited autonomy. Instead, employees lack the opportunity to be creative and simply follow the orders of the decision-makers. Hence, the skills and value of employees are not exploited.
- Demotivating – Employees may lack motivation since they feel less valued.

Decentralized structures

The alternative structure is to use decentralized decision-making, whereby some decision-making authority and responsibility is passed onto others in the organization (see Figure 2.2j). For example, departments or regional offices may be empowered to make decisions on behalf of the organization. However, key decision-making power is still centralized, i.e. concentrated in the hands of the senior management team.

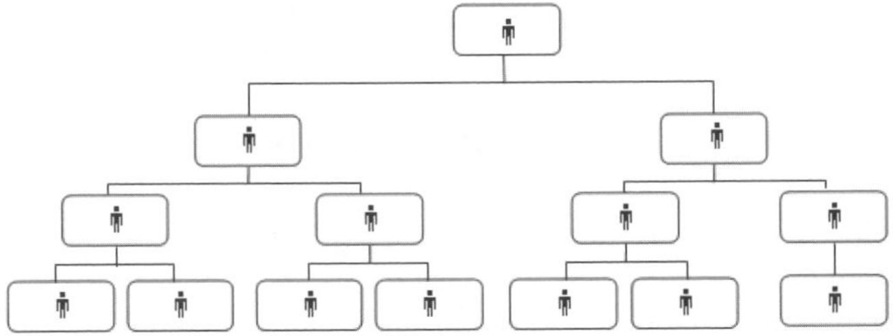

In this example, there are three levels of management that have decision-making authority and responsibility. Hence decision-making is more decentralized.

Figure 2.2j The decentralized structure

The **advantages** of decentralized structures include:

- Input from workforce – Firms can benefit from the development and exploitation of the skills of employees, especially their middle managers.
- Speedier day-to-day decision-making – Planning and execution become faster and more efficient since there is delegation of authority and responsibility.
- Higher morale – Empowered staff are more likely to feel motivated. Workers feel more valued since they have some input into decision-making. The autonomy also means that they can use their initiative and feel a sense of ownership for their work. Hence, their productivity is also likely to improve.
- Improved accountability – Staff are held directly accountable for their input and this can lead to improvements in the quality of their work.

- Encouragement of teamwork – A feature of decentralized structures is the presence of collaborative work across teams and departments. Hence, the sharing of ideas can generate innovative ideas as well as promoting harmonious relationships.

However, the **disadvantages** of decentralized structures include:

- Loss of control – By decentralizing decision-making, authority is diluted. This means that senior management have less direct control over the operations of the business.
- Greater chance of mistakes – Decentralizing authority and responsibility will only work if the empowered person is sufficiently competent. In addition, the more people who are involved in decision-making, the more likely it is that there will be conflicting opinions and this may lead to mistakes being made. With more decision-makers, it may become more difficult to track where mistakes were made or where things went wrong.
- Greater reliance on effective communication – By decentralizing decision-making power, there is a greater need for efficient communications. This may require additional time and resources, thereby adding to the costs of the business.
- Duplication of functions – In decentralized organizations, middle and junior managers may carry out duplicate functions as there is no overview of what everyone else is doing.

So the question is whether businesses ought to become more centralized or decentralized. The decision will depend on several factors:

- The size of the organization – The larger the firm becomes, the greater the need for decentralization. Multinational conglomerates for example cannot be efficiently operated by highly centralized structures.
- The scale of importance of the decision – Generally, decisions that have high cost implications and/or consequences will be centralized.
- The level of risk – High-risk decisions will again remain in the hands of the key decision-makers, i.e. remain centralized.
- The corporate culture – Organizations such as computer software companies that rely on the creative and innovative skills of employees will tend to be more decentralized. The culture of the organization will influence expectations about the degree to which senior management will delegate power and responsibility.
- Management attitudes and competencies – Managers that have a positive outlook towards worker attitudes and abilities are more likely to pass down authority and responsibility. By contrast, some managers are unwilling to let go of control or status and will therefore centralize decision-making authority.
- The use of information and communication technologies – Firms that adapt up to date methods of ICT are able to delegate to a greater extent. For example, firms that have a significant number of teleworkers (see Unit 2.1) empower their employees to work from home.

Question 2.2.5

Ferrari

Ferrari, the Italian sports car manufacturer, was founded in 1947 by Enzo Ferrari. The company prides itself on the outstanding build quality of its prestigious cars. Workers are exceptionally skilled and have a high degree of decision-making power. According to Ferrari, 88.5% of its 2,685 workers in Maranello (Italy) have attended training programmes to develop their managerial and professional skills. In 2007, Ferrari topped the rankings in the *Financial Times* annual '100 Best Workplaces in Europe' report. Over 1,000 European companies took part in the highly respected survey, so coming first was a major achievement for Ferrari. The rankings are mainly based on employee responses to questions regarding work practices, remuneration and organizational culture.

a Explain why skills training is important to a firm such as Ferrari. *[4 marks]*

b Analyse the factors that influence the amount of centralization and decentralization in a business such as Ferrari. *[6 marks]*

HIGHER LEVEL EXTENSION: MATRIX STRUCTURES / PROJECT TEAMS

The **matrix structure** refers to the flexible organization of employees from different departments within an organization temporarily working together on a particular project. Therefore, in a matrix structure, functional departments still exist except a team of workers (known as the **project team**) has the opportunity to work on projects with colleagues from other departments. Each project team is led by a *team leader* (or *project manager*). This means that each member in the matrix is held accountable to two managers – their departmental manager and the project manager.

For example, suppose that a project team was set up to look into the best way to launch the opening of a new store. The members of the project team might consist of one representative from each of the following sections of the company: board of directors, marketing, finance, human resources, production and security. One of these members may also be selected as the project manager. Figure 2.2k shows that the team members communicate using an all-channel network (see Unit 2.3) rather than the traditional channels of communication found in hierarchical structures.

Advantages of matrix structures include:

- A culture of teamworking and collaboration is created in the organization.
- Experts from different parts of the business can be brought together to work as a project team. This should enhance the chances of accomplishing the project successfully.
- Good career and personal development opportunities are provided for team members and the project manager.
- Projects can be spread out among various teams, thereby reducing the pressures on senior management.
- The ability to work on different projects adds interest and variety to the work and increases staff motivation.

Disadvantages of matrix structures include:

- Since team members have two line managers, there may be a conflict of interest, such as loyalty and prioritization of workloads. There is a limit to the amount that a person can do, so members of a project team may neglect their departmental roles (temporarily) in favour of dealing with the project that they have been assigned.
- There is also the potential that team members will not get on with one another. Since project teams are formed on a temporary basis, there is less of an obligation to make sure that team members get along with one another. This is especially the case if members of the project team come from departments with different cultural norms (the way that things are done in particular departments).
- Consequently, project managers may have a difficult task in controlling team members who have conflicting interests and priorities.

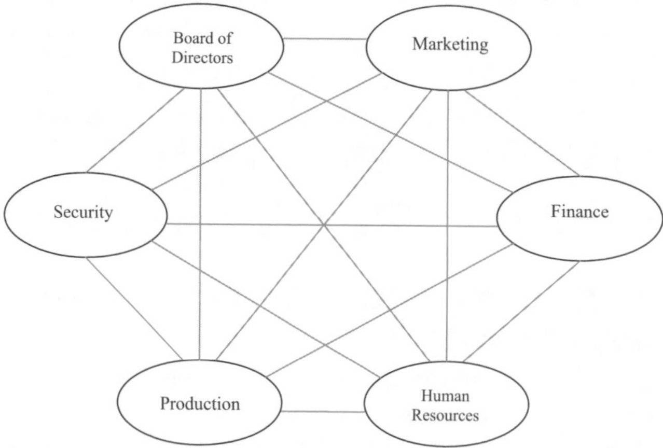

Figure 2.2k Matrix structure

Matrix structures tend to work best in organizations with a relatively flat hierarchical structure where there is a wide span of control. Staff also work better in project teams if there is no need for the team leader to micro-manage, i.e. the team members are highly skilled and experienced. Hence, in matrix structures, it is the capability of team members that is important, rather than their formal rank in the formal organizational structure.

HIGHER LEVEL EXTENSION: FLEXIBLE STRUCTURES

Organizational structures are important to a business since they determine how decisions are made and how things are done in the workplace. Traditional hierarchical structures may be unsuitable for today's business environment since they have too many layers of management and are too rigid to react to sudden changes in the economy. By contrast, a flexible organizational structure should enable a business to adapt when there is a need to respond to rapid change. This should then allow the business to be more successful.

Another feature of a flexible organization is the development of a **multiskilled** workforce. This involves training workers to carry out more than one function so that they can be switched to another operation as and when needed. For example, staff in the bakery and delicatessen departments of a large supermarket might be trained to operate tills at the checkout. They can then be redeployed as cashiers during peak periods at the checkouts or substitute a cashier who may be absent from work for reasons such as sickness.

Re-engineering is a radical form of organizational flexibility. It involves the redesign of organizational structures due to the driving forces of customers, competitors and change. Organizational structures are redesigned from scratch, rather than making incremental changes from its current structure, to better suit the changing needs of the business. For example, financial services company American Express claims to have reduced its annual costs by $1 billion by re-engineering. However, due to the drastic and disruptive nature of change caused by re-engineering, most large firms would not tend to adopt it.

Two key contributors to the development of flexible organizational structures are Henry Mintzberg and Tom Peters.

Henry Mintzberg

Henry Mintzberg suggested that the internal structure of an organization depends on both the complexity and the pace of change. Mintzberg argued that a business can only remain successful if its organizational structure is flexible enough to deal with rapid changes in the market. He suggested that organizational structures can consist of up to six basic parts (see Figure 2.21).

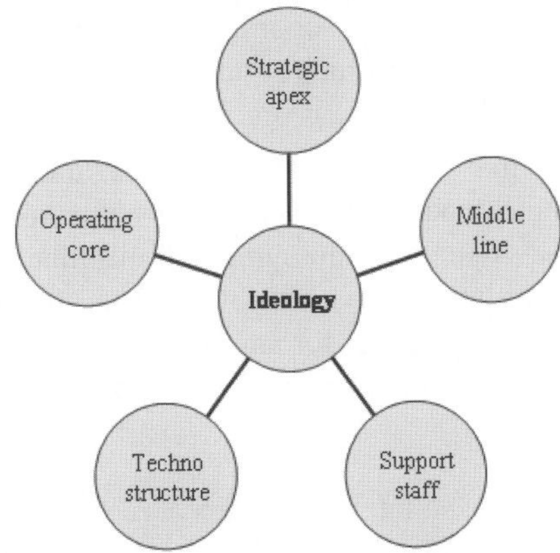

Figure 2.21 Mintzberg's framework of organizational structures

1. *Ideology* refers to the culture (beliefs, values and traditions) of the organization.
2. *Strategic apex* refers to the senior management team, i.e. the key decision-makers.
3. *Middle line* refers to the team of middle management in an organization.
4. *Operating core* refers to the operational processes within the organization.
5. *Techno structure* refers to the technical support team and systems.
6. *Support staff* refers to the team of auxiliary staff support outside of operational processes and technical support, such as clerical staff and those working in public relations.

From the above assumption, Mintzberg came up with six organizational configurations. He suggested that all of these may be present within an organization, although one structure is likely to dominate.

1. *Innovative organizations or adhocracy.* This system requires people being split into small project teams (called 'silos') that deal with a specific task or problem, such as an advertising agency. There is decentralized decision-making. There are no standardized procedures for dealing with routine problems. As these teams work on individual and independent projects, the organization becomes very flexible and adaptive to change.
2. *Entrepreneurial organizations.* Decision-making power in such organizations is retained by the strategic apex. There is direct supervision of staff and decision-making is centralized, meaning that flatter hierarchical structures exist. Mintzberg argued that centralized decision-making means that the strategic apex is flexible and quick in responding and adapting to organizational change.

HIGHER LEVEL

3 *Machine organizations.* Coordination is done by specifying the work processes of people, such as those in the operating core or technostructure. Work is based on what Mintzberg called 'machine bureaucracy', i.e. specialization and standardization. Procedures are formalized so communication is clear and reliable. However, the fixed processes and procedures means the organization is inflexible which may be problematic if market conditions unexpectedly change.

4 *Divisionalized organizations.* Coordination is through the middle line who ensure that their teams achieve standardization of output. Since there is standardization, such structures are inflexible in responding to rapid change. However, Mintzberg suggested that effective decentralization and delegation of decision-making power to divisions can lead to a high level of flexibility.

5 *Professional organizations.* In this structure, professionals with standardized skills tend to make up most of the operating core. They rely on their prior knowledge and learnt skills. However, professional bureaucracy is inflexible since this system uses highly specialized staff (such as brain surgeons or astronauts) who are not adaptable to other roles.

6 *Missionary organizations.* This refers to coordination through the standardization of organizational norms (the ideology). In such structures, every individual works on the same set of beliefs and norms rather like religious organizations.

Mintzberg's research suggested that there are different organizational configurations to suit different businesses. For example, machine bureaucracy is better suited to capital-intensive organizations that rely very heavily on the employment of machinery. He argued that adhocracy and entrepreneurial organizations are the most flexible, and are therefore the most suited to embracing change. Mintzberg suggested that for any structure to work effectively, employees must believe in the organization's common values (ideology).

Tom Peters

American management guru and consultant Tom Peters argues that flatter organizational structures are more successful since there are better channels of communication, greater opportunities for delegation and empowerment, and greater flexibility in adapting to change. He believes that flexible and flatter organizations promote innovation and commitment from the workforce. His research on 43 highly successful companies, reported in his book *In Search of Excellence* (1982), recognized that a motivated workforce is one of the key factors in determining the performance of an organization. Two key features of these successful companies also surfaced, which contributed to the development of flexible structures:

- The *removal of bureaucracy* would eliminate constraints on the organization caused by unnecessary or excessive company rules and regulations. Removal of bureaucracy would, by definition, also make the organization more flexible.
- The *use of project teams* (matrix structures) should lead to more innovative and creative ideas being generated.

Peters is a strong believer in people being an organization's core asset. Placing them under strict internal rules and regulations only serves to constrain and demotivate staff. He argued that workers are the ones who have daily contact with customers, and hence it is the employees who are best suited to learn from the customer. Therefore, Peters recommended that managers should adopt flatter and more flexible structures so that organizations are better positioned to respond to the changing needs of customers.

HIGHER LEVEL EXTENSION: THE INFORMAL ORGANIZATION

The formal organization of staff is shown in an organizational chart. However, relationships also exist beyond the formal groups that are established by a business. **Informal groups** within a business consist of people who have become friends and/or share similar interests. This is rather similar to schools where students are placed in form groups (formal organization) but arrange friendship groups of their own with people who are not in their tutor group (informal organization).

David Krackhardt and Jeffrey Hanson (1993) found three types of informal organizational networks that can exist in the workplace:

- *Advice networks* – people sought after for their ability to provide guidance and to help solve problems
- *Trust networks* – people who can be relied upon for their loyalty, dependability and trustworthiness
- *Communication networks* – people who talk to each other on a normal basis as friends.

These relationships exist between staff across different departments, functional areas and ranks. It has been suggested that businesses ought to acknowledge and support the use of informal organizations for several reasons:

- Motivation – Informal organizations can help to promote a sense of belonging in the workplace. This can have positive effects on the level of motivation in the organization (see Unit 2.5).
- Facilitates communication – Informal groups are a good source of spreading and receiving messages.
- Assists decision-making – Quite often, informal groups are the ones who come up with the most innovative and original solutions for a problem. Knowledge is unevenly spread out in an organization and the use of informal networks can help to identify and exploit different sources of knowledge.

HIGHER LEVEL EXTENSION: OUTSOURCING, OFFSHORING AND THE MIGRATION OF HUMAN RESOURCES

Outsourcing and offshoring are modern and rather radical methods of changing the organizational structure of a firm.

Outsourcing refers to the act of moving non-core activities away from internal operations by finding an external party to carry out such functions. The purpose is to reduce costs by using specialist parties that can carry out the function more efficiently and cost effectively. Typical operations that are outsourced include: office cleaning, accounting, real estate management, call centres, customer support and ICT maintenance. The business can then focus on developing its core competencies.

However, there are four main limitations or concerns regarding outsourcing:

- Outsourcing requires effective two-way communication and careful coordination.
- There must be mutual trust between the outsourcer and the other parties (its clients). Any conflict can be potentially damaging to the functioning of the business.
- The quality of the outsourced service is passed onto an external agent. Hence, there may be concerns regarding whether the expected standards will be met.
- It can cause uncertainty among the workforce due to restructuring and the likelihood of staff redundancies.

Offshoring is an extension of outsourcing that involves relocating business functions and processes overseas. The two categories of offshoring are *production offshoring* (such as manufacturing) or *services offshoring* (such as call centres). These often take place in less economically developed countries where labour costs are low. Offshoring has brought about many benefits for host countries, such as job creation and relatively higher wages (which should lead to higher standards of living in these poorer countries). Recently, China and Vietnam have proved to be popular locations for production offshoring whilst India has emerged as a magnet for services offshoring.

Question 2.2.6

Offshoring in India

Indian software firms have benefited from the influx of European and American companies that have been **offshoring** their operations in order to cut costs. For instance, Bangalore-based Wipro offers services in ICT, software development and call centre services to foreign customers such as Cisco Systems and Nortel. Foreign companies are attracted by the relatively low wage costs and the plentiful skilled labour in India. British and American companies are also lured by India's large English-speaking workforce.

a Define the meaning of **offshoring**. *[2 marks]*

b Evaluate the reasons for and against businesses choosing to offshore some of their functions to external organizations located overseas. *[8 marks]*

Migration refers to the international movement of labour. A recent BBC report revealed that over half a million Eastern European migrant workers resided in the UK following the enlargement of the European Union (see Unit 1.9). The influx of workers from overseas can provide many opportunities for businesses. Some of the advantages include:

- Easing of skills shortages – Hiring skilled migrants has two advantages to a business. First, they take on the jobs that cannot be filled by domestic workers, perhaps due to a lack of willingness or skills (ability). Secondly, as a skills shortage is prevented, the pool of migrant workers helps to keep wage costs down.
- Flexible work structures – Unit 2.1 explained the trend in businesses being able to open for longer hours due to workforce flexibility. Migrants add to the supply of workers willing to work part-time or shift work. This is good news for businesses which have outlets that open 24-hours a day, such as 7-Eleven, McDonald's, bars and hotels.
- Marketing opportunities – Migrant workers are likely to have different habits and tastes from the mass population. This can provide niche marketing opportunities, such as the provision of cultural goods and services. Examples are as varied as Polish beer being sold in Britain, to Malaysian spicy noodles in Finland and Chinese cuisine in Denmark.
- Personnel opportunities – The supply of migrant workers allows a business to employ a more flexible and dynamic workforce. They may bring new ideas, experiences and ways of thinking. The result is that the firm is more likely to be able to adapt to changing market conditions. In addition, skilled migrants may pose a threat to less-skilled workers in the country. This form of competition can therefore raise the standard of skills in an economy as domestic workers update their skills in order to retain their own jobs.

- Net social benefits – The vast majority of migrants are of working age. This means that they are likely to pay income tax (good news for the government and the general public). It also means that they will have disposable income to spend on goods and services (good news for marketers).

Studies have consistently shown that migrant workers contribute net benefits to an economy. Not only do they raise taxes for the government and provide marketing opportunities, they also contribute to the economic prosperity of the economy.

ORGANIZATIONAL STRUCTURE AND BUSINESS STRATEGY

There is little doubt that human resources are essential to the running of a business. However, effective control and organization of people is a challenging task for any manager. The consequences of an inefficient organizational structure include reduced staff motivation, duplication of effort, communication problems, difficulties in coordination and ineffective decision-making.

Formal organization of human resources can be shown in an organizational chart. An organization chart is important since it allows employees to see:

- The overall structure of human resources in the business
- Who their line manager is, i.e. the person that they are accountable to
- Those who must report to the liner manager, i.e. the manger's responsibility for subordinates
- The formal chain of command.

As an organization grows, it is inevitable that new job roles will be created. Hence, the increased need for human resources means that managers may have to restructure their organization. It is likely that larger organizations require longer chains of command and taller hierarchical structures.

Tall hierarchical structures, which were popularized in the 1930s, have given way to flatter structures in many large organizations today. Delayering not only cuts down costs and unnecessary management roles (financial rewards for managers are typically based on their rank in the hierarchy), but also leads to a shorter chain of command. Delegation of decision-making authority is also pushed down and spread out amongst those lower in the hierarchy. As a result, productivity should improve. Japanese companies, for example, have found that matrix structures and quality circles (see Unit 5.4) create synergy and save time, thereby improving the overall efficiency and competitiveness of businesses.

Although there has been extensive research into the optimal organizational structure, the conclusion is that there simply isn't a model that suits all organizations. Each model has its own strengths and weaknesses and every business is unique in its character and culture. The 'best' structure for an organization will depend on several key factors, including:

- The size of the business – Larger firms will require more formal structures that are likely to be relatively tall.
- Employee competencies – Organizations with highly skilled workers can adopt relatively flat, informal or matrix structures, whereas those with unskilled workers will require a more formal and rigorous structure.
- Management attitudes – Managers that are able to trust their staff and are willing to relinquish decision-making power are more likely to support flatter and flexible work structures.
- The history and culture of the business – For example, innovative firms that are accustomed to change may opt for more flexible structures.

Managers that have a positive outlook of their workforce (known as *Theory Y managers*) believe that employees are generally capable of doing far more than may be believed. If this proves to be the case in a particular business, then it should consider more decentralized structures in order to take advantage of the capabilities of its staff.

In today's fast-paced business environment, flexibility is a key factor to an organization's level of performance. Since many decisions and actions need to be spontaneous, the decision-making process can no longer be heavily centralized. For example, if businesses choose to adopt Charles Handy's concept of the *shamrock organization* (see Unit 2.1), the internal structure of the business will need to be reviewed.

REVIEW QUESTIONS 2.2

1 What is an 'organizational chart' and what is its purpose?

2 How does the role of a director differ from that of a manager?

3 What is the difference between a 'formal organization' and an 'informal organization'?

4 What does it mean to set SMARTER delegated tasks?

5 Explain three advantages of delegation.

6 What is meant by a 'wide span of control'?

7 Explain the difference between 'flat' and 'tall' hierarchical structures.

8 What is the difference between 'delayering' and 'downsizing'?

9 What is meant by a 'decentralized organization'?

Higher Level extension

10 Explain the link between 'delegation' and 'accountability'.

11 What is 'bureaucracy'?

12 Use examples to explain the meaning of 'flexible structures'.

13 What are 'informal groups' and why might they be important to a business?

14 Outline three advantages and two problems of using a matrix structure.

15 What is the difference between 'outsourcing' and 'offshoring'?

16 What opportunities do migrant workers bring to businesses?

Accountability describes the extent to which a person is held responsible for the success or failure of a task.

Bureaucracy refers to the official administrative and formal rules of an organization that govern business activity.

Centralization occurs when the vast majority of decision-making is done by a very small number of people, usually the senior management team, who hold onto decision-making authority and responsibility.

Chain of command refers to the formal line of authority, shown in a firm's organizational chart, through which orders are passed down in an organization.

Decentralization occurs when some decision-making authority and responsibility is passed onto others in the organization.

Delayering is the process of removing one or more levels in the hierarchy in order to flatten out the organizational structure.

Delegation refers to the passing on of authority to a person lower down in the organizational structure.

Directors or **executives** are elected by the shareholders of a company to run the business on their behalf.

Flat organizational structure means that there are only a few layers in the organizational hierarchy and hence managers have a wide span of control.

Flexible structures are not based on the traditional hierarchical organization of human resources. Instead, such structures enable a business to adapt their human resources when there is a need to respond to rapid change.

Formal groups refers to the official organization of people based on the needs of the business, such as by function or department.

Informal groups consist of people at work who have formed their own associations based on friendship and/or common interests.

Matrix structure refers to the flexible organization of employees from different departments within an organization temporarily working together on a particular project.

Offshoring is a form of outsourcing that involves relocating business functions and processes to another country.

Organizational chart refers to the diagrammatic representation of a firm's formal organizational structure.

Outsourcing is the act of finding external people or businesses to carry out non-core functions of a business, such as cleaning and ICT maintenance.

Re-engineering is the radical redesign of organizational structures to better suit the changing needs of the business.

Responsibility refers to who is in charge of whom, such as the Marketing Manager of an organization being responsible for the team of marketers.

Span of control refers to the number of subordinates that are controlled by a manager, i.e. the number of people who are directly accountable to the manager.

Tall organizational structure means that there are many layers in the organizational hierarchy and hence managers have a narrow span of control.

Communication

UNIT 2.3

Think like a wise man but communicate in the language of the people.

William Butler Yeats (1865–1939), Irish poet

Key topics

- Methods of communication: oral, written, visual, non-verbal, formal and informal
- Information and communication technology
- Choice of communication methods
- Barriers to effective communication
- Consequences of poor communication

Higher Level extension

- Communication networks

Note: Students need to be able to prepare different forms of communication, such as reports and executive summaries. (© IBO 2007)

INTRODUCTION

Communication refers to the transfer of information from one party to another. Managers allocate a significant part of their time to communications, both within an organization and beyond. The purposes or objectives of communication include to instruct, clarify, interpret, notify, warn, receive feedback, review and, above all, to inform.

Effective communication is vital to the success of any business so that:

- Staff are aware of their roles and expectations.
- Managers can gather and act upon feedback from employees, customers and other stakeholders.

In other words, effective communications enable managers to have a better understanding and control of their businesses.

Internal communication refers to communication within the same business organization, e.g. the store manager of a local McDonald's liaises with Head Office about a forthcoming promotional campaign. Communication that is conducted between one organization and another is known as **external communication**, e.g. the sales manager of Firm A contacts its suppliers, Firm B, regarding an order.

All forms of communication, except oral communication, come under the category of non-verbal communication. This includes the written and visual communication methods but also includes the use of information and communication technology.

This Unit examines the different forms of communication used by businesses and their relative merits.

ORAL COMMUNICATION

This method of communication, also known as **verbal communication**, involves parties talking and listening to one another. Oral communication is quick because the sender and receiver are usually in direct contact with each other. When something is not understood, questions can be asked, i.e. feedback and clarification can be gathered. However, whether a message is communicated well orally will depend on how good a speaker the sender is, such as their use of jargon or their tone of voice.

Some examples of verbal communication include:

- When a person gives instructions or information to others, such as a manager announcing and explaining a major change in the organization
- When people discuss problems
- Business meetings, which are formal meetings that follow a set *agenda* (see Figure 2.3a)
- Job interviews for the recruitment and selection of staff
- Job appraisals and feedback (see Unit 2.1), where staff are assessed on their level of performance
- Oral presentations
- When people are simply talking to each other.

Agenda for IB Business & Management Staff Meeting

Date: 24th September
Time: 3:30 p.m.
Venue: Room 346

1. Apologies for absences
2. Minutes of last meeting – any issues arising?
3. Mock examinations update
4. Internal Assessment update
5. Extended Essay titles
6. A.O.B.

Each agenda item will be discussed in turn with time for 'any other business' (AOB) at the end. A record of the meeting (called the **minutes**) is recorded for future reference.

Figure 2.3a Example of an agenda for a formal meeting

Advantages of oral communication include:

- Detailed questions can be asked.
- Questions can be answered without hardly any delay, i.e. feedback is very quick and spontaneous.
- There is very little, if any, cost involved.
- Some oral methods, such as interviews or presentations, are a good way to judge an employee's ability to communicate.
- Facial reactions and body language, along with tone of voice, can often be judged.

Disadvantages of oral communication include:

- The information given may not always be truthful.
- There is usually no permanent record of the conversation for future reference. (Hollywood popularized the saying, "A verbal contract isn't worth the paper it's written on.")
- Confidential messages may be difficult to communicate verbally, especially when many people are involved.
- Meetings and interviews can be very time consuming.

NON-VERBAL COMMUNICATION

All forms of communication, except oral communication, come under the category of non-verbal communication. This includes the written and visual communication methods discussed above but also includes the use of information and communication technology (see 'Information and communication technology' on page 236).

Written communication

Written communication refers to communications made via paper-based methods. The main methods of non-verbal communication are explained below.

Letters

Business letters follow a set format in which the layout and language used are considered to be important. For example, letters should:

- Indicate the name and address of the sender
- Include the date
- Have a reference (a focal point or a reference number), if appropriate
- Include proper salutations: 'Dear Sir/Madam… Yours faithfully' and 'Dear Mrs. Francis… Yours sincerely'.

Letters can be used for *internal communication*, such as when chain stores have branches in different locations or when confidential information is passed to an employee.

As with all forms of written communication, letters provide a hard copy that can be kept for future reference. They are also specific and can address issues in great detail. However, letters can be time consuming to produce and it may take a while to get a response from the receiver.

Memorandum

A memorandum (memo) is a note from one person to another. It can be a formal typed note or simply a hand-written message. Memos are used for internal purposes, such as when managers wish to call a meeting, to send a reminder or when people want to pass on a quick message without much fuss (see Figure 2.3b for an example).

Memo

To: All Heads of Department

From: Margaret Boon (Chief Finance Officer)

Date: 5th October

Re: HOD Meeting - 6th Oct in Conference Room

Dear all,
Just a quick reminder that our rescheduled meeting will take place tomorrow at 1:30 p.m. in the Conference Room.
Margaret

Figure 2.3b Example of a memorandum

A memorandum can be very quick to produce. Also, as the message is short and specific, it is easy to understand. They are not intended or useful for long messages or for passing on complicated information.

Reports

Reports are a formal method of written communication whereby information about something that has been researched is presented. Business reports follow a specific format and will tend to have:

- A front title page which may include information such as: the name of the author of the report, the audience it is targeted at and the date of the report
- An *executive summary* of what the report is about and the purpose of the research (see below for more details on executive summaries)
- A contents page with page numbering
- An introduction to the report
- Parts of the report separated by section headings
- Conclusions and perhaps recommendations
- A bibliography listing all sources of reference
- An appendix with supplementary evidence, such as quantitative research data.

Business reports are prepared in detail for a specified audience and this makes communication direct and easy to understand. However, it can take a long time to investigate and write the report, by which time any findings or recommendations made may be outdated.

Note: Higher Level Business & Management students are expected to write a 2,000 word report for their Internal Assessment (see IB B&M syllabus guide page 51 for more details and the format to be followed).

Notices

Notices are used when a message needs to reach a range of people, perhaps by postings on staff notice boards or on a company website. Notices may be formal, such as notices highlighting training opportunities or fire evacuation procedures. They can also be informal to the business, such as sponsorship notices for a charity event.

Notices are useful for passing on messages so that everyone can see. They can contain a lot of important information that can be left as a reminder to staff. However, notices are not confidential and old notices are often ignored.

Executive summaries

The striking increase in the amount of information available on most topics has generated growth in the size and number of reports. The internet's popularity has undoubtedly accelerated this phenomenon. Like all summaries, executive summaries are written to provide a condensed version of a report's content. Executive summaries are, however, written for someone who most likely does not have time to read the original report. Executives do not have the time to read so many reports but still need easy and fast access to information, so this is where executive summaries prove their use. A typical executive summary follows the format below:

1. Scope and purpose of report.
2. Methodology.
3. Main results and findings.
4. Conclusions and recommendations.

Executive summaries provide the main findings in the reports and often come with recommendations. The reader of an executive summary is a decision-maker who may have to decide on a course of action related to the contents in the report. Hence, all executive summaries must be written with this need in mind. They must be accurate as they are stand-alone documents and managers may make decisions based on the content of the executive summary without reading the original report.

> **Note:** Higher Level Business & Management students are expected to write an Executive Summary (maximum of 200 words) as part of their Internal Assessment (see IB B&M syllabus guide page 51 for more details).

Abstracts

Abstracts are similar in their purpose to executive summaries. An abstract is written as a condensed version of a report without losing the original message of the reports, i.e. it is a shortened version of a report. It differs slightly from an executive summary in that abstracts do not directly provide any recommendations to aid decision-making. An executive summary not only provides a summary of a report, but also the main findings and recommendations. In essence, a manager could do without reading the report if there is an executive summary provided. This is not possible with an abstract alone. A further difference is that executive summaries tend to be longer than abstracts.

> **Note:** Business & Management Extended Essay students are expected to write an Abstract as part of their EE (Criterion J).

Research proposals

A research proposal is a planning document. It sets out the key issue(s) to be investigated in a Report. The proposal may contain details of primary and secondary methods of research, an action plan with dates and identification of any foreseeable problems likely to be encountered in the investigation.

Note: Higher Level students are expected to write a Research Proposal as part of their IB B&M Internal Assessment (see pages 49–50 of IB B&M syllabus guide for more information).

Exam Tip!
Students are expected to be able to prepare different forms of written communication, such as memoranda, reports and executive summaries. There are usually marks allocated for displaying an understanding of the correct format of these written methods.

Visual communication

It is said that "A picture paints a thousand words" (Napoleon Bonaparte) and that images speak louder than words. What this implies is that visual aids can be used to enhance communication. Visual communication can be beneficial because images:

- Can be understood relatively easily
- Can often communicate ideas quicker than words
- Are often cheaper to produce than a page full of words
- Cater for the visual learner as some people understand better through the use of images rather than through verbal or written communication
- May have a longer lasting impact, which is why marketers often use powerful images in their promotional campaigns.

Different images are used for different purposes. For example:

- *Bar chart* – useful for showing frequencies and for ease of comparison
- *Pie chart* – for expressing percentage figures
- *Line graph* – to show time series data, such as sales figures during the past twelve months
- *Histogram* – useful for showing trends over time.

Other examples of visual aids include photographs, symbols, tables, maps, sketches and diagrams. Whichever image is used, it is important to remember *why* it is being used and what purpose it will serve.

Other forms of visual communication include **sign language** and **body language**. Sign language is used for those individuals with hearing or oral difficulties. Body language can tell you a lot about a message, for example, is the recipient staring into the sky or maintaining good eye contact during a conversation?

A major disadvantage of all forms of written communication is that of storage space. Managers need to be guided in this aspect – how long do they hold records for? In addition, many forms of written communication are slow and if the receiver does not understand the written message, there will be more delays.

Question 2.3.1

The importance of body language

The key factor to good communication is to pay attention to what others have to say. Good communicators are not those who simply speak at others. In business, effective communication is all about establishing a rapport with customers, colleagues and management. Not listening to customers can be a costly mistake – dissatisfied customers will result in a loss of sales and less loyalty to the organization.

In addition to listening skills, good communicators also show positive body language. Research has shown communication is 7% dependent on spoken words, 38% on the tone of the voice whilst the remaining 55% is on non-verbal signals.

a Using the above case study, outline two benefits of good communication skills to a business. *[4 marks]*

b Examine the importance of non-verbal communication as a tool for marketing a firm's products. *[6 marks]*

Formal and informal communication channels

The term **channel of communication** refers to the method(s) of communication. For example, in order to announce an end-of-season sale, managers of large retail businesses may choose to use television and/or newspaper advertising. Communication channels can be categorized as formal or informal methods.

Informal communication refers to all unofficial channels of communication that exist among informal groups (see Unit 2.2). These groups tend to form naturally because members share similar interests, not because they are formally part of the organization. An example of informal communication is **grapevine communication**, which simply translates to 'gossip' in the workplace. There is gossip in every company, especially in larger organizations. Informal communication does not necessarily relate directly to work matters, such as staff arranging a social function.

Some managers see informal communication, especially grapevine communication, as a hindrance to efficiency and productivity in the workplace. In addition, the informal group norms may not support the objectives held by management. Other managers however see informal communication in a more positive manner, suggesting that there are several benefits:

- Informal communication can foster a sense of belonging in the workplace. People from different departments of the organization can talk about non-work issues over lunch breaks, for example. This can help to meet their social needs, which Maslow (see Unit 2.5) argued is an important factor in affecting the level of motivation in the workplace.
- It can also foster a sense of security and mutual support. People can talk to colleagues who are seen as friends, for example. This can help an employee to have messages passed on from management clarified by other people and/or help to deal with any concerns or anxieties that the worker might have.
- The pooling of ideas can help to generate solutions that may not have occurred through more formal channels of communication. People are more likely to be open during informal discussions. Formality itself can constrain what people say or do in a meeting.

Formal communication refers to all official channels of communication, such as information being passed between managers and their subordinates. Written communication methods tend to relate to formal channels of communication. Formal communication is directly related to work matters, such as a discussion about who is the best candidate for a job vacancy.

Information and communication technology

Some examples of Information and communication technology (ICT) used to aid communication are explained in this section.

Electronic mail (email)

Electronic mail refers to the process of using computer wide area networks (WAN) as a mailing system. Data is electronically transmitted from one computer to another computer. Email connections require a modem for data conversion and a telephone line for transmitting the data. It is a very fast method of communication because all the data (text, graphs, charts, images) are already in electronic form. Very large quantities of data can be transmitted in a very short time, and sent to many different recipients at the same time. This saves on telephone and fax bills and on stationery costs.

However, the set-up costs for the purchase of a computer and the other peripherals that are required can be high. There is also the ongoing cost of using the internet service provider's telephone line. Moreover, data is not always secure if it is transmitted using the telephone system as it can be hacked into. This is one reason why many people still shy away from e-commerce and using their credit cards for online shopping (see Unit 4.8). Computer systems and networks can also go wrong (or 'crash') and, subsequently, there is communication failure.

Question 2.3.2

Email usage at work

Research has shown that most emails are accessed at work as many people can access the internet free of charge at their place of work. However, many of the emails sent are personal messages, such as arranging a social gathering, rather than work-related issues. Research has also suggested that **electronic mail** usage in the workplace varies from country to country. For countries where electronic communication is widely used, the result has been an increase in the number of people who are using the internet to communicate with their work colleagues. Some people argue that using email in the workplace can improve overall efficiency whilst others believe that it is open to abuse and an excuse to avoid talking to people.

a Define what is meant by **electronic mail**. *[2 marks]*

b Describe how email might encourage informal communication. *[2 marks]*

c To what extent does email improve the efficiency of communication in the workplace? *[7 marks]*

Facsimile (fax)

A facsimile (fax) machine converts text and images into electronic form for transmission. The receiving fax machine then converts the transmission back into images and text and prints out a hard copy. Faxes can be a quick and convenient method of communication and can be used even if the receiver is not by their fax machine. Today, fax machines are less popular because email can be used instead which is even faster and has other benefits. For example, emails can be a cheaper form of communication as there is no need for fax paper and ink cartridges.

Video-conferencing

Video-conferencing can be used as an example of oral communication, but it can only happen with the use of ICT. Video-conferencing uses a combination of telephone, computer and video technology. It allows meetings to take place when staff are in different locations, thereby cutting out travel time and costs. Video-conferencing allows people to talk to each other and see each other as they are also being filmed (rather similar to an online conversation using a web cam).

More and more multinational corporations are using this method for interviewing overseas recruits.

Once the initial start-up costs have been paid for, video-conferencing has the advantage of being much quicker and cheaper than bringing people together in one location. An added advantage over ordinary face-to-face meetings is that video recordings of the discussion can be made for future reference.

One major disadvantage of the system, however, is that video-conferencing systems are expensive to set up. Meetings may also be more difficult to conduct due to the over-reliance on technology. There is also usually a small time lag between sending and receiving messages, so large meetings involving many people from numerous locations may have a slightly different feel.

Telephones and mobile phones

The traditional telephone is still immensely popular as a means of communication in business organizations. More recently, mobile telephones (or cell phones) have taken over in terms of popularity and ownership. For example, the top four mobile phone producers surpassed the one billion sales figure for the first time in 2007. The average person in Finland owns more than two mobile phones; whilst the average Japanese person replaces his/her mobile phone every nine months. Mobile phones are used by managers and employees that are increasingly 'on the go', such as estate agents, sales representatives, insurance brokers and teleworkers (see Unit 2.1). Technological progress, such as digital music and camera technology, has also further popularized the use of mobile phones.

In summary, electronic methods of communications are of growing importance in the global business world. ICT has allowed for faster yet cheaper communication over long distances. However, using ICT can mean the need to purchase and maintain expensive equipment. Although email can be cost effective, the use of faxes or mobile phones for international calls is still rather expensive. Businesses that rely heavily on the use of ICT find that things tend to come to a halt when electronic equipment fails.

FACTORS INFLUENCING THE CHOICE OF COMMUNICATION METHOD

The choice of communication methods used by a business can be based on any combination of the following factors which can be remembered by the mnemonic POSSESS LUC:

- **Personal preferences** – Some people may prefer to chat to others about problems, whereas other people may prefer to put their thoughts and feelings in writing.
- **Organization structure** – A tall organizational structure (see Unit 2.2) requires more formal and sophisticated systems of communication.
- **Security issues and concerns** – For example, hard copies of important records are often kept in case computer files get damaged by a virus.
- **Skills and training** of the users – Many schools, for example, now have interactive whiteboards and projectors to enhance teaching and learning. However, unless the teachers have received proper training to use the equipment, such investment could be a waste of money as the resources are not fully utilized.
- **Ease of use** – Some people may prefer to use a sketch as part of their presentation rather than using software such as PowerPoint. Sending out flyers to potential customers will also be easy for many people in comparison to setting up their own website to convey the same message.
- **Size of business** – Large firms may find that the use of emails serves their communication purposes, whereas a small firm may prefer to primarily use verbal methods of communication.

- **Storage issues** – An order placed by a customer needs to be recorded whereas a conversation about organizing a staff social event does not need any formal documentation.
- **Location** of sender and receiver – Time zone differences in Australia and France, for example, may mean that an email is preferred to a telephone call.
- **Urgency** – Time and speed may mean a firm prefers to use a courier service such as FedEx or DHL instead of using the normal postal system.
- **Cost** – The use of written communication methods tends to be cheaper than methods that rely on ICT systems. Also, parcels sent by sea mail are obviously cheaper to send than those sent by air mail.

In reality, businesses will use a combination of communication methods to fit their requirements. The type of communication method chosen will depend upon a mixture of the above factors. Overall, businesses will look at *value for money* in their choice of communication methods. For a large multinational company, as an example, the use of email is likely to be more cost effective than the use of faxes for external communications.

BARRIERS TO EFFECTIVE COMMUNICATION

The term **noise** is used to refer to any barrier to effective communication. Communication may fail due to any combination of the following reasons:

- **High costs** hinder effective communication as firms do not have sufficient finance to set up good communication networks. Costs also include the necessary training for staff to become effective communicators.
- **Technological breakdowns**, such as computer failure, viruses and crashes.
- **Language** skills are proving to be a highly valued communication skill in today's ever-more competitive labour market. For example, English is the official business language in much of South East Asia but fluency in native languages such as Malay and Mandarin are also vital in many occupations in this part of the world.
- Similarly, **accents** can hinder communication as different pronunciations and tone of voice can cause messages to be misinterpreted or misunderstood.
- Technical language, known as **jargon**, is used to speed up communication. However, when jargon is used for non-specialists, this can cause communication problems. For example, a student's report written by a teacher may contain a lot of subject-specific vocabulary and examination criteria that mean very little to some parents. Hence, jargon can become a barrier to effective communication when managers fail to identify situations when it is inappropriate.
- HSBC's slogan "The world's local bank" suggests that they are aware of the different **cultures** in the countries in which they operate. Ignorance of cultural issues can cause offence. For example, KFC's slogan "We do chicken right" is literally translated into Chinese as 'It's correct to be a prostitute' – not exactly the best of slogans for a family-orientated restaurant. Unit 4.7 deals with culture and international marketing in more detail.
- Some people have a poor **attitude** or prejudice towards the use of ICT, whilst others are simply ignorant or unfamiliar and cannot effectively use ICT for communication purposes.
- **Geographical location** and distance mean that remote areas have limited communication access such as mobile phone reception. There tends to be a positive correlation between distance and the cost of communication. Hence, geographical distance between the sender and receiver can be another barrier.
- **Internal politics** occur when there is conflict within an organization. This can generate rumours and gossip within the workplace and a general resistance to cooperate with fellow colleagues and/or management.

- **Poor presentation skills** mean that listeners will lose interest and may not understand the contents of the message being conveyed.
- Poor or **negative body language** may result in listeners being put off as they focus on the negative vibes being displayed rather than listening to the speaker.
- '**Chinese whispers**' exist within tall hierarchical structures. Messages have to be passed through many layers so communication tends to slow down and messages may get distorted. If the chain of command is very long, then there may also be a failure from some people to pass on information.
- **Physiological barriers** such as hearing or sight disability will also hinder effective communication.

Question 2.3.3

The global office

Evermore multicultural communities are making a presence in the business world. The driving forces behind this trend include globalization, greater cross-border labour mobility and government laws that prevent racial discrimination in the workplace. Whilst the global office can provide many benefits, there is the potential for disastrous misunderstandings to occur due to communication barriers such as differences in language, mannerism, expectations and cultures.

a Outline why foreign language might be a hindrance to effective business communication. *[2 marks]*

b Explain how an awareness and knowledge of multiculturalism in the 'global office' can improve communications in the workplace. *[4 marks]*

CONSEQUENCES OF POOR COMMUNICATION

Poor communication hinders businesses in four ways:

- Low morale will exist as staff feel out of touch, lose confidence and sense of direction. They may also feel under-valued.
- Errors and reworking will rise as staff are not fully aware of what they have to do. Hence, work may need to be revisited so this represents wastage and thus increases costs. On an international scale, for example, communication problems may occur due to language barriers and this may hinder trade. Marketing errors not only cost money, but may harm a firm's image if marketing messages are offensive to other cultures (see Unit 4.7).
- There will be a loss of competitiveness due to the lower productivity caused by both lower morale and the increase in errors and reworking.
- A lack of control may transpire as subordinates may need clear instructions from their line managers. Equally, managers will need feedback from their staff in order to fulfil organizational objectives.

To solve communication problems, managers must first look at the *causes* of the communication breakdown. A recent trend in many large organizations has been **delayering** of the organization (see Unit 2.2). This means removing layers of supervisors and management from the hierarchy. This is done not only to reduce costs but also to improve the speed and accuracy of communication flows.

Another example of dealing with communication problems on an international scale is to recruit bilingual or multilingual employees. This trend has been fuelled by the huge growth in world tourism which has led to language skills being in high demand in many tertiary sector industries. Disneyland Tokyo employs staff who speak both Japanese and English to cater for domestic and most of their foreign visitors. In Paris, Disneyland employs staff who are fluent in both French and English. Similarly, staff at Hong Kong Disneyland must be trilingual in English, Cantonese and Mandarin. This reduces the impact that language may have as a barrier to effective communication in business.

Question 2.3.4

OCR's examination paper blunder

The Oxford, Cambridge and Royal Society of Arts (OCR) Examination Board is one of the main examination boards in the UK. In 2006, some 6,400 A Level Geography students were forced to sit an incomplete exam paper because OCR failed to send schools copies of a map that was required for a question worth 16 marks. The blunder by the examination board meant that students had to overlook the question that was worth more than 20% of the exam paper. This enraged teachers and parents since OCR's error placed extra stress on students. OCR responded by stating that the question would be ignored during the marking process and launched an investigation into how the slip-up occurred.

a Explain two barriers to effective communication. *[4 marks]*

b Examine the importance of effective communication to an organization such as the OCR Examination Board. *[6 marks]*

HIGHER LEVEL

HIGHER LEVEL EXTENSION: COMMUNICATION NETWORKS

A **communication network** shows the routes (links) that allow different parties to communicate a message, i.e. the actual communication structures within the business. Networks can be used to examine the effectiveness of communication between people. This is important for a manager to know because the success of an organization depends on the efficiency and productivity of its people. Communication networks are therefore a crucial factor in determining the effectiveness of the workforce.

There are two broad types of communication networks – centralized and decentralized networks.

Centralized networks

Centralized methods of communication involve a key player (or team of people) that holds decision-making power. Examples of such networks include *Wheel*, *Chain* and *Y-Chain*, where the information must pass via a central person.

Wheel network

The wheel network uses an experienced person or team leader at the hub (centre) (see Figure 2.3c). Others communicate primarily through the person in the centre. Such networks give control to the person at the hub of the wheel, yet allow other people to have some input. The wheel system is suitable when quick decision-making is required.

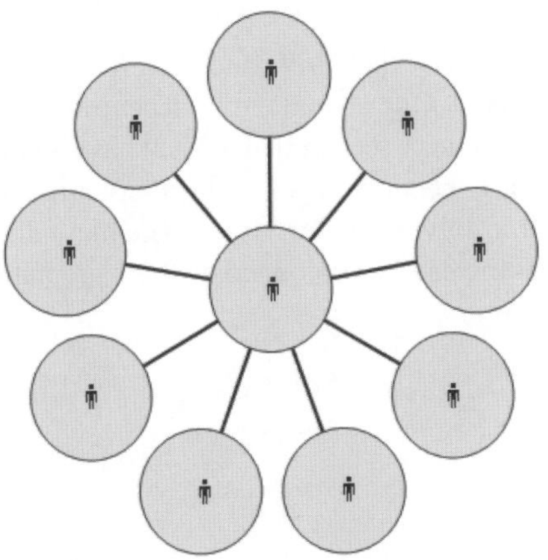

Staff communicate with and through the decision-maker, i.e. the person at the centre of the wheel.

Figure 2.3c Wheel network

Chain network

The chain network structure is used by organizations with a tall hierarchy. A large multinational, such as McDonald's, uses this system to pass on information from regional managers to area managers and then finally to branch managers. The main advantage of this system is that there is direction from the leader or coordinator at the top of the chain (see Figure 2.3d). The main disadvantage is that there can be distortions of the original message if the chain is very long.

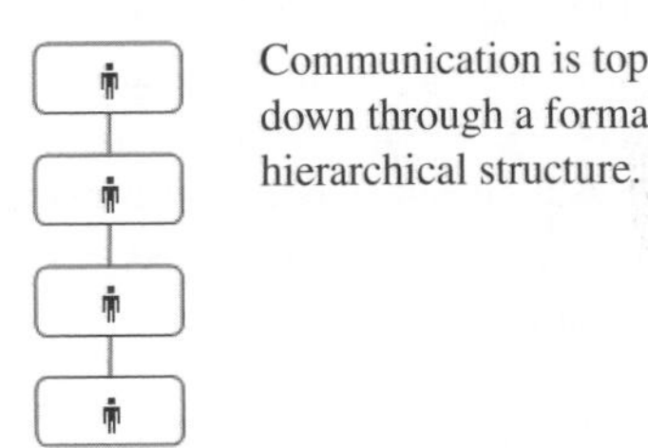

Communication is top-down through a formal hierarchical structure.

Figure 2.3d Chain network

Y-chain network

The Y-chain structure is similar to the chain method except that the information is passed onto several different parties (see Figure 2.3e). For example, in a school, the principal may pass on information to her two deputy principals. A larger organization may pass on the same information about a change in its services to its shareholders and to its customers. The main drawback of the wheel and Y-chain networks is that the central person can become overloaded. The chain and Y-chain (centralized networks) also have the disadvantage that other people in the organization lack any input and those lower down the organization may feel rather isolated.

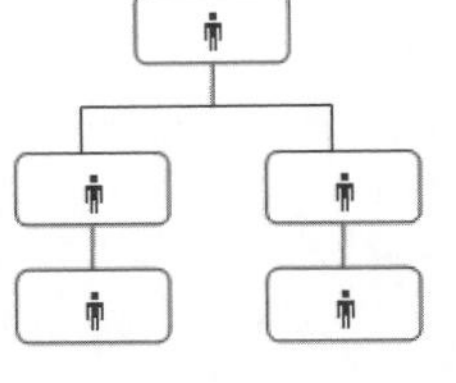

The Y-chain is a variation of the chain network found in formal hierarchical structures.

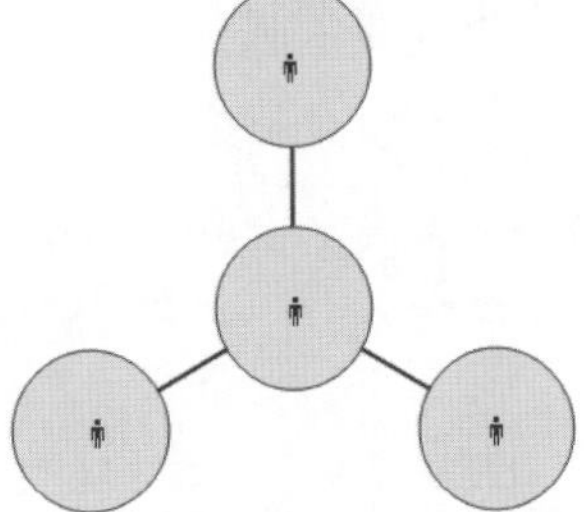

Figure 2.3e Examples of Y-chain networks

Decentralized networks

Decentralized methods of communication include the *Circle* and *All Channel* networks, where information passes round from person to person. One advantage of decentralized networks, especially the all channel system, is that people may feel valued as they have an input in planning and decision-making. The open nature of these networks also means that more ideas can be generated, so such networks are often used to solve complex issues. The main drawback of decentralized networks is that decision-making can be prolonged as there are many people involved in the process.

Circle network

The circle communication network may be used for team-based tasks or a group of middle managers communicating with one another. It is a useful network when working on complex problems. However, as shown in Figure 2.3f, each person only communicates with two others. Communication is conducted on a sequential basis. The main disadvantage of this network is that there is no formal leader established so decision-making or formulation of business strategy might be prolonged.

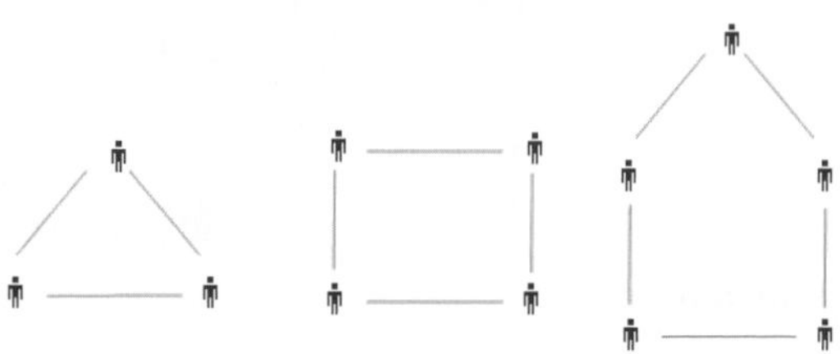

Figure 2.3f Examples of a circle network

All channel network

The all channel network, sometimes called the **web network**, allows people to communicate with whomever they feel is necessary in order to meet their needs (see Figure 2.3g). An example of an all channel network is communication via brainstorming during a meeting. Ideas bounce off person to person, in all directions. This method therefore allows everyone to participate. It is useful when dealing with highly complex tasks. Charles Handy suggests that this network is the most ideal when dealing with complex and/or open-ended tasks.

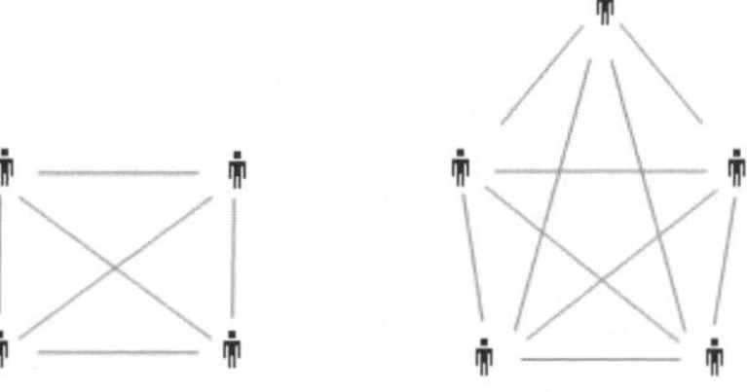

Figure 2.3g Examples of the all channel network

Question 2.3.5

Networking

Identify and explain which type of communication network would be most effective in each of the following cases: *[12 marks]*

- **a** Organizing a staff social party.
- **b** Outbreak of fire in a factory.
- **c** Announcement to regional managers of a change in the board of directors.
- **d** Working on the design and name of a new brand.

COMMUNICATION AND BUSINESS STRATEGY

The art of communication is crucial to an organization's success. Unless managers and leaders can communicate effectively, organizational goals are unlikely to be accomplished. In their attempt for continuous improvement, managers seek to improve communications in the workplace. The objectives of introducing new or improved communication systems into an organization include:

- Improved speed, access and accuracy of communication
- Greater potential for communication to reach a wider audience; hence the phenomenal growth in the number of companies that have their own websites
- Improved motivation and productivity as the use of ICT reduces errors, reworking and workloads (in theory at least).

However, there are disadvantages of introducing changes to communications systems:

- Cost – New equipment may not be compatible with existing software or hardware and this represents wastage or a need for more capital expenditure to replace obsolete equipment.
- Threat to security – The growing importance of and reliance on ICT in business organizations also brings about its threats (see Unit 4.8).
- Need for change management – Any change needs to be managed effectively, although this can be a highly complex task (see Unit 1.8).

Furthermore, managers must be aware that **information overload** can be demotivating in the workplace. This happens when staff are swamped with too much communication. For example, this often happen to new members of staff during their induction training. In addition, if information is passive or documents are too lengthy, then staff may view such communications as *hygiene factors* (factors that can cause dissatisfaction in the workplace).

On the one hand, the internet and e-commerce (see Unit 4.8) have reduced the cost of domestic and international communication. However, communication problems can still occur on an international level where language and culture may present barriers to effective marketing (see Unit 4.7).

Professor Albert Mehrabian's research has provided managers with insight into the relative importance of non-verbal and verbal communication. His theory suggests that:

- *Visual Liking* – Facial expression and body language accounts for 55% of how a message is understood or interpreted.
- *Vocal Liking* – Tone of voice and paralinguistic cues account for 38% of how a message is understood or interpreted, i.e. the way that the message is said, such as signs of anxiety, enthusiasm or sarcasm.
- *Verbal Liking* – Only 7% of a message is understood or interpreted by the actual words spoken.

Mehrabian's theory (sometimes referred to as the *7-38-55* rule or the *Three V's*) suggests that the way in which a message is said is far more influential than what is actually said. If this is the case, certain jobs such as sales people or newsreaders have to be highly effective communicators since viewers will be assessing *how* things are said and not just *what* is being said. Likewise, appearance is vital, given that Mehrabian's findings suggest visual interpretation is the most significant of the three factors. Critics of the model suggest that the figures are rather non-conclusive since such observations are over-simplistic and cannot be applied to all cases of communication. For example, Mehrabian's research cannot be accurately applied to telephone communication since there is little, if any, opportunity for visual stimuli.

Today, most managers and leaders would agree that it is often important to listen to the views of their staff, especially if workers are viewed as a firm's best assets. For motivational reasons, it is important to listen to their views. Staff are employed for their expertise and having their input in decision-making can sometimes generate new ideas. Indeed, Japanese businesses have been using such methods successfully for many years (see Unit 5.4 on Quality Circles). Management guru Peter Drucker argued on similar lines that the most important things are sometimes simply the messages not being communicated.

REVIEW QUESTIONS 2.3

1 In a business context, explain what is meant by 'communication'.

2 Why is effective communication important for the running of a business?

3 Explain, using examples, the difference between 'written communication' and 'oral communication'.

4 What is the difference between a 'research proposal' and an 'executive summary'?

5 Distinguish between 'formal' and 'informal' methods of communication.

6 How has the use of information communication technology (ICT) improved business communication?

7 State five factors that affect the choice of communication methods used by businesses.

8 State five barriers to effective communication.

9 What is meant by 'information overload'?

10 State three consequences of poor communication.

Higher Level extension

11 What is a 'communication network'?

12 Distinguish between 'centralized' and 'decentralized' communication networks.

13 Outline Albert Mehrabian's *7-38-55* theory.

Communication is the transfer of information between different people and between business organizations.

Communication channels (also known as **channels of communication**) refer to the methods or routes through which information is passed from the sender to the recipient. **Open channels** are used when information is not confidential and can be shared by anyone. **Restricted channels** of communication are used when information is confidential and is directed only to those who need to know.

Communication network refers to a diagram representing the communication structure within an organization, e.g. the wheel, the chain, the Y-chain and the circle.

Delayering is a method of improving communication by reducing the number of levels in an organizational hierarchy.

Formal communication refers to the official channels of communication that are established by an organization.

Informal communication refers to unofficial channels of communication naturally established by people from within an organization, often based on their common interests.

Minutes are a written record of the issues discussed in a business meeting.

Noise refers to barriers to effective communication, e.g. jargon, ignorance or computer failure. These barriers cause communication breakdown.

Non-verbal communication is any form of communication other than oral communication. Examples include: electronic systems (such as email), written methods (such as letters) and visual stimulus (such as body language).

Verbal communication, also known as **oral communication**, refers to communication via the use of spoken words, such as meetings, interviews and appraisals.

Video-conferencing is a communication method that allows meetings, or conferences, via telecommunications networks. The parties can see and hear each other via the electronic equipment.

Visual communication refers to communication methods that use visual images and stimuli, such as poster displays and a person's body language.

Leadership and Management

UNIT 2.4

Some are born great, some achieve greatness, and some have greatness thrust upon 'em.

William Shakespeare (1564–1616), English playwright

Key topics

- Nature of leadership
- Leadership and management styles

Higher Level extension

- Trait theories: Likert, Fiedler, Blake and Mouton, and Tannenbaum and Schmidt
- Contingency and Situational theories
- Differences between leadership and management
- Functions of management: theories of Fayol, Handy and Drucker

INTRODUCTION

A leader is a person who influences and inspires others to get things done. An effective leader will promote loyalty, motivation, respect and trust from the workforce. **Leadership** is the process of influencing and inspiring others to achieve a goal, from completing a task to achieving corporate objectives. Leaders tend to focus on achieving broader goals or visions with no definite time frame in mind.

Management is essentially about problem-solving based on reasoning, rather than on emotions. Managers are involved in complex organizational tasks including planning, organizing, budgeting and controlling. Management theorist Mary Parker Follett (1868–1933) famously defined management as "the art of getting things done through people". In other words, management refers to the process of planning, organizing and coordinating human and capital resources of a business in order to achieve organizational objectives. Managers are likely to focus on the attainment of specific goals within a definite time frame.

Within an organization, there tends to be three broad levels of management:

- **Senior management** refers to the team of higher-ranking managers or directors that plan and oversee the long-term aims and strategies of the organization. They are responsible for the middle managers.
- **Middle management** refers to the group of managers in charge of running individual departments of the organization. They set the departmental objectives (which are in line with the firm's overall aims) and are responsible for implementing appropriate strategies to achieve these goals. Middle managers are accountable to the senior management team and responsible for their departmental staff.
- **Junior management** or **supervisory management** refers to lower-ranking managers who are in charge of monitoring and controlling day-to-day and routine tasks. They are accountable to the middle managers and responsible for their team of workers.

Leaders and managers are not necessarily the same people, as managers are officially appointed to a position of power. Leaders become known as the best person to handle a given situation, such as a crisis or during a period of significant change. Leaders do not have to be the people at the top of an organization.

This Unit looks at the nature of management and leadership, the various styles and their relative merits.

NATURE OF LEADERSHIP

Leadership is concerned with influencing other people to achieve a vision or target. In business, this means that effective leaders are crucial if employees are to be inspired and motivated to achieve the aims and objectives of their organization.

An **official leader** (also known as a formal leader) is established by an organization and therefore has the authority to give orders to other people within the organization. An **informal leader** is not in an official role but has natural flair or charisma in influencing other people. Hence all leaders have the 'power' to influence, although the source of power is different for official and unofficial leaders.

Professor Warren Bennis found that successful leaders take an interest in what is happening within their organization. Having studied managers working for profit and non-profit organizations, Bennis found that there is no single correct way to lead an organization, but that leaders have to find the style that best suits them. However, Bennis did suggest general characteristics (or *core competencies*) of successful managers:

- *Management of attention* – Managers and leaders need to have a clear vision or dream of where they want the business to be.
- *Management of meaning* – Managers and leaders need to be able to communicate this vision or dream to others in the organization and beyond.
- *Management of trust* – Managers and leaders need to be consistent, dependable and honest to gain people's trust. An environment must be created to allow people to openly disagree but still work together professionally.
- *Management of self* – Managers and leaders need to be self-reflective of their strengths and weaknesses, and be able to accept constructive criticism in order to deal with their weaknesses.

Henry Mintzberg

Henry Mintzberg disputed the idea of the customary management ***roles*** of planning, organizing, monitoring and controlling. Instead, he argued that a manager has three main roles (functions or responsibilities): interpersonal roles, information role and decision-making roles.

- **Interpersonal roles** are the formal parts of a manager's job. Mintzberg described these as *leader role* (being in charge of employee-related issues such as recruitment and retention strategies), *figurehead role* (being a representative or ambassador of the business) and *liaison role* (being a communicator for the business with external stakeholders).
- **Informational role** refers to the manager acting as a communication channel between departments and senior management. For example, a Head of Department in a school may feed back information to his or her team following a Middle Management meeting.
- **Decision-making role** refers to the tactical and strategic decisions made by managers. They have access to the necessary information to take such decisions and have the formal authority to do so.

In addition to identifying the roles of management, Mintzberg's research also recognized the ***work*** (tasks or activities) of managers:

- **Routine tasks** are the daily or frequently recurring tasks of managers. These tasks tend to be formal ones such as attending meetings and conducting staff appraisals. This finding challenges the idea that managers do not have set tasks because they delegate all the work to other people.
- **Planning tasks** refer to the timetabling and preparation of daily tasks. It also includes forecasting and setting up of systems to deal with urgent or unforeseen tasks.
- **Communication tasks** refer to the sharing and passing on of information. Mintzberg suggested that managers find using verbal communication more effective on a day-to-day basis since it is quicker and easier to understand. Instant feedback can also accelerate the decision-making process.

Modern management thinking suggests that to get the best out of the workforce, people need to be led, rather than simply managed as subordinates. Successful leaders such as Sir Richard Branson try to do this by motivating and inspiring their people to gain their loyalty and commitment. In terms of approach to people, the use of coercion has lost any form of priority to the use of consultation and persuasion. Ken Blanchard, author of *The One Minute Manager*, believes that effective managers offer support and encouragement rather than act as an evaluator or critic of their subordinates.

Question 2.4.1

Donald Trump

Donald Trump (b. 1946) is the CEO of the Trump Organization and the host of the highly successful television show *The Apprentice*. He has a diverse portfolio of businesses, which include: real estate, hotels, casinos, restaurants, bottled water, vodka, ice cream and golf courses. Trump is often reported in the press as being an outspoken and flamboyant **leader**. His high profile makes him one of the highest paid public speakers in the world, demanding up to $1 million for each lecture.

a Outline what it means to be a **leader**. *[2 marks]*

b Explain why Donald Trump might be classed as an effective leader. *[4 marks]*

LEADERSHIP STYLES

Management and leadership style refers to the way in which managers and leaders behave or reveal their behaviour in different ways. The preferred style of a manager or leader will depend on many factors such as cultural styles of leadership. For example, a **consensus model** of leadership is found in countries like Japan and the Netherlands where group decision-making is the norm. In other countries such as the UK, USA or Australia, we can observe the **charismatic model** of leadership where there is a tradition and expectation of leaders to make decisions with decisiveness and transparency. Whatever the causes of a particular style, there are several common types of leadership and management styles, which are considered below.

Autocratic

An autocratic leader or manager is one that makes all the decisions and prefers not to delegate any responsibility to their subordinates. Instead, an autocratic leader (also known as an **authoritarian**) simply tells employees what to do. This style is suitable in situations that require quick decision-making or when critical decisions need to be made by the leader, such as during a crisis or when dealing with a hostile takeover. Autocratic management is also seen as appropriate when the workforce is unskilled and depends on the directions and instructions of leaders.

One drawback of this style of leadership is that communication is top-down, so there is no prospect of feedback for the leader. The opinions and suggestions of workers are totally ignored. This can cause resentment amongst employees who want to be part of decision-making. Hence, an autocratic leadership or management style can demotivate and alienate the workforce.

Democratic

A democratic leader is one who prefers to discuss with and involve employees in decision-making. Managers and leaders consult staff and take into account their views before making any final decision. This style can lead to better morale and motivation amongst the employees, as they are able to express their views and have some input into decision-making. The sharing of ideas can also lead to improved decision-making. A democratic style of leadership may work more effectively if the leader cannot always be around to ensure that employees remain on task.

However, the main limitation of this approach is that it can delay decision-making because more people are involved in the process. Furthermore, such a style is not suitable when dealing with a very large workforce (since communication would be severely affected) or when there is a high dependence on clear leadership, such as dealing with trade union strike action (see Unit 2.7) or a public relations crisis.

Laissez-faire

A laissez-faire leader or manager is one who prefers to have minimal direct input into the work of the employees. Instead they leave their subordinates to make their own decisions and to complete tasks in their own way. The leader will set the objectives but then it is up to the employees to decide how best to achieve the objectives using the resources available to them.

This style of leadership can lead to high levels of motivation as staff may feel trusted and highly valued by their employer. Employees also feel that they have control over their work and can contribute to the success of the organization. It is suitable in businesses or situations where creative ideas are important, such as in computer software firms or advertising agencies.

One key limitation of this style is that coordination and decision-making can be very time-consuming since there is a lack of supervision or direction. Execution of strategies can therefore be prolonged, so this style is unsuitable for businesses or situations that require quick decision-making. In addition, laissez-faire management relies heavily on people's goodwill and teamwork to achieve the organization's goals. This style may also encourage *slack*, i.e. people choose to be less proactive as they know they are not being directly monitored by senior management.

Situational leadership (contingency management)

Situational leadership is a leadership style that, unlike the others above, is not based on any single approach to leadership because employees and businesses are all very different in so many ways. In essence, it is about using the right person and the right style for the right situation. For example, a crisis will call for a more authoritarian leadership style whereas a laissez-faire approach can be adopted for managers with highly skilled and empowered staff.

Situational leadership also suggests that managers and leaders must be able to change and adapt their style to different situations. 'CLOTS' is a useful acronym for remembering the factors that may affect situational leadership styles:

- ***Culture*** – For example, what type of culture exists within the organization and what are the group norms?
- ***Leader*** – For example, how much trust do leaders have in their subordinates and what is their preferred (or natural) leadership style?
- ***Organization*** – For example, are there tall or flat hierarchical structures?
- ***Task*** – For example, to what extent are the tasks difficult, urgent and important?
- ***Subordinates*** – For example, what are the level of skills, motivation and unity of the employees? How many employees are there?

Question 2.4.2

Explain which form of leadership and management style would be most appropriate for the following organizations: *[9 marks]*

a A small local restaurant with 13 employees.

b The armed forces (military).

c A typical secondary school (high school).

Exam Tip!

If a theorist is mentioned by name in the guide (for example, Porter) students should be familiar with the nature of his or her work and its appropriate application in a business setting.

If a theorist is not mentioned by name in the guide, students do not need to know his or her work, although teachers may wish to cover relevant business theory and/or theorists in addition to those listed in the guide. © IBO, *Further clarifications to the Business and management guide* (March 2007)

HIGHER LEVEL EXTENSION: TRAIT THEORIES

Trait theorists argue that leadership and management styles depend on the personal characteristics (traits) of individual leaders and managers. For example, an extrovert and confident manager is likely to adopt a different style of management from one who is more introvert and insecure. As a consequence, trait theorists do not come to a conclusion about what makes an effective leader as the same traits cannot be found in all effective leaders and managers (see Box 2.4a for some examples). Peter Drucker analysed the traits of different leaders and came to the same conclusion, i.e. that there were no exact traits that could be applied to all leaders.

Box 2.4a Examples of leadership traits

Listening skills to hear the views of others
Enthusiastic about and driven by their goals
Ambitious in their aims
Decisive in execution of strategy
Enterprising (entrepreneurial)
Recognition and approval from followers
Seeing the bigger picture
High standards of integrity
Influential and inspiring others to have the same vision
Prudence in decision-making

Are leaders born (natural born leaders) or can leadership be learnt by developing different traits? There is much debate over this question and there is no consensus on this to date.

Some analysts argue that leaders are born experts. Subordinates know immediately when a leader is incompetent and is simply putting on an act. These theorists and psychologists have argued that it is more or less impossible for someone to change their basic character to become whatever they think an effective leader should be. The Chinese have a proverb: "It is easier to move a mountain than to change one's personality." On similar lines, Stephen Covey author of *The Seven Habits of Highly Effective People*, argues that there are two sides to leadership: a person's *character* and their *competence* (what she or he does). Effective leaders will set an example for others to follow, thereby establishing their own credibility. Psychologists have shown that people unconsciously imitate the behaviour of those they most admire.

By contrast, other leading theorists believe that most people can learn to become good leaders, even if this means by trial and error. Warren Bennis argues that the notion of born leaders is a myth, i.e. people are not simply born with or without certain leadership qualities. Instead, Bennis believes that leaders can be made. His in-depth studies have shown that there is no single right way to lead and that leadership is a skill that can be developed. Similarly, John Adair (the world's first professor of leadership studies) believes that leadership qualities can be cultivated and developed through practise and experience. However, Adair also suggests that good leaders should possess some key qualities: integrity, enthusiasm, warmth, calmness and a combination of toughness and fairness. Some of the more popular trait theories are considered below.

HIGHER LEVEL

Likert

Rensis Likert (1967) identified four styles of management and leadership:

- **Exploitative autocratic**. These authoritative leaders do not trust or have confidence in their subordinates. Subsequently orders and decision-making comes from the senior management who put pressure on performance by using threats and punishments.
- **Benevolent autocratic**. These managers and leaders have some compassion and trust in their subordinates and so will seek their ideas and opinions at times. Rewards are preferred to threats. Essentially, this management style is **paternalistic** meaning that the leader acts like a father (or parent or guardian). Such leaders consider the needs of their staff and make decisions that they believe are in their best interests.
- **Participative**. Such managers and leaders place a great deal of trust and have confidence in their workforce and people. They will frequently seek the views and opinions of subordinates, but ultimately retain decision-making power, i.e. they are consultative.
- **Democratic**. These leaders have absolute confidence and trust in their subordinates. They are actively asked for their suggestions and opinions and these are frequently acted upon. Employees feel responsible for the achievement of organizational objectives and there is a substantial amount of teamworking.

The research findings of Likert suggest that both participative and democratic styles are most successful. One criticism of this though is that the theory ignores situations where the autocratic styles may be more suitable and more effective.

Fiedler

Fred Edward Fiedler's contingency theory (1967) is one of the best known situational theories of leadership. As with all situational theorists, Fiedler found that there is no one best way of leading. He suggested that the effectiveness of leaders depends on their personality and the situation under consideration. Some leaders may be effective in certain situations but not equally so in all situations. Fielder's theory rests on three principles that determine the most effective leadership style:

- Relationships – how well leaders and subordinates get along with and trust one another. This will ultimately determine how willing people are to follow the instructions and directions of the leader.
- Situation – the nature of the task itself, the level of difficulty of the task and whether it is structured or subject to change.
- Authority – how much power or authority the leader has.

The model then showed eight possibilities which were very favourable, moderately favourable or very unfavourable. So, for example, if there are good relationships at work, structured tasks and a high degree of authority then leaders are more likely to achieve their objectives.

One of the largest implications of Fiedler's research is that it suggests almost anyone can be a leader if his or her leadership style can be correctly matched to the task or situation. However, one weakness of Fiedler's theory is that it ignores other situational factors that affect leadership effectiveness, such as the experience and training of the leader.

Blake and Mouton

The **Managerial Grid model** was devised by Robert Blake and Jane Mouton (1964). It is a model that shows a range of five different leadership styles. Their two- dimensional grid (see Figure 2.4a) shows the range of management styles based on the *concerns for people* on the *y*-axis and the *concern for completing the task* at hand on the *x*-axis. The axes range from 1 (low) to 9 (high) in the degree of concern held by a manager. Blake and Mouton's managerial grid highlights five styles of management.

Impoverished management style (1,1)

In this style, managers adopt a laissez-faire approach and have little concern for either people or the task. Such managers put in the minimum effort required to keep the task running. Managers may use this style to avoid being held responsible for any mistakes.

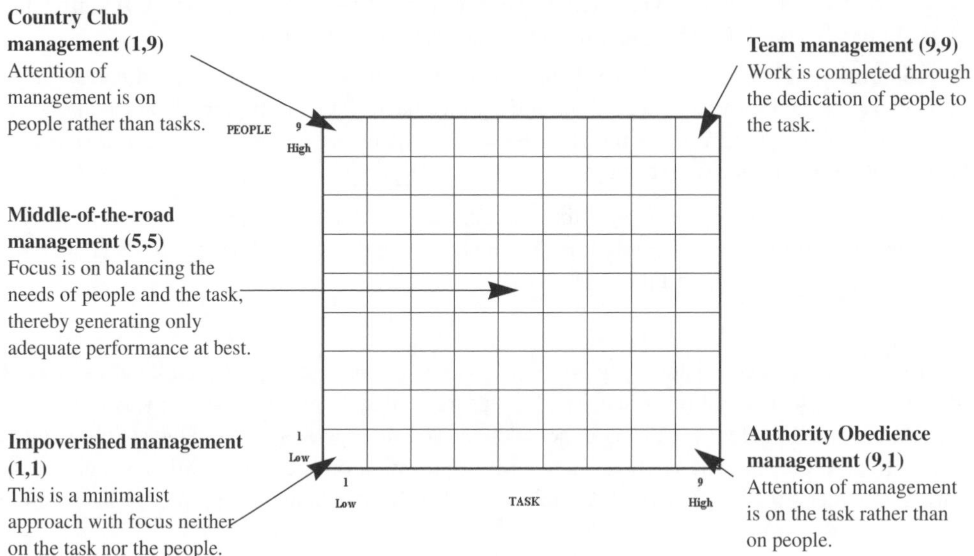

Figure 2.4a Blake and Mouton managerial grid

Country Club management style (1,9)

Leaders adopting this style focus on people's concerns and feelings whilst there is a low concern for completing the task. Managers may strive to create a safe and comfortable working environment. Conflict is minimized in hopes that this would create a friendly working environment and to increase overall performance.

Authority Obedience management style (9,1)

This style of management is the opposite to that of the 'country club' style in that there is utmost concern for production and a low concern for people. This is an autocratic style used by managers whose priority is on completion of the task. Such managers see workers as a means to an end, i.e. they are paid to complete the task at hand and their needs are not relevant or important. This style is based on McGregor's Theory X (see Unit 2.5). It is commonly observed when companies face a major crisis that threatens their survival. Hence this style is also known as the '*produce or perish*' management style.

Team management style (9,9)

With this management style, there is high concern for both people and for the completion of the task. Similar to McGregor's Theory Y, managers adopting this style will involve employees in decision-making, encourage teamwork and make employees feel valuable to the organization.

HIGHER LEVEL

Middle-of-the-road management style (5,5)

Managers that adopt this style aim to balance the goals of a business and the needs of its workers. Such managers are likely to make compromises in order to achieve acceptable performance. However, Blake and Mouton believed that such managers are unable to get the best out of people or to effectively complete the task. Hence, the ultimate consequence is underperformance due to an ineffective management style.

Blake and Mouton concluded that the least effective management style is that of the 'middle of the road' (5,5 on their grid). They also concluded that '*team management*' is the ideal management style. They also found that many leaders tend to switch between styles depending on different situations, despite most people having a preferred style. Donald Trump, real estate mogul and television celebrity, also prefers this style of leadership. In recruiting leaders for his Trump Organization, he looks for two things in a person: a team player who is an effective leader.

Tannenbaum and Schmidt

Robert Tannenbaum and Warren Schmidt (1973) put forward the concept of a **leadership continuum** showing a range of leadership and management styles. The leadership continuum model acknowledges that the chosen style depends on the leader's personality, the qualities of peers and subordinates, and situational factors (such as the degree of urgency and the corporate culture).

At one extreme of the continuum (see Figure 2.4b), managers and leaders exercise full use of their authority and subordinates have no freedom in decision-making. At the other extreme, management allow employees to have full responsibility for decision-making.

Figure 2.4b Tannenbaum and Schmidt leadership continuum

The model also highlights a range of leadership and management styles:

- **Tells** – This style is adopted by autocratic managers and leaders. They will present the final decision to subordinates without any form of consultation with, or participation from, the workforce.
- **Sells** – Leaders and managers adopting this style use persuasion to win support or compliance from subordinates, although the decision itself has already been made.
- **Consults** – This style involves asking subordinates for their opinions before making a final decision. However, this does not necessarily mean that their opinions are acted upon.
- **Participates** – This style absolutely involves employees in the decision-making process. For this to happen, there must be trust and delegation and managers must be willing to let go of their use of authority. This style would tend to be adopted by a highly democratic or laissez-faire manager.

In deciding on the best style, managers and leaders should consider the qualities of the workforce such as their experience and their ability and willingness to take responsibility for decision-making. These factors will help determine the level of confidence that a manager places in the capabilities of the employees and therefore affect his or her ability to reduce the use of authority.

HIGHER LEVEL EXTENSION: CONTINGENCY THEORY AND SITUATIONAL THEORY

Contingency theory

The essence of **Contingency theory** is that there is no single best way to manage an organization or to lead people because what might work in one situation does not necessarily work in other circumstances. The 'best' style depends on internal and external factors that affect the situation, such as the size, knowledge and experience of the workforce.

These theories see leadership as being more flexible in order to adapt to varying circumstances. For example, if the nature of change is immense (such as relocating operations to an overseas country) then this would require a different approach to situations where change is negligible. Hence, these theories differ from traditional styles that are 'fixed', such as democratic, autocratic and laissez faire. Box 2.4b outlines some of the main factors that affect the particular style of management used in different circumstances.

Box 2.4b Factors influencing management and leadership style

- The organizational **culture**, e.g. are staff accustomed to change?
- The **attitudes** of senior managers, e.g. are they optimistic or pessimistic about the abilities of their workers?
- The **traits** of managers, e.g. what are their levels of motivation, experience and know-how?
- **Subordinates**, e.g. how many staff members are there to be managed, and what are their temperament and their experiences?
- The **task** that needs to be performed by staff, e.g. it is a routine or unfamiliar task; is it challenging or straightforward?
- **Time constraints**, e.g. is the deadline imminent or is there enough time to complete the task?

The most predominant contingency theory is that of Fred Fiedler (see 'Fiedler' on page 253). Fiedler argued that a leader's own personality has a large impact on leadership effectiveness, i.e. the performance of the workforce is contingent (dependent or reliant) on the personality of the leader.

Most commentators agree that the best or most successful managers can adapt their management style to suit different situations. They also acknowledge, however, that people will naturally prefer and therefore portray one style.

Situational theory

Situational theory is similar to contingency theory in that both assume there is no optimal style of management or leadership for all businesses. A key difference is that situational theory places greater focus on the behaviour of effective managers and leaders. Contingency theory takes a broader approach and considers the internal and external factors that affect leader ability.

One of the best known situational theories of recent times is that devised by Kenneth Blanchard and Paul Hersey (1969). The **Blanchard and Hersey model** built on the work of Blake and Mouton and used the same criteria – concern for people and concern for the task. They also built in one of Fiedler's variables, namely the *ability* and *willingness* of subordinates to achieve the task set.

Their work showed four possibilities ranging from subordinates being unable and unwilling to being able and willing to complete the task at hand. Subsequently, in each of the four situations with their varying degrees of competence and commitment of staff, a different leadership style was required based on the amount of support and direction needed:

- **Telling/directing style** – This autocratic style is necessary when employees are unable and/or unwilling to complete tasks. Workers have to be told what to do and communication is one-way.
- **Selling/coaching style** – This style of leadership is used when employees have some ability but are not committed, so they therefore need persuading and coaching in order to accomplish targets. This means leaders and managers need to have concern for both task and people (a feature of the Blake and Mouton model). Communication is more two-way than with the telling/directing style.
- **Participating/supporting style** – With this style, the manager or leader acts as a facilitator. Workers have a high degree of competence but an inconsistent commitment. The manager's role is to oversee and encourage rather than to direct their staff.
- **Delegating style** – This style is used if both ability and willingness of staff are high. The manager or leader can feel assured in delegating tasks or jobs. Similar to the above style, the manager or leader acts as a facilitator who is held accountable for the work that is delegated.

Out of these four styles, there is no single best style for any leader. Instead, Blanchard and Hersey found that effective leaders need to be flexible in adapting themselves to a given situation. Nevertheless, individual leaders tend to have a preferred or a natural style that they revert to when situations return to normal. However, they believed that it is the role of the leader to adapt, rather than the follower.

Blanchard and Hersey also suggested that worker attitudes are situational. For instance, although workers might be highly skilled, committed and confident in what they do, they would not necessarily feel this way when faced with tasks requiring skills that they don't have. The role of the manager or leader in this instance is to determine the development level of their team or followers.

One key criticism of Blanchard and Hersey's situational model is that it fails to distinguish between management and leadership. After all, leadership is more about inspiring people rather than about problem solving and decision-making.

The **Path-Goal theory** devised by Robert House (1971) is another situational theory. House identified four different leadership styles which dominate depending on the situation in question:

- **Directive leadership** – The leader gives specific orders and guidelines to subordinates who are expected to follow these instructions.
- **Supportive leadership** – The leader takes a more sympathetic and caring approach by showing their concern for their subordinates' well-being.
- **Participative leadership** – The leader involves subordinates in decision-making by getting them to share their ideas and opinions. This consultative approach means that leaders will consider the suggestions of subordinates before making any final decisions.
- **Achievement-orientated leadership** – The leader has faith in the ability of subordinates and therefore sets challenging goals, with expectations of high-level performance.

HIGHER LEVEL

Again, the model assumes that leaders can adapt to changing situations. In particular, House argued that leaders need to take account of two types of situational factors:

- *Subordinate personality* – Leaders need to consider the traits of the subordinates, e.g. their attitudes, experiences, abilities and level of willingness. For example, directive leadership is unlikely to be suitable for workers who are highly talented and competent.
- *Characteristics of the environment* – In adapting their style, leaders should consider the background and surroundings of the situation, such as nature of the task, the resources available to complete the task and time pressures.

Question 2.4.3

Using situational leadership theories, explain how the following situations may be handled by an effective manager or leader. *[9 marks]*

a Bob is seeking permission to take two weeks off work to look after his father who is critically ill.

b Leona is highly demotivated and is not putting in much effort, causing huge concerns for her team.

c Paolo has complained that his line manager is using bullying tactics and is not observing the equal opportunities policy of the organization.

A final situational theory of leadership is Professor John Adair's **Action-centred leadership model**. Adair believes that managers and leaders are not necessarily 'born leaders'. Instead, he feels that anyone can take charge of a team and develop leadership skills, even if this is through trial and error. Action-centred leadership is based on the appropriate use of authority relevant to the situation in question. Adair identified four types of authority:

- *Position* – authority that comes from the official position of a manager or leader in the organization
- *Knowledge* – authority possessed because of a person's knowledge and access to important information, data and/or acquaintances. It may also originate from someone's experience or familiarity with the particular situation
- *Personality* – authority that exists because of someone's appealing character, personal qualities and/or charisma
- *Moral persuasion* – the art of being able to convince or persuade others to act in a particular way or to make sacrifices for the benefit of others.

Adair concluded that managers and leaders need to understand the particular circumstances of a situation in order to choose the most appropriate type of authority to implement.

HIGHER LEVEL EXTENSION: THE DIFFERENCE BETWEEN LEADERSHIP AND MANAGEMENT

The terms *management* and *leadership* are often used interchangeably because they serve similar purposes. At times, this is acceptable. However, there are some significant differences between their true meanings and it is important to consider these when referring specifically to either management or leadership. Managers and leaders differ on several issues, such as:

- *Time and devotion* – Management consultant and author Gregory P. Smith suggests that management is an 8 a.m. to 5 p.m. obligation whereas leadership is about being responsible 24-hours each day. Warren Bennis argued that managers have a short-term view whereas leaders have a much longer term perspective. In essence, the manager deals with the tactical decisions of an organization whereas the leader takes care of the strategic decisions (see Unit 1.3).

- *Roles and responsibilities* – Leaders are accountable for a much broader range of responsibilities. They deal with *what* and *why* questions, such as the direction of the organization. Hence, leaders are innovative in their way of thinking. For example, Steve Jobs constantly reminds his staff at Apple that they are "changing the world". Managers, on the other hand, deal with the more routine *how* and *when* questions. For example, managers know how best to administer the day-to-day operations of a business. Leaders, however, know what the best thing to actually do is.
- *Influence on others* – Instructions and orders from managers are listened to because they are in an official position of authority. Leaders, however, inspire and motivate their followers through action. They also focus on people and their emotional feelings, rather than concentrating on tasks or rationality (see Figure 2.4c). Hence, leaders are much more socially involved than managers. Warren Bennis argues that the key to competitiveness rests with the ability of leaders to generate *intellectual capital* (the skills and competencies of the workforce). This means that people can no longer be seen as resources that are simply managed. In fact, Bennis suggests that such an approach would be as difficult as 'herding cats' – an expression which means that it is impossible to manage the unmanageable. Instead, leaders inspire and entrust creative and talented people to help the organization move forward.

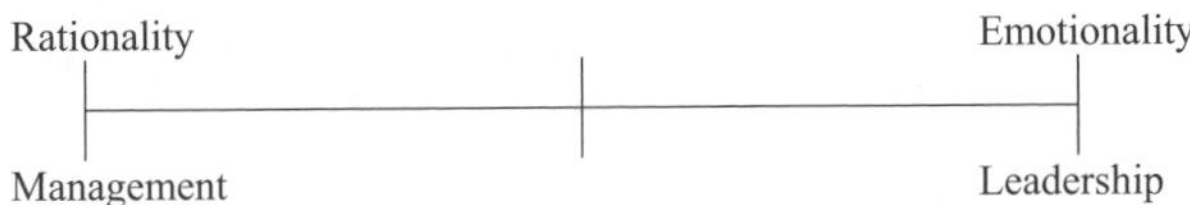

Figure 2.4c The management–leadership continuum

- *Risk taking* – Managers follow predetermined rules and policies set by the organization. They tackle a particular task by keeping order and control. Their focus tends to be on accomplishing tasks. They set an example to their subordinates and this shapes part of the organization's culture. Leaders are more radical in their thinking. They will challenge the status quo (the norms within the organization) in order to move the organization forward.
- *Vision* – Some theorists argue that it is the **vision** that leaders have that separates them from managers. French emperor Napoleon Bonaparte (1769–1821) once said that "a leader is a dealer in hope". Leaders create a culture of hope, getting their people to where they have not been before, whereas managers abide by the procedures and culture of an organization. Manager can do well in stable business environments, but leaders are the ones who shine during times of change.

Despite their differences (see Table 2.4a for an overview of the differences), both management and leadership are essential for a business to be successful. Of course, it is possible for a manager to also be a leader (and vice versa) but this is not necessarily desirable. They provide different traits and strengths to enable an organization to meet its objectives.

HIGHER LEVEL

Table 2.4a Differences between the skills and roles of managers and leaders

Management	Leadership
Do things right	Do the right thing
Doing what's right	Knowing what's right
Directing and controlling others	Motivating and inspiring others
Delegating tasks to subordinates	Empowering 'followers'
Follow orders from senior executives	Inspire others to follow a shared vision
Conform to norms of the organization	Create and foster a change culture
Problem solvers	Innovators
Official position of responsibility within the organization	Traits within people, irrespective of their rank
Position	Action
Planning, directing and monitoring	Strategic decision-making
Listened to by others	Respected, appreciated, liked and trusted by others
Achievement of objectives through compliance of others	Achievement of objectives through acceptance and willingness of followers
Analysis	Decisiveness
Learned skills	Natural instincts
Organization of staff, e.g. supervision and training	Support and guidance for followers

In essence, the difference between management and leadership can be explained by the differences in their characteristics, roles and outcomes. Large businesses in particular rely on both management and leadership to ensure the efficient running of their organizations.

Question 2.4.4

School leadership and management

Schools are typically led by a Principal (the Head Teacher) and a senior leadership team. Middle managers are recruited to fill posts such as Heads of Department and Heads of Year. There might also be a Business Manager whose role is to administer the non-teaching aspects of a school, such as buildings maintenance and management of the non-teaching staff.

a Using examples, comment on how the roles of a manager and a leader differ in organizations. *[4 marks]*

b Apply leadership and motivation theory to discuss how different management and leadership styles can influence the level of staff motivation in organizations such as schools. *[8 marks]*

HIGHER LEVEL EXTENSION: KEY FUNCTIONS OF MANAGEMENT

Functions of management refers to the responsibilities and tasks carried out by managers, i.e. the planning, organizing, directing and controlling of business operations. This section looks at the theories of Fayol, Handy and Drucker, all acclaimed writers in the field of management.

Henri Fayol

Henri Fayol (1841–1925), a French economist, investigated the scientific management of labour organization and production. He argued that a manager's task evolved around planning and execution to ensure its success. He identified the five functions of management in business activity as:

- **Planning**. Managers are responsible for setting the course of action to achieve corporate objectives. Managers are involved in setting both tactical plans (short-term plans) and strategic plans (long-term plans).
- **Organizing**. Managers organize resources in order to achieve corporate objectives. This might include delegating or allocating tasks to workers to ensure that deadlines are met.
- **Commanding**. Managers give instructions and orders to their teams and subordinates in order to achieve business objectives.
- **Coordinating**. Managers have the responsibility of ensuring that all sections or departments strive to achieve the main goals of the business. This means there is a universal or harmonious approach to achieving corporate objectives.
- **Controlling**. Managers are responsible for the performance and health and safety of their teams. Corrective measures must take place if targets are not being met.

Much of Fayol's research was based on his own management experience. He suggested that effective management would entail 'principles of management' which include:

- Division of labour to develop skills and specialization
- Formal lines of authority and wide spans of control, rather like in the military
- An authoritarian style of management being vital so that managers have the authority to give orders. This also meant that decisions were made from the top of the organization only.
- Unity of command because Fayol felt that employees should only have one line manager and that this would improve communication and productivity
- Equity in treatment of employees to ensure that they are committed rather than resentful
- 'Esprit de corps' (creating harmony and unity within teams and groups at work) since Fayol firmly believed in building team cohesiveness in the workplace.

Fayol also believed that management should ensure that there was discipline in the workplace to prevent slack or disobedience. However, he also emphasized the use of equity of treatment so that workers would receive a decent payment for their services, reflective of their input to the production process.

Charles Handy

Charles Handy (born 1932) is renowned for being one of Britain's greatest management gurus, having been credited in 2001 as the second most influential management thinker. A graduate from Oxford University, Handy argued that trying to define a manager is less meaningful than examining what a manager actually does.

HIGHER LEVEL

Handy suggested that there are a number of common characteristics present in most effective managers and leaders:

- **Intelligence**. Handy argued that managers and leaders should have a good level of intelligence (but not necessarily outstanding ability). Managers who think that they are more intelligent (superior) than others or have poor 'people skills' often find that they do not get on very well with their subordinates.
- **Initiative**. Managers and leaders need to be proactive, creative and able to take on risks in order to identify business opportunities.
- **Self-assurance**. Managers and leaders must set an example for others to follow. At the same time, they should show respect for their colleagues. Handy suggested that self-assured managers and leaders bring out the best in people.

Handy also outlined three key roles of management:

- **Managers as general practitioners**. Handy compared the art of management with a person's health. He compared personal health problems with the well-being of a firm, such as the level of staff turnover, productivity and customer satisfaction. If there are health problems in the business, then managers must deal with these. For example, if low productivity is a concern, then managers may hire more people, retrain staff and/or dismiss unproductive employees. Alternatively, low productivity may be a result of poor morale so financial incentives might be used to deal with this.
- **Managers as confronters of dilemmas**. Handy suggested that managers are relatively well paid because they have to deal with a constant flow of dilemmas (problems). For example, managers are required to let go of some authority when delegating work to their teams, but they must also retain control of the assigned tasks. The dilemma is that managers may need to let go in order to gain the trust of their staff.
- **Managers as balancers of cultural mixes**. Much of Handy's theories concentrated on organizational culture (see Unit 2.6) in the workplace. He argued that it is the manager's role to balance the cultural mix in an organization in order to get the best out of each individual. Fayol would have suggested a hierarchical and formal organizational structure to shape and embrace the culture of an organization. However, Handy argued that organizations should become flatter. He suggested that this would improve communications thereby enhancing management decision-making.

Handy suggested that effective management requires a *helicopter factor*, i.e. managers and leaders need to be able to rise above situations to see the 'bigger picture'. Mismanagement or ineffective management, he argued, takes place when there is *micro-managing* in an organization, i.e. managers and leaders get caught up or over-involved in every small part of the business. Instead, managers and leaders need to be able to delegate by being generalists rather than specialists.

Peter Drucker

Peter F. Drucker (1909–2005) is widely credited as the father of modern management. In fact, during the course of his career as a management consultant and university professor, Drucker had written 35 books in his 65 years of writing.

Drucker believed that people are the key to the success of a business. He argued that managers should not get too involved in the daily activities of employees as he believed that they have more knowledge in certain areas than their line manager or other colleagues. Hence, *decentralization* (see Unit 2.2) is encouraged in the workplace.

Drucker considered that managers carry out five basic functions:

1. **Setting organizational objectives**. Managers are involved in setting and communicating organizational objectives (see Unit 1.3).
2. **Organizing tasks and people**. Managers establish systems to ensure the different functional areas of the business are integrated to achieve the organizational objectives. An appropriate organizational structure (see Unit 2.2) must also be used to ensure that all the various tasks and roles are carried out efficiently.
3. **Communicating with and motivating employees**. In order for the workforce to be efficient and productive, managers must build teams that are motivated in achieving organizational objectives.
4. **Measuring performance**. Drucker suggested that job performance should be measured through a system known as 'Management by Objectives' (see Box 2.4c). He believed that each and every employee's job performance can be measured by the extent to which s/he meets the objectives that have been set.
5. **Developing people**. Managers are responsible for bringing out the best in their people. This may be done through giving employees opportunities to take on responsibilities, for example.

Drucker suggested that effective communication with staff and the development of people could prevent a '*them and us*' culture at work (a psychological divide between management and subordinates). He went on to argue that employees need to be given opportunities to develop personally and that they should be managed in a way to suit their needs. This, in turn, would mean that employees would yield greater results for the business. Hence, managers and workers are dependent on each other to fulfil their functions. This notion formed the basis of Drucker's model of management by objectives (MBO), a system based on regular feedback and participation between managers and employees in the setting of objectives. The outcome should therefore include increased productivity, quality and performance in the workplace.

Drucker's Management by Objectives also introduced the setting of SMART objectives (see Unit 1.3). Objectives, whether they are set by management or employees, should be **S**pecific, **M**easurable, **A**greed, **R**ealistic and **T**ime-related.

Often, objectives are not set in this manner and Drucker argues that this leads to mismanagement. Drucker suggested that MBO only works if the people involved clearly know what the objectives are (which he thought was not usually the case).

Drucker also believed that all managers should be involved in **strategic planning**, especially as the business environment is always undergoing change (see Unit 1.8). Drucker felt that businesses ought to recognize the importance of change and embrace change. However, he also argued that businesses should avoid meaningless change, especially since change can be highly expensive. Furthermore, pointless change or change that is not communicated clearly to employees can cause major demotivation among the workforce.

HIGHER LEVEL

Box 2.4c Management by Objectives (MBO)

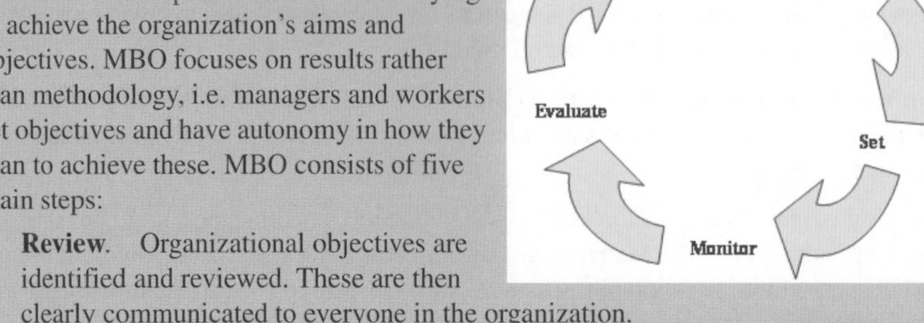

Management by Objectives is a management tool that tries to ensure each person within a business has a clear understanding of their own roles and responsibilities towards trying to achieve the organization's aims and objectives. MBO focuses on results rather than methodology, i.e. managers and workers set objectives and have autonomy in how they plan to achieve these. MBO consists of five main steps:

1 **Review**. Organizational objectives are identified and reviewed. These are then clearly communicated to everyone in the organization.
2 **Set**. Workers set their own goals and targets, enabling them to work towards meeting the organization's aims and objectives.
3 **Monitor**. The progress of employees is checked to ensure that they are likely to meet their goals and targets.
4 **Evaluate**. The performance of workers is evaluated. Feedback on areas of strength and suggestions for improvement are made for the next round of MBO.
5 **Reward**. Employees who achieve or exceed their targets are recognized and rewarded for their contributions towards the organization.

Question 2.4.5

Wilkinson Textiles Ltd

Wilkinson Textiles Ltd is a clothing manufacturer that employs 50 people in its factory. Starting wages at the firm exceed the national minimum wage and staff have come to expect annual pay rises. The current management team, who adopt a laissez-faire approach, have expressed their desire to export the firm's products overseas to gain higher sales and market share. However, mismanagement over the years has led to falling profits and poorer competitiveness. Part of the problem is that many of the staff have become complacent as there is very little supervision.

The new incoming Managing Director of Wilkinson Textiles Ltd has hinted at restructuring the organization. She intends to introduce a system whereby staff are remunerated based on their attainment of certain targets. Pay increments would no longer be a right but a reward for improved performance.

a Apply the theories of authors such as Fayol, Handy or Drucker to explain the functions of management. *[6 marks]*

b Examine how management by objectives might help to improve the competitiveness at Wilkinson Textiles Ltd. *[6 marks]*

LEADERSHIP AND MANAGEMENT AND BUSINESS STRATEGY

The management and leadership styles adopted by a business will have a direct effect on the levels of morale and motivation in the workplace. In turn, this will affect the productivity and profitability of the organization. Hence, it is important for a business to have effective managers and leaders.

The trend for modern organizations is a shift away from an autocratic style of leadership, as advocated by the likes of Fayol and Taylor, towards a more democratic style of leadership; although this does not imply that other organizations have not thrived under a more autocratic leadership system. Effective managers and leaders have been observed to trust their staff rather than to micro-manage their work. Responsibility and power have been delegated to subordinates. Modern management practices see employees having a role in the decision-making process. Mahatma Gandhi (1869–1948) said, "I suppose leadership at one time meant muscles; but today it means getting along with people." This is not seen as a weakness of leaders but an amplification of their ability to lead others.

The Chinese proverb "Talk does not cook rice" suggests that managers and leaders must set an example to subordinates by action, rather than through talk alone. Most people agree that managers and leaders should lead by setting an example. The children's fable in Box 2.4d is an example of why this is important.

Box 2.4d Children's tales and leadership

A mother crab disliked and disapproved of her offspring for walking sideways. Confused, the little crab asked the mother crab for a demonstration on how to perfect his walk. Eventually, the mother crab had to apologize for criticizing the little crab as she herself was unable to walk straight.

From a business viewpoint, theorists such as Fiedler, Blake and Mouton and Blanchard and Hersey have pointed out that it is evidently advantageous to develop subordinates to increase their morale, competence and commitment. Furthermore, delegation of authority spares up the time of leaders and managers so that they can fulfil other strategic tasks. However, it is important to remember that not everyone is suitable or wants to take on extra responsibility. Furthermore, managers still retain overall accountability for the delegated work so must be proactive in monitoring or reviewing the progress of their subordinates.

Management by walking about (MBWA) is a more proactive style of management. Rather than managing operations from an office, MBWA emphasizes the importance of being in physical contact with people, such as by face-to-face conversations.

Management consultant and author, Wally Bock suggests there are 5 P's of effective leadership:

- *Pay Attention To What's Important.* Like Handy, Bock suggests that leaders need to concentrate on what's most important, rather than getting bogged down in the minute details of the organization. He uses the **Pareto 80/20** rule to suggest that 20% of the things done by a manager or leader get 80% of the results.
- *Praise What You Want to Continue.* Praise should be genuinely and sparingly used to get employees to take positive action in continuing to do certain (desirable) things.
- *Punish What You Want to Stop.* By contrast, sanctions should be used to prevent undesirable things from happening.

- *Pay For the Results You Want.* Praise alone will not get results. Pay is a tangible method of rewarding people for doing a good job. The German proverb "Good pay makes happy workers" can be applied here. Motivation theory also suggests that other forms of motivation (see Unit 2.5) can be applied to reward people.
- *Promote People Who Deliver The Results You Want.* Bock suggests that effective people (those who deliver results) should be promoted to help the organization become even more successful.

Bock believes that the five P's of leadership will also help an organization to head towards positive organizational change.

Leadership styles stem from a whole range of factors such as the behaviours and attitudes of subordinates. These in turn can be influenced by the personality and experiences of the manager or leader. Warren Bennis, who has devoted all of his professional life to the qualitative study of leadership, showed that leaders find their own style that suits them best. Although effective managers and leaders may have a natural or preferred style, it is unlikely that they will use a single style since different situations require them to adapt. This will depend on several factors such as the:

- Traits and personality of the manager or leader
- Level of skills, experience, motivation and confidence of the employees
- Time frame, i.e. how quickly decisions need to be made
- Degree of importance of the decision, e.g. tactical or strategic decision-making
- Degree of difficulty of the task, e.g. whether it is routine or a crisis.

However, managers and leaders differ in their approach even when faced with the same task or situation. Hence, the above factors are subjectively weighted by individuals when they adopt a particular style.

The occurrence of *globalization* (see Unit 1.9) brings additional complexities to selecting and using the most appropriate management or leadership style. Using the style that they prefer may not be appropriate in a foreign country where language, cultures and habits are different. Geert Hofstede studied the links between international cultures and organizational cultures (see Unit 2.6) and found that people in different cultures expect different things from a leader. He concludes that knowledge and understanding of the differences that exist can largely affect how managers and leaders behave in a cross-cultural situation.

Despite the distinction made between leaders and managers, they are not mutually exclusive given that the skills required to be an effective leader or manager are essentially the same. After all, managers have to lead their teams in order to achieve the objectives of the organization.

REVIEW QUESTIONS 2.4

1. Outline the qualities of effective managers.
2. Explain the meanings of 'leadership' and 'management'.
3. What are the three levels of management?
4. What are the three main roles of management as advocated by Fayol?
5. Distinguish between 'autocratic', 'democratic' and 'laissez-faire' styles of management and leadership.
6. What five factors affect situational leadership styles? (*Hint*: think of the mnemonic CLOTS.)
7. Outline the difference between 'contingency theory' and 'situational theory'.

Higher Level extension

8 What is the difference between 'trait theory' and 'content theory'?

9 Name the four types of situational styles identified by R. Likert.

10 Outline the findings of F. Fiedler.

11 What did Blake and Mouton mean by 'team leadership'?

12 Outline the four types of leadership and management styles as outlined by Tannenbaum and Schmidt.

13 What are the differences between 'management' and 'leadership'?

14 Compare and contrast the functions of management according to Fayol and Drucker.

Autocratic refers to managers and leaders that adopt an authoritarian style by making all the decisions rather than delegating any responsibility to their subordinates. Instead, the autocratic simply tells others what to do.

Contingency theory is a leadership model based on the belief that the 'best' leadership style for a business depends on a range of interconnected factors, such as the size, skills and abilities of the workforce. There is no single style that suits all businesses and all employees all of the time.

Democratic leader refers to a decision-maker who takes into account the views of employees. Decision-making can therefore be decentralized.

Fayol's theory of management approaches the study of management by looking at the functions of management. Henri Fayol's research found that the main functions of management included planning, organizing, commanding, coordinating and controlling.

Functions of management refers to the tasks of managers, such as the planning, organizing, directing and controlling of business operations.

Leadership is the skill of getting things done through other people by inspiring, influencing and motivating them.

Management is the practice of achieving an organization's objectives by using the available resources of the business, including its human resources.

Management by Objectives (MBO) is a management technique whereby employees set their own objectives, with the help and advice of their manager. Subordinates then decide how they will achieve these targets. Progress towards meeting these objectives is then tracked with follow-up meetings with the manager.

Management style refers to the way in which managers tend to operate, such as in an autocratic, paternalistic, democratic or laissez-faire manner.

Paternalistic managers and leaders treat their employees as if they were family members by guiding them through a process of consultation. In their opinion, they act in the best interest of their workers.

Situational leadership refers to the belief that there is no distinct or unique approach to leadership and management which suits all organizations and all employees. The 'best' style depends on different situations, such as the culture and attitudes of managers and workers.

Motivation

UNIT 2.5

I'm a great believer in luck, and I find the harder I work, the more luck I have.

Thomas Jefferson (1743–1826), 3rd president of the USA

Key topics

- Intrinsic and extrinsic needs and rewards (non-financial and financial)
- Content theories of motivation: Taylor, Maslow, McGregor and Herzberg
- Motivation in practice: financial packages and non-financial rewards

Higher Level extension

- Content theories of Mayo and McClelland
- Process theories of Vroom and Adams

INTRODUCTION

Motivation refers to the desire, effort and passion to achieve something. In business terms, it is often referred to as the willingness to complete a task or job with enthusiasm. The UK Institute of Management defines motivation as "getting someone to do something you want or, on an individual basis, wanting to do something for yourself for a particular reason".

Many businesses argue that people are their most valuable and expensive asset. If this is the case, then it makes sense that the business seeks to gets the most out of their human resources. This Unit looks at *how* managers seek to motivate their workforce to maximize job satisfaction, morale and labour productivity. Box 2.5a outlines some of the benefits of a motivated workforce. This then implies that mangers need to understand the driving forces of their staff in order for the business to achieve its organizational objectives.

Box 2.5a Generic benefits of increased worker motivation

- Higher morale and job satisfaction (which leads to improved productivity and quality)
- Improves corporate image (which helps to attract both customers and potential employees)
- Better industrial relations (reduces the chances of conflict in the workplace)
- Lower staff turnover (reduces the costs of hiring staff)
- Lower absenteeism (staff have incentives to turn up for work)
- Higher profits (generated from all of the above factors)

By contrast, a demotivated workforce will hinder the performance of a business. Signs of poor motivation are summarized in Box 2.5b.

Box 2.5b Warning signs of poor motivation in the workplace

- High absenteeism rates – percentage of workforce that miss work without valid reasons
- High labour turnover rates – number of staff who leave as a percentage of the total workforce
- High wastage level – a high percentage of defected output or work that needs to be redone
- Low quality output – workers are more likely to make mistakes and care less about quality
- Increasing number of customer complaints – because of the poorer quality of output
- Poor punctuality – poor timekeeping and lateness
- Increasing number of disciplinary problems – corrective measures are put into place to deal less productive staff

Motivation can be classified as being either *intrinsic* or *extrinsic*. People are likely to be motivated by a combination of both intrinsic and extrinsic factors.

Intrinsic motivation occurs when people engage in an activity out of their own desire, such as enjoyment of pursuing a hobby or an interest. Activities are undertaken because the person finds them to be challenging, stimulating or satisfying. For example, intrinsically motivated students would want to master a subject rather than rote learn the subject simply to get good test or examination grades. Intrinsic motivation can also occur due to altruistic reasons because there is a sense of commitment to others, such as teams in an organization or to people in the local community.

Extrinsic motivation occurs when people participate in an activity because of the benefits and rewards associated with the activity. These rewards may be tangible (such as wages, salaries, and bonuses) or intangible (such as recognition and praise). Extrinsic motivation can also come about from the threats and pressures imposed by senior management, i.e. workers engage in an activity to avoid punishments.

MOTIVATION IN THEORY

Taylor

Frederick Winslow Taylor (1856–1915) was an American engineer and inventor who advocated the use of piece-rate payment systems. Taylor's **principles of scientific management** (1911) assumed that employees are primarily motivated by money: "What the workmen want from employers beyond anything else is higher wages." Taylor believed that higher productivity could be accomplished by setting output and efficiency targets related to pay.

In Taylor's view, it was the duty of a manager to decide how each and every individual task should be completed. This could be done by analysing the way a task was being done and devising ways to maximize output without jeopardizing efficiency. As a result, Taylor also advocated repetitive tasks based on the **division of labour** and **specialization** in the production process. Taylor suggested, "In the majority of cases, man deliberately plans to do as little as possible." He felt that it was the manager's role to plan, direct and control. Shop floor workers, he assumed, were ill equipped to plan their own work and only sought to maximize their economic rewards from work. The nature of motivation itself can be seen to be subjective since what motivates one worker may not necessarily motivate another. One benefit of Taylor's theory is that it is objective rather than subjective in rewarding workers for their efforts.

Another part of Taylor's scientific management was the introduction of **differentiated piecework**. With this payment system a worker would receive payment based on a standard level of output and receive another rate if the worker exceeded that level. Essentially, this acted as an incentive scheme that rewarded highly productive workers. Furthermore, he recommended that workers ought to be scientifically selected for jobs, based on their abilities rather than managers subjectively making decisions based on their friendship groups.

Taylor's ideas were highly influential in the 1920s. They were most famously adopted by Henry Ford (1863–1947) who used conveyor belt technology in the mass production of the Ford Motor Company's Model T cars. Today, McDonald's Restaurants still use a system of scientific management. Their catering procedures, such as cooking temperatures and cooking times, are the same throughout the world. McDonald's even have their own university to ensure that senior managers are trained to perform their tasks in exactly the same way, wherever they work in the world. It is the managers who routinely carry out inspections to the production processes in their restaurants to ensure that things are running smoothly. Waged-staff are paid using a differentiated piecework system, have no input into how things are done, and most of these workers would say that it is the money that motivates them to work at McDonald's.

Taylor's theory has been criticized for ignoring the *non-physical* contributions of workers. Economists define labour input as the *mental* and physical human efforts used in the production process. Unlike Taylor's studies, it is not easy to measure the 'output' of certain professionals, such as teachers, doctors and social care workers. Therefore, any system of scientific management of such professionals would be ineffective. Furthermore, subsequent studies have shown that people are not only and simply motivated by money. Taylor's theory ignored the *non-financial factors* that motivate employees. Due to the higher levels of educational attainment in modern societies, workers do not simply want to be told what to do but prefer to have a say in how things are done at work. Workers can be innovative and be independent thinkers, something that was not acknowledged in Taylor's study. A final criticism is that scientific management can lead to repetitive and monotonous tasks, thereby leading to job dissatisfaction rather than motivation. Although Taylor's system rewards hard work, employees today do not necessarily feel that financial compensation is sufficient for the drawbacks of such a system.

Nevertheless, Taylor's research on how to increase the levels of productivity and efficiency has stood the test of time. Introduced in the early twentieth century, Taylor's work proved to be highly influential and relevant to the business environment at the time. Firms introducing mass production in the USA employed low skilled migrants who were probably most interested in the pay. Today, many businesses throughout the world, such as in China, Indonesia and India, still use Taylor's approach to motivation. The culture, values and beliefs of the Chinese, especially those in poorly paid occupations, make it idea to use a Taylorite approach. Taylor assumed that people are rational (sensible) so would not work for nothing. By the same argument, this would then mean that a rational person would work harder if they were better paid. The very nature of some jobs, such as factory workers in less economically developed countries, means that the principles of scientific management still apply in the present day.

Maslow

American psychologist Abraham Maslow (1908–1970) focused on the psychological (emotional and mental) needs of workers since he believed that people are motivated by more than just money. He argued that these needs must be met in order to motivate the employee. His research revealed five levels of needs, which he called the **hierarchy of needs** (1943) (see Figure 2.5a).

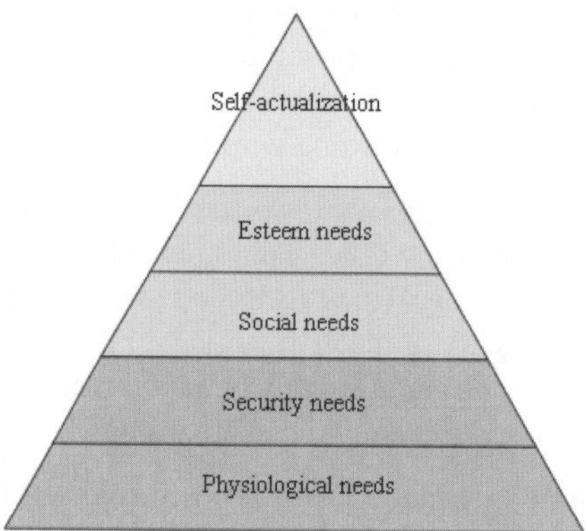

Figure 2.5a Maslow's hierarchy of needs

Workers, it was suggested, would need to be satisfied with all the lower level needs being met before they could progress to higher level needs. For example, a person suffering from hunger would not worry about trying to satisfy recognition or self-esteem needs. Maslow's research suggested that businesses ought to offer incentives to workers in order for them to fulfil each level of need in sequence. The five levels of Maslow's hierarchy of needs are considered below.

1. **Physiological needs** refer to the needs that must be met in order for people to survive. This includes the need for water, food, air, warmth and sleep. In terms of business, how much money a person earns determines the extent to which they are able to meet these fundamental needs.
2. **Security needs**, also known as **safety needs**, refer to the desires necessary to make people feel safe and stable. Once the physiological needs have been met, people can then concentrate

on trying to achieve this next level of needs. Security will include predictability (daily structure and routine) and order (protection from harm). Business applications of safety needs include job security, sick pay, maternity leave and pensions (retirement income).

3 **Social needs**, also known as **love and belonging needs**, refer to the human need to be accepted as part of a friendship group or a family. These needs can be satisfied by communications, social gatherings, weddings, having children and any other opportunity to meet and bond with people. It is human nature to want to be loved and accepted by others. Business applications of this human need include opportunities for interaction and teamwork and recognition of trade union membership. Anti-discrimination legislation (see Unit 2.1) can also help businesses to promote a sense of worth and belonging in the workplace.

4 **Esteem needs**, also called **ego needs**, refer to the desires for recognition and being able to have self-respect. Esteem needs can be *internal* which indicates that people feel good about themselves, perhaps due to a sense of achievement. Alternatively, esteem needs can be *external* (recognized by others) such as having status in the workplace. Professionals such as lawyers, architects and actors strive greatly to meet this level of needs. Job titles, such as 'Head of Department' or 'Regional Director', can help to boost internal and external ego needs. Sincere praise and positive reinforcements is also another method of boosting the ego of employees. Internal promotion of staff, rather than recruiting someone from outside the organization, may also improve staff morale since this shows that employers have faith in the existing workforce. Training and development opportunities also suggest that the business values its people. Giving workers some input into the decision-making process can also increase their level of morale.

5 **Self-actualization** is the highest level in Maslow's hierarchy of needs. It refers to the forces that drive a person to become the best that they can be. Businesses can encourage this by providing opportunities for personal development and promotion. Maslow argued that people who achieve self-actualization are democratic in their outlook rather than authoritarian. This is because in order to reach self-fulfilment, a person must have the freedom over what they do in order to exploit their talents in the job that they excel at and in a way that only they know best. Maslow explained this by saying, "A musician must make music, an artist must paint, a poet must write, if he is to be ultimately happy."

In reality, it may not be feasible for an organization to aim to motivate *all* workers up the hierarchy of needs. In a large department store or supermarket, for example, it may be more realistic to satisfy only physiological and security needs of the sales workforce. It may be more appropriate to concentrate on meeting the higher level needs of key personnel such as senior managers.

Critics of Maslow's theory put forward the following arguments:

- Levels of needs are somewhat difficult to measure. Maslow was a psychologist and not a scientist or mathematician. How accurate can businesses measure the quantitative level of security, ego, esteem and love or belonging in the workplace?
- Maslow assumed that everyone is motivated in the prescribed order of his model. However, do freelance artists and writers or volunteer workers fit this model? Homeworkers and self-employed drivers do not get the social interaction of working in an office, but this does not mean that they cannot be highly motivated or that motivation has to follow a chronological order. Other workers may be willing to sacrifice pay and financial benefits for better working conditions and job security. Indeed, subsequent studies by the Minneapolis Gas Company from 1945–1965 found that both men and women placed security needs as their number one motivator. These extensive studies revealed that advancement, the type of work and being proud of working for the company were the next three key motivators (the latter two do not feature in Maslow's model).

- There is no explanation of what motivates people once they have achieved self-actualization. What drives those who have perhaps already reached self-actualization, such as the likes of Bill Gates, Richard Branson, Lakshmi Mittal and Donald Trump? What motivates them to continue in their lines of business if they have already achieved so much in their prolific careers? What encourages wealthy people who are past retirement age, such as Warren Buffet and Li Ka-Shing, to continue working?

Question 2.5.1

The world's richest people

	Billionaire	Net worth ($US)	Company
1	Warren Buffett	$62 billion	CEO of Berkshire Hathaway (conglomerate)
2	Carlos Slim Helú	$60 billion	CEO of Telmex (telecommunications)
3	William Gates	$58 billion	Founder of Microsoft
4	Lakshmi Mittal	$45 billion	CEO and Chairman of Mittal Steel Company
5	Mukesh Ambani	$43 billion	Chairman of Reliance Industries (India's largest company)
6	Anil Ambani	$42 billion	Chairman of Reliance Group (conglomerate)
7	Ingvar Kamprad	$33 billion	Founder of IKEA (home furnishing)
8	Kushal Pal Singh	$30 billion	President of DLF Universal Limited (real estate)
9	Oleg Deripaska	$28 billion	Chairman of Rusal (energy and aluminium)
10	Karl Albrecht	$27 billion	Founder of Aldi (multinational supermarket chain)
11	Li Ka-Shing	$26.5 billion	Chairman of Cheung Kong Holdings (conglomerate)

Source: adapted from *Forbes* magazine World's Richest People Survey (www.forbes.com)

a Describe what is meant by 'motivation'. *[2 marks]*

b Apply the theories of Taylor and Maslow to comment on whether people are simply motivated by money. *[6 marks]*

c It is difficult to say whether the world's richest people have truly reached self-actualization. Discuss the factors that drive them to continue working in business despite their age or their wealth. *[7 marks]*

McGregor

Douglas McGregor devised **Theory X** and **Theory Y** (1960) to represent the different assumptions that managers have about their employees. McGregor argued that the beliefs managers have about worker attitudes directly influences their management style. Hence, strictly speaking, McGregor's theory is focused on management attitudes rather than motivational theory.

McGregor used the term 'Theory X' to explain the negative management attitude about the workforce. Such managers see their workers as being lazy people who avoid work if possible. They believe that workers need to be given clear instructions and to be supervised because employees do not enjoy work and lack ambition. Theory X managers are most likely to adopt an authoritarian management style where the emphasis is on output and productivity, rather than on the people in the organization. As such, Theory X managers are likely to follow the scientific management approach advocated by F.W. Taylor.

Theory Y managers take a more positive approach and assume that employees are able to achieve organizational objectives out of their own accord and initiative. They believe that workers can gain satisfaction from work and that they are able to take on responsibility. Demotivation,

McGregor argued, is caused by a lack of challenge in a job. Hence, theory Y managers take a more democratic and decentralized approach in their management style.

Exam Tip!
Theory X was used by McGregor to explain managerial thoughts of worker attitudes based on negative assumptions, such as a lack of desire to work or to seek personal professional development. Hence, there are only Theory X (and Y) managers rather than Theory X (and Y) workers.

McGregor concluded that managers ought to adopt a Theory Y approach. He suggested that if managers take on a Theory Y approach, then workers respond accordingly with positive results for the whole organization. US Army General George S. Patton (1885–1945) said, "Never tell people how to do things. Tell them what to do and they will surprise you with their ingenuity."

Herzberg (1959)

Professor Frederick Herzberg (1923–2000) carried out research that focused on investigating the factors that caused satisfaction and dissatisfaction at work. Like Elton Mayo (see 'Mayo' on page 277), Herzberg focused on the sociological and psychological aspects of work. His research was conducted by a series of interviews with accountants and engineers that resulted in two categories of factors affecting the level of motivation in the workplace: *hygiene factors* (mainly physical aspects) and *motivators* (mainly psychological aspects). A list of his findings is shown in Box 2.5c.

Hygiene factors, also known as **maintenance factors**, are the aspects of work that do not motivate but must be met to prevent dissatisfaction. He cited organizational rules, regulations, policies, supervision, working conditions and pay as examples of hygiene factors. The hygiene factors are the factors that meet people's basic needs. Hygiene factors cause job dissatisfaction if they fall below a level considered as being acceptable by the workforce. So, for example, a business that pays less than average wages, offers no job security and has poor working conditions will negatively affect its employees. Herzberg suggested that a pay rise does not in itself motivate, at least not in the long term, because workers can come to expect further pay rises in the future. Furthermore, Herzberg suggested that hygiene factors become an expectation and are taken for granted, such as employer contributions to a worker's pension fund. Hence, maintenance factors do not motivate an employee to work any harder.

Motivators are the factors that can lead to the psychological growth of workers and hence increase satisfaction and performance at work. Herzberg showed that achievement, recognition, responsibility and advancement of the worker led to increased worker satisfaction. He argued that the use of motivators would help to improve the nature and content of the job.

Herzberg believed that firms ought to motivate employees by using a democratic management style. Businesses, he argued, should train employees to perform tasks that they were not capable of doing when they were recruited. He suggested that managers could achieve worker motivation through three key areas:

- **Job enlargement** – Giving workers more variety in what they do, which should make the work more interesting. This does not necessarily mean that the work is any more challenging though.
- **Job enrichment** – Giving workers more complex and challenging tasks, which should contribute to workers feeling a sense of achievement as they are able to exploit their potential.
- **Job empowerment** – Delegating decision-making power to workers over their areas of work, which should help to boost their overall morale.

In addition to coining the terms 'hygiene factors' and 'motivators', Herzberg's theory looked at the crucial difference between what he called 'movement' and what he understood by the term 'motivation'. **Movement** occurs when a person does something because she or he *needs* to, perhaps because it is part of their job description or because the person feels obliged to do so, i.e. movement is based on extrinsic motivation. **Motivation**, on the other hand, happens when a worker does something because she or he actually *wants* to (but the person doesn't have to do it), i.e. it is based on intrinsic motivation. Unlike other theorists who believed that people are motivated by rewards, Herzberg felt that workers are motivated by being responsible for their work, i.e. the work itself can be rewarding.

Figure 2.5b Rules are hygiene factors

Herzberg's theory allowed managers to think in a different manner from previous motivational theorists. The existence of hygiene factors means it may be better for management to ensure that employees are not demotivated, rather than trying to hypothesize what might motivate the workforce. Herzberg's arguments also present problems for managers as he claimed that individuals are unique and therefore what motivates one worker does not necessarily motivate others. He further suggested that a person's mood and priorities affect the level of motivation, so what motivates someone today does not necessarily motivate them tomorrow.

Critics of Herzberg's two factor theory argue that it does not apply to many occupations, especially those in low-skilled and low-paid jobs, where job enrichment and job empowerment are not a feature of the work. Herzberg used professional workers and skilled engineers in his research sample, so the findings may not be representative of less skilled workers. Furthermore, some employees may not want enriched jobs as this involves having extra responsibility and stress. His research also ignored the role of team working in motivating the workforce.

Box 2.5c Herzberg's findings of motivators and hygiene factors

Motivators (causes of satisfaction)	Hygiene factors (causes of dissatisfaction)
• Achievement • Advancement • Interesting tasks • Opportunities for promotion • Personal growth • Recognition • Responsibility • Work itself	• Company policy, rules and regulations • Relationship with peers, subordinates and supervisors • Salary and wages • Security • Status • Supervision and coordination • Working conditions

Question 2.5.2

Richer Sounds

Julian Richer is the Chairman and owner of Richer Sounds, a hi-fi retailer specializing in audio equipment, such as DVD players and amplifiers. He opened his first store in London Bridge at the tender age of nineteen. In 1994, his flagship store in London Bridge set a new Guinness World Record for the highest sales per square metre of any retail outlet in the world – a staggering £195,426 (over $380,000) per square metre.

richer SOUNDS

Richer believes that it is very important his staff 'have fun' and enjoy their work. The top three sales people each month get to use Richer's personal Bentley or Rolls-Royce for the weekend. He also only promotes people internally. Richer argues that businesses with demotivated staff face higher absenteeism, labour turnover, theft and customer complaints.

Sources: www.richersounds.co.uk, www.richerstudentszone.co.uk and *The Richer Way* by Julian Richer

a Explain how motivation can lead to improved labour productivity. *[4 marks]*

b Examine how the views of managers, such as Julian Richer, can affect the successful implementation of motivation in the workplace. *[6 marks]*

HIGHER LEVEL EXTENSION: CONTENT THEORIES OF MAYO AND MCCLELLAND

Motivation theories can be categorized as either *process theories* (covered later in this Unit) or *content theories*. **Content theories** of motivation seek to explain the specific factors that actually motivate people, i.e. *what* motivates people. Such theories acknowledge that human needs tend to change over time and hence factors that motivate people are also likely to change. The theories of McGregor, Maslow and Herzberg (all explained above) are examples of content theories. The theories of Elton Mayo and David McClelland are further examples of content theories of motivation.

Mayo

Professor Elton Mayo (1880–1949) was an Australian psychologist who conducted his experiments on motivation at Hawthorne, USA. Mayo disputed the ideas of Taylor that labour productivity is influenced purely on scientific management methods. Instead, Mayo believed that workers are motivated by a more humane approach to management whereby human relations at work are the key factor. Mayo is credited as establishing the **Human Relations** school of thought on motivation (1927).

The Hawthorne experiments, which lasted over four years, concluded that non-financial factors at work can be more of a motivator than financial incentives. Contrary to Mayo's initial belief that working conditions would affect motivation levels at the Hawthorne factory, his findings showed that any increase in output was simply due to people working together better. Workers performed better when there was scope for discretion, creativity and teamwork. Mayo's research also found that businesses benefited from a more motivated and productive workforce when management take an interest in the welfare of their workers. Staff who feel that their views or efforts are recognized and have a sense of belonging in the organization will be most motivated. His findings were later named the **Hawthorne effect**.

Mayo's findings were instrumental in changing workforce planning and personnel management. Businesses began to see the value in establishing teamworking and setting up social events for staff, realizing that workers enjoy interacting with their colleagues. Mayo acknowledged that teamworking can be obstructive and negative as well as being constructive. He therefore suggested that managers should work to promote and manage **team spirit** (loyalty and unity of team members) and **group dynamics** (exploiting the skills and expertise of each team member). Furthermore, the recruitment process started to look at people's attitudes and personalities rather than just their educational background and skills. It also became accepted that if managers simply showed that they were concerned for the well-being of their staff, this would usually drive workers to perform better.

Critics of Mayo's theory argue that the findings are far too generic. They feel that many workers, particularly those who lack experience or skills, actually want and welcome direction and control from management.

McClelland

American psychologist David McClelland (1917–1998) put forward the **theory of needs** (1961). From his study of 500 managers working in 25 American companies, he concluded that there are three types of motivational needs that must be satisfied in order to boost morale: n-Ach (the need for achievement), n-Aff (the need for affiliation) and n-Pow (the need for power). McClelland believed that these three needs are present in all people although the relative intensity of each one varies from one person to the next. As with all theories of motivation, if managers are aware of these needs and how they affect employees, then the business can allocate jobs and tasks more suitably to boost morale and productivity.

- **Need for achievement** – McClelland found that people who are driven by a need to achieve tend to be moderate risk takers. Low risk activities are too easy to accomplish so n-Ach people do not feel they have genuinely achieved anything. At the same time, achievement-motivated people do not take high risks because the outcome is largely based on chance and luck, rather than through their own efforts. Such people also prefer to work on tasks where they hold the key responsibility or to work alongside high achievers. They are more concerned with personal achievement, rather than any extrinsic reward that recognizes their achievement. This could mean that high achievers may prefer not to delegate tasks. They also tend to self-reflect on their performance in order to find ways to further improve. McClelland suggested that the major causes of n-Ach are parental influences, cultural factors and educational experiences.
- **Need for power** – Power-motivated people like to influence the behaviour of other people so tend to be very strong-willed managers. Power in an organization can take two forms: personal or institutional. People who seek *personal power* do so to pass on instructions or orders to others. This might make the manager feel more important, given their authoritarian approach, but it often makes others resent the manager who is seen by others as a 'power freak'. Staff will have to do as they are told, whether they agree with the manager or not. By contrast, people who have *institutional power* strive to make others work harder in order to achieve corporate aims and objectives. They use their authority to try and bring out the best in their staff. Hence, McClelland argued that these people are more likely to be successful. He also suggested that any good leader needs to have at least moderate n-Pow since leadership is about influencing the behaviour of others.
- **Need for affiliation** – People who need affiliation are those who seek to have a good social and working relationship with their colleagues and the management team. This will make them happier at work, thereby helping to increase their morale and productivity. Such people tend to conform to group norms and avoid conflict in order to be accepted as part of a group. Unlike n-Ach people who may prefer to work alone, n-Aff people prefer work with opportunities for social interactions, such as teamworking or customer relations.

McClelland's main contribution to the Human Relations school of thought is that people with different kinds of needs are motivated differently. People with high n-Ach ought to be given achievable but challenging tasks. They also need frequent feedback, often reflected in the level of their salary (even though money is not a key motivator for them). People with high n-Pow should be given opportunities to manage and lead a team of people. Finally, those with n-Aff should be provided with a cooperative and collaborative working environment in order to gain their best performance.

HIGHER LEVEL EXTENSION: PROCESS THEORIES OF MOTIVATION

Process theories of motivation look at the decision-making processes and behaviour of people to determine motivation. Instead of focusing on *what* motivates (content theories), process theories look at *why* people behave in a certain manner and *how* motivation can be maintained or stimulated. Process theories suggest that people have a choice in how they tackle tasks, perhaps in either a positive or contrived manner, in order to meet a desired goal. These theories look at what people think about when deciding whether to put in effort to complete a task. Two widely known process theories of motivation are Vroom's Expectancy Theory and Adams's Equity Theory.

Vroom's Expectancy theory

Victor Vroom suggested that people will only put in effort to do a task when they expect that their role will help to achieve the required result (1964). If workers feel that they lack the ability, expertise or skill to achieve a target, then their level of effort will be lower (which reflects a lower level of motivation).

Vroom's work shows that a variety of factors affect a person's approach to work. However, it is assumed that the worker will choose the route that offers the greatest probability of achieving their goals. Not surprisingly, Vroom found that there is a positive correlation between a person's efforts and his or her level of performance. He acknowledged that a worker's performance is based on personal factors such as experience, skills, knowledge and self-belief.

Vroom also argued that when faced with alternative approaches to dealing with a certain task, individuals choose the option with the greatest *motivation force*. Motivation force is composed of three parts:

- **Expectancy** – People have different expectations about their experience, capability and level of self-confidence in tackling a task. There are also different perceptions about the level of difficulty of the task.
- **Instrumentality** – People hold the perception that if they meet performance expectations, then they will be rewarded accordingly (or what they think is desirable as an award). Managers need to ensure that promises are upheld to gain people's trust and therefore their level of motivation.
- **Valence** – People place different values on different rewards. In tackling a task, they will think about whether it is worth the extra effort in terms of both intrinsic rewards (such as satisfaction and ego) and extrinsic rewards (such as money and promotion). Hence, Vroom suggested that managers need to find out what their staff value.

Adams's Equity theory

John Stacey Adams's Equity Theory (1963) suggests that workers will naturally compare their efforts or rewards to those of others in the workplace (subordinates, peers and superiors). Each worker should receive a *remuneration package* (salary plus fringe benefits) that reflects his or her efforts. Adams argued that workers will only be motivated if their remuneration package is seen to be fair in relation to others in the workplace. The degree of equity (fairness) in rewarding efforts will have an impact on the level of motivation. There is inequality if those who put in more effort (or have to contribute more as part of their job) are paid a lower salary. This might be due to poor *job analysis* and *job evaluation* (see Unit 2.1). Inequality is therefore likely to mean the disgruntled employees (who are paid less but do at least the same or more work as others) will reduce their efforts and contributions.

Adams proposed that businesses strive to ensure that their employees perceive equality in the workplace. Staff who feel that they are under-compensated may become demotivated and subsequently withdraw any goodwill and reduce their effort. If inequity is allowed to continue then **absenteeism** may increase thereby increasing costs (see Box 2.5d). In more extreme cases, staff may even resign from their jobs.

Box 2.5d Costs of high absenteeism

- Hiring temporary staff to cover for absent workers.
- Overtime costs and disruptions to staff who take on the work of absent staff members.
- Lower productivity since the absent worker's expertise is missed.
- Understaffing which causes detrimental effects on staff morale and customer service.
- Loss of output if a worker's position or role cannot be replaced by another worker.

Table 2.5a Summary of motivational theorists and their main findings

Theorist	Theory	Main findings
F.W. Taylor	Scientific Management	Pay, above all, is the main source of motivation
A. Maslow	Hierarchy of Needs	Levels of human needs, from physiological to self-actualization
F. Herzberg	Two Factor Theory	Hygiene factors (which do not motivate alone) and Motivators
D. McGregor	Theory X and Theory Y	Management perceptions of the attitudes of their workers
E. Mayo	Human Relations	Motivation is improved by better human relations at work
D. McClelland	Theory of Needs	Managers have varying degrees of n-Ach, n-Pow and n-Aff
V. Vroom	Expectancy Theory	Motivation depends on expectations of effort needed and the rewards
J.S. Adams	Equity Theory	Workers are motivated if there is fairness in remuneration packages

MOTIVATION IN PRACTICE

This section looks at what managers do and use in practice to achieve motivation. **Financial motivation** refers to the payment methods that are used by businesses to motivate their workforce, such as by using wages, salaries and bonuses. **Non-financial motivation** refers to all other forms of motivation, such as praise, recognition and teamworking.

Financial motivation

Financial methods of motivation are the ways that businesses can motivate workers by using some form of monetary reward, such as profit-related pay. The main methods of financial payment systems are considered below.

Wages (time and piece rates)

One category of payment system is the **time-based payment system**, which refers to payments made to staff based on the time they have devoted to their work. **Wages** are usually expressed as the hourly rate of labour, although wages can be paid on the basis of a daily or weekly rate. The vast majority of unskilled workers in developed countries are paid by hourly wages. The wage rate is likely to depend on the worker's age, experience and responsibilities. In many countries, a *national minimum wage rate* is set by the government and all employers must pay their workers no less than the stated rate. Those who earn wages are likely to be paid **overtime** (hours in excess of a worker's contracted time) for any extra hours that they work. This extra work attracts a higher rate of pay per time period to compensate the employee for sacrificing more leisure time in order to work. It is quite common for overtime rate to be paid at *time and a half* (50% extra pay per hour) or *double pay* (100% extra pay per hour).

The advantage of using wages as a payment system is that it is a straightforward method which is easily understood by the workforce. The key disadvantage, however, is that workers are not rewarded for their efforts but their time. This may encourage slack and poor productivity.

Piece rate

Piece rate is a payment system that can be used to get around the problem of wages by rewarding workers that are more productive. This payment system, advocated by Frederick W. Taylor, pays workers for each item that they produce or sell in a given time period. This helps to ensure that workers are paid for the amount of work they actually do. Taxi drivers, for example, are paid using this method; the more customer rides they complete, the higher their income becomes. Piece rate is also commonly used for paying factory workers. The key advantage is that employees have an incentive to work hard in order to maximize their incomes. However, there may be a trade off between quantity and quality of output and hence there tends to be a need for supervision and quality control. In addition, staff may be demotivated by piece rate systems due to the uncertain level of incomes, often caused by factors beyond their control such as machinery failure (which would affect their productivity and hence their pay).

Salary

Salaries are set at a fixed annual rate but paid at the end of each month. For example, a person earning $30,000 per year is paid $2,500 per month. Salaries help to improve a firm's cash flow since workers are only paid once a month, usually directly into the worker's bank account. This is also safer and more convenient since there is no need to pay workers in cash. By contrast, those earning wages may be paid in cash on a daily basis. Salaried workers often have to work more than their contracted hours but they are not likely to be paid for this extra work (just ask your teachers!) since any overtime is usually considered to be part of the job.

Salaries are an example of time rate payment systems. These are used where output or productivity is not easy to measure and where linking pay with speed may lead to lower standards, e.g. as in the case of teachers and doctors. However, time-based payment systems suffer from two key disadvantages:

- It is not easy to distinguish the efforts or output of different workers. Therefore, it is difficult to reward those who are more efficient and productive.
- There is little, if any, incentive to work hard since people are paid the same amount for their time. This may encourage slack or 'skiving' in the workplace.

The way to deal with these problems is to introduce a system of *performance management* and *performance appraisal* (see Unit 2.1).

Exam Tip!

The terms 'salary' and 'wage' are often used interchangeably by students. However, to a firm, salaries are seen as a fixed cost whereas wages are a variable cost. Instead, it might be better for students to use the term **earnings** which is often used to describe the amount of payment received from employment. The total amount earned during a period of time is known as the **gross earnings**. From the gross earnings, there are several *deductions* that need to be made, such as personal income tax and pension contributions. The government also allows people to earn a certain amount of money (known as the **tax allowance**) before they pay income tax. The amount received after all deductions are made is known as **net earnings** (the take-home pay).

Commission

Apart from time-based payment systems, businesses can use **output-based payment systems**. The most common types of output-based payment systems are *piece rate* (see 'Piece rate' on page 281) and *commission*. Under these systems, workers are paid a certain amount of money based on their level of output, i.e. how much they produce or sell. **Commission** pays workers based on a proportion (percentage) of sales or output contributed by a worker whereas **piece rate** is a fixed amount per unit sold or produced. For example, an estate agent may get paid 1% (known as the *commission*) of the value of each property that she or he sells. By contrast, if a machinist working in a clothing factory gets paid $1.20 per garment (known as the *piece rate*) and manages to produce 200 items of clothing in a week, then the gross earnings would be $240.

Piece rate and commission are commonly found in jobs that pay a low basic wage or when payment acts as an incentive to sell more. Insurance brokers, for instance, receive a percentage of the premium paid on policies that they have arranged for the company.

In reality, it is common for those paid by piece rate or commission, such as sales personnel, to receive a basic salary. To some extent, this helps to meet their physiological needs so even if the sales person does not manage to sell anything, then she or he will still be paid the basic amount. However, for each item sold the sales person will earn commission thereby boosting their overall earnings.

Piece rate and commission as payment methods can overcome the problems of time-based systems. However, they suffer from their own limitations:

- Speed in production or aggressive selling techniques do not necessarily correlate with high quality output or customer care.
- There is added pressure on workers to sell more or to perform at a faster pace.
- Tasks can be quite repetitive and monotonous, thereby causing boredom.
- Since payments depend on fluctuating sales or output levels, there is a lack of security (staff do not know how much they will be paid).
- There may be a need to hire more quality controllers, especially in manufacturing processes.

Question 2.5.3

a Sarah earns $5 per hour as a part-time worker at a fast-food restaurant. Her contracted hours are 12.5 hours per week. Calculate her weekly gross pay. *[2 marks]*

b Michael earns $2,400 per month. Income tax rate is 15% and his tax allowance is $15,000 per year. Use these figures to calculate Michael's:

i annual gross income. *[2 marks]*

ii annual taxable income. *[2 marks]*

iii annual take-home pay. *[2 marks]*

c Linda works in an office and earns $12,500 per calendar month. Calculate how much she earns per week. *[2 marks]*

d Steve is a sales person who earns a basic salary of $1,000 each month. Last month, he managed to sell goods to the value of $15,000 on which he earns a commission of 5.5%. Calculate his gross pay for the month. *[3 marks]*

e Use examples to distinguish between time-based and output-based payment systems. *[3 marks]*

Profit-related pay

Some businesses try to motivate their workforce by linking pay to the level of profits in the firm; the higher the amount of profit made, the greater the pay received by employees. This method of payment is known as **profit-related pay** or **profit sharing**, and it is usually paid as an annual bonus. Wal-Mart, the world's largest retailer, announced in 2007 that it was to bring back annual bonuses as part of its remuneration to staff. The American firm stated an average payout of $651 to its 1.3 million hourly-paid workers. Similarly, many airlines pay a thirteenth month bonus, paid along with the employee's December salary. The amount paid will usually be linked to the employee's salary and length of service, so those on higher salaries and who have been with the firm the longest are rewarded the most. This is seen to be a fairer way to share any profits of the business with its workers.

Profit-related pay is used to strengthen employee loyalty and to foster team working (since profits for the business can only be made by combined team efforts rather than by efforts of an individual). Hence, profit sharing should boost labour efficiency and limit the possibility of labour conflict. Another advantage of profit sharing is that it can help to break down a 'them and us' culture (see Unit 2.6) since management and employees work together to achieve higher levels of profit.

However, profit-related pay suffers from several key drawbacks. The first is that the share of profits given to employees is often seen as too small to provide an incentive to work any harder. Also, individual efforts are not explicitly recognized by this reward system, so there is no incentive for any individual to improve their performance. In reality, profit sharing tends to be used as a reward system for senior management rather than for the whole workforce, especially since most individuals lower down in an organization feel that they have no influence in changing the level of a firm's profits.

Performance-related pay

Performance-related pay (PRP) is a little more flexible than profit-related pay as a payment system. PRP rewards those employees (as individuals, teams or as a whole workforce) who meet certain goals. These goals may be related to sales targets, competence in a job or successfully completing a contract. It is common that the goals are evaluated and reviewed in performance appraisal meetings (see Unit 2.1).

There is a variety of ways in which PRP can be paid:

- *Performance bonus* – Paid to workers who have reached output or quality targets. Sales staff, for example, may receive a cash bonus for reaching their sales targets.
- *Loyalty bonus* – Paid to workers who have stayed with a firm for a certain length of time. Many businesses pay a Christmas bonus (or a 13th month bonus) for their loyalty to the business.
- *Pay rise* – An increment in a person's pay due to meeting or exceeding their performance management targets.
- *Gratuity* – Paid to staff who complete their employment contracts. For instance, international schools typically pay teachers that have been recruited from overseas a 20% gratuity (end-of-contract bonus based on an employee's annual salary).

The main advantage of PRP is that it should create incentives for people to work and perform better. Workers can also focus better if targets for each individual are clearly set out. It is also seen as a fairer system since hard work is rewarded (see 'Adams's Equity theory' on page 279). Furthermore, a system of performance management helps to develop a performance culture where people strive to achieve their targets (in return for the benefits of PRP, such as opportunities for promotion or a financial bonus).

However, PRP does suffer from several disadvantages:

- Targets may be unrealistic or unachievable and this will cause resentment and hinder job performance.
- Stress caused by the pressure imposed on workers to meet their targets (especially if their pay scale is linked to meeting set targets).
- Non-financial motivators are ignored.
- PRP is not appropriate for some professions where quality is seen as more important than quantity, e.g. it is not easy to use PRP for rewarding public sector doctors and teachers since it is difficult to quantify their level of performance.
- It may not promote teamwork since individual targets are set in a performance appraisal meeting (even though team targets can be set). This can lead to workers feeling rather alienated especially if they feel they are being treated unfairly and their colleagues are being better rewarded.

Question 2.5.4

The Hong Kong Football Association

In 1996, the Hong Kong Football Association offered a HK$100,000 ($12,850) bonus for each goal scored in the match between local club Instant-Dict and European football giants AC Milan.

a Define 'performance-related pay'. *[2 marks]*

b Explain the problems of paying staff who work as a team, such as professional football players, by a system of performance-related pay. *[4 marks]*

Employee share ownership schemes

This payment system rewards workers, managers and directors by giving them shares in the company. Alternatively, shares in the company can be sold to these groups at a discounted price. It is an alternative to profit sharing or awarding a cash bonus.

The reasons for using share ownership schemes is that staff will have a more direct interest in the well-being of the organization by also being shareholders of the company. A more profitable business will tend to translate into a higher market price for the company's shares. In addition, employers who offer such schemes tend to benefit from lower rates of absenteeism and staff turnover (see Unit 2.1).

In reality, share ownership schemes tend to be used for rewarding those in the senior management team. The majority of employees do not qualify for share ownership, and even if they did the amount distributed is hardly sufficient to sustain their level of motivation. Hence, this payment system may prove to be impractical for many companies.

Fringe payments

Fringe benefits, or **perks**, are the payments and benefits to an employee in addition to his or her wages (or salary). These will vary from one firm to another and depend on the position of an employee in the organization. Examples of fringe benefits include: subsidized meals, private health insurance, housing allowance, employer contributions to the employee's retirement fund, staff discounts and company cars. For instance, Timberland (the American boots and outdoor apparel company) offers a $3,000 subsidy to its employees who buy a hybrid motor vehicle. Timberland's outdoor brand image is coupled with its aim to preserve the environment by offering this fringe benefit for its workers wishing to purchase environmentally friendly cars. In contrast, the top executives at Google have access to a corporate jet.

One important advantage of using fringe benefits is that it helps to encourage employee loyalty. Fringe benefits can help to meet an employee's safety needs (see 'Maslow' on page 272). They can also make employees feel valued because the employer provides these extra benefits to enhance the well-being of their workers.

The key disadvantage of using fringe benefits is the potentially huge cost. For example, it is likely that every employee will receive basic fringe benefits, such as free uniforms, private medical cover and staff discounts (when purchasing the firm's products). In addition, senior managers will qualify for further benefits, such as company cars and business-class air travel. These expenses all add up and can be a huge burden on a firm's cash flow position.

Question 2.5.5

Citic International School

Citic International School (CIS) was set up in 1992 and has become a highly successful independent fee-paying school. The school employs teachers, mainly from overseas, on a two-year finite contract. In addition to their salaries, staff earn a 20% gratuity at the end of their contracts and other benefits in excess of industry norms.

Dave Sanda, the new principal who joined a year ago, has decided that there needs to be some radical changes to ensure that CIS remains competitive. Annual pay increments would now be based on a performance appraisal carried out by line managers, i.e. performance related pay. Dave Sanda also stated that CIS teachers would get a 5% pay cut, to bring salaries in line with other international schools. This would also allow the school to cut tuition fees by up to 3% within the next year.

a Using motivational theory, examine the possible consequences following implementation of the principal's plans. *[6 marks]*

b Evaluate the principal's proposal to remunerate teachers by using performance appraisals. *[8 marks]*

Non-financial motivation

Non-financial motivators are non-monetary factors that motivate people by offering psychological and intangible benefits, i.e. these factors are not directly linked to money. Mayo, Maslow and Herzberg were all advocates of non-financial rewards as a means of motivation in the workplace. Examples of non-financial motivators are explained below.

Job enrichment

Herzberg emphasized that one way to improve motivation was by making a job more interesting or challenging. **Job enrichment**, also known as **vertical loading**, gives workers more *challenging jobs* with more *responsibilities*. It aims to give workers greater independence and power in their work. Therefore, workers have better opportunities to express and develop their own ideas. This could result in psychological growth for the worker and better execution of the work carried out. The ability to do a range of tasks also means that workers have a better sense of achievement and hence they become more committed to their work. Therefore job enrichment, Herzberg argued, would be beneficial for an organization.

The limitation of job enrichment is that time and money need to be spent training the worker to fulfil these extra aspects of their job. Furthermore, managers must ensure that jobs are not be too challenging for the task holder. Setting tasks that are too complex for an employee who does not have the right skills will not only lead to disastrous outcomes, but can also destroy the confidence and morale of the worker.

Job enlargement

Job enlargement refers to broadening or increasing the *number of tasks* that an employee performs in order to motivate. The idea is to increase the variety of tasks, thereby reducing the monotony (repetitiveness) of tasks that can cause boredom and demotivation. So a communications officer employed to answer telephone calls might be given extra duties, including filing, photocopying, typing and other clerical tasks. Job enlargement can add interest to a job as there is more variety and involves the worker having an enlarged role within the organization.

Job rotation is a form of job enlargement that involves workers performing different tasks at the same level of complexity (known as **horizontal loading**). This method is systematic as it involves employees performing a number of different tasks in order. Again, the idea is to provide more variety to avoid the problems of over-specialization (such as boredom caused by performing the same tasks over and over).

Empowerment

This involves granting workers the *authority* to be in charge of their own jobs, to make decisions and to execute their own ideas. Hence, subordinates have some autonomy in decision-making and can decide for themselves the best way to deal with a task, an issue or a problem. It is thought that such an approach can boost motivation as empowered employees have a say in how things are done at work and they can feel a sense of achievement when tasks are successfully accomplished. For example, empowerment is commonly found in the teaching profession where the head teacher or head of department allows subject teachers to deliver lessons in a way that they see most appropriate.

However, empowerment must be used appropriately. Delegating tasks and empowering staff can only be successful if the workers have adequate skills and have received the necessary training to independently tackle given tasks. Managers are still held accountable for the tasks that they delegate to their subordinates, so inappropriate use of empowerment can lead to expensive mistakes being made.

Teamworking

Teamworking is where staff have the opportunity to work alongside fellow employees. Examples include:

- *Cell production* – Team members work on part of the production process.
- *Quality circles* – Members meet regularly to discuss solutions to problems regarding quality within the production process.
- *Departmentalized teams* – Labour is divided by organizing people into functional departments.

Working in groups can reduce boredom (of working alone) and help to meet the social needs of employees. From the employer's perspective, teamworking can help workers to build a sense of belonging, thereby helping to reduce absenteeism and staff turnover whilst boosting labour productivity. Furthermore, it can lead to greater flexibility and multiskilling as workers learn from other team members. This means workers can cover for one another during times of absences without delaying the production process or the quality of service being delivered.

The **Adair model** of team building (named after Professor John Adair) shows that there are three parts to effective teamworking:

- *Tasks* must be challenging enough to maintain the interest of individual team members.
- The *team* must work collectively to successfully complete the task.
- The team caters for the needs of each *individual* member of the group.

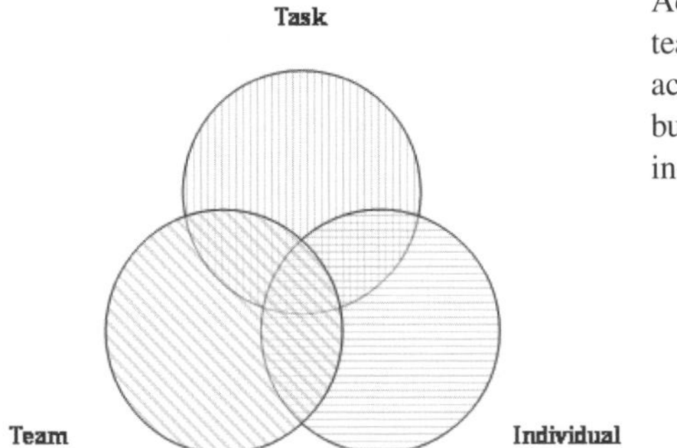

Adair found that effective team leaders strive to accomplish challenging tasks, build teams and develop the individual.

Figure 2.5c The Adair Teamworking model

The Adair model presents an ideal situation for successful teamworking. Adair argued that too often, teams focus on performance and achieving goals, with little attention being paid to individuals within the team. Hence, **group dynamics** (the range of individual problem-solving skills and experiences) are not exploited. Effective management of teams requires recognition and reinforcement of the importance of every member's input. This will help to keep every team member enthusiastic and improve the atmosphere in the workplace.

The **Belbin model** of teamworking (named after Dr. Meredith Belbin) considered the behaviour of managers from all over the world. These managers were put into different teams and given a series of psychometric tests and complex management exercises. Their different personalities, intellect and conduct were assessed during the tests. Over a period of almost a decade, different clusters of behaviour were identified as underlying the success of different teams. The findings showed the emergence of nine patterns of behaviour (or **team role**):

- Action orientated – *Shaper*, *Implementer* and *Completer Finisher.*
- People orientated – *Coordinator*, *Teamworker* and *Resource Investigator.*
- Cerebral orientated – *Plant*, *Monitor Evaluator* and *Specialist.*

Belbin argued that different team roles yield different benefits (what he called **contributions**) and that a person's overall strongest roles are the ones most appreciated by other people. For example, a 'monitor evaluator' (see Table 2.5b) has the strength of being able to make objective judgements. However, by having the characteristics of a monitor evaluator, Belbin argued that this comes at a price (what he called **allowable weaknesses**).

Belbin's model can give some insight to how an individual feels and behaves in a group. Belbin's research showed that a balanced team – one with the greatest chance to succeed – would contain a balance of team roles. Furthermore, every team goes through phases during which some team roles are better able to contribute than others. Belbin's model allows a group to analyse its collective strengths and weaknesses in team role terms and objectively plan to capitalize on those strengths and minimize the negative impact of its allowable weaknesses.

Table 2.5b Belbin's team role model

	Team–Role Type	Contribution (Benefits)	Allowable Weaknesses	Suggested task allocation
Action orientated	Shaper	Challenging, dynamic, thrives on pressure; drive and courage to overcome obstacles; Directing team attention to objectives and priorities.	Prone to provocation. Offends people's feelings.	Person best suited to overcome obstacles and opposition; create a sense of urgency and ensure that talk is turned into action.
	Implementer	Disciplined, reliable, conservative and efficient. Turns ideas into practical actions; out agreed plans systematically and efficiently.	Somewhat inflexible. Slow to respond to new possibilities.	Appointed as organizer, responsible for procedures and practical steps to be taken once team reaches significant decisions.
	Completer Finisher	Thorough, conscientious, anxious. Searches out errors and omissions. maintains sense of urgency within team and delivers on time.	Inclined to worry unduly. Reluctant to delegate. Slow to respond to new possibilities.	Should ensure team's work meets necessary deadlines and conforms to highest standards. Responsible for ensuring no inaccuracies or errors.

Table 2.5b Belbin's team role model (cont.)

	Team–Role Type	Contribution (Benefits)	Allowable Weaknesses	Suggested task allocation
People orientated	Coordinator	Mature, confident, good chairperson; clarifies goals; promotes decision-making; delegates well; recognizes where team's strengths and weaknesses lie.	Can often be seen as manipulative. Off loads personal work.	Best person to coordinate group effort; ensure that everyone has a useful role and that team works towards common goal.
	Team worker	Cooperative, mild, observant and diplomatic. Listens, builds, averts friction Supports members in their strengths; e.g. building on suggestions, fostering team spirit generally.	Indecisive in critical situations.	Should play a floating role, using versatile qualities to help where others cannot manage. Should use diplomatic skills to overcome conflict.
	Resource Investigator	Extrovert, enthusiastic, communicative. Explores and reports on opportunities, and resources outside the group.	Over-optimistic. Loses interest once initial enthusiasm has passed.	Should be responsible for developing external contacts and exploring new opportunities; needs a chance to conduct negotiations but must report back to group.
Cerebral orientated	Plant	Creative, imaginative, unconventional; solves difficult problems; redefines problems; advances new ideas and strategies.	Ignores incidentals; too preoccupied to communicate effectively.	Deal with most problem solving or be responsible for generating new strategies or ideas and proposing solutions to the rest of the team.
	Monitor Evaluator	Objective, impartial and good at carefully weighing up all possibilities to make the right decision; judges accurately.	Lacks drive and ability to inspire others; can come across as unenthusiastic or boring.	Responsible for ensuring all worthwhile options are considered; needs a key role in planning; an arbitrator in event of controversy.
	Specialist	Single-minded, self-starting, dedicated. Provides technical knowledge and skills in rare supply. Contributes professional viewpoint on subject under discussion.	Contributes only on a narrow front; Dwells on technicalities.	Should provide focus on technical issues confronting team; should provide knowledge and techniques in short supply.

Question 2.5.6

European studies show that 'soft' interpersonal skills such as communication, coaching and mentoring are being increasingly demanded by employers. A recent survey showed that employers in the UK value teamworking above leadership and problem-solving skills in a workforce.

a Examine the advantages to businesses that encourage teamworking. *[6 marks]*

b To what extent do non-financial motivators increase the productivity of a workforce? *[8 marks]*

Others

Other forms of non-financial motivation include the use of:

- **Recognition and praise** – Henry Ford once said, "There is no happiness except in the realization that we have accomplished something." Employees feel a sense of accomplishment when they are recognized and praised for the tasks that they have done. Professional sports people win trophies and other honours in recognition of their achievements. The same applies in the workplace. Schemes such as 'employee of the month' may or may not come with a financial reward, but for many people the recognition is likely to be more important than any financial gain. Charle, a Japanese lingerie maker, pay for an all-expenses annual visit to one of Disneyland's theme parks (including flights, entrance and hotel costs) for over 5,500 members of its staff. This is in recognition of the contributions of the firm's workers during the year.
- **The working environment** – Having a pleasant and well-resourced workplace will help to make workers feel more comfortable at work, thereby boosting their morale. For instance, being able to work in a nice office can certainly help to raise productivity levels. Staff at Google's head office are never late for work or do not mind working overtime since there are free breakfast, lunch and dinner buffet canteens for all employees, irrespective of their rank. Staff can also relax when not working by using Google's on-site staff gym, sauna and swimming pool facilities.
- **Continuous professional development** (CPD) opportunities – Employers who provide opportunities for their staff to undertake ongoing training tend to find that the costs of providing CPD are far less than the benefits reaped from having a more loyal and productive workforce. Workers feel more important and valued if the firm provides them with training and development opportunities. Furthermore, managers can delegate more responsibilities to staff who have been appropriately trained. This can help workers to climb up the career ladder and to fulfil their potential.
- **Delegation** – This occurs when managers pass on responsibility to their subordinates. This allows the subordinate to take charge of a task and to take credit for his or her accomplishments. Managers must ensure that subordinates have the competence (ability) and desire (willingness) to take on extra responsibility. In addition, they must make sure that staff are given sufficient time and resources to accomplish the delegated tasks. Successful delegation can therefore help to improve staff morale and help people to progress in their careers by gaining invaluable experiences.
- **Worker participation** – This occurs when employees have opportunities to participate in decision-making. Managers may ask workers for their ideas and suggestions when dealing with a particular task or problem. Participation allows people to become more involved and interested in their work. This can be done through various means such as employee suggestion schemes and the use of quality circles (see Unit 5.4).

Finally, it is important to remember that there are potential problems with the use of non-financial methods of motivation. The key problem associated with implementing non-financial motivators is that of costs. Even methods of non-financial motivation can be expensive, such as the provision of training opportunities for the whole workforce. Praise and recognition may not be as costly but will still take up management time if such practice is to be valued by the workforce. Furthermore, some people are better suited to a system of scientific management, such as those in unskilled jobs in a manufacturing plant or a fast food chain. Theory X managers do not see any value in using non-financial motivators for workers who do not want responsibility or lack skills and ambition. Managers must therefore weigh up the costs of these methods in relation to the expected benefits such as increased productivity.

Note: Higher Level students need to be able to evaluate alternative methods of non-financial rewards in different circumstances in the workplace. (© IBO 2007)

Question 2.5.7

Pfizer

Pfizer, the multinational pharmaceutical giant, employs 160 staff in Hong Kong. The firm uses the motto "CANI" (Continuous and Never Ending Improvement) as a guiding principle to motivating the workforce. Pfizer uses both financial and non-financial methods to encourage employee loyalty. Having a relatively small workforce, it is quite easy for the company to devise individual development plans for each worker's training and development needs. The firm claims that 80% of management positions are internally filled. The culture is one of encouragement and risk-taking rather than name and shame (blame).

a Comment on the likely benefits for Pfizer in using internal recruitment for filling 80% of its managerial positions. *[4 marks]*

b Explain why a culture of risk-taking is important to pharmaceutical firms such as Pfizer. *[4 marks]*

c To what extent do managers over-estimate the importance of using financial rewards to motivate their employees? *[7 marks]*

MOTIVATION AND BUSINESS STRATEGY

There is a saying, "You can take a horse to water but you cannot force it to drink the water." This is because the horse will only drink if it is thirsty. By the same token, people will only perform their jobs well if they are motivated to do so. Motivation is undoubtedly a key management issue, especially as people are such an important aspect of any business. Productivity is dependent on an employee's level of ability *and* motivation. Failure to motivate workers can lead to a range of problems for a business, such as higher absenteeism, increased labour turnover, poor customer service and low quality work. By contrast, improved motivation leads to better labour retention and its associated benefits (see Box 2.5e).

However, there is no general rule or model for how best to motivate employees. This is largely because each and every worker is different in what motivates them. Despite these difficulties, The Institute of Management (IoM) in the UK has observed three key characteristics of successful motivators:

- They are **positive thinkers** (the glass is half full, rather than half empty). Henry Ford said, "If you think you can do a thing or think you can't do a thing, you're right." Having a positive attitude can go a long way in helping to achieve the aims and objectives of an organization.

- They have and show **gratitude** and **appreciation** to their staff. By doing so they help to promote harmony and trust in the workplace, thereby helping to bring out the best in their employees.
- They believe in the **self-worth** of all workers. It is human nature to yearn for acceptance and love (see Maslow's theory). When each employee's self-worth is boosted through motivators, the business will be more likely to flourish.

Box 2.5e Benefits of higher staff retention

- Lower costs of recruitment, selection, induction and training of new staff.
- Better corporate image, thereby making it easier to recruit new staff when necessary.
- Skills and knowledge are kept within the organization.
- Greater labour productivity as there is greater stability.
- Better delivery of customer service, leading to improved customer satisfaction and loyalty.
- Improved competitiveness, due to the above reasons.
- Ultimately, helps to improve the firm's profitability.

In reality, motivating the workforce can be an extremely difficult task for any manager because there are so many different factors that affect the level of motivation of each and every individual, such as: working conditions, the desired degree of autonomy and responsibility, the level of pay and other benefits, job security, promotional opportunities and the state of professional relationships in the workplace.

A. Milligan and S. Smith (2002) suggested in their book *Uncommon Practice* that motivation is subject to the forces of change. What motivates one person does not necessarily motivate another. Even the same person is not necessarily consistent. What motivates a person today may not necessarily motivate the same person tomorrow. The threat of redundancies, for instance, can be both a motivator and a demotivator. For some people, the fear of losing their job may bring about a driving force to ensure that they keep their jobs. For other people, the insecurity will not motivate (refer to Maslow's safety needs). On similar grounds, American motivation author Zig Ziglar argues that employee motivation is not long-lasting and therefore it is important for managers to motivate their staff on a daily basis.

Finally, the manager's role in implementing motivation is fundamental. Chris Argyris's **Maturity and Immaturity theory** suggests that if managers treat workers as adults, they behave as rational adults. However, if managers treat workers as children by using corporate restraints (such as tedious company policies) and unfair payment systems, then workers will behave like immature children. It is important to remember that motivation is not an isolated issue. Like most aspects of Business & Management, motivation is an integral part of the complex nature of managing people within an organization.

REVIEW QUESTIONS 2.5

1 Distinguish between 'intrinsic' and 'extrinsic' methods of motivation.

2 What are the signs of a demotivated workforce?

3 Distinguish between the theories of Taylor, Maslow and Herzberg.

4 What is McGregor's Theory X and Theory Y?

5 State five methods of financial and five methods of non-financial ways to motivate individuals.

6 What are the benefits to a firm in having a highly motivated workforce?

7 What are the impacts of financial reward packages on job satisfaction, motivation and productivity?

8 Explain how different methods of non-financial rewards work in different circumstances.

9 What, according to Professor John Adair, are the three key elements of effective teams?

Higher Level extension

10 Distinguish between 'content theories' and 'process theories' of motivation.

11 Differentiate between the theories of Elton Mayo and David McClelland.

12 Differentiate between the theories of Victor Vroom and John Stacey Adams.

Absenteeism measures the percentage of the workforce not present at work in a given period of time. A high level of absenteeism is a possible sign that there are low levels of motivation and job satisfaction.

Content theories of motivation explain the actual factors that motivate people, i.e. *what* motivates workers. Herzberg, for example, looked at hygiene factors and motivators, whilst McClelland studied the need for achievement, affiliation and power.

Delegation refers to managers passing on tasks or responsibilities to their subordinates. This can motivate workers who wish to be entrusted with assigned tasks and recognized for their abilities.

Empowerment is a form of non-financial motivator which involves a line manager giving his or her subordinates some autonomy in their job and the authority to make various decisions.

Fringe benefits are the benefits received in addition to a worker's wages or salaries, such as free uniforms, subsidized meals, housing benefit, pension fund contributions and company cars.

Herzberg's two factor theory looked at the factors that motivate employees, namely motivators and maintenance (hygiene) factors.

Hygiene factors are parts of a job that Herzberg referred to that do not increase job satisfaction but help to remove dissatisfaction, such as reasonable wages and working conditions.

Mayo's Hawthorne effect (experiments) found that workers are most motivated and productive when they are able to have some social interaction with their fellow workers and when management take an interest in their well-being. This philosophy formed the basis of the *human relations management* school of thought on motivation.

Motivators are the factors that Herzberg considered to increase job satisfaction and motivation levels, such as praise, recognition and responsibility.

Job enlargement refers to increasing the *number of tasks* that an employee performs, thereby reducing or eliminating the monotony of repetitive tasks.

Job enrichment is a form of job enlargement that involves giving workers more *challenging jobs* with more *responsibilities*. Therefore, workers have better opportunities to express and develop their own ideas.

Job rotation is another form of job enlargement that entails giving workers a number of different tasks of the same level of complexity in a prescribed order. This helps to reduce the problems caused by performing repetitive tasks.

Maslow's Hierarchy of Needs is a motivation theory that outlines the five levels of needs, from the requirement to satisfy basic physiological needs through to self-actualization. Maslow argued that until a lower order need is met, people cannot progress onto the next level of needs.

McGregor's Theory X and Theory Y is a theory based on management perceptions of worker attitudes in the workplace. Theory X managers are authoritarian and assume that employees need to be supervised. Theory Y managers assume that employees seek recognition and praise for their contributions and achievements.

Motivation refers to the inner desire or passion to do something.

Performance-related Pay (PRP) is a payment system that rewards people who meet set targets over a period of time. The targets can be on an individual, team or organizational basis.

Piece rate is a payment system that rewards employees based on the amount that he or she produces or sells. Pay is therefore directly linked to the productivity level of staff, such as sales people.

Process theories of motivation look at *why* people behave in a certain manner and how motivation can be maintained or stimulated. These theories look at what people think about when deciding whether or not to put in the effort to complete a task.

Productivity measures the level of output per worker. It is a measure of motivation because employees tend to be more productive with increased levels of motivation.

Remuneration means the overall package of pay and benefits offered to an employee.

Scientific management was developed by F.W. Taylor who believed that specialization and division of labour would generate greater levels of productivity. Taylor introduced a piece-rate payment system to link pay with productivity levels.

Theory X is McGregor's term for describing managers that perceive their employees in a pessimistic way, i.e. subordinates need constant supervision, prefer to be told what to do, avoid work if they can, and do not seek any responsibility.

Theory Y is an optimistic management stance towards worker attitudes, as described by McGregor. Theory Y managers believe that employees do have initiative, want praise and recognition for their achievements, and like taking on responsibility at work.

Time rate is a payment system that rewards employees for the time (rather than output or productivity) that they put into work. Payment is expressed per period of time, e.g. $10 per hour or $5,000 per month.

Organizational and Corporate Culture

UNIT 2.6

I don't want tradition. We want to live in the present.

Henry Ford (1863–1947), founder of the Ford Motor Company

Key topics

Higher Level only

- Importance of organizational culture
- Determinants of organizational culture
- Theories of organizational/corporate cultures
- Impacts of culture
- Consequences of cultural clashes within and between organizations

INTRODUCTION

Culture can be defined as what is considered 'normal' to a business organization and what guides the way that workers behave within the organization. Corporate culture may be based on a set of beliefs and values held by the management and employees, which will have a large influence on the behaviour of managers and staff. It can include a range of things such as the attitude towards punctuality at the workplace, dress code or whether smoking is acceptable. Some people suggest that corporate culture represents the character or personality of an organization.

Culture can help people to 'fit' in to an organization, based on its traditions and routines. Understanding the culture of a department or an organization is important to any manager who wishes to have any influence in implementing change within the business. Managers that are aware of and understand the corporate culture have at least a chance of trying to interact with it.

In reality, although one culture might dominate in a particular organization, there may be other groups that conform to subcultures. These groups may have different viewpoints, beliefs and interests. This discrepancy among subgroups can also cause a **culture gap** (the difference between the desired culture of a business and the culture that actually exists). Strategies used to close culture gaps are outlined later in this Unit.

One of the most common ways used to establish a corporate culture is by using a mission statement (see Unit 1.3). This issue is outlined later in this Unit.

HIGHER LEVEL

THE IMPORTANCE OF UNDERSTANDING ORGANIZATIONAL CULTURE

Cultural intelligence, or **cultural quotient** (CQ), is the ability of an individual to blend into occupational, corporate and national cultures. The term was coined by Christopher Earley and Elaine Mosakowski (2004). CQ is important in a business context as it measures the ability of workers to understand and adjust to unfamiliar situations.

Culture also applies to the attitude of the workforce towards change. Businesses are exposed to the constant forces of change (see Unit 1.8). If the organization's employees are not interested in pursuing change, then this could harm the business's success. A negative and undesirable culture can lead to increased absenteeism and lateness, thereby escalating the costs for the business. By contrast, a culture of acceptance to change and cooperation with management will aid a business in responding to the changing needs of the market. Cultural harmony within an organization can only come about if all staff understand and share the values of the culture. This can be achieved, to some extent, by using induction for new staff and training for existing staff.

A challenging task for any manager is to deal with organizational culture in a rapidly changing and diverse business setting. For example, when growing through mergers and takeovers (see Unit 1.7), corporate culture clashes may present major problems for the organization.

Fostering improved culture

The main problem for managers in trying to foster a desired culture is that its culture is established over long periods of time. Culture is largely formed by the subjective views of people and it becomes ingrained in the workers' minds of how they see the organization. Of course, it is not always easy to change the views of people and this task is more difficult for an organization with a large workforce. There can be considerable resistance to change of corporate culture as workers argue that 'things have always been done that way here'. Earley and Mosakowski suggest that employees who are rational, motivated and attentive can attain an acceptable level of cultural intelligence. This should therefore help to foster the desired corporate culture.

INFLUENCES ON ORGANIZATIONAL CULTURE

The acronym NORMS can be used to remember the interrelated determinants of the culture that exists in an organization:

- **Nature of the business** – The nature of an organization is dependent on its mission, aims and objectives (see Unit 1.3). Culture is shaped by the purpose and direction of the organization. For example, there is likely to be a very different culture in a not-for-profit organization (such as charities), than one found in an organization that thrives on aggressive selling (such as real estate agencies). The philosophy of the founders of the organization may also affect the organizational culture.
- **Organization structure** – A firm with tall structures will tend to have small teams that work well independently. By contrast, flatter structures are more likely to benefit from collaborative team working. Organizations made up of highly skilled and innovative staff will have a different culture from those with highly demotivated workers who have no input in the decision-making process.
- **Rewards** – If employees are appropriately remunerated for their efforts, the organization is more likely to develop a strong culture. This means that a motivated workforce will result in a culture of workers who strive to achieve organizational objectives.
- **Management styles** – Firms that adopt a Theory Y management style (see Unit 2.5) will experience a completely different culture from those that use a Theory X approach. The culture in firms that have theory Y managers will tend to benefit from workers being able to deal with most problems themselves, rather than taking their problems to management. Conversely, in firms where managers use a theory X style, the use of threats and sanctions is the norm. In extreme versions of this culture, much of management time is spent on checking employee emails, their use of the internet, monitoring their telephone calls or even using surveillance cameras to keep an eye on the staff.
- **Sanctions** – An organization with few sanctions may encourage staff to be slack at work, e.g. to be late for work, or even miss work, and to deliver poor customer service. However, if an organization is too rigid in its policies and is extremely harsh in reprimanding workers, then staff may feel resentful of management.

The strength of an organization's culture depends on the degree of unity among the staff. If staff are unified in their beliefs and values, then the stronger the corporate culture tends to be, i.e. a strong culture exists when the staff support the vision and mission of the organization. By contrast, a weak culture exists if there is little if any alignment with organizational values. This means that management will need to exercise control through formal and perhaps bureaucratic procedures.

There are advantages to a business that has a strong corporate culture:

- It creates a sense of belonging and security for staff because they feel as though they are part of the business. This can help to improve team work and to raise motivation in the organization.
- Mistakes and misunderstandings may be minimized since staff are familiar with the processes at work.
- It promotes team cohesiveness whereby people do things because they simply feel that it is the right thing to do.
- Problems associated with a culture gap, such as conflict between different groups (see Unit 2.7), are minimized.

Cultures develop and strengthen over time. Beliefs, norms, attitudes and values are more likely to be shared within the organization if they are given the time to do so. This will make any attempts at changing the culture a more difficult task. Nevertheless, as markets become more competitive and globalized, organizations are forced into being more adaptive to change (see Unit 1.8). In addition, political, economic, social, technological and legal changes may require organizational cultures to adapt and embrace the changes.

Cultures may also change when there is a joint venture, merger or takeover. In theory, mergers should help the organizations concerned to gain from economies of scale and synergies (see Unit 1.7). However, some mergers often fail due to a culture clash (such as different management styles). Even if the merger goes ahead, what tends to happen is that the culture of the more dominant firm prevails or a new hybrid culture develops in the organization. In reality, those that cannot adapt to work in the new culture are likely to leave the organization.

Question 2.6.1

Wahaha and Danone's joint venture

China's largest drinks producer, Wahaha, formed a joint venture with France's largest foods company, Danone, in 1996. When Wahaha's founder stepped down in 2007, several disputes broke out between the two companies, such as the choice of a new chairman for the joint venture. Danone also claimed that the Chinese had illegally copied some of its drinks whilst Wahaha had accused its French partners of harming its reputation on the international circuit. Both companies wanted their own representative to take over as the new chairman. Under the joint venture agreement, Wahaha is not allowed to make products that directly compete with Danone's range of drinks products. Danone also faced pressures from Chinese officials when thousands of bottles of its Evian water were seized on accusations that the products contained unsafe microorganisms.

a Describe what is meant by 'corporate culture'. *[2 marks]*

b Analyse the importance of understanding corporate and international cultures for the success of a cross-border joint venture. *[6 marks]*

THEORIES OF ORGANIZATIONAL AND CORPORATE CULTURES

Organizations are vastly different in the way that they operate. Hence there is no single overriding organizational or corporate culture that exists. Various theorists have put forward models of organizational culture and these are considered below.

Charles Handy

In his book *The Gods of Management* (1978) Professor Charles Handy argued that different cultures are needed for different business activities. He stated that the culture used to run an efficient chocolate plant is different to that used to run a primary school or a construction site. Handy described four types of organizational culture:

- **Power cultures** occur when there is one dominant individual or group who hold decision-making power. The organizational structure (see Unit 2.2) is likely to be flat with a relatively wide span of control for the decision-makers. Formal job titles or positions may not be highly regarded because decision-making power only exists with the very few. Decision-making in such organizations is therefore very swift. This type of culture is often found in small businesses. Signs of power cultures can come in various forms, such as private toilets (washrooms) and/or parking spaces reserved only for senior executives.

- **Role cultures** occur in highly structured organizations with formal rules and procedures. Job roles are clearly stated in formal job descriptions. Power is devolved depending on the formal position that the individual holds in the organization.
- **Task cultures** occur in organizations where the focus is on getting results from the work done. Unlike power cultures, there is no single source of power. Hence, individuals and teams are empowered and have discretion over their responsibilities. Unlike in role cultures, formal job titles are seen as less important than the contribution that individuals make to completing tasks. Such cultures promote problem solving through flexible and dynamic teams in a matrix organization (see Unit 2.3), made up of representatives from different departments based on their individual expertise and talents.
- **Person cultures** occur in organizations when staff in similar positions, with similar expertise and training form groups to share their knowledge and to enhance their own skills. This type of culture is found in larger organizations with different branches, such as in commercial retailing, or in certain professions such as accountants, surgeons and lawyers. Such cultures only exist for the benefit of the individuals involved, although the organization can benefit from the creativity and the sharing of good practice amongst the group members.

Edgar Schein

Professor Edgar Schein is credited for coining the term *corporate culture*. He argues that there are three levels of corporate culture:

- **Artefacts** are superficial aspects of an organization that can be easily detected by our senses. Examples include the organization's facilities, buildings, dress code and how people are seen to interact with each other.
- **Espoused values** deal with culture of the staff themselves. Metaphors and symbols, such as the organization's mission statement, brands or slogans, can be used to express its culture among the staff. It can also be established by interviewing the staff or using questionnaires to study the attitudes of the employees.
- **Basic assumptions and values** represent the deepest level of culture entailing culture that is unseen and not easily identified. This will include elements of corporate culture that are considered unthinkable to discuss inside the organization. Such cultures are invisible to those new to the organization and only those who have acclimatized over time will understand this level of culture in an organization. Schein argued that it is at this level that culture drives an organization.

Deal and Kennedy

Terrence Deal and Allan Kennedy (1982) described corporate culture as the way things get done within an organization. Their research was based on a two-dimensional framework:

- **Feedback and reward** was the first dimension and looked at the speed of feedback and the level of rewards within an organization. If feedback is rapid (immediate) it will quickly remove any unproductive conduct. For example, those who are lazy at work will be dismissed. In a competitive team sports match, feedback and reward will be rapid. For a business exploring new technologies, feedback and reward is likely to be slow. Deal and Kennedy argued that rapid feedback and reward is likely to lead to a consistent corporate culture.
- **Risk** is something that either drives workers or something that demotivates people. High-risk organizations are more likely to employ people with a high-risk profile such as stock market brokers. These can be very stressful organizations to work in, such as the emergency services, so those that do not fit the culture will not last very long in their job.

Feedback and Reward

Risk		Rapid	Slow
	High	Tough-guy macho	Bet-the-company
	Low	Work hard, play hard	Process

Figure 2.6a Deal and Kennedy's organizational culture model

From their two-dimensional framework, Deal and Kennedy suggested four types of organizational culture:

- **Tough-guy macho culture** occurs in organizations where feedback is rapid and risks are high. This culture often applies to fast-paced financial markets, such as the trading on the stock exchange. It is also present in the police force and amongst surgeries. It can be very stressful to work in such a culture as there are high risks.
- **Work-hard, play-hard culture** exists where there is rapid feedback with low or few risks being taken. Such a culture is typical in large organizations. It is also apparent in fast-pace customer-orientated businesses such as restaurants and hotels. Stress is more likely to come from the quantity and pace of work rather than risk or uncertainty.
- **Bet-the-company culture** occurs in organization that take high risks but without rapid feedback or immediate rewards. An example would be an oil company exploring for alternative energy sources, where it may take many years before getting any results. It can also be stressful working in such organizations as there is a high degree of risk and uncertainty as results can take a long time to materialize, if at all.
- **Process culture** exists in organizations where there is slow, little or no feedback with low risks. Bureaucracy exists and people become caught up with *how* things are done rather than focusing on achieving the aims and objectives of the organization. There is a low level of stress and a high degree of security. Government establishments and departments are often given as examples of organizations with a process culture.

Kotter and Heskett

In their 1992 book *Corporate Culture and Performance* John Kotter and James Heskett put forward two types of corporate cultures:

- **Adaptive cultures** are receptive to change and exist in organizations that are open and adapt themselves to change. Staff and management are encouraged to be entrepreneurial and to take risks by not having a culture of blame. This culture is often found in innovative organizations.
- **Inert cultures** are resistant to change and exist in organizations that hold negative values of any change to their culture. Such organizations, directly or indirectly, promote inertia (disinterest and opposition) rather than being proactive to changes in the business environment.

Goffee and Jones

Rob Goffee and Gareth Jones devised the *Double-S Model* of organizational culture, which looks at two dimensions of culture: Sociability and Solidarity. They argue that the ideal culture exists when there is both high sociability and high solidarity.

- **Sociability** refers to the extent to which people have concerns for their colleagues. Cultures with *high sociability* tend to focus on 'people' whereas *low sociability* cultures place greater focus on completing 'tasks'.
- **Solidarity** refers to the degree of cohesiveness or unity in an organization, such as whether people share the same values and have common interests. Hence *high solidarity* aids harmony and efficiency in the workplace, whereas *low solidarity* implies self-interest takes priority. This is detrimental as it can promote high levels of internal conflict, uncooperative behaviour and/or inefficiency.

Question 2.6.2

Warwick Park School

Warwick Park School (WPS) failed its school inspection in 2008. The government inspectors had commented that teachers and students at the school failed to engage in active teaching and learning. Examination results were very poor with only 15% of the students achieving the national required standards. Although the school was a happy community, staff and students had grown accustomed to failure when it came to examinations. Ellis Gregory, the new 'super head teacher', was hired to improve the quality of teaching and learning at WPS. Gregory was known for his outstanding vision and entrepreneurial ability to turn around the fortunes of failing schools. At his first staff meeting, Gregory announced his radical plan for change, which included:

- restructuring the senior management team
- introducing a system of bimonthly staff performance appraisals
- performance management systems to be linked to pay
- lesson observations to be carried out on a random and unannounced basis
- changes to the school timetable to allow for more meetings, planning and extra-curricular activities.

Not surprisingly, the teachers at WPS were worried about job losses, the manner in which change was imposed and the way in which staff were to be managed.

a Outline the term 'organizational culture' with reference to WPS. *[2 marks]*

b Explain why Ellis Gregory felt the need to change the organizational culture at WPS. *[4 marks]*

c Comment on how the concerns of staff could be dealt with to foster the desired change in organizational culture. *[4 marks]*

Geert Hofstede

Unlike the other theorists mentioned above, Geert Hofstede, a Dutch expert on corporate culture, studied the links between international cultures and organizational cultures. He found five dimensions of culture:

- **Power distance** – This measures the extent to which subordinates (or citizens) expect and accept unequal distribution of power within the organization (or country). A low power-distance rating, as found in Scandinavian countries, reflects the society's view that people should have equal rights. Hofstede found that high power-distance cultures tend have centralized decision-making, whereas low power-distance cultures tend to be decentralized and feature delegation and empowerment of subordinates.

HIGHER LEVEL

- **Individualism versus collectivism** – This measures the extent to which people feel they should care for themselves (individualism) or be cared for by the family network and society (collectivism). It also looks at the extent to which a person feels it is his or her responsibility to look after others or whether he or she feels that this is the responsibility of others in society.
- **Masculinity versus femininity**. This dimension focuses on the extent to which a culture conforms to traditional gender values. *Masculinity* refers to values usually dominated by males, e.g. aggressive, competitive, ambition, selfishness and materialistic. *Femininity* refers to values traditionally associated to be held by females, such as placing more focus on relationships, the family network and overall quality of life.
- **Uncertainty avoidance**. This measures the extent to which people in an organization or country prefer structured routines (predictability) over flexible structures (or uncertainty). Hofstede found that high uncertainty avoidance cultures have strong customs and habits. As a result, they tend to favour formal structures, rules and regulations. Those who hold a high degree of uncertainty avoidance tend to remain loyal to their employers.
- **Long-term versus short-term orientation**. This final dimension of culture looks at the extent to which a particular culture values making sacrifices today for the benefits to be reaped in the future. Cultures with long-term orientation will invest for the future, have a high degree of perseverance and are patient with the results.

Hofstede's research gives some insight into how organizational cultures may differ from one country to another. National culture will have a direct impact on organizational culture. It is important for organizations with operations in overseas markets to consider the cultural differences that exist. What works well in one culture or country does not necessarily apply to others (also see Unit 4.7).

IMPACTS OF CULTURE

Corporate culture can have a direct impact on both organizational structures and staff motivation.

There is a strong link between corporate cultures and *organizational structures* (see Unit 2.2) within a business. For example, a *power culture* requires centralized decision-making whereby mangers keep hold of authority and control. Hence, the organizational structure is likely to be tall with a narrow span of control.

By contrast, in *adaptive cultures* where workers are receptive and adaptive to change, more flexible or decentralized structures are likely to be found. Such structures will then facilitate employees and managers to adopt a more entrepreneurial role. Similarly, flatter organizational structures are likely to exist in *innovative cultures*. This exists in organizations that empower workers to take important decisions and to act on their own initiative. Flexible structures are also likely to be found in *task cultures* where the focus is on using the talents of various team members, often from different departments, to achieve organizational objectives.

There are also links between organizational culture and *motivation* (see Unit 2.5). For example, in power cultures, where employee input is not really valued, it may prove difficult for individuals to fulfil their higher level motivation needs. In such cultures, managers may also see staff training and development needs as irrelevant since the staff do not have any decision-making rights. Similarly, if staff are earning low wages or salaries, then they may develop a culture of low or no risk taking since they feel that they are not being paid enough to justify making such important decisions.

To some extent, each classroom has its own culture. The culture is largely influenced by the members of the group (the students) and the attitude of the group leader (the teacher). Students may work better in some classes than others because of the group dynamics and different expectations set by teachers. By contrast, in a department with a carefree manager where staff see work as an excuse for gossiping, then both motivation and productivity are likely to be low.

The organization's culture will also affect its approach to **ethical business behaviour**. For example, if recycling is part of a school's culture, then staff and students are more likely to conserve the use of energy and other resources as this is the expected approach in the organization. On the other hand, a profit-focused business may take a completely different stance on ethical questions.

Question 2.6.3

The Body Shop

The Body Shop was founded by Dame Anita Roddick in 1976. The company prides itself on its 'green' and socially responsible approach to business. This ethical stance has led the company to expand its operations to over 55 countries around the world, serving over 77 million customers each year. The Body Shop has five core values that are instilled in everything the company does:

- Against animal testing
- Support community trade
- Activate self-esteem
- Defend human rights
- Protect our planet

Source: adapted from www.the-body-shop.com and reproduced with the kind permission of The Body Shop International plc

a Based on the above information, describe the corporate culture at The Body Shop. *[2 marks]*

b Examine how ethical business behaviour can shape corporate culture *and* provide The Body Shop with a commercial and competitive advantage. *[6 marks]*

CONSEQUENCES OF CULTURE CLASHES

Culture clash exists when there is conflict between two or more cultures within an organization. This may exist, for example, when two firms integrate via a merger or takeover, or when a firm expands overseas and is ignorant of international cultural differences.

In April 1992 when Euro Disney first opened, management faced huge problems with the unhappy workforce. The media reported staff protests and a *walk-out* (see Unit 2.7). A large part of the problem was that Disney managers insisted on English being the language of communication at meetings. Furthermore, they enforced a strict dress code, based on American practices, but something that is not obligatory in the workplace in France. Many analysts blamed the huge losses made by Disneyland Paris in 1994 were due to this major cultural clash. Not surprisingly then, Disney's management subsequently adopted French working practices whilst keeping the core product 'American'. In October 1994, the theme park was renamed Disneyland Paris. Happily for the Disney Corporation, the fortunes have turned around and Disneyland Paris continues to be highly profitable. However, this case study highlights the fact that businesses that ignore cultural differences do so at their peril.

Changing corporate strategy, which is inevitable following a takeover or merger for instance, may prove difficult for a number of reasons. Such constraints include:

- **Costs** of implementing change may be very high. Training costs, for example, may be necessary for retailers that change from having a physical presence to having an online presence (see Unit 4.8).
- **Resistance to change** from the workforce because staff are likely to resent changes to the culture that they are used to. This may be due to reasons such as fear of the unknown or a lack of understanding of the benefits of a changed culture.
- **Public opinion** such as the perception of an organization's expected values may also hinder changes to organizational culture. Stakeholders would not expect (or perhaps accept) doctors to be inert or high risk takers, for example.
- **National cultures** may be so strong that any attempts to change the way how things are done may cause resistance and resentment. Cosmetic firms, for example, may find it difficult to expand into Muslim countries because the attitudes towards female liberation and freedom of expression are still very conservative.

Question 2.6.4

Lenovo

Lenovo, founded in 1984, is China and Asia's largest computer manufacturer. In 2005, the computer giant bought IBM's personal computer division for $1.25 billion. Workers at the Lenovo production plant in China are used to stringent manufacturing systems, with only 18 seconds to add components before they are moved on in the assembly line. This means that more than 400 ThinkPad laptops are produced each hour. Workers are also expected to show respect to their seniors (higher ranked staff). Unlike in Western economies, Lenovo's employees are not generally encouraged to voice their opinions or to think independently. They would certainly shy from questioning the decisions of senior management. Hence, mergers and joint ventures with Western firms have often proved difficult due to such **cultural differences**.

a Outline the meaning of **cultural differences**. *[2 marks]*

b Examine the problems that Lenovo may have faced in the integration of two different corporate cultures. *[6 marks]*

ORGANIZATIONAL CULTURES AND BUSINESS STRATEGY

Edgar Schein argued that cultural understanding is desirable for everyone in an organization. He further suggested that cultural understanding is a prerequisite to effective management and leadership. Management are often viewed by others as people who establish the corporate culture. It is the management that set the rules, beliefs and norms within an organization. The way in which culture is developed is quite often determined by the actions of senior management. Managers seek to shape the culture of the organization. This can done through various means such as determining the extent to which employees can contribute their ideas or interact as team members.

HIGHER LEVEL

There are several interrelated steps to creating a positive and harmonious culture:

- Develop a sense of history – Large and well established organizations create a sense of belonging by developing historical accounts of their businesses. Past successes are glorified in publications and literature. Photographs and artefacts are prominently displayed within the organization. The history of most companies can now be found on the internet. Multinationals such as Coca-Cola and Cadbury's have their own museums. This all helps to connect the past to the present and to shape the future direction of the organization.
- Create a sense of unity – Managers and leaders of an organization can create a sense of harmony and unity by establishing SMART objectives (see Unit 1.3) for the business and the workforce. This can help to foster a culture of collaborative teamworking and mutual understanding.
- Promote a sense of value – A strong and positive culture is more likely to prevail if there are established systems to appropriately reward and recognize the input of workers. For instance, an organization might encourage the use of internal promotions (see Unit 2.1) to help workers manage their careers. Organizations that strive to promote a *total quality culture* (see Unit 5.4) will also need to invest in the training and development of their staff.
- Encourage a sense of responsibility – Employees need to feel dedicated and responsible for their work. This is more likely to happen if there is a sense of unity. There are many ways that managers can do this, from creating opportunities to work in interdepartmental teams to organizing social events for people to get to know each other better. This should therefore increase a person's sense of responsibility for others in the organization. It is often argued that a business built on friendship groups is a recipe for disaster, whereas friendship groups that stem from within a business can only help to further strengthen the organization.

In fostering a desired culture, management will usually use mission statements (see Unit 1.3) to provide a common purpose and clear direction for the staff. The mission statement usually provides some indication of the corporate culture. If this mission is shared and accepted by the staff, then they are more likely to work together to help achieve the aims and objectives of the organization, thereby helping to establish its culture. Without a clear mission statement or effective management, a culture may develop which prevents the organization from achieving its aims and objectives.

An understanding and awareness of corporate culture may also be important during the recruitment process. Many argue that in order for a business to reduce staff turnover and to employ the correct staff, there is a need to employ people who will fit in with its culture or who are able to positively develop the culture.

Finally, it is important to recognize that it may not be possible to have just one culture within an organization, especially in large ones where subcultures may exist. Managers need to realize that not all parts of an organization have the same culture. Indeed, the dominant culture may not be suitable for certain groups or individuals within the organization. This point is further complicated when organizations operate on an international scale. A recent report from the UK and Hong Kong Chambers of Commerce found that 20% of jobs in developed societies are directly tied to international trade (a proportion that is continually increasing). Competitiveness is therefore centred on being able to work effectively with those in other countries. Hence an understanding and appreciation of different cultures is essential. After all, there is no right or best culture for all organizations, especially as businesses are constantly exposed to the forces of change. An awareness of the differences that exist can better equip managers to deal with human resource management issues.

REVIEW QUESTIONS 2.6

1 What is meant by 'organizational culture'?
2 What is a 'culture gap'?
3 Explain the meaning of 'cultural intelligence' and why high CQ is important.
4 What are the five determinants of organizational culture? (*Hint*: NORMS)
5 How might organizational culture be affected following a takeover or merger?
6 Outline Charles Handy's four types of organizational cultures.
7 Outline the main findings of Geert Hofstede's investigations into international cultures.
8 How might corporate culture affect motivation and organizational structures?
9 What is 'culture clash' and how might it affect an organization?
10 How might a mission statement be used to communicate corporate culture?

Adaptive cultures exist in organizations that are receptive to change. Such organizations tend to be innovative and are able to foster change.

Corporate culture, or **organizational culture**, describes the traditions and norms within an organization, such as: dress code, work ethos and attitude towards punctuality.

Cultural quotient (CQ), also known as **cultural intelligence**, measures the ability of an individual to blend into occupational, organizational and national cultures. CQ is important in a business context as it measures the ability of workers to cope with change.

Culture clash occurs when there is conflict between two or more cultures within an organization. This may exist, for example, when two firms integrate via a merger or takeover.

Culture gap refers to the difference between the existing culture of an organization and its desired culture. Management will use different strategies to reduce this gap.

Inert cultures are the opposite of adaptive cultures. As its name suggests, inertia is present in such cultures where people are negative about and resistant to change.

Innovative cultures exist in organizations that empower workers to make important decisions and to act on their own initiative.

Person cultures exist in organizations when staff in similar positions, with similar expertise and training form groups to share their knowledge and to enhance their own skills.

Power cultures exist when there is one dominant individual or group who hold decision-making power. Hence, the organizational structure is likely to be flat with a relatively wide span of control for the decision-makers.

Role cultures exist in highly structured organizations with formal rules, policies and procedures. Job roles are clearly stated in formal job descriptions and power is devolved to middle managers.

Task cultures exist in organizations where the focus is on getting results from the work done. Individuals and teams are empowered and have some discretion over their responsibilities.

HIGHER LEVEL

Employer and Employee Relations

UNIT 2.7

The voice of the people is louder than the boom of a canon.

Armenian proverb

Key topics

Higher Level only

- Negotiations and collective bargaining
- Methods used by employees in pursuit of their objectives
- Methods used by employers to achieve their objectives
- Sources of conflict
- Conflict resolution

INTRODUCTION

Managers will usually strive to ensure that there are good working relationships at work. This is often much easier to do in theory than in practice. Poor working relationships will often lead to lower morale and the possibility of conflict (disagreements). Subsequently industrial unrest will arise, i.e. relations between the employer and employees will worsen. This means that workers are displeased with issues at work, such as pay and working conditions, which can lead to protests being undertaken by the employees. Extreme actions taken by the disgruntled workforce may include strike action or even rioting.

This Unit looks at the sources of conflict between employers and employers and how their representatives can resolve any disputes.

NEGOTIATIONS AND COLLECTIVE BARGAINING

Negotiation is a bargaining process whereby two or more parties attempt to achieve a mutually acceptable outcome. The ultimate and ideal goal of negotiation is a 'win-win' situation for the parties concerned. For example, employees via their union representatives may promise higher levels of productivity in return for better financial rewards. The outcome benefits both the employees and the employer.

Some individuals may not wish to negotiate alone so they will use 'agents' such as a lawyer or a trade union representative to act on their behalf. **Collective bargaining** describes the process of negotiation between management (the employer's representative) and trade union representatives. The negotiations are most likely to focus on the terms and conditions of employment, such as wage rates, hours of work and working conditions.

Negotiations are not technically a form of industrial action, although failure in the negotiation process is likely to lead to further industrial disputes and action. In reality, any negotiation or process of collective bargaining is likely to involve a degree of compromise; otherwise there will be a **stand-off** (also known as a **deadlock**). This means that there is a failure to reach a satisfactory compromise and therefore commencement of a dispute is likely to follow.

There are three levels of negotiations:

- **Management negotiations** refer to the day to day negotiations concerning the internal affairs of a business. An example would be management and their subordinates establishing new production and sales targets.
- **Commercial negotiations** take place between different organizations. An example would be a business negotiating delivery times and prices with its supplier.
- **International negotiations** are an extension of commercial negotiations which involve consideration of cross-border cultural and language differences. Therefore this often requires a different stance to be taken in the negotiation process.

There are six stages in the negotiation process, which are outlined in Table 2.7a.

Table 2.7a The negotiation process

Stages of negotiation	Examples of processes during each negotiation stage
1. Preparation	• Identify objectives and issues that can or cannot be compromised • Gather all necessary facts and information • Anticipate possible problems • Prepare alternative proposals, known as a BATNA (Best Alternative To a Negotiated Agreement) • Assign roles for key negotiators • Consider consequences of not striking a deal
2. Proposal	• Put forward the case, preferably in order of priority • Listen to the proposal of the opposition • Ask questions for clarification of proposals
3. Debate	• Each party discusses the points in their case • Find inconsistencies in arguments • Further questioning and reiteration of main points or proposals
4. Bargaining	• Discussions to find a mutually beneficial outcome • Compromise without a 'win–lose' situation • Convincing the other party to compromise • Aim to make, rather than to win, a deal
5. Closing	• Choosing a way forward, i.e. strategy • A final offer from each party is proposed • Formalize and summarize agreements in writing
6. Review	• Review each stage of the negotiation process to see what went well and what could have been improved • Reflect on the whole process in order to learn how to achieve a better outcome in future negotiations

There are different views about negotiation. These varying opinions will affect the approach used by people to the negotiation process.

- *Avoidance approach* – Advocates of this approach suggest that the best way to resolve a dispute is to avoid it in the first place. For example, people should resist the temptation to respond in a rude or inappropriate way during the negotiation process. Critics of this approach argue that avoidance usually leads to a lose-lose situation for both parties because the underlying issues are not dealt with.
- *Level playing field approach* – This view of negotiation sees both parties being equal. If this were not the case, then the relatively stronger party would dictate the outcome of the negotiation. In other words, there would be no negotiation at all unless the parties were equal.
- *Winner takes all approach* – The traditional view on negotiations is that one person's gain is another person's loss, i.e. a win-lose situation.
- *The win–win approach* – In his book *The Art of Negotiating* (1968) Gerard I. Nierenberg advocated the philosophy that everyone could win from the negotiation process. Nierenberg suggested that this approach yields more successful outcomes than the 'winner takes all' approach.

Employees are usually represented by a **trade union** (also known as a **labour union**). A trade union is an organization that consists of worker-members who unite to protect the rights and welfare of its members. An individual is unlikely to have much bargaining power in comparison to a union of workers, i.e. there is strength in numbers. From an employer's perspective, it is also cheaper and quicker to bargain with just one trade union representative than many individual workers. Box 2.7a describes the main types of labour unions.

Box 2.7a The main types of trade unions

Craft unions. These were the original labour unions with members sharing a particular skill or craft, such as engineers or printers.

Industrial unions. These unions accept members from the same industry, irrespective of their skills, qualifications, ranking or the nature of their work.

General unions. Such unions accept members from any industry, regardless of their skills or qualifications, and so they tend to have a very large number of members. An example is the UK's Transport and General Workers Union (TGWU). The TGWU's members include transport drivers, hotel workers and retail employees.

White-collar unions. These unions admit clerical, administrative and professional staff, i.e. members are non-manual workers. White-collar unions exist in professions such as teaching and banking.

Each member of the trade union must pay an annual fee. This contributes towards the costs of running the labour union, i.e. the support services that are provided for its members. Union subscription fees might, for example, cover the costs of legal advice and representation for an individual or group of members in a grievance dispute.

The primary role of any labour union is to protect the interests of its members, i.e. the employees who belong to the union. This is done mainly through bargaining on behalf of their members for improved pay and working conditions and/or through persuading governments to pass legislation in favour of employees (such as a national minimum wage). Some examples of the main issues that labour unions are occupied with include:

- Improving the conditions of work for its members, such as reduced hours of work or a better work-life balance
- Negotiating with employers for increased pay and benefits
- Proving members with necessary legal advice, as and when needed (e.g. as in the case of grievances)
- Providing financial support to members who may have been unfairly dismissed or made redundant
- Supporting the right of its members to have continuous professional training and development
- Pressuring employers to ensure that equipment and machinery at work are safe for its members to use, i.e. that health and safety concerns are dealt with.

The outcome of the negotiation and collective bargaining process will depend on the bargaining strength of the employer and employee representatives. These, in turn, depend on several factors, including:

- Experience and skills of the representatives as effective negotiators
- Number of members and the degree of unity within the trade union. Generally, a union is more powerful if members are united in their cause and if there is a large percentage of the workforce belonging to the union.
- State of the economy. If there is high unemployment, for example, then employees are in a weaker position to negotiate pay deals.
- Demand for labour deriving from the demand for the product or service that labour will be used to supply. If, for example, the long-term prospects for a good or service is unfavourable, the demand for labour is unsustainable. This would then weaken the bargaining power of union representatives.

- Degree of substitution between labour and capital. if unions continually push for pay rises without benefits to a firm, then the business is more likely to use *capital-intensive* methods of production or to make staff redundant due to its higher costs of production.
- Public and media opinion. support for the business or labour union may determine which party has stronger negotiating powers.
- Government involvement. Government rules and regulations will often direct the parameters within which negotiations take place.

METHODS USED BY EMPLOYEES TO ACHIEVE INDIVIDUAL AND GROUP OBJECTIVES

Workers may have any combination of the following objectives:

- Increased pay (see Box 2.7b) or the prevention of pay cuts
- Improved remuneration, such as fringe benefits and paid holidays
- Better working conditions
- Training and development opportunities
- Enhanced terms of employment, such as hours of work
- Better-quality staff facilities, such as an improved canteen or office.

Box 2.7b Reasons why workers may demand a pay rise

Trade unions demand higher wages on behalf of their members due to a combination of reasons:

- The *cost of living* has increased (due to inflation in the economy) which effectively reduces the real income of their members.
- Workers in similar occupations in the industry have received a pay increase.
- The increased profits in the business, largely contributed by the input of workers, is a 'justification' for a higher return to labour.
- The productivity of labour has increased so workers should be rewarded accordingly.
- A significant increase in the *staff turnover* rate means that a pay rise may be needed to recruit and retain the best workers for the business.

Trade unions and individuals can use the following methods to help achieve their objectives: negotiations, go-slow, work-to-rule, overtime bans and strike action.

- **Negotiations**. Individual employees are unlikely to be in a position to negotiate well with management. However, this weakness is removed when the workforce is united in their cause, via trade union representation. Subsequently, management will be more pressured to listen to the views of the workforce. A united workforce is likely to benefit from an increase in its collective bargaining power during the negotiation process.
- **Go-slows**. Under this form of industrial action, employees work at the minimum pace allowable under their employment contract. This will reduce productivity of the workforce yet employers will find it difficult to discipline staff who work at a slow but contractually acceptable pace. Overtime work will be avoided and 'hustling' by staff will cease as employees seek to minimize the speed of their work. Go-slows can be highly effective as a form of industrial action when firms face imminent deadlines or during periods of high seasonal demand since the organization becomes extremely disrupted.
- **Work-to-rule**. This occurs when employees do the absolute minimum required according to the rules set by the employer. Workers adhere precisely to all rules and regulations in order

to slow down production and to reduce productivity. Any goodwill from staff is likely to be withdrawn; workers will not do any more than they absolutely need to. For example, office staff may refuse to answer telephone calls during lunch breaks and to leave work as soon as their shift finishes. This method of industrial action is considered less disruptive than *strike action* as workers are simply just obeying rules and regulations. Hence, employers will find it more difficult to discipline employees who work to rule.

- **Overtime bans**. This refers to a directive from the employees' representatives to its members to disengage in any overtime activity. Overtime is not usually part of a worker's employment contract. By prohibiting overtime work, unions cause disruptions to business activity in the hope that management will listen to the views of the union. Like go-slows, overtime bans can be highly effective during peak seasons and when businesses have impending deadlines.
- **Strike action**. Strike action, commonly known as a **strike**, refers to the refusal of employees to work. This is usually the result of major industrial unrest such as pay disputes or serious grievances. A strike is only considered to be official if it has the backing of the majority of members of a trade union. The union usually carries out a vote on strike action beforehand and then give notification of such intent to all of the members and to the management. Workers carry out strike action in the hope that an agreement with management can be reached.

  A **walk-out** is often used in conjunction with strike action. This happens when workers collectively leave (or walk out of) a meeting or place of work as a sign of protest or disapproval of management decisions and actions. However, unlike strike action, a walk-out usually occurs spontaneously and does not necessarily involve all employees.

Strike action used to be a powerful weapon used by unions to get their demands met. However, changes in attitudes and legislation have meant that, in extreme cases, employers may sue employees who strike for breach of contract. In many countries there are laws to protect employers and businesses from the potential power and threat of trade unions. Strike action can obviously be very disruptive to a business and governments try to ensure that businesses can operate fairly and competitively, without the added pressures imposed by trade unions. For example, in many countries, it is illegal for a union to call for strike action from its members without giving prior notice to the employer. This allows the management to formulate a contingency plan (see Unit 2.8) as its business will obviously be disrupted by the proposed industrial action.

Whichever method of industrial action is implemented, workers and trade unions attempt to reduce the output and efficiency of the business. This therefore reduces competitiveness and profits of the organization, with the intention of making the employer listen to the demands of the workforce.

However, trade unions have steadily declined in popularity across all modern societies. Fewer people tend to be joining unions, for a variety of reasons. For instance, automation and mechanization in some organizations have led to redundancies in the manufacturing sector (traditionally the largest segment of union workers). In addition, a range of government rules and legislation has led to weakening trade union powers, thereby making them less attractive to members. Finally, more women and part-time employees in the workforce have also led to the decline in union membership (since these groups tend not to be unionized). As a consequence, many organizations have developed **staff associations**. A staff association has similar roles to a trade union except that it operates only within the organization. Hence, the issues dealt with by a staff association will be more relevant to the workers, although their bargaining strength is weaker than that of a labour union.

Question 2.7.1

The **public sector** is an important employer in Portugal, directly accounting for over 20% of the economy's gross domestic product (GDP). In 2007, a coalition of trade unions called for a general strike over discontent with the government's public spending cuts and failure to deliver promised labour reforms. Unions presented the government with data suggesting that Portugal had the lowest rate of economic growth of any country in the Europe Union, stating that even relatively new member states such as Slovenia and Malta had overtaken Portugal in terms of **GDP per head**. Unions were also displeased that unemployment had hit a 20-year high.

Public services that were disrupted included public transport, refuse collection, hospitals, schools and international flights. The government responded by saying that the industrial action was only temporary and had limited consequences on the economy. It further argued that public spending cuts were in the best interest of the country in the long term.

a Define the terms **public sector** and **GDP per head**. *[4 marks]*

b Examine how a general strike will affect the economic prospects of a country such as Portugal. *[6 marks]*

METHODS USED BY EMPLOYERS TO ACHIEVE THEIR OBJECTIVES

Employer objectives may include:

- Lower costs of production in order to remain competitive
- Improved levels of productivity
- Lower rates of absenteeism and staff turnover.

The objectives of workers, if they are to be met, will raise the costs of production for an organization. Hence, employer objectives are likely to conflict with those of employees. Employers are usually represented in the negotiation process by a management team. Alternatively, organizations can be represented by **employers' associations**. These are organizations that represent the general views and interests of all businesses within a certain industry. Their function is to influence government action, rather like a pressure group, and to negotiate with trade unions and the media. Employer associations may also offer business-related and advisory services.

The senior management team and employers' associations are likely to consist of highly skilled negotiators who are likely to use any combination of the following tactics: negotiations, public relations, threat of redundancies, changes to employment contracts, closures and lock-outs.

- **Negotiations**. Negotiations differ from other forms of conflict management and conflict resolution in that they do not require the involvement of third parties to establish a win-win situation. Skilled negotiators representing the employers often use deadlines as a tactic. Setting short deadlines often gives the opposition little time to prepare or fight for their case.
- **Public relations**. Public Relations (PR) is the function of a business that deals with comments, complaints and criticisms from the general public, including the firm's customers. PR specialists (whether internally or externally hired) are used to deal with the media and are responsible for issuing press releases and other information that portray the business in a positive manner. PR is different from advertising in that it aims to achieve favourable publicity without the cost and it does not primarily aim to boost sales. Instead, PR is more about raising awareness and building goodwill.

HIGHER LEVEL

- **Threats of redundancies**. Some negotiators will also use intimidation as a tactic to pressure or threaten employees. For example, during times of conflict, senior management may use the threat of redundancies to jolt workers into complying with their demands. This does not, however, mean that employers can mistreat or exploit employees as they are protected under employment rights legislation (see Unit 2.1).
- **Changes of contract**. It may be legally possible to change people's contracts of employment, if administered fairly. For example, if staff are on finite contracts, then it is possible to change the terms and conditions of pay when offering the next contract. This gives the business a degree of flexibility in its pay structure. However, this method can be seen as a form of coercion since people who do not accept the new terms and conditions of the contract are simply denied the opportunity to extend their employment contract.
- **Closure**. One way that management can deal with strike action is to close the business. This can be a rather extreme case which is used when other methods have been exhausted and when unions reject the employer's final offer. Closure, at best, means that workers will not receive any wages. In the worst case scenario, closure will mean that workers are made redundant. This ultimatum might be enough to persuade employees to renegotiate or to settle for a compromise.
- **Lock-outs**. A lock-out occurs when an employer stops employees from working. This is different from a strike where it is the employees who refuse to work. A lockout takes place when only some union members choose to strike, or take considerable industrial action, whilst other employees continue to work. However, this may mean that some tasks cannot get done as businesses may rely on teamwork and division of labour. Hence, a business may cease production until the union declares an end to strike action. Another purpose of a lockout is to put pressure on a trade union by trying to win the support of those who are willing to work. A divided trade union soon becomes a dysfunctional union.

Question 2.7.2

Chilean miners

In the summer of 2006, Chilean miners went on strike as they rejected an improved pay and benefits offer from BHP Billiton, the world's largest privately-owned copper mine. Workers in Escondida, Chile turned down the offer of a 4% pay rise over three years and demanded a 10% pay rise (they had originally demanded a 13% rise). World copper prices had soared, fuelled by rising demand from China and India, and workers argued that they should get a share of the firm's record-breaking annual profits of $10 billion. The dispute led to **closure** of the mines because protesters had blocked access roads, thereby causing potential health and security risks.

a Describe what is meant by a **closure** in the context of industrial disputes. *[2 marks]*

b Examine *two* alternative methods that BHP Billiton could use to protect its interests. *[6 marks]*

CONFLICT

The term **conflict** refers to a situation of friction or mutually exclusive goals between two or more parties, such as employees and employers. It is caused by disagreements or incompatibilities between these groups and results in a lack of cooperation. Conflict can arise at different levels, ranging from *interpersonal conflict* between individuals to *international conflict* between nation states.

Sources of conflict

Conflicts can arise from any of five interrelated causes:

- *Needs and wants.* Conflicts arise when people's needs and desires are ignored. For example, workers need job security and would like attractive remuneration packages. Conflict in the workplace often arises due to differences in opinions over rates of pay and working conditions. Introducing flexible working practices (see Unit 2.1) may suit some people, such as part-time staff, but not others who may face restructuring or redundancies.
- *Perceptions.* Different people interpret things differently. What annoys one person does not necessarily annoy others. Misunderstandings and misperceptions can easily lead to conflict. Some people, for example, are quite receptive to change, whilst others are opposed to change perhaps due to a lack of understanding. Hence, there is a crucial role for effective communication to unite perceptions if conflict is to be minimized.
- *Values.* Conflict can arise when people hold incompatible beliefs or principles. If people are unwilling to compromise, this can make the management of conflict a very challenging task.
- *Power.* Conflict can arise when people in a position of power try to make others do something against their will or benefit. The unfair or exploitative use of power will cause friction in the workplace. For example, managers might place pressure on employers to meet unrealistic sales targets. Management styles will also influence how conflict is managed in the organization.
- *Feelings and emotions.* Conflict often occurs because people ignore the feelings of others in the organization. It is quite natural for a person to feel let down or upset when others disagree with their ideas or arguments. It is not easy to simply separate professional life from personal life matters so feelings and emotions can become a major influence over how people deal with conflict. For example, grievances in the workplace (see Unit 2.1) or gossiping (see Unit 2.3) often lead to permanent conflict as people find it hard to forget and forgive those who have been unjust.

Conflict, if not managed properly, can become a problem because it can:

- Hinder productivity as there is less focus on the task
- Reduce the level of staff morale
- Cause inappropriate conduct (behaviour at work)
- Fuel the internal politics of an organization (incompatible differences in the workplace)
- Hamper opportunities for collaborative teamworking.

The approach taken to deal with conflict depends on people's concern for their own outcomes and the concern for the other party. This means that there are five possible outcomes (see Figure 2.7a).

HIGHER LEVEL

Concern for Others	Low (Concern for Self)	Moderate (Concern for Self)	High (Concern for Self)
High	Surrender		Collaborate
Moderate		Compromise	
Low	Avoidance		Compete

Concern for Self

Figure 2.7a Outcomes of conflict

- High concern for personal outcome leads people to compete for a win only outcome.
- High concern for others only means surrendering, which leads to a win situation for the other party.
- Low or no concern for either party's outcomes simply means there is an avoidance of the conflict.
- High concern for the outcome of both parties leads to collaboration to find a mutually beneficial solution.
- Moderate concern for the outcome of both parties leads of some sort of compromise being made.

Most theorists believe that high concern for the outcome of both parties (and hence efforts to find a mutually beneficial resolution) leads to the most satisfactory result. Note that each strategy will be appropriate in different circumstances, at different times. Collaboration, for example, does not work for all cases of conflict.

Question 2.7.3

Deutsche Telekom

Deutsche Telekom AG, Europe's largest telecommunications company, was privatized in 1996. Although the German company had experienced short-term **walk-outs** in the past, it had not experienced full **strike action** until 2007 when over 10,000 employees went on strike over proposed pay cuts and increased working hours. Deutsche Telekom, which owns mobile phone giant T-Mobile, argued that the proposals were necessary since more than half a million customers had left its fixed-line business, having switched to cheaper rivals.

a Distinguish between a **walk-out** and **strike action**. *[3 marks]*

b Explain how the aims and objectives of Deutsche Telekom may have changed following its privatization. *[4 marks]*

c Comment on the source(s) of conflict at Deutsche Telekom. *[4 marks]*

Finally, it is important to point out that conflict is not necessarily a negative thing. Some people believe that conflict is often needed in an organization. For instance, conflict can help to raise and address real problems that are bothering people. It can also help people to recognize and benefit from their personal differences. Having a better understanding of each other's differences and needs can actually foster better working relationships in the future. Conflict itself is not the true problem; it is the way in which conflict is managed that can become a problem.

CONFLICT RESOLUTION

Conflict resolution refers to the course of action taken to resolve conflict and differences in opinion. Conflict resolution is considered to be successful if each party's interests are addressed, resulting in a satisfactory outcome for all sides. Given that employers and employees tend to have conflicting interests, it may be difficult for both sides to reach a settlement.

There are several ways to approach conflict resolution, including conciliation and arbitration, employee participation and industrial democracy, no-strike agreements and single-union agreements.

Conciliation and arbitration

Conciliation is a process whereby the parties involved in a dispute agree to use the services of an independent mediator. This person then meets with the parties separately (a practice known as **caucusing**) in an attempt to resolve their dispute and differences. The conciliator's role is to encourage the parties to negotiate and compromise in order to reach a solution that is mutually acceptable (see Figure 2.7b). The parties in conflict are unlikely to ever actually face each other so it is important for conciliators to be highly skilled negotiators and effective communicators. Conciliation is often referred to as **mediation**.

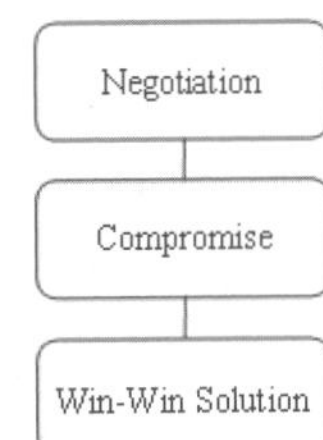

Figure 2.7b The three-step conciliation process

Conciliators, or mediators, will almost always get the parties to commit their compromise in writing, which makes their commitment to the resolution legally binding.

Arbitration is similar to conciliation in that an external party is used as a form of conflict resolution. However, the process involves the independent arbitrator deciding on an appropriate outcome. The arbitrator will act rather like a judge by listening to and examining the arguments put forward by both parties before making a final decision and recommendation. The arbitrator's final decision becomes legally binding.

An extreme case of arbitration is known as **pendulum arbitration** which requires the arbitrator to decide completely in favour of one party or the other, i.e. there is no compromise or negotiation that takes place. The theory behind this approach is that both parties in the dispute are forced to make more realistic and/or conservative demands. For example, suppose that there is conflict over the rate of pay rises, with the labour union pushing for 6% but employers arguing for only 3%. The arbitrator will need to assess both sides of the argument. If the arbitrator the feels that 4% is the correct level of pay increments, then this is closer to the 3% advocated by the employer and therefore the decision will be to raise pay by 3%.

Employee participation and industrial democracy

Employee participation is an example of *industrial democracy.* This means that employees are given responsibilities and authority to complete tasks and are involved in the decision-making process. An example of employee participation is team working (see Unit 2.5). Motivation theorists such as Maslow and Herzberg (also see Unit 2.5) point out that employee participation and industrial democracy helps to increase productivity levels because workers are more involved and happier. Furthermore, employers will benefit from a more cooperative workforce that is less likely to engage in industrial disputes. Employees benefit from higher levels of morale and an increase in job satisfaction. As a result, absenteeism and labour turnover rates are also likely to fall. All these benefits lead to a 'win–win' situation for both the employers and the employees.

No strike agreements

Trade unions have been negatively affected by their image for being disruptive to the business community. In addition, union membership throughout the world has been declining. In response to these trends, many unions have tried to improve their image by having a *no-strike agreement*, i.e. members agree not to take strike action as a form of industrial action. In the UK, for example, the Association of Teachers and Lecturers has a no-strike policy. This has helped the union to attract more members and reassured employers and other stakeholder groups that the teachers and lecturers will not take strike action at the expense of their students.

Single-union agreements

This refers to the organization agreeing to participate in the collective bargaining process with a sole labour union that represents the workers. The benefit is that this causes fewer disruptions to the employer, since there is no need to spend as much management time and resources in dealing with a multitude of problems from various inter-union disputes.

Consultation

This refers to the process of the management team asking employees for their views on key issues or problems before negotiations take place in order to execute a decision. This process therefore allows employees to have some input and influence in decision-making. Consultation only works if staff believe that their ideas will be listened to seriously. If ideas are continually ignored, then employees will see little point in the process.

Litigation (lawsuits)

Litigation is a form of conflict resolution that involves using the law and order system to seek a legal remedy to a conflict. Litigation can be used, for example, when employees are filing for grievances at work and are seeking compensation from their employers. However, this is likely to lead to a win–lose situation.

Expectations

A common source of conflict between managers and employees is that unrealistic expectations are often set. If expectations are set too high (or even too low), then managers will not get the desired results, which leads to conflict. Therefore, setting SMART targets (see Unit 1.3) can help to resolve this source of conflict.

Avoidance

This refers to a case of 'agreeing to disagree' where the parties in conflict do not reach a resolution. Remember that some conflict is healthy; there is nothing wrong with people having different opinions. Critics of this approach argue that avoidance does not resolve the underlying conflict and therefore leads to a 'lose-lose' situation.

Question 2.7.4

Human Rights Watch and Wal-Mart

Human Rights Watch is an international **non-governmental organization** based in New York. In 2007, it carried out its first ever survey on how American companies treat their workers (having previously conducted studies in other foreign countries). The group found that Wal-Mart, the largest employer in the USA, had violated federal laws by its aggressive efforts to shut out trade unions. The report found that none of the 1.3 million Wal-Mart workers were found to be associated with a labour union. Independent reports also suggested that Wal-Mart employees were disgruntled over its lack of corporate social responsibility, especially the poor pay and working conditions.

Wal-Mart responded by defending its labour policies. The retailer argued that it provided open channels of communication to allow employees to express their ideas, comments and concerns. Wal-Mart also claimed that their labour practices meant that none of the workers needed to join labour unions, further testifying that the accusations made in the Human Rights Watch report were outdated and misleading.

a Define the meaning of a **non-governmental organization**. *[2 marks]*

b Explain how a perceived lack of corporate social responsibility at Wal-Mart can cause conflict. *[4 marks]*

c Evaluate alternative approaches to conflict resolution at Wal-Mart. *[9 marks]*

EMPLOYER–EMPLOYEE RELATIONS AND BUSINESS STRATEGY

Industrial relations will depend very much on the dominant leadership and management styles within an organization. Blake and Mouton's managerial grid (see Unit 2.4) focuses on the concerns of managers for their people and their concern for achieving tasks. They suggest that there are five different styles of management and each of these will have varying effects in industrial relations. For instance, managers that have low concern for people and only focus on completing tasks tend to foster poor employer-employee relations.

Corporate culture (see Unit 2.6) also has a role in affecting industrial relations. Some organizations may develop a culture that values the importance of consultation in the decision-making process. Such businesses value the contribution that workers can make in order to come up with more informed judgements. It has also been recognized that consultation and employee participation can reduce the likelihood of industrial action. Better still, consultation and industrial democracy can improve industrial relations by motivating people since they feel more valued.

Due to their varying and often conflicting interests, employees and employers often face disputes and conflict. The key to successful negotiation is that all parties need to gain something of value for the compromise that they make. If negotiations (win-win situations) do not work, businesses can resort to more aggressive methods, such as intimidation and threat of dismissals. For example, Cathay Pacific Airways fired 49 of their 1,500 pilots in 2001 caused by industrial unrest. The purpose was to send a warning to all other union members to refrain from taking industrial action.

A union might be able to succeed in promoting the priorities of some or most of its members, but there are likely to be some members who are not catered for. This is because not everyone necessarily agrees with the industrial action advocated by the union. A challenge facing many trade unions is the sharp decline in membership numbers.

HIGHER LEVEL

It is also important for management to be aware of cultural differences when trying to deal with conflict at work. For example, American and European companies are used to dealing with confrontational issues, whereas the Japanese find outright confrontation a barrier to negotiations. Another example is that of gestures such as shaking hands; in some cultures the shake of hands means 'farewell' or 'nice to meet you' but in other situations it also means 'we have a deal'. In some Asian countries, physical contact between men and women is discouraged, but this should not be seen as being unfriendly mannerism. International business etiquette is covered in Unit 4.7.

Finally, it is imperative for managers to remember that if people are an organization's most valuable asset, then they should be considered and treated in an appropriate manner. After all, it is the employees who persuade and serve customers in order for them to part with their money. Open and trusting employee–employer relations will therefore enhance the prosperity of a business.

REVIEW QUESTIONS 2.7

1 Distinguish between 'negotiations' and 'collective bargaining'.
2 What are the three levels of negotiation?
3 Outline the six steps used in the negotiation process.
4 Distinguish between the 'winner takes all' and 'win–win' approaches to negotiations.
5 The outcome of any negotiation or collective bargaining process will depend on several factors. State five of these factors.
6 What is a 'trade (labour) union' and what is its main purpose?
7 Distinguish between 'go-slow' and 'work to rule'.
8 Differentiate between 'lock outs' and 'closures'.
9 What is meant by 'conflict' and why does it become a problem if not managed properly?
10 Distinguish between 'conciliation' and 'arbitration'.
11 Why might employee participation and industrial democracy lead to a win–win outcome?
12 How might no-strike agreements help to improve the image of a labour union?
13 What is 'litigation'?
14 Outline why avoidance is not often regarded as an ideal method of conflict resolution.
15 How do management and leadership styles affect employee–employer relations?

Arbitration is a process that involves an independent person or body, known as the arbitrator, deciding on an appropriate outcome to a dispute. The arbitrator's final decision becomes legally binding.

Collective bargaining is the negotiation process whereby trade union representatives and employer representatives discuss issues with the intention of reaching a mutually acceptable agreement.

Conciliation, also known as **mediation**, is a process whereby the two parties involved in a dispute agree to use the services of an independent mediator to help in the negotiation process.

Conflict refers to disagreements that result from differences in the attitudes, beliefs, values or needs of people. It can also arise from past rivalries and personality clashes (collectively known as *internal politics*).

Conflict resolution refers to the course of action taken to resolve conflict and differences in opinion.

Deadlock, also known as **stand-off**, refers to a situation when there has been a failure to reach a satisfactory compromise in the negotiation process. Hence, deadlocks will tend to lead to industrial disputes.

Employers' associations are organizations that represent the general views and interests of all businesses within a certain industry by influencing government action and negotiating with trade unions.

Go-slow is a form of industrial action that involves employees working at the minimum pace allowable under their employment contract.

Industrial action refers to the activities taken by employees who are disgruntled by working conditions and practices, such as hours of work or pay disputes. Examples of such action include: go-slow, work-to-rule, strike action and overtime bans. Industrial action is a result of poor employer–employee relationships.

Industrial democracy means that employees are given responsibilities and authority to complete tasks, i.e. they have opportunities to be involved in the decision-making process.

Negotiation is a bargaining process whereby separate parties attempt to achieve a mutually acceptable outcome, i.e. a 'win–win' situation for those involved.

Single-union agreement refers to an organization agreeing to participate in the collective bargaining process with a single trade union that represents the workers.

Staff associations have a similar role to trade unions (upholding the welfare of their staff members) except that they operate only within an organization. Hence, the issues dealt with are more relevant to the staff, although their bargaining strength is weaker than that of a trade union.

Strikes are a form of industrial action that involves employees refusing to work. This is usually the result of major industrial unrest such as pay disputes or serious grievances.

Trade union (also known as a **labour union**) is an organization that consists of worker members who unite to protect their rights and well-being in the workplace.

Walk-out is a form of industrial action that happens when employees independently or collectively leave (or walk out of) their place of work as a sign of protest or disapproval of management decisions and actions.

Work-to-rule occurs when employees do the absolute minimum required, as stated in their contracts of employment, i.e. they adhere precisely to all rules and regulations in order to reduce productivity.

HIGHER LEVEL

Crisis Management and Contingency Planning

UNIT 2.8

A crisis is an opportunity riding the dangerous wind.

Chinese proverb

Key topics

Higher Level only

- Crisis planning and contingency planning
- Costs and benefits of contingency planning
- Crisis management

HIGHER LEVEL

INTRODUCTION

A **crisis** is a situation of instability which results in major problems for a business. Crises are usually unexpected and often unpredictable. In the event of an actual crisis materializing, it is probable that costs to the business will be significant in terms of both time and money. At the extreme, a crisis can threaten the survival of a business. All businesses, irrespective of size and sector, run the risk of experiencing a crisis. Hence, managers plan for such events in order to minimize the damage that crises can cause to their organizations.

Box 2.8a shows some examples of real crises in the business world. Some broader examples of crises include:

- A lack of working capital to pay wages and suppliers
- Damaging media publicity
- Computer hacking
- Soaring levels of staff turnover
- Accidents such as fire damage to stock
- Natural disasters such as floods
- No power due to a blackout or power cut
- Terrorist attacks
- Delayed flights due to computer failure at airports
- Food poisoning at a chain of restaurants.

Crisis management refers to the response of an organization to a crisis situation. This Unit looks at how businesses can set up measures to allow instantaneous and constructive action to be taken in response to crises, such as those mentioned above.

Box 2.8a Business crises

- 1985 – Coca-Cola, partly in response to the infamous Pepsi Challenge, launched a replacement product for regular Coke called New Coke. With 40,000 written complaints each day about the new product, Coca-Cola was forced to bring back the original-flavoured Coke.
- 2004 – Coca-Cola introduced its bottled 'natural still water' called Dasani in the UK. It was later discovered that the water came from a tap in Sidcup, England and contained prohibited levels of bromate (a chemical compound that can cause cancer).
- 2006 – Sony recalled almost six million of its lithium-ion laptop batteries from its clients Dell and Apple (see Question 2.8.2 on page 328). Sony announced that the recall would cost the firm up to 20% of its net profits for the year.
- 2006 – Disney oversold tickets for its first Chinese New Year season at the Hong Kong Disneyland theme park. Tourists from China were turned away even though they had valid tickets. The poor public relations that followed meant Disney fell short of their annual attendance target (see Question 2.8.5 on page 331).
- 2006 – Cadbury's suffered a £30 million ($59 million) loss when a burst pipe in its UK factory caused salmonella contamination to one million bars of chocolate.
- 2007 – The world's largest toy store, Toys 'R Us, removed all *Thomas The Tank Engine* products from its shelves, following findings that the paint on the wooden toy trains contained traces of toxic lead that is harmful to young children. In North America alone, over 1.5 million units were recalled.

HIGHER LEVEL

CRISIS PLANNING VERSUS CONTINGENCY PLANNING

Crisis planning is about being *reactive* to events and changes that might cause serious damage to a business. In extreme cases, a crisis can lead to the closure of the business. The first five years of the 21st century saw events such as the terrorist attacks of September 11 in the USA, the deadly SARS outbreak and a tsunami in SE Asia, world oil prices hitting historical highs and a global pandemic of avian flu. Crises can also be unique to a business, such as a sudden announcement of a hostile takeover from a rival company or a fire in the office. Businesses will usually find it extremely difficult to plan for such unpredicted and unquantifiable risks, which can have profound impacts on their operations. Such plans consist of thoughtful processes to anticipate the complex nature of an actual or perceived crisis. If a business finds itself faced with a crisis, then **crisis management** is required to minimize the impact on the business. Radical measures and an autocratic style of leadership are likely to prevail.

Crisis planning involves forecasting potential crises. By contrast, contingency planning looks at how to deal with such crises to ensure the continuity of the business. Managers can then plan appropriate action to deal with these events. In the case of a crisis, such as a health and safety scare related to a firm's products, then the plan has to deal with a large number of issues. For example, the brand image and reputation must be protected, customers must be reassured and shareholders must be convinced of the firm's ability to overcome the catastrophe. All these issues, and more, must appear in the business continuity plan.

Contingency planning is about being *proactive* to changes in the business environment. It involves developing a plan before an unwanted and unlikely event occurs by using 'what if?' questions to identify all probable threats. Anyone working in the insurance industry will testify that the future is not easy to predict. Things are likely to turn out different from what may have been predicted. However, to reduce the risks and impacts of encountering a crisis, businesses carry out contingency planning. Management will examine what might happen and assess their effects on the business, such as a downturn in the economy, the loss of electricity and power, extreme poor weather conditions or strike action being taken by the workforce. Contingency plans are designed to help managers cope with unwanted and unlikely problems that might arise. Most contingency plans are based on the worse case scenario in order to better prepare businesses to deal with crises.

Most organizations will have a contingency plan for the eventuality of a fire in the workplace. The plan will include procedures for evacuation of the buildings (including the use of emergency exits) and contacting the emergency services (fire, police and ambulance). Deciding on the key duties of people in such circumstances will also appear in the plan. The plan also needs to be tested, i.e. fire drills are carried out to test the contingency plan. This might include actions such as response rates (how efficiently people evacuated the building) and other tests performed under safe conditions. A review is then conducted and a report submitted to the management team with recommendations for further improvements to the contingency plan.

The more quantifiable the possibility, the more effective a contingency plan is likely to be. For example, the Hong Kong government has contingency plans and arrangements for the onslaught of tropical typhoons and torrential rain. Each year, Hong Kong is likely to be hit by a typhoon and/or heavy rain. Warnings signs are broadcast on the radio, internet and television to inform people of the situation. In extreme cases, such as 'Typhoon signal 8 or 10' (the latter being the highest warning signal) or a 'black rain' warning, businesses and schools are closed as the severe weather threatens people's safety. Similarly, in Middle Eastern countries such as Dubai and Qatar, severe heat warnings are signalled by the government. Schools and businesses will be closed for the day if the heat proves too dangerous for people to be outdoors for extended periods of time. Hence, effective contingency plans enable a business to be better prepared to manage a crisis (proactive), rather than being totally unprepared to cope with the crisis when it occurs (reactive or passive). This is easier to do if risks and crises are quantifiable.

Advantages of contingency planning include:

- Careful planning can help to reduce risks since most if not all eventualities have been accounted for.
- It can reduce the impact of a crisis on the organization since there is a well thought out plan to follow in the event of a disaster.
- It can help to reassure staff and hence satisfy the safety needs of employees, as advocated by A. Maslow (see Unit 2.5).
- Contingency planning necessitates effective communication between management and employees, thereby helping to enhance productivity and motivation.

Disadvantages of contingency planning include:

- Contingency planning uses up valuable management time and resources, thereby increasing costs.
- Crises may never happen and therefore the time and money invested into contingency planning could have been better used elsewhere.
- If plans are based on outdated or inaccurate data, then inappropriate action may be taken if and when a crisis occurs.
- No amount of planning can prevent the totally unexpected, such as a tsunami or other natural disasters.

Exam Tip!

It is wrong to assume that insurance is the solution to a crisis. Indeed, insurance can help to recover some of the damages caused by a crisis, such as floods or fires. However, some risks are simply unquantifiable, such as financial losses due to terrorist attacks. Hence, not all risks can be covered by insurance.

Carrying out crisis and contingency planning does not eliminate all eventualities of a problem occurring. Nevertheless, careful planning can mean that the number and extent of surprises are reduced.

Question 2.8.1

H5N1 bird flu

In 2006, the World Health Organization (WHO) confirmed the outbreak of the deadly avian flu in Turkey, the first case in Europe. Health experts believed that the H5N1 virus could quickly spread from birds to humans, thereby harming the global economy if sick employees across the world were forced to stay away from work. It is no wonder then that Turkey's lucrative tourism industry was badly hit by the news.

Many international businesses, such as HSBC, responded to the threat of a global outbreak by devising **contingency plans** to deal with the potential outbreak. Even schools in Japan, Singapore and Hong Kong (all highly densely populated countries) drew up plans to respond to a possible pandemic. Schools had trained their staff to work from home, via telecommunications and internet technologies.

a Define the term **contingency plan**. *[2 marks]*

b Examine the costs and benefits to organizations such as banks and schools in devising contingency plans. *[6 marks]*

CRISIS MANAGEMENT

Crisis management refers to the management of operations before, during and after the event of a crisis.

Successful managers have the ability to respond to any significant disruption to their business by implementing a contingency plan to restore its business operations. Hence, crisis management is sometimes referred to as **disaster recovery**.

Effective crisis management requires directors and managers to detect and deal with potential crises in a swift manner before they escalate into a real problem for the business. By doing this, the media never get to hear about the crisis and hence key stakeholders are not worried by such events.

An essential step in successful crisis management is to ensure that measures are in place to avoid crises altogether. This might minimize exposure to a crisis, but external shocks are inevitable in today's business environment. Effective crisis management can then make the difference between survival and disaster for a business.

Crisis management will entail the use of **business continuity plans** to minimize the disruptions and damages (physical, psychological and financial) caused by a catastrophe. These plans will generally consist of six key stages:

1. Select a team of staff who are trained to deal with crises. This should include a senior executive and someone who will be good with the press (media). All external enquiries relating to the crisis are dealt with by this team to ensure that the correct or desired messages are being portrayed in a consistent manner.
2. The team analyses and assesses the potential threats. They consider 'what if' scenarios and analyse the impact that these might have on the organization. User-friendly plans are devised to deal with these crises. To be of any use to a business, risk analyses must be up to date.
3. The team then develops and implements alternative tactics. There should be plans to ensure that critical business functions are protected in the event of a crisis. This will also require sufficient resources to be deployed to maintain its core activities.
4. Information and decisions are systematically communicated to those who are involved and/or affected. In the event of a real crisis, the first few hours are the most critical, especially as there is so much ambiguity in the initial moments following a crisis. When the September 11 terrorist attacks took place in New York, the whole world was waiting to hear a response from the US President.
5. Resume normal business operations once the crisis has been dealt with.
6. Reflect on the experiences in order to better deal with crises in the future by updating the business continuity plan.

Some risks are uninsurable since they are so difficult to quantify. This makes crisis and contingency planning even more challenging. Nevertheless, careful and effective planning can help a firm to become better prepared and resilient to any major catastrophes. Although some people argue that the plans may be unnecessary, given the low probability or unquantifiable nature of crises, most people believe that businesses would become extremely exposed to the dangers of crises if they have no plan to follow. As the saying goes, if we fail to prepare, then we are preparing to fail.

Question 2.8.2

Sony laptop batteries

In the summer of 2006, Apple had to recall 1.8 million batteries used in its laptop computers due to overheating problems. Apple claimed that the batteries, made by Sony, did not meet its safety and performance standards and was quick to blame the crisis on Sony. Apple said that its key priority was to replace the batteries free of charge to its customers. In the same year, Dell had recalled more than 4 million laptop batteries, also made by Sony. The Japanese company forecast that the recall would cost it between ¥20 billion and ¥30 billion yen (approximately \$165 million to \$250 million). Not surprisingly, Sony's shares on the stock market slipped in value on this news.

a Describe, in the context of the case study, the meaning of a 'crisis'. *[2 marks]*

b Analyse how crisis management can help Sony to deal with such a crisis. *[6 marks]*

Most experts believe that it is best to be open and honest during a time of crisis. In 1990 for example, authorities in the USA found traces of benzene in Perrier bottled mineral water. The producers tried to hide the truth from the general public but this only served to damage their image of supplying purified water from its springs. The mass media saw Perrier putting profits before the interest of people and this led to the recall of some 160 million bottles of Perrier. The lesson to be learnt is that in times of such crises, acting in a socially irresponsible way is more likely to cause a firm long-term damage than if it had accepted responsibility and taken necessary corrective measures from the outset. Box 2.8b outlines some of the benefits of spontaneously and openly responding to crises.

In addition, crisis management often includes a strong focus on **public relations**. A crisis may have damaged the corporate image of a business and reduced the confidence of its stakeholder in the business. Managers need to rectify this and assure stakeholders that recovery is imminent. Public relations experts can be hired to help in this process (see Unit 4.5).

Box 2.8b Benefits of open crisis management

- *Corporate social responsibility* (CSR) – Acting in a socially responsible way (see Unit 1.3) can be a source of competitive advantage. The general public can be quite forgiving, especially if crises are way beyond the control of a business. Untruthful and deceitful cover-up stories are frowned upon by the public and the media.
- *Minimize negative reaction* – Similarly, by taking appropriate action, critics have fewer opportunities to react negatively to the crisis. This can also help to prevent poor publicity of the way in which the crisis was managed.
- *Reduce personal liability* – In the event of a catastrophic loss (such as injury or death to people), then the directors, managers or employees of the organization may be held personally or severally liable if certain guidelines were not followed, such as the non-compliance of health and safety legislation.
- *Handling staff concerns and anxieties* – Immediate actions, such as communications with the organization's personnel can help to alleviate or minimize staff concerns.
- *Minimize financial losses* – Prompt action is imperative to the recovery process. Delays in responding can allow problems to escalate beyond repair.

Ultimately, these benefits will enhance the chances of the firm's survival during a time of crisis.

Question 2.8.3

Bausch & Lomb

In April 2006, American eye-care company Bausch & Lomb (B&L) had $500 million wiped off its stock market value following findings that the company's top-selling 'ReNu' contact lens solutions were linked to an unusual eye infection. Shipments of the contact lens solution from its South Carolina factory were halted by the US Centre for Disease Control and Prevention.

a In the context of the case study, describe what is meant by 'crisis planning'. *[2 marks]*

b Discuss how far it is possible for a business, such as B&L, to plan for a crisis. *[8 marks]*

Exam Tip!
Worked example

Question: The management at a manufacturing plant have estimated that, in the worst case scenario, a crisis would cost the firm $100 million. To what extent should the firm spend $1 million today in order to prevent this crisis, knowing that it might never happen? *[10 marks]*

Answer: Remember to start with definitions, in this case, define the meaning of 'crisis' (a sudden and unexpected threat to the survival of the business) and give an example. Then present both sides of the argument.

Arguments for spending the $1 million:

- It limits the damage caused by an actual crisis.
- The $1 million only represents 1% of the costs in the worst case scenario, i.e. not spending this money can actually cost the firm much more if there is a crisis.
- It can give management and workers a sense of security (piece of mind).

Arguments against spending the $1 million:

- Spending the money does not prevent the crisis from occurring.
- The $1 million will diminish the firm's cash flow.
- There is an opportunity cost to the $1 million, such as diversification to spread risks.
- The likelihood of a crisis occurring is perhaps too low to justify the spending.

Since the question requires the candidate to address the *extent* to which the $1 million is justified, some sort of decision or judgement must be made. This will depend on several factors such as:

- the probability of the crisis occurring.
- the nature, scale and severity of the crisis.
- the nature of the business and its operations, e.g. whether it has a flexible workforce, the size of the firm and its financial strength.
- management traits and experiences.

Answers, as always, must be written in the context of the concerned business and the various functions of the firm.

HIGHER LEVEL

Question 2.8.4

Peugeot

In October 2006, French car producer Peugeot was forced to recall 10,500 of its Peugeot 307 models in Denmark because of a technical problem. The risk was linked to the aggressive Danish weather with high humidity which could cause a short circuit in the car, thereby sparking a fire. In June 2005, Peugeot also blamed the cold and humid Scandinavian weather for nine of its cars that had burst into flames. No fires had been reported in Denmark, but Peugeot were not taking chances with their reputation at stake.

a Explain why product recalls can be damaging to a firm's corporate reputation. *[4 marks]*

b Evaluate whether it would be in Peugeot's best interest to spend money on contingency planning or improving the quality of its cars. *[8 marks]*

CRISIS MANAGEMENT, CONTINGENCY PLANNING AND BUSINESS STRATEGY

Crises represent a threat to businesses. Crisis management is about dealing with threats and disasters by acknowledging the potential for crises and establishing contingency plans to deal with them in an open and instantaneous manner. With any crisis management situation, it is the planned prevention (crisis planning) and the proactive response (contingency planning) of managers that minimizes the impacts of a crisis. The crisis coordinator, usually a senior executive, works closely with colleagues and external agencies (such as lawyers, the press and emergency services) to develop an effective crisis management system. The plans must be properly and regularly monitored, tested and updated accordingly.

During the outbreak of a crisis, it is important to act fast. The mistakes of businesses such as Perrier have shown that immediate and transparent action can allow the firm to take control of the situation. However, such actions require both careful crisis and contingency planning and an effective crisis management team. For example, only people who have been properly trained should be used to handle the media. Such a person is often credited as the firm's media spokesperson.

The crisis management team will need to investigate the root causes of the crisis. Various tools can be used for this, such as *Ishikawa's cause-and-effect model* (see Unit 1.6). Although no two crises are exactly the same, there is much to be learnt from one situation which can help the firm to deal with future crises. The *Pareto principle* can also be a useful tool for crisis management (also discussed in Unit 1.6). This principle states that 80% of a task is completed in 20% of the time. In other words, careful planning takes time, but can really save managers a lot of time if a crisis does materialize. Crisis experts will also use their plans to create opportunities out of a threat. John F. Kennedy (1917–1963), the 35th president of the USA, famously pointed out that the Chinese word for 'crisis' is composed of two characters – danger and opportunity.

So just how far should a business go in planning for a crisis? This Unit has looked at how planning can be vital for business survival. Yet, it is questionable whether and how much time and resources managers should devote to planning for events that may never happen. Moreover, some risks are simply not quantifiable, so devoting time and resources to crisis planning and contingency planning may not be very cost effective. Even if a plan exists, given the unpredictable nature of crises, it is possible that management do not act according to plans once they actually face a crisis (see Question 2.8.5).

Nevertheless, with some sort of crisis and contingency planning in place, managers are better served to deal with the uncertainties and dynamics of change in the ever-transforming business world. Albert Einstein said, "Intellectuals solve problems; geniuses prevent them." Effective managers must be both geniuses (by having measures to prevent crises) and intellectuals (by having contingency plans in place to solve crises as they develop).

Perhaps the words of American politician and ambassador Benjamin Franklin (1706–1790) can sum up the purpose of proper crisis and contingency planning, when he said, "By failing to prepare, you are preparing to fail."

Question 2.8.5

Chaos at HK Disneyland

The first year of operations proved problematic for Hong Kong Disneyland, with some major **public relations** setbacks. The Park ran into trouble with labour unions after staff complained of being overworked and underpaid. The company also faced complaints from international conservationists who forced Disneyland caterers to remove sharks fin soup from its menus.

However, the general public were most outraged during Chinese New Year when thousands of ticket holders were denied access to the Park due to overcrowding reasons. Despite holding valid prepurchased tickets, many customers who had travelled from China were turned away at the gates. Hong Kong lawmakers said that Disneyland's decision to refuse ticket holders entry was a breach of contract.

The company apologized for the disaster, claiming that it was placing public safety as a priority. It also announced extended opening hours to cater for more visitors. Disneyland admitted to underestimating the level of customer demand as it had not predicted the huge influx of tourists during the Chinese New Year holiday week.

a In the context of the case study, outline what is meant by **public relations**. *[2 marks]*

b Examine two strategies that Disneyland could have used in order to deal with the poor public relations that it faced. *[6 marks]*

c Justify whether you feel that Disneyland could have been better prepared for dealing with the large number of visitors to its theme park. *[7 marks]*

REVIEW QUESTIONS 2.8

1 Use two examples to explain what is meant by a 'crisis'.

2 What is 'crisis management'? Why is it of value to businesses?

3 Differentiate between 'crisis planning' and 'contingency planning'.

4 Outline two advantages and two disadvantages of contingency planning.

5 What is 'disaster recovery'?

6 Summarize the key stages in the crisis management process.

7 Why is it important to take immediate action when a crisis occurs?

8 Why is it important to be open and transparent about issues and concerns during a time of crisis?

9 Outline the role of public relations during a crisis.

10 Why do some people question the financial value of crisis and contingency planning?

HIGHER LEVEL

Business continuity plans are used as part of crisis management in order to minimize the disruptions and damages (physical, psychological and financial) caused by a catastrophe in order for the firm to retain its core operations.

Contingency planning looks at how to deal with a crisis to ensure the continuity of the business. It is about being *proactive* to change by using 'what if?' questions to identify probable threats.

Crisis management refers to the responses of an organization's management team to a crisis situation. It involves setting up measures to allow instantaneous and constructive action to be taken in the event of a crisis.

Crisis planning is about being *reactive* to events and changes that might cause serious disruptions and damage to a business. In extreme cases, a crisis can lead to the closure of the business.

Personal liability means that directors, managers or employees of an organization can be held legally responsible for any catastrophic loss if certain laws and guidelines are not followed, such as ignoring health and safety legislation in the workplace.

Quantifiable risks, often referred to as **insurable risks**, are definite and financially measurable threats to a business, such as fire damage to an organization.

Unquantifiable risks, often referred to as **uninsurable risks**, are threats to a business that are impossible or prohibitively expensive to examine and measure.

HIGHER LEVEL

ACCOUNTS AND FINANCE

UNIT 3

UNIT

Sources of Finance

UNIT 3.1

A business that makes nothing but money is a poor kind of business.

Henry Ford (1863–1947), founder of the Ford Motor Company

Key topics

- Capital and revenue expenditure
- Internal sources of finance: personal funds, family and friends, working capital, retained profits, selling of assets and investing extra cash
- External sources of finance: share capital, loan capital, overdrafts, trade credit, government grants and subsidies, donations, sponsorships, debt factoring, leasing, hire purchase, debentures, venture capital and business angels
- Short-term, medium-term and long-term finance
- Sources of finance for public sector organizations

INTRODUCTION

All businesses need money to finance business activity. This can be for the initial setting up of the business, for its day-to-day running or for expansion purposes. Businesses can obtain their finance from a range of sources, such as loans from a financial institution or by selling unused assets.

The choice of which source(s) to use depends on several factors, including the size and type of business organization, the time scale involved and the purpose of the finance. For example, a sole trader is likely to use personal finance for setting up the business, whereas a multinational may seek other sources of finance to expand in overseas markets.

This Unit examines the range of sources of finance that can be obtained by different types of business organizations.

THE NEED FOR BUSINESS FINANCE

Business finance can be categorized in terms of its *purpose*.

Capital expenditure

Capital expenditure is the finance spent on purchasing **fixed assets**. Fixed assets are items of a monetary value which have a long-term function and can be used repeatedly, such as land, buildings, equipment and machinery. These determine the scale of the firm's operations. Such assets are not intended for resale in the short term but for the purpose of generating money for the business. Since the purchase of fixed assets tends to be expensive, the sources of finance for capital expenditure tend to come from medium and long-term sources. Fixed assets can provide *collateral* (financial guarantee) for securing additional loan capital, but most types of fixed assets tend to depreciate in value with use.

Revenue expenditure

Revenue expenditure refers to payments for the *daily running* of a business, such as wages, raw materials and electricity. Revenue expenditure also includes the payment of *indirect costs* (see Unit 5.2), such as rent, insurance and advertising. Costs must be controlled in order for a business to generate enough revenue to make a profit.

Different businesses have different access to an array of business finance (see Table 3.1a on page 345). For example, a sole proprietorship needs finance to set up the business. The owner is likely to have some personal funds but will usually also need to borrow money to start the business. Typically, the main source of finance for sole traders is their personal savings. On the other hand, larger and more established businesses may seek sources of finance for expansion purposes. They may, for example, seek sources from further *share issues* or by selling *debentures* (see 'Debentures' on page 342).

Question 3.1.1

Olympic Games 2012

The UK construction industry has been very optimistic since London was announced as the host of the Olympic Games in 2012. News media reported an estimated half a million new recruits to the industry in preparation for the global sporting event.

a Use examples to distinguish *revenue expenditure* from *capital expenditure*. *[4 marks]*

b Analyse the benefits for UK businesses of the Olympic Games being held in London. *[6 marks]*

INTERNAL FINANCE

Sources of finance can also be categorized as *internal* or *external* sources. Internal sources of finance come from *within* the business, such as profits that have been retained for business use or from the sale of goods and services that earn money for the business. The main types of internal sources of finance are considered below.

Personal funds

This is the main source of finance for a *sole trader* and for *partners* going into business together. For example, Jamie Oliver, the famous British celebrity chef who hired fifteen unknown recruits for his restaurant 'Fifteen', used £500,000 (just under $1 million) of his own money to finance the project.

Family and friends

Borrowing from family and friends is another source of finance that is popular amongst sole proprietorships and partnerships. Borrowing is often reasonably straightforward and inexpensive compared to borrowing from a bank which may require collateral before authorizing a loan. However, this source of finance is usually very limited and borrowing from family and friends often provokes arguments and fallouts.

Working capital

Working capital (see Unit 3.3) refers to the money that is available for the day to day running of a business. It comes from the sale of goods and services. It is a vital source of finance as working capital is needed to pay for everyday costs such as wages, utility bills and payment to suppliers.

Retained profits

This is the value of profits that the business keeps hold of (after paying taxes to the government and dividends to its shareholders) to use within the business. Retained profits are also known as **internal profits** or **ploughed-back profits**. It is often used for purchasing or upgrading fixed assets. Some retained profit may also be kept in a *contingency fund* (see Unit 2.8) in case of emergencies and unforeseeable expenditure in the future. The benefit of using retained profits as a source of finance is that the business does not have to rely as much on borrowing (which incurs interest charges). However, retained profits alone may not be sufficient for a firm to conduct its business, so other sources may still be needed. In addition, keeping more of the profit for business use means less of it is available for distributing to shareholders.

Selling assets

Businesses can sell their **dormant assets** (unused assets). This might include selling machinery that has been replaced, such as computer equipment, or it could include selling off out-of-season stock at discount. If a business has chosen to relocate, it may be able to raise finance through the sale of land and buildings. In more extreme cases, businesses can sell some of their *fixed assets* to raise finance in order to survive a liquidity problem.

Investing extra cash

Cash that does not need to be spent imminently can be placed in an interest-bearing savings account. This earns interest for the business, and so acts as another source of finance. Although the return does not tend to be very high, cash-rich companies such as Toyota can earn a significant amount of interest on their cash deposits. In addition, there is an opportunity cost to keeping cash at hand rather than at the bank, i.e. the interest that could have been earned by placing the money in the bank.

EXTERNAL FINANCE

External sources of finance come from *outside* the business. Examples include the selling of shares to shareholders or obtaining loans from a bank. With most types of external sources of finance, the providers of finance, such as shareholders and banks, will demand a financial reward, such as dividends and interest payments. The main types of external sources of finance are considered below.

Share capital

Share capital tends to be the main source of finance for a limited company. Share capital is the money that has been raised from selling shares in the company, as shown in the firm's *balance sheet* (see Unit 3.5). An advantage of issuing shares is that it often provides a huge amount of capital. *Private limited companies* cannot sell their shares to the general public whereas *public limited companies* can issue their shares on a stock exchange. The stock exchange, or stock market, refers to any place for buying and selling **securities** (the collective name for stocks and shares). Its main functions are to enable companies or governments to raise capital and to provide a market in second-hand shares and government stocks. The London, Tokyo and New York Stock Exchanges are among the biggest in the world.

Many businesses decide to 'go public' by floating their shares on a stock exchange for the first time. This is known as an **Initial Public Offering** (IPO). Popular IPOs are several times oversubscribed and this pushes up the share price. However, by issuing shares, ownership and control of the business becomes diluted. In addition, share issuance involves many legalities and administrative procedures, with their associated costs.

There are two main types of share capital:

- **Preference shares**. Preference shareholders earn a fixed dividend from a company's profits and they are paid before all other shareholders. Preference shares may be *cumulative* which means that if dividends cannot be paid in a particular year, perhaps due to poor profits, cumulative preference shareholders will get twice the dividend payments in the following year. Preference shares provide a relatively safe income stream and are a low-risk investment in comparison to ordinary shares. However, they are often non-voting shares and preference shareholders do not benefit to the same extent as ordinary shareholders during highly profitable periods.
- **Ordinary shares**. Also known as **equity capital**, ordinary share capital forms the vast majority of shares. The return (dividends) is unknown beforehand because it is based on the level of profits made by the company, and will fluctuate from year to year. Ordinary shareholders receive dividend payments *after* preference shareholders have been paid. However, most ordinary shareholders are granted voting rights based on the number of shares they hold. As their return is not fixed, ordinary shares carry more risk than preference shares but holders tend to gain more dividend payments during good trading periods.

Exam Tip!

When shareholders sell their shares, the company does not receive any of this money as these shares are traded on the secondary market of the stock exchange; no new shares have been issued by the company. Students often write that a drop in the company's share price affects its level of profits as the firm has less money. It is more likely to be the other way around; the poor performance of a company will lead to a fall in its share price as the value of the company declines. In addition, a decline in the company's share price may harm its reputation and will make it more vulnerable to a takeover.

Question 3.1.2

Industrial and Commercial Bank of China (ICBC)

In October 2006, Industrial and Commercial Bank of China (ICBC) launched its **initial public offering** (IPO) in Shanghai and Hong Kong, raising close to $22 billion. Despite the turmoil in Asian stock markets and fears that Chinese bank stocks were overvalued, investors poured money into China's largest lender. The flotation (IPO) proved to be the world's largest ever, beating the previous record of $10.6 billion set by the IPO of AT&T Wireless Services in April 2000.

a Define the term **initial public offering**. *[2 marks]*

b Comment on why ICBC might have decided to float its shares on the stock market. *[4 marks]*

c Explain why investors might have been so keen to buy shares in ICBC, despite the uncertainty and havoc in Asian stock markets at the time. *[4 marks]*

Loan capital

These are loans that are obtained from commercial lenders such as banks. Loans tend to be medium to long-term sources of finance. Interest charges are imposed and can be fixed or variable, depending on the agreement between borrower and lender. Loans are sometimes referred to as *fixed-term loans* because the amount borrowed is paid back in instalments over a definite and predetermined period, such as 5, 10 or 25 years. An example is a **mortgage** which is a secured loan for the purchase of property such as land or buildings. If the borrower *defaults* on the loan (fails to repay the loan), the lender can repossess (take back) the property. Another example of a commercial loan is a **business development loan**. As its name suggests, these loans are catered to meet the specific development needs of the borrower. Businesses may use these highly flexible loans to start or expand their business, to purchase equipment and other assets, or even to boost working capital.

Overdrafts

An overdraft facility allows a business to temporarily overdraw on its account, i.e. to take out more money than it has from their bank account. Overdrafts are commonly used when businesses have minor cash flow problems. Although overdrafts can demand a relatively high rate of interest, they are usually more cost effective than bank loans. This is because, unlike bank loans, overdrafts are used as a short-term source of finance and interest is charged on a daily basis if, and only if, a business overdraws on its account. Overdrafts are suitable when there is a need for a huge cash outflow, such as retail outlets stocking up for the Christmas holiday trading period. They are also suitable for businesses that have sold items on credit and are awaiting payments from their customers. However, a major disadvantage is that overdrafts are *repayable on demand* without prior notice from the lender. Nevertheless, an overdraft facility provides flexibility for a business that may face cash flow problems from time to time.

Trade credit

Trade credit allows a business to 'buy now and pay later'. Although a sale is made at the time of purchase, the seller or credit provider does not receive any cash from the buyer until a later date. Organizations that offer trade credit (known as **creditors**) usually allow between 30–60 days for their customers (known as **debtors**) to pay. This relieves cash outflows for the debtors, which can help to improve their cash flow management.

Government grants

The government may offer financial aid to support business activities. This may be for small business start-ups or to help stimulate economic activity in regions or industries that may be facing particular problems, such as high unemployment in a particular area of the country. Grants are usually offered to eligible businesses as one-off payments. Unfortunately for most businesses, this source of finance is very hard to obtain.

Government subsidies

This source is similar to government grants in that the purpose is to reduce the costs of production, although the focus of subsidies is to provide benefits to *society*. For example, farmers are often provided subsidies so that food prices can be stabilized. They are often provided for essential products and services in order to keep prices down for the consumer. Subsidies, if they can be obtained, are great for businesses as they do not cut into profit margins. Although firms charge lower prices, the lower earnings are made up by the government subsidy. Moreover, with a cut in price, businesses are likely to face increased demand for their goods and services.

Donations

Donations are financial gifts from individuals or organizations to a business. There are usually no direct benefits to the donor (except that they feel good about themselves in donating to a worthwhile cause), although some donations have terms and conditions attached, such as an appropriate display of the donor's name in recognition of their gift. This source of finance is not a likely source for most private sector businesses. Charities, schools, hospitals and universities often receive donations to boost their finances.

Sponsorships

Sponsorship occurs when an organization gives financial support, in the form of cash, products or services, for another business in return for prominently displaying the sponsor's company brand or logo. In essence, sponsorship is a form of promotion. For example, Nike and Adidas have contracts to supply many of the world's top sporting teams and celebrities with apparel. This reduces the cost of buying equipment and clothing for sports clubs and therefore acts as a source of finance for them. Many local events are sponsored by businesses that may believe in exerting social responsibility (see Unit 1.3). For most businesses, however, it is difficult to obtain this source of finance.

Question 3.1.3

Manchester United Football Club

In April 2006, Manchester United Football Club (MUFC) chose to reject a huge sponsorship deal with Mansion, an online gambling company, worth up to £70 million ($140 million). Instead, MUFC signed a four-year sponsorship deal with insurance giant American International Group (AIG) worth £56.5 million, after having terminated ties with its previous sponsors Vodafone.

a Explain the *opportunity cost* of MUFC declining the larger sponsorship offer from Mansion. *[2 marks]*

b Explain why businesses such as Vodafone or AIG might want to sponsor a large football club. *[4 marks]*

c Justify the view that management at MUFC were correct to select AIG as their new sponsor. *[6 marks]*

Debt factoring

The key to understanding debt factoring is the concept of **debtors**. Debtors are people or organizations that owe the business money. For example, a business may have sold supplies to a customer on 30 days credit. This means that the business will not receive any payment until the following month. There is a danger, however, for businesses that give credit to too many of their clients. The more credit that is given to customers, the higher is the chance of facing **bad debt** – debtors who are unable to repay the money owed, perhaps due to their own financial problems. Banks, for example, often see an increase in their bad debts when there is a sudden and unexpected increase in unemployment. The resulting loss of incomes for many people means that they cannot repay the money that they borrowed.

Debt factoring is a financial service that allows a business to raise funds based on the value owed by their debtors, i.e. customers who have bought on credit. Most factoring service providers will offer between 80–85% of the outstanding payments from debtors within 24 hours once the application has been approved. This is a major advantage over receiving money in 30 or 60 days time – typical credit periods. Hence, debt factoring can act as an immediate source of finance for businesses facing cash flow problems. This service can also help the business to save time and money, since the service provider takes over the responsibility of chasing up debtors for payments.

Another advantage of using a factoring service is the option of **non-recourse factoring** for the provision of *bad debts*. Ordinarily, factoring providers do not hold responsibility for bad debts so the business has to absorb these as losses. However, with the added feature of non-recourse, even if debtors don't pay, the factoring service provider will absorb the loss or insure itself against any losses; either way, the business does not suffer any losses from bad debts. This therefore helps to reduce the risk of doing business. Of course, there is an additional charge for this service but it may give a business piece of mind over the issue of dealing with bad debts.

The main disadvantage of this source of finance is the high fees charged by the financial institutions that offer debt factoring services. The basic fees are comparable with those of overdrafts (see 'Overdrafts' on page 339). However, there are additional charges for management, administration and maintenance of accounts. The larger the value of debtors and the riskier the business seems to be, the higher the charges tend to be. In addition, not all businesses are eligible to use the service, especially smaller firms.

Question 3.1.4

Tiffany Stones Ltd.

Tiffany Stones Ltd. has a forecast cash flow deficit of $140,000 in two months time. It also has debtors totalling $180,000. The firm decides to use a factoring service that advances 80% of the debtor balance.

- Calculate and explain whether this decision would resolve the cash flow problem for the business. *[3 marks]*

Leasing

Leasing is a form of hiring whereby a contract is drawn between a leasing company (known as a **lessor**) and the customer (known as the **lessee**). The lessee pays rental income to hire assets from the lessor, who is the legal owner of the assets. Hence, the rental income is a source of finance for the lessor. It can be cheaper to lease assets such as machinery, vehicles and buildings, especially in the short to medium term. Therefore, leasing is suitable for business customers that do not have the initial capital to pay for such assets. This consequently releases cash for other purposes within the business. Another benefit to the lessee is that added services, such as maintenance and upgrading, are provided by the leasing firm. Finally, since spending on leased equipment is classed as a business expense, the tax bill of the lessee is reduced. The main disadvantage to the customer is that in the long term, leasing is more expensive than outright purchase of the assets.

Hire purchase (HP)

Hire purchase means that a business can pay for items in instalments, perhaps over 12 or 24 months. Once all payments have been made, the item then belongs to the business but in the interim the asset is legally the property of the HP firm. Quite often, a deposit (also known as a **down payment**) is required in order to secure a HP deal from the lender. In addition, if the buyer defaults on the agreement, i.e. they fall behind on paying their instalments, then the lender can repossess the asset. Essentially, HP is a form of buying on credit, so interest is charged by the lender on the amount borrowed. It is different from leasing because the buyer eventually owns the asset on payment of the last instalment.

Debentures

Debentures are essentially long-term loans. They are similar to shares in that a certificate is issued to all debenture holders, be they members of the public, the government or other businesses that have purchased debentures. However, unlike shareholders, debenture holders do not usually have ownership or voting rights in how the business should be run. Debentures are used by a vast range of organizations, from Arsenal Football Club for its Emirates Stadium in London to private independent schools in Hong Kong (see Question 3.1.5 on page 344).

The benefit to debenture holders is that they receive interest (which can be fixed or variable depending on the type of debenture) before shareholders would receive any dividend. Perhaps more importantly, debenture holders receive interest payments even if the business makes a loss. Buying debentures is therefore relatively low risk in comparison to holding shares. Not all debentures pay interest, however, such as those used by sports clubs. They, instead, may offer their debenture holders exclusive privileges such as VIP seating or 'free' annual passes. The safest type of debenture is a **secured debenture** where the loan is tied to the financing of a particular fixed asset. This then means that the debenture holder has a legal interest in the asset, rather like a mortgage with collateral.

For a business, debentures provide the benefit of a long-term source of finance, without losing any control in the business (as debenture holders do not usually have any voting rights). One disadvantage is that issuing debentures increases a firm's *gearing* (see Unit 3.6). This means that the firm has more borrowing as a percentage of its capital employed and therefore this not only raises interest repayments to the lender, but also increases the risk to the business if interest rates increase.

Venture capital

Venture capital is high risk capital, usually in the form of loans or shares, invested by venture capital firms or individuals, usually at the start of a business idea. Venture capital firms seek to invest in small to medium sized businesses that have the potential of earning high profits. There is a considerable chance of business failure but also significant returns if the business venture succeeds. Hence, venture capital is often perceived as a high risk strategy for the investor. Businesses that aim to raise venture capital must present a coherent and convincing business plan with supporting data to show the investors that the risk is worth taking.

Venture capitalists and *business angels* (see below) will look at a number of criteria before committing their capital in an investment project, including:

- **Return on investment** – Investors demand a return on their capital. Venture capitalists know that a huge majority of business start-ups will fail outright, so each business in their portfolio has to have good potential to be highly profitable in order to cover any losses.
- **The business plan** – The business plan should outline the long-term aim and purpose of the business venture. The purpose creates *direction* and an *identity* for the business, which is central to securing finance from investors. Investors must feel confident that the business fully understands the market in which they operate. Investors want to see that the idea will allow the business to operate in a high-growth market with few competitors. Innovative and original ideas in the business plan may be enough to convince investors to part with their capital.
- **People** – It is extremely difficult for any individual person to have all the skills, experience and contacts required to run a business successfully. Essentially, no matter how good an idea might be in the business plan, success will only materialize if the business has a good team of people to run it. Ineffective people management is a major cause of business failure (see Unit 1.2) and this is one aspect of business operations that venture capitalists will examine carefully.
- **Track record** – Venture capital firms will also assess the historical track record of a business and its management before investing any capital. This might include an investigation into the firm's ability to pay back previous investors and lenders of capital as well as the success record of the entrepreneurs.

Business angels

Some private investors are extremely wealthy and choose to invest in businesses that offer high growth potential. These tend to be high risk, high return business ventures. Such investors are known as **business angels**. These highly experienced entrepreneurs are likely to take a proactive role in the setting up or running of the business venture. This means that the owner of the business loses some control to the business angel. Another possible disadvantage of using this source of finance is that the business may eventually have to buy out the stake owned by the business angel. However, with the wealth of experience and financial backing, business angels can be a major advantage to the survival and success of a new business.

Question 3.1.5

Yew Chung International School

In mid 2006, Yew Chung International Secondary School in Kowloon Tong (Hong Kong) introduced a cut in fees of around 15% but also introduced plans for a debenture. The timing coincided with the school's move to a new campus in 2007 with its much improved facilities such as an indoor swimming pool, larger classrooms, specialist music rooms and an art gallery. Parents of children at the school in Years 7–11 pay HK$112,000 ($14,395) under the new scheme instead of HK$131,780 ($16,940). The fees for Year 12–13 students were also reduced by a similar amount.

However, parents also need to pay a debenture of HK$200,000 ($25,700), which is refundable when students eventually leave the school. Parents with more than one child at the school would get a small discount. Critics say that the new campus cost twice as much as building the average secondary school in Hong Kong.

Source: adapted from www.ycis-hk.com

a Describe why Yew Chung International School decided to sell debentures. *[2 marks]*

b Explain why most parents might agree to purchase the debentures. *[3 marks]*

c Explain the potential drawbacks to a school that chooses to raise finance through the sale of debentures. *[4 marks]*

d Examine two alternative sources of finance that the school could have used. *[6 marks]*

Question 3.1.6

MG Rover

In May 2000, four British businessmen, nicknamed the Phoenix Four, bought MG Rover from previous owners BMW for just £10 ($19.50). They each put in £60,000 ($117,000) of their own money but were also given £1 billion in cash and assets from BMW (who were losing £1 million from MG Rover each day). The British saw them as heroes, having saved the former British company from extinction.

However, five years later, the business announced that there were to be 5,000 job losses. The Phoenix Four were condemned for their gross mismanagement of MG Rover and for their extravagant financial rewards. Some analysts say that £1 billion was not enough to save MG Rover which was struggling to survive in a highly competitive and rapidly changing industry. Whilst BMW retained the highly successful Mini, Range Rover was sold off to Ford Motor Company. MG Rover is now owned by Chinese firm Nanjing Automobile.

a Describe why the members of the Phoenix Four might be classed as 'business angels'. *[2 marks]*

b Explain the dangers outlined in the article concerning the use of business angels. *[4 marks]*

c Analyse how the profitability of a business, such as MG Rover, affects its ability to raise external sources of finance. *[6 marks]*

Table 3.1a Summary of business ownership and sources of finance

	Sole Trader	Partnership	Private Limited Company	Public Limited Company	Non-profit Organizations
Business Angels	✓	✓	✓		
Donations / Gifts					✓
Factoring	✓	✓	✓	✓	
Grants	✓	✓	✓	✓	✓
Leasing and Hire purchase	✓	✓	✓	✓	✓
Loans	✓	✓	✓	✓	✓
Mortgage	✓	✓	✓	✓	✓
Overdraft	✓	✓	✓	✓	✓
Personal funds	✓	✓			
Retained profit	✓	✓	✓	✓	
Shares			✓	✓	
Trade credit	✓	✓	✓	✓	
Venture capital	✓	✓	✓		

SHORT-TERM, MEDIUM-TERM AND LONG-TERM FINANCE

Effective managers pay careful attention to the cash-flow situation of their business. They strive to balance the cash coming into the business (from sales revenue) with the cash going out (for costs). However, they will inevitably face problems from time to time so must consider different forms of finance to deal with short-, medium- and long-term changes.

Different sources of finance are used to deal with different situations. However, they all serve the same purpose – to aid business operations. This is very important because serious cash-flow problems (when a business is unable to pay its short-term debts) can cause liquidation or bankruptcy. This is especially the case if creditors chase for the money owed but the business does not have the finance to immediately repay its creditors.

Business analysts do not have a common definition for the short, medium and long term. However, it is quite safe to use the following definitions, which are pretty much in line with accounting terminology.

Short term refers to the current tax (or fiscal) year. In terms of external sources of finance, this means anything that has to be repaid to creditors and lenders within the next twelve months.

Medium term refers to the time period of more than twelve months but less than five years. It is quite common for many businesses and governments to have medium-term plans (or five-year plans). In terms of sources of finance, medium-term sources might therefore include commercial loans or hire purchase agreements in excess of a year but repayable within five years.

Long term refers to any period after the next five years. The longer the time period in question, the harder it becomes to plan effectively. Managers might well know which sources of finance are needed within the next 6–12 months, but are less likely to understand how much is required in ten years time. Examples of long-term sources of finance include mortgages and debentures.

Nevertheless, it is important to remember that these definitions will tend to vary from business to business and industry to industry. What is important is how these definitions link to the overall aims and objectives of a business. Industries that are heavily involved in research and development such as space technology or pharmaceuticals, for example, may view the medium term as the next ten years, whereas fast-paced industries such as ICT might see five years as relatively long term.

Table 3.1b categorizes, in a simple way, the different sources of finance under the headings of the short, medium and long term.

Table 3.1b Summary of sources of finance

	Short term	Medium term	Long term
Internal sources			
Cash at bank	✓		
Retained profits	✓	✓	
Sale of fixed assets (divestment)	✓		
Selling dormant assets	✓		
Working capital	✓		
External sources			
Business angels	✓	✓	✓
Debentures			✓
Debt factoring	✓		
Donations	✓		
Government subsidies and grants	✓	✓	✓
Hire purchase	✓	✓	✓
Leasing	✓	✓	✓
Loan capital		✓	✓
Overdrafts	✓		
Share capital			✓
Sponsorships	✓	✓	
Trade credit	✓		
Venture capitalists	✓	✓	

SOURCES OF FINANCE FOR PUBLIC SECTOR ORGANIZATIONS

Certain public sector organizations may directly charge for their services. For example, Japan's postal service, owned by the government, gets revenue mainly from selling stamps, but also offers other services such as savings and travel insurance. The BBC, owned by the British government, charge annual license fees for its services.

However, in addition to charging customers, public sector organizations also get funding from the government. This will help to keep business costs lower than would otherwise be the case. Schools and hospitals usually qualify for some kind of financial support from central government. This money is, of course, funded from government tax revenues. Donations are another important source of finance for many public sector organizations.

SOURCES OF FINANCE AND BUSINESS STRATEGY

Business failure is largely attributed to the lack of financial planning and control. Effective financial management is essential for the successful daily running of a business and for its long-term prosperity. As with so many aspects of business, it is important for students to be aware that managers have to consider various factors in order to make a rational decision. Hence, managers have to consider a number of interlinked factors when deciding between alternative sources of finance. These closely related factors include:

- **Purpose of finance** – Will the source of finance be used for short-term purposes (for the day-to-day running of the business) or for the replacement of fixed assets over a longer time? Overdrafts, for example, will be more suitable for improving working capital whereas hire purchase may be more suitable for buying expensive equipment.
- **Cost** – Managers will need to consider not only the purchase cost of assets but the associated costs such as administrative charges, service and maintenance charges, and short- and long-term consideration of interest rates. As with most business decision-making, managers also need to bear in mind the *opportunity cost* of their final choice, i.e. the sacrifices incurred once a final decision is made.
- **Amount required** – Large amounts of finance might be raised through share issues or through secured loans from financial institutions. These can be financed by paying the lender in regular instalments to spread the high cost of finance. If only a small amount is needed, perhaps for dealing with a short-term liquidity problem, then an overdraft might be sufficient.
- **Time** – If the finance is needed for a long period, such as for the purchase of new buildings, long-term sources of finance such as mortgages or debentures are suitable. If the finance is needed to help fund working capital, short-term sources such as trade credit will be more appropriate.
- **Status and size** of the firm – A well-known and large multinational corporation will find it much easier to raise finance from a wider range of sources than a sole trader. Despite a stock market crash during mid-2006, ICBC was able to raise the most substantial amount of finance for any initial public offering in the history of the world's stock markets (see Question 3.1.2 on page 339). This was largely due to consumer and business confidence in the share issue of China's largest lender. In addition, large organizations are able to obtain finance cheaper due to *financial economies of scale* (see Unit 1.7), especially as they are able to offer higher levels of collateral than smaller firms.
- **Financial situation** of a firm – Businesses with poor cash flow will find it more difficult to raise finance as they represent a higher risk to investors and lenders. In addition, lenders will assess the existing *gearing* (long-term external borrowing as a percentage of capital employed) of the business before granting any finance. Firms with a high gearing ratio represent a relatively high risk as they have existing debt commitments and are more vulnerable to any increase in interest rates (which raises their interest repayments to banks). Lenders will be aware that any increase in short-term liabilities will reduce working capital.
- **External factors** – Factors beyond the control of a business may have a huge impact on the choice and availability of finance. Managers will be affected by the state of the economy and business confidence levels (see Unit 1.5). Investments for expansion plans are more likely to take place during prosperous economic times. Changes in interest rates and stock market volatility also affect the level of consumer and producer confidence levels, thereby affecting the level of business investments.

Like so many aspects of business, managers will be aware that the choice of finance will have repercussions on the firm's financial accounts. The choice, and hence the associated costs, of finance will impact directly on the firm's Profit and Loss Account, Cash Flow statement and Balance Sheet. It is the figures that appear in these financial documents that reveal, in quantitative terms, the degree of success of a business.

REVIEW QUESTIONS 3.1

1 Give three reasons why businesses need finance.
2 Distinguish between 'internal' and 'external' sources of finance.
3 State three sources of internal finance and five sources of external finance.
4 What are the differences between 'hire purchase' and 'leasing'?
5 What are the advantages and limitations to a business in using debentures as a source of finance?
6 What criteria do business angels and venture capital firms use when deciding whether to invest in a business?
7 What is the difference between short-term, medium-term and long-term borrowing?
8 What factors do managers need to decide on before choosing their source(s) of finance?

Business angels are wealthy and entrepreneurial investors who risk their money in small to medium sized businesses that have high growth potential. Their hands-on approach, experience and financial investment can have a large impact on the success of business start-ups.

Capital expenditure is spending by businesses on fixed assets such as the purchase of land and buildings. Such expenditure is seen as vital to the growth and survival of businesses in the long run. This type of expenditure is also known as **investment expenditure**.

Creditors are individuals or organizations that the business owes money to that needs to be settled within the next 12 months. Examples include money owed to a bank for an overdraft or to suppliers for the purchase of stock bought on credit.

Debentures are a type of long-term loan to a business with the promise of fixed annual interest payments to the debenture holders. The vast majority of these loans are also repayable on maturity, although some are indefinite so are classed as permanent capital to the firm as there is no maturity date.

External financing means getting sources of finance from outside the organization, such as through debt (for example, overdraft, loans or debentures), share capital, or funding from the government.

Factoring is a financial service whereby a factor (such as a bank) collects debts on behalf of other businesses, in return for a fee. The factor will pay, in cash, most of the outstanding debts owed to the business and then chase its debtors for payments.

Leasing (or hiring) is suitable if a firm needs to use expensive assets such as equipment or vehicles. The leasing company owns the equipment and hires it out to the customer. As a result, lessees do not have to commit large amounts of their own capital.

Non-recourse debt factoring refers to a financial service where a debt factor, such as a bank, protects its customer against bad debts that they might incur.

Overdrafts are a service offered by financial institutions that allow a business to spend in excess of the amount in its account, up to a predetermined limit. This is the cheapest and most flexible form of borrowing for most businesses.

Revenue expenditure refers to spending on the day-to-day running of a business, such as rent, wages and utility bills.

Sources of finance is the general term used to refer to where or how businesses obtain their funds, such as from working capital, commercial lenders and/or government assistance.

Working capital, also known as **net current assets**, is the day to day money that is available to a business. It is calculated as the difference between a firm's liquid assets (the value of cash, stocks and debtors) and its short-term debts (such as creditors, tax and overdrafts).

Investment Appraisal

UNIT 3.2

Never let a poor man advise you on investments.

Spanish proverb

Key topics

- Quantitative investment appraisal methods:
  Accounting Rate of Return (ARR) and Payback Period
- Qualitative investment appraisal

Higher Level extension

- Quantitative investment appraisal methods:
  Discounted Cash Flow (DCF) and Net Present Value (NPV)

INTRODUCTION

In simple accounting terms, **investment** refers to the purchase of an asset with the potential to yield future financial benefits. For economists, the term refers to sacrificing consumption expenditure today in order to purchase capital that will further production levels in the future. Examples of investments might include the purchase of an office or the upgrading of expensive computer equipment. With such investments, resources are risked in a venture that might bring about future advantages – but not necessarily. For example, the Hollywood movie *The 13th Warrior* starring Antonio Banderas, cost £107.8 million to produce in 1999. However, it proved to be a poor investment since world box office sales only amounted to £39.5 million (source: MSN Entertainment). On a social level, adults are increasingly aware of the escalating costs of raising a child; *The Independent* newspaper reported in November 2006 that the average cost of raising a child in the UK was £180,000 ($360,000). The high *opportunity cost* of raising children has led to a decline in birth rates in developed economies.

Investment appraisal is the general term referring to the quantitative techniques used to calculate the financial costs and benefits (i.e. the potential net gains) of an investment decision. There are four main methods of investment appraisal: the payback period, the accounting rate of return, discounted cash flows and net present value. The actual method(s) used will depend on the circumstances facing the business.

This Unit looks at the different methods used by managers to assess the risks involved in investment decision-making.

PAYBACK PERIOD

The **payback period** refers to the period of time for an investment project to earn enough profits to repay the cost of the initial investment. The formula for calculating the payback period is:

$$\frac{\text{initial investment (\$)}}{\text{contribution per month (\$)}}$$

For example, a firm may be considering the purchase of new photocopier equipment at a cost of $10,000. The anticipated financial gain that this would bring is $6,000 of revenue per year after maintenance costs are paid for. Hence the payback period would be:

$$\frac{\text{\$10,000 for purchase}}{\text{(\$6,000 / 12 months)}}$$

$$= 20 \text{ months}$$

Most investment projects will only be considered if they have a relatively short payback period. In the above example, 20 months may be seen as acceptable for a short payback period; the business does not want to purchase the expensive photocopying equipment and find that it is obsolete before the payback period.

In reality, it is unlikely that the income stream will be constant each year. It is still possible though to work out the payback period using the *cumulative cash flow* method, as demonstrated in the Exam Tip worked example on page 351.

Exam Tip!
Worked example

Question: Suppose, the construction of a new sports complex that costs $1,000,000 is expected to generate the following net cash flows over the first four years:

Year 1 $210,000
Year 2 $350,000
Year 3 $480,000
Year 4 $450,000

What is the payback period?

Answer: It is clear that the project will not reach its break-even in the first year (the cash outflow was $1 million whereas the net cash inflow in Year 1 is only $210,000). By calculating the cumulative cash flow, we get the following figures:

	Net cash flow	Cumulative cash flow
Year 1	$210,000	$210,000
Year 2	$350,000	$560,000
Year 3	$480,000	$1,040,000
Year 4	$450,000	$1,490,000

We can now see that the payback period (for the initial $1 million) happens between years 2 and 3, i.e. within the third year. To work out the payback period:

a Calculate the difference between the cumulative net cash inflow in year 2 and the amount invested, i.e. $1,000,000 minus $560,000 = $440,000.

b Calculate the average monthly cash inflow in year 3, i.e. $480,000 divided by twelve months = $40,000 per month.

c Divide **a** by **b** to find the number of months, i.e. $440,000 into $40,000 = 11 months.

Therefore, the payback period for the sports complex is forecast to be 2 years and 11 months.

Question 3.2.1

Chelsea Football Club

Chelsea Football Club (CFC) has gained a lot of titles since Russian oil tycoon Roman Abramovich took over the sports club in June 2003. He poured in an estimated £440 million ($858 million) into the club that year. Abramovich had no intention of cutting back either as he released a further £240 million for the purchase of new players in 2006. However, huge financial losses have weighed down CFC, with reported annual losses of £140 million, £88 million and £80 million in his first three years as owner of the club. CFC estimated that they would break-even by 2010.

a Identify two factors that might have influenced Roman Abramovich's decision to buy CFC. *[2 marks]*

b Explain, using the above case study, why investment can be risky. *[4 marks]*

c Comment on how application of the payback period might be useful for CFC. *[4 marks]*

The **advantages** of using the payback period as a method of investment appraisal are that it:

- Is the simplest and quickest method of investment appraisal; hence it is the most commonly used method.
- Can be useful for firms with cash flow problems as such firms can identify how long it will take for the cash to be recouped.
- Allows a business to see whether or not it will break-even on the purchase of the asset(s) before it needs to be replaced. This can prove important in today's fast-paced technological environment.
- Can be used to compare different investment projects with different costs by calculating the quickest payback period of each option.
- Helps to assess projects which will yield a quick return for shareholders.
- Assesses only the short term, so payback calculations are less prone to forecasting errors.

The **disadvantages** of using the payback method as a method of investment appraisal are:

- It may encourage a **short-termism** approach to investment, i.e. managers only focus on the short-term benefits and ignore the potential gains in the longer term. Property developers, for example, have to risk a huge amount of capital when building on a new site; the costs are unlikely to recouped for several years to come. Hence, payback may not be the most suitable method of investment appraisal for such firms.
- The contribution per month is unlikely to be constant as demand is prone to seasonal fluctuations, and hence the payback period may take longer to realize.
- Payback focuses on time as the key criterion for investment, rather than on profits – the main aim of most private sector businesses.

Exam Tip!

Students often conclude that because something is 'high risk' or 'risky' it should be avoided by the business. This is not reflective of the real business world where managers have to make regular decisions which involve an element of risk. Many businesses and entrepreneurs have become highly successful by taking huge risks. The decision is not whether to take risks in business but whether the benefits of the risk are likely to outweigh the costs involved.

ACCOUNTING RATE OF RETURN (ARR)

The accounting rate of return (ARR) calculates the *average profit* on an investment project as a percentage of the amount invested. Hence, the ARR is also known as the **average rate of return**. The formula for calculating the ARR is:

$$\frac{\text{total profit during project's lifespan} \div \text{number of years of project} \times 100}{\text{initial amount invested (\$)}}$$

The ARR is expressed as a percentage to allow managers to compare the rates of return on other investment projects. As a basic benchmark, the ARR can be compared with the base interest rate to assess the rewards for the risk involved in an investment. For example, if the ARR of a project for a large established multinational such as McDonald's is 8% whilst the interest rate on savings is 5%, then the real rate of return is 3%. This may well be worth the risk for the multinational. However, if it were for a new firm entering a niche market selling horse saddles, then a 3% real return may not be enough to convince decision-makers to implement the investment plan, especially if banks are offering a (guaranteed) 5% return.

Exam Tip!
Worked example

Question: As a worked example, suppose the purchase of a new computer system that costs $400,000 is forecast to generate the following net cash flows over the next five years (when it needs to be replaced):

Year 1 $100,000
Year 2 $200,000
Year 3 $180,000
Year 4 $120,000
Year 5 $100,000

Calculate the ARR for this project. *[4 marks]*

Answer: There are several steps needed to calculate the ARR for this project:

- Total net cash inflow over the five years is $700,000
- Project profit = $700,000 minus $400,000 for the initial investment = $300,000
- Average annual profit = $300,000 ÷ 5 years = $60,000 per year
- Hence the ARR = $60,000 ÷ $400,000 = 15%

Comparing this figure with the base interest rate allows us to see whether the project is worth the risk. If banks are offering a 5% return, then this particular investment project seems relatively attractive.

The main advantage of the ARR method is that it enables easy comparisons (in percentage terms) of the forecast proceeds of different investment projects, thereby aiding business decision-making. For example, if two projects are forecast to yield the same accounting rate of return, then the relatively cheaper project may be more desirable given that it carries less financial risk.

However, a weakness of the ARR method is that it ignores the timing of cash inflows and hence is prone to forecasting errors when considering seasonal factors. In addition, the project's useful life span (which might be a pure guess) is needed before any calculations can be made. Finally, as with all time-based forecasts, errors are more likely the longer the time period that is under consideration. We may know what is likely to happen today and tomorrow but we are less sure about the events in five years from now.

Question 3.2.2

Study the information in the table below and then answer the questions that follow.

Year	Net cash flow	
	Project Atlanta ($)	**Project Boston ($)**
0	(130,000)	(130,000)
1	80,000	60,000
2	60,000	60,000
3	20,000	60,000

a Identify the cost of the investment projects under consideration. *[1 mark]*

b Calculate the **payback period** for both projects and comment on your findings. *[4 marks]*

c Calculate the **Accounting Rate of Return** on both projects. Assuming that the base interest rate is 5.25%, comment on your findings. *[5 marks]*

d Considering all relevant factors, explain which project you would prefer and why. *[5 marks]*

HIGHER LEVEL EXTENSION: DISCOUNTED CASH FLOW

Discounted cash flow (DCF) is a technique based on the concept of the **opportunity cost** of money and future cash flows. Suppose you had the option of receiving a university scholarship to the value of $30,000 in either one lump sum today or over a three-year period. Which would you opt for? Most people would go for the first option rather than the deferred payment option. The reason is linked to the popular phrase 'time is money'. Money received today can be invested (or simply saved in a bank to earn compound interest) whereas money received in the future will have lost some of its value.

For example, if you have $100 and decide to place it into a bank account paying 5% interest, at the end of the year you will have $105. Therefore, the *present value* of $105 in a year's time is $100, i.e. $105 in a year's time is worth the same as $100 today. If the money was saved for a further year, then the present value would be $110.25 (i.e. $105 plus another 5% interest). Discounted cash flow is used to calculate today's value of the estimated future net cash flows from an investment project.

Discounting cash flow is the reverse of calculating compound interest. A **discount factor** (see Table 3.2a and Box 3.2a) is used to convert the future net cash flow to its present value today. Given that receiving money today is worth more than it is in the future, the discount factor can represent either inflation or interest rates.

Table 3.2a Discount factors

	1%	2%	3%	4%	5%	6%	7%	8%	9%	10%
Year 1	0.9901	0.9804	0.9709	0.9615	0.9524	0.9434	0.9346	0.9259	0.9174	0.9091
Year 2	0.983	0.9612	0.9426	0.9246	0.9070	0.8900	0.8734	0.8573	0.8417	0.8264
Year 3	0.9706	0.9423	0.9151	0.8890	0.8638	0.8396	0.8163	0.7938	0.7722	0.7513
Year 4	0.9610	0.9238	0.8885	0.8548	0.8227	0.7291	0.7629	0.7350	0.7084	0.6830
Year 5	0.9515	0.9057	0.8626	0.8219	0.7835	0.7473	0.7130	0.6806	0.6499	0.6209
Year 6	0.9420	0.8880	0.8375	0.7903	0.7462	0.7050	0.6663	0.6302	0.5963	0.5645
Year 7	0.9327	0.8706	0.8131	0.7599	0.7107	0.6651	0.6227	0.5835	0.5470	0.5132
Year 8	0.9235	0.8535	0.7894	0.7307	0.6768	0.6274	0.5820	0.5403	0.5019	0.4665
Year 9	0.9143	0.8368	0.7664	0.7026	0.6446	0.5919	0.5439	0.5002	0.4604	0.4241
Year 10	0.9053	0.8203	0.7441	0.6756	0.6139	0.5584	0.5083	0.4632	0.4224	0.3855

As an example, suppose an organization expects to receive $10,000 in three years time whilst today's interest rate is 5%. What is the present value of the $10,000?

From Table 3.2a, we can see that the discount factor for 5% interest over 3 years is 0.8638. Hence, the present value of the $10,000 in 3 years' time is: $10,000 × 0.8638 = $8,638

Box 3.2a Calculating discount factors

- Determine the interest rate, e.g. 5%
- Work out the cumulative interest rate, e.g. 5% for 3 years = $(1.05)^3$
- Place this value as the denominator, with 1 as the default numerator: $1 / (1.05)^3 = 0.8638$ (to 4 d.p.).

Note: Students will not be expected to calculate discount factors; discount tables will be given for examination questions.

Whilst DCF can be a useful decision-making tool, even small changes in interest rates can result in a large change in the value of future net cash flows. Today, there are several dedicated software programs to help managers calculate DCF of investment projects.

HIGHER LEVEL EXTENSION: NET PRESENT VALUE

Net Present Value (NPV) takes discounted cash flows one step further. Money received in the future is worth less than if it were received today, i.e. the longer the time period under consideration, the lower the present value of that future amount of money. The NPV is calculated by the sum of all future expected net cash flows minus the investment cost:

NPV = Sum of Present Values – Cost of Investment

The original amount invested is often referred to as the **principal**. The Net Present Value will be positive, i.e. greater than the principal, if the discounted (future) cash flows are enough to justify the initial investment. Likewise, if the NPV is negative, then the investment project is not worth pursuing. A worked example of how to calculate NPV is shown below.

Exam Tip!
Worked example

Question: Suppose that new mechanization for a firm is estimated to cost $400,000 and should last for five years. It will cost an estimated $50,000 per annum to maintain but will increase the value of the firm's output by an estimated $150,000. Base interest rates are currently 5%. Work out the NPV on the proposed investment.

Answer: Working out: figures in $.

The net cash flow in each year is simply the total cash inflow minus the total cash outflow, i.e. $150,000 minus $50,000 = $100,000

Period	Net cash flow	Discount factor	Present value
Year 1	100,000	0.9524	95,240
Year 2	100,000	0.9070	90,700
Year 3	100,000	0.8638	86,380
Year 4	100,000	0.8227	82,270
Year 5	100,000	0.7835	78,350
Total	500,000		432,940

Notice that although the net cash flow is expected to be the same throughout the life of the project, a sum of $100,000 received in 5 years time is worth a lot less than the same amount received this year.

Next, add the total present value figures and minus the initial investment cost.

i.e. NPV = $432,940 – $400,000 = $32,940.

Notice that without using DCF the estimated return would be much higher at $100,000 (i.e. $500,000 – $400,000). In reality, however, the NPV method shows us that each of the $100,000 net cash flow received in the future is worth less than the value today, i.e. the real return is lower at only $32,940.

In the above table, since the NPV is a positive value of $32,940, the investment should go ahead. However, the business must take care not to over-rely on the NPV figure, as it would be *reduced* if interest rates were to go *up* during the next five years.

The disadvantages of this method are that calculations can be complex and that results are only comparable if the initial investment cost is the same between projects.

Question 3.2.3

a Calculate the **Net Present Value** by completing the data in the table below. Discount factors for 5% are given to 4 d.p. Both projects cost $300,000. Explain which project should be pursued. *[5 marks]*

Year	Investment Colorado			Investment Detroit		
	Net cash flow ($)	**Discount factor**	**Present value ($)**	**Net cash flow ($)**	**Discount factor**	**Present value ($)**
0	(300,000)	1.00			1.00	(300,000)
1	50,000	0.9524		100,000	0.9524	
2	100,000	0.9070		200,000	0.9070	
3	200,000	0.8638		200,000	0.8638	
4	200,000	0.8227		50,000	0.8227	
NPV						

b Comment on what other information you would consider before making a final choice over which investment project to pursue. *[5 marks]*

HIGHER LEVEL

Question 3.2.4

Study the data below and answer the question that follows. Each project costs $30,000. You will need to refer to Table 3.2a on page 354 for the relevant discount factors. Assume the average interest rate is 4%.

Year	Net cash flow ($)	
	Project HK	**Project UK**
1	10,000	10,000
2	12,000	20,000
3	15,000	15,000
4	20,000	10,000
Total	57,000	55,000

- Using relevant investment appraisal methods, recommend which of the above projects would be the most attractive to investors. *[10 marks]*

Exam Tip!

Students are expected to be able to calculate the Payback Period, ARR, DCF and NPV from given data. More importantly, as this is not an accounts or finance examination, students are also expected to be able to analyse the results of their calculations and assess their implications for business decision-making.

From time to time, students will be asked directly to use a method of investment appraisal. For example, students may be asked to calculate the payback period, ARR and NPV (to 2 decimal places). It is more important, however, to be able to interpret the calculations. Students can be asked to evaluate specified investment options and to recommend to the management which investment option to choose.

QUALITATIVE INVESTMENT APPRAISAL

The methods discussed above are all **quantitative investment appraisal** techniques. Numerical data do not necessarily show us the full picture so it is important to consider other factors. **Qualitative investment appraisal** methods do not focus on numerical data. Qualitative factors that affect investment decisions can be remembered by the mnemonic PORSCHE:

- **Predictions** (or gut feelings) – Investment decisions are often based on the intuition of changes in the future, such as predictions of changes in interest rates and income levels.
- **Objectives** – A profit-seeking firm, for example, will prefer to use quantitative methods but a firm with a strong ethical stance may not give financial data such a high priority.
- **Risk profile** – Firms with a low risk profile are less likely to opt for high-risk, high-return investments, choosing instead to opt for lower risk projects with more certain returns. This approach will protect the business if the risk does not pay off.
- **State of the economy** – If consumer and producer confidence levels are high, for example, then higher risk projects might be undertaken. However, if interest rates are forecast to rise over the medium to long term, then managers may put off many investment plans.
- **Corporate image** – Managers need to consider how an investment project might affect its public relations and corporate image. For example, will the attention and response of pressure groups such as Greenpeace be an issue if the investment project goes ahead?
- **Human relations** – For example, will automation cause mass redundancies? How will the change affect staff morale levels and the corporate image?
- **Exogenous shocks** – Hurricanes and other natural disasters of unquantifiable risk may also have to be considered when making investment decisions.

Question 3.2.5

Deregulation in India

Deregulation of markets in India has allowed foreign retailers to own their own stores in the country. Before the liberalization, foreign business activity was heavily regulated as a way of protecting domestic jobs and businesses. The change presents many investment opportunities for multinationals such as Nike, Reebok and Marks & Spencer.

India is opening up to western cultures and has huge market potential for businesses. Foreign firms will have a larger role in supporting the rapid development of the country's retail, tourism and aviation industries.

a Explain the risks involved for multinationals, such as Nike, Reebok and Marks & Spencer, wishing to set up businesses in developing countries like India. *[4 marks]*

b Examine the opportunities that might exist for businesses that plan to invest in a country such as India. *[6 marks]*

INVESTMENT APPRAISAL AND BUSINESS STRATEGY

Quantitative investment appraisal can be a useful management tool as decision-making becomes more objective. Risks are not eliminated but at least decisions are less prone to inaccuracies. The use of such techniques can be used by managers to justify their capital expenditure.

In assessing the value of investment projects, it is important to remember the value of money over time. Cash received in the future is not of the same value as if it were received today because the money could have been invested. In addition, inflation over time will reduce the value of money in the future. So, it is important to know how to calculate the present value of money in order to distinguish between the yields of investments over different time periods. Ralph Waldo Emerson (1803–1882), an American poet and philosopher, made this point clear in his famous quote, "Money often costs too much."

Nevertheless, the quality of the outcome of any quantitative investment appraisal is only as good as the reliability of the data used to compile the investment appraisal. As the saying 'garbage in, garbage out' implies, the use of inaccurate data will reduce the validity of the estimated figures. In addition, changes in interest rates will affect the outcome (potential net gains) of any quantitative investment appraisal technique. A final point is that an investment appraisal may not capture all the relevant costs and benefits, whether financial or otherwise; and again this reduces the value of such calculations.

In summary, it is necessary for managers to remember that decision-making is not purely based on numerical calculations. Even if an investment appraisal suggests that a project is financially feasible, other qualitative factors may be important in making a final decision. For example, in 2006 the shareholders of Manchester United Football Club voted against a £70 million ($140 million) sponsorship deal with Mansion, an online gambling company. They felt that although the deal was lucrative, it went against the principles of the Club. Hence, when it comes to decision-making, it is necessary to consider the wider context and the impacts on the various stakeholders of the organization.

REVIEW QUESTIONS 3.2

1 What is meant by the term 'investment appraisal'?

2 What is the 'payback period' and how is it calculated?

3 State three benefits and two limitations of the payback period as a method of investment appraisal.

4 What is the 'average rate of return' and how is it calculated?

5 Distinguish between quantitative and qualitative investment appraisal.

6 What does the mnemonic PORSCHE stand for when referring to qualitative investment appraisal?

Higher Level extension

7 What is meant by a 'discount factor'?

8 What is 'net present value' and how is it calculated?

Accounting rate of return is an investment appraisal technique that calculates the average annual profit of an investment project. It is expressed as a percentage of the initial sum of money invested.

Discounted cash flow is an investment appraisal technique that reduces the value of the money that a business receives in future years. This is done as there is an opportunity cost to money (which loses its value over time) and in order to give a current (present-day) value for the expected future returns.

Investment appraisal is a financial decision-making tool that helps managers to assess whether certain investment projects should be undertaken based mainly on quantitative techniques.

Net present value is an investment appraisal technique that calculates the total discounted cash flows, minus the initial cost of an investment project. If this figure is positive, then the project is viable and should be undertaken (on financial grounds).

Payback period is an investment appraisal technique which estimates the length of time that it will take to recoup the initial cash outflow of an investment project.

Qualitative investment appraisal refers to judging whether an investment project is worthwhile through non-numerical means, such as whether an investment decision is in line with the corporate culture. It is based on intuitive rather than scientific decision-making.

Quantitative investment appraisal refers to judging whether an investment project is worthwhile through numerical (financial) means, such as payback period, accounting rate of return and net present value.

Working Capital

UNIT 3.3

Don't empty the water jar until the rain falls.

English proverb

Key topics

- Working capital and the working capital cycle
- Cash flow forecasts
- Causes of cash flow problems
- Managing working capital (dealing with liquidity problems)

INTRODUCTION

It is often said that cash is the lifeblood of a business. This is because every business needs cash in order to keep functioning. Cash is needed to pay for daily costs such as wages and electricity charges. Failure to pay suppliers and utility bills may eventually result in a business being declared bankrupt.

Cash is a current asset. It is the money that a business receives from the sale of goods and services. Cash can be either held 'in hand' (actual cash at the business) or 'at bank' (cash held in a bank account). The other two main current assets are *stocks* and *debtors*. Therefore, **current assets** can be expressed as the sum of:

Current assets = Cash + Stocks + Debtors

The term **liquidity** refers to how easily an asset can be turned into cash. Highly liquid assets are those that can be converted to cash quickly and easily without losing their monetary value. For example, cash deposits at a bank would be classed as highly liquid assets. Raw materials, on the other hand, would be classed as relatively illiquid assets as they cannot be changed into cash as easily or quickly.

Evidence from around the world has consistently shown that insufficient working capital is the single largest cause of business failure, rather than a lack of profitability. A lack of working capital will lead to **insolvency** (a situation where working capital is insufficient to meet current liabilities). This can lead to either voluntary closure of the business or compulsory closure (since creditors have taken legal action to recoup their money). This will then lead to the **liquidation** of the firm, i.e. it will need to sell off all its assets in order to repay as much of the money owed to its creditors.

This Unit looks at the various methods that can be used to prevent or to deal with working capital problems. Working capital management is an essential part of a manager's role to ensure the prosperity and survival of the business.

THE WORKING CAPITAL CYCLE

Working capital refers to the money that is available for the daily running of a business. Working capital is also known as **net current assets** and is calculated by using the formula:

Working Capital = Current Assets – Current Liabilities

The amount of working capital shows the funds that are available for a business to pay for its immediate costs and expenditure (known as **running costs**). It can be used to pay for raw materials, stocks, wages, or any other running costs of a business. A lack of working capital means that the firm has insufficient cash to fund its routine operations, such as paying suppliers. One of the main reasons why businesses collapse is due to a lack of working capital. This is true even for profitable organizations.

Current assets are resources that belong to a business that are intended to be used within the next twelve months. Current assets are also known as **liquid assets**. There are three main types of current assets:

- **Cash** – This is the money that is held in the business or at the bank.
- **Debtors** – This term refers to people or other organizations that owe money to a business as they have purchased goods on credit. Businesses (the creditors) often allow their customers (the debtors) a credit period, i.e. to buy now and pay later. The figure for debtors is classed as an asset because it is money that the business is owed.

- **Stocks** – These are unsold stocks of raw materials, semi-finished goods or finished goods used in the manufacturing process. Finished stocks are relatively liquid in comparison to raw materials. Stocks are also called **inventories**.

Current liabilities refer to the money that a business owes that needs to be repaid within the next twelve months. Some of the more common examples include:

- **Overdrafts** – This short-term source of finance needs to be repaid quickly as interest rates on overdrafts tend to be higher than those placed on longer term bank loans.
- **Creditors** – Suppliers need to be repaid for items that have been purchased on credit.
- **Tax** – Businesses will need to pay a variety of taxes to the government, such as corporation tax and stamp duty (see Unit 1.5). It is possible to delay some tax payments, but these still represent a current liability.

For most businesses, there is a delay between paying for costs of production, such as the purchase of stock and payment of wages, and receiving the actual cash from the sale of the product. This is because the production process takes time. Consider the time difference between placing an order for a Ferrari and actually receiving the cash once the car is finally produced and handed over to the customer. This then means that businesses must manage their working capital very carefully. This time lag between cash payments for the costs of production and receiving the cash from customers is known as the **working capital cycle** (see Figure 3.3a). If a business has insufficient working capital, then it is likely to struggle to continue financing its operations.

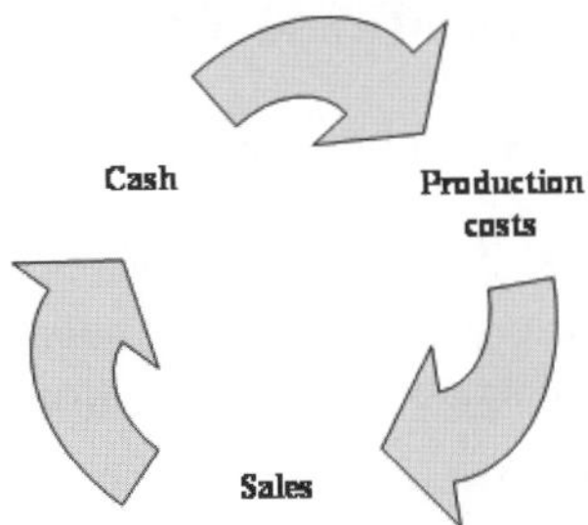

Figure 3.3a The working capital cycle

Whilst it is important for firms to have sufficient working capital, it does not mean that they should have 'too much' liquidity. Holding too many current assets in the business can be regarded as being wasteful. This is because the assets, such as stocks and cash, could have been used more productively and profitably elsewhere, e.g. to expand the business.

A common measure of liquidity is the **current ratio** (see Unit 3.6). This ratio compares the value of current assets with the value of current liabilities. For example, if current assets were $3 million and current liabilities were $2 million, then the current ratio is 1.5:1. This means that for every $1 of current liabilities the firm has $1.5 of liquid assets. If the ratio is below 1:1, the organization has a liquidity problem because it cannot meet all its current liabilities.

Question 3.3.1

Le Royal Meridien Hotels

Le Royal Meridien is a luxury hotel chain that operates in many parts of the world, such as Ko Samui (Thailand), Mumbai (India), Bristol (UK), Hamburg (Germany) and Toronto (Canada). The parent company, Starwood Hotels & Resorts, has set plans for continued expansion in the world's top cities. However, the construction of a typical hotel takes between 2–3 years. This means that the hotel group must maintain sufficient **working capital** at all times.

Le Royal Meridien in Dubai

a Define the term **working capital**. *[2 marks]*

b Explain why Le Royal Meridien needs better cash flow management when there is a long cash flow cycle during the construction of new hotels. *[4 marks]*

THE DIFFERENCE BETWEEN CASH AND PROFIT

Profit in its simplest form is the positive difference between a firm's total sales revenue and its total costs of production, i.e. Profit = Revenues minus Costs. When a sale is made, this contributes towards paying the costs of the firm. When enough products are sold to pay for all the costs of production, the firm has reached its *break-even point* (see Unit 5.3). Any sales beyond a firm's break-even point will then generate profits for the firm.

When customers pay for the purchase of products, they may have several payment options: cash, cheque, direct debit (from the customer's bank account) or trade credit. The last option means that customers can buy now, but pay later. A credit period of 30 days, for example, means that customers do not need to pay for their purchase until a month later. This can attract customers to the business, but can cause cash flow problems for the firm since it will need to survive without immediate payment from its credit customers.

When a firm sells products on credit, it will automatically make a profit on the sale (assuming that price exceeds the unit costs of production). However, since customers pay on credit, the firm does not receive the cash at the time of purchase. Hence profit is made before the cash is received, i.e. profit is not the same as cash. For example, if a firm sold $5,000 of goods in a week, with 60% of its customers paying by cash, then only $3,000 cash is received. The other 40% (or $2,000) is not received until the end of the credit period. Hence, the sales revenue ($5,000) is not the same as the cash inflow ($3,000) at the end of the trading week.

In addition, there is a key difference between sales revenues and cash inflows. The former comes from a single source, i.e. customers. Cash inflows can come from sales revenues but there are also other sources that are not limited to trading. For example, a firm can sell off its dormant (unused) assets. This generates cash but is not classed as sales revenue. Other sources of cash inflow include bank loans, donations and grants from the government.

It is therefore possible for a firm to be profitable but cash deficient. The classic reason is because the firm offers credit to its customers (in some cases, there is poor credit control and therefore this damages the cash flow position of the business). Another case is when a profitable business tries to expand too quickly, so runs out of cash. Seasonal variations in sales may also mean that there are certain times in the year when demand is low and therefore the firm may experience some short-term liquidity problems. Ultimately, a business cannot remain profitable without sufficient cash to pay its employees, suppliers and financiers, i.e. a lack of cash will eventually lead to a firm going bankrupt.

Conversely, it is also possible to be cash rich but unprofitable. The initial hype for a new product may bring in plenty of cash for a business. However, unless the firm is able to control its costs of production, including the fixed and indirect costs (see Unit 5.2), then the business will not be profitable. Therefore, all businesses, however profitable, must manage their working capital and cash flow position in order to survive.

Question 3.3.2

McDonald's

In keeping with the times, fast food giant McDonald's has revamped its menus since 2003. It has added healthier options such as salads, pastas, soups and bottled water. The company's strive to gain more revenue led to its global "I'm lovin' it" slogan, extended opening hours and new facilities to allow customers to pay with their credit cards. In April 2006, McDonald's reported annual sale revenues had increased by 6% to $5.1 billion, although profits were down by 14%.

a Explain, with reference to the working capital cycle, how it is possible for McDonald's to report a 6% increase in sales but a 14% fall in profits. *[5 marks]*

b Explain how the use of credit cards might help to increase sales yet at the same time prolong the working capital cycle for McDonald's. *[5 marks]*

CASH FLOW FORECASTS

A cash flow forecast is a financial document that shows the expected movement of cash into and out of a business, per time period. It is based on three key concepts:

- **Cash inflows** – Cash inflows usually come from sales revenue, when customers pay for the products that they have purchased. Calculations of cash inflows require an accurate sales forecasts (see Unit 4.2) for the period in question. Cash inflow can also come from payment by debtors, loans from a bank, interest received from bank deposits, the sale of assets and rental income charged on property owned by the business. Cash inflows are often referred to as **receipts**.
- **Cash outflows** – Cash usually leaves a firm when bills have to be paid. A cash flow forecast therefore requires a detailed operations budget with itemized expenses such as: labour, purchase of stocks, rent, taxes, payments to creditors, advertising, interest repayments and dividends. Cash outflow is also known as **payments**, **expenses** or **outgoings**.
- **Net cash flow** – This refers to the difference between cash inflows and cash outflows, per period of time. Ideally, the net cash flow should be positive, although a firm may be able to temporarily survive if it suffers from negative net cash flow. A firm might be profitable, but it can only survive in the long run if receipts are greater than cash outflows.

For example, Rowlands Digital Ltd might buy imported cameras from Japan at an average cost of $120 and sell these at an average price of $250. Each camera sold means that the company makes $130 gross profit (i.e. $250 minus $120), irrespective of how customers pay. However, if some customers pay by credit, then this will reduce the value of cash inflows for this particular trading period.

Exam Tip!
Cash flow statements

A cash flow statement is a financial document that shows the details of *actual* cash inflows and outflows for a business over a twelve month period. For organizations that must produce annual reports, cash flow statements appear as part of the final accounts (see Unit 3.5). It can also be used to prepare a cash flow forecast for the forthcoming year. Cash flow forecasts are largely based on the results from the cash flow statement of the previous year.

Reasons for cash flow forecasts

- Banks and other lenders require a cash flow forecast in order to help them better assess the financial health of the business seeking external finance.
- Cash flow forecasts can help managers to anticipate and identify periods of potential cash deficiency. This can then allow the business to better deal with liquidity problems, such as by arranging for a bank overdraft. Alternatively, the firm might choose to adjust the timing of receipts (cash inflows) and payments (cash outflows) to avoid cash flow problems.
- Cash flow forecasting aids the planning process. Good financial control is not only socially responsible but can help a business to better achieve its aims and objectives. Forecasts can be compared with actual figures to improve future predictions and planning.

Constructing cash flow forecasts

Consider the following numerical example which shows a simplified six-month cash flow forecast for San & Fung Trading Company. Assume that the firm receives $4,000 of rental income in November. It is conventional to show negative numbers in brackets.

Table 3.3a Simplified cash flow forecast for San & Fung Trading Co.

	Jul	Aug	Sept	Oct	Nov	Dec
Opening balance	5,000	3,000	300	(1,400)	(2,600)	600
Inflows						
Cash sales revenue	6,000	5,000	6,500	6,800	7,500	9,500
Other income	0	0	0	0	4000	0
Total cash inflows	6,000	5,000	6,500	6,800	11,500	9,500
Outflows						
Stocks	2,500	2,200	2,700	2,700	3,000	3,300
Labour costs	3,500	3,500	3,500	3,500	3,500	3,500
Other costs	2,000	2,000	2,000	1,800	1,800	2,200
Total cash outflows	8,000	7,700	8,200	8,000	8,300	9,000
Net cash flow	(2,000)	(2,700)	(1,700)	(1,200)	3,200	500
Closing balance	3,000	300	(1,400)	(2,600)	600	1,100

In addition to the three key components in a cash flow forecast, there are two other important parts:

- **Opening balance** – This refers to the amount of cash at the beginning of a trading period. For instance, the cash balance at the beginning of July is $5,000. Notice that the opening balance is the same value as the preceding month's closing balance, e.g. at the close of business on 31st July, the cash balance was $3,000. Hence it is logical that the opening balance on 1st August is the same value, i.e. $3,000.

- **Closing balance** – This refers to the amount of cash at the end of a trading period. It is calculated by the formula: Closing balance = opening balance plus net cash flow. For example, in July, although the net cash flow is negative $2,000 (since cash outflow exceeds cash inflow for the month), the closing balance is positive $3,000 when we take account of the opening balance.

Notice also that in the months of September and October, the company has a negative closing balance. A business cannot survive without sufficient cash and therefore the cash flow forecast can help the firm to devise plans to deal with cash shortages. It might, for example, seek to take out a bank overdraft (see Unit 3.1) as a short-term measure to deal with the liquidity problem.

Exam Tip!
Worked example

Question: Study the cash flow forecast below to complete the missing values for (**a**)–(**e**). *[5 marks]*

	Jan ($)	Feb ($)	Mar ($)	Apr ($)
Cash sales	2,000	2,000	**(d)**	4,000
Stock purchases	600	600	900	1,200
Rent	1,000	0	1,000	0
Other costs	600	600	800	1,000
Opening cash balance	1,000	**(c)**	1,600	1,900
Net cash flow	**(a)**	800	300	1,800
Closing cash balance	**(b)**	1,600	1,900	**(e)**

Answer:

a Cash inflow in January is $2,000. The total cash outflow is $2,200 (the sum of stocks, rent and other costs). Since net cash flow is the difference between cash inflows and cash outflows for the month, the value of **a** = **($200)**, i.e. there is negative net cash flow.

b The closing balance = opening balance plus net cash flow, i.e. the value of **b** = $1,000 + ($200) = **$800**.

c The opening balance in February is the same value as the closing balance in January, i.e. **c** = **$800**.

d The total cash outflow in March is $2,700 (i.e. $900 + $1,000 + $800). The net cash flow is given as $300. This means that cash sales must have exceeded the cash outflow figure by $300 and hence **d** = **$3,000**.

e The closing balance at the end of April is worked out in the same way as question **b**, i.e. the sum of the opening balance and the net cash flow for the month. Hence the value of **e** = $1,900 + $1,800 = **$3,700**.

Question 3.3.3

Cottam Stationers

David Cottam has recently received his license to set up a stationery outlet, Cottam Stationers. His main clients would be from the business sector, such as schools and offices. He plans to commence trading on 1st August and has initial capital of $5,000 that he puts into a business bank account. In preparing for his business, David Cottam has gathered the following information:

- Sales for the first four months are forecast to be: $2,000 (Aug), $5,000 (Sept), $2,000 (Oct) and $3,000 (Nov).
- Stock purchases are expected to cost exactly half the value of sales each month.
- Rent is paid every two months, starting in September. Each payment is $2,000.
- Utility bills are predicted to average $500 per month.
- Other expenses are expected to be $2,000 for the first month and $1,000 per month thereafter.

a Construct a cash flow forecast for Cottam Stationers based on the above information. *[6 marks]*

b Comment on the liquidity position of the firm in its first four months of trading. *[4 marks]*

CAUSES OF CASH FLOW PROBLEMS

All businesses must have healthy cash flow in order to generate sufficient working capital to pay their employees, suppliers, financiers and landlords. A problem with long working-capital cycles is that businesses have to pay for their expenses well in advance of receiving any cash inflows. If this problem is prolonged or not dealt with it can lead to a liquidity crisis. The main causes of cash flow crises for a business include:

- **Overtrading** – This situation occurs when a business attempts to expand too quickly (or aggressively), without the sufficient resources to do so. For example, a firm might take on more orders than it can possibly handle. The excess orders will add to the costs of production without any corresponding revenue (which only come later after the product has been manufactured and sold to consumers). Rapid expansion will also consume a lot of cash when purchasing fixed assets. This then leaves very little cash left for the day to day running of the business. This was a major reason for the collapse of Hong Kong's budget carrier Oasis Airlines.
- **Overborrowing** – Firms that are *highly geared* (see Unit 3.3) often find that they cannot afford to meet their monthly loan repayments. The larger the proportion of capital raised through external sources of finance, the higher will be the cash outflow on interest payments. During times of rising interest rates, cash outflow on loan interest will increase, putting further pressure on a firm's liquidity position.
- **Overstocking** – This means that the firm holds too much stock. Overstocking is the result of an ineffective stock control system (see Unit 5.7). Stocks cost money to buy, produce and store. In addition, stock surpluses are a waste of scarce resources, i.e. the money could have been better spent elsewhere. The costs of overstocking are explained in more detail in Unit 5.7.

- **Poor credit control** – Cash flow problems can arise when a firm allows too much credit to its customers. For example, the credit period might be too generous so the business has to continue trading longer without cash inflows. It can also mean that too many customers are offered credit and this can lead to more bad debts being experienced, i.e. the number of debtors who fail to pay money to the business.
- **Unforeseen changes** – Unexpected and erratic changes in demand may cause major cash flow problems. Conversely, seasonal fluctuations in demand will cause a temporary, but perhaps predictable, cash-flow issue. This will affect firms that face highly seasonal demand, such as producers of Valentine's cards, Easter eggs, Halloween products, fireworks and Christmas trees. Another example of unforeseen changes might be machinery breakdown, which lengthens the working capital cycle.

Question 3.3.4

Charlotte Davies Perfume Boutique

Charlotte Davies is planning on opening a perfume boutique which will commence business at the beginning of August this year. Consider the following information and then answer the questions that follow.

- Charlotte has $5,000 from her personal bank account that she wishes to use for her business in August.
- She estimates that the first four months of sales revenue will be: $4,000, $6,000, $8,000, and $12,000
- The expenditure on buying the perfumes is estimated to cost: $2,000, $2,400, $3,200 and $4,800 respectively.
- Her anticipated expenditure on advertising is $1,000 for the first month and $500 every month thereafter.
- Charlotte intends to hire five members of staff who will each earn a salary of $800 per month.
- Other costs (such as rent and utility bills) amount to an average of $600 per month.

a Complete the cash flow forecast for Charlotte Davies by using the format below. *[5 marks]*

	Aug ($)	Sept ($)	Oct ($)	Nov ($)
Opening balance				
Receipts (Inflows)				
Total receipts				
Payments (Outflows)				
Variable costs				
Advertising				
Staffing				
Others				
Total payments				
Closing bank balance				

b Examine the cash flow position faced by Charlotte Davies. *[5 marks]*

MANAGEMENT OF WORKING CAPITAL (DEALING WITH LIQUIDITY PROBLEMS)

Improving the cash flow position of a business requires effective working capital management. This means the business must successfully manage its current assets (cash, debtors and stocks) and its current liabilities. Quite often, the solution to a problem is to deal directly with the cause of that problem. There are numerous ways to deal with liquidity problems. These can be split into three main categories:

- Seeking alternative sources of finance
- Improving cash inflows
- Reducing cash outflows.

Seeking alternative sources of finance

If a firm is able to seek alternative sources of finance (see Unit 3.1), then this should boost its liquidity position. Such methods include:

- **Overdrafts** – These are banking services that allow a business to temporarily take out more money that exists in its bank account. This gives the firm immediate access to cash during times of negative net cash flow. However, the key drawback is that the firm will need to pay interest on the amount that has been overdrawn. In addition, firms facing a liquidity crisis might find it difficult to get an overdraft approved by lenders.
- **Sale and leaseback** – This method involves a business selling its fixed assets, such as buildings or vehicles, and then directly leasing these assets. Sale and leaseback therefore generates cash (from the sale) yet the firm continues to use the resources sold. For instance, a cash deficient firm on the verge of bankruptcy could sell its premises, such as its head office, and then lease it back on a long-term basis.
- **Selling off fixed assets** – The sale of *dormant assets* (obsolete or unused assets) can generate some much-needed cash. This source of finance can generate a considerable amount of cash for the business, although it is only a one-off (since the asset cannot be resold by the business). However, selling fixed assets is not advisable, unless unavoidable, since these are needed for a business to operate and to expand.
- **Debt factoring** – This financial service involves an external party taking over the collection of money from debtors. The debt factor will pass on the money owed to its client (less the commission charges) thereby giving the business immediate access to cash. The costs and benefits of using debt factoring are outlined in Unit 3.1.
- **Government assistance** – Some businesses will qualify for state grants, subsidies or low-interest loans. This can help to boost the cash flow position of a business at minimal cost. Governments are often reluctant to ignore struggling businesses since this could lead to job losses and higher social welfare payments.
- **Growth strategies** – These methods (covered in Unit 1.7) refer to strategies used to enhance the size of a business. This could be through growth strategies such as strategic alliances, joint ventures, mergers and takeovers. In fact, many firms that face liquidity problems become a natural target for takeovers.

Improving cash inflows

- **Tighter credit control** – Firms can limit trade credit to their customers or reduce the credit period that customers are granted, i.e. reduce the debtor period. Both methods mean that the business will receive cash sooner so this helps to improve cash flow and working capital. However, customers who receive deteriorating trade credit terms may switch to a rival supplier. Alternatively, debtors can be encouraged to pay earlier or on time by offering incentives, such as price discounts. Accepting interim payments will also help both the business and its debtors. In some rare cases, it might be best to write off a debt as bad debt rather than to lose a valuable and loyal customer.
- **Cash payments only** – An alternative to credit control is to only accept payments by cash. This removes the delay in receiving cash from credit sales. However, the drawback is that customers may prefer to buy from a rival that offers preferential credit terms. After all, if business customers paid by cash, this could negatively affect their own cash flow position.
- **Change pricing policy** – Cutting prices can help to convert stocks into cash. In addition, it can help to offload excess stocks. This tactic will work for *price elastic* products (see Unit 4.4).
- **Improved product portfolio** – By providing a wide and varied product portfolio (see Unit 4.3), a business is more likely to generate sales from a range of market segments. Poor sales in one product market can be offset by better sales in other markets. Limitations with this approach are that diversifying the product portfolio increases costs and risks, and it does not guarantee higher net cash inflows.
- **Improved marketing planning** – Effective marketing planning (see Unit 4.2) can help a business to better meet the needs and wants of customers, thereby helping to improve the firm's cash inflows. For example, more thorough market research can help a business to anticipate and respond to market changes in fashion and tastes.

Reducing cash outflows

These methods of improving the cash flow position of a firm deal with reducing costs and/or delaying the payment of costs.

- **Seek preferential credit terms** – A business can negotiate extended credit terms, i.e. to lengthen the time taken to pay its suppliers and creditors. Alternatively, it can seek alternative suppliers who can offer preferential credit terms. One limitation with this approach is the administrative costs and the time needed to investigate and negotiate better deals, which might not result in significant differences to the cash flow position of the firm.
- **Seek alternative suppliers** – Different suppliers may be able to offer stocks at more competitive prices. This will help to reduce cash outflows. However, cheaper raw materials and stocks may equate to lower quality output so the firm may need to change its marketing strategies as a result of this.
- **Better stock control** – Reducing stock levels by using a just-in-time system (see Unit 5.7) can help to reduce liquidity being tied up in stocks. This tactic works well for manufacturers of mass market products such as motor vehicles and consumer electronics. However, such methods will not work as well for businesses that only offer a service and do not hold much stock, such as airline carriers and hair salons.
- **Reduce expenses** – Investigating and scrutinizing expenses can help to identify costs that can be reduced, without compromising quality. Airline companies, for example, have saved huge amounts of money by reducing the number of drinks and snacks that are available on economy class travel. Some business costs may not be necessary at all, such as extravagant (non-essential) 'expenses accounts' for senior executives.

In reality, firms are most likely to use a combination of cash boosting and cost-reducing methods in order to improve their working capital. Whatever course of action is taken, the important thing is that it is implemented quickly and monitored carefully to avoid a cash flow crisis. The **Pareto principle** (also known as the **80/20 rule**) suggests that forward-looking businesses ought to focus 80% of their time and resources to boosting cash inflows and only 20% on cost cutting methods. In addition, firms are likely to set up or have a **contingency fund** which sets aside cash for unexpected and emergency use. The greater the level of uncertainty faced by a business, the higher its contingency fund tends to be.

Note: Since cash flow forecasts and cash flow statements do not show the profitability of a firm, the above suggestions are based purely on working capital problems (rather than profitability problems). Instead, the profitability of a firm can be seen in its profit and loss account (see Unit 3.5) and via ratio analysis (see Unit 3.6).

Table 3.3b Preventing and dealing with cash flow problems

Alternative Sources	Raise cash inflows	Lower cash outflows
Overdraft	Tighter credit control	Preferential credit terms
Sale and Leaseback	Cash payments	Alternative suppliers
Debt factoring	Change of pricing policy	Stock control
Sale of fixed assets	Broaden product portfolio	Lower expenses
Government assistance	Marketing planning	
Growth and evolution		

An alternative approach to dealing with cash flow problems is to take measures from the outset to minimize the risks and impacts of cash flow problems on the business. These measures might include:

- Spreading risks by having a wider customer base, which should generate more sources of cash inflows. In addition, it avoids the reliance on a few large customers. If one of these switches supplier or has its own cash flow problems, then the firm's cash flow will not be as badly affected.
- For large and extended projects, such as construction of property, sending out demands for part-payments at certain key dates as the project progresses will help to improve cash inflows. Establishing this agreement in a contract can therefore help to prevent cash flow problems.
- Similarly, establishing systems to pay large bills in regular instalments can help to prevent huge cash outflows during certain times of the year. Paying by instalments tends to be less disruptive to a firm's cash flow position.
- Ensuring that quality management systems (see Unit 5.4) are in place. Poor quality is likely to lead to customer complaints and delays or disputes in payment. For example, customers may demand price discounts for substandard quality or late deliveries.

Exam Tip!
Watch out for credit sales
When dealing with credit sales, be aware that the cash from such transactions will not be received until the end of the credit period. For example, if $10,000 of goods were sold in July with 30 days credit, then the cash for this is not received until August. Hence, the $10,000 cash inflow is recorded under the accounts for August (not July).

Question 3.3.5

Ducie's Dance Studios Ltd.

Marj Ducie runs a profitable dance company. However, she is concerned about the latest cash flow forecast for the business. Marj used the following data to prepare her cash flow forecast:

- Sales revenue: $10,000 in March; $10,000 in April; $8,000 in May; $12,000 in June.
- Payment from customers for sales are 50% paid for in cash whilst the other 50% is paid for on one month's credit.
- Direct costs: $3,000 in April; $5,000 in May, and $4,000 in June.
- Indirect costs are $6,000 per month.
- The opening cash balance in April is $1,000.

a Outline a possible reason for profitable firms to experience cash flow problems. *[2 marks]*

b Construct a cash flow forecast for Ducie's Dance Studios Ltd. for the period April to June. *[5 marks]*

	April ($)	May ($)	June ($)
Cash sales			
Credit sales	5,000		
Cash inflows			
Direct costs			
Indirect costs			
Cash outflows			
Net cash flow			
Opening balance			
Closing balance			

c Evaluate the options available to Marj Ducie in dealing with her liquidity problems. *[8 marks]*

LIMITATIONS OF CASH FLOW FORECASTING

Sam Goldwyn, a movie mogul, once joked that making predictions is difficult, especially if it concerns the future. Cash flow forecasting attempts to predict the liquidity position of a business in the future, based on certain assumptions. Inaccuracies can occur due to a number of internal and external reasons:

- **Marketing** – Inaccurate or poor market research may lead to incorrect sales forecasts. A distasteful or undesirable marketing campaign may put off customers, thereby harming the firm's cash flow position.
- **Human resources** – A demoralized workforce becomes a less productive workforce that delivers poor customer service. Disputes that are not managed may lead to industrial action. The result of unmanaged conflict in the workforce will be an unfavourable effect on the firm's cash flow position.

- **Operations management** – Machine failure, for example, may cause production delays to the detriment of a firm's cash flow. Initial production delays to the Airbus A380 (the world's largest commercial aircraft) caused Airbus to pay out huge sums of compensation to its customers such as Singapore Airlines and Emirates Airlines. This subsequently forced the break-even level of sales of the A380 to increase by almost 70%.
- **Competitors** – The behaviour of rival firms, especially market leaders, can be difficult to anticipate but is likely to directly a firm's level of success. Toyota's aggressive yet appealing marketing strategies in the USA has further threatened the sales and cash flow position of American giants General Motors and Ford Motor Company.
- **Changing fashion and tastes** will cause a change in demand – A favourable change means cash flow forecasts will be more positive than originally predicted, vice versa. Some products may become unpredictably popular and this will boost their cash flow.
- **Economic changes** – Changes in economic variables will also present opportunities or threats to a business (see Unit 1.5). For instance, lower interest rates tend to encourage borrowing from the private sector which boosts consumer expenditure and investment expenditure. Over time, this should encourage economic growth and reduce unemployment, thereby boosting sales and cash flow for businesses. By contrast, higher rates of inflation or a poor international trade balance may damage consumer and producer confidence levels, possibly leading to a downturn in the economy.
- **External shocks** – Events such as a war, an oil crisis, stock market crashes or a health scare will make initial cash flow forecasts less accurate.

There is no guarantee that predictions and assumptions made in a cash flow forecast will materialize. Hence, forecasts tend to be for the immediate and foreseeable future only because forecasts for the distant future tend to be highly inaccurate and therefore meaningless. Cash flow forecasting is also a continuous, ongoing process with regular revisions being made to the forecasts when necessary. This will therefore help to ensure that the cash flow position is carefully monitored to identify potential problems before they occur.

WORKING CAPITAL AND BUSINESS STRATEGY

This Unit has shown that managing working capital and cash flows is crucial to the running of any business. Businesses that do not clearly understand the differences between profit and cash flow will tend to run into financial difficulties causing problems for employees, customers, suppliers and investors of the organization. More often than not, businesses fail because of cash flow problems rather than profitability problems.

Working capital is essential for all parts of a business. For example:

- Human resources – Working capital is essential to ensure that staff are paid on time. Motivation theory (see Unit 2.5) suggests that pay is a key motivator for many people. Indeed, a lack of pay is seen as a demotivator and can lead to industrial disputes (see Unit 2.7). Therefore, even if the firm is profitable, insufficient working capital will lead to a demoralized and unproductive workforce.
- Marketing – Marketing activities ranging from new product development to extension strategies (see Unit 4.3) require plenty of cash. Only the largest firms can afford to advertise via the mass media such as television and national newspapers (see Unit 4.5). Marketing activities can be funded from products, known as *cash cows*, which generate a large and regular stream of cash (see Unit 4.3). In addition, cash is required to pay suppliers to ensure that there is efficient *supply chain management* (see Unit 4.6).
- Production – Manufacturers with long working capital cycles, such as producers of luxury yachts or commercial property, need huge amounts of cash in order to complete their projects.

Cash flow forecasting can be an effective management tool in managing and controlling the working capital of a business. However, it is important to remember that such forecasts and calculations are static, i.e. they only represent the cash flow situation of a firm at one point in time. Changes in the business environment will alter the forecasts, perhaps in a detrimental way. Hence, the results of any cash flow forecast must be handled with some caution. Indeed, forecasts should be updated regularly to ensure that decision-making is based on the most up to date and relevant information. The critical factor is to ensure that the firm has sufficient liquidity in order to meet its costs and current liabilities, such as the money owed to suppliers, financiers and tax authorities.

However, managers face a dilemma in balancing the conflict between the desire for sufficient working capital and the desire for profits. Larger profits can be made by granting credit to more customers, to encourage them to buy. However, this will prolong the working capital cycle and possibly lead to more bad debts. Demanding cash payments only from all customers will ultimately drive away many customers. The balance then depends on customer expectations and the actions of competitors in the market. For example, competition has led customers to expect credit facilities for purchases of expensive consumer durables such as jewellery, motor vehicles and home furniture. Since credit incurs administrative charges, it will not tend to be offered for inexpensive purchases. This is why many retailers require customers to spend a minimum amount of money before they can benefit from paying by credit.

In summary, working capital is regarded as being more important than profit in the short run. Profitable firms will not survive in the long run if they lack sufficient working capital. There is no doubt that profit is vital and that it leads to the long-term prosperity and survival of a business. However, working capital problems can happen at any time, thereby causing huge disruptions or crises to even the most established firms (see Unit 2.8 on crisis management).

REVIEW QUESTIONS 3.3

1 Define the term 'liquidity'.

2 What are the three components of current assets?

3 Distinguish between 'insolvency' and 'liquidation'.

4 What is meant by 'working capital'?

5 Briefly explain the stages in a simple working capital cycle.

6 Distinguish between 'current assets' and 'current liabilities'.

7 What are the differences between 'cash' and 'profits'?

8 Distinguish between 'cash inflows', 'cash outflows' and 'net cash flows'.

9 Why do businesses produce cash flow forecasts?

10 Explain the link between a firm's closing balance and its opening balance in a cash flow forecast or cash flow statement.

11 What are the five main causes of cash flow problems?

12 What are the three generic ways in which a firm can deal with cash flow problems?

13 What does it mean if a firm has 'tighter credit control'?

14 Why do many firms hold a contingency fund?

15 Outline four limitations of cash flow forecasts.

Assets are items owned by a business and have a monetary value. They can either be *fixed assets* (owned and not intended for resale within the next 12 months) or *current assets* (owned and expected to be used up within the next 12 months).

Cash is the actual money a business has received from selling its products. It can exist in the form of *cash in hand* (cash held in the business) or *cash at bank* (cash held in a bank account). It is the most liquid of a firm's current assets.

Cash flow refers to the transfer or movement of money into and out of an organization. *Cash inflows* mainly come from sales revenue whereas *cash outflows* are for items of expenditure.

Cash flow forecast is a financial document that shows the predicted future cash inflows and cash outflows for a business over a trading period.

Cash flow statement refers to the financial document that records the actual cash inflows and cash outflows for a business over a specified trading period, usually 12 months. It is often used to prepare a cash flow forecast for the subsequent trading period.

Closing balance refers the value of cash left in a business at end of the month, as shown in its cash flow forecast or statement. It is worked out by the formula: Closing balance = Opening balance plus Net cash flow.

Current assets are resources that belong to a business that are intended to be used within the next twelve months, such as cash, debtors and stocks.

Creditors are businesses that have sold goods or services on credit and will collect this money at a future date. Creditors are often referred to as **accounts payable** by accountants.

Debtors are private customers or commercial customers who have purchased goods or services on credit, so therefore owe the business money that must be paid at a later date. In accounting terms, 'debtors' are often recorded under the heading of **accounts receivable**.

Expenses are the spending in the working capital cycle of a business, i.e. costs of production such as salaries, raw materials, rent, advertising and distribution.

Liabilities are debts owed by a business. *Current liabilities* are short-term debts, such as an overdraft, which need to be repaid within twelve months from the balance sheet date. *Long-term liabilities*, such as mortgages and bank loans, are repayable over a longer period.

Liquidity is the ability of a business to convert assets into cash quickly and easily without a fall in its value.

Liquidity crisis refers to a cash flow emergency situation where a business does not have enough cash to pay its current liabilities (short-term debts).

Net cash flow refers to the cash that is left over after cash outflows have been accounted for from the cash inflows. If it is positive, then this means the value of cash inflows exceeds that of cash outflows. Net cash flow can be negative, in which case a business may need to apply for an overdraft.

Overheads are the costs not directly associated with the production process but necessary for providing and maintaining business operations, e.g. lighting, rent, security, insurance and maintenance.

Stocks, or **inventories**, are the physical goods that a business has in its possession for further production, (raw materials and unfinished goods) or for sale (finished goods).

Working capital is the amount of finance available to a business for its daily operations. Also known as **net current assets**, it is calculated as Current Assets minus Current Liabilities.

Budgeting

UNIT 3.4

If you buy things you don't need, you'll soon be selling things you do.

Filipino proverb

HIGHER LEVEL

Key topics

Higher Level only

- The purpose and importance of budgeting
- Setting budgets
- Limitations of budgeting
- Variance analysis

INTRODUCTION

A **budget** is a financial plan for expected revenue and expenditure for an organization or a department within an organization, for a given period of time. It is an essential part of the way in which an organization is coordinated and managed. Budgets can also be stated in terms of financial targets such as planned sales revenues, costs, cash flow or profits.

Budgets should be set in line with the aims of the business and allow managers to assess whether they are achieving their organizational objectives. They allow resources (financial and otherwise) to be allocated according to the expected level of business activity for a specified period of time, usually one year. If a budget holder, such as a head of department, is not operating within the allocated budget, then corrective measures can be taken to improve the situation.

This Unit examines the role and importance of budgeting in business organizations. Good budgets should set challenging and realistic targets. At the same time, budgets should be regularly monitored for variances. The quantitative technique of variance analysis is covered in the latter part of this Unit.

THE PURPOSE AND IMPORTANCE OF BUDGETING

HIGHER LEVEL

As a forward-looking financial plan, a budget is prepared in advance of a period of time, usually on a monthly, quarterly or annual basis. The purpose of budgets will depend largely on the type of budget used within an organization (see Box 3.4a).

Box 3.4a Types of budgets

Within an organization, there is likely to be a range of different types of budgets such as:

Sales budget – The focus is on forecasting how many products a business aims to sell over the next year and the likely revenue to be received from these sales. In other words, sales budgets are a breakdown of the planned volume and value of sales.

Staffing budget – This plan translates to the monetary costs of staff that are required throughout the organization for the next twelve months. It will set a limit in terms of the number of staff and the overall cost of labour.

Production budget – This is the plan for the level of output over the next year, including forecasts for the level and cost of stocks that need to be purchased. Overhead costs that the business will incur in the forthcoming year will also feature in a production budget. The production budget can then be used to help plan and manage capacity utilization in the organization (see Unit 5.7).

Marketing budget – This refers to the forecast of how a business intends to achieve its budgeted sales through marketing activities, such as the amount planned for advertising and sales promotion expenditure.

Zero budgeting – This method sets each budget holder's account to zero, per time period. The budget holder, such as a Head of Division, must then justify the money that they apply for, i.e. there must be prior approval for any planned expenditure. Zero budgeting helps the organization to identify areas or departments that require large amounts of essential capital expenditure and those that require minimal expenditure. However, it does involve a lot of management and administrative time in comparison to other types of budgets.

(cont.)

Flexible budget – This type of budget enables a business to adapt to changes in the business environment. Rapid and sudden unexpected changes will result in actual outcomes being very different from budgeted outcomes. For example, flexible budgets allow production and sales budgets to change according to sudden changes in the level of customer demand.

In practice, whichever type of budget is used within an organization, these budgets are consolidated into the overall budget, known as the **master budget**. The Chief Financial Officer (CFO) will have general control and management of the master budget, including financial plans for capital expenditure on fixed assets that the firm intends to purchase over the next accounting year.

Budgets are produced for four interrelated reasons:

Planning and guidance

A budget informs managers whether they are going in the right direction, financially. All businesses have organizational objectives (see Unit 1.3) so budgeting helps to measure the progress made towards achieving these targets. Budgeting requires managers to plan for the future and to anticipate financial problems before they arise. This should therefore help the organization to be better prepared to overcome such problems should they arise.

During the planning stage of budgeting, the following questions might be asked:

- How much should the firm spend on marketing activities in the forthcoming year?
- How many workers are needed and how much will they cost the organization?
- How much money is set aside as a **contingency fund**? This is a reserve budget set aside for emergency and back-up use.

These questions, plus many more, will help in the allocation of budgets to different departments and divisions of the organization. They can also help to provide some guidance for managers and budget holders in their decision-making.

HIGHER LEVEL

Question 3.4.1

Michael Cahill is a college student who has plans to visit Prague with his friends in the summer holidays. The cost of the vacation is expected to be around $500, all inclusive. Michael has a part-time job working in a local fast-food restaurant for which he is paid $150 per week. His outgoings average $110 per week, although some of this is flexible. There are ten more weeks until the summer holidays.

a Calculate whether Michael Cahill is likely to be able to afford his overseas holiday. *[3 marks]*

b Outline how budgeting can help Michael in his financial plans for the summer holidays. *[4 marks]*

HIGHER LEVEL

Coordination

A budget enables managers to control the firm's money, instead of the money controlling the organization.

Effective budgeting requires managers to match budget allocations with the aims of the organization. This will be understood and seen as being fair to all those in the business. In a school, for example, the annual budget allocated to the Science and ICT departments is, understandably, greater than that planned for the Psychology or History departments.

A budget helps the entire workforce to focus on common goals. Without proper **budgetary control** (corrective measures taken to ensure that actual performance equals the budgeted performance), budget holders might make decisions that conflict with those made in other departments. For example, the marketing department might budget to boost sales unknowingly beyond the productive capacity of the business. Likewise, the production department might budget to expand beyond the financial means of the organization. Hence, coordinated and controlled budgeting leads to consistent and complementary actions being taken by different budget holders.

Control

Just as a person cannot continually live beyond their means (i.e. spend more than they earn), budgeting helps to control business expenditure to prevent liquidity problems. Many businesses do not have proper cost control and, therefore, end up overspending. Without budgeting, managers are not held accountable for their actions. This subsequently leads to all sorts of financial and cash flow problems (see Unit 3.3).

Budgets are used to keep better overall financial control of an organization. Budget holders are constrained in what they can do and are held accountable for their actions. Budgetary control and variance analysis (covered later in this Unit) help to identify areas where a department is perhaps overspending. By having tighter control over finances, managers can help to prevent a business going into debt. This is especially important in large organizations that delegate budgets to their middle and senior managers. As part of their annual performance appraisal (see Unit 2.1), budget holders will discuss their budgets with the appraiser. This provides an opportunity for the budget holder to express particular areas of concern. It also helps the organization to have better overall financial control since budget holders are held accountable for the management of their designated budgets.

Motivational

According to motivational theorists such as E. Mayo and F. Herzberg (see Unit 2.5), recognition, responsibility and employee participation can be used to motivate. Delegating budgetary control to budget holders can therefore boost their level of morale since they feel valued and trusted by the organization. In addition, involving staff in the budgeting process helps to promote teamworking and employer–employee relations (examples of non-financial motivation). This should then lead to benefits such as higher productivity levels and reduced absenteeism.

For the business, budgetary control can act as a method of allocating and clarifying responsibilities in the organization; more senior managers will be placed in charge of larger budgets. It can also be linked to performance management, as mentioned above, in order to recognize and reward the achievement of organizational objectives. This can be a further source of motivation, thereby possibly giving the business a competitive advantage over its rivals.

Ultimately, these four purposes provide benefits that lead to the improved operational efficiency of an organization. Having to work within a realistically set budget encourages managers to seek efficiency gains in their operations by drawing attention to wastage and inefficiencies.

Question 3.4.2

Tsingtao Brewery Company

The Tsingtao Brewery Company (Tsingtao for short) is China's largest and most famous brewery. Founded in 1903, the company has been export orientated since the 1980s with sales in more than 50 countries worldwide. The barley used in its beer is imported from Canada, Australia and France. According to *Forbes* magazine, Tsingtao is the number one brand of consumer products exported from China. To further enhance its brand awareness and development, Tsingtao secured budgetary funds to officially sponsor the 2008 Beijing Olympics.

a Define the term 'budgeting'. *[2 marks]*

b Examine the importance of budgeting to Tsingtao Brewery Company. *[6 marks]*

SETTING BUDGETS

Bearing in mind the purpose of budgeting, there are several ways that an organization might set its budgets:

- Available finance – This factor is an obvious one since the greater the financial strength of a business, the greater the amount of funds that is available. This will affect the amount of budgeted expenditure for each budget holder.
- Historical data – Budgets are often based on what has happened in the past, such as last year's budgeted figures. If economic forecasts are positive, then budgets may be set at a certain percentage above last year's figures.
- Organizational objectives – If a business is planning external growth, then budgets will need to be raised accordingly since the marketing and production budgets will need to be set at a significantly higher level.
- Benchmarking – This means setting a firm's budget based on the budgets of its nearest competitors. So if Cadbury's budgets for a $2 million marketing campaign, rival firms Nestlé and Mars are likely to follow in the same direction.
- Negotiations – Some budgets are set by discussions between budget holders and the senior manager in charge of the master budget.

LIMITATIONS OF BUDGETING

Despite their potential benefits to help a business in its planning, coordination and control, there are numerous potential limitations and drawbacks of budgeting:

- As with all forms of quantitative forecasts, there are likely to be unforeseen changes that can cause large differences between the budgeted figure and the actual outcome. This can make budgets unrealistic and unachievable.
- There is a natural tendency for budget holders to overestimate their budgets. The simple reason for this is that by inflating budgets, it becomes easier to meet targets. However, an over-generous budget can cause complacency and wasteful or excessive expenditure.
- Budgets are often not allowed to be carried forward to the following year. This means that any surplus is simply discounted in the subsequent budget. Such practice gives no incentive for budget holders to under spend.

- In many organizations, budgets are set by senior managers who have no direct involvement in the running of the department. This can cause resentment and discontent since the senior manager may not fully understand the needs of the department. Ideally, the senior manager and budget holder should discuss and set the budget together, although in reality this only happens to some extent.
- Rigid and poorly allocated budgets can result in lower quality. For example, a lower production budget might lead to the use of substandard raw materials and components being used. Lower quality output will affect sales and probably damage the reputation of the business. Cutting the staffing budget can lead to pay cuts and/or job losses and this can create poor industrial relations (see Unit 2.7).
- The process of planning, setting, controlling, monitoring and reviewing budgets can be extremely time consuming.
- Since finances are limited, one person's gain is another's loss. Budget holders will compete to increase their own budgets, at the expense of their colleagues. Hence, budgeting can limit the degree of staff cooperation within an organization.
- Budgeting ignores qualitative factors that affect the financial performance of an organization. By placing too much emphasis on budgetary control, businesses may neglect non-financial issues such as corporate social responsibilities (see Unit 1.3); responsibilities towards the natural environment (see Unit 1.5); non-financial motivation of staff (see Unit 2.5); customer relations management (see Unit 4.2) and brand development (see Unit 4.3).
- Critics of budgeting argue that the process is often far too inflexible in today's fast-paced and constantly changing business environment. They therefore believe that budgeting is an inappropriate management tool.

Question 3.4.3

Ryanair

In the summer of 2007, Ireland's budget no-frills airline Ryanair bought 27 Boeing 737 aircraft worth £960 million (approximately $1.9 billion). The company has enjoyed double-digit growth rates each year for well over a decade. In 2005, to celebrate its 20th birthday, Ryanair issued 100,000 tickets at just 99 pence (under $2!). With around 500 routes to more than 25 countries, Ryanair is Europe's largest airline as measured by passenger numbers.

Source: www.ryanair.com

a Other than by calculating the number of customers, state two other ways to measure the market size of airline companies. *[2 marks]*

b Explain two limitations of using budgeting at Ryanair. *[4 marks]*

VARIANCE ANALYSIS

As mentioned earlier in this Unit, budgetary control refers to the use of corrective measures taken to ensure that actual performance equals the budgeted performance or outcomes. If there is a difference between the budgeted figure and the actual outcome, in the sales budget or marketing budget for example, then this is known as the **variance**. Budgetary control requires managers to investigate the cause(s) of any variance, which is worked out by using the formula:

$$\text{Variance} = \text{Actual outcome} - \text{Budgeted outcome}$$

All budget holders are expected to monitor and review the actual outcomes against the budgeted outcome (the planned outcome or target). Two types of variances can exist: favourable and unfavourable.

- **Favourable variances** – A favourable variance exists when the discrepancy is financially beneficial to the organization. For example, a favourable variance exists if the actual costs of marketing turn out to be less than the planned expenditure. So, if actual marketing costs were valued at $220,000 but the budgeted value was $250,000, then the firm has a favourable variance of $30,000. Alternatively, the actual sales outcome might exceed the budgeted sales target, which is beneficial to the business. For example, if sales revenue were budgeted at $500,000 for a specified period of time, but the actual sales were $520,000, then there would be a favourable variance of $20,000.
- **Unfavourable variances** – An unfavourable variance, also known as an **adverse variance**, exists when the variance is financially detrimental to the organization. It occurs when actual costs are higher than expected (i.e. overspending) or when actual revenue is lower than budgeted revenue (i.e. underselling).

Budget holders will need to investigate the causes of any variance. For example, if an adverse variance is the result of overspending, then senior management will demand an explanation. There could be valid reasons for this, such as a supplier hiking prices after the budget had originally been set or because the firm switched to using better-quality inputs in the production process (which costs more money than budgeted).

Exam Tip!
Favourable or positive?

There is no such thing as a positive (or negative) variance. Mathematically, a 'positive' variance exists when the actual outcome exceeds the planned or budgeted outcome. However, this might not be a good thing for the business if we are referring to production and marketing budgets (since this would mean incurring higher costs than planned). Therefore, for reasons of clarity, we only talk about favourable (and unfavourable) variances.

Variance analysis helps managers to monitor and control budgets. Adverse variances provide warnings of falling revenues and/or rising costs. Managers can then implement corrective measures to offset these unfavourable variances. In addition, variance analysis helps in the review and revision of annual budgets. Discrepancies can be investigated to identify the root cause(s) and to allocate appropriate funding in the future. For example, if there is an adverse variance in the production budget due to rising raw material costs, then more funds may be allocated to the production department.

To illustrate this management tool, consider the data in Table 3.4a which shows the budgeted and actual figures for Meigh Visual Arts Company. It is common in variance analysis to use the abbreviations (F) for favourable variances, and (A) for adverse variances.

Table 3.4a Variance analysis for Meigh Visual Arts Company, period ending 30th June

	Actual value ($)	Budgeted value ($)	Variance ($)
Sales	55,000	50,000	5,000 (F)
Raw materials	18,000	15,000	3,000 (A)
Staffing	23,000	25,000	2,000 (F)
Marketing	14,000	12,000	2,000 (A)
Rent	20,000	20,000	0

HIGHER LEVEL

From the table, we can see the following:

- Sales are $5,000 higher than budgeted (planned), so this is financially beneficial to the organization, i.e. there is a favourable variance.
- There is an adverse variance of $3,000 for raw materials because Meigh Visual Arts Company had only planned to spend $15,000 but actually spent $18,000.
- Staffing costs were budgeted for $25,000 but the firm only spent $23,000 thereby saving $2,000 (a favourable variance).
- Since there is overspending on the marketing budget by an extra $2,000, this represents an adverse variance for Meigh Visual Arts Company.
- Finally, the planned expenditure on rent matches the actual spending on rent and therefore no variance exists in this instance.

Variances do not have to be expressed in monetary terms (see Exam Tip below). Some businesses prefer to use percentage figures to show discrepancies between budgeted and actual values. In the above example, the sales variance for Meigh Visual Arts Company is 10% (F) higher than the budgeted figure. Either way, once the variances have been calculated, it is the manager's role to investigate the causes of any variances and to implement measures to improve these figures. In reality, it is common practice for managers to place greater emphasis on investigating the areas with larger variances.

Exam Tip!
Worked example

Question: Complete the missing figures in the 'Variance' column and state whether the variance is adverse or favourable. *[5 marks]*

Budget variances for The Wok Express			
	Budgeted figure ($'000)	**Actual figure ($'000)**	**Variance**
Sales	500	495	
Cost of sales	200	210	
Gross profit	300	285	
Expenses	100	90	
Net profit	**200**	**195**	

Answer:

Budget variances for The Wok Express			*Answer 1*	*Answer 2*
	Budgeted figure ($'000)	**Actual figure ($'000)**	**Variance ($'000)**	**Variance (%)**
Sales	500	495	5 (A)	1% (A)
Cost of sales	200	210	10 (A)	5% (A)
Gross profit	300	285	15 (A)	5% (A)
Expenses	100	90	10 (F)	10% (F)
Net Profit	200	195	5 (A)	2.5% (A)

HIGHER LEVEL

Question 3.4.4

Laptops-R-Us – variance analysis

a Complete the table below for Laptops-R-Us and identify variances as adverse or favourable. *[5 marks]*

Variable	Budget	Actual	Variance
Sales of product A (units)	250	180	
Sales of product B (units)	250	260	
Production costs ($'000)	120	150	
Output per worker (units)	20	22	
Labour costs ($)	100	115	

b Use your answers from above to explain why variances are referred to as favourable or adverse rather than as positive or negative variances. *[4 marks]*

c Calculate the variance, in financial terms, for each of the cases below. Show your working.

i Laptops-R-Us had budgeted for $6,000 operating costs in 100 machine hours. However, actual operating costs totalled $5,850 in 100 machine hours. *[2 marks]*

ii Laptops-R-Us had budgeted production of 250 units of Product A in 10 machine hours. Variable costs are $100 per machine hour. In fact, 250 units are produced in 8 machine hours. *[3 marks]*

BUDGETING AND BUSINESS STRATEGY

Budgeting helps to ensure that managers plan ahead. They are required to anticipate the costs and revenues of different business activities for the forthcoming trading period. This also involves managers agreeing on priorities and targets. In addition, budgetary control is an important function of managers. This role encourages regular monitoring and review of budgets in order to deal with any variances. Therefore, budgeting has a central role in business strategic planning.

The way in which budgeting is handled within a workplace depends largely on the firm's organizational culture (see Unit 2.6). Organizations that adopt an authoritarian culture will tend to be arranged by a tightly controlled budgetary system, such as a zero budgeting arrangement. Targets will also be imposed upon budget holders without any discussion or negotiation. By contrast, organizations that have an open and entrusting culture will tend to use budgeting as a form of employee recognition and motivation.

Since budgets are financial plans used to achieve organizational objectives, **SMART budgeting** requires budgets to be:

- *Specific* – Budgets should be set in line with the strategic vision of an organization.
- *Measurable* – Any budgeting system should ensure that budget holders are held accountable for their successes or shortcomings. Variance analysis can help in this respect.
- *Agreed* – For budgeting to work properly, the budgets should be set through a process of negotiations and discussions to ensure that more appropriate budgets are set.

- *Realistic* – Only realistically set budgets can motivate people to reach their set targets. Under funding will hinder output, whilst over funding is likely to lead to complacency.
- *Time constrained* – Since budgets are financial plans for the foreseeable future, there must be a time constraint. Some organizations allow budget holders to carry forward any unspent funds, whilst other firms do not encourage any funds to be carried forward.

We have seen in this Unit that budgeting is a process, as summarized in Figure 3.4a. However, budgeting does not come without its problems. For instance, the budgeting process might be too rigid. This means that the business will not be in a position to respond to changes in the internal and external business environment. In addition, budgets can lose their meaning if they are unfairly and inappropriately set. For example, *sales forecasting* (see Unit 4.2), which is a prerequisite to setting the sales budget, is only as accurate as the quality of the data used to make the sales predictions. Finally, budgets can give managers access to huge funds. In the wrong hands, this could lead to misuse and abuse of the budgeted funds. Take the case of Enron as an example. Enron was the seventh largest American company and had been voted by *Fortune* magazine as the "Most innovative company" for six consecutive years. However, in 2001, the company went bankrupt due to accounting fraud which left employees and investors with absolutely nothing. Similarly, in 1995, Barings Bank (which was established in 1762) collapsed due to illegal insider trading from one of the bank's employees Nick Leeson who lost $1.4 billion on the stocks and futures exchange. The bank was subsequently acquired by Dutch financial services provider ING Group for a nominal fee of just £1 ($2).

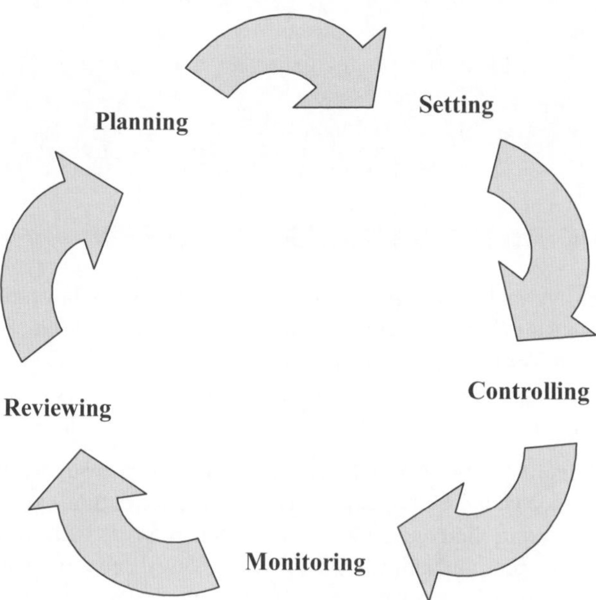

Figure 3.4a The budgeting process

Nevertheless, most people argue that there are significant benefits in using budgets. Budgeting can be used to motivate managers and budget holders, to foster responsibility and accountability and to aid financial control. Ultimately, effective budgeting avoids inefficient expenditure, thereby helping to enhance the competitive strength of an organization.

REVIEW QUESTIONS 3.4

1 What is meant by a 'budget'?

2 Outline four types of budgets.

3 What is a 'master budget'?

4 State the four main reasons for producing budgets.

5 Why do many businesses hold a contingency fund?

6 What is 'budgetary control' and why is it important to an organization?

7 Outline three ways by which an organization might set its budgets.

8 Briefly explain five limitations of budgeting.

9 What is 'variance analysis' and why is it an important management tool?

10 Distinguish between 'favourable' and 'adverse' variances.

11 How is it possible to deduce organizational culture from a firm's use of budgeting?

12 What is meant by 'SMART budgeting'?

Budget refers to a financial plan for expected revenue and expenditure for an organization (or a department within an organization), for a given period of time.

Budget holder refers to a person who has been placed in charge of a budget. The budget holder is then responsible and accountable for all revenue and expenditure within the allocated funds.

Budgetary control refers to the use of corrective measures taken to ensure that actual performance equals the budgeted performance.

Contingency fund is the name given to a reserve budget that is set aside for emergency and back-up use.

Master budget is the overall or consolidated budget, comprised of all the separate budgets within an organization. The Chief Financial Officer (CFO) will have general control and management of the master budget.

SMART budgeting refers to budgets that are specific, measurable, agreed, realistic and time constrained. This set of criteria helps to ensure that budgets are appropriately set in order to facilitate budgetary control.

Variance refers to any discrepancy between actual outcomes and budgeted outcomes. Favourable variances exist when the variance is beneficial for the business, such as sales being higher than budgeted or costs turning out to be lower than expected. The opposite is true for adverse (unfavourable) variances.

HIGHER LEVEL

Final Accounts

UNIT 3.5

Nothing speaks more eloquently than money.

French proverb

Key topics

- Income statements: trading, profit and loss and appropriation accounts
- Balance sheets
- Window dressing

Higher Level extension

- Depreciation: straight-line and reducing balance methods
- Intangible assets: patents, copyrights, goodwill and trademarks
- Stock valuation: last in, first out (LIFO) and first in, first out (FIFO)

Note: Students will be expected to construct and amend accounts from given information but will not be tested on the Manufacturing Account or double entry. (© IBO 2007)

INTRODUCTION

All businesses need to keep a record of their financial statements. For some businesses, proper accounting simply lets them have better financial planning and control, whilst for others it is a legal requirement. Where there is a divorce of ownership and control (see Unit 1.2), much of the firm's finances will have probably come from shareholders. Final reporting acts as a way to account for all monies of the firm, whether it belongs to the owners, investors or lenders. In other words, having to produce final accounts ensures that all payments and receipts of a business have to be officially accounted for.

All companies or corporations (i.e. businesses owned by shareholders) must provide a set of final accounts consisting of three statements:

- *Profit and loss account* – This account shows the trading position of a business at the end of a specified accounting period.
- *Balance sheet* – This account shows the assets and liabilities of a business at a specific point in time.
- *Cash flow statement* – This document shows the sources of cash inflows of a business and where it has been spent. Cash flows are covered separately in Unit 3.3.

It is a legal requirement in most countries for companies to have their final accounts audited by independent and chartered accountants who certify the accounts as being truthful. However, since there is no uniform method to present the final accounts, there is some degree of flexibility in reporting the 'true' financial position of a company and much of this interpretation comes down to the auditor's professional judgement.

This Unit looks at **financial accounting** (public and disclosed), rather than **management accounting** (internal and confidential). There is an examination of the various components of the profit and loss account and the balance sheet. Both are essential, not just to comply with legal requirements, but for the organization's strategic planning.

THE PURPOSE AND USERS OF FINAL ACCOUNTS

Incorporated businesses are legally obliged to produce final accounts, which act to ensure transparency in their use of funds. There are various users of final accounts:

- *Shareholders* – The owners of a company will be interested to see where their money was spent and, more importantly, how well their investments have performed. Based on the financial performance of a company, shareholders can decide whether to hold, sell or buy (more of) their shares.
- *Employees* – Staff will be interested in their organization's financial accounts to assess job security and the likelihood of pay increments.
- *Managers* – Managers can use financial accounts to judge the operational efficiency of their organizations. In addition, financial analysis can be useful for target setting and strategic planning.
- *Competitors* – Rival firms will be interested in the final accounts of a business in order to make comparisons of their financial performance (see Unit 3.6).
- *Government* – The tax authorities will want to examine the accounts of businesses, especially large multinationals, to ensure that businesses are paying the correct amount of tax.

- *Financiers* – Financial lenders such as banks or business angels (see Unit 3.1) will scrutinize the accounts of a firm before approving any financial backing. Suppliers can examine a firm's accounts to decide whether trade credit should be approved.
- *Potential investors* – Private and institutional investors will use final accounts to assess whether an investment would be financially worthwhile. They will use methods such as ratio analysis (see Unit 3.6) in their assessment.

The various stakeholders of a business will have different, but complementary, demands on a firm. This, therefore, adds pressure to the business to ensure that its final accounts are impressive.

Question 3.5.1

Nestlé

Nestlé is a multinational food company founded by Henri Nestlé in 1860. Many of the Swiss company's brands are internationally renowned, such as Kit Kat (confectionery), Necafé, Nestea and Perrier (beverages), Dreyer's (ice cream) and Gerber (baby food products). A significant proportion of Nestlé's revenues come from the sale of confectionery, a market also dominated by rival brands such as Mars (with brands such as Snickers and M&Ms) and Cadbury's (which owns brands such as Time Out, Crème Eggs and Diary Milk). Nestlé is listed on the Swiss stock exchange in Zurich. It also owns a large share in L'Oreal, the world's largest cosmetics company.

a Identify two stakeholder groups of Nestlé from the case study. *[2 marks]*

b Analyse the importance of final accounts to both stakeholder groups mentioned above. *[6 marks]*

TRADING AND PROFIT AND LOSS ACCOUNTS

The trading, profit and loss account (sometimes referred to as an **income statement**) is a financial statement of a firm's trading activity over a period of time, usually one year. Most businesses that operate in the private sector aim to make a profit. Even for non-profit organizations and those in the public sector, it is important to make a surplus for the business to survive. The main purpose of producing this account is to show the amount of profit or loss that a business has made during a particular trading period.

Profit creates an incentive for most businesses to do well. If a business does not earn profit, it will struggle to survive in the future. Profit, in its simplest form, is the difference between a firm's revenues and its costs. **Revenue** refers to the inflow of money to the business from ordinary trading activities. Revenue can come in the form of cash sales, credit sales, fees and royalties. **Costs** represent the outflow of money from a business due to its operations. Costs of production are likely to include wages, salaries, rent and the purchase of stock.

Different stakeholders may use this set of accounts for their own purposes. For example, the government may use the profit and loss (P&L) account to assess tax liabilities of the business. Shareholders will look at the profit figures to assess the likely return on their investment in the business. Employees may use the accounts to assess job security and the likelihood of pay increments. Managers might use the profit and loss account as a guide to their financial performance during the year, such as their ability to control overhead expenses. In addition, they might use the P&L account to help plan for future expansion. Stakeholders can also use the account to assess the **profit quality** of a business. This refers to the long-term prospects of a business in making and sustaining a good level of profit. Firms that sell inferior products at relatively high prices will have low profit quality.

There are three sections to a Trading, Profit and Loss Account: the Trading Account, the Profit and Loss Account and the Appropriation Account.

Trading account

The trading account represents the top section of the P&L account and shows the difference in sales revenue and the direct costs of trading. In essence, the trading account is used to show the **gross profit** of a business. It is the difference between the sales turnover (the value of products sold to customers) and the cost to the business in producing or purchasing those products. Sales turnover will include the value of goods sold even if payment for them has yet to be received. The formula for working out gross profit is:

$$\text{Gross profit} = \text{Sales revenue} - \text{Cost of goods sold}$$

The cost of goods sold (COGS) is the accountant's term for direct costs of the goods that are actually sold, such as raw materials and wages for direct labour. COGS is also known as **cost of sales** and is worked out by the formula:

$$\text{Cost of sales} = \text{Opening stock} + \text{Purchases} - \text{Closing stock}$$

Calculating the cost of sales can be quite tricky because the distinction between 'price' and 'cost' is often overlooked. For example, if a business opens trading this morning with $1,000 of stock (the cost value) and receives a delivery of stock for which it pays $2,000, then the business has costs of stock valued at $3,000. Assume that after the trading day it has $1,800 of the stock (at cost value) remaining. Using the formula, the calculation of cost of sales then becomes:

$$\text{COGS} = \$1{,}000 + \$2{,}000 - \$1{,}800$$

Thus the cost of sales is $1,200. Assume that the stocks sell for three times their cost – this would then generate sales revenue of $3,600. Gross profit is then:

$$\$3{,}600 - \$1{,}200 = \$2{,}400$$

Using the example from above, the trading account can be shown in the following format:

Trading Account for Company Y
for year ended 1st April 20XX

	$	$
Sales		3,600
Cost of Goods Sold		
Opening stock	1,000	
Purchases	2,000	
Closing stock	1,800	
		1,200
Gross Profit		2,400

A business can improve its gross profit in a number of ways:

- Use cheaper suppliers – This will help to reduce the cost of sales, although finding cheaper suppliers without hindering quality may be more problematic.
- Increase selling price – This will raise the value of each item of sale, but will also be likely to lead to a fall in the volume of sales.
- Use marketing strategies – Methods such as promotions and repackaging can be used to make the product more appealing. This will, however, raise the expenses to the organization.

Question 3.5.2

The information below represents data for Bags-R-Us Ltd.:

– 3,000 bags sold at $35 each

– Closing stock is valued at $20,000

– Purchases totalled $50,000

– Stock at 1st April 2007 was valued at $15,000

- Construct a Trading Account for Bags-R-Us Ltd. for the year ended 31 March 2008. *[4 marks]*

It is important to note that the final gross profit figure may be revised at a later date to reflect any adjustments, such as customers returning faulty products. Furthermore, gross profit is not the profit that a business gets to keep. This is because gross profit does not account for the fixed costs of production, such as rent, insurance and advertising costs. To see what profit is left after both direct and indirect costs are accounted for, accountants produce the Profit and Loss account.

Profit and Loss account

The profit and loss account, sometimes referred to as the **profit statement**, shows the **operating profit** and **net profit** (or loss) of a business at the end of a trading period. The gross profit, calculated from the trading account, is used to deduct all expenses (indirect costs) to calculate operating profit. Hence, the formula for working out operating profit is:

$$\text{Operating profit} = \text{Gross profit} - \text{Expenses}$$

This means that operating profit is the surplus, if any, from sales revenues after all **operating costs** (both direct and indirect costs) are accounted for. Hence **operating profit** is the actual profit made from a firm's normal trading activities. Expenses are the indirect or fixed costs of production (see Box 3.5a). Although the P&L account shows the total figure for expenses, a business must provide accompanying notes to the accounts to show a breakdown of the expenses, such as directors' salaries, accountancy fees and donations made to charitable organizations.

Box 3.5a Examples of business expenses

Expenses are regular or ongoing indirect costs for a business. They will vary from business to business but will invariably include:

- Administration charges
- Utility bills, e.g. gas, electricity, telephone and water charges
- Insurance premiums, e.g. for buildings, vehicles and stock
- Interest on bank loans
- Marketing costs, such as advertising expenses
- Rent for land and property
- Management salaries
- Stationery costs
- Transportation and distribution costs

Suppose, for example, that a small florist company sold $200,000 of stock with a market value of $450,000 for the fiscal (tax) year ended on 31st December 2008. Rents payable amounted to $80,000 whilst utility bills for gas, water, electricity and telephone usage added up to $50,000. Other overheads added up to $30,000. The trading, profit and loss account could then be presented as:

Profit and Loss Account for Florists-R-Us
year ended 31st December 2008

	$	$
Sales Revenue		450,000
Cost of Sales		200,000
Gross Profit		250,000
Less **Expenses**		
Rents	80,000	
Utility bills	50,000	
Other overheads	30,000	
		160,000
Operating Profit		90,000

There are several ways in which a business might try to reduce its expenses, or overheads, to increase its net profit figure. The method used will depend on the type of overhead that needs to be reduced. For example:

- Rent charges could be negotiated or the firm could move to cheaper premises; although relocation may not prove feasible due to *industrial inertia* (see Unit 5.5).
- Fuel consumption for heating and lighting could be reduced. For instance, businesses could turn down the heating temperature during the winter, use less air conditioning in the summer and turn off lights when not required. This should help reduce their electricity bills and could give them a better corporate image with environmentalists.
- Administration costs could be examined by reviewing the work of clerical staff to reduce costs. This could be achieved by, perhaps, combining jobs or employing fewer people to carry out such tasks.

Businesses may also add income from other activities, known as **non-operating income**, to the P&L account. Such incomes might come from the business collecting payment from renting out their property, interest gained from its deposits at a bank or dividends earned from holding shares in other companies. This gives *Operating Profit plus Non-operating Income*, and is shown as **profit before interest and tax** in a P&L account.

Interest charges and tax levies, despite being expenses, are shown as a separate item on profit and loss accounts. This is because interest rates and tax rates change over time and are beyond the control of the business. Profit may be lower this year simply because interest rates were raised, despite the business making more gross profit. This practice then allows a business to compare like with like and to make historical comparisons of performance.

Interest payable is a cost as it represents the charge that a business pays to its lenders for loans. **Interest receivable** is a source of revenue from investments and cash deposits at the bank. **Corporation tax** is the tax payable on a company's profits. Suppose that Florists-R-Us earns $5,000 from the sale of a fixed asset but has $8,000 of interest to repay to the bank. By including non-operating income and interest payments, the format of the profit and loss account shows the **net profit**:

Profit and Loss Account for Florists-R-Us, year ended 31st December 2008

	$
Sales Revenue	450,000
Cost of Sales	(200,000)
Gross Profit	250,000
Less Expenses	(160,000)
Operating Profit	90,000
Plus non-operating income	5,000
Profit before interest and tax	95,000
Less Interest payable	(8,000)
Net Profit	87,000

Note: If a business does not declare non-operating income or interest charges, the operating profit is equal to the net profit.

Question 3.5.3

Masks-R-Us Ltd.

An extract of this year's financial data for Masks-R-Us Ltd. for the period ended 31st August is shown below:

- Sales turnover 15,000 masks @ $8 each
- Opening stock $9,000
- Purchases $40,000
- Closing stocks $8,000
- Overhead expenses $18,000

a Construct a Trading, Profit and Loss account for Masks-R-Us Ltd. *[5 marks]*

b Interpret the findings from your answer above and comment on whether the financial performance of Masks-R-Us can be judged solely on this information. *[5 marks]*

Appropriation Account

The third part of the Trading, Profit and Loss Account is called the **appropriation account**. This section of the accounts shows how the net profit is distributed. There are three parts to this account:

- **Taxation** – This represents the compulsory levy imposed by governments on company profits. This figure will be transferred to the balance sheet and shown as a *current liability.*
- **Dividends** – This figure shows the share of net profit that is distributed to the owners of the business (the shareholders). This figure is also transferred to the balance sheet and shown under *current liabilities.*
- **Retained profit** – This shows how much of the net profit is kept by the business for its own use, such as reinvesting in the business or to expand the business. This figure is transferred to the *capital and reserves* section of the firm's balance sheet.

Firms have little power over taxation as corporation tax rates are compulsory levies set by the government (see Unit 1.5). However, they are free to decide on the share of net profits after tax that is distributed to shareholders and how much is retained for internal business use. The share of profits allocated to shareholders is based on the decision of the board of directors and is approved at the company's annual general meeting. If dividend payments are approved, it is usual for the business to pay these biannually. An *interim dividend* is paid approximately half-way through the year and then the *final dividend* is declared and paid at the end of the firm's financial year. In addition, businesses will retain a share of the profits for investment and precautionary purposes.

In reality, the three parts of the Trading, Profit and Loss and Appropriation Account are combined into one account and termed the **Profit and Loss Account**. It is also a legal requirement for existing firms to report their P&L account for two consecutive years for benchmarking purposes. It is not always clear where the three separate sections start and end. For example, in some accounts, the appropriation account shows net profits being distributed in *two* ways, dividends and retained profit, whilst taxation is shown as a business expense. The important thing is that a business produces the accounts in a consistent format to enable historical comparisons.

Combining all three parts of the account will produce a P&L account like this:

Profit and Loss Account for Florists-R-Us, year ended 31st December 2008

	$	
Sales Revenue	450,000	Trading Account
Cost of Sales	(200,000)	
Gross Profit	250,000	
Less Expenses	(160,000)	
Operating Profit	90,000	
Plus non-operating income	5,000	Profit and Loss Account
Profit before interest and tax	95,000	
Less Interest expenses	(8,000)	
Net profit before tax	87,000	
Less Taxation	(15,000)	
Net profit after interest and tax	72,000	Appropriation Account
Dividends	22,000	
Retained Profit	50,000	

At times, it may be necessary to show **exceptional items** on a P&L account. Exceptional items are one-off transactions that affect the profit (or loss) of a firm and are not expected to recur. For example, an extremely large bad debt may need to be written off, which would cause profits to decline significantly. On the other hand, the sale of fixed assets will increase the revenue figure for the period in question.

Exam Tip!
What's the correct format?

Different firms use slightly different methods to present their P&L accounts. Usually in the exams, the following format is presented. Remember that it is important to place an appropriate title at the top of the P&L account.

Profit and Loss Account for (Company name), for year ended (Date)

	($'000)
Sales revenue	***
Cost of sales	***
Gross profit	***
Less Expenses	***
Plus Non-operating income	***
Net profit before interest and tax	***
Less Interest	***
Less Tax	***
Net profit after interest and tax	***
Dividends	***
Retained Profit	***

Question 3.5.4

Ahmed Educational Books Ltd.

Study the data below and answer the questions that follow.

**Profit and Loss Accounts for Ahmed Educational Books Ltd.
for year ended 31st December 2008**

	Year 2 ($'000)	Year 1 ($'000)
Sales	**(i)**	450
Cost of sales	200	**(ii)**
Gross profit	300	270
Expenses	100	90
Net profit before interest and tax	**(iii)**	180
Interest Payable	10	0
Taxation	48	**(iv)**
Net profit after interest and tax	142	135
Dividends	10	15
Retained Profit	132	**(v)**

a Complete the missing figures in the above profit and loss account. *[5 marks]*

b Discuss whether the shareholders of Ahmed Educational Books Ltd. would be pleased with the performance of the company. *[8 marks]*

The profit and loss account is important as it shows the profit (if any) that is generated after *all* costs (such as advertising, utility bills and salaries) are accounted for. The gross profit may be appealing, but if the expenses are higher than the gross profit, the business has made an overall loss. Clearly, a business cannot survive for long without making any profit.

However, profit and loss accounts have several limitations:

- As with most financial accounts, the P&L account shows the historical performance of a business rather than what is likely to happen in the future. There is no guarantee that future performance is linked to past performance or successes. Nevertheless, with data for several years it may be possible to forecast trends in a firm's profit or loss.
- *Window dressing* (legal manipulation of the accounts to make them look financially more attractive) can take place. This means that the 'true' figures are hidden. For example, a firm may include the sale of some fixed assets or non-operating income to increase the value of profits to impress its shareholders.
- As there is no standardized format for producing a P&L account, it may be difficult to compare the profit or loss of different firms, be they in the same or dissimilar industries.

BALANCE SHEETS

A balance sheet is one of the three annual financial statements that companies are legally required to produce for auditing purposes. It is a record of an organization's financial position at a specific date, usually the end of the trading year. The balance sheet will therefore contain information on the value of an organization's assets, liabilities and the capital invested by the owners. Since it represents the financial position of a business on one day only, it is often described as showing a 'snapshot' of the financial situation of the organization.

It is called a balance sheet because the financial document shows a firm's sources of finance (shown as the *capital employed*) and where that money has been spent (shown as the *assets employed*), i.e. it shows where a firm's money has come from (capital and liabilities) and what it has been spent on (assets). This helps to ensure that all monies within the organization are properly accounted for.

A balance sheet must contain three essential parts: *assets*, *liabilities* and *capital and reserves*.

Assets

Assets are items owned by or owed to a business and hold a monetary value, such as cash or buildings. To purchase assets, firms will need different sources of finance (see Unit 3.1), which can also be inferred from a balance sheet. Assets can be classified as being fixed assets or current assets.

A **fixed asset** is any asset that is purchased for business use, rather than for selling, and is likely to last for more than 12 months from the balance sheet date. Fixed assets can be further split into three groups:

- **Tangible fixed assets** – These are physical fixed assets such as equipment, machinery, property (land and buildings), fixtures and fittings, and motor vehicles. Apart from land and buildings, tangible fixed assets tend to depreciate (fall in value) over time.
- **Intangible fixed assets** – These are non-physical fixed assets such as brand names, goodwill, trademarks, copyrights and patents. These may prove to be a firm's most valuable assets although it is usually very difficult to place a value on intangible assets.
- **Investments** – These are medium- to long-term financial investments that the business has. Businesses can hold shares and debentures in other companies, for example. Although this may generate some short-term income for the firm, such as dividend or interest payments, investments are held for long-standing strategic reasons.

A **current asset** refers to cash or any other liquid asset that is likely to be turned into cash within twelve months of the balance sheet date. In Unit 3.3, it was explained that there are three main kinds of current assets: cash, debtors and stocks.

Liabilities

A liability is a legal obligation of a business to repay its lenders or suppliers at a later date. It is recorded on the balance sheet and can be interpreted as the amount of money owed by the business at the balance sheet date. Like assets, there are also two main classifications of liabilities: long-term liabilities and current liabilities.

- **Long-term liabilities** are debts that are due to be repaid after twelve months, i.e. they are sources of long-term borrowing. Examples of such liabilities include debentures, mortgages and bank loans (see Unit 3.1). In the balance sheet, these liabilities are often placed under the heading of '*Accounts payable: amounts falling due after one year*'.
- **Current liabilities** are debts that must be settled within one year of the balance sheet date. Examples include paying tax to the government, dividends to shareholders and interest to the bank for loans and overdrafts. Accruals are another example as these are expenses that have been accumulated during the year but are yet to be paid. Current liabilities are often shown in a balance sheet as '*Creditors: amounts falling due within one year*'.

The value of a firm's **net assets** is then the total value of all assets minus its current liabilities. This must be equal to (balance with) the *Capital Employed* section of a balance sheet. Net assets or **assets employed**, can be calculated by using the formula:

Net assets = Fixed assets + Working capital

Note: Some firms prefer to use the alternative method of calculating net assets by subtracting the value of all liabilities from the sum of all assets,
i.e. Net assets = Fixed assets + Working capital – Long-term liabilities.
If this approach is taken, net assets must be equal to (balance with) the Capital and Reserves section of a balance sheet. However, this is not the approach used in this book.

Capital and Reserves

This section of the balance sheet appears towards the bottom. It may appear in a balance sheet as **shareholders' funds** (for limited companies) or as **owners' equity** (for businesses other than limited companies). There are three main sections to this part of the balance sheet:

- **Share capital** refers to the amount of money raised through the sale of shares. The figure shows the value raised when the shares were first sold, rather than their current market value. For businesses with preference shareholders, this section is usually listed as **called-up capital** and shows the figures for both ordinary shares and preference shares.
- **Retained profit** is the amount of net profit after interest, tax and dividends have been paid. This money is then reinvested in the business for its own use. This money, of course, belongs to its owners so appears as Owners' Equity or Shareholders' Funds. The figure for retained profits comes from the firm's Trading, Profit and Loss account.
- **Reserves** will record any proceeds from retained profits in previous trading years. It may also include capital gains in the value of fixed assets. This will raise the value of property compared to its purchase price, so appears as a **revaluation** in the Reserves section of the balance sheet. Since depreciation (see 'Depreciation' on page 403) is catered for elsewhere in the balance sheet, there is no need to record depreciation in the value of fixed assets in this section.

Capital and reserves, in essence, show the internal *sources* of funds for a business. Since the capital and reserves belongs to its owners, it is often described as a liability. However, it differs from current and long-term liabilities in that there is no definite date by when they have to be repaid. Instead, they are viewed as being sources of permanent capital.

From a balance sheet, we should be able to see that:

Net Assets = Long-term Liabilities + Owners' Equity

This means that the *use* of funds matches the value of the sources of funds. Likewise, rearranging the above equation gives us another condition shown in a balance sheet:

Owners' Equity = Net Assets – Long-term Liabilities

This simply means that the owners of the business own the value of the assets of the business after deductions have been made for the business's debts.

It is common practice, and a legal requirement in many countries, to report the balance sheet figures for two consecutive years. This allows comparisons regarding the performance of the business to be made. The example on page 401 shows a balance sheet for Jasmine Restaurants, a hypothetical chain of restaurants, for one particular year. It serves to illustrate the format and concepts used to construct a vertical balance sheet. Some of the key terms are explained to the right of the balance sheet.

Exam Tip!
What's the correct format?

Different firms use slightly different methods to present their balance sheets. Usually in the exams, the following format is presented. Remember that it is important to place an appropriate title at the top of the balance sheet.

Balance Sheet for (Company Name) as at (Date)

	$'000	**$'000**
Fixed assets		***
Less Depreciation	***	
Total (net fixed assets)		***
Current assets		
Stocks	***	
Debtors	***	
Cash	***	
		***
Current liabilities		
Creditors	***	
Short-term borrowing	***	
		***
Net assets		***
Financed by:		
Loan capital		***
Share capital	***	
Retained profit	***	
		***
Capital employed		***

The balance sheet of sole traders and partnerships will differ slightly from those produced by limited companies. For example:

- Sources of finance will differ. For instance, limited companies can raise finance through the sale of debentures, whereas this source of funds will not appear on the sole trader's balance sheet.
- Shareholders funds may be replaced by *owner's equity* or *personal funds* as these businesses do not have shareholders.
- Since there are no shareholders, dividends will not appear under the firm's current liabilities. Instead, the sole trader or partner might take out funds from the business for their personal use (known as **drawings** to accountants).

Balance sheet for Jasmine Restaurants Ltd.
as at 30th Sept 20xx

	$'000	$'000	
Fixed assets			Fixed assets are items owned by a firm that are not intended for resale within the next 12 months but are used to generate output and sales, e.g. the physical restaurant (premises), tables, chairs, drinks machines, fridges, cookers, cash registers, lighting equipment and so forth.
Premises	1,500		
Machinery and Equipment	500		
		2,000	
Current assets			Current assets are items owned by a firm that are in the form of cash or what it intends to change into cash within one year. Examples include stocks of goods (food and drinks) and debtors (customers who have paid by cheque or credit card).
Stocks	250		
Debtors	30		
Cash at bank	200		
	480		
Current liabilities			Current liabilities are debts that the business must repay to its creditors within 12 months of the balance sheet date, e.g. money owed to its suppliers of food and drinks (trade creditors), to the bank for short-term borrowing, corporation tax owed to the government, and dividends owed to the company's shareholders.
Trade creditors	250		
Short-term borrowing	15		
Taxation	35		
Dividends	20		
	320		
Net current assets (Working capital)		160	Net current assets, also known as working capital (see Unit 3.3) is calculated as the difference between a firm's current assets and its current liabilities.
Net assets		**2,160**	The net assets figure refers to the sum of total assets less current liabilities. This figure must be matched with (or balanced with) the capital employed figure.
Financed by:			
Long-term liabilities			Long-term liabilities are the debts owed by a business which are payable after 12 months from the balance sheet date. Examples include a mortgage and debentures (see Unit 3.1) to purchase the premises and outstanding bank loans (which may have been used to purchase the machinery and equipment).
Mortgage	500		
Debentures	500		
Bank loans	100		
		1,100	
Capital and Reserves			The capital and reserves section of the balance sheet shows the money that belongs to its shareholders. In this case, 1 million shares were issued at $1 each, thereby raising $1 million for the restaurant (note that this has nothing to do with the current market price of the shares). Retained profit refers to the profit appropriated to the company in the previous year.
Ordinary share capital (1,000,000 shares at $1)	1,000		
Retained profits	60		
		1,060	
Capital Employed		**2,160**	Capital employed refers to the funds available for the purchase of a firm's assets, i.e. it is equal to all forms of long-term loans, share capital and reserves.

Exam Tip!
The balance sheet of a sole proprietorship or partnership is different from that of limited companies. The main difference is that share capital does not appear in the Capital and Reserves section, because these businesses do not have shareholders. Most examination questions will ask you to interpret the balance sheet of a limited company.

The uses of balance sheets

In addition to showing the assets and liabilities of a business, a balance sheet can be used for several other purposes:

- The difference between current assets and current liabilities shows us the **net current assets** or the **working capital** (see Unit 3.3). This is an indication of the short-term liquidity position of the business and shows the amount of money available for the day-to-day running of the business.
- The **asset structure** can be analysed. For example, an increase in the value of fixed assets may suggest that the business is undergoing expansion. A significant increase in the value of stocks might suggest that a firm is overtrading.
- The **capital structure** can be examined to see the sources of finance. Examples might include shareholders' capital, debentures and current liabilities.
- The firm's **capital employed** can give an indication of its size. The higher a firm's capital employed, the greater its market value tends to be.

Limitations of balance sheets

There are several limitations to the use of balance sheets:

- Since balance sheets are static documents, the financial position of a business may be very different in subsequent periods. The value of capital and reserves can change the next day due to the business using the funds for expansion purposes, for example.
- The figures given in a balance sheet are, at best, only 'accurate' estimates of the value of assets and liabilities. The market value of an asset is not necessarily the same as its **book value** (the value of an asset as shown on a balance sheet). The true market value of a fixed asset, for example, is only known once the item has been sold. The value of stock will depend on the method of stock valuation used (see 'Stock valuation' on page 408), and this will therefore alter the value of current assets. Also, the values shown do not show a breakdown of a firm's assets, so the information given is somewhat incomplete.
- Since there is no specific format required for producing a balance sheet, different businesses (or their accountants) will produce balance sheets in different formats and include varying assets and liabilities. This can make it difficult to compare the financial position of different businesses, even those that operate in the same industry.
- Not all assets, especially the intangible assets and the value of human capital, are necessarily included in a balance sheet. For example, football clubs do not include the market value of their players in their balance sheet. To do so would be a difficult task as each organization, such as Chelsea, Real Madrid and AC Milan, would need to determine which players to include in their valuation. Similarly, the manager or coach has a market value that is not shown on a balance sheet. If the saying "Workers are a firm's most valuable assets" is true, it means that the financial position of a business is not really accurately represented in a balance sheet.

Question 3.5.5

Zawada Electronics Ltd.

Zawada Electronics is a Canadian importer and exporter of consumer electronics, specializing in the trade of computer accessories. Selected financial data from the company on 31st December are shown below.

	2010 ($'000)	2009 ($'000)
Bank overdraft	20	10
Cash	25	20
Creditors	50	50
Debentures	50	50
Debtors	70	50
Fixed assets	250	250
Long-term liabilities	50	80
Retained profit	75	75
Share capital	200	150
Stocks	100	95

a Identify one example of fixed assets and one example of stocks for Zawada Electronics. *[2 marks]*

b Construct a balance sheet for Zawada Electronics for both years. *[6 marks]*

c State the values of the firm's working capital for both years. *[2 marks]*

HIGHER LEVEL EXTENSION: DEPRECIATION

Property and land tend to rise in value over time. This increase in the value of fixed assets is known as **appreciation**. However, most fixed assets tend to depreciate over time. **Depreciation** refers to the fall in the value of fixed assets over time. Depreciation spreads the **historic cost** (purchase cost) of a fixed asset over its useful lifespan. Fixed assets may depreciate for two main reasons:

- **Wear and tear** – This means that fixed assets, such as computers and motor vehicles, fall in value as they are used over and over. This causes the assets to wear out and increases maintenance costs. They may also need to be replaced earlier than planned. These factors make such assets less valuable to a buyer and so the value is depreciated.
- **Obsolete assets** – This means that newer and better products become available and this reduces the demand for existing fixed assets. Obsolete assets are then out-of-date assets, such as old versions of computers or software. These will fetch very little, if any, value if sold. Hence their value needs to be depreciated.

The changes in the value of fixed assets are shown by reassessing the value of the assets on a balance sheet. Depreciation needs to be recorded in order to:

- Calculate the value of a business more accurately. Revaluing assets that have appreciated is likely to increase the net asset figure on a balance sheet. Similarly, depreciating fixed assets will reduce the value of net assets to better reflect the true value or financial position of a business.

HIGHER LEVEL

- Realistically assess the value of fixed assets over time. The historical or purchase cost of fixed assets, such as property or vehicles, is unlikely to be equal to its current market value.
- Plan for the replacement of assets in the future. Provisions are made in order to replace the cost of purchasing new fixed assets. In reality, money is not put away to pay for the purchase of new fixed assets, but depreciation is recorded as an expense (on the profit and loss account) as it reflects the fall in the value of fixed assets that will eventually need to be replaced.

The amount of depreciation has to be accounted for when placing the value of fixed assets on a balance sheet. This will then show the actual book value (as shown on a balance sheet) of the fixed asset.

HIGHER LEVEL EXTENSION: METHODS OF CALCULATING DEPRECIATION

There are two main methods of calculating the depreciation of fixed assets: the straight-line method and the reducing balance method. In practice, it does not really matter which method is used. However, in order to allow for meaningful and historical comparisons of the accounts, it is better to be consistent in the choice of method.

Straight-line method

This is the simplest and most commonly used of the two methods. It is popular amongst British companies. To calculate the annual rate of depreciation, three key variables are needed: the life expectancy of the asset (how long it is intended to be used before it needs to be replaced), the scrap or residual value of the asset (how much it is worth at the end of its useful life) and the purchase cost of the asset. The formula for calculating the straight-line depreciation is:

$$\text{Annual depreciation} = \frac{\text{Purchase cost}}{\text{Lifespan}}$$

For example, if an electronic security system is bought for \$25,000 and is expected to last five years (i.e. when it will be replaced) then using the straight-line method, the purchase cost is simply divided by the expected lifespan of the asset. This then gives an annual depreciation of \$5,000 (\$25,000 / 5 years). The value of the asset at the end of each time period is shown in Table 3.5a and represented diagrammatically in Figure 3.5a.

Table 3.5a Straight line depreciation at $5,000 per annum

Year end	Depreciation ($)	Book value ($)
0	–	25,000
1	5,000	20,000
2	5,000	15,000
3	5,000	10,000
4	5,000	5,000
5	5,000	0

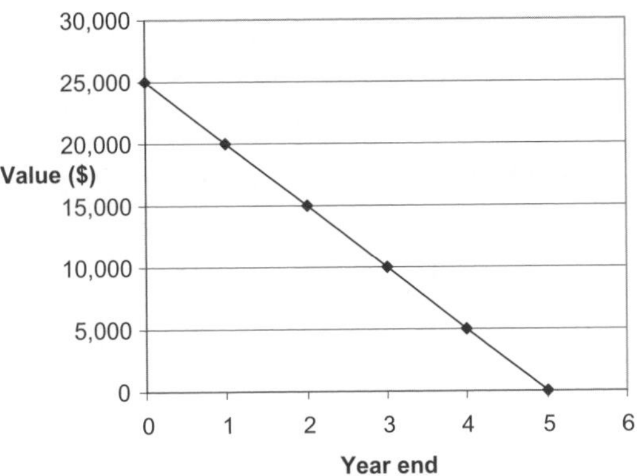

Figure 3.5a Straight-line depreciation

The **residual value** is an estimate of the scrap or disposal value of the asset at the end of its useful life. Many firms simply use a zero residual value since estimates may well prove to be inaccurate. However, it is unusual for a fixed asset to lose all of its value because it can fetch a minimal price when sold. If this is the case, then the formula for working out the straight-line depreciation becomes:

$$\text{Annual depreciation} = \frac{\text{Purchase cost} - \text{Residual value}}{\text{Lifespan}}$$

So, if the electronic security system is expected to fetch a second-hand value of $5,000 in 5 years time, then the annual amount of depreciation is worked out as ($25,000 – $5,000) / 5 years = $4,000 per annum, i.e. a fall of $1,000 in the depreciation charge each year when compared to the charge if there is no residual value.

The key advantage of the straight-line method of depreciation is that it is straightforward and simple to understand. The main weakness, however, is that fixed assets are depreciated by an equal amount each year, which is not realistic. Motor vehicles, for example, lose a much larger percentage of their value at the beginning of their useful life.

Reducing balance method

The reducing balance method depreciates the value of an asset by a predetermined percentage. This percentage is used for each year, thereby reducing the value of an asset by a larger amount in the earlier years of its useful life. This approach is preferred by most American companies.

The book value of the asset is then calculated by deducting the cumulative depreciation from the historic cost (or purchase cost) of the asset, i.e.

$$\text{Net Book Value} = \text{Historical cost} - \text{Cumulative depreciation}$$

The reducing balance method of depreciation is also known as the **diminishing balance method** or the **declining balance method**. This method is more realistic in representing the declining market value of fixed assets. However, it is not as easy to calculate. It is also unnecessary if the purpose is to simply spread the cost of an asset over its useful life.

Continuing with the above example, assume the business chose to use the reducing balance method to depreciate the security system at an annual rate of 25%. The depreciation charge of 25% at the end of each year would give the data in Table 3.5b (figures rounded to nearest $). The graphical representation of this is shown in Figure 3.5b.

HIGHER LEVEL

HIGHER LEVEL

Table 3.5b Reducing balance depreciation at 25% per annum

Year end	Depreciation ($)	Book value ($)
0	–	25,000
1	6,250	18,750
2	4,687	14,063
3	3,516	10,547
4	2,637	7,910
5	1,977	5,933

This method leaves a residual value of $5,933 for the electronic security system after 5 years (see Figure 3.5b).

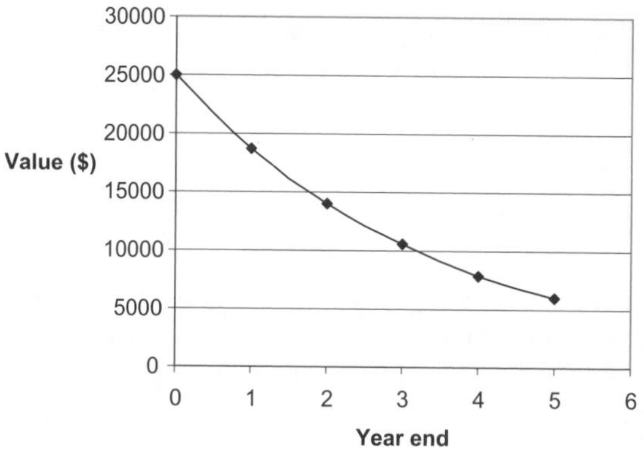

Figure 3.5b Reducing balance depreciation

The reducing balance method is more representative in that fixed assets lose a larger amount of their value in earlier years. However, it is more troublesome to calculate and deciding on the rate of annual depreciation is not always a simple task.

Amortization is similar to depreciation but is used to reduce the value of non-physical fixed assets. It is the process of reducing the value of a firm's intangible assets (see 'Intangible assets' on page 407) on a balance sheet. As copyright or patents near their expiry date, for example, the value of such intangible assets will tend to fall and these need to be reflected in its accounts.

Question 3.5.6

Satine Enterprise Ltd

Satine Enterprise Ltd. recently bought a new company car for $25,000. The firm expects to replace it in five years time. The current market resale value of the car in five years time is $2,900. The company uses an annual depreciation rate of 35%.

- **a** Use the reducing balance method of depreciation to calculate the book value of Satine Enterprise Ltd.'s asset after the first *two* years. *[3 marks]*
- **b** Calculate how much the car would have depreciated in the same period if Satine Enterprise Ltd. had used the straight-line method of depreciation. *[3 marks]*
- **c** Explain which method of depreciation would reduce the net book value of the car the most by the end of the *third* year. *[4 marks]*
- **d** Examine the strengths and weaknesses of both methods of depreciation for Satine Enterprise Ltd. *[5 marks]*

HIGHER LEVEL EXTENSION: INTANGIBLE ASSETS

Intangible assets differ from other types of fixed assets because they are **non-physical assets** owned by a business. Like physical fixed assets though, intangible assets generate income and add value to a business and are not intended for sale within twelve months of the balance sheet date.

There are several examples of intangible fixed assets that may appear in a balance sheet:

- **Patents** are a form of legal protection for inventors to prevent others from copying their creation for a period of time, usually around 20 years. Compact discs were patented by electronics firm Philips, for example. Patents act as an incentive to stimulate innovation. If rival companies could simply copy the invention, there would be little need for them to spend large amounts of money on research and development. Patents can then allow the inventor to have exclusive rights over the production of the product for a limited period of time. Other firms must pay a fee to the patent holder if they wish to use or copy the ideas, processes or products created by the inventor.
- **Copyrights** provide legal protection for the original artistic work of a creator, such as an author, photographer, painter or musician. Media sources, such as newspapers, sound recordings, computer software and movies are examples of such works. Anyone wishing to reproduce or modify the artist's work must first seek permission from the copyright holder, usually for a fee.
- **Goodwill** is the value of an organization's image and reputation. It may also include the value of a firm's customer base and its business connections. A firm that treats its workers well will be likely to see a lot of goodwill from its staff, i.e. employees are loyal to the firm and consequently add greater value to the organization. Goodwill is then the sum of customer and staff loyalty and can provide a major competitive edge for any business. As American entrepreneur Marshall Field (1834–1906) once said, "Goodwill is the one and only asset that competition cannot undersell or destroy."
- **Registered trademarks** are distinctive signs, such as the Nike 'swoosh' mark, that uniquely identify a brand, a product or a business. Trademarks can be expressed by names, symbols, phrases or an image. Like copyrights and patents, trademarks provide legal protection against those who may try to copy their creations and inventions. Registered trademarks can be sold

and ownership of trademarks can be transferred for appropriate fees (which should be reflected in the firm's balance sheet). For instance, Volkswagen bought the Bentley (luxury automobiles) brand for £430 million ($860 million) in 1998.

Intangible assets serve to increase the competitiveness of a business. Since they have the ability to earn income for a business but their value may be difficult to measure, they are often referred to as **intellectual property rights** (IPR).

Intangible assets are not always shown in a balance sheet. The main reason for this is that they are very difficult to value. For example, what are the Coca-Cola brands and logos really worth? How do we value the goodwill of staff in a school or hospital? No two firms are likely to answer these questions in exactly the same way.

This suggests that the subjective nature of placing a value on intangible assets renders it unnecessary or even impossible to place on a balance sheet. For example, goodwill is only truly realized when a takeover or merger has taken place with the buyer paying a premium for the purchase of the business. This premium represents the goodwill – the difference between the value of the business and the purchase price. Critics go as far as suggesting that placing intangible assets on a balance sheet is a form of window dressing to artificially inflate the value of a business. Vodafone managed to turn a €11 billion loss into a €10 billion profit in 2006 by the legal use of creative accounting to include goodwill. There is no disagreement about intangible assets adding value to a business beyond its book value; the argument lies in how to place an accurate figure on such assets.

Question 3.5.7

Harry Potter (J.K. Rowling)

J.K. Rowling was unemployed at the time when she wrote her first Harry Potter fantasy novel back in 1994. She has certainly come a long way since then. In 1998, Warner Bros. purchased the rights for film adaptations of the Harry Potter novels. In 2007, Warner Bros. and Universal Studios announced the construction of 'Harry Potter World' at the Universal Islands of Adventure theme park in Orlando, Florida. Prior to the release of Rowling's seventh and final instalment of the series, global sales of her books had already exceeded 325 million copies. The phenomenal commercial success and high market value of the Harry Potter franchise means that Rowling, her publishers and Warner Bros. are keen to protect their **intellectual property rights**.

a Describe what is meant by **intellectual property rights**. *[2 marks]*

b In the context of the case study, explain two benefits of protecting copyrights. *[4 marks]*

c Comment on how the 'high market value of the Harry Potter franchise' might be affected by the subjective nature of valuing intellectual property rights. *[4 marks]*

HIGHER LEVEL EXTENSION: STOCK VALUATION

For many businesses, stocks (or inventories) represent a significant proportion of assets and hence these must be accurately valued in the balance sheet. **Stock valuation** refers to the technique used to measure the value of a firm's inventories, be they raw materials, work-in-progress or finished stocks. Stock valuation is important when stocks are difficult to distinguish in terms of purchase date and costs. For example, crude oil and copper prices change on a daily basis but it is difficult for a business to distinguish between different batches of such stocks. This means that a firm's inventories will consist of different batches of deliveries, valued at different purchase costs.

Even in a supermarket, it is not always possible to distinguish between different batches of the same product on the shelves (some of the inventories are likely to have been purchased by the business at different prices from its different suppliers). Supermarkets use a **stock rotation** system whereby the newest stocks go to the back of the shelves to ensure that the older batches are bought first. It is particularly important for perishable stocks, such as fresh milk or eggs, to be rotated on a last in, last out basis. This helps to prevent older stocks going out of date, which would mean the product becomes unfit for sale. However, for financial controllers, measuring the cost of such stocks can become a problem if the batches were bought at different prices.

The dilemma facing financial controllers of a business is how to measure the cost value of stocks. There are two main methods of stock valuation: **LIFO** (last in, first out) and **FIFO** (first in, first out).

Last in, first out (LIFO)

This method of stock valuation involves using the most recent batches of stocks first. It is a suitable method for businesses that do not need to rotate their stocks since there is no 'sell by' (expiry) date on the stocks, such as supplies of coal, copper, aluminium and oil. The result is that the older stock, which is usually valued at a lower cost, will remain, i.e. closing stock is valued at a lower value. The implication of this is that there may be some tax benefits. To explain this, consider the way in which we calculate the Cost of Goods Sold (COGS) and gross profit:

Cost of goods sold = Opening stock + Purchases – Closing stock

and

Gross profit = Sales revenue – COGS

Hence, if closing stock is low, then the COGS will tend to be higher. Since gross profit is calculated from sales revenue less COGS, then a higher COGS value will result in a lower figure for gross profit. This has the benefit of less corporation tax being applied to the business, although there is no fundamental difference to the business in using this method of stock valuation. Similarly, on the revenue side, prices may have risen due to inflationary pressure, so the use of LIFO can help to raise the value of COGS, thereby reducing tax liabilities.

Businesses that use the LIFO approach generally have quite large inventories, for which costs are likely to rise steadily in the future. This is because tax payments will fall during times when inventory costs are rising, assuming all other factors remain constant.

The method is best explained through a numerical example. Suppose that Gadgets-R-Us makes gadgets for teenage children for which they charge an average price of $50. The cost of stock varies from week to week since its supplier operates in a foreign country so costs are exposed to exchange rate fluctuations. Its transactions and production schedules for March are as follows:

1st March:	30 units bought @ $25 per unit
5th March:	20 units issued for production @ $25 per unit
8th March:	20 units bought @ $30 per unit
10th March:	15 units issued for production

The stock valuation for Gadgets-R-Us in using LIFO is shown in Table 3.5c.

HIGHER LEVEL

Table 3.5c Stock valuation using LIFO method for Gadgets-R-Us

Date	Stock bought	Stock issued	Remaining Stock	Stock valuation	
1st March	30 units @ $25 p/u		30 × $25		$750
5th March		20 units @ $25 p/u	10 × $25		$250
8th March	20 units @ $30 p/u		10 units @ $25 20 units @ $30	$250 $600	$850
10th March		15 units @ $30 p/u	10 units @ $25 5 units @ $30	$250 $150	$400

Explanation of Table 3.5c (LIFO):

- At the beginning of March, Gadgets-R-Us bought 30 units of stock at $25 each; therefore the stock valuation is $750.
- Four days later, 20 units were required for production. This means there are 10 units of stock remaining, valued at $250.
- On 8th March, the firm paid its supplier for the delivery of another 20 units. However, adverse exchange rate movements mean that each unit now costs $30, therefore giving a valuation of $600. Once this is added to the opening stock of $250, the stock valuation as at 8th March is $850.
- On 10th March, 15 units are issued for production. The LIFO method means that all 15 units issued are valued at $30 (the most current cost value). This leaves 5 units left, valued at $30 each, giving a valuation of $150. Once added to the unused batch of the earlier stock, valued at $250, the stock valuation as at the close of business on 10th March is $400.
- The total value of stocks purchased equals $1,350 (i.e. $750 on 1st March and another $600 on 8th March).

First in, first out (FIFO)

This is a method of stock valuation whereby stock is valued based on the order in which it was purchased by the business, i.e. last in, last out. This method ensures that any unsold stock is more realistically valued at its current or replacement cost, i.e. closing stock is valued at the most recent purchase cost. It is therefore suitable for businesses that regularly rotate their stocks.

The benefit of using FIFO is that the value of a firm's stocks (as shown on the balance sheet) is more realistic and representative of the current market value of stocks. However, this method will boost the value of gross profit compared to using LIFO, which will therefore lead to demands for higher tax by the government. Higher profit figures can also lead to shareholders demanding higher dividend payments.

Keeping with the example of Gadgets-R-Us, if the firm used the FIFO method of stock valuation the figures would be as shown in Table 3.5d. Recall the following information:

1st March:	30 units bought @ $25 per unit
5th March:	20 units issued for production
8th March:	20 units bought @ $30 per unit
10th March:	15 units issued for production

Table 3.5d Stock valuation using FIFO method for Gadgets-R-Us

Date	Stock bought	Stock issued	Remaining Stock	Stock valuation	
1st March	30 units @ $25 p/u		30 × $25		$750
5th March		20 units @ $25 p/u	10 × $25		$250
8th March	20 units @ $30 p/u		10 units @ $25 20 units @ $30	$250 $600	$850
10th March		10 units @ $25 p/u 5 units @ $30 p/u	15 units @ $30	$450	$450

So, comparing the two methods, the closing stock values as at 10th March are:

LIFO = $400 FIFO = $450

Recall that the gadgets sell for $50 each. Given that Gadgets-R-Us has sold 35 units, the total revenue is $1,750. The impact on profits of using different stock control methods is shown in Table 3.5e.

Table 3.5e Effect of LIFO and FIFO on the trading account

Trading Account for Gadgets-R-Us (up to 10th March)				
		LIFO ($)		FIFO ($)
Sales		1,750		1,750
Cost of goods sold				
Purchases	1,350		1,350	
Closing stock	400		450	
		950		900
Gross profit		**800**		**850**

As can be seen from Table 3.5e, LIFO and FIFO yield different values for closing stock for the same business, and therefore have different effects on the firm's gross profit figure. As mentioned earlier, the LIFO method will generate a larger value for COGS and therefore will result in a lower gross profit figure (beneficial for tax purposes). Of course, if prices are falling over time then the opposite effects would be true.

Choosing between LIFO and FIFO

If there were no price increases over time (i.e. no inflation), the stock valuation using either LIFO or FIFO would give the same results. However, in reality, inventory prices tend to rise over time due to inflation. This then makes the choice of stock valuation method important since it can affect the reported level of profits.

However, once a particular method is chosen, laws prevent businesses from switching between LIFO and FIFO methods (such as using LIFO during inflationary times and FIFO during periods when prices fall). Presenting the final accounts by using LIFO for the government (to benefit from tax reductions) means that the company also has to use LIFO when reporting final accounts to shareholders (who will be less pleased with relatively lower levels of profits).

In some countries, such as the UK and Canada, businesses are not generally permitted to use LIFO for tax purposes, although this practice is allowed in other countries such as the USA. The important thing for a business is to use a consistent method in reporting the final accounts, year after year.

Exam Tip!
Worked example

The inventory for Boyd Wines Company (BWC) is shown below. The market price per unit is $20.

Month	Stock purchased (units)	Cost p/u ($)	Stock issued (units)	Value of stock purchased ($)
January	1,000	10	1,000	10,000
February	1,000	11	1,000	11,000
March	1,000	12	1,000	12,000
Total	3,000			33,000

Note: Opening stock in January = 1,000 units at $9 each (giving a total of 4,000 units in the given time period).

Question: Using LIFO and FIFO stock valuation methods, construct a profit and loss account to show the effects on BWC's trading profit.*[6 marks]*

Answer:

Profit and Loss Account for BWC (simplified: Jan–Mar)

	LIFO ($)	FIFO ($)	Notes
Sales	60,000	60,000	3,000 units sold @ $20 each
Opening stock	9,000	9,000	1,000 units @ $9 each
Purchases	33,000	33,000	$10k + $11k + $12k = $33,000
Closing stock	9,000*	12,000#	
COGS	33,000	30,000	COGS = Opening + Purchases – Closing stock
Gross profit	**27,000**	**30,000**	Gross profit = Sales – COGS

* LIFO uses the most recent units bought and hence the oldest inventories remain, i.e. 1,000 units @ $9 = $9,000

\# FIFO uses the oldest units first, leaving the newest inventories for closing stock, i.e. 1,000 units @ $12 = $12,000.

Question 3.5.8

Crystal Arts

Crystal Arts is a producer of expensive crystal chandeliers. Each chandelier sells for $1,000. During this month, the firm has taken orders for 15 chandeliers. It has 10 units as **opening stock**, purchased at a cost of $500 each. Crystal Arts replenishes its stock by ordering another 10 units, but inflation has raised costs to $600 per unit. Operating expenses are $1,000 per month and the rate of corporation tax is 30%.

a Define the term **opening stock**. *[2 marks]*

b Using both LIFO and FIFO methods of stock valuation, construct a simplified Profit and Loss account for Crystal Arts to show the effects on gross profit and net profit. *[8 marks]*

WINDOW DRESSING

Final accounts must be handled with some caution. Since there is no single accounting standard that is universally accepted, accountants can be creative in the compilation of final accounts. **Creative accounting**, or **window dressing**, is the legal manipulation of accounting statements based on the accounting principles and rules of that country in order to make the figures look more flattering. Examples might include:

- Show an overdraft that is repayable after twelve months as a long-term liability to improve the working capital figure of the business. This is perfectly legal since, in practice, the firm could apply for an extension in repaying the overdraft.
- A firm wishing to window dress its accounts would include a realistically optimistic valuation of its intangible assets. In other words, *how* firms treat and value intangible assets will affect the values shown in their balance sheets.
- Using sale and leaseback (see Unit 3.1) just before the final accounts are due will show a sudden hike in the liquidity position of a firm, although leasing fixed assets will cost the company more in the long run. Similarly, some fixed assets might be sold just before the reporting date in order to improve working capital.
- Outstanding loans and other bills that are about to be paid off may be postponed until a few days after the date of the accounts. This allows a firm to benefit from tax concessions due to the lower profits that are reported.
- Declare sales revenues (in the P&L account) for items paid on credit for which payment has yet to be received. This will boost the profit figures of the company, much to the delight of its shareholders.
- The choice of method will affect the reported value of fixed assets (straight-line versus declining balance methods of depreciating fixed assets – covered earlier in this Unit). In addition, delaying depreciation charges until after the balance sheet date will mean a higher reported value for the firm's fixed assets.
- Use LIFO and FIFO methods of stock valuation to affect the reported level of gross profit.

Creative accounting does not cover illegal misrepresentation of financial records. Instead, this would be classed as fraudulent and unlawful.

It is important to be aware of creative accounting since it can hide shortcomings in a firm's financial performance. For example, window dressing to make working capital look more impressive does not actually do anything to solve the underlying liquidity problem.

Limitations of final accounts

In addition to window dressing, when looking at financial accounts it is important to consider the following limitations:

- A set of final accounts must be used together. Using a single account in isolation is of no value since there is no way of judging financial performance. Instead, a series of accounts would be more useful to show any trends over time.
- Human resources are totally ignored. It is often argued that people are an organization's most valuable asset, yet this is not represented in the final accounts. The skills, creativity, loyalty and motivation of staff are overlooked in financial analyses. The inability to retain or motivate staff can have major repercussions on the future financial position of a firm.
- Final accounts do not reveal anything about the organization's non-financial matters. Qualitative factors can be equally important when making decisions. For example, ethical objectives and the location of industry are affected by both financial and non-financial factors.

- There needs to be access to the accounts of other businesses in order to benchmark performance (see Unit 5.4).
- Whilst final accounts must be lawfully produced, it does not mean that they report the whole truth. Companies will limit, within reason, the financial information that they reveal since their accounts will be in the public domain and hence accessible by their rivals. This means that final accounts must be treated with some caution.
- Profit and Loss accounts, Balance sheets, and Cash flow statements are a historical account of the financial position of an organization. Past performance is not necessarily indicative of current or future performance. By contrast, management accounts (for internal use only) are forward looking, but these are not disclosed to external stakeholders or the general public.

FINAL ACCOUNTS AND BUSINESS STRATEGY

Companies that produce their own set of final accounts must have these audited by an external verifier. **Auditing** is the process of examining an organization's financial statements to ensure that they give an accurate and truthful view of the financial position of the business.

A valuable business strategy is to develop the intellectual property rights (IPR) of an organization. The use of IPR, such as patents and copyrights, can act as an effective form of barrier to entry. Global businesses such as Coca-Cola, McDonald's, Toyota and The Walt Disney Company have used IPR to erect artificial entry barriers to protect their market share. Aristotle Onassis, a Greek business mogul, once said that the secret to corporate success is to know or have something that no-one else does. This means that innovation and new product development (see Unit 4.3) are important business strategies for long-term survival of the business. The legal protection of new products, designs and processes can therefore help to boost the value on a firm's balance sheet. In today's evermore competitive environment, many organizations no longer see IPR as a defensive strategy, but rather as an offensive business strategy for corporate success.

However, one problem facing multinationals is that different countries have different laws governing IPR (i.e. intangible assets). The United Nation's World Intellectual Property Organization (WIPO) has gone some way to encourage and promote the protection of IPR around the world. However, non-complying and non-participating countries, such as Taiwan, present somewhat of a challenge for multinationals and the WIPO. The accusation by the USA of China's poor governance of IPR is another example.

When looking at the final accounts of a business, it is useful to consider the working capital and liquidity of the organization (see Unit 3.3). The balance sheet will reveal the ability of the firm to meet its daily running costs. Indeed, the balance sheet and profit and loss accounts are often used by a business to secure external funding for growth and expansion (see Unit 1.7).

In addition, when analysing the final accounts of a firm, *ratio analysis* is usually used (see Unit 3.6). This is a set of management tools for analysing and judging the financial performance of a business by using historical and inter-firm comparisons of key financial information. Ratio analysis can help a firm to better gauge its level of profitability, efficiency and liquidity.

Ultimately, the final accounts are important for two key reasons: disclosure and accountability of financial matters of the business. Used correctly, they can reveal the profit quality of a business. If profit has been reported due to a one-off sale of fixed assets such as land and property, then there is likely to be low profit quality. Conversely, high profit quality can be seen if the final accounts reveal a series of healthy trading profit figures.

Finally, as always with quantitative techniques, it is important to look beyond the financial figures. When evaluating financial data, managers will consider qualitative issues such as organizational objectives (see Unit 1.3) and the state of the economy (see Unit 1.5). Moreover, the final accounts are only one part of the quantitative analyses required to give an accurate appraisal of the financial position of a business. Budgeting (see Unit 3.4) is an important consideration for the daily operation of a business, whilst investment appraisal (see Unit 3.2) looks at the financial returns on growth and expansion plans. As such, the importance of any single financial statement should be handled with prudence. Nevertheless, the careful use of the Balance sheet, Profit & Loss account and Cash flow statement of a business can certainly give a clearer overall impression of its financial health.

REVIEW QUESTIONS 3.5

1 Name the three final accounts that all companies are obliged to report to their shareholders.

2 Distinguish between 'financial accounting' and 'management accounting'.

3 Outline four stakeholder groups that might make use of financial accounts.

4 What is an 'income statement'?

5 What are the uses of a profit and loss account?

6 What is 'profit quality'?

7 Outline the difference between 'gross profit' and 'operating profit'.

8 What are the three ways to appropriate net profits?

9 What is a 'balance sheet' and why it is said to be a static financial document?

10 What is 'window dressing'?

11 Outline four limitations of final accounts.

Higher Level extension

12 Why do firms depreciate the value of their fixed assets?

13 Distinguish between the 'reducing balance' and the 'straight-line method' of depreciation.

14 Describe three examples of intangible assets.

15 Distinguish between LIFO and FIFO as methods of stock valuation.

Appropriation account refers to the final section of a profit and loss account which shows how the net profits of a business are distributed. Profits are appropriated in three ways: taxation, dividends and retained profits.

Balance sheet refers to the financial statement showing a firm's assets and liabilities at a specific point in time. It shows the sources of funds, such as long-term loans and owners' equity, which must be balanced with the uses of funds, such as the purchase of fixed assets.

Book value is the value of an asset as shown on a balance sheet. The market value of assets may be higher than its book value because of intangible assets, such as the reputation and brand value of the business.

Capital employed is the value of all long-term sources of finance for a business, such as bank loans, share capital and any reserves that the business holds. This represents the total amount of capital available to business.

Cost of goods sold (COGS) is shown in the Trading Account section of a Profit and Loss Account. It represents the direct costs of producing or purchasing a particular level of stock that has actually been sold to customers. The term is also known as the **cost of sales** or the **cost of stock sold**.

Depreciation is the fall in the value of fixed assets over time, such as motor vehicles, computers or machinery. The main cause of depreciation is wear and tear (loss of value due to the asset being used) although some assets can become obsolete (outdated or out of fashion).

Final accounts, also known as **published accounts**, are the annual financial statements that all limited companies are legally obliged by the authorities to report. These include the Balance Sheet and the Trading, Profit and Loss Accounts.

First in, first out (FIFO) is a method of stock valuation whereby stock is valued based on the order in which it was purchased by the business. This method ensures that any unsold stock is more realistically valued at its replacement cost.

Fixed assets are items of monetary value that are owned by a business but are not intended to be sold within the next twelve months. They can be used repeatedly to generate revenue for the business. Examples include land, premises and machinery.

Goodwill is when the value of a firm exceeds its book value (the value of the firm's net assets). It is an example of an intangible asset. Examples of goodwill include the value of a firm's business contacts (customer base and suppliers) and its reputation. Goodwill therefore raises the value of a business.

Gross profit is the difference between the sales revenue of a business and its direct costs incurred in manufacturing or purchasing the products that have been sold to its customers. Gross profit is calculated by using sales revenue minus the cost of goods sold. Gross profit is also called **trading profit**.

Intangible assets are a type of fixed asset but do not exist in a physical form. Examples include: goodwill, copyrights, brand names and registered trademarks.

Last in, first out (LIFO) is method of stock valuation that uses the most recent batches of stock first. It is a suitable method for stock that does not need to be rotated, i.e. it has a very long shelf life. This method raises the value of cost of goods sold, thereby giving some tax benefits as gross profits will be relatively lower.

Net assets show the value of a business by calculating the value of all its assets minus the long-term liabilities. It is often referred to as **assets employed** and represents the use of funds.

Net profit is the surplus (if any) that a business makes after all expenses (indirect costs) have been paid for out of gross profit. It is therefore calculated by taking expenses away from the gross profit figure.

Profit and Loss Account is a financial statement of a firm's trading activity over a period of time (the balance sheet by contrast shows the financial position of the business at a specific point in time). The profit and loss account is split into three parts: the Trading Account, the Profit and Loss Account and the Appropriation Account.

Shareholders' funds show the sources of finance of a firm less its long-term liabilities. It includes the capital invested by shareholders (known as share capital), retained profit plus any reserves which it may have accumulated over time.

Trading account appears at the top section of the Profit and Loss Account and shows the difference between a firm's sales revenue and its direct costs of trading. In essence, the trading account is used to show the gross profit of a business.

Window dressing, also known as **creative accounting**, refers to the legal act of manipulating financial information to make the results look more flattering.

Ratio Analysis

UNIT 3.6

Many of the things you can count, don't count. Many of the things you can't count, really count.

Albert Einstein (1879–1955), Nobel Prize for Physics

Key topics

- The purpose of ratio analysis
- Types of financial ratios
- Financial ratios: profitability ratios, liquidity ratios, efficiency ratios, gearing ratio
- Uses and limitations of ratio analysis

Higher Level extension

- Efficiency ratios: debtor days and creditor days
- Shareholders ratios: earnings per share and dividend yield

Note: Ratio formulae are given in the first Appendix item of the Syllabus Guide and a copy of which will be provided to candidates in the examinations. (© IBO 2007)

INTRODUCTION

In its simplest sense, a ratio is one number expressed in terms of another. For example, suppose that in an organization there are 50 employees, 30 of whom are females. This means that the male to female ratio is 2:3, i.e. for every two male employees, there are three female employees. **Ratio analysis** is a management tool for analysing and judging the financial performance of a business. This is done by calculating financial ratios from a firm's final accounts (namely the balance sheet and the profit and loss account).

In order to assess whether financial performance has improved, figures are normally compared with the previous years' figures, expressed as a ratio. Alternatively, the same figures can be compared to those of competitors to judge whether the business has improved against its rivals.

This Unit examines the various types of financial ratios, their uses and limitations.

Exam Tip!

Don't just simply learn the formulae for the ratios without *understanding* what they actually mean. Instead focus on *why* or *how* the ratios could be used in the context of the given organization. Address issues such as:

- How the business is performing (based on financial grounds)
- How the business has performed over time (trends)
- What else needs to be considered that is not presented in the data, such as business objectives and external constraints on business activity.

THE PURPOSE OF RATIO ANALYSIS

Ratio analysis serves several purposes:

- To aid analysis of a firm's financial position, such as its short-term and long-term liquidity positions
- To assess a firm's financial performance, such as its ability to control expenses
- To compare actual figures with projected or budgeted figures (known as variance analysis)
- To aid decision-making, such as whether investors should risk their money in the business.

Ratios are compared in two ways:

- *Historical comparisons* involve comparing the *same ratio* in two different time periods for the *same business*. Such comparisons over time show *trends* which, in turn, help managers to assess the financial performance of a business.
- *Inter-firm comparisons* involve comparing the ratios of businesses in the *same industry*. For example, two businesses may have the same amount of profit although their sales revenue might be quite different. Ratio analysis can therefore show the relative financial performance of a business.

In reality, firms will use both historical and inter-firm comparisons when analysing their financial ratios. However, it is important to remember that the exercise of comparing financial ratios is only of real use if managers compare *like with like*. For example, McDonald's should only compare their financial ratios with rivals of similar size in the same industry. There is little value in McDonald's comparing their financial ratios against a sole trader who runs a fast-food restaurant or comparing the figures to manufacturers of furniture.

Exam Tip!
When learning the different financial ratios, make sure that you understand the various *units of measurement* used. Some ratios will be expressed as a number in terms of another (e.g. 2:1), whilst others are shown as a percentage, or a currency (e.g. $1 per share) and yet others may be shown as 'number of days'. The important thing is to understand the meaning of the ratio and to be able to put the ratio into context.

TYPES OF FINANCIAL RATIOS

There are five types of ratios, all of which are examined in more detail in the next section. Ratios can fall into the following categories:

- **Profitability ratios** examine profit in relation to other figures, such as the ratio of profit to sales revenue. Profitability ratios help to assess the financial performance of a business. These ratios will tend to be relevant to profit-seeking businesses rather than for not-for-profit organizations. Managers, employees and potential creditors and investors will be interested in these ratios since they show how well a firm has performed in financial terms.
- **Liquidity ratios** look at the ability of a firm to pay its short-term liabilities, such as by comparing working capital to short-term debts. Creditors and financial lenders will be interested in these ratios to help them assess the likelihood of getting back the money they are owed. Shareholders and potential investors may also be interested in these ratios since they may reveal a firm's ability to repay its debts.
- **Efficiency ratios** show how well a firm's resources are used. For example, a business may wish to calculate the average number of days it takes to collect money from its debtors or how long it takes for a firm to sell its stocks. Supermarkets will sell their stock faster than luxury jewellers, for instance.
- **Shareholders ratios** measure the returns to shareholders in a company. Shareholders will be interested in the dividends they earn in relation to the purchase price of the shares. Potential shareholders will be interested in the possible earnings of each share.
- **Gearing ratio** looks at the long-term liquidity position of a firm. Creditors and investors will be interested in the level of gearing of a firm. A high degree of gearing could mean inadequate long-term liquidity since the firm is committed to repaying its loans with interest to financial lenders. Highly geared firms are also considered to be risky businesses since they are more vulnerable to increases in interest rates due to their large debts.

Exam Tip!
Examination questions have typically asked students to use financial ratios to comment on a firm's:

a Profitability.
b Liquidity position.
c Efficiency position.
d Gearing.
e Ability to satisfy shareholders.

These are the main categories of ratios! Make sure that you know their meaning and the different types of ratios within each category.

PROFITABILITY RATIOS

Profit is a key objective for most businesses and acts as a measure of a firm's success. Profit is defined as the surplus earnings of a firm once all costs have been deducted from sales revenue. Profitability ratios measure profit in relation to other variables such as sales turnover or capital employed. The main profitability ratios are the gross profit margin (GPM) and net profit margin (NPM).

The absolute amount of profit, as declared in a profit and loss account, tells us little about the financial performance of a business (see Exam Tip below). For example, if a business makes $1 million profit is this seen as being financially successful? The answer might be 'yes' for a small partnership selling computer accessories but the answer would be a definite 'no' for a much larger business such as Dell or IBM. We can draw this conclusion when comparing the ratio of profit to the huge sales turnover of, or the amount invested by, Dell and IBM. Hence, to assess the profitability of a business, it is important to compare and relate profit to other financial aspects of the business. A key limitation of using profitability ratios is that the ratios only apply to profit-orientated businesses.

Exam Tip!
When dealing with finance, it is important to look at the bigger picture and put the figures into context. Take the following example. In February 2007, Puma (the sportswear manufacturer) announced a 26% drop in its profits to €38.2 million ($43 million). Does this represent poor performance? Not necessarily. This very limited information can, on its own, be misleading. In fact, Puma was undergoing expansion and was using its profits to finance the growth (hence the fall in its declared profits). Puma's sales had actually increased by more than 33%.

Gross profit margin (GPM)

The ratio for gross profit margin shows the value of gross profit as a percentage of sales revenue. The figures for working out the GPM can be found in the firm's profit and loss account and by using the formula:

$$\text{GPM} = \frac{\text{Gross profit}}{\text{Sales revenue}} \times 100$$

The GPM ratio is expressed as a percentage. For example, if a business has a gross profit of $120 million from sales of $200 million, then the GPM is 60%. This figure shows that for every $100 of sales, $60 is gross profit (with direct costs of production accounting for the other $40). Clearly, the higher the GPM ratio, the better it is for a business as gross profit goes towards paying the overheads and expenses of the business.

Gross profit margin can be improved by financial and non-financial strategies in two main ways.

- **Raising revenue**
  - Increasing the selling price for *price inelastic* products (see Unit 4.4) – If customers are not highly responsive to changes in price, due to there being a lack of substitutes for example, the firm can gain more sales revenue by raising price.
  - Decrease the selling price for *price elastic* products – If there are many rival products, then the firm may gain a competitive advantage by reducing its prices.
  - Marketing strategies to raise sales revenue – Strategies such as sales promotion (see Unit 4.5) may be used to try and boost sales.
  - Producing or selling products with a higher gross profit margin – This will enable the firm to gain a higher amount of gross profit per unit sold, thereby raising its GPM ratio.

- **Reducing costs**
  - Reduce direct material costs – This might be achieved by, perhaps, using cheaper suppliers or by using cheaper materials. Airline companies, for example, have saved millions of dollars each year by cutting back on the number of chocolates or olives that they offer onboard. However, cost cutting may have a negative impact on the perceived quality of the product.
  - Reduce direct labour costs – This strategy will involve reducing the cost of staffing by reducing the number of staff or by getting staff to do more (for the same pay). Either way, the productivity of staff may increase, thereby reducing unit labour costs. However, this strategy may cause resentment and a lack of motivation among the workforce.

In reality, a business is likely to strive to raise GPM by a combination of strategies to reduce costs and to raise revenues.

Net profit margin (NPM)

Net profit margin shows the percentage of sales turnover that is turned into net profit. For example, a NPM ratio of 35% means that for every \$100 of sales, \$35 is net profit. This is the profit that is left after all costs of production (both direct and indirect costs) have been accounted for. The formula for working out NPM is:

$$\text{NPM} = \frac{\text{Net profit}}{\text{Sales revenue}} \times 100$$

Note: If required, it is common practice to use 'Net Profit *before* interest and tax' to calculate the NPM. This is because it allows historical comparisons to be made, since net profits are subject to change caused by fluctuating interest and tax rates (factors that are beyond the control of a business).

The NPM ratio is a better measure of a firm's profitability since it accounts for both cost of sales and expenses. The difference between a firm's GPM and its NPM represents the expenses; therefore, the larger the difference between these two ratios, the more difficult overhead control tends to be. As with the GPM, the general rule is that the higher the NPM ratio, the better it is for the firm. A higher net profit margin means that firms will have more profit to distribute to shareholders and to reinvest in the business.

It is common for high volume products, such as confectionery and fast food, to have a relatively low profit margin. However, the high sales volume compensates for this. Conversely, for low volume products, such as aircraft and luxury wines, the profit margin tends to be relatively high to compensate for the lower number of sales.

Net profit margin can be improved by financial and non-financial strategies such as those mentioned above for the gross profit margin. However, costs can be examined further to reduce business expenses. For example, it may be possible to:

- Negotiate preferential payment terms with creditors and suppliers – By delaying payment, for example, a business may be able to improve its working capital. Alternatively, it may be possible to negotiate discounts for paying creditors on time.
- Negotiate cheaper rent – Trustworthy and creditable businesses may be able to negotiate lower rents or delay payment of rent to improve their cash flow.
- Reduce indirect expenses – An examination of the structure of business expenses may reveal areas where costs can be cut without creating damaging effects to a business. For example, many businesses no longer allow their senior managers to fly on first-class air travel, choosing business-class or economy-class travel instead. A business may also investigate whether other overheads can be reduced, such as advertising, stationery and insurance premiums.

To calculate financial ratios, such as the GPM and the NPM, it is usually necessary to use a **Balance Sheet** and a **Profit and Loss Account** (see Unit 3.5). For illustrative purposes, the numerical questions that follow in the rest of this Unit will refer to the figures given in Tables 3.6a and 3.6b for JKL Ltd., a fictitious textiles company.

Table 3.6a Balance Sheet for JKL Ltd. as at 31 December (figures in $'000s)

	Year 2	Year 1
Fixed Assets	600	500
Current Assets:		
Stocks	350	250
Debtors	150	200
Cash	200	50
	700	500
Less Current Liabilities	300	200
Net Current Assets	400	300
Assets Employed*	**1,000**	**800**
Financed by:		
Ordinary share capital (@ $2 per share)	500	500
Retained profits	250	50
Debentures	250	250
Capital Employed	**1,000**	**800**

* Assets employed = Fixed Assets plus Net Current Assets

Table 3.6b Excerpts from Profit and Loss Account for JKL Ltd. for years ending 31 December ($'000s)

	Year 2	Year 1
Sales Turnover	1,000	850
Cost of Sales	500	450
Net Profit before Interest & Tax	400	360
Tax	100	90
Dividend	50	220
Retained Profits	250	50

Question 3.6.1

a State the value of JKL Ltd.'s gross profit and its expenses for Year 2. *[2 marks]*

b Calculate the GPM and the NPM ratios for JKL Ltd. in both years (show your working) and explain your findings. *[6 marks]*

c Comment on further information that could be used to analyse the profitability of the firm. *[4 marks]*

Question: Explain how a price reduction for a product could reduce the gross profit margin (GPM), but actually boost the net profit margin (NPM). Use a numerical example to help explain your answer.

Answer:
For example:

	Before ($)	After ($)	
Turnover	1,000	1,200	
Cost of goods sold	600	740	
Gross profit	400	460	
GPM	40.0%	38.3%	↓
Indirect costs	300	300	
Net profit	100	160	
NPM	10.0%	13.3%	↑

The fall in price will automatically reduce the profit margin, other things being equal. However, the price reduction has attracted more customers and since indirect costs are constant, the NPM has increased.

LIQUIDITY RATIOS

It might be quite easy to sell off buildings and vehicles quickly, but only by simply offering these at hugely discounted prices. However, this would generally be highly undesirable. Liquidity ratios assume that certain assets of a business can be turned into cash quickly, without losing their value, in order to meet its financial commitments. These assets are known as **liquid assets** and can be in the form of cash itself (either as cash in hand or cash at the bank) or as assets that can be turned into cash quickly and easily (such as finished goods, ready for sale).

Short-term liquidity ratios calculate how easily a firm can pay its short-term financial obligations from its current assets. These are important ratios as they reveal the level of liquidity with which firms can meet their everyday financial obligations. The two main short-term liquidity ratios are considered in more detail below.

Current ratio

The current ratio deals with the liquid assets and short-term liabilities of a firm, i.e. its working capital. It shows the relationship between a firm's current assets and its current liabilities, and is calculated by the formula:

$$\frac{\text{Current Assets}}{\text{Current Liabilities}}$$

The ratio helps to reveal whether a firm is able to use its liquid assets to cover its short-term debts. For example, if a business has current assets (cash, debtors and stocks) of $300,000 and current liabilities (such as overdrafts and trade creditors) of $120,000, then the current ratio would be 2.5:1. This means that for every $1 of current liabilities, the firm has $2.5 of current (liquid) assets.

It is generally accepted that a current ratio of 1.5 to 2.0 is desirable. This is to allow for a safety margin because in reality it may not be possible to sell assets quickly without losing some value.

It also means that there is likely to be sufficient working capital. Clearly, if the current ratio is below 1:1, that means the short-term debts of a business are greater than its liquid assets, which could spell disaster for its survival if creditors demand payment. Equally though, a firm can have *too high* a current ratio. A high current ratio suggests that there is too much cash (which could be better spent in generating more trade), too many debtors (which increases the likelihood of bad debts) or too much stock (which increases storage and insurance costs). Nevertheless, it is always important to put ratios into context. Supermarkets that hold a huge amount of stock, for example, may have a current ratio of over 2:1 but this is acceptable as its stocks are highly liquid.

The current ratio can be improved by a combination of raising the value of current assets and reducing the value of current liabilities. For example, overdrafts can be reduced by securing long-term loans that offer more attractive rates of interest. This will also free up working capital in the short term. However, this option may, of course, affect the long-term liquidity of the firm.

Acid test ratio (quick ratio)

The acid test ratio, also known as the quick ratio, is similar to the current ratio except that it ignores stock when measuring the short-term liquidity of a business. The formula for calculating this is:

$$\frac{\text{Current Assets less Stock}}{\text{Current Liabilities}}$$

Many people argue that this approach is more meaningful than the current ratio because stocks cannot always be easily converted into cash, i.e. not all stocks are highly liquid assets. For example, *work-in-progress* (semi-finished) goods do not have much *value added*, so will not fetch a very good price. Highly expensive stock, such as Boeing jumbo jets, also cannot be turned into cash quickly.

As a general guideline, it is recommended that the acid test ratio should be at least 1:1. A quick ratio figure of less than 1:1 suggests that the firm may experience working capital difficulties or a **liquidity crisis** (a situation where a firm is unable to pay its short-term debts). As with the current ratio, too high an acid test figure may suggest that the firm is holding onto too much cash rather than using it more effectively. As always, however, this ratio must be put into the context of the business and the industry in which it operates.

Potential investors and short-term lenders, such as banks, are likely to be interested in a firm's acid test ratio. Since the ratio measures the ability of a firm to cover short-term debts with its cash and debtors, this will help reduce the level of risk exposed by investors and lenders.

Mathematically, the quick ratio can be improved by either raising the level of current assets (cash or debtors) or lowering the amount of current liabilities. It can be dangerous for a firm to increase debtors since this increases the likelihood of bad debts being incurred. There is also a potentially large opportunity cost in holding too much cash. Therefore, a business is most likely to concentrate on reducing the level of short-term liabilities, such as overdrafts and creditors. It may be possible, for example, to negotiate delayed payment to creditors.

Question 3.6.2

- **a** Refer to the accounts for JKL Ltd. shown in Tables 3.6a and 3.6b and calculate the current ratio and acid test ratio for both years. *[4 marks]*
- **b** Comment on the liquidity position of JKL Ltd. *[4 marks]*
- **c** Explain what other information would be needed in order to judge the liquidity position of JKL Ltd. *[4 marks]*

EFFICIENCY RATIOS

Efficiency ratios look at how well a firm's financial resources are being used. There are four main efficiency ratios: *stock turnover, return on capital employed, debtor days* and *creditor days*.

Stock turnover

The stock turnover ratio measures the number of times a firm sells its stocks within a time period, usually one year. The ratio therefore indicates the speed at which a firm sells and replenishes all its stock. There are two alternative ways to calculate stock turnover:

$$\frac{\text{Cost of goods sold}}{\text{Average stock}}$$

or

$$\frac{\text{Average stock}}{\text{Cost of goods sold}} \times 365$$

When looking at stock turnover, *cost of sales* is used rather than sales turnover since stocks are always valued at *cost* of purchase rather than selling *price*. For example, if a business has *cost of goods sold* equal to $100,000 and an *average stock level* valued at $20,000, the stock turnover ratio is 5 times a year (or every 73 days on average). This means that the business sells all of its stock, which is then replenished, five times a year. In general, the higher the ratio the better it is for the business. This is because the higher the stock turnover, the more stock is being sold and therefore the more profit the firm is likely to generate. In addition, a high stock turnover ensures that perishable stocks do not expire and durable stocks do not become outdated.

There are several ways to increase the stock turnover ratio:

- Holding lower levels of stock will require stocks to be replenished more regularly which can have both advantages and disadvantages (see Unit 5.7).
- Divestment (dispose) of any stocks that are slow to sell, such as unpopular product lines or obsolete stock.
- Reduce the range of products that is being stocked by only keeping the better selling products.

When comparing this ratio, it is important (as always) to compare like with like. Different businesses will have different benchmark figures for stock turnover. For example, a restaurant should expect a significantly higher stock turnover figure than a supplier of luxury motor vehicles. A stock turnover rate of 5 is perhaps acceptable to suppliers of consumer durables, but unacceptable to a florist or fresh fish monger. In addition, the figure must be put into context; a low stock turnover rate is not necessarily a bad sign. For example, to have a high stock turnover, businesses may need to hold very little stock but this reduces their ability to benefit from *purchasing economies of scale* (see Unit 1.7).

Return on capital employed (ROCE)

The profit and loss account shows the amount of profit that a business makes at the end of its trading year. However, this figure alone does not have much substance without making inter-firm or historical comparisons. Would a firm that makes $10 million profit have performed well? This depends on how well other firms have performed in the same time period and also on the historical profit levels of the firm. In addition, it would depend on the size of the business itself, as measured by the capital employed. Ten million dollars profit for a small textbook publisher would be very welcome, but the same amount of profit for Sony, Nike or Microsoft would outrage their shareholders.

The return on capital employed (ROCE) is an efficiency ratio that measures the financial performance of a firm compared with the amount of capital invested. ROCE is also an indicator of the profitability of a firm. It is calculated using the formula:

$$\frac{\text{Net profit before interest and tax}}{\text{Capital employed}} \times 100$$

The figure for capital employed can be found on a firm's balance sheet. Capital employed is the sum of shareholders' funds plus reserves plus long-term liabilities. The ROCE figure shows profit as a percentage of the capital used to generate it. The higher the ROCE figure, the better it is for the business. Some sources refer to a 20% ROCE as being a target benchmark, although this needs to be put into the context of the business and the industry in which it operates. A 20% ROCE figure shows that for every $100 invested in the business, $20 profit is generated. As a general rule, the ROCE should at least exceed the interest rate offered at banks; otherwise, it would simply be better to deposit the capital in an interest-bearing bank account. In addition, bank deposits would probably carry less risk compared with other investment projects. Hence, ROCE must be high enough to create an incentive for investors to part with their money.

ROCE is calculated by using *net profit before interest and tax* as this allows for better historical comparisons (since interest and tax rates are subject to change over time and are beyond the control of the business). Many people regard the ROCE as the single most important financial ratio since it measures how well a firm is able to generate profit from its sources of funds. Hence, the ROCE is often referred to as the **key ratio** or the **primary ratio**.

The ROCE ratio can be increased mainly by strategies to boost net profits (see above). In theory, the ratio will also increase if capital employed falls whilst net profits remain constant; although in reality this is probably not desirable.

Question 3.6.3

a Calculate the ROCE ratio for the textile company JKL Ltd. for both years. *[3 marks]*

b Explain what the figures suggest about the efficiency and profitability of JKL Ltd. *[4 marks]*

HIGHER LEVEL

Debtor days (Higher Level extension)

The debtor days ratio, also known as the **debt collection period** measures the number of days it takes a firm, on average, to collect money from its debtors. Debtors are the customers who have purchased items on credit from the business and therefore owe money to the firm. The formula for the debtor days ratio is:

$$\frac{\text{Debtors}}{\text{Sales revenue}} \times 365$$

For example, if a firm's debtors (shown on its balance sheet) totals $1 million whilst its sales turnover is $5 million, then the ratio is 73 days. This means that, on average, it takes the business 73 days to collect debts from its customers who have bought items on credit. The higher the ratio, the longer the credit period customers have. Logically, the less time it takes on average for customers to pay their debts, the better it is for the business. There are two reasons for this: first, the business improves its cash flow if customers are able to pay on time and second, due to the opportunity cost of holding onto the money, the business could invest this money in other revenue-generating projects.

However, a ratio that is too high or too low can also be bad for a business. Although firms may allow customers to buy on credit, it is important that the credit period granted is not too long, otherwise, the businesses may face liquidity problems (see Unit 3.3). Equally, too low a ratio is also undesirable because customers may seek other suppliers if the credit period given to them is uncompetitive. Other things being equal, clients would prefer to purchase from a business that offers better credit terms. A low ratio does mean, however, that the firm receives all the cash from its sales revenue sooner rather than later.

It is quite common to allow customers 30–60 days credit. Hence, it should be possible for a business to collect its money from debtors in this period, making a debtors day ratio of between 30 to 60 days acceptable. Too low a figure may suggest that there are not enough customers buying on credit and too large a figure may damage the firm's cash inflow. The firm's ability to collect debts within a suitable time frame is known as **credit control**. A business is generally seen as having good credit control if it can collect debts within 30–60 days.

Businesses can improve their debt collection period in several ways:

- Impose surcharges on late payers. Banks, utility companies and many other organizations add a fine to those who pay their bills late. In some countries, such as Hong Kong, the government will impose a surcharge on income tax bills for all late payers.
- Give debtors incentives to pay earlier, such as a discount to those who pay their bills before the due date. Many firms now encourage their credit customers to use *direct debit* or *autopay* to settle their bills. These are financial services that involve settling money owed to creditors by using funds directly from the client's bank account on designated days. This saves the customer having to remember when to pay their bills and hence avoiding penalties for late payment.
- Refuse any further business with a client until payment is made. This may include stopping supplies to a customer or suspending an order until payment is received.
- Threaten legal action. The threat of taking a customer to court is a rather more extreme approach but is often used for clients who repeatedly pay late.

As always, it is important to put the ratio into context. Some businesses, such as suppliers of expensive luxury goods, will rely more on credit sales than others. Hence, for these businesses it is more acceptable to have a higher debtor days ratio. Supermarkets, on the other hand, have customers paying for their goods at the time of purchase so their debt collection period would be much lower.

Creditor days (Higher Level extension)

A business may offer its clients credit. Equally, other suppliers may offer the business credit. The creditor days ratio measures the number of days it takes, on average, for a business to pay its creditors. The formula for this ratio is:

$$\frac{\text{Creditors}}{\text{Cost of sales}} \times 365$$

For example, if a firm has $225,000 owed to its suppliers (as seen from its balance sheet) with $1.75 million worth of costs of sales (also known as the *cost of goods sold*), the creditor days is 47 days. This means, that on average, the business takes 47 days to pay its debts to suppliers. It is common to provide customers with 30–60 days credit, and therefore a creditor days ratio in this range would be seen as acceptable.

In general, the higher this ratio, the better it is for the business as it means that repayment is prolonged. This may help to free up cash in the business for other uses in the short term. However, a high ratio may also mean that the business is taking too long to pay its creditors so suppliers may impose financial penalties for late payment. In this case, a high creditor days ratio will harm the firm's cash flow position. Hence, it is important to put the ratio into the context of the industry in which the firm operates.

HIGHER LEVEL

The efficiency position of a firm can be enhanced by improving any of its efficiency ratios, i.e. reducing debtor days and increasing stock turnover and creditor days. Strategies to achieve this might include:

- Develop closer relationships with customers, suppliers and creditors. This should help to reduce debtor days and extend the period of credit.
- Introduce a system of just-in-time production (see Unit 5.7). This should help to reduce the need to hold large amounts of stock and to improve stock control.
- Improve credit control, i.e. reduce the debtor days ratio at the same time as increasing creditor days. This will help to improve the firm's working capital. Giving customers an incentive to pay earlier or on time will also help to reduce the likelihood of experiencing bad debts.

Question 3.6.4

a Calculate the stock turnover, debtor days and creditor days ratios for JKL Ltd. *[6 marks]*

b Given your answer for the above question, evaluate the efficiency position of JKL Ltd. *[8 marks]*

c Analyse the ways in which JKL Ltd. could improve its efficiency position. *[6 marks]*

HIGHER LEVEL

HIGHER LEVEL EXTENSION: SHAREHOLDERS RATIOS

Shareholders generally buy shares in a company for two main reasons:

- **Capital gain** – The difference between the buying and selling price of a company's shares represents the capital gain (or loss). Shareholders hope for an increase in the value of the shares held. Share prices tend to go up if a company is making more profit or the stock market expects the company to do well in the future.
- **Dividend** – This is the payment to shareholders from a company's after-tax profits. The higher the net profit of a firm, the higher the dividend payments tends to be. Dividends are usually paid to shareholders in two instalments each year.

Potential shareholders are likely to use shareholders ratios to assess the worth of a company. This can help them to make more informed choices before buying shares in certain companies. Two key shareholders ratios are the **earnings per share** and the **dividend yield**.

Earnings per share (EPS)

The earnings per share ratio shows the maximum dividends that could, in theory, be paid to shareholders. It is calculated using the formula:

$$\frac{\text{Net profit after interest and tax}}{\text{Number of ordinary shares}}$$

For example, if a business has a net profit after tax of $10 million (seen from its profit and loss account) and has 20 million ordinary shares issued (seen from its balance sheet), then the firm's EPS is $0.50. This means that each ordinary share can earn a maximum dividend of 50 cents. This, however, assumes that the firm chooses not to retain any profit but to pay out all after-tax profits to its shareholders. Hence, the EPS figure is unlikely to materialize, although the higher the EPS ratio the higher will be the probability of shareholders receiving a large dividend payout per share. The ratio can therefore give a good indication of the value of the company's shares. It is called earnings per share since the ratio shows how much each share has earned for its owners (recall that retained profit of a company also belongs to its owners even though it is used for reinvestments in the business).

Dividend yield

The dividend yield ratio measures the return on a share (dividend) in relation to its current market price. If two firms pay out the same dividend but the shares of the first company are half the price, it represents a better investment for shareholders. The ratio is calculated by using the formula:

$$\frac{\text{Dividends per share}}{\text{Market price of each share}} \times 100$$

Dividends per share is calculated by dividing the value of dividends (shown in the balance sheet) by the number of shares in the company. For instance, in JKL Ltd.'s case, for Year 2, the dividends per share is \$0.20 (i.e. \$50,000 ÷ 250,000 shares).

Taking this one step further, if dividends per share is \$0.20 and the current market price of the share is \$4, the dividend yield is 5%. This ratio can then be compared with historical or inter-firm figures to make an assessment of the performance of the company in satisfying shareholder returns. Note that although dividends are usually paid biannually, it is the total annual dividends figure that is used for calculating dividend yield.

In general, the higher the ratio the better it is for shareholders – at least in the short term. As always, it is important to put the ratio into context and to ask further questions such as how the ratio compares to the interest rate offered at the bank or the potential return from other investment projects. Furthermore, it is important to consider *why* the ratio might not be high. Dividend yield may be low for two main reasons:

- The *dividends per share* is low. This may not be all bad if the company has decided to invest for the future rather than to please shareholders through large dividend payments in the short term.
- The market share price is high. A high market price for the share will reduce the dividend yield, but the higher share price is a good thing for existing investors who aim for capital growth in the business.

Hence, a low dividend yield may initially look bad, but as with all ratios the figure should be put into context.

Question 3.6.5

a Calculate the earnings per share for shareholders of JKL Ltd. for both years and comment on your findings. *[5 marks]*

b Calculate the dividend yield for Year 1, assuming that the market price was \$8 per share at the time. Comment on what your answer reveals and does not tell about the company. *[5 marks]*

GEARING RATIO

The gearing ratio is used to assess a firm's *long-term liquidity* position. This is done by examining the firm's capital employed that is financed by long-term debt, such as mortgages and debentures (see Unit 3.1). The gearing ratio formula is:

$$\frac{\text{Long-term liabilities}}{\text{Capital employed}} \times 100$$

or

$$\frac{\text{Loan capital}}{\text{Capital employed}} \times 100$$

For example, a firm with long-term liabilities totalling $5 million whilst its capital employed is $15 million has a gearing ratio of 33.3%. This means that one-third of the firm's sources of finance come from external interest-bearing sources, whilst the other two-thirds represents internal sources of finance. The higher the gearing ratio, the larger the firm's dependence on long-term sources of borrowing. This means that the firm incurs higher costs due to debt financing, such as interest repayments to banks or debenture holders. Other things being equal, this will tend to reduce the net profit for the firm. A firm is said to be *highly geared* if it has a gearing ratio of 50% or above.

Furthermore, firms with a high gearing ratio are more vulnerable to increases in interest rates. This situation is similar to an individual who has a large mortgage with a bank. A rise in interest rates will mean such individuals will have higher monthly interest repayments on their outstanding mortgages. Similarly, a highly geared business will be more exposed to interest rate increases. In addition, the person with a large mortgage and a business with high gearing are highly exposed if there is a downturn in the economy, as their loan repayments remain high whilst cash inflow from sales will tend to fall in a recession. Other financiers are less likely to lend money to firms that are already highly geared. Highly geared firms, with their large loan commitments, will tend to experience financial difficulties and may collapse or even be taken over by larger rivals.

Shareholders and potential investors will be interested in the gearing ratio as it helps to assess the level of risk. Since financiers have to be repaid first (with interest), the amount of return paid to shareholders and the amount retained for reinvestments may therefore be reduced. However, if the profitability of the firm is high, potential returns can be very attractive even in highly geared firms.

Although gearing can make profits more volatile, businesses may need external funds to finance their expansion. The business saying the 'you need money to make money' suggests that external financing can help businesses to grow in size. Property tycoon Donald Trump made his wealth largely through high gearing since internal sources of finance are rarely sufficient to finance the rapid growth of a business. The problem facing finance managers is how much debt the company can handle before the benefits of growth outweigh the costs of high gearing and financial risk. The level of gearing that is acceptable to a firm may depend of several factors, such as:

- The size and status of the business – Generally, there is a positive correlation between a firm's size and status and its ability to repay long-term debts. Most stakeholders would not really worry too much if McDonald's had a gearing ratio of 50% as it is likely to be able to repay these debts.
- The level of interest rates – If interest rates are low, businesses are less vulnerable (at least in the short term) even with high gearing. For example, during Japan's recession in the 1990s,

interest rates were close to zero per cent. This would minimize the interest repayments on long-term external finance.

- Potential profitability – If firms have good profit quality (long-term prospects of making profit), high gearing is less likely to be a problem. This applies to many firms in high-tech industries that invest heavily in research and development. They may need external sources of finance to fund the expenditure on R&D but the potential for high returns can minimize their exposure to gearing.

Question 3.6.6

a JKL Ltd. has issued debentures valued at $250,000. Outline what is meant by 'debentures'. *[2 marks]*

b Calculate the gearing ratio for JKL Ltd. for both years. *[3 marks]*

c Explain what the gearing ratios tell you about JKL Ltd.'s long-term liquidity position. *[4 marks]*

d Examine whether high gearing can actually be beneficial to a business. *[6 marks]*

USES AND LIMITATIONS OF RATIO ANALYSIS

Ratio analysis is useful for anyone who has a direct interest in the financial performance of a business. These people or organizations are known as the **stakeholders** of the business (see Unit 1.4). For example:

- *Employees and trade unions* can use financial ratios to assess the likelihood of pay rises and the level of job security (perhaps by examining profitability and liquidity ratios).
- *Managers and directors* can also assess the probability of getting management bonuses for reaching profitability and efficiency targets. They can also use ratios to identify areas of weakness that need corrective measures.
- *Trade creditors* will look at short-term liquidity ratios to make sure that the customer (i.e. the business) has sufficient working capital to repay them.
- *Shareholders* will use shareholders ratios to assess the return (capital gain and dividends) of their investment relative to holding other investments, such as purchasing shares in other companies or placing the money in a bank account.
- *Potential financiers* will use a variety of ratios to consider if the business has sufficient funds and profitability to repay any loans that may be approved.
- The *local community* can use a range of financial ratios to gauge job security and opportunities for local residents. The community may also use ratios in an attempt to secure funding from businesses for local community projects or events.

Essentially, stakeholders use financial ratios to assess the relative strengths and weaknesses of a company to aid their own decision-making. Shareholders, for example, can use financial ratio analysis to decide whether to purchase certain shares. Financiers will use profitability and liquidity ratios to decide whether to lend money to a business.

However, financial ratio analysis has its limitations.

- Ratios are a historical account of a firm's performance. They do not indicate the current or future financial situation of a business (although they can give an indication of the financial health of the firm).
- Changes in the external business environment can cause a change in the financial ratios without there being any underlying change in the performance of a business. For example, higher interest rates will reduce profitability, although sales revenues may have actually increased. Higher prices over time, caused by inflation in the economy, will change the financial figures of a firm.
- There is no universal way to report company accounts and this means that businesses may use different accounting policies. For example, some firms use the *straight-line method* whilst others use the *reducing balance method* for depreciating assets (see Unit 3.5). This makes inter-firm comparisons difficult and perhaps meaningless.
- Qualitative factors that affect the performance of a firm are totally ignored. For example, the level of staff motivation and the state of public opinion are not considered in ratio analysis.
- Organizational objectives differ between businesses, so results from a ratio analysis may be misleading. For example, there should be some reservations in the comparison of the financial performance of a state-owned airline with that of a private sector airline company.

As with all financial analyses, such as cash flow forecasts and investment appraisal, ratio analysis is only partial analysis, i.e. it does not provide a complete picture of a company. There are other quantitative and qualitative factors that stakeholders ought to consider to make a better assessment of a company's financial performance. Such considerations include:

- *Historical comparisons* – The same ratio should be compared year on year to identify any trends and, perhaps more importantly, the reasons for such trends. This can help stakeholders to assess any improvement or deterioration in the firm's financial performance.
- *Inter-firm comparisons* – Ratios should be benchmarked (compared) with those of close rival businesses to assess the relative performance of the company. A firm's ratio analysis may reveal pleasing results, but this may not be so pleasing if it has been outperformed by its competitors.
- *The nature of the business* and its *aims and objectives* – A profit-seeking multinational company may understandably have very different ratios from those of not-for-profit organizations. Firms that have a predominant social and ethical stance will perhaps have somewhat lower profitability ratios.
- The *state of the economy* – A firm's financial performance may at first seem to have deteriorated but when put into the context of the business cycle (booms, recessions and slumps) it may paint a different picture.
- *Social factors* – A firm's activities may be highly profitable but there is no consideration for the environment or society under financial ratio analysis. For example, side-effects of a firm's activities may include air pollution, excess packaging and job losses; none of which are revealed when analysing financial ratios.

Whilst financial ratio analysis certainly aids management decision-making, there are limitations to what this management tool can do and reveal. It is therefore important to consider other quantitative and qualitative factors when attempting to measure the performance of a business.

Exam Tip!

Often in financial ratio analysis questions it is just as important to consider what data are *not* given rather than just to assess the financial data provided. Good management decision-making considers a range of information, both quantitative and qualitative in nature.

Table 3.6c Ratio analysis summary

Type	Ratio	Formula
Profitability	Gross profit margin	$\frac{\text{Gross profit}}{\text{Sales revenue}} \times 100$
	Net Profit Margin	$\frac{\text{Net profit before interest and tax}}{\text{Sales revenue}} \times 100$
Liquidity	Current ratio	$\frac{\text{Current assets}}{\text{Current liabilities}}$
	Acid test	$\frac{\text{Current assets} - \text{stocks}}{\text{Current liabilities}}$
Efficiency	Stock turnover	$\frac{\text{Cost of goods sold}}{\text{Average stock}}$ or $\frac{\text{Average stock}}{\text{Cost of goods sold}} \times 365$
	Return on capital employed	$\frac{\text{Net profit before interest and tax}}{\text{Capital employed}} \times 100$
	Debtor days	$\frac{\text{Debtors}}{\text{Sales revenue}} \times 365$
	Creditor days	$\frac{\text{Creditors}}{\text{Cost of sales}} \times 365$
Gearing	Gearing	$\frac{\text{Loan capital}}{\text{Capital employed}} \times 100$
Shareholders	*Earnings per share*	$\frac{\text{Net profit after interest and tax}}{\text{Number of ordinary shares}}$
	Dividend yield	$\frac{\text{Dividends per share}}{\text{Market price of each share}} \times 100$

Note: Ratios in *italics* are for Higher Level students only.

Question 3.6.7

Study the data below regarding the performance of two hypothetical companies, Pia and Hayman, then answer the questions that follow.

		Years		
	Firm	**1**	**2**	**3**
Gross profit margin (%)	Pia	50	45	40
	Hayman	50	40	45
Net profit margin (%)	Pia	20	20	20
	Hayman	19	18	20
Return on capital employed (%)	Pia	15	13	14
	Hayman	12	10	15
Quick ratio	Pia	2.5	2.2	1.5
	Hayman	1.5	1.9	1.1
Earnings per share ($)	Pia	0.5	0.6	0.7
	Hayman	1.2	1.5	0.8

Note: SL students are not expected to use the Earnings Per Share ratio in this question.

a Outline the difference between gross profit and net profit. *[2 marks]*

b Discuss the relative attractiveness of the two companies to potential investors. *[9 marks]*

c Comment on why it is important for potential investors to consider non-financial factors when making investment decisions. *[4 marks]*

RATIO ANALYSIS AND BUSINESS STRATEGY

Ratio analysis is a management tool that can be used to assess the financial health of a business. Its financial position will depend on a combination of profitability, liquidity (both short-term and long-term) and financial efficiency.

Many managers today place great emphasis on short-term liquidity ratios, since a lack of working capital is the main cause of business failure. However, all categories of financial ratios are important since they are interrelated. For example, adequate gearing and sufficient liquidity should help a firm to increase its profitability. Profitable firms that lack sufficient liquidity (see Unit 3.3) are unlikely to survive in the long run. Hence, it is the firm with good overall financial performance, in all aspects of ratio analysis, which succeeds and survives in the long run.

As financial ratios can be used to judge the success of a business, they pose a slight problem for judging the success of non-profit organizations such as state schools and hospitals. So what qualitative and non-financial ratios could we use to judge the degree of success of schools? Since state schools are not run to make a profit, non-profit factors need to be considered. The most apparent factor to look at could be the students' examination results to judge their attainment. If the school has achieved better results over time, it could suggest that the school has improved its performance. Another measure could be to look at how well the school operates within its allocated budget.

Nevertheless, in judging the performance of any business, there is a need to consider a range of qualitative factors and not just financial factors. In addition, it may be difficult to compare like with like since schools can be different in so many ways. There are religious schools, different levels of funding, different catchment areas, demographics, selective and non-selective schools, and so on. Hence, schools are all likely to have different organizational objectives. Since we judge 'success' by the degree to which objectives are met, the criteria for judging success in non-profit organizations will vary inevitably from those used for profit-seeking businesses.

Finally, it is important to be reminded that when looking at the financial performance of a business, the calculations should be put into the context of the market in which the firm operates. A stock turnover rate of 2 days is perhaps acceptable to a supermarket, whereas 100 days may be acceptable to a business that sells solar panel units to property developers. The context also includes consideration of the economic, social and political environments (see Unit 1.5) in which the business operates. Poorer liquidity is expected during a recession, for example. When assessing the financial performance of a business, ignoring the external environment in which it operates would result in less valid conclusions being drawn.

When looking at the return on capital employed, it is important for managers to put the figures into perspective. A high figure is not necessarily indicative of good financial performance as the ratio should be compared with historical performance, inter-firm performance, interest rates offered by banks and the returns from alternative projects if the capital had been used elsewhere.

REVIEW QUESTIONS 3.6

1. What is meant by 'ratio analysis'?
2. What are the main purposes of carrying out financial ratio analysis?
3. Outline the two ways in which ratios can be compared.
4. When conducting ratio analysis, why is it important to compare like with like?
5. Differentiate between the main categories of ratios: profitability, efficiency, gearing and liquidity.
6. What do the GPM and NPM ratios tell us about a firm's profitability?
7. Why do many businesses prefer to use the acid test ratio rather than the current ratio?
8. Why do firms prefer a high figure for both the stock turnover and the return on capital employed ratios?
9. Outline why it is generally considered that highly geared firms are risky.
10. Outline how any four stakeholder groups might be interested in financial ratio analysis.
11. Summarize three limitations of ratio analysis.

Higher Level extension

12. Explain whether a high or low figure is preferable for the:
    - i debtor days ratio
    - ii the creditor days ratio.
13. What are the two reasons for investors buying shares in a company?
14. What are 'shareholders ratios'?
15. How might changes in the external business environment affect the financial performance of a business?

Acid test ratio is a liquidity ratio that measures the ability of a firm to meet its short-term debts. It differs from the current ratio in that stocks are ignored from the calculation. This is because not all stocks, such as supplies of Ferrari cars or Boeing jumbo jets, can be easily and quickly turned into cash.

Creditor days ratio is an efficiency ratio that measures the number of days it takes, on average, for a business to pay its creditors. The higher this ratio is, the better it tends to be for the business.

Current ratio is a short-term liquidity ratio that calculates the ability of a firm to meet its debts within the next twelve months. It is worked out by the formula: current assets divided by current liabilities.

Debtor days ratio is an efficiency ratio that measures the average number of days it takes for a business to collect the money owed from its debtors. The lower this ratio is, the better it tends to be for the business.

Dividend yield is a type of shareholders ratio which shows the dividends received as a percentage of the market price of the share. Investors often use this to compare the relative attractiveness of shares in different companies. They can also compare the ratio to interest rates that can be gained from a bank to assess the risks of investment.

Earnings per share (EPS) is a shareholders ratio which shows the amount of money that stockholders could receive per share *if* the company allocated all its after-tax profits to the shareholders. The higher the EPS, the higher the potential return to shareholders.

Gearing is a long-term liquidity ratio that measures the percentage of a firm's capital employed that comes from long-term liabilities, such as debentures and mortgages. Firms that have at least 50% gearing are said to be *highly geared.*

Gross profit margin (GPM) is a profitability ratio that shows the percentage of sales revenue that turns into gross profit, i.e. the proportion of sales revenue left over after all direct costs have been paid.

Liquid assets refer to the assets of a business that can be turned into cash quickly, without losing their value, i.e. cash, stock and debtors.

Liquidity crisis refers to a situation where a firm is unable to pay its short-term debts, i.e. current liabilities exceed current assets and, therefore, the acid test ratio is less than 1:1.

Net profit margin (NPM) is a profitability ratio that shows the percentage of sales revenue that turns into net profit, i.e. the proportion of sales revenue left over after all direct and indirect costs have been paid. The difference between a firm's GPM and its NPM indicates its ability to control business expenses.

Ratio analysis is a management tool that compares different financial figures. It requires the application of figures found in the Balance Sheet and Profit and Loss account of a business. Ratios can be classified into five categories: profitability, efficiency, liquidity, gearing and shareholders ratios.

Return on capital employed (ROCE) is an efficiency ratio (although it also reveals the firm's profitability). ROCE measures the profit of a business in relation to its size (as measured by capital employed). The higher the ROCE figure, the better it is for a business as it shows more profit being generated from the amount of money invested in the firm.

Stock turnover is an efficiency ratio that measures the number of times a firm sells its stocks within a year. It can also be expressed as the number of days it takes, on average, for a firm to sell all of its stocks. In calculating the stock turnover, the *cost of goods sold* (rather than the selling price of the stocks) is used.

MARKETING

UNIT 4

UNIT

The Role of Marketing

UNIT 4.1

The greatest pleasure in life is doing what people say you cannot do.

Walter Bagehot (1826–1877), British journalist

Key topics

- The market: characteristics, market size, market growth and market share
- Definition of marketing and nature of marketing
- Market orientation and product orientation
- Marketing of goods and the marketing of services
- Marketing of non-profit organizations
- Marketing plans

Higher Level extension

- Social marketing and asset-led marketing

INTRODUCTION

People have different needs and wants. **Needs** are the essential necessities that all humans must have in order to survive: food, shelter, warmth and water. **Wants** are the desires that humans have. Irrespective of a person's income or wealth, it is argued that we all have infinite wants.

Marketing exists to address people's needs and wants. It is about making customers want to buy the products of a business rather than those of rival businesses. It therefore looks at the reasons behind people's decisions, such as the price, colour, size, or special features of the product. Ultimately, marketing must serve to meet the needs and wants of the customer. This is essential for all businesses aiming to make a profit.

Legendary reggae songwriter and singer Bob Marley (1945–1981) famously said that he did not need a BMW (what he described as an expensive car). This sums up the challenge facing marketers who must tempt customers to buy their goods and services.

The marketing department of an organization tends to have four main or generic objectives:

1 Ensure that the right **products** are supplied to fulfil the needs and wants of customers.
2 Set the correct **price** so that customers can afford to buy the product and to ensure that they do not buy from a rival business.
3 Distribute the products to a **place** that is convenient for the customer to make the purchase.
4 Ensure that there is adequate and effective **promotion** to convince customers to buy from the business.

This Unit looks at the characteristics that define a market and the varying roles of marketing. For example, the marketing of goods differs somewhat to that of services. Also, marketing tools used in profit organizations differ to those used by non-profit seeking organizations. These issues are developed in the latter parts of this Unit.

THE MARKET

A **market** is a place or process whereby customers and suppliers trade. A market exists where there is demand for a particular product, such as textbooks, flowers, motor vehicles or plasma televisions, and where there is a willingness from businesses to supply these products. Note that the customers can be private individuals, other businesses or the government. Markets that cater for private individuals (i.e. the general public) are known as **consumer markets**, whilst those that cater for organizations (businesses and the government) are known as **industrial markets** or **commercial markets**.

Within any particular market, there is likely to be a number of rival products and suppliers that can be used to satisfy the needs and wants of the consumer. In the luxury consumer clothing industry, for example, the market consists of competitors such as Gucci, Armani and Dior.

A business will be interested in three elements of the market in which they operate: the *size* of the market, the *growth* rate within the market and the firm's *share* of the market.

Market size

Markets differ in their size. The market for fast food is huge and there is room for growth, especially in overseas markets. The market for horse saddles is much smaller. Market size can be measured in a number of ways:

- **Customer base** – This measures the total potential number of customers. Multinationals have been expanding into China and India partly because they account for a third of the world's population. The internet has also broadened the customer base for many industries. Market size can also be measured in terms of the *value*, not just the volume, of what customers purchase. Using this method, the size of the mobile phone market is larger than the market for textbooks or badminton equipment.

- **Barriers to entry** – These determine the number of suppliers in the market and can also be a measure of a market's size. In markets such as oil and aircraft manufacturing, the entry barriers are extremely high: there are huge set-up costs and existing firms dominate with their market power and huge economies of scale. In other markets where entry barriers are relatively low, there tends to be a lot more firms that operate on a much smaller scale.
- **Location** – Some markets focus on a particular area, country or region. Adidas, for example, is the market leader in the supply of equipment for Taekwondo (a popular form of martial arts), with around four-fifths of the world's black belt holders residing in Korea. Another example is the one billion vegetarians who reside in India. By contrast, other markets, such as motor vehicles or mobile telephones, target an international audience. International trade and globalization have meant that the size of a market is not confined to the domestic market. In fact, they have led to the growth in the export of many cultural products, such as sushi (Japanese rice cuisine) and kimchi (Korean pickled vegetables), since location becomes less of an issue.

Market growth

Market growth refers to an increase in the size of a market over a period of time, usually per year. This can be measured by an increase in the value or volume of sales in the market. It is usually expressed as a percentage to indicate the extent of market growth. For example, if the sales revenue in a particular market rises from $100 million to $110 million, the market is said to have experienced 10% growth.

Market growth is likely to lead to more suppliers entering the market as they are attracted by the potential profits that can be made. The number of mobile phone operators has grown immensely following the huge growth in the market in recent years.

Market share

Since there is likely to be a number of rival products and rival firms within any market, a business contributes to a share of that market. Market share refers to an organization's share of the total value of sales of all products within a specific market. It is measured by expressing the firm's sales as a percentage of the total market value:

$$\text{Market share} = \frac{\text{Sales revenue of firm}}{\text{Total sales revenue in market}} \times 100$$

For example, if sales revenues for a business are $100 million in an industry that is worth a total of $400 million, then the firm's market share is 25%.

Evidence has shown that there is a positive relationship between market share and profits, although the firm with the largest market share is not necessarily the most profitable. Nevertheless, high market share has other benefits such as the status enjoyed from being a dominant market player and the ability to gain further economies of scale. Such firms are known as **market leaders**. For example, Nike and Adidas are market leaders in the mass market sports apparel industry.

In general, a firm with high market share has better pricing power and is less threatened by competition. Hence, a common objective of established firms is to increase their market share. This might be achieved in a number of ways:

- Promotion of brands (see Unit 4.3)
- Product development, improvements and innovation (see Unit 5.6)

- Motivation and training of the workforce (see Unit 2.5) to deliver better customer service
- Establishment of property rights through the use of copyright and patents (see Units 3.5 and 5.6)
- Use of more efficient channels of distribution (see Unit 4.6).

Market share information can be used to measure the level of concentration in a particular market. **Market concentration** measures the degree of competition within a market by calculating the market share of the largest firms in a market. The sum of these market shares is known as the **concentration ratio**. For example, an industry with a three-firm concentration ratio of 98% means that the top three firms in the market account for 98% of the industry's output (usually measured by sales revenue per time period). Hence, this would not be a very competitive industry since other firms would only account for 2% of the overall sales of the market.

In reality, most industries within a country are dominated by a few large businesses. Such businesses are said to be **oligopolists**. Each dominant firm accounts for a large proportion of the industry's overall sales revenues. Some businesses grow so large that they are able to remain oligopolists even on a global scale. For example, the market for mobile phone handsets is dominated by manufacturers such as Nokia, Motorola, Samsung and Sony-Ericsson.

However, calculating market share is not necessarily straightforward as it is not always easy to define the market. When calculating market share in the transport market, for example, which markets should be included – road, rail, sea or air? Sales data are out of date (simply because they show a period in the past) and may not necessarily represent the current position.

Sales data are also old or out of date so any market share information will represent a historical situation and not necessarily the current position.

Question 4.1.1

Nokia

Nokia is the world's largest mobile phone producer, with approximately 35% **market share**. The Finnish company's market share is almost double that of its nearest rival, Motorola. Sales of Nokia handsets have soared recently mainly due to rising demand in India, China and Eastern European markets.

a Calculate the approximate two-firm concentration ratio in the mobile phone industry. *[2 marks]*

b Outline what is meant by **market share** and show how it might be calculated. *[4 marks]*

c Explain two advantages that Nokia might enjoy by having a larger market share than its rivals such as Motorola. *[4 marks]*

DEFINITION AND NATURE OF MARKETING

There is no single definition of the term marketing that is universally accepted because it is a complex process and differs from one type of organization to another. The marketing objectives and strategies of charitable and non-profit organizations, for example, differ from those of large multinational companies.

Probably the most widely used and accepted definition is provided by the Chartered Institute of Marketing which defines marketing as "the management process involved in identifying, anticipating and satisfying consumer requirements profitably".

This definition is commonly used as it covers the nature of marketing:

- Marketing is a management process so it requires people to take responsibility for decision-making.

- Marketing involves identifying the needs and wants of customers. This can be done through market research and data analysis, for example.
- Marketing involves anticipating or predicting what customers might want in the future. For example, market research and product development have created markets for mobile phones, laptops and high-definition plasma televisions. The movie industry is constantly trying to produce films that audiences may want to see. Product development and innovation (see Unit 5.6) are therefore important features of marketing for many businesses.
- Marketing seeks to satisfy the consumer. Products must satisfy the consumer's need or want. Products must represent value for money. Price, availability and quality are essential elements that consumers consider when assessing value for money. Satisfied customers are more likely to become loyal customers rather than those who switch to products offered by competitors.
- Marketing is about making a profit. Prices must therefore cover the costs of production. Motor manufacturers would not use promotions such as 'buy one, get one free' as part of their marketing. Non-profit organizations must ensure that the benefits of marketing outweigh their costs.

Professor Philip Kotler suggests that marketing is about satisfying consumer needs and wants through exchange. Kotler argues that customers will buy products from the firm that offers the highest value for money (what he called **customer delivered value**). This is the difference between the benefits and costs to the customer purchasing the product.

Marketing is fundamental to the success of a business as it will affect the sales and profits of the organization. However, marketing alone does not ensure success since other aspects the business must also be considered. In reality, a business will use marketing alongside its other functional areas, such as:

- **Operations management** – The production department will work closely with the marketing people in using sales forecasts (from market research) to prepare their production schedules. The departments will also need to work directly with each other to research, develop and launch products to meet the needs of customers. There may, however, be some conflict between the two departments since production managers would prefer a longer time period in which to test and develop products whereas marketing managers would urge for a quick launch in order to maximize sales revenues. Delays in launching a product not only means a loss in sales, but can also be damaging to the organization's image. Hence, this would weaken the messages that the marketing department are trying to portray.
- **Finance** – The marketing department will work closely with the finance department in order to set appropriate budgets. Again there may be conflict between these departments. For example, marketers may wish to exceed their budget in order to get maximum marketing exposure. However, the finance people will want all departments to work within their allocated budgets. It is likely that the finance department would want prices to cover costs of production in order to generate a profit for the organization. However, marketers may feel that low prices (that do not necessarily cover all costs) are necessary in the short term to get a foothold in the market. Marketers may also want to use extended credit facilities (such as interest free-credit instalment plans) to entice customers. However, the finance department will be conscious of the fact that extended credit can lead to all sorts of liquidity problems (see Unit 3.3) for the business. Hence, both departments will need to work collaboratively to strike a balance between their potentially conflicting interests.
- **Human resource management** – Marketing data can help the HRM department to identify staffing needs. For example, the introduction of a new product may require recruiting extra production staff. In addition, more marketing staff may be required, such as sales personnel. The HRM department's role is to ensure the business has the right quantity and quality of workers through effective workforce planning (see Unit 2.1) in order to meet the needs of their customers.

MARKET AND PRODUCT ORIENTATION

The nature and focus of marketing has changed over the years as new ideas, markets and external influences have evolved. Marketing used to focus on getting customers to buy the products that businesses felt their clients needed or wanted. This approach became known as **product-orientated marketing**.

Today, most marketing activities are used to gain a competitive advantage over rivals by focusing on meeting the actual needs and desires of their customers. Such an approach is termed **market-orientated marketing**.

Product orientation

Product orientation is a marketing approach adopted by businesses that are *inward* looking. They focus on selling products that they make, rather than making products that they can sell. The heart of such an approach is on the production of a good. Businesses believe, or hope, that customers will then buy them. Many hi-tech products that are used in daily life were created using a product orientation approach. Innovative products such as the automobile, television, mobile phone, the internet and MP3 players were all 'unknown' to the mass market during their initial launch. Even Henry Ford did not originally realize that the automobile would become a mass market product, worldwide.

Economists use Say's law ("supply creates its own demand") to describe how product orientation might be successful. The idea is that creative and innovative products are launched onto the market and customers will be tempted to buy these. Of course, not all products launched will be successful. The usual result is that these products are hit-and-miss, i.e. producers are not really sure if the products will sell.

Many product-orientated businesses today concentrate on producing high quality products. The belief is that customers are willing to pay a higher price for exclusivity and luxury products. In general, product-orientated businesses will supply products that they have an expertise in, such as Ferrari producing sports cars or Airbus producing aircraft. The main advantage of product orientation is that quality can be assured. The firm also has more control over its activities.

However, product-orientated firms are often described as inward-looking firms because they assume they know what customers want. Customers do not simply want an improved version of an existing product. Since the needs of the market are ignored, such as changes in fashion and tastes, the high failure rate of businesses that use product orientation suggests that this strategy is highly risky. The money spent on research and development of products without taking the customer into consideration often proves fruitless.

Question 4.1.2

Sony

Sony Corporation, the Japanese electronics giant, had built up a reputation of being a leader in innovation since its beginnings in 1946. However, its complacency during the late 1990s meant that the company had to play catch-up. In 2003, Sony launched its luxury line of gadgets under the brand name of Qualia. This included a ¥380,000 ($25,700) digital camera and a ¥1.5 million ($101,500) audio system.

The big problem, however, was that Sony seemed to be more obsessed about the pricey technology than what their consumers wanted. The Qualia line of products was not well received by customers, especially with the growing competition from the likes of Samsung and Apple. For example, in 2006, Apple's iPods were outselling Sony's digital music players by a ratio of 5 to 1. Critics argued that Sony was losing touch with its consumers.

(cont.)

a Outline why Sony might be described as a 'product-orientated business'. *[3 marks]*

b Explain two disadvantages of product-orientated marketing to a business such as Sony. *[4 marks]*

Market orientation

Market orientation, also known as **consumer orientation**, is a marketing approach adopted by businesses that are *outward* looking. They focus on making products that they can sell, rather than selling products that they can make. It focuses on the consumer in order to identify, design, develop and supply products that meet their needs and wants. Information can be gathered from *market research* (see Unit 4.2) to identify the needs and wants of customers, instead of what the business thinks its customers want. For instance, decisions concerning pricing are taken after information about customers, such as their level of income, are considered. Market research and analysis are therefore central to this approach.

A market-orientated, or **market-led**, business will therefore place its focus on the consumer, rather than a product. Market changes, such as the increased use of the internet, have forced most businesses to be more sensitive to the needs and wants of consumer. If the consumer is ignored, firms are likely to lose competitiveness in the market with devastating results in the long term. It has become increasingly common for retailers such as Ikea, for example, to provide added facilities to meet the needs of their customers, such as restaurants, adult-supervised play areas for children (whilst their parents go shopping), changing rooms and free parking. In customer relations management terms, businesses do not worry about the cost of doing things for the customer; instead they consider the cost of *not* doing these things.

The two main advantages to a business in being market orientated are:

- **Flexibility** – Firms can respond quicker to changes in the market as they will have access to relevant data and information. Market-orientated businesses are also more able to anticipate changing markets and hence prepare for such changes.
- **Less risk** – Firms can be more confident that their products will sell and be successful. Without proper market research and analysis, the sale of a product is much more likely to be a gamble. Since products are deliberately catered to meet the requirements of consumers there is a higher chance of success.

The main disadvantage of market orientation is that market research tends to be very expensive. In addition, given the dynamic nature of the business environment and the uncertainty of the future, there is no guarantee that this approach will lead to success.

Whether a business decides to adopt a product or market-orientated approach depends on several factors, such as the:

- Market – Producers of highly technical products, such as digital camera phones, tend to start off as product-orientated businesses. In mass consumer markets, a more market-orientationed approach tends to be adopted.
- Organizational culture – Businesses that believe 'the customer is always right' are more likely to be market orientated.
- Nature of barriers to entry – Firms without much competition tend to be less customer-focused. Such firms hold *monopoly power* in pricing and distribution decisions and can therefore be more product orientated.

HIGHER LEVEL

HIGHER LEVEL EXTENSION: ADDITIONAL MARKETING ORIENTATIONS

Social marketing

The Social Marketing Institute defines social marketing as "the planning and implementation of programs designed to bring about social change using concepts from commercial marketing". Social marketing is then the use of mainstream marketing methods to achieve the benefits of social change, such as informing the public about the dangers of under-age drinking. Commercial marketing might support the tobacco industry by arguing that smoking can help people to relax, that it is people's choice to smoke and that it creates jobs. Social marketing focuses on benefits from a different stance, e.g. smoking bans in public areas will mean reduced air pollution, less litter and a more pleasant environment for everyone. Social marketing is similar to commercial marketing in that all forms of marketing aim to influence action. However, most organizations that focus on social marketing tend to get their sources of funds through donations or governmental grants.

Philip Kotler (1971) is credited as the founder of social marketing. He defined social marketing as any activity that seeks to influence social behaviour to benefit the target audience and society as a whole. This differs markedly from commercial marketing, which focuses on benefits for the marketer or business. Kotler believed there were benefits to non-profit organizations in using social marketing to market their services. Social marketing, he argued, could be used to affect the behaviour of people in order to enhance the lives of all individuals in society. Aids awareness, anti-smoking and unwanted teenage pregnancies are examples of social marketing campaigns.

The challenge facing social marketers is getting people to change their customary behaviour. Nicotine in tobacco is addictive so getting smokers to change can be difficult. The same applies to drivers who claim they 'need' to drive rather than use public transport.

The clients of social marketing agencies tend to be non-profit organizations, such as charities, and government organizations. However, companies that believe in social responsibility (see Unit 1.3) will also carry out activities such as sponsoring events in the local community. This could also help to enhance their corporate image.

Market research has an important role in social marketing. For example, in order to change people's behaviour, marketers must discover people's perceptions of the issue or problem in question. This will help to determine the action that might be taken to deal with the social problem. If people do not feel that recycling is a convenient option, then this problem must be corrected by taking appropriate action such as lobbying governments to educate people about the benefits of recycling.

When considering pricing decisions in social marketing, marketers tend to refer to the net benefits, i.e. the difference between the benefits and the costs of taking action. If people believe that the benefits are greater than the costs, then social marketers are more likely to achieve their objectives. In countries where littering is heavily fined, such as Singapore and Hong Kong, people are more likely to refrain from doing so as the cost of littering far outweighs any benefit.

Place is also an important part of the marketing mix for social marketing. It must be convenient for people to donate money to charity, for example. Many charities now accept credit card and online payments. Charities and pressure groups in many countries have also managed to persuade their government to give tax reduction benefits to those who donate money to charity.

Question **4.1.3**

Singapore's littering policy

Singapore is considered to be one of the cleanest countries in the world. However, clean cities do not simply come about by chance. Singapore imposes strict laws against littering of any kind. Chewing gum, for example, is totally banned in the country. First-time offenders face a fine of up to S$1,000 ($650) but repeat offenders can be fined up to S$5,000 ($3,265). In addition, offenders are placed under the Corrective Work Order (CWO). The CWO requires litterbugs, who are made to wear bright jackets to draw public attention, to spend up to 12 hours of community service cleaning a public place. The government also 'names and shames' offenders by inviting the media to cover the spectacle. Litter laws are taught in schools and promoted by the government to ingrain Singapore's culture of cleanliness.

a Define the meaning of 'social marketing'. *[2 marks]*

b Examine the role of social marketing for the success of the Singaporean government in dealing with litter problems. *[6 marks]*

Asset-led marketing

Asset-led marketing is a strategy based on the **core competencies** (key strengths) of a business. Core competencies can include human, physical or non-physical assets. Coca-Cola has used their globally recognized name to launch products such as Coke Light, Diet Coke, Cherry Coke and Coke Zero. Such businesses use their core asset, or strength, to develop and launch new products. Yao Ming, the famous Chinese basketball player, has helped the Houston Rockets and the National Basketball Association (NBA) to promote basketball throughout SE Asia, especially in China. Similarly, football clubs have use their most famous players, such as David Beckham, to help sell merchandise.

Asset-led marketing enjoys the benefits of both product and market orientation. It emphasizes the product or firm's key strengths yet makes decisions based on the needs of the market. Businesses that use this approach tend to use the product name or brand image to extend their presence in existing markets or to enter new markets. Toyota's excellent reputation for quality and reliability of its automobiles enabled Lexus, one of it subsidiaries, to enter the luxury car market. Nissan and Honda have also done the same with their respective Infiniti and Acura brands. Many of the global chocolate manufacturers, such as Cadbury, Nestlé and Mars, have also used their names to diversify into the ice cream market.

Not only is asset-led marketing used in mass markets such as football or soft drinks, it is often used to enter **niche markets**. These are small and specialist market segments, such as the market for minority sports. Marketers identify and satisfy the needs of customers in these small but often lucrative markets. Adidas uses it brand name to dominate in the market for martial arts apparel. Lady Linda McCartney (late wife of The Beatles's Sir Paul McCartney) used her name in the early 1970s to launch the highly successful Linda McCartney brand of frozen vegetarian meals.

The main advantage of using asset-led marketing is that the firm can capitalize on its strengths to gain a competitive advantage. This advantage is maximized when a firm can offer better quality products, at attractive prices and available through a wide range of distribution channels. Asset-led marketing is also suitable in extending the life of a product by diversifying into new markets. The main drawback of using asset-led marketing is that firms will tend to overlook markets in which they do not hold any core competencies. This means that weaknesses may never be turned into strengths and potential market opportunities are ignored.

THE MARKETING OF GOODS AND SERVICES

A **service** is an intangible product such as a bus ride, a visit to the cinema or a haircut. Unlike physical goods, purchasers of services do not actually take anything away with them after payment is made. This then implies that there is no ownership of the product and that the product is perishable (as it cannot be kept) even after payments have been made. Services are also heterogeneous, i.e. each customer gets a different experience each time and, unlike mass market goods, the quality is therefore varied.

Customers pay for services in order to fulfil their wants and needs, such as to gain support or advice. Banking, counselling and tutoring are examples of services. Product differentiation is therefore important for the marketing of services. Banks, for example, may offer a range of different services such as tax-free savings accounts, overdrafts or mortgages. They will use marketing tools to entice customers to these different services.

In addition to the traditional marketing mix for goods, which consists of *price*, *product*, *promotion* and *place* (see Unit 4.2), the marketing of services includes three additional elements: people, processes and physical environment. Together these form the **7 P's** in the marketing mix of services. The three additional elements were first suggested by Bernard Booms and Mary Bitner in 1981.

People

The provision of services relies on the goodwill of all employees. Schools require teachers who are passionate about their subjects to deliver good education to students. Hotel staff are crucial in helping holiday makers to enjoy their vacation. However, people are not consistent and countless factors affect the behaviour and motivation of staff, which may change from one day to another (see Unit 2.5).

The effectiveness of people in delivering a service may be measured in a number of ways:

- **Appearance and body language** of the staff – Uniforms and formal clothing are worn in many occupations to give a more professional image to customers. For example, newsreaders on television dress conservatively to portray a formal and serious image. McDonald's have a 'Smiles are free' policy to ensure that their customers are greeted with a friendly smile.
- **Aptitudes and attitudes** – Managers will ask a range of questions concerning the capability and behaviour of their staff, such as: whether staff have sufficient product knowledge; whether they proactive, i.e. whether they are attentive to the needs of their clients; and whether they are caring, courteous and confident. If the answers to all these questions are 'yes', it is highly likely that customers will be happy with the service being delivered.
- **Feedback** – Comments made by various stakeholder groups can also provide useful information regarding the effectiveness of people in delivering good customer service. Schemes such as 'employee of the month', suggestion schemes and records of customer complaints can also provide useful feedback.
- **Efficiency** – Staff who do not keep customers waiting and who do not make mistakes will help the business to gain a better reputation of reliability. For instance, many restaurants and cinemas have staff to assist customers to their seats. By contrast, late deliveries and long waiting times (before customers are served) will render poor customer care.

Processes

Process refers to the way in which a service is provided or delivered. It can be difficult for a business to demonstrate the benefits of services to its customers. Insurance brokers, for example, often have a challenging task in convincing clients to buy insurance policies as the process is quite complex. Businesses selling physical goods, however, tend to have a relatively easier task in demonstrating and convincing the public of the benefits.

Processes in the marketing of services include:

- **Payment methods** – Businesses may offer their customers the convenience of different methods of payment (such as cash, cheque or credit card). This makes the process more convenient for customers.
- **Waiting time** – There can be a large opportunity cost to businesses that do not manage the waiting time of their customers. These consequences include a poorer image, complaints and disgruntled customers. Many pizza companies will offer a discount or will not charge the customer if the product is delivered late. Diners may switch to another restaurant if they have to wait too long for a table.
- **Customer services** – This refers to the degree of attentiveness and politeness of staff towards their customers. Feedback on the quality of customer service can be obtained from customer service satisfaction surveys, suggestions schemes or comment cards.
- **After-sales care** – A business can gain a competitive edge if they provide after-sales services. These are services that are offered following the sale of the product, such as maintenance or help desks. Guarantees and warranties are further examples of such services.

Physical evidence (or physical environment)

The physical environment refers to the tangible aspects of a service. In a 5-star hotel, for example, we might expect to see a clean lobby with nice décor and well-groomed hotel staff. The restaurants and hotel facilities should also be pleasing to the eye. The rooms should be clean with fresh towels and bed sheets. These all help the customer to feel happy with the overall service provided by the hotel. Many businesses use **peripheral products** in delivering their services. These are additional products, such as drinks or magazines offered to clients in a hair salon, which are used to enhance the overall experience for customers.

In modern societies, it is usual for the majority of the workforce to be engaged in the services, or tertiary, sector of the economy (see Unit 1.1). This heightens the importance of marketing services and the use of the three extra P's in the marketing mix.

Managing the provision of services can prove to be a challenging task in comparison to managing the marketing of physical goods. Challenges facing managers in delivering quality customer services include:

- **Correcting mistakes** – It can be relatively easy, albeit costly perhaps, to correct mistakes made during the manufacturing of physical goods. However, with the provision of services it can be very difficult to correct any mistakes. Indeed, a poor image caused by appalling and inattentive customer service may be irreversible.
- **Measuring productivity** – How can we measure the output of teachers, doctors and actors? They all provide a service although it may be difficult to measure their productivity in the same way as we can measure the output of workers in the manufacturing of physical products. Since it is difficult to measure the output of intangible products, it might be difficult to reward the staff who are more productive.
- **People management** – The provision of services tends to be labour intensive. This can be costly to an organization. Lawyers, architects and accountants are paid well for their skills and expertise. Managing people in such professions requires effective leadership. In service industries that require a large workforce, such as supermarkets and fast-food restaurants, it may be difficult for managers to ensure that all staff are consistent in their delivery of customer service. The lack of motivation from just one worker, for example, could be enough to tarnish the reputation of the business.

Question 4.1.4

Wallington High School for Girls

Wallington High School for Girls, located in Surrey (UK) is a selective grammar school for girls. Selection is based on an academic entrance exam. There are several other selective and private fee-paying schools in the proximity. Surrey has the reputation of having the 'best' schools in the UK. Like all schools, Wallington High School for Girls is involved in marketing. Each year, the management team of the school will deliberately run events to market their organization. These events include: parents' information evenings, charity events, celebration evenings, music concerts and drama productions. Wallington High School for Girls gained its Engineering Status in 2004 (which gives it extra funding from the government) and proudly markets this achievement. The school also communicates its outstanding examination results to all key stakeholders.

Source: www.wallingtongirls.sutton.sch.uk

a Explain two reasons why marketing is important to Wallington High School for Girls. *[4 marks]*

b Analyse how people, process and physical evidence are vital elements of the marketing mix in the marketing of schools. *[6 marks]*

MARKETING IN NON-PROFIT ORGANIZATIONS

Most definitions of marketing refer to activities that are profitable for the business. This does not necessarily apply to **non-profit organizations** such as charities, religious organizations and government departments. The government, for example, may use television advertisements for reminding citizens to complete their tax returns on time, or to persuade drivers not to drink and drive. These forms of marketing are not primarily profit related.

It may seem clear that profit-seeking organizations must market their products successfully. Without market research to create a desirable product, at the right price, promoted effectively and available in the right places, a business is unlikely to survive for long. This is, however, also true for not-for-profit organizations. Marketing remains an integral part of their strategy in order to raise awareness of their cause.

Marketing in non-profit organizations is, nevertheless, somewhat different to some of the more commonly used definitions of marketing. Marketing in non-profit organizations tends to be more informative (so does not necessarily intend to increase sales) as opposed to being persuasive.

Non-profit organizations tend to use **social marketing** strategies rather than the market-led strategies used by profit-seeking organizations. The main aim of social marketing campaigns is not to make a profit at the end but for the public to take action, such as donating money to a specific charity or providing their support in recycling household products. For many non-profit organizations, the marketing is not about selling a physical product but a mission, vision or cause. The Chartered Institute of Marketing reported that in 2002 the Multiple Sclerosis Society's £4 million ($8 million) marketing budget had resulted in a £5 million ($10 million) 'profit' for the organization to further fund its charity work. This example shows that even non-profit organizations need to undertake marketing to survive. In their book *Principles of Marketing* Philip Kotler *et al* suggest that many charities have moved away from traditional ways of collecting funds, opting to employ some fairly sophisticated marketing techniques. Government agencies and departments such as the Army and Police Force in many countries also use marketing to enhance their image and to help in hiring new recruits. Governments are also adopting social marketing techniques to encourage recycling and protection of the environment.

Another strategy that is popular is to use memorable **catchphrases**, better known as **slogans**. For example, The Dogs Trust, an animal welfare charity based in the UK, is best known for its advertising slogan "A dog is for life, not just for Christmas". Politicians and governments also use slogans to promote their causes. One of the best known advertisements worldwide, with many variants that followed, showed a picture of Britain's Lord Kitchener calling for recruits to fight in World War I with the now infamous slogan "Your Country Needs You".

Management and marketing guru Philip Kotler coined the term **de-marketing** to mean the use of marketing to reduce the demand for socially undesirable products, such as tobacco. Government agencies use marketing strategies to inform or to persuade citizens to act in a particular way or to change their behaviour. Government warnings about the dangers of smoking or drink driving are examples.

A traditional problem for non-profit organizations is the tight constraint on their marketing budgets (largely because of they lack sufficient sources of finance). Additional sources of funds and a better corporate image may be brought about by using **public relations** (see Unit 4.5). For example, charities often hold fund-raising events, such as the annual Flora London Marathon. The more prominent charities also use celebrities or heroes to endorse their cause. Public relations can also be improved by holding press conferences to get marketing messages in the media. Alternatively, firms can use representatives of the organization to give talks at schools to communicate their organization's causes to students and teachers.

Other marketing tools that are being increasingly used by non-profit organizations are **internet technologies**. Firms are using the internet to promote their cause or mission in a cost-effective way. For example, newsletters are published online and there may be facilities to make online donations.

Non-profit organizations will also strive to increase their **distribution channels** (see Unit 4.6) just like any private sector firm. The Red Cross, for instance, has donation boxes in retail outlets such as shops and supermarkets in many parts of the world. They will tend to focus more on promoting the *image* (rather than the product) of the organization for its long-term survival.

In summary, marketing in non-profit organizations takes many forms, some of which are non-convention methods. Examples of their approach include the use of: social marketing, slogans, de-marketing, public relations (such as fund-raising events), celebrity and hero endorsement, sponsorship and the use of internet technologies.

Question 4.1.5

Unicef & FC Barcelona

On the evening of 17th May 2006, Spanish football giant FC Barcelona won the Champions League trophy, the second most lucrative soccer competition after the FIFA World Cup. Four months later, the Club signed a five-year **sponsorship** deal with Unicef (the world's largest children's charity, set up by the United Nations). The Club, which is well known for its moral values and not just its football, agreed to donate 0.7% of its annual revenue to Unicef and to wear the Unicef logo on the front of its football shirts. The agreement was symbolic with the Club's **social values** and motto that it is "More than a club".

Source: FCBarcelona.com

a Define the terms **sponsorship** and **social values**. *[4 marks]*

b Most football clubs are sponsored *by* commercial supporters. Explain why FC Barcelona might have decided to sponsor Unicef, a non-profit organization. *[4 marks]*

c Discuss how the effectiveness and efficiency of non-profit organizations might be increased by using marketing strategies. *[7 marks]*

ELEMENTS OF A MARKETING PLAN

A **marketing plan** is a document outlining a firm's marketing objectives (see Unit 4.2) and the marketing strategies to be used in order to achieve these objectives. Successful marketers advocate planning a firm's marketing objectives and strategies, rather than adopting an ad hoc and uncoordinated approach.

A marketing plan is usually preceded by a **marketing audit**. This is a review of the current position of a firm's marketing mix, in terms of its strengths, weaknesses, opportunities and threats. The review may address questions and issues such as the intensity of competition in the market, the firm's product portfolio (see Unit 4.3) and an assessment of the effectiveness of the firm's marketing.

From the marketing audit, managers can then produce a marketing plan. This is likely to include details of the following:

- SMART marketing objectives (specific, measurable, agreed, realistic and time constrained), such as the expected market share or sales volume within a specified time frame
- Methods of market research to be used to identifying target markets
- An assessment of the strengths and weaknesses of competitors in the market
- Outline of the marketing mix, such as the product design, channels of distribution to be used, anticipated price(s) and promotional strategies to employ
- Details of the marketing budget
- Outline of the likely problems that may be encountered and strategies to deal with them.

It is also usual for PEST and SWOT analyses to be shown in a marketing plan. These will help the firm to assess the internal and external factors affecting the business and its marketing objectives.

The main advantage of using marketing planning is that it improves the chances of success. The plan does not, of course, guarantee success but it can help managers to identify and deal with likely problems to be encountered. In addition, the various functional areas of a business will have a clearer idea of the organization's objectives and the constraints in which they are to operate. This allows senior managers to have better control of the business.

However, marketing planning does have several limitations. For example, many small firms do not have the time, resources or expertise to plan their marketing. Subsequently, they react to, rather than anticipate, changes in the marketplace. Even for large firms, management will need to devote appropriate resources (time, people and money) to marketing planning. Marketing plans can also become outdated quite quickly or instill inflexibility in the organization since they do not allow for sudden changes in market conditions. This is especially the case in high-tech and fast-paced industries.

THE ROLE OF MARKETING AND BUSINESS STRATEGY

Marketing is about understanding the market(s) in which a business operates in order to develop strategies to influence the action of others. The marketing department has a crucial role in the running of any business. Marketing allows a business to be forward looking as it involves investigating potential opportunities in the marketplace, customer needs and requirements, pricing possibilities, and appropriate promotional activities.

Different businesses approach marketing in different ways. Businesses that take a market-led approach to their marketing put the customer at the top of their priority. Economists call this **consumer sovereignty**, whereby the consumer is ruler and is always right. This approach may well suit the marketing of services although it is not necessarily the best approach for the marketing of hi-tech goods that require extensive product research and development. Research has shown that most businesses adopt market orientation, especially since customers are increasingly more knowledgeable and have greater access to alternative suppliers. Hence, businesses are more perceptive of their customers' needs and wants.

For many services, the location of businesses (see Unit 5.5) is of vital importance to the customer. Hairdressers, vets, cinemas and schools are examples of businesses that need to be located near their markets. However, the emergence of e-commerce (see Unit 4.8) has meant that the location decision for some service providers, such as banks, is no longer such a difficult one. Even so, businesses must still ensure an overall service package that meets the needs of their customers, such as the convenience and reliability of online transactions.

Marketing is often associated with the practices of large companies like McDonald's, Coca-Cola, Microsoft and Toyota. They have the financial resources and expertise to carry out effective marketing planning. However, the principles of marketing are increasingly important to small and non-profit organizations too. Professor Kotler argues that almost any business can use informal and low-cost alternatives to market research. This is especially the case with developments in internet technologies. Marketing is about informing, reminding and persuading, whether the purpose is to sell more products to make more profit or to promote a cause, such as donating money to charities or to reduce under-age drinking. The growing number of non-profit organizations in society can therefore provide many opportunities and challenges to marketing agencies.

Businesses often fail due to a lack of proper planning. For example, they may not have considered the extent of competition in the marketplace or changes in market conditions. Marketing planning can help to reduce the risks of doing business. It gives a sense of direction to the business and ensures that marketing is properly coordinated and managed. It allows managers to identify likely problems so that they can be avoided or dealt with beforehand. However, a dilemma facing managers is that the nature of business is dynamic and always exposed to the forces of change. This means that managers will need to build some flexibility into their marketing plans so that marketing tactics and strategies can be altered spontaneously. In their book *Uncommon Practice* A. Milligan and S. Smith (2002) argue that the fastest way to build a name in business is to command attention to a firm's products or services. In essence, this is the role and challenge of marketing.

REVIEW QUESTIONS 4.1

1. Distinguish between consumer 'needs' and 'wants'.
2. What are the four generic objectives of marketing?
3. What is a 'market'?
4. What is the difference between 'market size' and 'market share'?
5. Explain two ways in which market size might be measured.
6. State four external factors that might affect the growth rate of a market.
7. What is meant by the term 'marketing'?
8. Outline three marketing techniques used by non-profit organizations.
9. Distinguish between 'market-orientated' and 'product-orientated' marketing.
10. Explain how the marketing of services differs from the marketing of goods.
11. What is a 'marketing audit'?
12. What is likely to feature in a typical marketing plan?

Higher Level extension

13 Distinguish between 'social marketing' and 'asset-led market orientation'.

14 What are 'core competencies'?

15 What is a 'niche market'?

Asset-led marketing is a business strategy based on the core strengths (or core competencies) of the firm. Businesses that adopt this approach use their core assets, such as the brand name, to develop and launch new products.

Market leaders are firms that dominate the market share in a particular market. The business that has the largest market share in an industry, as measured by value or volume of sales, is called the market leader.

Market orientation is an approach adopted by businesses that are *outward* looking. They focus on making products that they can sell, rather than selling products that they can make.

Market share measures the value of a firm's sales revenues as a percentage of the industry total. Hence, a business with 35% market share means that for every $100 sold in the industry, the firm earns $35 of the sales revenue.

Market size refers to the magnitude of an industry, usually measured in terms of the value of sales revenue from all the businesses in a particular market, per time period. Hence, the market size of motor vehicles is greater than that of fresh pineapples.

Marketing is the management role of predicting, identifying and meeting the needs and wants of customers in a profitable manner. The activities can be summed up as the eight P's: product, price, promotion, place, people, physical evidence, process and packaging.

Marketing audit refers to a review of a firm's current marketing mix, in terms of its strengths, weaknesses, opportunities and threats.

Marketing mix refers to the main elements of a firm's marketing strategy. It consists of the 4 P's – *product*, *price*, *promotion* and *place*.

Marketing plan refers to the document outlining a firm's marketing objectives and strategies for a specified time period.

Marketing strategy is any medium- to long-term plan for achieving the marketing objectives of a business.

Product orientation is a marketing approach adopted by businesses that are *inward* looking. They focus on selling products that they can make, rather than making products that they can sell.

Social marketing refers to any activity that seeks to influence social behaviour to benefit the target audience and society as a whole.

Marketing Planning

UNIT 4.2

> *You generally hear that what a man doesn't know doesn't hurt him, but in business what a man doesn't know does hurt.*
>
> E. St.Elmo Lewis (1872–1948), American author

Key topics

- The marketing mix
- Ethics of marketing
- Marketing audits
- Marketing objectives
- Market research
- Market segmentation and consumer profiles
- Targeting and the marketing mix
- Positioning: corporate image, position maps, and unique selling point (USP)
- Marketing strategies and tactics

Higher Level extension

- Porter's five forces analysis
- Methods of sampling: quota, random, stratified, cluster and snowballing
- Sales forecasting and trends

INTRODUCTION

Marketing planning is a systematic process concerned with devising marketing objectives and appropriate marketing strategies to achieve these goals. It requires the collection and analysis of information about a particular market, such as market research data on existing and potential consumers.

To achieve a marketing objective, such as sales growth, a business must decide how to achieve this goal. This is the role of marketing planning. The typical marketing planning process is outlined below:

- Marketing audit – This refers to an examination of the current climate in which a business operates. Market research will be integral to this investigation.
- Marketing objectives – The marketing audit will enable the firm to set marketing goals and targets, such as increased market share.
- Marketing strategies – This refers to the plan and use of the marketing mix to achieve the marketing objectives. Marketing strategy also covers the marketing mix and issues of ethical marketing.
- Monitoring and review – This is a continual process of checking and assessing that targets are being met. Subsequently, marketing strategies may need to be adjusted accordingly.
- Evaluation – This refers to an examination of the extent to which the firm has succeeded in achieving its marketing objectives. This will aid decision-making and planning in the next annual marketing audit.

All these issues are explained in this Unit which covers the diverse range of activities linked to marketing planning.

THE MARKETING MIX

The **marketing mix** is a combination of the elements needed to successfully market any product. The marketing mix is at the heart of marketing planning. It is used to review and develop marketing strategy. These elements are commonly known as the **Four P's** of marketing, a term coined by Jerome McCarthy in 1960:

- Product – A product is the good or service being marketed to meet the needs and wants of the consumer.
- Price – Price refers to how much the customer is charged for the product.
- Place – Place refers to the distribution channels used to get the products to the customer.
- Promotion – This is the process of informing, reminding and persuading customers to buy the product.

No marketing plan can work without all four elements of the marketing mix. This is because the four P's are interdependent. A high price for a low-quality product without any promotion and with limited distribution networks is a recipe for failure.

Product

A product is a physical good or an intangible service. Motor vehicles and motor insurance are examples. In the eyes of customers, products serve one purpose – to fulfil the needs or wants of the consumer. What differentiates one product from another are the collective and relative customer benefits of purchasing that product, such as the brand image, packaging, functions and after-sales care.

There are several categories of products (see Unit 4.3). The marketing strategy used will depend on the type of product.

- **Producer products** are industrial products such as raw materials, machinery and components that are sold to other businesses to further the production process. For example, Mittal Steel Company (the world's largest steel producer) sells their products to other businesses, such as rail and motor companies.
- **Consumer products** are those that are sold to the end-user such as private individuals. Consumer products can be further classified as *convenience products* (or fast-moving consumer goods) such as food, *consumer durables* (long lasting) such as furniture, or *speciality products* (expensive items) such as diamonds.

Some products, such as personal computers and motor vehicles, are sold to both industrial and private customers.

To maximize profits, a business tends to have a collection of related products, known as a **product line**. Honda, for example, produces a range of cars from its best-selling Honda Civic to its Acura NSX super car. To increase the customer base even further, many businesses produce more than one type of product, choosing instead to provide a wide variety known as a **product mix**. The product mix of Samsung, the largest company in South Korea, includes mobile phones, televisions, home entertainment systems, digital cameras and MP3 players. The topic of 'Product' is covered in more detail in Unit 4.3.

Price

Pricing can be one of the most difficult decisions in the marketing mix. If a product is over-priced, customers will not buy the product, no matter how good it might be. Customers will feel that they are being 'ripped off' and sales will be minimal. However, products can also be priced too low, which means they are perceived by customers as lacking in quality. Economists define the 'correct' price as the **equilibrium price** where buyers and sellers agree on an appropriate price for the product. Buyers want a price to reflect value for money and sellers want a price that exceeds their costs of production to earn sufficient profit.

The pricing decision depends on a number of factors:

- Demand – The higher the ability and willingness of customers to pay, the higher the price can be. For example, the prices of airline tickets soar in the summer due to the higher levels of demand.
- Supply – The lower the supply of a certain product on the market, the higher its price tends to be. Diamond suppliers can charge higher prices than suppliers of bottled water due to the relative scarcity of diamonds.
- Business objectives – Charities and non-profit organizations (see Unit 1.2) will price differently from firms seeking to maximize profit.
- Competition – The higher the degree of competition, the more price competitive (prices being similar to those set by rivals) firms tend to be.
- Costs of production – The higher the costs of producing a product, the higher the price tends to be.
- Corporate image – Businesses with a prestigious and exclusive image, such as Lamborghini or 5-star hotels, charge higher prices for their products.

There are numerous pricing methods that a business might use as part of its marketing strategy, and these are covered in Unit 4.4.

Place

Place is the term used to describe the ways of distributing products to customers, such as via the internet or in retail outlets. Coca-Cola, for example, uses a range of methods from wholesalers to vending machines to get their drinks to the customer. Place can also refer to the **channels of distribution** which are the intermediaries used to get a firm's products to the consumers.

Traditionally, the channels of distribution start at the factory of the manufacturer, who then sells the product to wholesalers. Wholesalers buy in bulk to reduce the cost per unit of the product. The product is then sold in smaller units to retailers. The final channel is then from the retailers to the consumers. Each intermediary will add on a profit margin to the cost paid to its supplier. Changing wants and needs of the market, such as swift deliveries and lower prices, mean that the traditional channels of distribution are less popular today. The fewer intermediaries there are in a transaction, the lower the price tends to be. Buying property directly from the seller will be cheaper than having to go through real estate agents who will charge for their services.

The topic of 'Place' is covered in more detail in Unit 4.6.

Promotion

Promotion refers to the strategies used to attract customers to a firm's products. Branding, for example, helps to differentiate a product from its rivals. Promotion is usually classified as being either *above the line* or *below the line*. The former refers to promotional activities that use mass media such as television, newspapers and radio. Below the line refers to all other promotional tactics, such as packaging, sponsorship and direct mail. In reality, most businesses use a combination of both types of promotion.

There are many examples of promotional activities (see Box 4.2a). The topic of 'Promotion' is covered in more detail in Unit 4.5.

In addition to the traditional four P's of marketing, the marketing of services includes an extra three P's (see Unit 4.1). These extra elements of the marketing mix for services are: people, process and physical evidence.

Box 4.2a Examples of promotional activities

Advertising – This tends to be the most expensive form of promotion. Advertisements are commonly carried via television, radio, newspapers, magazines, posters and the internet.

Sales promotion – This is a temporary way of boosting sales. Examples include price reductions, gift vouchers, competitions and free gifts or samples.

Sponsorship – This refers to financial gifts or donations in support of an event or a business venture in return for a prominent display of the sponsor's name. Coca-Cola is one of the main sponsors of the Olympic Games and its brand, logo and slogans appear throughout the promotional period.

Publicity – This is the marketing process of getting good press and media coverage. This might be achieved through using famous celebrities to endorse a firm's products, for example.

People (customer relations management – CRM)

The attitudes and aptitudes of the people employed by a firm will determine the experience and quality of service given to customers. The Chinese have a saying, "A man without a smiling face must not open a shop." A highly motivated and competent sales team is more likely to deliver good customer service than a demotivated and incompetent team. Happy customers are more likely to stay loyal to a business and can also be a good source of marketing through positive *word-of-mouth promotion* (see Unit 4.5) to their friends and family. Customer service does not simply stop after sales are made; in fact, a firm that provides relatively better after-sales customer support can gain a competitive advantage over its rivals.

Customer relations management (CRM) involves setting standards for, and training staff to deliver, good customer service. CRM also emphasizes *customer lifetime value* (the profitability that can be gained during the lifetime of a positive relationship with customers) rather than the profits made from a single transaction with the customer. Business analysts argue that it is cheaper to keep existing customers than to find new ones. If this is the case, then CRM has a massive role to play in the marketing of goods and services.

Process

Process refers to the methods and procedures used to give clients the best possible customer experience. For instance, businesses will try to keep their promises to customers or handle their complaints effectively. Process can help to build customer loyalty by fulfilling the needs and wants of customers.

For example, customers are constantly in search of improved convenience. Not all items that are bought are taken away by the customer at the time of purchase. Examples of items that may need delivering to a customer include heavy items (such as furniture or fridge-freezers) and mail-order items (such as books, DVDs and clothes). It would be inconvenient for the customer to have to wait a long time for these items to be delivered. Online retailers, such as Amazon.com, provide different shipment options such as free delivery (for which the customer accepts a longer delivery time) and next-day delivery (for which the customer has to pay a premium price for the service). Customers are kept informed about their orders, which can be tracked using a reference number once an order has been paid for. Other firms, such as Ikea, charge their customers for delivery, claiming that there is no such thing as 'free' delivery (since this essentially adds to the costs of a firm). Instead they charge for their deliveries but compensate customers by charging relatively lower prices for their products.

Physical evidence

Physical evidence refers to the image portrayed by a business (or perceived by customers) regarding its tangible and observable features. In particular, businesses that offer services rather than physical products (such as hotels, schools, restaurants and banks) must pay careful attention to this element of the marketing mix. Businesses positioned in prime locations, with welcoming reception areas and well-groomed staff portray good quality and standards. When visiting a restaurant, customers will not be willing to pay high prices if the ambience is wrong (such as clutter, disorderly seating, poor hygiene and unwelcoming and untidy looking staff). Playwright and novelist Oscar Wilde (1854–1900) once said, "It is only shallow people who do not judge by appearances." Looks certainly do count when it comes to marketing a product (also see 'Packaging' below).

Finally, marketers also suggest that packaging, as an eighth P in the marketing mix, can be critical in the marketing of many products (see Figure 4.2a).

Packaging

Packaging refers to the ways in which a product is presented to the consumer. It is a form of product differentiation. Packaging can be important if a product's design, functions or features cannot be easily differentiated from others on the market. Psychologists have shown that people's moods are affected by things such as colour, texture and appearances. Businesses have used this idea in packaging to entice customers by using different colours, shapes, sizes and material in their packaging. For example, most jewellers will offer a wrapping service.

Packaging can be very important in the marketing mix due to its varied functions:

- Packaging has a profound impact on customer perceptions of a product or brand. For example, imagine buying jewellery from Tiffany & Co. or perfume from Christian Dior and receiving the contents in a simple plastic carrier bag! Customers perceive quality packaging with a quality product.
- Similarly, packaging acts as a form of differentiation. Free gift-wrapping services offered by retailers, especially during the Christmas trading period, may be enough to sway customers away from rivals that do not offer such a service.
- Packaging protects a product against damage during transportation of the product. Imagine buying a 100 inch (250 centimetre) high-definition plasma television or a crystal chandelier and having it delivered without any form of packaging.
- Labelling can be used to provide information. This might be to meet legal obligations, such as health warnings on cigarette boxes, or for a variety of promotional purposes, such as competitions on cereal boxes.
- Packaging makes the distribution of products easier for a business. Boxes can be stacked on top of each other, thereby making distribution easier, safer and faster.
- Packaging can be used to encourage **impulse buying** (unplanned purchases). Confectionery and other food items sold in supermarkets often have eye-catching packaging or enticing messages such as '20% extra free' to make customers buy the product.
- Finally, packaging is used to advertise the brand or the business. For example, carrier bags usually incorporate the name of the firm or brand.

One drawback of packaging is the cost. Customers, of course, are the ones who ultimately pay for the privilege of attractive packaging. Environmentalists would also argue that marketing creates excess packaging, at the cost of environmental damage. A report in *Fortune* magazine in November 2006 stated that Wal-Mart saved $2.4 million and one million barrels of oil per annum in shipping costs by eliminating excess packaging.

Some people argue that packaging should not be seen as a separate element of the marketing mix because it is essentially a form of promotion. Nevertheless, there is no doubt that packaging *does* affect costs, prices, customer perceptions and consumer demand.

Figure 4.2a The 8 P's of marketing

Question 4.2.1

Del Monte Foods

Del Monte is an American foods company based in San Francisco. Its products, which include canned fruits and vegetables, fruit snacks, fruit sorbets, tuna, and pet foods, are sold all over the world. According to Del Monte's website, over 55% of American families have a dog and/or cat and the firm is keen to capitalize on this market. Its **vision statement** states that the company is "committed to enriching the lives of today's family – everyone in the family, including pets".

Source: adapted www.delmonte.com/company

a Define the meaning of **vision statement**. *[2 marks]*

b Evaluate how the marketing mix helps a business such as Del Monte achieve its organizational objectives. *[8 marks]*

ETHICS OF MARKETING

Ethics are the moral principles that guide business behaviour (see Unit 1.3). Marketing ethics refers to the moral aspects of a firm's marketing strategies. Unethical marketing behaviour exists when moral codes of practice are not adhered to and when such actions are offensive to members of the general public.

For example, **bait-and-switch** marketing techniques are considered to be unethical. Bait and switch is a controversial marketing method used to entice customers by advertising deals that are simply too good to be true. Once customers are hooked onto the deal (the bait), they discover that it is no longer available and change to purchasing another more pricey alternative (the switch) from the business. High-pressure sales tactics are used to ensure that the captured audience makes the switch. Examples of businesses that use bait and switch include:

- Airline companies advertise cheap flights from $10, when in fact only several seats are available at this price. Once they are sold, and quite often to their own staff, the promotion is continued although there are no more seats left at the advertised price. Customers therefore end up paying higher prices.
- Mobile phone retailers advertise a new product, but it is very limited in supply or simply out of stock. Customers have to end up buying higher priced models.
- Real estate companies launching new developments often use advertisements such as 'Apartments from just $250,000 with just $1,000 deposit needed' when in fact only one apartment is being sold at that price. It is likely to have already been sold before the advertisement even goes out to print!

It was reported in *The Times* newspaper that the people of Britain pay up to £1 billion ($2 billion) every year because of dubious marketing tactics such as bait and switch. Other examples of misleading, deceptive or unethical advertising techniques include:

- Health fraud, such as unsubstantiated promises of overnight medical cures
- 'Get rich quick' schemes using promotional activities that offer people the opportunity to get rich in a very short time span with minimal effort
- Travel fraud involving misleading information being given to travellers, such as descriptions of hotel facilities and supposedly 'sea view' rooms
- *Product misrepresentation* using brand names similar to well-known trademarks, such as China's Rasonic and JNC (both variations of Japan's Panasonic and JVC)

- Exploitation of weaknesses using fear tactics that prey on people's vulnerability or pre-empting urgency such as 'limited stocks only'
- Unsubstantiated claims using promotional declarations that cannot be proved, such as '9 out of 10 tests prove…' or '4 out of 5 people prefer…'
- *Pester power* involving using children to pester their parents into buying certain products, such as toys, fast food and automobiles, and choosing certain holiday destinations
- *Confusion marketing* using a marketing strategy that involves businesses swamping customers with excessive price information. Being inundated with such confusing information prevents customers from making informed choice, with the aim that customers won't be bothered switching to products of rivals firms. This method is commonly found when marketing mobile phone subscription plans and mortgage deals.

The factors that affect the ethical stance (or approach) of a business will depend on the moral principles that are held by management, the organization and society as a whole. However, whether an act is deemed as ethical can often be rather subjective. This is because what is offensive to one person or group of people may not be to another. The above examples are regarded by most people to be rather unethical. However, the examples in Box 4.2b may be seen as unethical business behaviour by some, whilst others are not offended at all by such acts.

Box 4.2b Ethical marketing?

Would you consider the following marketing campaigns as unethical and/or offensive?

- In 2002, advertising producers 2DTV had two of their advertisements banned. One featured President George W. Bush putting a video cassette into a toaster and the other featured football celebrity David Beckham asking his wife how to spell 'DVD'.
- Would you consider McDonald's marketing of their 'Happy Meal' as unethical? Some people argue that by targeting children, especially in an age of growing child obesity in many parts of the world, parents face unnecessary pressure to buy their children fast-food products.
- China recently relaxed their rules on nudity in magazines and newspapers.
- It is still legal to use television and radio advertising of cigarettes and tobacco products in some countries.
- In 2005, Daimler Chrysler released its luxury motor vehicle, the $2.6 million armoured Maybach. The Hong Kong marketing campaign featured mock kidnappers shooting at the bullet-proof car.

Question 4.2.2

Banning pester power

Pester power is a marketing tool that aims to put pressure on parents by targeting advertisements at children. A 2007 European Union (EU) directive banned pester power techniques in all member countries. The EU also banned businesses from using bait-and-switch marketing, which it claims is misleading and can offend members of the public.

The rationale behind the EU's change in legislation, which replaced all national consumer protection laws at the time, is to force companies to trade more fairly.

a Examine whether it is ethical to market products directly at children. *[6 marks]*

b Discuss the likely outcome of marketing campaigns designed to shock, and possibly offend, members of the general public. *[9 marks]*

The use of unethical marketing, whether deliberate or otherwise, is a high-risk strategy. Marketing tactics that are misleading or offensive can backfire and make customers boycott the products of a business. Furthermore, pressure has been placed on governments to intervene to ensure that the general public is protected from immoral business activity. Therefore, most businesses abide by certain rules for ethical marketing. These rules are known as an ethical code of practice. The guidelines on ethical marketing in the **ethical code of practice** help to serve three main functions:

- Identify acceptable business practices.
- Foster internal management and control.
- Avoid confusion regarding what is and what is not acceptable.

In most countries, governments have controls on marketing activities of businesses. In the UK, for example, advertising is carefully monitored through certain measures including:

- Regulation of television and radio advertisements by the Office of Communications (Ofcom). This government agency's main duties are to promote healthy competition in the industry and to ensure that citizens are protected from unethical advertising. All advertisements are screened before authorization is given for broadcasting.
- Regulation of advertisements and sales promotions by the independent Advertising Standards Authority (ASA) agency. The ASA is funded by the advertising industry rather than by the government. The self-regulating industry empowers the ASA to ensure that all broadcast and non-broadcast advertisements must be "legal, decent, honest and truthful" and that they must not cause grave or widespread offence.
- Consumer protection legislation to uphold the rights of consumers. For example, the *Weights and Measures Act* stops businesses from misrepresenting the weight or size of the products being traded. So, a 500 ml bottle of water must contain that amount of content and not, for example, 400 ml. Under the *Trade Descriptions Act*, businesses must not make false or fabricated claims about their products either.
- Careful monitoring of restrictive trade practices, such as price fixing, by the Office of Fair Trading (OFT). Multinationals are able to use advertising expenditure as a form of barrier to entry to an industry. For example, in February 2005, Chanel spent $250 million on promoting its new 14,000 square feet (1,300 square metres) store in Japan. This can make it very difficult for smaller firms trying to compete in the industry. The OFT will intervene in business activity, if necessary, in order to prevent unfair and restrictive competition.

Question 4.2.3

Offensive advertising: a strategy?

Is unethical marketing a business mishap or an intentional strategy? A business may provoke a calculated 'reverse reaction' from customers through deliberately offending a particular **segment** in the market. For example, Nestlé's Yorkie chocolate bar used the slogans 'It's *not* for girls' and 'It's *not* for handbags'. This may have offended many females, but the resulting increase in the sales of Yorkie bars suggests that, if carried out effectively, offensive marketing may not only increase brand awareness but also increase demand for the product.

a Define the term **segment** as used in a marketing context. *[2 marks]*

b Discuss whether firms should act ethically in their advertising campaigns or whether offensive marketing is simply an effective marketing strategy. *[8 marks]*

MARKETING AUDIT

A marketing audit is a systematic review of the current strengths and weaknesses of a firm. Marketing audits help to clarify the marketing opportunities and threats facing a business, and allow managers to make any necessary changes to their plan. The review will examine internal and external issues such as:

- The business's marketing objectives and strategies
- The existing products and brands sold by the business
- An assessment of the effectiveness of the firm's recent marketing activities
- The firm's market share (It is rising or falling? Are markets growing?)
- Competitor analysis (Which are the largest of its rivals? How much of a threat do they pose?)
- An update on the demographic profile(s) of the firm's customers.

The information found in a marketing audit give managers an overview of their current marketing situation. The audit can then be used to aid marketing planning. It can also help in decision-making by applying the information in the audit to management tools such as SWOT analysis and PEST analysis (see Units 1.5 and 1.6).

HIGHER LEVEL

HIGHER LEVEL EXTENSION: PORTER'S FIVE FORCES ANALYSIS

Management guru Michael Porter has been a highly influential writer. One of his most famous theories, called **five forces analysis**, looks at assessing the nature of competition within an industry (see Figure 4.2b). Hence, this theory is also referred to as **competitor analysis**. The theory gives managers some insight into the degree of competition within the industry they operate so as to identify the important issues that need addressing.

An industry can be defined as a group of rival businesses that operate within the same market. Their products are seen by customers as substitutes for one another. Honda, Nissan and Toyota are firms in the automobile industry. Virgin Atlantic, British Airways, Air France and Lufthansa all operate in the airline industry.

Porter suggests that there are five competitive forces that determine the long-term attractiveness and profitability of an industry:

- Threat of *new entrants* to an industry
- Threat of *substitutes*

- Bargaining power of *suppliers*
- Bargaining power of *buyers*
- Extent of rivalry among *existing competitors*.

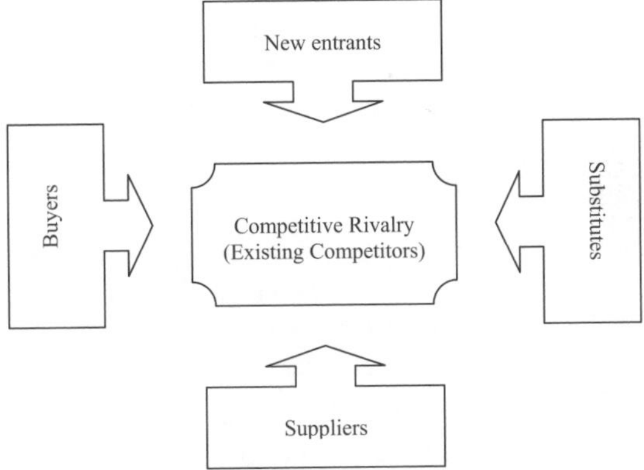

Figure 4.2b Porter's five forces analysis

Threat of new entrants

The threat of new entrants to an industry will usually intensify competition in an industry. Whether new firms can enter an industry depends on government legislation and the nature of **barriers to entry**. High barriers to entry exist in certain industries, such as the airline industry. The existence of high entry barriers prevents new entrants from being attracted to the market. In other industries, such as the catering industry, entry barriers are low and so a larger number of firms exist in the market.

Barriers to entry may be classed as natural or artificial. **Natural entry barriers** exist due to the nature of an industry, such as the high set-up costs in the fuel and power industries. **Artificial entry barriers** are hurdles and obstacles deliberately set up by existing firms to prevent others from entering the market. In reality, it is not always clear whether some barriers, such as trade secrets and know-how, are natural or artificial. The main barriers to entry include:

- *Economies of scale* (see Unit 1.7) – Existing firms may operate on such a large scale, thereby enjoying huge economies of scale, that it would be very difficult for a new firm to compete on price. For example, soft-drinks giant Coca-Cola would face little, if any, threat as they are likely to be able to undercut the price of any new entrant to the industry.
- *Legal barriers* – Government legislation is a potentially large barrier to entry. Setting up in the catering industry will require businesses to adhere to hygiene, health and safety laws. This is relatively easier than obtaining the right qualifications to set up a law firm or a health clinic. Businesses may also find legal problems when trying to operate in overseas markets. Products may also be protected by patents and copyrights (see Unit 3.5).
- *Start-up costs* – Most businesses start off on a small scale, usually set up as a sole proprietorship or as a partnership. This is because the cost of raising capital is difficult for new businesses. In industries with high start-up costs, there is less likely to be many new entrants as they lack the financial ability to enter such industries.
- *Know-how and trade secrets* – Trade secrets and expertise also help to give existing firms a competitive advantage over any new entrants. It is a high risk strategy for any business to enter markets in which it does not have any expertise. Believers in asset-led marketing (see Unit 4.1) argue that businesses should only focus on their core competencies rather than to diversify into the unknown. This is partly why many large firms have a huge research and development budget.

- *The threat of retaliation* – Existing firms are likely to strike back at the threat of new entrants taking away their market share. Market leaders in the industry will have the financial and intellectual resources to fend itself against competition. This may therefore prevent new firms from trying to penetrate the market.
- *High market standing* – Some businesses may be so well established that they have a large and loyal customer base. Having high market standing means that the business stands out from the competitors in the industry. This could be due to the reputation and trust that they have generated over a long period of time. Subsequently, this can make it very difficult for new firms to compete.

Threat of substitutes

The existence of substitute products in an industry can lower the attractiveness and profitability of an industry. The larger the degree of choice for customers, the lower the profit margins tend to be as firms will have less pricing power. The extent to which substitutes are a threat (i.e. the ability of customers to make a switch to rival products) depends on:

- *Brand loyalty* for existing products – The stronger the brands in an industry, the larger the threat they will be. This will tend to lower the profitability for other firms in the industry as customers are unwilling to switch between brands.
- The *relative price* of substitutes – The more competitive the price, the higher the likelihood of substitution tends to be. A small difference in price might be enough to entice some customers to switch from one product or brand to another.
- The *costs of switching* to substitute products – Some businesses use the strategy of making it difficult for customers to switch brands. For example, manufacturers of digital cameras and mobile phones use different formats for their memory cards. This means that the owner of a Canon IXUS digital camera cannot use peripheral products (such as the memory cards, battery charger and cables) if they switch to rival brands such as Sony's CyberShot or Olympus's Stylus. Hence, this makes substitution more costly and troublesome for the customer.

Bargaining power of suppliers

Suppliers are businesses that provide stocks (raw materials, manufactured products and finished goods) to businesses in a particular industry. For instance, McKey Food Services Ltd provides the chicken nuggets and burger meats to McDonald's Restaurants in much of South East Asia. Foxconn produces a large range of mobile phones for Nokia and Motorola.

The bargaining power of a supplier will directly affect the cost of the items that a business buys from the supplier. Large multinationals will tend to have significant power over its suppliers, such as Yue Yuen Holdings which supplies sports shoes to companies such as Nike and Adidas. Multinational businesses will be in a better position to dictate prices and delivery times. However, if suppliers hold most of the bargaining power, such as Coca-Cola, then they are likely to charge relatively higher prices. Retailers may rely on the supplier's products in order to attract customers to their stores. Hence, the bargaining strength of existing suppliers will tend to make the industry less attractive for any new entrants.

A supplier will tend to have strong bargaining power if it has some degree of monopoly power, i.e. it is the only provider or one of a few suppliers in an industry with many buyers. In addition, suppliers of products that are highly differentiated will also tend to have strong bargaining power. Product differentiation (see Unit 4.3) helps to attract customers and ensures that prices are higher than would otherwise be the case. Examples include products such as Rolex watches, Ferrari cars, Nike sportswear, Jimmy Choo shoes and Ritz-Carlton hotels.

Bargaining power of buyers

Buyers are the customers, both private individuals and businesses, who purchase products in a market. They therefore form the level of demand in an industry. If buyers have high bargaining power it means that they have a large degree of influence over the decisions made by a business. Buyers tend to have greater bargaining power in highly competitive markets, where customers can switch to other suppliers if they are unhappy with a firm's price, quality and/or level of service.

Buyers will tend to have greater bargaining power over their suppliers when:

- There are many suppliers in the industry. The greater the number of sellers, the greater the choice available to buyers. This therefore raises the relative bargaining strength of buyers.
- There are a few dominant buyers. Businesses that rely on several key buyers are in a weaker bargaining position. For example, Airbus relies heavily on orders from a few buyers such as Emirates and Singapore Airlines. Hence, the few dominant buyers will have greater bargaining power over their supplier.
- Products in the market are homogeneous (or standardized). This gives buyers stronger bargaining power since the products can be purchased from other suppliers with relative ease. Homogeneity helps to keeps costs down for the supplier, but standardization of products means that prices are also relatively lower.

Intensity of rivalry (existing competitors)

This final force refers to the degree of competitive rivalry in an industry. Intensity of rivalry refers to both the degree of competition and the type of competition. For example, there is very little competition facing dominant market leaders such as Microsoft (computer software industry). By contrast, the degree of competition in the airline industry is much more intense. For example, airlines often engage in price wars whereby firms attempt to undercut the prices of each other (see Unit 4.4). They will also compete by using *non-price competition*, such as the use of loyalty schemes (known in the airline industry as 'frequent flyer' programmes).

The intensity of rivalry in an industry will depend on two key factors:

- The nature of barriers to entry – Rivalry is more intense in markets that have low entry barriers, where there are lots of small-sized firms. By contrast, monopolists do not have much, if any, competitive rivalry.
- The degree of product differentiation – Businesses that are able to successfully differentiate their products face less competitive rivalry, whereas firms that provide homogeneous products will need to rely on price competition.

The five forces allow businesses to identify the various areas that need strategic focus. For example, the threat of new entrants would be low for Nokia whereas the bargaining power of buyers would be strong. The intensity of rivalry from existing competitors such as Motorola, Samsung and Sony-Ericsson would also be high. Hence, Nokia is likely to focus on price and non-price competition in order to attract buyers.

Exam Tip!
If asked in an exam to design a **marketing plan**, this is an open question and students are expected to use relevant theory that is applicable to the business in question. These may include the marketing mix, the Ansoff matrix, the Boston matrix, position mapping and Porter's five forces analysis.

MARKETING OBJECTIVES

Marketing objectives are the targets that the marketing department wishes to achieve. These objectives should be compatible with the firm's overall objectives (see Unit 1.3). For example, if growth were an organizational objective, the marketing department may consider entering overseas markets and/or launching new products. As with all organizational objectives, marketing objectives should be specific, measurable, agreed, realistic and time constrained.

Marketing guru Philip Kotler suggested that the fundamental objective of marketing is to create customer satisfaction in a profitable way. Hence, setting marketing objectives is important because the targets can:

- Provide a sense of purpose, direction and motivation for the marketing department
- Allow progress to be monitored and success to be assessed
- Help in the planning and development of appropriate marketing strategies.

Marketing objectives may include, amongst many others, any combination of the following:

- Maintain/increase **market share** – This can be achieved through *market penetration* strategies (see Unit 1.7) that allow the business to increase sales revenues and profits.
- **Market leadership** – This means that the firm aims to have the greatest market share in an industry.
- **Product positioning** – This refers to attempts to change the image of the organization held by consumers (see section on *position maps* later in this Unit).
- **Consumer satisfaction** – Ensuring that the consumers are content with issues such as the quality of the product and its price.
- **Diversification** – This refers to the objective of successfully marketing new products in new markets. This is a high-risk strategy that only tends to be used by financially stable businesses.
- **Market development** – The objective of selling existing products in new markets, such as through the use of international marketing (see Unit 4.7).
- **New product development** – This involves businesses aiming to sell new products in existing markets. This is a common marketing objective for firms operating in high-tech industries.
- **Product innovation** – This refers the objective of launching a totally original or new product onto the market. This can help a firm to gain a *first-mover advantage* in establishing itself in the market.
- **High market standing** – Market standing refers to the extent to which a firm has a presence in the marketplace. It is largely based on an organization's image and reputation, which can be maintained or enhanced by effective marketing strategies.

Constraints on achieving marketing objectives

There are numerous constraints or limitations faced by firms trying to achieve their marketing objectives. These include both internal constraints (those within the control of the business) and external constraints (those beyond the firm's control). Some examples include:

- Finance – The size of the firm's marketing budget will determine the marketing activities that can be undertaken in order to achieve its marketing objectives.
- Costs of production – The firm's costs (and its ability to exploit economies of scale) determine its capacity to compete on price and/or quality.
- The size and status of the firm – Firms that do not have high market standing might be unable to achieve their marketing objectives as they are relatively unknown.
- Social issues – The attitude of those in society can also dictate the level of success of any marketing strategy. For example, it may not be socially acceptable to market certain products

such as cigarettes or children's war toys. A shift in consumer fashion and tastes will also affect the success of any marketing campaign.

- Time lags – There will be a delay between an organization's marketing activities and its expenditure having any impact on customers. This means that the organization may face short-term liquidity problems (see Unit 3.3).
- Activities and reaction of competitors – Rival businesses might launch new or improved products which hinder the success of the firm's marketing. In addition, competitors are likely to respond to the marketing of the business, such as engaging in price wars (see Unit 4.4).
- The state of the economy – It will be much harder for a business to achieve its marketing objectives during a global recession, since consumers and businesses are more careful about their spending. A high exchange rate (see Unit 1.5) will also present problems for international marketers.
- The political and legal environment – Government rules and regulations can limit the extent to which marketers can achieve their targets. For example, it is not possible for fast-food firms operating in the European Union to advertise on children's television programmes.

THE ROLE OF MARKET RESEARCH

Market research refers to marketing activities designed to discover the opinions, beliefs and feelings of potential and existing customers, i.e. it serves to identify and anticipate the wants and needs of customers. Market research involves collecting primary and secondary data and information to gain some insight and understanding into the structure of a market. For example, a business may need to gather information on competitors, the state of the economy and the level of demand in order to assess the current situation facing the firm and the outlook for its future. There are two main categories of market research: ad hoc and continuous market research.

- **Ad hoc market research** takes place on an 'as and when necessary' basis. The focus of the research is on specific marketing problems or issues. Ad hoc research tends to be on a one-off basis. For example, firms may test a new product on a sample of customers in order to gauge their reactions in order to perfect their launch campaign. Perception mapping (see 'Position (perception) maps' on page 488) is also researched using ad hoc methods.
- **Continuous research**, unlike ad hoc research, takes place on a regular and ongoing basis. Research is carried out over and over, perhaps on a monthly or yearly basis. For example, governments usually calculate the cost of living based on the price changes of a representative sample of products bought by a typical household. Market research firms report annual 'league tables' containing information, such as the most popular brands in a certain country, region or the world. Broadcasting companies record and report viewer and audience numbers on a regular basis. The movie and music industries also compile weekly 'Top 10' lists based on sales figures.

Uses of market research

The role of marketing research serves several purposes:

- Gives businesses up-to-date and accurate information. This is particularly important in fast-paced industries that are always changing, such as the fashion and consumer electronics industries.
- Allows a business to see whether current products meet the needs of customers. Customer tastes and preferences change over time and market research can help firms to gather this information.
- Allows businesses to improve their marketing by using a distinct marketing mix for each customer target group (known as *market segment*).

- Assesses potential customer reactions to a new product by testing it on a small group of customers. This can prevent huge losses incurred if an unsuccessful product is launched on a mass scale.
- Gives businesses an understanding of the activities and strategies used by their competitors.
- Helps businesses to predict what is likely to happen in the future. Understanding the likely trends will enable firms to react accordingly in order to maximize future opportunities.

Market research is frequently carried out when a business plans to launch a new product. Effective market research will help to reduce the risks of failure by investigating the needs and wants of customers. If research findings show that customers react negatively to the product, the business can either make necessary adjustments or scrap the project altogether (without having spent huge amounts of money on a national launch of the product). Such market research could be used to establish answers to the following questions:

- Are customers likely to buy the product?
- Which customer groups are interested in the product?
- How often are they likely to purchase the product?
- Which brands do customers see as being a rival to the marketed product?
- How much are they willing to pay?
- What are the preferred (most effective) types of promotion?
- Where and how should the products be sold?

Drawback of market research

The general limitations of market research are:

- Information and findings are only as good as the research methodology used. Directly asking customers whether they are willing to pay higher prices will generate obvious responses. Similarly, asking smokers only whether smoking should be banned from public areas will generate pointless results. In business terms, this is known as **garbage in, garbage out** (GIGO) whereby unreliable or inaccurate input data generates poor quality output of information.
- Data and information can also be inaccurate or unreliable due to **bias**. Company annual reports or company websites, for example, will obviously report on the more positive aspects of business performance. Interviewer bias will also distort research findings.
- The **cost** of good market research is often very high. Postal and telephone questionnaires, for instance, can be very expensive. Data analysts also need time and financial rewards to generate the findings from market research.

Ultimately, market research helps to reduce business risks. Being able to accurately forecast future market trends will give a business greater chance of success, although there must be some consideration for the limitations of drawbacks of market research.

PRIMARY AND SECONDARY RESEARCH

Primary research

Primary research is market research that involves gathering new data first-hand for a specific study. For example, if an organization wanted to know how staff felt about their working environment, primary research would be used. Primary research, also known as **field research**, is often used by firms to gather data and information directly from customers to identify their buying patterns and to anticipate changes in their behaviour. There are several methods of conducting primary research, such as: questionnaires, observations, experimentation and online surveys.

Questionnaires

Questionnaires are the most common method of primary research. A questionnaire is a document that contains a series of questions in order to collect primary data for a specific purpose. Questionnaires can be used in a variety of ways:

- *Self-completed questionnaires* – These are questionnaires that are completed by a sample of people who then return them to the researcher or business. Many hotels and restaurants, for example, have feedback questionnaires to gather the views of their customers. Businesses can then use this information to identify problems, trends and suggestions for improvement.
- *Personal questionnaires* – These are face-to-face questionnaires conducted as an interview, perhaps in an office or in the street. This method benefits from the interviewer being able to address any questions that may arise from the questionnaire (such as clarifying to the interviewee what certain questions mean). It is also quicker for the interviewer to complete the survey due to his or her familiarity with the questionnaire.
- *Postal questionnaires* – These are questionnaires sent to people's homes or office addresses for them to complete in their own time. One disadvantage of this method is that people may simply see such questionnaires as junk mail and hence ignore them. Postal questionnaires also have to be returned to the researcher. To create an incentive for people to return postal questionnaires, businesses often offer free postage (the business pays for the postage) and some will offer prizes or gifts as incentives. This will obviously add to the costs of the business.
- *Telephone questionnaires* – These are similar to personal questionnaires but the interviewer uses telecommunications technology rather than conduct a face-to-face interview. The benefit of this is that a larger number of people in a wider geographical spread can be covered in the research. The main disadvantages are the relatively higher costs of such research and the low response rate since a large number of people are not willing to take part in telephone interviews.

Due to the potential benefits of using questionnaires and their high cost, good questionnaire design is of real importance to a business. Good questionnaires should:

- Avoid *bias* in order to collect meaningful and useful data. The wording of questions should not distort answers from respondents. Asking people how much they like Coca-Cola is not as good a question as asking them which brand of cola they prefer. Asking smokers for their views of anti-smoking campaigns will produce inappropriate data.
- Avoid *jargon* (technical language) so that respondents understand the questions. This will prevent misrepresentative answers being put forward.
- Include both *closed* and *open-ended* questions. Closed questions, such as 'yes or no' questions, multiple choice options or a sliding scale, make it easier and quicker to complete questionnaires. They also aid quantitative analysis, such as the percentage of those surveyed who hold a particular view posed in the questionnaire. Open-ended questions allow the researcher to obtain qualitative answers, such as the reasons why respondents chose a particular answer. They may also provide ideas or suggestions that enable the firm to make better decisions.
- Allow all relevant data to be collected so that the *objective* of the questionnaire is met. For example, unnecessary questions should be avoided and the length of the questionnaire should be limited as far as possible.

Question 4.2.4

Questioning questionnaires

Study the questionnaire below and answer the questions that follow.

Questionnaire Research

Is it feasible to open another branch of Lightning Greeting Cards in Fo Tan Town Centre?

1. Name ……………………..

2. Age: Under 10 ❑ 10–15 ❑ 15–25 ❑

26–35 ❑ 36–64 ❑ 65+ ❑

3. Gender:

4. Where do you live? ……………………..

5. Do you shop in Fo Tan? ………… 6. How often? …………

7. Do you shop in Lightning Greeting Cards? …………8. Why? ……………

9. What item(s) do you buy there? ……………………………….

10. If a new Lightning Greeting Cards store were to open in Fo Tan Town Centre, would you use it? Yes ❑

Thanks!!!

a Identify and explain any **three** mistakes in the questionnaire. *[6 marks]*

b Use examples to distinguish between quantitative and qualitative questions. *[4 marks]*

Before using a questionnaire as market research, it is common for a questionnaire to be trialled (tested) with a small group of people. This can help to correct any errors or omissions in the questionnaire so that the results from the final questionnaire better serve the needs of the researcher.

Questionnaires have the benefit that they can generate quantitative and qualitative answers specific to the needs of the researcher. If designed properly, they can also be very simple to complete thereby making the process easier for respondents. However, questionnaires can be a very costly and time-consuming process since it is necessary to use a large sample to get statistically representative answers. There might also be reservations with the findings from a questionnaire due to bias or dishonest responses.

Observations

This method of primary research involves watching how people behave and respond in different situations. It can be done under controlled conditions (rather like a laboratory test) or as real-life situations (where people do not know that they are being observed). Observations can be carried out using surveillance filming, photographic evidence or by using a survey. Traffic audits, for example, use all three of these methods to measure the flow of traffic on certain roads or in certain areas. Observations are often used by businesses such as restaurants, hotels, theme parks and the post office to measure the average time it takes to serve a customer (queuing times).

Observations are beneficial in that they record people's actual behaviour rather than what people say they would do, as in the case of a questionnaire. However, observations do not necessarily reveal *why* a person behaves or responds in the way they do. The only way to establish the reasons behind a person's motivation is to ask them, either in a direct or indirect way. One final point about observation is that the researcher needs to consider the ethical issues surrounding their research. The use of photography or audio-visual recordings has broadened the information that can be gathered by the researcher. However, the use of such technology can be seen as an invasion of privacy, especially if inappropriately used in the workplace to observe employees.

Experimentation

Experimentation is the process of introducing marketing activities to a group of people to measure their responses and reactions. For example, an ice cream manufacturer may give out different samples to customers in a shopping mall to see which flavours they prefer. Experimentation is often referred to as **piloting** or **test marketing** and can save a business a lot of time and money by identifying errors or areas in need of improvement. It can help to provide useful information to the business before it launches the product on a much larger scale. This also helps to reduce risks and uncertainties.

Online surveys

Online surveys using email or dedicated software programmes, such as Zoomerang.com, are an increasingly popular way of gathering primary data. Many schools, for example, use online surveys to find out the views of staff and students on a range of issues, such as getting feedback on school uniform and staff induction programmes. Hotels use online surveys to get feedback from their customers and employees. The findings can then help the organization to improve its products, customer service and level of staff motivation.

Online surveys are much cheaper than other methods of primary research such as paper-based questionnaires or telephone interviews. Dedicated software can also be used to help the researcher to collate quantitative research data, thereby saving a lot of time and resources.

Advantages of primary research. Businesses might spend money on conducting primary research for several reasons:

- Up to date – Secondary research data tends to be more dated and therefore less reliable than primary research findings.
- Relevance – Primary research is carried out for the specific purpose of the business and therefore directly addresses the questions which need to be answered. Conversely, secondary research data is not always in a format that can be easily used by a firm.
- Confidential and unique – Since the research is done first-hand, no-one else (including rivals) has access to the information.
- Objectivity – Primary research data and information helps to provide hard facts and figures to aid decision-making.

Disadvantages of primary research. These include:

- Time consuming – It can be a very tedious and lengthy task to collect primary data that is accurate and representative. This will then delay decision-making and could mean that marketing opportunities are not exploited.
- Costly – Collecting primary data is usually quite costly. This might be due to the time involved to collect quality data or because the data is difficult to collect. This is why many businesses hire specialist research agencies to conduct market research on their behalf.
- Validity – Due to the high cost of collecting primary research, data is often collected from a sample of the population. However, faults in market research including poor questionnaire design or too small a sample size will lead to misleading results. In addition, people are not always honest in their responses to certain questions (such as age, income level or their ability to pay certain prices for a product). Cultural differences and people's suspicion of the intention of the researcher may also be factors that affect the responses given.

Secondary research

Secondary research, also known as **desk research**, involves the collection of second-hand data and information, i.e. the data or information already exists in another form. This means that the data and information, such as reports in a newspaper or magazine, have been gathered by others.

Secondary research data tends to be cheaper and faster to collect than primary research data because the data is already available. However, the data or information have not been specifically collected for the study in question so only has some relevance. Furthermore, secondary data and information can be outdated and the reliability of the source may be questioned.

Secondary research can be collected from internal and external sources. Internal sources are those that have already been gathered by the organization itself, such as company annual reports and sales records. External sources of secondary research come from outside the organization and include sources such as government data, information from competitors, newspaper articles, encyclopaedias and the internet.

Advantages of secondary research. These include:

- If the data or information exists, it is generally cheaper and faster to collect and analyse than primary research.
- There is a huge range of sources that the researcher can use, making secondary data usually more accessible than primary data.
- Secondary research often provides an insight to changes or trends in a whole industry, such as whether customers are spending more money on household goods, automobiles and tourism. This allows a business to develop strategies in response to these changes.

Disadvantages of secondary research. These include:

- Second-hand data may be out of date or can become outdated quite quickly.
- The data or information may be in an inappropriate format for the researcher because it has been collected for another purpose. Therefore, the data and information need to be further adapted or manipulated to suit the specific needs of the business.
- Secondary research may only provide partial information as it was produced for a different purpose; hence, it does not address all the questions sought by the researcher.
- Unlike primary research, the data and information is widely available to competitors.

In reality, it is common for both primary and secondary research methods to be used. This is because neither method is necessarily better than the other as it depends on what data or information a firm needs to collect. Secondary research is generally quicker and cheaper to gather but may be out of date or may not be sufficiently appropriate. Primary research findings may contain errors or bias, but can provide information not available through secondary data sources.

QUALITATIVE AND QUANTITATIVE MARKET

In addition to primary and secondary research, market research can also be classified as being qualitative or quantitative.

Qualitative market research

Qualitative market research is a form of research that involves getting non-numerical answers and opinions from respondents. It is commonly used as part of primary research. The main purpose of a researcher using qualitative market research is to understand the behaviour, attitudes and perceptions of customers or employees. 'Soft' answers (people's views rather than hard facts or objective evidence) are sought by the researcher. This might be done by using in-depth interviews or by asking open-ended questions, for example. The two main types of qualitative research methods are *focus groups* and *in-depth interviews*.

Focus groups

Focus groups involve getting small discussion groups together to provide an insight into the attitudes and behaviour of customers. The group may, for example, be asked to discuss the merits of alternative advertisements or to give feedback on the prototype of a product. Detailed questions are often asked to the group during the research. The group is typically made up of several participants who share a similar customer profile. It is argued that by using a group approach, participants are more likely to engage in discussions and generate more insightful information.

One drawback of using focus groups is that only extroverts tend to take part; those who shy from group discussions and debates are unlikely to participate and therefore their views are unregistered. Furthermore, there may be some pressure for group members to conform to the majority view rather than to advocate their own opinions. Another potential limitation is that participants usually have to be paid, either in cash or in lieu such as a free meal, for their time and contributions. This expense will add to the overall research costs.

It is common for focus groups to be used in conjunction with observations and audio-visual recordings of the discussions and behaviour of group participants to aid research analysis. The use of focus groups could provide important information to the marketing department in devising and refining their marketing strategies. Hence, focus groups are often used when a business plans to launch a new brand or new product.

A variation of focus groups is to use **consumer panels**. These consist of small groups of consumers within a business's target market who are used for regular market research. By using the same panel, it saves the business from having to find new respondents (as in the case of focus groups). In addition, since panellists are usually specialists, they are particularly useful for conducting research that requires specialist knowledge rather than using a random sample. For example, car manufacturers often use consumer panels formed by a group of loyal and specialist customers prior to launching new models.

In-depth interviews

In-depth interviews involve an interviewer and a customer having a one-on-one interview to find out more about the interviewee's personal situation and opinions. These interviews are usually carried out in person (face to face) although in-depth telephone interviews can also be used. The findings from all interviews are then analysed to identify the views that customers share. Identifying the differences can also be important though as it may help a business to refine its marketing. In-depth interviews are often used when a business is planning to introduce change and new initiatives. They can be used to investigate the views of respondents to a new proposal. Beliefs, attitudes and feelings can also be examined in detail.

However, interviews will provide a range of non-quantifiable information which may prove to be difficult to analyse or to make any extrapolations from. In addition, interviews tend to be lengthy as a method of research. There is also huge scope for interviewer bias which can have an effect on the way in which respondents answer.

Advantages of qualitative research. These include:

- Qualitative research is better than quantitative research to explore the driving (motivators) and restraining forces (demotivators) concerning the behaviour and attitudes of employees or customers.
- Information gathered from qualitative research can be very rich in depth. Unlike a questionnaire or a survey, there is flexibility in the process to gather additional and useful information from interviewees.

- Due to the low number of respondents involved in qualitative market research, it can be inexpensive yet provide useful information to the marketing department.
- With one-to-one interviews, respondents are not under the pressure of conforming to the views of the majority. This should therefore help to generate more realistic and representative responses.

Disadvantages of qualitative research. These include:

- Due to the small sample size typically used in qualitative research, the findings cannot be used to represent the whole population. Further research, both primary and secondary, may therefore be necessary.
- It can be very time consuming to conduct and to interpret the findings. Quantitative responses (such as the percentage of staff that support an initiative at work) are easier and quicker to collate than qualitative responses (such as the reasons why staff do not support the initiative). Hence, analysis of the results can also be rather subjective.
- A high level of interviewing expertise is required to engage and encourage respondents. The cost of hiring skilled interviewers can be high.
- Interviewer bias can be easily introduced to serve the researcher's own purpose. If this is the case, the validity of the findings becomes questionable.

Quantitative market research

Unlike qualitative market research, quantitative market research relies on a much larger number of responses to get 'hard' answers (factual and measurable information rather than people's opinions) to aid statistical analysis. It involves using a representative sample to gauge the views of the population. Examples of quantitative primary market research include surveys and questionnaires, which typically feature the use of two techniques:

- *Closed questions* – These questions allow respondents to choose from a given list of options. Examples include questions on gender, age, income level, true or false questions, and multiple choice questions.
- *Ranking or sliding scales* – For example, in a survey, customers may be asked to rank their favourite television programmes or to state the extent to which they agree with a given statement (using a scale from 'strongly agree' to 'strongly disagree').

Secondary research methods can also supply a wealth of quantitative data such as market share, sales figures or forecast changes in consumer income levels.

The advantages and disadvantages of quantitative market research are the opposite of those for qualitative methods, as outlined above. For instance, quantitative market research methods do not have the flexibility of qualitative methods because pre-set questions are used. However, since the findings can be represented numerically, the results are easier to analyse.

Question **4.2.5**

Toys 'R' Us

Toys 'R' Us is the world's largest supplier of toys, with over 13,000 chain stores around the world. It stocks toys that are based on all the latest and classic trends, such as Barbie dolls, and Star Wars and Disney characters. The toy industry is a massive business. CNN reported in late 2006 that Americans spend over $221 billion a year on toys – and that's just the figure for children aged between 8 and 12 years (known as preteens or 'tweens'). Toy manufacturers are often keen to investigate the television programmes and movies watched by children and the magazines that they read.

a Explain why Toys 'R' Us might be interested in the television programmes or magazines viewed by children. *[4 marks]*

b Analyse how market research can allow Toys 'R' Us to differentiate itself from its competitors. *[6 marks]*

HIGHER LEVEL EXTENSION: SAMPLING METHODS

All the potential customers of a particular market make up what researchers call the **population**. Since a market comprises thousands or even millions of potential customers, such as the market for textbooks or personal computers, researchers lack the time and finance to carry out market research on every person in the population. Statisticians would even argue that asking the whole population is unnecessary to get statistically valid results. Instead, a sample of the population is selected for research. **Sampling** is the practice of selecting a small group (or sample) of the population for a particular market for primary research purposes.

There are numerous methods used to choose a particular sample. The key questions to ask when deciding on the type of sampling to use are: who to ask, what to ask and whether the costs of the research can be justified. The 'best' sampling method will entail research from a large enough sample to generate representative responses.

The five main methods of sampling are: quota, random, stratified, cluster and snowballing.

Quota sampling

Quota sampling is based on market segmentation, i.e. grouping research respondents according to shared characteristics such as their age, gender or occupation. It is the most commonly used sampling method in market research. A certain number of people (known as the quota) from each segment is then selected to be part of the sample. For example, in a firm with 1,000 workers a researcher may want to interview 50 junior managers and five senior managers about a certain work-related issue. A certain number of male and female workers of different age groups may also be interviewed.

The advantage of using quota sampling is that a relatively representative sample can be obtained quickly and cheaply. The findings will be more reliable than simply asking anyone on a random basis to participate in the research.

The disadvantage of quota sampling is that the number of people interviewed in each segment and how randomly they are chosen for interview are not always representative of the population. For example, if a researcher had a quota of 100 female customers to interview, the first 100 female customers may be asked to take part in the research, without considering whether these respondents are representative of the population. Sampling errors are therefore likely to occur since not everyone gets an equal chance to be sampled.

HIGHER LEVEL

Random sampling

Random sampling, also known as **probability sampling**, involves giving everyone in the population an equal chance of being selected for the sample. The respondents are often randomly chosen by a computer using information from a database.

Random sampling is useful when all members of a population have the same or very similar characteristics. Airlines might use this method, for example, to get feedback from its business and first-class passengers. Parents of children in a school may be randomly selected to get their views on school uniform and other school-related issues.

The advantage is that everyone has an equal chance of being selected so this may help to minimize bias or unrepresentative samples being judgementally selected (as in the case of quota samples). Furthermore, it is quite easy to get a sample using this method.

The main drawback of random sampling is that it is indiscriminate, i.e. it may select people who are not part of the target group. Due to the non-discriminatory nature of random sampling, sample sizes also need to be large enough to get representative results.

Stratified sampling

Stratified sampling is similar to quota sampling in that it involves segmentation. The population is likely to be heterogeneous so needs to be subdivided into segments (known as strata) that share homogeneous or very similar characteristics. However, the difference between quota sampling and stratified sampling is that the latter method chooses a number of respondents from each stratum that is proportional to the population as a whole and then randomly selects them for interviewing. So for example, if the retired population of a country accounted for 20% of the overall population, then one in five respondents chosen for the sample would be a retired person.

This method benefits from using samples that are more representative of a particular market segment. Sampling is usually random (known as stratified random sampling) but with clearer focus so the findings will be more relevant and with less sampling errors.

One disadvantage of stratified sampling is that it can be difficult to select relevant strata, especially if the subgroups of a population are largely homogeneous. It can also be an expensive task to generate accurate information about the population and then to further subdivide this into representative subgroups.

Exam Tip!
Worked example

Assume that the management at a secondary school (high school) is proposing to change the timing of the school day. This will involve an earlier start to the day, but an earlier finish too. The management are seeking the views of staff and wish to use a stratified sample of 30 from a total of 100 teachers. The demographics of the staff are as follows:

- Full-time teachers: 40 male and 30 female staff
- Part-time teachers: 10 male and 20 female staff

Question: In order to get their stratified sample, calculate how many people should be sampled from each segment according to the above information. *[4 marks]*

Answer:

Step 1: Calculate the percentage of staff in each group.

Step 2: Stratify each group according to the percentages found in Step 1 (see table below).

Category of staff		Percentage	Stratified sample size
Full-time	Males	(40/100) = 40%	40% of 40 = 16
	Females	(30/100) = 30%	30% of 30 = 9
Part-time	Males	(10/100) = 10%	10% of 10 = 1
	Females	(20/100) = 20%	20% of 20 = 4
Total		100%	30 staff

The above analysis then tells the management to select the sample of 30 from each of the following strata:

- 16 male full-time teachers who represent 40% of the teaching population
- 9 female full-time teachers who represent 30% of the population
- 1 male part-time teacher who represents 10% of the teaching staff
- 4 female part-time teachers who represent 20% of the teachers.

Cluster

Cluster sampling is used when getting feedback from respondents involves too much time, travelling or money. For instance, it would be too time consuming and costly for a multinational to randomly interview people across all the countries that it operates in. Instead, it is more cost effective to select several geographical areas (known as clusters) and then randomly interview people within each of the chosen clusters. A firm selling travel insurance might, for example, choose to survey people living in towns near sea ports or airports. The opinions from the selected clusters are used to represent the views of the population.

The advantages of using cluster sampling are that it is quicker, easier and cheaper than other methods of sampling if the population is widely dispersed over different geographical areas. Where characteristics of customers are homogeneous, it is not necessary to sample people from every location.

The main potential drawbacks of using cluster sampling are bias and sampling error. By selecting and using just a few locations, the results may be biased because people living in the same area are likely to share homogeneous views or characteristics, such as lifestyle and social status. Increasing the number of clusters in the sample would reduce bias and sampling errors but will clearly add to costs and prolong data analysis.

Snowballing

Snowballing refers to surveys or interviews carried out with individuals who then suggest other friends, family or colleagues to increase the sample. Businesses use this technique when they are unable to get hold of appropriate respondents since the population is not clear. Snowballing is common in the financial services sector, such as health insurance, motor vehicle insurance and personal financial planning. These firms can gain access to a massive number of potential subjects for research or marketing purposes from an individual's acquaintances. Essentially, this sampling method takes a 'word of mouth' approach to develop the sample size.

The main advantage of using this sampling method is that it is cheap to get hold of the research subject's contact details. However, due to the nature of respondent-driven sampling, it is extremely difficult to make unbiased estimates from the sample. For example, a wealthy person's acquaintances are likely to have similar lifestyles and attitudes thereby enlarging potential bias in the sample.

Exam Tip!
So which sampling method is the best method? Each method has its own strengths and weaknesses. With all forms of sampling, there is a risk that the sample may not represent the population. Sampling errors such as bias or an inadequate sample size will hinder the validity of the findings. The 'best' method of sampling for a business depends on its size, financial resources, the purpose of its research and the extent to which customers have homogeneous or heterogeneous tastes. It is important, as always, to put your answers into the context of the business.

HIGHER LEVEL EXTENSION: LIMITATIONS OF SAMPLING AND SAMPLING ERRORS

HIGHER LEVEL

Sampling is not a perfect science and the findings from a sample may not be absolutely reliable. There is always the chance that respondents do not give representative or truthful answers. The larger the sample size, the more statistically reliable the answers are in reflecting the views of the population. Careful **sample design** can also help to reduce sampling errors. Sample design refers to the process of sample selection, sample structure and the plans for interpreting the results.

There are two potential types of errors when using sampling. The first type, caused by human error or human behaviour, is known as **non-sampling errors**. These arise from the researcher's mistakes in recording, processing or analysing data. Furthermore, non-sampling errors can occur because respondents do not always give truthful and honest responses. Such errors will distort the final results of the research. Statisticians use *confidence levels* in order allow for a margin of error. This measures the extent to which certainty can be attached to market research findings. Most statisticians accept nothing less than 95% confidence levels, i.e. there is only a 5% chance (2.5% either way of the predictions or findings) that the results are inaccurate.

The second type of error is known as **sampling errors** and these arise from mistakes made in the sample design. Sampling errors may arise from many different sources:

- The sample size is too small to get statistically valid responses within desired confidence levels and margins of error. If the sample size is too small, perhaps due to financial or time constraints, there will be large *sampling discrepancies* (differences in the views of the actual population and the selected sample).
- The sample selected is not representative of the population. Due to poor sample design, the sample chosen for research might be unrepresentative of the views of the population. Asking only smokers about their views on banning smoking in public places will produce highly biased findings.
- An inappropriate sampling method is used. Random sampling will, in theory, have little bias since everyone has an equal chance of being selected, but snowballing is less likely to produce results representative of the population.
- There is bias present in the research. This usually comes from bad sample design, but bias can also be introduced from poor research design such as misleading questions being asked in an interview or questionnaire.

MARKET SEGMENTATION AND CONSUMER PROFILES

A market for a particular product consists of different types of customers which can be subdivided into market segments. For example, there are many markets that exist to meet the needs and wants of children: schools, entertainment, toys and food being obvious examples. A **segment** refers to a distinct group of customers with similar characteristics, such as age or gender, and similar wants or needs. By dividing the market into different segments, it is easier for a business to analyse which group of customers buy the product and then to target these customers more distinctively. **Targeting** means that each distinctive market segment can have its own marketing mix. This might be done by producing products aimed more specifically at different market segments or by making marketing more relevant to these groups. For example, business and first-class air travellers are targeted in a very different way to those who travel by economy class. Overseas teaching vacancies are advertised in *The Times Educational Supplement* (and on its website www.tes.co.uk), a dedicated weekly newspaper for those in the teaching profession.

Consumer profiles are the characteristics of customers and consumers in different markets, such as their age, gender, income and purchasing habits. The typical pensioner, for example, may be described as someone who is above 60 years of age on a fixed income (their pension) who has paid off their mortgage. The consumer profile for Suzuki motorbikes might be males aged between 20–45 years. Knowledge of consumer profiles will help a business to identify the needs and wants of its customers and to identify any segments that may be overlooked by the firm. For example, Coca-Cola realized that health-sensitive male customers were reluctant to purchase Diet Coke or Coke Light as these products tend to be associated with female customers. This gap in the market led to the launch of Coke Zero, nicknamed Bloke Coke in countries such as the USA, UK and Australia.

Market segmentation is the process of splitting a market into distinct groups of buyers in order to better meet their needs. The main methods of market segmentation are based on demographic, geographic and psychographic factors.

Segmentation by demographics

Demography is the study of the characteristics of the human population within a certain area or region. It looks at a range of variables including:

- *Age groupings* – Each age group tends to have similar wants and some will have similar financial circumstances (such as retired pensioners). Teenagers and middle-aged adults, for example, have very different spending patterns.
- *Gender* – Male and females can have very different wants and spending habits. For instance, there is a huge market for women's fashion in comparison to men's fashion (just take a look at the floor space area devoted to female clothing compared to that allocated to male customers in a typical shopping mall).
- *Race and ethnicity* – Different races of people have different cultures and this affects their demand for different products. Chinese people will demand rice as part of their staple diet whereas the Irish may prefer a different food. Due to the globalization of markets (see Unit 1.9) there have been many opportunities for businesses to sell cultural exports to reach a wider customer base.
- *Marital status* – More and more people are delaying marriage, perhaps due to the soaring costs of a wedding and due to career aspirations. Divorce rates in western societies are also increasing. Such trends can present both opportunities and threats to business.
- *Religion* – Jewish people, for instance, buy kosher food. Muslims do not eat pork. McDonald's has had to alter its menu in countries such as India where beef is rarely eaten.

- *Language* – Businesses may cater for different customers based on their mother-tongue language. For example, IBO courses and examinations exist in three main languages: English, Spanish and French. Many famous tourist destinations, such as Stonehenge in the UK or Tokyo Disneyland, cater for their international visitors.
- *Income and socio-economic class* – Very wealthy people tend to have different spending patterns from the rest of the population. The American upper-middle class, for example, refers to people who earn in excess of $65,000 per year. The UK uses a similar model (see Box 4.2c). The level of income of different segments can affect the pricing policy of a business. For example, a cinema or theme park will charge different prices for adults, children, students and pensioners.

Marketers have invented many creative acronyms and names for various demographic groupings. Examples include DINKY (double income, no kids yet); NILK (no income, lots of kids); OINK (one income, no kids); GLAM (greying, leisured, affluent, middle aged); OPAL (older people with active lifestyles); WOOF (well-off older folk); RAP (retired affluent people); SINBAD (single income, no boyfriend and desperate); SITCOM (single income, two children, outrageous mortgage); Kidults (adults who purchase products that are mainly aimed at children, such as certain toys or computer games) and Tweenagers (children aged between 7–12).

In reality, different combinations of these demographic factors are used for marketing purposes. For example, there are cards for numerous occasions such as birthday cards produced specifically for girls, boys, teenagers, parents and grandparents, and different cards for Thanksgiving, Christmas, Hanukkah, Diwali and Chinese New Year.

Box 4.2c Socio-economic groups (UK model)

Socio-economic group	Socio-economic class	Description and examples of occupations
A	Upper-middle class	Senior managerial, administrative or professional workers, e.g. company directors, diplomats, barristers and surgeons
B	Middle class	Middle managerial, administrative or professional workers who tend to be highly educated and salaried staff, e.g. teachers, nurses and accountants
C1	Lower middle class	Skilled non-manual, e.g. supervisory (junior managerial), administrative or clerical workers
C2	Skilled working class	Skilled manual workers, e.g. self-employed plumbers and electricians
D	Working class	Semi-skilled and manual workers, e.g. assembly line factory workers and cleaners
E	Subsistence	Unskilled and casual workers, pensioners and the unemployed

Segmentation by geographic factors

The geographic location of customers can have implications for segmentation. Note that some demographic factors, such as race, language and religion, are largely influenced by geographic issues. Geographical factors affecting market segmentation come in two broad categories:

- *Location* – Different areas and regions of a country may have different cultures and attitudes. Singapore and Malaysia, for example, are very multicultural and most businesses cater for the three main cultures – Chinese, Malay (or Singaporean) and Indian.
- *Climate* – The typical weather in an area can have a large impact on business activity. Warm clothing product lines, such as scarves, hats, socks and coats are unlikely to meet the needs of people living in regions with tropical climate. Hence, many businesses are likely to adjust the products they sell in different parts of the world.

Segmentation by psychographic factors

Psychographic factors are those that consider the emotions and lifestyle of customers, such as their habits, hobbies, interests and values.

- *Status* – Some people are very conscious of social and economic status. A feeling of status can come about by the *feel-good factor* of owning certain assets, such as designer outfits, luxury jewellery or sports cars.
- *Values* – This refers to people's beliefs, morals and principles. Ethically responsible businesses such as The Body Shop cater for people who are against testing on animals. Special interest groups (see Unit 1.4) such as Greenpeace try to rally people to support their cause. Religion can also be a big source of business. For example, it is estimated that there are over 2 billion Christians in the world – a figure not overlooked by marketers.
- *Culture* – The culture and buying habits of different ethnic groups can provide immense opportunities for marketers, such as the increased trade in *cultural exports* (see Unit 4.7).
- *Hobbies and interests* – An understanding of the different hobbies and interests of customers can provide plenty of marketing opportunities for a business. For example, the sports industry is huge, catering for customers that actively participate in and/or watch sports.

Advantages of segmentation

- Better understanding of customers – Segmentation can allow a firm to better understand the needs of its various customer groups. This will aid its numerous marketing strategies since marketing is largely about satisfying the needs of customers. A clearer marketing focus therefore reduces the likelihood of a business wasting resources on marketing its products in the wrong places and to the wrong people.
- Increase sales – Being able to cater for a wider range of customers can help a business to sell more products, and hence to earn more profit.
- Growth opportunities – Effective segmentation can help firms to identify new opportunities at home and abroad.
- Gives support to product differentiation – Having a better understanding of different market segments allows a business to effectively differentiate its products in order to spread risks.

It is not always be possible for a business to effectively carry out market segmentation. Marketers often use the acronym DAMAS as a set of criteria for ensuring successful segmentation:

- Differential – Segments must be unique and respond to the different marketing mixes of the business
- Actionable – Businesses must be able to provide suitable products to cater for each segment.
- Measurable – The size and purchasing power of each segment must be quantifiable.
- Accessible – The business must be able to reach customers in a cost-effective way.
- Substantial – Each market segment must be sufficiently large in order to generate profits.

Question 4.2.6

The business of international students

International students provide large business opportunities. In addition to their direct costs of education, international students also improve domestic tourism, especially with visiting friends and relatives. World Bank figures show that international students account for a significant proportion of service export earnings in countries such as Australia, New Zealand and the United States.

The international mobility of students is being fuelled by three main factors: the phenomenon of **globalization**; new technologies that are making education more accessible to people from around the world, and the intensity of competition between universities to attract foreign students.

a What is meant by **globalization**? *[2 marks]*

b Examine how knowledge of market segmentation might help universities to have more cost-effective marketing activities to attract foreign students. *[6 marks]*

TARGETING

Once a market has been segmented, targeting becomes the next stage in marketing planning. Targeting refers to the market segment(s) that a business wishes to sell to. Appropriate marketing strategies are then developed for these target markets. There are three broad targeting strategies that a business can use: *niche marketing*, *mass marketing* (undifferentiated), or *differentiated marketing*.

Niche marketing

Niche marketing, also known as **concentration marketing**, targets a specific and well-defined market segment. An example is businesses that cater for minority sports, such as horse riding and Tae Kwon Do. Businesses that provide speciality goods (such as Louis Vuitton handbags, Armani suits, Ferrari cars and Cartier watches) also operate in niche markets, catering for consumers interested in high-end luxury goods.

Advantages of niche marketing

- There is better marketing focus since a specific market segment is being targeted. By contrast, mass marketing has little focus and aims to market products at the 'average' customer.
- Since there is less competition, businesses can charge higher prices for their exclusive products. This will help the business to gain higher profit margins on its products.
- Firms become highly specialized in meeting the needs and wants of their niche target market. This not only helps to deliver first-rate customer service, but also encourages customer loyalty. This can therefore give such firms a competitive advantage.

Disadvantages of niche marketing

- Most niche markets are very small and hence this limits the number of customers in the market. By contrast, mass marketing caters for a much wider customer base.
- Due to the small market size, businesses operating in niche markets have very few opportunities to exploit economies of scale.
- Highly successful and profitable niche markets may attract new entrants into the industry. The threat of larger firms entering the market may therefore endanger the survival of the organization.

Undifferentiated marketing

Undifferentiated marketing, also known as **mass marketing** or **market aggregation**, is the strategy that ignores targeting individual market segments. Instead, a large number of different market segments are targeted in order to maximize sales volume. Coca-Cola, Nokia, Nike, Apple and Microsoft all use this strategy to target all market segments in the same way. Governments also use this strategy when communicating public announcements such as anti drink-driving campaigns.

Advantages of undifferentiated marketing

- Huge potential economies of scale from being able to supply products in a mass market.
- There is no need to tailor different marketing mixes for different segments since the whole market can be addressed with a single marketing campaign. This can save the business a lot of time and resources.
- Catering for larger markets also means that the business can establish a bigger customer base in order to earn more profits.

Disadvantages of undifferentiated marketing

- Mass marketing is not suitable for all businesses because there are high entry barriers for mass production (see Unit 5.1).
- Competition can become quite fierce as customers must be persuaded to buy the firm's product rather than to buy from a rival business.
- Since there is a lack of focus, mass marketing can be quite wasteful as specific customers are not being directly targeted.

Differentiated marketing

Differentiated marketing, also known as **selective marketing** or **multi-segment marketing**, is the targeting strategy that tailors a marketing mix to each market segment. Marketers will often use *position maps* (see 'Position (perception) maps' on page 488) in order to identify how different customers think and feel about a particular product or brand. This can then help the marketers to devise appropriate strategies for each market segment.

Advantages of differentiated marketing

- Customers can enjoy a more satisfying experience since a tailored marketing mix caters for their specific and individual needs and wants.
- Risks are spread out by focusing on several market segments. Hence, a decline in one market segment has less of an impact on the overall business.

Disadvantages of differentiated marketing

- Differentiated marketing is costly. Only large companies have the financial resources to target all segments in a market.
- Marketing economies of scale cannot be fully exploited since there are additional marketing costs involved when catering for different segments.
- Excessive differentiation can drain a firm's resources and confuse customers.

In reality, many businesses will have operations that use all three targeting strategies. For example, Pinault-Printemps-Redoute (PPR), which owns luxury brands Gucci and Yves Saint Laurent, developed its portfolio by taking over Puma in order to spread risks. PPR also owns FNAC, the largest French consumer electronics retailer that operates throughout Europe.

Question 4.2.7

Pink Ladies

Pink Ladies is a unique women-only, private car hire service, driven by women for women. The firm was founded in 2006 by Tina Dutton and Andrea Winders who had concerns for lone women travellers and the dangers of the many unlicensed taxi drivers in London. The firm's vehicles, which of course are pink, are equipped with satellite navigation devices and are driven by women trained in self-defence. To bolster security even further, the firm has a 'no cash in the car' policy.

Market research from their pilot of the service showed that women generally feel happier with a female driver.

Source: adapted from www.pinkladiesmembers.co.uk

a Outline what is meant by a 'niche market' in the context of the case study. *[2 marks]*

b Explain two advantages for Pink Ladies operating in a niche market. *[4 marks]*

c Comment on the importance of a **pilot** scheme for Pink Ladies. *[4 marks]*

d Explain two other market research techniques that Pink Ladies were likely to have used. *[4 marks]*

POSITIONING

Market positioning is an analytical tool that ranks different products, services or firms in relation to others in the market according to the views of the general public. For example, in the cosmetics industry, Chanel is seen to be of higher quality and price compared to Rimmel. Similarly, most customers perceive Evian and Perrier as superior brands of bottled water.

There are three stages to positioning:

- *Identify* the competitive advantages of the product.
- *Decide* on which aspects of these strengths should be marketed.
- *Implement* the desired positioning by using an appropriate marketing mix.

Corporate image

Corporate image plays a vital part in the success of businesses. In 2007, Pakistan International Airlines was banned from flying to European Union countries due to safety concerns. In the same year, America also raised concerns over the poor image of Garuda Airways, the Indonesian airline carrier, due to its poor safety record. A poor image will not only drive customers away, but it can also impose damage that is irrevocable.

One of the most famous corporate bloopers in business history was made by Gerald Ratner in 1991. His company, Ratners, was the UK's largest mass market jeweller, with 80% market share. However, in a speech to over 6,000 members of the Institute of Directors back in 1991, Ratner joked that his firm's earrings were "total crap" and added that a prawn sandwich from Marks & Spencer would cost more *and* lasted longer! Subsequent media coverage effectively ended the company's value, which dropped by an estimated £500 million ($1 billion). Other corporate leaders have also committed blunders that have severely harmed the image of their companies (see Box 4.2d).

There are vast possibilities for a firm to improve its corporate image, such as through implementation of *corporate social responsibility* (CSR) (see Unit 1.3). Some CSR activities include providing educational support for schools, colleges and universities. Firms might also sponsor environmental projects to enhance their corporate image.

Alternatively, businesses may seek to market their **unique selling point** (USP). A unique selling point, or **unique selling proposition**, is any aspect of a product that makes it stand out from those offered by competitors. The USP explains *why* customers buy the product over rival brands, for example, its appealing packaging. A USP can be a major source of competitive advantage and therefore firms will want to emphasize their product's USP in order to attract customers, such as Pink Ladies which offers a taxi service for females only (see Question 4.2.7 on page 486). This again can help develop a firm's image and to differentiate itself from competitors.

Michael Porter proposed three generic (or basic) competitive strategies for businesses to achieve positioning success:

- **Cost leadership** refers to businesses that aim to excel as low cost suppliers of particular products.
- **Differentiation** refers to businesses that produce distinct products by using methods such as branding to differentiate their products from those supplied by rivals firms.
- **Focus** refers to businesses that pay close attention to a particular market segment.

Porter argued that businesses that attempt to be good at everything are unrealistic and are rarely good at anything in particular. He suggested that a firm cannot, logically and simultaneously, provide cost leadership and high quality. Porter's generic strategies are covered in more detail in Unit 1.7.

Box 4.2d Corporate blunders... how to get the wrong image

- July 2001 – David Shepherd, Marketing Director of the UK's mass market clothes retailer Topman, called his customers "hooligans or whatever", joking that they bought suits either for a job interview or for attending court.
- March 2003 – EMI's chief executive, Alain Levy, said that there were not many people from Finland who could sing, and so the firm was to cut the number of Finnish recording artists.
- Oct 2003 – Matt Barrett, chief executive of Barclays - the owners of the UK's largest credit card company – criticized the Barclay Card stating that he would never use it because it was just too expensive.

Question 4.2.8

J.D. Power & Associates

J.D. Power & Associates is the motor industry's benchmark for judging the quality of new motor vehicles. Lexus, Toyota, BMW and Porsche often dominate the annual quality awards conducted by J.D. Power & Associates. Such brands tend to use the J.D. Power & Associates ratings in their marketing campaigns.

a Explain how quality awards and ratings, such as those awarded by J.D. Power & Associates, can provide car manufacturers with a **unique selling point**. *[3 marks]*

b To what extent does having a unique selling point in a highly competitive market, such as the motor industry, help a firm to achieve its objectives? *[7 marks]*

Position (perception) maps

A **position map** is a visual tool which shows the customers' perception of a product or brand in relation to others in the market. The term, created by Jack Trout in 1969, is often known as a **perception map**. The two-dimensional diagram plots customer perceptions using variables such as price and quality (see Figure 4.2c).

- **Premium brands** are products that are of high quality and high price. Examples include brands such as Lexus, Mercedes-Benz and BMW.
- **Economy brands** are products that are of low quality but appropriately priced. Supermarkets often supply 'no-frills' products to lure price-sensitive customers.
- **Bargain brands** are those that are of high quality but with low prices. This is not sustainable and the approach is only used as a short-term tactic to boost sales.
- **Cowboy brands** are products that are of poor quality but highly priced. These products are positioned to deceive customers and are therefore only used as a short-term tactic to gain revenue.

A major advantage of perceptual mapping is that it is a simple way of presenting potentially complex market research findings. The maps are quick and easy to interpret by non-specialists. Perception maps can direct management attention to market opportunities and threats.

Price \ Quality	High	Low
High	Premium brands	Cowboy brands
Low	Bargain brands	Economy brands

Figure 4.2c Perception map (price and quality)

Box 4.2e lists the ten most admired companies in the USA, as perceived by consumers.

Uses of position maps

- Position maps allow a business to identify any gaps in its product portfolio. For example, Mercedes-Benz introduced their A-Class cars in 1997 after having found that there was a market for smaller cars that featured the luxury brand name. Similarly, BMW identified a gap in the market for luxury 4×4 sports utility vehicles and subsequently introduced its X-class line of cars in 2000.
- They can be used for targeting strategies. For example, if customers perceive a brand to be of high price and high quality, then appropriate market segments can be targeted.
- They can also inform businesses of a need for **reposition** their products. If an undesired perception exists, then the organization will need to devise strategies to change (reposition) that perception. British Airways, for example, revamped its image to appeal to younger and less affluent customers after findings that the airline company was associated with wealthy and elderly travellers only. Alternatively, *product development* (see Unit 4.3) could be pursued to better meet the needs and wants of consumers.

Box 4.2e Ten of America's most admired companies

1. General Electric
2. Starbucks
3. Toyota Motor
4. Berkshire Hathaway
5. Southwest Airlines
6. FedEx
7. Apple
8. Google
9. Johnson & Johnson
10. Procter & Gamble

Source: adapted from *Fortune* magazine's annual survey of 'America's Most Admired Companies' (http://money.cnn.com/magazines/fortune/mostadmired/)

Question 4.2.9

The hotel industry, London (UK)

Study the data below regarding perceptions about hotels in London and then answer the questions that follow.

Hotel	Price	Quality of Service	Quality of Location
Savoy Hotel	High	High	High
Premier Travel Inn	Medium	Medium	Medium
Travelodge	Low	Low	Low
Holiday Inn	Medium	Medium	High
Raddison	High	Medium	High
Shaftsbury Hyde Park	Low	Medium	High
Britannia International	High	High	Medium
Peckham Hotel	Medium	Low	Low

a Construct a position map for the hotel industry in London based on the information above. *[6 marks]*

b Explain the benefits of position maps to both Savoy Hotel and Peckham Hotel. *[4 marks]*

DEVELOPMENT OF MARKETING STRATEGIES AND TACTICS

This Unit has referred to the terms 'tactics' and 'strategy' many times. Marketing tactics (short-term plans) and strategies (medium- to long-term plans) are used in order to achieve the marketing objectives of an organization.

Marketing tactics include, among many others covered in subsequent Units on marketing:

- Promotional tactics such as sponsorship or buy-one, get-one-free deals (see Unit 4.5)
- High-pressure sales tactics such as bait and switch methods
- Dubious marketing tactics such as misleading, deceptive or unethical marketing
- Bargain brands that are used as a short-term tactic to boost sales
- Short-term price reductions to entice customers (see Unit 4.4).

Marketing tactics are used to achieve the marketing strategies of an organization. Marketing strategy usually consists of three key phases:

- Market research – using primary and secondary research techniques to identify the needs and wants of customers
- Product planning, design and development – producing products to meet the needs and wants of customers (see Unit 4.3)
- Implementation – execution of the strategy through an appropriate marketing mix, within the marketing budget.

In developing a marketing strategy, marketing managers may choose from an array of tools, such as:

- Perception mapping – product positioning and repositioning techniques
- Porter's five forces analysis – competitor analysis (covered earlier in this Unit)
- Porter's generic strategies – marketing strategies for competitive advantage (see Unit 1.7)
- Ansoff matrix – marketing strategies for growth (see Unit 1.7)
- Boston matrix – development of a firm's product portfolio (see Unit 4.3)
- SWOT analysis – identification of a firm's marketing strengths, weaknesses, opportunities and threats
- Force Field analysis – method used to successfully implement and manage organizational change (see Unit 1.8).

Successful marketing tactics and strategies are carefully planned out in order to achieve the organization's marketing objectives. The marketing strategy is implemented through an appropriate marketing mix. Professor Robert Lauterborn (1990) argues that successful marketing strategy entails examining the marketing mix from the perspective of consumers. He called this the **4 C's of marketing**: Customer solution (product), Cost to the customer (price), Communication (promotion) and Convenience (place). Execution of the marketing strategy should be done in a cost-effective way without the organization having to overspend its budget.

HIGHER LEVEL EXTENSION: SALES FORECASTING AND TRENDS

Sales forecasting is a quantitative technique that attempts to estimate the level of sales a firm expects to achieve, over a given period. It is an essential tool for managing a business since sales forecasts can help a firm to identify problems and opportunities in advance. However, trying to predict what will happen in the future can be very difficult because there are so many variables that may render the forecasts inaccurate. Therefore, in order to make realistic and accurate forecasts, managers will use a range of forecasting techniques, such as:

- **Extrapolation** – This technique is used to predict what is likely to happen in the near future by identifying the trend that exists in past data and extending this trend to predict future sales. For example, if a firm's sales have been increasing by an average of 5% each year for the past five years, then it might be expected that this trend will continue for the next year or two. Graphically, the trend can be identified by a 'line of best fit' and extrapolation simply extends this line to make predictions of the near future (see Figure 4.2d).

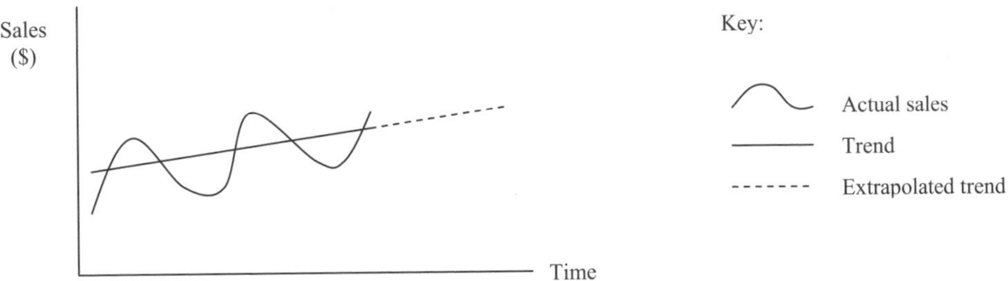

Figure 4.2d Extrapolation of sales trend

- **The Delphi technique** – This method involves using a panel of independent experts who discuss and come to a consensus on the forecasting of sales in the distant future. For example, Nokia and Motorola have used this technique to predict sales in emerging markets in Eastern European countries.
- **Market research** – Identifying and establishing the future purchasing intentions of consumers can be vital to a firm's prosperity and survival. For example, despite being the top global producer of cars for 76 years, General Motors grew complacent and overproduced cars and failed to recognize the changing demands of customers. With soaring oil prices and greater concerns for the environment, Toyota took over as the top motor manufacturer in 2006, with its highly successful fuel efficient and hybrid vehicles. Similarly, market research data allowed Thai Beverage Plc to expand its range of non-alcoholic drinks in response to health-conscious consumers and tighter laws in Thailand to limit sales of beer and spirits. Market research techniques have been covered earlier in this Unit.
- **Time series analysis** – This technique attempts to predict future sales levels by identifying the underlying trend line from a sequence of actual sales figures recorded at regular intervals in the past. There are five elements to time series analysis:
  - *Trends* – the underlying growth (or decline) in sales
  - *Erratic* or *random fluctuations* – unpredictable fluctuations in sales
  - *Seasonal fluctuations* – seasonal variations in demand, such as the summer holidays or Christmas season
  - *Cyclical factors* – variations linked to the economic cycle of booms and slumps
  - *Responses* – deliberate actions taken to affect sales, such as the use of sales promotions.

In practice, businesses are likely to use a combination of forecasting methods. The choice will depend on several factors, such as:

- How accurate forecasts need to be – The greater the degree of certainty needed, the more thorough the methods of sales forecasting that is required. For example, it would be more meaningful to use monthly or quarterly data to forecast the sales of ice cream; using annual figures would not reveal seasonal fluctuations in demand. This will, however, involve more time and resources, i.e. incur higher costs.
- How far ahead forecasts need to be – It is relatively easy to forecast sales for the next day, week or month. However, to predict sales levels over the next five years is much more ambitious. Extrapolation, for example, will only be useful if predictions apply to the near future.
- The availability and cost of data and information – Widespread access to a wealth of information at no or very little cost can make forecasting more accurate. However, if it proves difficult to find appropriate and up-to-date information, or if access to information is highly expensive, the choice of forecasting method will be affected.
- The stage in a product's life cycle – Market research rather than time series analysis, for example, will be used during both the 'Research and Development' and 'Launch' stages (see Unit 4.3). More data and information will become available during the growth and maturity stages of the product life cycle.

Benefits of sales forecasting

Businesses that are able to carry out accurate sales forecasting can reap important benefits, such as:

- *Improved working capital and cash flow* (see Unit 3.3) – Sales forecasting can help a firm to identify seasonal fluctuations in demand and its implications for the cash flow position of the organization.
- *Improved stock control* – The firm will have better control over its stock levels. Accurate sales forecasts will help to ensure that the correct levels of stocks are available for use in production at different times of the year.
- *Improved productive efficiency* (see Unit 5.7) – The ability to plan for the correct level of production means better use of a firm's resources. The labour supply, for example, can be adjusted to suit the level of sales. Many retailers will temporarily hire part-time staff during the Christmas trading season due to the high seasonal demand. Accurate sales forecasting therefore allows managers to devote time to strategic planning to develop the business, rather than to use their time in dealing with operational problems caused by a lack of planning.
- *Helps to secure external sources of finance* – Accurate, realistic and positive sales forecasting can help a business to obtain external financing from investors and lenders. This is especially important for new businesses as sales forecasts are often a requirement in a business plan (see Unit 1.6).

Essentially, the combination of these benefits should help a firm to operate more efficiently and profitably.

Statistical analysis techniques

There are many statistical techniques that can be used to analyse sales data:

- *Mean* – The arithmetic mean refers to the sum of all items divided by the number of items in a set of data.
- *Median* – When all numbers are ranked in numerical order, the median refers to the middle number in a set of data.

- *Modal* – This refers to the number that occurs more frequently than any other value in a set of data.
- *Range* – This refers to the numerical difference between the highest and the lowest numbers in a set of data.
- *Standard deviation* – This measures the difference (or digression) of a variable from the mean value in a set of data.

Question **4.2.10**

Paisey B&B

Roz and Richard Paisey own and run their own bed and breakfast boarding house in New Plymouth, New Zealand. Located near the waterfront, Paisey B&B booms in the summer season but suffers from a lack of tourists in the winter months. Their sales forecasts for the next twelve months, based on past data, are shown below.

	Mar	Apr	May	Jun	Jul	Aug	Sept	Oct	Nov	Dec	Jan	Feb
Sales ($)	3,500	3,000	3,000	2,500	2,800	2,600	2,900	3,000	3,600	4,500	4,000	4,000

a Calculate the mean, median and modal averages from the sales data above. *[3 marks]*

b Calculate the range and comment on your findings. *[3 marks]*

c Explain how the above calculations may be of use to Roz and Richard Paisey. *[4 marks]*

Moving averages

The most frequently used method of calculating averages is the arithmetic mean. However, **moving averages** are a more accurate method of identifying trends so are, perhaps, more useful for sales forecasting. To illustrate this point, consider the data below for an imaginary clothes retailer.

	Year 1	Year 2	Year 3	Year 4	Year 5	Total
Sales ($)	100,000	110,000	120,000	95,000	130,000	555,000

The arithmetic mean value is the sum of the sales figures ($555,000) divided by the number of items in the data set (in this case, there are five). Hence, the arithmetic mean is $111,000 per annum. The moving average helps to identify the trend that exists within a set of data (as above) by smoothing out fluctuations that may exist. For example, to calculate a '3-year moving average' requires the following steps:

1. Work out the mean for the first 3 data items, i.e. (100k + 110k + 120k) / 3 = $110,000
2. Repeat this for the next 3 data items, i.e. years 2, 3 and 4. This gives a mean of (110k + 120k + 95k) / 3 = $108,333
3. Continue this process for the final 3-year period in the data set (i.e. years 3, 4 and 5). This gives a figure of (120k + 95k + 130k) / 3 = $115,000

Whilst more time consuming to calculate than the simple arithmetic mean, moving averages show how the underlying trend has moved over the five-year period, by smoothing out irregular fluctuations in the series of data.

HIGHER LEVEL

HIGHER LEVEL

Question 4.2.11

Yoshiko Travel Ltd.

Yoshiko Travel Ltd. is a London-based company that specializes in travel services for Japanese customers from around the world who are interested in The English Premier League (the world's most watched and lucrative sports league). A football fan herself, CEO of the company, Yoshi Sano has built a wide customer base of wealthy clients who mainly fly from Japan, Holland and Italy. Actual sales turnover figures for the latter part of the football season last year are shown below:

	Jan	Feb	Mar	Apr	May	Jun
Sales ($'000)	30	28	32	35	28	0

a Outline why Yoshiko Travel Ltd. might be described as operating in a niche market. *[2 marks]*

b Calculate 3-month moving averages for Yoshiko Travel Ltd. for the period shown. *[4 marks]*

c Construct an appropriate graph to show the actual sales figures and the moving averages. *[5 marks]*

d Comment on the trend and seasonal fluctuations from your graph and outline how such fluctuations might affect the company. *[4 marks]*

MARKETING PLANNING AND BUSINESS STRATEGY

Marketing planning is important since businesses operate in a dynamic and changing environment. Changes can come about for all sorts of reasons beyond the control of an organization, such as changes in technology, fashion and economic conditions. Marketing planning ensures that managers monitor and respond to these changes. It also helps to reduce the risks since marketing planning and research can help to provide more informed decision-making. Technological advances have made market research much easier and cost-effective for many firms. For example, online surveys can help to capture a large sample, with the software being able to compute the results from the survey. Effective marketing planning will involve segmentation, targeting and positioning. However, it is highly unlikely that smaller businesses will have the financial and human resources to target all segments. Essentially, effective marketing planning can help to ensure the firm's longevity. A summary of marketing planning is shown in Figure 4.2e.

Segmentation is about anticipating the needs of different customers. BMW is an example of a firm that has used market segmentation and consumer profiling to increase sales revenue. Its range of cars caters for literally all potential customers. Their cars come in all sorts of sizes and styling to suit different customer needs. They also appeal to both female and male customers of different nationalities.

Market research can also help businesses that operate in overseas markets. Differences in language, culture and etiquette can present both opportunities and threats. For example, Durex is a highly popular brand of condoms in the UK and many parts of Asia. However, Durex is also a registered brand in Brazil for adhesive tape; in Mexico it is a brand of socks; in Canada it is the name of a steel company, and in the USA it is also a brand name of badminton rackets! Hence, careful market planning is important in communicating the correct messages to consumers. A potential problem for market researchers is how to get truly representative and reliable results.

Much of this comes down to effective marketing planning such as the choice of sampling method and sample size, given the budget that has been allocated to market research.

However, marketing planning and research data are not perfect. For example, samples are not often representative of the population and results often contain bias. In other words, the quality of the outcome of marketing planning is only as good as the quality of the input. This condition is known as **garbage in, garbage out (GIGO)**. A lack of quality inputs (including human effort) will lead to second-rate outputs, such as substandard products, wastage, costly errors, reworking and disgruntled customers. Nevertheless, effective use of market research will help to prevent a business from becoming too inward looking and losing touch with what consumers really want.

Figure 4.2e Aspects of marketing planning

Ethical marketing is a growing part of marketing planning. It refers to the social and moral responsibilities of marketers. Ethical marketing can present a moral dilemma for businesses. If they sell products aimed at children that are perfectly legal, such as war toys or fast food products, why shouldn't businesses be allowed to market these? Marketers could argue that advertising can be informative, not just persuasive or pressuring. Marketing can also help customers to make better and more informed decisions. Finally, businesses would also argue that using inappropriate and unethical marketing strategies can damage their firm's brand image, so this shouldn't be an issue.

Marketing planning is an essential prerequisite to marketing strategy. Strategy refers to the ways in which the business intends to achieve its marketing objectives. Strategic decisions will affect the direction of the organization and determine its future prosperity. The remaining Units on marketing in this book look at the different aspects of marketing strategy, with a focus on the four main elements of the marketing mix (see Units 4.3 to 4.6), international marketing issues (see Unit 4.7) and the growing importance of e-commerce (see Unit 4.8).

REVIEW QUESTIONS 4.2

1 What is meant by 'marketing planning'?

2 What is the 'marketing mix'?

3 What are the three additional P's needed for the marketing of services?

4 What is meant by 'ethical marketing' and how can it present both opportunities and threats to a business?

5 Give four examples of lawful but unethical marketing activities.

6 What are 'marketing audits'?

7 What are the 'five forces' in Michael Porter's theory of competitive advantage?

8 State five examples of marketing objectives.

9 Differentiate between 'primary' and 'secondary' research.

10 Using examples, explain the difference between 'quantitative' and 'qualitative' research.

11 Explain why segmentation might be of value to a business.

12 What are the three main ways of targeting?

13 What is 'positioning' and why do businesses care about it?

14 State three uses of perception maps.

15 Distinguish between 'marketing strategies' and 'marketing tactics'.

Higher Level extension

16 What is meant by 'sampling'?

17 Outline three common methods of sampling.

18 Explain what is meant by 'sales forecasting'.

19 When analysing statistical data, explain why the calculation of moving averages is more meaningful than simply calculating the arithmetic mean.

20 How might marketing planning help businesses that operate in overseas markets?

Customer relations management (CRM) refers to the use of people in the marketing mix. CRM focuses on what can be gained during the lifetime of a positive relationship with customers.

Ethical marketing refers to the moral aspects of a firm's marketing strategies. It can be encouraged by the use of moral codes of practice.

Five forces analysis refers to Michael Porter's model of assessing the nature of competition within an industry by examining five variables (or forces): new entrants, existing competitors, substitutes, suppliers, and buyers.

Market research refers to the range of marketing activities designed to discover the opinions, beliefs and feelings of potential and existing customers to identify and anticipate the needs and wants of customers.

Marketing audit refers to a systematic examination and review of the current position of a firm in terms of its strengths and weaknesses.

Marketing mix refers to the four main elements of marketing strategies: product, price, promotion and place. Hence, the marketing mix is often referred to as the **4 P's of marketing**.

Packaging is the eighth 'P' in the marketing mix which focuses on the ways in which a product is presented to the consumer.

Physical evidence refers to the image portrayed by a business (or perceived by customers) regarding its observable and tangible features such as the cleanliness and physical size of a business or the presentation of its staff.

Position map refers to a visual aid that shows the customers' perception of a product or brand in relation to others in the market. Position maps are often referred to as **perception maps**.

Primary research, also known as **field research**, involves data being collected by the researcher since the information does not currently exist.

Process is part of the extended marketing mix which refers to the methods and procedures used to give clients the best possible customer experience.

Qualitative research focuses on the comments, suggestions and opinions of respondents. Qualitative research data are not statistical but can generate in-depth findings.

Quantitative research focuses on the collection and interpretation of statistical and numerical data for market research purposes.

Quota sample is a sampling method that involves segmenting the population and then selecting a certain number (the quota) of people in each market segment.

Random sample is a sampling method that gives every person in the population an equal chance of being selected.

Repositioning is a strategy that involves changing the market's perception of a product or brand relative to those offered by rival firms.

Sales forecasting is a quantitative technique that attempts to estimate the level of sales a business expects to achieve, over a given time period.

Sampling is the practice of selecting a representative group (known as the sample) of a population for primary research purposes.

Secondary research, also known as **desk research**, involves using data and information that has already been collected by another party, i.e. the data or information already exists.

Segmentation refers to the process of categorizing customers into distinct groups of people with similar characteristics (such as age or gender), and similar wants or needs for research and targeting purposes.

Targeting means that each distinctive market segment can have its own marketing mix. Different markets can also be targeted, depending on whether they operate in niche, differentiated or mass markets.

Unique selling point (USP), or **unique selling proposition**, refers to any aspect of a product that makes it stand out from those offered by rival businesses.

Product

UNIT 4.3

It is not the employer who pays wages – he only handles the money. It is the product who pays the wages.

Henry Ford (1863–1947), founder of the Ford Motor Company

Key topics

- Classification of products: product line, mix and range
- Consumer and producer products
- Innovation, technological change and research and development
- New product design and development
- The product life cycle
- Product differentiation
- Product portfolio analysis: The Boston Consultancy Group matrix

Higher Level extension

- Branding
- Types of branding
- Branding in a global market

INTRODUCTION

A **product** can be defined as any good or service that serves to satisfy the needs or wants of customers.

Products can be **tangible** (physical products such as computers) or **intangible** (services such as education). They can be sold to private individual customers, to business customers or to the government.

Every year, there are thousands of new products launched in both consumer and commercial markets. Most new products fail but a special few may succeed to become a global success. Before customers part with their money, they ask themselves whether the product offers value for money. The benefits of consumption must outweigh the costs in order for the customer to make a purchase. Products must have **value added** (see Unit 1.1) in order to stand any chance of success in the marketplace. Marketing has a large role in adding value to a product, perhaps through the use of production differentiation methods such as quality, packaging and/or branding.

Value added can come in two broad forms. **Functional value** refers to what the product actually does for the customer. For example, Coca-Cola helps to quench people's thirst whilst Apple's iPod lets consumers listen to music. The second form of value added is called **emotional value**. This refers to the psychology and feel-good factor behind the purchase of a product, such as feeling proud of owning a particular brand. The customer may also find that the design of a product suits his or her personal style and taste. This means that product strategy, such as design and branding, is vital in adding value to a product.

CLASSIFICATION OF PRODUCTS

There are several ways in which to categorize products. One method is to class a business's products by *line*, *mix* and *range*.

Product line

A product line refers to a variety of the same product that a business produces for customers of a particular market. For example, Samsung produces different television sets such as LCD and plasma televisions. Its product line will include all the different sizes and types of televisions that Samsung manufacture. Crisps (potato chip snacks) made by manufacturers such as Walkers come in different flavours to meet the needs of different customer tastes within the same market. Products in a product line typically differ in colour, size, price or quality so that there is a greater chance that each product meets the needs of different customers.

Most businesses will change their product line due to changes in the market. Some products will be entering their decline phase in the product life cycle, and will therefore be discontinued, whilst other products will be introduced in new markets and hence be a new addition to a firm's product line.

Product mix

The product mix, also known as the **product assortment**, describes the variety of the different product lines that a business produces. Honda produces automobiles and motor bikes. Unilever produces food, beverages, personal care and cleaning products. Its brands include Axe, Vaseline, Persil, Cif, Flora, Ben & Jerry's, Lipton, PG Tips, Pot Noodle, Marmite and Slim Fast. Ikea's product mix includes sofas, beds, desks, indoor and outdoor plants, carpets and food.

By having a wide product mix, sometimes referred to as the **product portfolio**, businesses should be able to increase overall sales as a variety of products are sold to a larger customer base. Adidas, for instance, can sell its sports shoes to one group of customers and sell its clothing or sports equipment to other groups of customers. In addition, a wide product mix allows a business to spread risks; a downturn in one particular product line may be offset by increased sales in other product lines.

Product range

The product range of an organization refers to all product lines of a firm's product mix, i.e. all the products sold by the business. For example, Apple Macintosh sells different types of computers (product line) and laptops, accessories and iPods. These collectively form Apple's product mix; all the range of Apple computers, laptops, iPods and so forth form the company's product range.

If there are two firms with the same product mix, such as Sony and Samsung, the business with more products in each product line (the firm with a wider product range) is likely to have higher risk bearing.

Question 4.3.1

Mattel

Mattel is the world's largest manufacturer of toys. The American firm has profited from product lines such as *Barbie* dolls and *Elmo* cuddly toys (of *Sesame Street*). Their brands include Fisher Price, Hot Wheels, Matchbox, Tyco, UNO, Pictionary and Scrabble. Mattel credited its pleasing performance to other products in its **portfolio** such as strong sales of toys based on Pixar's animated films *Cars* and *Toy Story.*

a Explain the meaning of **portfolio** in the context of the case study. *[2 marks]*

b Examine the importance of a diversified product portfolio for a business such as Mattel. *[6 marks]*

Products can be also generally classified as either **consumer products** or **producer products**.

Consumer products

These are products that are purchased by private individuals for their own personal use. Consumer products can be further classified into four categories:

- ***Fast-moving consumer goods*** (FMCG) are everyday convenience products that are sold in retail outlets such as supermarkets. Examples include personal health care products, groceries, newspapers and confectionery. Due to the low profit margins on many convenience products, businesses tend to rely on the high sales volume and turnover of such products.
- ***Consumer perishables*** are products that do not last for a very long time, such as fresh flowers or fresh seafood. They are different to FMCGs in that purchases are not necessarily as frequent or stable and that they may carry a high profit margin. Consider the price of flowers just before Mothers' Day and Valentine's Day; businesses are able to exploit the high capacity and willingness of consumers to pay a high price for flowers during these peak periods. However, perishables do not last long, so at the point when fish and flowers, for example, are no longer seen as 'fresh', businesses will tend to reduce prices significantly to get rid of the stock. This is one reason why Christmas trees are often sold so cheaply – or sometimes even given away free of charge – at the close of business on Christmas Eve; it would cost the business money to get rid of any excess stock.

- ***Consumer durables*** are products that are purchased irregularly because they tend to last for a relatively long time and/or take up a relatively large proportion of a consumer's income. Examples of consumer durables include furniture, electronic appliances and automobiles. Due to the low frequency of purchase, businesses often charge a high profit margin on such products. Consumer durables are sometimes further separated into *white goods* (electronic devices for home use, such as fridge-freezers, cookers and microwaves) and *brown goods* (home entertainment devices, such as televisions, DVD players, personal computers and games consoles). A subcategory of consumer durables is ***soft goods***. These are products that have a relatively shorter life cycle as they wear out more quickly than most consumer durables. Examples of *soft goods* include clothes, shoes and batteries.
- ***Speciality consumer products*** are exclusive and very expensive products that often require a large amount of commitment in both money and time. This is because such purchases will usually take up a very large percentage of the income of the consumer. Examples of such products include the purchase of designer jewellery, residential property and exclusive motor vehicles such as Porsches and Ferraris. Due to the relatively low *price elasticity of demand* (see Unit 4.4) for these products, businesses are usually able to charge a premium price for such prestigious products to earn very high profit margins.

In addition, marketers often talk of ***LIP*** and ***HIP products***. A LIP (Low Involvement Product) is a product that does not require too much thought before the customer makes a purchase. FMCGs and consumer perishables are examples of LIPs. A HIP (High Involvement Product) is a product that requires a high degree of thought before customers make a purchase, usually because of the price. Consumer durables and other luxury products would be examples. Due to the different market conditions in LIP and HIP markets, businesses will tend to use different marketing strategies in these respective markets.

Producer products

Producer products or **industrial goods** are those that are purchased by businesses, rather than aimed at consumers. They are used in the production process to help the running of the business. Examples include the purchase of raw materials and components which are used to make other products. The category of producer goods also includes the purchase of **fixed assets** (see Unit 3.1) such as land, machinery, tools and other equipment.

In reality, many products (such as stationery, furniture and computers) cater for both private individuals and businesses. Their classification difference is only based on who buys the product, rather than the physical make-up of the product.

NEW PRODUCT DESIGN AND DEVELOPMENT

Most businesses will change their product portfolio from time to time. This could be due to internal driving forces, such as the desire to launch new products to cater for a larger number of customers. Alternatively, the drive for introducing new products could come from changing consumer tastes and preferences.

The design of a new product tends to be crucial to its success. In marketing terms, the term **design** does not only refer to the physical appearance of a product. Instead, design refers to the process of **adding value** to a product. This can be done through a *value analysis triangle* (see Figure 4.3a) which sees design consisting of three components: the physical design, performance and reliability of a product. These three elements are analysed carefully in order to see where and how value can be added to a product. As with all aspects of marketing, design must also consider the costs of producing or supplying the product. Firms that are able to take these factors into consideration stand a much better chance of launching successful products.

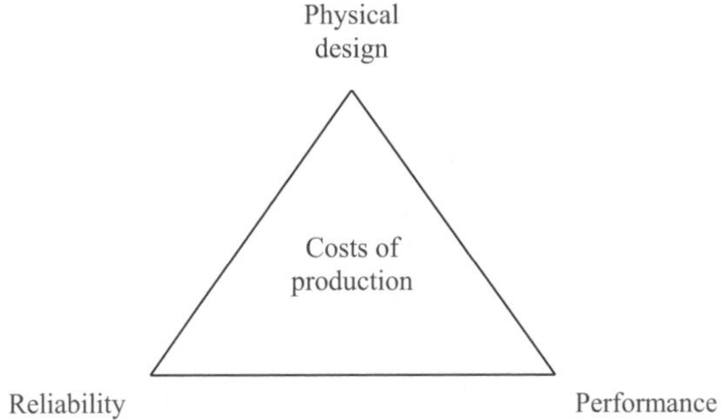

Figure 4.3a Value analysis triangle

Tom Peters, management guru and author, suggests an alternative model for gaining a competitive advantage, again by adding value to a product. Peters suggested that a small increase in costs of production can generate a disproportionate increase in value added or customer appeal. The question that managers must address is how to sustain or develop this competitive advantage. This can be done by any combination of four methods (see Figure 4.3b):

- *Raise* – Look at the features of a product that should be improved to exceed industry norms.
- *Create* – Examine the unique features of a product that should be included to outclass rivals.
- *Reduce* – Investigate the features of a product that can and/or should be cut back.
- *Eliminate* – Explore the ways in which certain features of a product can be removed.

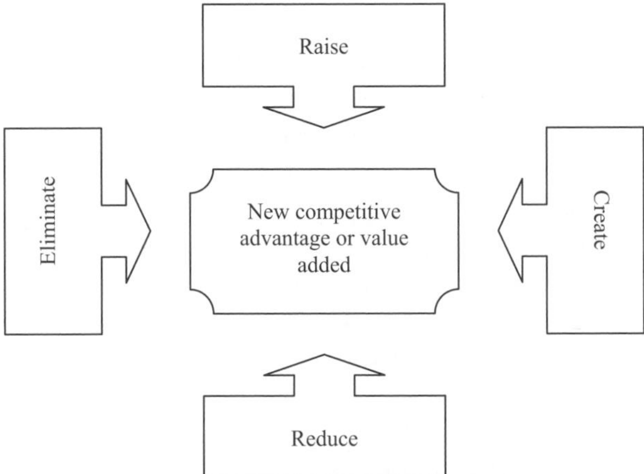

Figure 4.3b Tom Peters's sources of value added

In addition, the launch of a new product must be carefully planned in order to give it the best chance of being a success. This can be a costly exercise in itself. For example, in 2002 the movie producers of the first Spider-Man motion picture spent $50 million on its launch in the USA to boost its chances of being a hit. The producers hoped that this would also ensure that the Spider-Man sequels would also stand a better chance of success. Similarly, Sony announced that the launch of its PlayStation 3 in 2006 led to a staggering ¥100 billion ($926 million) operating loss for the year.

Ideas for new products can come from various sources, such as customers, competitors, staff and research and development. However, research has shown that most new products fail to succeed. Matt Haig author of *Brand Failures* claims that there is only a one in ten chance of a product becoming a long-term success. Hence a structured plan for developing new products is crucial.

Stages of new product development (NPD)

Before a new product can be sold in a market, it must first go through several stages.

1. **Market research**. This will involve carrying out primary and secondary research to establish where there are gaps in the marketplace that customers want to be filled. Market research will also involve brainstorming to generate ideas. Suggestions and discussions will take place and cover important issues such as: whether the new product complies with the corporate culture, whether there is spare capacity and resources to develop a new product and the implications of the change on staff. Market-orientated firms will also seek the views of potential customers by using various marketing planning techniques (see Unit 4.2). This can help to prevent large sums of money being spent on products that may have a short product life cycle.
2. **Product development and testing**. The second stage involves the business making **prototypes** (trial products). This will also enable the business to physically examine the product and to make any necessary alterations. The prototypes are also tested to ensure that they fulfil their purpose. For instance, motor vehicle manufacturers will test their new cars to ensure that they pass strict standards such as steering, braking and crash tests. Perfecting the prototype may be a very time-consuming process since any alterations at a later date will be very costly to a business. Testing also includes **test marketing** when samples of the new products are trialled with a small but representative number of potential customers. Feedback from these potential customers then allows a business to assess the reactions to the new product and to further refine its marketing mix to enhance the chances of success if the product is to be fully launched. Most products do not succeed beyond the first two stages of the NPD process.
3. **Feasibility study**. At this stage, management will look into the legal and financial viability of launching the new product. Costs of production and pricing decisions need to be examined to allow the business to forecast profits from launching the new product. Legal issues, such as safety standards, copyright and patent legislation, will also need to be considered.
4. **Launch**. Assuming that the product has passed the first three stages, it will enter its 'introductory' stage of its product life cycle. The products will be distributed to retail outlets to sell to customers. There will be a marketing campaign to launch the new product, perhaps on a local, national or international scale. New Hollywood blockbuster movies, for example, use extensive *above-the-line promotional strategies* (see Unit 4.5) and tend to have their own dedicated website for potential customers to obtain more information or to see trailers of the new movie.

Sources of new product development

Ideas for new product development can come from several sources. These include:

- **Market research** – This refers to the process of businesses collecting and analysing relevant data and information to better meet the needs of their customers (see Unit 4.2). Market research can therefore reveal opportunities for product design and development.
- **Product extensions** – This refers to the use of existing brands, especially the more successful ones, in order to design and develop new products. Coca-Cola, for example, has successfully launched Coke Light (also called Diet Coke in some parts of the world) and Coke Zero by using the original Coca-Cola brand name.
- **Research and development (R&D)** – Technological and scientific research helps to generate a flow of new ideas and processes.
- **'Me too' developments** – This occurs when businesses rely on other firms to be innovative and then simply copy their ideas legally. This approach tends to be used by relatively unestablished firms and/or those that have an insufficient R&D budget.

Although the focus of NPD is clear, it is important to remember that managers also look at all other elements of the marketing mix in order to increase the chances of successfully launching the new product. This therefore means that NPD can be extremely expensive.

PRODUCT LIFE CYCLE

The **product life cycle** shows the different stages that a product is likely to go through from its initial design and launch to its decline (and its eventual withdrawal in most cases). Its life cycle is measured over time in terms of the differing levels of sales. The use of a product life cycle (PLC) allows managers to identify any changes that may be needed in the product's marketing strategy. It also alerts the firm to take appropriate action to deal with the issues raised.

Some specific products, such as different models of mobile phones, have a relatively short life cycle whilst other products have very long life cycles. For example, Coca-Cola, Levis Jeans and Colgate toothpaste were established over 100 years ago. Moët & Chandon (a well-known brand of champagne) has existed since 1743. Other products, such as textbooks, certain children's toys or pop music bands, may have a much shorter life cycle. The fashion industry is challenged constantly by change, perhaps more so than in most other industries. Shoes such as Uggs (Australian boots) and Crocs (lightweight American shoes) have been very popular but the life cycles were short lived. According to *Newsweek* magazine, mobile phones have a life cycle of 18 months in the USA before consumers replace their phones. The figure is 15 months in Europe and just 9 months in Japan, even though mobile phones are made to last for around 5 years (*Newsweek*, Jan 2007). Newer and better designed mobile phones are readily available on the market. However, the life cycle for mobile phones as a product itself has a much longer life cycle.

For most products, there are generally six stages to their life cycle: research and development, launch (introduction), growth, maturity, saturation and decline (see Figure 4.3c). Each stage of the product life cycle is likely to have a different marketing mix.

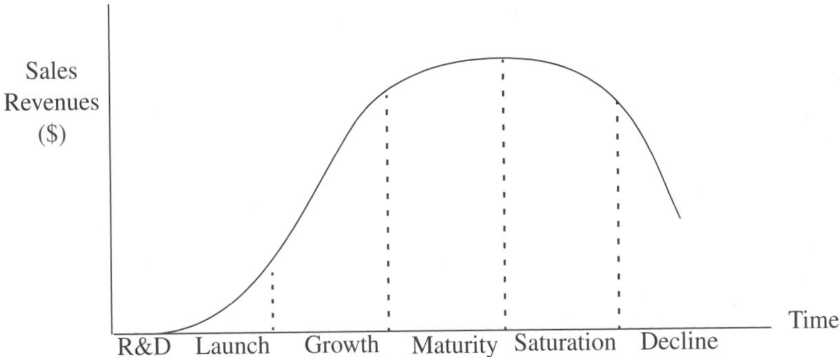

Figure 4.3c The product life cycle

1 **Research and development (R&D).** The R&D stage of a product's life cycle involves designing and testing the product. This tends to be a time-consuming task. A **prototype** (a trial product) will often be produced and test-marketed along with other methods of market research in order to assess the potential success of the product. **Test marketing** will usually take place. This involves trialling a new product with a sample of customers, perhaps in a limited geographical area, to determine reactions of customers and to gather valuable feedback. This helps to minimize costs (and embarrassment) if the product is unsuccessful, rather than having launched the product nationally without any test marketing. If the product is unsuccessful at this stage, then the business can either make changes, based on the feedback of customers, or discontinue the product. Advertising guru David Ogilvy suggests that the most important aspect of R&D is testing. He argues that if a firm pre-tests its product with

consumers and pre-tests its advertising, it will have a much higher chance of success in the market place. One danger in using test marketing, however, is that competitors may find out about the product before its launch. For example, the media often report new models of cars being tested by motor vehicle manufacturers. The R&D and testing phase will also incur high costs, thereby negatively affecting the net cash flow of a business. Studies have shown that most ideas at this stage do not proceed to the launch of the products, i.e. there is a high rate of failure. Products that are launched must be priced competitively yet high enough to recover the costs of R&D – for the successfully launched product and those unsuccessful products that never commercialized.

2 **Launch (introduction)**. The introduction stage requires careful marketing planning. Sales will be relatively low since customers are not fully aware of the product's existence. At the same time, however, costs are very high due to the costs involved in the launch stage (such as the costs of publicity, promotion and distribution). Hence, the product is unprofitable at this stage of its life cycle, although prices may be high in order to recover R&D costs as quickly as possible. The aim of managers is therefore to get the product to its next stage as soon as possible. This will be easier to achieve for some products (such as blockbuster Hollywood movies) but harder for others (such as new books by unknown authors). The customers who tend to buy the product during its launch are often referred to as **innovators** (people who like to be the first to own a certain product, perhaps due to prestige or because they are fanatics of the product, brand or company). Innovators have been observed queuing days before the launch of the Star Wars movies, Harry Potter books and Sony PS3 games consoles in order to be one of the first customers to purchase these products. Once customers are aware of the new product, through successful and extensive marketing campaigns, then the product will head towards its next phase in the life cycle.

3 **Growth**. The growth stage of a product's life cycle sees sales volume increasing. This is partly due to businesses using a wider distribution network to get the product to different customers in different locations. Brand awareness and loyalty amongst the customers (known as the **early adopters)** (see Unit 5.6) at this stage also help to boost sales. Profits may materialize due to sales revenue rising and the possibility of lower unit costs due to economies of scale in production. Businesses will aim to prolong this stage of the life cycle as far as possible. However, profits will attract rivals to the industry who may launch similar products. As a result, the pricing and non-pricing strategies of the firm may need to be reviewed.

4 **Maturity**. During the maturity stage of a product's life cycle, sales revenues continue to rise, but at a much slower rate. The firm is likely to have obtained significant market share since sales revenues are at their peak. Economies of scale will give the firm a competitive advantage, although there are likely to be many competitors in the market at this stage. Promotional activities tend to focus on reminding customers, rather than persuading them, about the product in an attempt to emphasize brand loyalty. Coca-Cola is an example of a product at its maturity stage – but it has been there for a very long time now!

5 **Saturation**. Saturation occurs when there are too many competitors in the market and sales have peaked or have started to fall. Price reductions and extension strategies (see 'Extension strategies and the product life cycle' on page 507) are likely to be used in order to maintain market share and to avoid sales falling even further. Promotional activities may become more aggressive to get existing customers to purchase the product. At this stage, managers may also look to exploit new market segments for the product.

6 **Decline**. The UK's largest electronics chain store, Dixons, sold its last batch of CRT (cathode ray tube) televisions during Christmas 2006, having opted to stock only LCD and plasma televisions. This represents the product's final stage of the product life cycle (before its withdrawal or 'death' happens). During decline, sales and profit of the product decline. This could be the result of changing customer demands (due to changing tastes and fashions),

new technology, and new replacement models being introduced either by the firm itself or by competitors (making the existing product obsolete). Promotional spending on the current product is cut and prices plummet. In reality, new products are ready to be launched before the previous product enters decline since this will help a business to maintain its cash flow and profitability.

The life cycle of a product will therefore have varying effects on a firm's level of investment, profits and cash flow (outlined in Table 4.3a).

Table 4.3a PLC and its relationship with investment, profit and cash flow

PLC stage	Investment level	Profit	Cash Flow
R&D	Very high (research and development)	None	Highly negative
Launch	Very high (marketing)	Little, if any	Negative
Growth	High (persuasive)	Yes, rising	Positive
Maturity	Less (mainly reminding)	High; but little or no growth	Positive
Saturation	Extension strategies	High, stable	Positive
Decline	Little, if any	Yes, but falling	Positive, but falling

EXTENSION STRATEGIES AND THE PRODUCT LIFE CYCLE

For many products that reach the saturation stage of their life cycle, various **extension strategies** can be implemented to prolong their sales revenue. Extension strategies are so called because they refer to any means of extending the product's life cycle and delaying its decline. Apple's highly successfully iPod was launched some five years before Microsoft's wireless Zune media player. To prolong the iPod's life cycle, Apple introduced variations of the original product (such as the tiny iPod Nano and matchbox-sized iPod Shuffle) and other iPod accessories. The effects of extension strategies on a product's sales and life cycle are shown in Figure 4.3d.

Some common extension strategies are outlined below.

- **Price reductions** – Lowering price will tend to raise the level of demand for a product. Businesses often use this extension strategy to get rid of excess stocks before they become obsolete.
- **Redesigning** – This involves introducing special features or 'limited editions' to a current product. This strategy **adds value** to the product and therefore can entice more customers to buy the product.
- **Repackaging** – Changing the packaging of a product, such as using more attractive colours or materials, can help to revive demand. The appearance of a product, including its packaging, can have a large impact on the level of demand.
- **New markets** – Trying to locate new opportunities for a current product can also extend its life cycle. Examples include trying to sell the product in new retail outlets, different regions or overseas.
- **Promotion** – Revised promotional activities such as advertising can help to remind customers about the benefits of purchasing the product. This can help to boost demand, at least for a little longer.

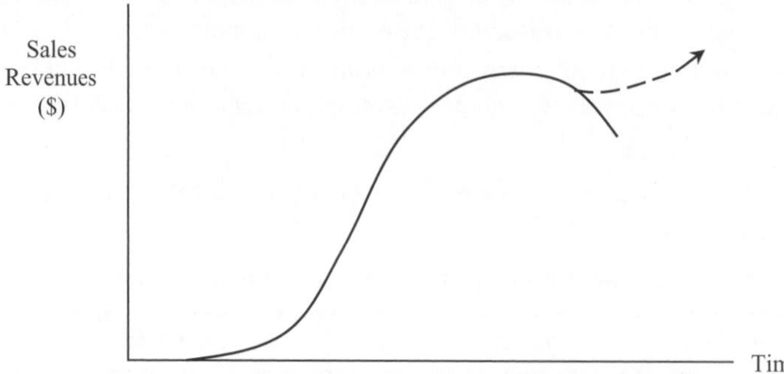

Figure 4.3d Extension strategies

PRODUCT DIFFERENTIATION

Product differentiation is a marketing strategy that involves making a product stand out from others, especially those offered by rival firms. By having a unique element to the products offered by a firm, it could help the business to withstand competition in the market. An example of product differentiation is **product branding**. Nike's swoosh or the three stripes of Adidas allow customers to instantly identify products from these firms. Successful product differentiation will require marketing support such as sales promotion. Other examples of how products could be differentiated are outlined in Box 4.3a.

There are several benefits to production differentiation:

- *Price advantages* – Products that are homogeneous act as strong substitutes and thereby are price elastic (see Unit 4.4). This means that the firm is unlikely to be able to raise price to increase sales revenue and profit margins because customers have many other substitute firms to choose from. By contrast, product differentiation allows a firm to charge a higher price than otherwise would be the case.
- *Consumer recognition and loyalty* – Brand recognition can be a valuable source of competitive advantage. Being able to recognize a branded product increases the chances of selling the product. This might be due to customer loyalty or simply because people feel more comfortable in purchasing a product that they are familiar with. By contrast, new products and non-differentiated products tend to lack customer recognition and loyalty.
- *Distribution advantages* – Retail space is limited so businesses will only stock the best selling brands. Therefore, successful product differentiation improves placement (distribution) of a firm's products.

Box 4.3a Methods of product differentiation

Colour – The different flavoured crisps (potato chips) found in supermarkets can be distinguished by their colour. Red and white combinations are used by many firms, such as Colgate, KFC, Virgin and Coca-Cola. Ikea's famous yellow and blue combination is symbolic of the Swedish flag.

Size – The physical size of a product can make it stand out. Large-sized plasma televisions or cars demand a higher price. However, miniaturization is preferred for other products such as mobile phones and MP3 players.

Quality – Motor firms use performance as a guide to the quality of a car. BMW will use the high performance and build quality of its cars to differentiate itself from rival firms.

Design – The design of Apple's iPod or Sony's PSP helps to attract more customers. Design plays an important role in the purchase of highly expensive products.

After-sales service – Customers who purchase consumer durables tend to receive some form of after-sales services, such as warranties, guarantees, installation and servicing. Businesses that offer after-sales care are more likely to satisfy their customers' needs. This method can also be a source of customer loyalty.

Packaging – Presentation plays an important part in the marketing of most products. It can add value to a product and it certainly acts as a form of differentiation. Japanese consumers are very particular about packaging.

Purchase terms – Many businesses will offer special purchase terms to attract customers. Popular schemes include 0% financing, hire purchase, part-exchange and 'buy now, pay later' plans.

Customer relations management – The level of customer care is very important, especially in the service industry. Hotels, airlines, banks and retail outlets rely on their staff to deliver a first-rate customer experience in order to maintain their market share.

PRODUCT PORTFOLIO ANALYSIS

Product portfolio means the range of products owned by a business. Mitsubishi, the Japanese multinational company, has a product portfolio that includes products as diverse as motor vehicles, consumer electronics and ballpoint pens. Product portfolio can also refer to **strategic business units (SBU)**. These are businesses or divisions owned by a firm, such as Volvo and Mazda (both owned by the Ford Motor Company). Similarly, PepsiCo is part of the same organization as Pizza Hut and KFC.

Product portfolio analysis allows a business to decide which products should receive more or less investment. For example, products that do not have high market share may be withdrawn or remarketed. The analysis also allows a business to develop growth strategies (see Unit 1.7) by adding new products to an existing or new range.

A diverse product portfolio is important for a firm's cash flow since selling to limited market segments will limit sales revenues for the business. It also helps to spread risks because a decline in sales for one product may be offset by favourable sales of other products in the portfolio.

The most popular model of product portfolio analysis is the **Boston Consultancy Group matrix** (or the **Boston matrix or BCG matrix** for short) devised by the USA's Boston Consultancy Group. The BCG matrix is a marketing planning tool which helps managers to plan for a balanced product portfolio. It looks at two dimensions, market share and market growth, in order to assess new and existing products in terms of their market potential (see Figure 4.3e).

		Market share	
		High	**Low**
Market Growth	**High (growing)**	Stars	Problem Children
	Low (mature)	Cash Cows	Dogs

Figure 4.3e The Boston matrix

A business would place each individual product in its product portfolio (or product range) onto one of the quadrants of the Boston matrix based on the product's relative market share and the product's market growth in the industry. There are four possible results from using the Boston matrix:

- ***Dogs*** are products with a low market share operating in a low growth market. Dogs do not generate much cash for the business as the market tends to be stagnant or declining, so businesses may try to dispose of these products. Firms that have too many products in this quadrant find that there is a lack of cash for the business.
- ***Problem child*** refers to products that operate in a high market growth sector, but have low market share. This can be a concern as problem children may represent inferior product quality or marketing to those of competitors. Given that the market has high growth, a business should analyse reasons for its low market share and then develop strategies to gain a higher share of the growing market. This means that problem children are the main users of cash in the BCG matrix. In the 1980s when personal computers saw huge market growth, Apple Mac computers were seen as a problem child. Steve Jobs, the CEO of Apple, led the company to profits by targeting the product at different consumers. Steve Jobs also changed the focus of Apple to incorporate multimedia products such as the iPod. Problem children are also known as **question marks** or **wild cards** because it is not always obvious whether a business should invest more in these products.
- ***Stars*** are products that operate in high growth markets and have high market share. Hence, stars are highly successful products that tend to generate high amounts of cash for a business. For this reason, businesses will tend to invest money in developing and promoting their stars. It is hoped that many stars will eventually turn into cash cows for the business. The cash generated from stars can also be used in an attempt to turn some of the wild cards into stars. Samsung, the South Korean electronics giant, has a huge amount of products in its portfolio. One of its stars is the Anycall brand of mobile phones which has taken away significant market share from its more established American rival Motorola and Finland's Nokia. With continued investment, Anycall is likely to become a cash cow for Samsung.
- ***Cash cows*** are products with high market share operating in a low growth market. These markets tend to be mature markets and the products are very well established, thereby generating superb net cash flow. Coca-Cola operating in the soft drinks market is an example. Cash cows provide businesses with large amounts of profits and have good *profit quality* (ability to earn long-term profits). However, some cash cows run the risk of becoming dogs, so businesses tend to use extension strategies to prolong their high earning potential.

The BCG matrix shows that the ideal product portfolio for a business is to have a balanced portfolio, which might include some stars, a few problem children and several cash cows. It is important for managers to note that the BCG matrix is not a static model. Managers are aware that the money generated from cash cows is used to turn the question marks into stars, otherwise they may become dogs. The term **rising star** is often used to describe problem children moving into the category of stars. Similarly, the stars may ultimately become cash cows. Some problem children may turn into stars whilst many others will turn into dogs. Appropriate marketing strategies need to be devised to foster these changes. Managers will also need to decide whether to spend money on reviving demand for dogs or whether to withdraw all investments in them, thereby releasing cash for other products. It is important then, that a business has a balanced range of products in the BCG matrix.

One of the main criticisms of this model is its assumption that higher profits come from higher market share. This is not necessarily the case. Euro Disney, for example, made huge losses between 2002–2006 despite receiving large amounts of revenue and having a high market share in the theme parks industry. The company even had to raise a further £175 million ($350 million) through share issues in 2005 to prevent it going into liquidation. Due to the attractiveness of its brand, the Disney Company gained a high market share quickly but still faced the problem of recouping its high redevelopment costs. In addition, whilst the BCG matrix can provide a quick synopsis of a firm's product portfolio, it fails to explain the root causes of the position of these products in the grid. The BCG matrix, as with any other business decision-making tool, should be used in conjunction with other planning tools such as the Ansoff Growth matrix (see Unit 1.7).

Note: Higher Level students must be able to use the BCG matrix to help in developing the future strategic direction of a business. (© IBO 2007)

Question 4.3.2

Virgin Group Ltd.

Virgin was set up in the early 1970s by British tycoon Sir Richard Branson. His entrepreneurial skills have led to the growth of the Virgin Group which now consists of over 200 companies. Some of his better known businesses include: Virgin Atlantic Airways, Virgin Blue, Virgin Trains, Virgin Cola and Virgin Mobile.

a Explain why a broad product portfolio might be important for business success. *[4 marks]*

b Examine the reasons why businesses such as Virgin need a different marketing mix for each of their distinct products. *[6 marks]*

BRANDING

Branding is a form of differentiating a firm's product from those of its competitors. A brand refers to a name that is identifiable with a product of a particular business (although the term can also refer to a sign, symbol, colour scheme, font or design). Interbrand, the internationally renowned branding consultancy, defines a brand as "a mixture of tangible and intangible attributes symbolized in a trademark". A trademark gives legal protection to the registered firm to exclusively use a brand name or brand mark. Microsoft's brand names, for example, include: Windows, XP, Explorer, Microsoft Word, Microsoft Excel, PowerPoint and Vista.

Research has shown that a well-known brand, such as Coca-Cola, can be so influential that it actually alters the consumer's feelings and/or their perception of the product's taste. It is important for marketers and managers to realize the importance of the roles and functions of branding. These in turn form the basis of the advantages of branding.

The role and advantages of branding

- *Branding as a legal instrument.* Brand names create a legal **identity** for a product by giving it a unique and recognizable name and image to differentiate it from other products. This can serve to meet the physical or psychological needs of employees, suppliers and customers. For instance, there are plenty of examples of businesses that use branding to give an upmarket image of their products, such as: Gucci, Versace, Rolex, L'Oreal and Rolls-Royce. As a legal instrument, branding gives lawful ownership of the product and protects it against imitations.
- *Branding as a logo.* This function stresses the importance of logos (visual representations of a brand) as a vital source of differentiation. Logos can provide huge cost advantages to a business, e.g. it is much cheaper for McDonald's to use its Golden Arches 'M' logo or for Kentucky Fried Chicken to use its abbreviated 'KFC' logo than for these firms to use their full names. Logos also have the advantage of being able to break international language barriers. Other highly recognized brand logos include Nike's swoosh (the tick), the Coca-Cola font and Mercedes-Benz's three-pointed star.
- *Branding as a risk reducer.* Brands can give new products a better chance of survival in the marketplace. They can create a sense of value for money and encourage **customer loyalty** or **brand loyalty**. There is plenty of research to show that customers remain devoted to the purchase of well-known brands. Brands can also help to prolong the product life cycle of a good or service. This will, however, require the business to invest money in promoting and sustaining the loyalty of the brand.
- *Branding as an image enhancer.* Brands that are successful allow a business to charge a **premium price** (see Unit 4.4). Customers are often willing to pay a substantially higher price for a 'good' brand. This allows the business to earn much higher profit margins on its products. Lexus, the luxury division of Toyota Motor Corporation, is able to charge premium prices due to the high-class image of its brand of cars. Psychologists and marketers have confirmed that purchasing decisions are not plainly based on the price or function of a product but also the 'feel good factor' associated with the purchase of a particular brand label.
- *Branding as a sales generator.* Branding can reduce the **price elasticity of demand** (see Unit 4.4) for the product. This means that consumer demand is less sensitive to changes in prices. Customers perceive the branded product as superior to others and will not tend to buy substitutes, even if the price is higher. Being able to charge a proportionately higher price without losing customers means that the firm earns higher sales revenues. In addition, brand loyalty can mean that customers stick to buying products from the same business. This makes brand extension strategies much easier to accomplish.

Ultimately, these interlinked advantages amount to one reason: to make more profits for the business. In the sports industry, for example, the strength of some brands has enabled sports clubs, such as Manchester United and Chelsea Football Club, to extend into merchandising in overseas markets as well as providing financial services and their own digital television channels. Marketers suggest that businesses that invest in and sustain their brands will tend to prosper. Those that fail to use branding effectively suffer from lower levels of profitability. However, developing a brand is very expensive and can take many years. Most brands fail to ever become established in the marketplace, whilst many existing brands need regular investment or must evolve in order to survive. For example, British Telecom announced that its latest logo, launched in 2003, would cost the company approximately £5 million ($10 million) in rebranding. The huge cost is partly because the British customers had become used to the previous logo, which had been around since 1991.

Question 4.3.3

Lexus

Toyota Motor's luxury brand Lexus is a relatively young brand, having been introduced in 1989. However, its success has been incredible and by 2005, Lexus had sold more luxury vehicles in the USA than any of its foreign and domestic rivals. Lexus has also secured significant market share in Singapore, Taiwan, South Korea, Thailand and Brunei. Lexus has been voted by drivers, time after time, as the most reliable cars in the world.

a Explain why Toyota might have chosen to label its luxury cars as Lexus rather than Toyota, a much more globally recognized brand name. *[4 marks]*

b Discuss the role and importance of branding to a multinational firm like Toyota. *[8 marks]*

Advocates of branding as a marketing strategy argue that a brand is far more important than a product because they differ in several ways:

- *Intangibility* – Brands are the intangible value that customers place on the actual physical product. Marketers argue that it is the brand that sells the product, not the other way round.
- *Uniqueness* – Brands are unique, whereas a product is quite easily copied.
- *Time* – Successful brands are timeless, whereas products themselves may become obsolete. Sony's Walkman personal stereo and first generation PlayStation games console were withdrawn in the late 1990s, but both brand names live on.

BRAND NAMES

Devising and choosing a brand name is a vital, albeit extremely difficult, part of a firm's marketing strategy. Effective brand names are easily recognizable, memorable and portray the desired image of the business. Nike, for example, was chosen by the company's founder and chairman, Phil Knight, because Nike is the name of the Greek goddess of victory. It is also a short name, so is easier to spell and remember. Good brand names also act as a stimulus for positive associations with the product or business. For example, United Parcel Service (UPS), the international courier service provider, chose its name to represent what the business does. Box 4.3b outlines some other examples of how famous brand names were created. Branding becomes even more difficult when dealing on an international basis. Examples of badly designed brand names from various parts of the world are outlined in Box 4.7a (see Unit 4.7). A final point is that branding must be free of copyright infringements.

There are different types of brand names:

- **Coined brands** are made-up brand names. Some will have no obvious meaning. For example the world's largest luxury ice cream producer, Haagen Dazs, was chosen by its American owners in 1961 who wanted to make the brand name sound 'foreign'. Coined brand names are quite easy to come up with but are usually very difficult to promote. Other examples include Google (search engine), Exxon (oil) and Xerox (commercial equipment). Some coined brand names have an implicit meaning. Examples include Microsoft (computer software), Hotmail (Microsoft's email service), FedEx (international courier formerly known as Federal Express) and Prittstick (glue stick). These names are relatively easier to remember and therefore promoting such brands is more straightforward.

- **Bona fide names** refer to real world names that are used in branding. Apple (computers and electronics), Royal Dutch Shell (petroleum), Caterpillar (industrial equipment) and Texas Instruments (semiconductors) are examples. They are the opposite of coined names. These names can be quite descriptive, such as British Petroleum, General Electric, Burger King or Toys 'R' Us. However, other bona fide names have no obvious association with the product, such as Total (petroleum), Legal & General (life and health insurance), Sharp (electronics) and Kingfisher (retailing). These brands are probably the most difficult to trademark since they are used in everyday language or are too generic to have legal protection (Steve Jobs did very well to get Apple!)
- **Acronyms** are abbreviations that stand for the name of a business. For example, multinational clothing company French Connection, United Kingdom uses the acronym FCUK. Other examples include D&G (Dolce and Gabbana), BMW (Bavarian Motor Works), KFC (Kentucky Fried Chicken), CNN (Cable News Network) and HSBC (Hong Kong & Shanghai Banking Corporation). Long brand names are harder to remember whilst vague abbreviations may mean little to customers. Hence, having well-designed acronyms can help a firm to get around these two problems.
- **Numbers** are the numerical symbols that are used in branding. Numbers are easily recognizable throughout the world. Examples include: 7-Eleven, Levi's 501, Chanel No. 5, Play Station 3, Nike 90 and Airbus A380. Car manufacturers tend to use numbers for branding their individual product lines. For instance, Z4, Z10, M3, M5, X5, 325i and 7 Series are all registered trademarks of BMW.
- **Personal names** are brands named after famous people or their founders. Computer giant Dell was named after its founder Michael Dell. Walt Disney, Johnson & Johnson, Ralph Lauren, Marks & Spencer, Sara Lee, Ford Motors, the Trump Organization and Levi Strauss are further examples. Marketers believe that this approach helps customers to feel a sense of association as they can easily identify the business to these famous people. Doctors, accountants and solicitors tend to use this method of branding. Unless very well established, individual names can be quite limiting. Associating a brand with a famous person can be a short-lived strategy. Nike dropped its highly successful 'Jordan' brand following the retirement of basketball legend Michael Jordan. If a celebrity becomes unfashionable or gets negative media coverage, this too may shorten the durability of the brand.

Johnson & Johnson

- **Place names** refer to brands that are named after a certain area, location or country. Nokia (mobile phones) gets its name from the Finnish town where the firm was founded in 1865, over a century before the introduction of the first generation mobile phone. Airline carriers often use this method, such as: Air China, China Air (Taiwan), Singapore Airlines, British Airways, Air France and Japan Airlines. Newspapers are also often named after their location, such as *The New York Times*, *The Washington Post* and *The Wall Street Journal*. Other examples of place names include: Japan Post (courier and delivery), American Express (financial services), China Mobile (mobile phone services), Zurich International (financial services), and Telecom Italia (telecommunications). These names are easily recognizable but may prove difficult to trademark.

Branding is often supported and developed with the use of corporate **slogans** (catchphrases). Examples include McDonald's "I'm lovin' it", Nike's "Just do it" and Nokia's "Connecting People". In non-profit organizations, political slogans have also been used for a very long time. "Make love, not war" was used during the Vietnam War, for instance. The British Conservative Party, led by Margaret Thatcher, used the slogan "Labour is not working" in 1978 to publicize the fact that the Labour Party government was highly unsuccessful in reducing unemployment in the economy.

Box 4.3b Behind the name of famous brands...

7-Eleven – Founded in 1927, the opening times of 7-Eleven convenience stores were originally from 7 a.m. to 11 p.m.

Adidas – The sports apparel giant gets its name from the founder of the company, ADI DASsler.

Amstrad – The electronics company Amstrad gets its name from the initials of its founder, the British business tycoon Sir Alan Michael Sugar, and the first three letters of TRADing.

Hotmail – Microsoft's free email service (HoTMaiL) was created by two ex-employees of Apple Corporation who worked on the project using the internet-based computer language called HTML. This gave them the inspiration for the name.

Ikea – The world's largest home furnishing firm, established in 1943 by Ingvar Kamprad, gets its name from the initials of the founder and Elmtaryd Agunnaryd, the farm and village where he grew up.

Intel – The leading producer of microprocessors and semiconductors was founded in 1968 as INTegrated ELectronics Corporation.

Mattel – The world's largest toy producer, which owns brands such as Fisher-Price, Tyco, Barbie, Matchbox, and Hot Wheels, gets its name from the founders of the company, Harold 'MATT' Matson and ELliot Handler.

Spam – Spam is a registered trademark of Hormel Foods Corporation. The name was changed from the original name of 'Hormel Spiced Ham' (luncheon meat), which didn't really catch on. Spam is derived from SPiced hAM.

Question **4.3.4**

Coca-Cola

Coca-Cola is the biggest brand in the world. The company claims that its brand name is the second most understood word in the English language (after 'okay'). In fact, Coca-Cola (also referred to by its trademark name of Coke) is synonymous with American culture. The company preserves the position of its brand by devoting a huge amount of money to its marketing. For example, Coca-Cola is one of the largest sponsors of sporting events such as the NBA (basketball), the NHL (hockey), the Olympic Games and the FIFA World Cup.

Source: www.cocacola.com

a Explain why a brand name is important to a business such as Coca-Cola. *[3 marks]*

b To what extent should firms devote time and resources to creating a 'big' brand name? *[7 marks]*

BRAND DEVELOPMENT AND BRAND LOYALTY

Brand preference means that customers favour a particular brand over rival brands. This could be due to customers being loyal to a certain brand. **Brand loyalty** is seen when customers buy the same brand of product time and time again. They must therefore have brand preference. Both brand preference and loyalty will help to sustain or improve a firm's market share. The firm with the largest share of the market is known as the **market leader** (or **brand leader**). Microsoft, Coca-Cola and Google are examples of market leaders in their respective industries.

There are numerous advantages for a business that tries to achieve brand loyalty:

- **Higher market share**. Market share is an indicator of the level of brand preference and brand loyalty. It is assumed that there is a strong and positive relationship between a firm's market share and the level of brand loyalty. Marketers try to improve this correlation by investing money into brand development, such as using persuasive advertising and other promotional methods.
- **Ability to charge premium prices**. Having brand loyalty and brand leadership not only brings in regular customers, but it also allows the business to charge higher prices for their products. Furthermore, market leaders are able to set their own prices whereas rivals are likely to be forced into charging prices determined by the brand leader. This is because customers feel that they are paying for the *added value* that the brand carries. The added value might, for example, be in the reputation of the brand, thereby giving customers reassurance that the product is genuine, reliable and trouble free.
- **Demand becomes more price inelastic**. Brand loyalty can also reduce the *price elasticity of demand* for the product, i.e. consumer demand is less sensitive to changes in price. This can help a business to protect itself against price competition from rival brands.
- **Fosters brand extension strategies**. Brand loyalty helps a business to develop and launch new products under the brand name. Cadbury's, Toyota and Sony are examples of successful businesses that have used their brand names to enlarge their product portfolios.
- **Higher barriers to entry**. Brand loyalty makes it more difficult for new firms to enter the market because customers are loyal to the existing brand. The dominance of brands such as Coca-Cola, Nike and Nokia have created huge problems for rival brands. These products can then enjoy the status of being *cash cows* (see page 510) for the business.

Brand development is part of a firm's long-term marketing strategy. It is the process of strengthening and building the name and image of a brand in order to boost its sale. This can be done through brand awareness techniques that focus on what makes a brand stand out from the crowd. This is likely to take a lot of time, perhaps years to establish. This will also mean that the costs of brand development are likely to be high.

Successful brand development will help to extend the maturity stage of a product's life cycle. Some firms are so successful in doing this (such as Coca-Cola and Colgate) that their products have stayed at this stage indefinitely.

Question 4.3.5

The top brands in the world

Interbrand, the world's largest branding consultancy firm, conducts annual rankings of the world's top brands. These brands must have a global presence, with at least 20% of sales coming from outside their home country. Interbrand assesses each brand based on its future earning potential. Some of the most valuable brands include: Coca-Cola, Microsoft, IBM, GE (General Electric), Intel, Nokia, Toyota, Disney, McDonald's and Mercedes-Benz.

Source: Interbrand.com

a Explain why globally recognized brands such as Coca-Cola, Microsoft and Toyota continue to spend huge amounts of money on brand development. *[4 marks]*

b Examine how the brand name might determine the future success of a business. *[7 marks]*

The opposite of brand loyalty is **brand switching**. This means that consumers turn to alternative branded products. This happens mainly because the original brand has lost something which was once its strength. For example, customers may switch to rival products that offer more competitive prices or special offers. Alternatively, the new product or brand may offer better functions and services than the existing brand. To prevent brand switching, businesses often use **customer loyalty schemes**. These are a form of sales promotion (see Unit 4.5) used to entice customers to stick to the purchase of their brands by rewarding their faithful customers. An example are the 'air miles' schemes that are used by most airline carriers.

Question 4.3.6

French Connection, UK

French Connection reported that 2005 was one of its most difficult years, after announcing that profits had fallen by a huge 53%. Customers, it seemed, were growing tired of the FCUK brand which has lost its **brand loyalty** and shock factor over time. In response, French Connection launched yet another potentially offensive marketing campaign in 2006 which featured two women kung fu fighting before they embrace one another.

a Define the meaning of **brand loyalty**. *[2 marks]*

b Explain why brand loyalty is important to a business such as French Connection. *[4 marks]*

HIGHER LEVEL EXTENSION: TYPES OF BRANDING

There are five main types of brands: family branding, product branding, corporate branding, own label brands and manufacturer's brands.

Family branding

Family branding refers to marketing a range of products under a single brand name, such as Sony, General Electric (GE), Hewlett–Packard, Cadbury's and Kellogg's. The family brand encompasses all products of the business. Essentially, it is a marketing strategy that is the opposite of individual branding which gives each product in the product mix a unique brand identity, such as Fanta, Sprite, Minute Maid and Bonaqua of the Coca-Cola Company.

Businesses that use family branding as a marketing strategy can benefit from **economies of scope** because a whole range of products can be promoted using a single advertisement. Family branding can also help new products to survive in the market place by using **brand extension strategies**. The Virgin Group, for example, uses their family brand when diversifying into new markets such as airlines, rail, mobile phones, car sales, books and drinks. A new product launched by established family brands has a higher chance of success and continued existence. A further benefit of family branding is that it can help to build consumer trust and loyalty.

However, family brands can equally create problems. One drawback of using family branding is that bad publicity for one product or the business itself can lead to huge problems for all products under the family brand. Maintaining consistency in quality across different products can also be problematic. Substandard quality of one product could lead to sales of all other products declining since customers relate the family brand to that of the poor quality product.

HIGHER LEVEL

Product branding

Within a family brand, there may be **individual brands**, also known as **product branding**. This refers to giving the brand a separate identity that is distinct from the family brand name. This strategy can help to reduce the limitation of family branding since the failure of the individual brand prevents the family brand from being harmed. Product branding also allows a business to launch a new product that is separate from its main target market. For example, Toyota was able to use Lexus to reposition itself to cater for more affluent customers, whilst Mercedes-Benz did the opposite with their Smart cars.

Popular brands are subject to takeover bids. The product brand may have established itself as a leading brand in a particular market segment but has been acquired by another company. BMW did exactly this when they bought out the Mini and Rolls-Royce brands. Despite its strong family brand name, BMW chose to leave the acquired product brands unchanged.

Company brand (Corporate branding)

Corporate branding is a type of family branding. It refers to the use of a business's name as the brand name. McDonald's, Nike, Disney and Virgin are examples. It uses the company name as a strategy to create brand recognition and loyalty.

Corporate branding has the benefit of potentially large *economies of scope* (see Unit 1.7) because a single advertisement can promote the whole range of products under the corporate brand. For example, Nike uses television advertising to promote the corporate brand rather than any individual Nike brand or product. Since corporate branding is a form of family branding, it also facilitates brand extension strategies, since potential customers are already familiar with the company brand name.

One main disadvantage of this strategy is that products under the corporate brand may not be treated as individual products with their unique core qualities. The company brand might be 'too' successful that the name becomes synonymous with the actual product (see Table 4.3b). This is a drawback because the company brand then loses its individual identity and copyright protection becomes meaningless.

Own label brand

Own label brands are the brands created and owned by distributors, such as warehouses and retailers. For example, supermarkets tend to have their own label brands for many of their products, such as Wal-Mart wines. These will be stocked in addition to more well-known manufacturers' brands. Own label brands are rarely produced by retailers themselves, but are manufactured on their behalf. Own label brands, also known as **private label brands**, will usually be priced lower than other more well-known brands. This is because packaging and promotion is often based on a 'no-frills' basis. In addition, retailers are able to benefit from huge purchasing economies of scale (being able to bulk buy enormous quantities directly from the manufacturer). These cost savings therefore allow the retailer to charge lower prices for own label products.

A key drawback of using own label branding is that private labels tend to be seen by the public as low quality products that are catered for price-sensitive consumers. Despite this disadvantage, own label brands have grown in popularity as consumers have learnt to trust own label brands that offer value for money. For instance, most Wal-Mart stores around the world stock more of its own-label products than any other brand.

Manufacturer's brand

Manufacturer brands are created and owned by the producers of a good or service. Examples include Heinz, Nestlé, Dell, Nokia, Intel and Microsoft. Most manufacturers protect their brands by using registered trademarks and copyright legislation. Some firms will actively take legal action to protect their brand identity against manufacturers, retailers or supermarkets that try to copy their brand name or logo. Some producers such as Kellogg's openly disclose that they do not produce products for other suppliers. This strategy informs the customer that the manufacturer's brand is different or superior from own label brands.

One drawback of using a manufacturer's brand is that consumers may not recognize it, especially as they tend to be used as components in manufacturing. For example, Sony manufactures batteries for Dell, Apple and Lenovo laptops (but the typical consumer is not aware of this). The same applies for car parts and components used in the motor manufacturing industry.

Note: It is not always clear which type of branding a trademark falls into. Coca-Cola, for example, is certainly a corporate brand (it's the most recognized brand in the world), but it may also be considered as a manufacturer's brand or a product brand.

Brand owners will clearly aim to maximize the popularity of their trademarks. Some brands become so famous (or 'genericized') that they are often mistaken for the name of the product itself (see Table 4.3b). Such brands are known as **generic brands**. This may signify the extent to which a brand is well known and successful. However, there is a danger that the generic use of a brand name leads to problems of enforcing copyright protection of the trademark.

Table 4.3b Brand or product?

Brand Name	Company	Product
Aspirin	Bayer AG, Germany	Acetylsalicylic acid (drug)
Astro Turf	Textiles Management Associates	Artificial lawn (or grass)
Band-Aid	Johnson & Johnson	Adhesive bandage
Biro	Invented by Laszlo Biro in 1938	Ballpoint pen
Blu-Tack	Bostik Findley, Australia	Reusable putty adhesive
Bubble Wrap	Sealed Air Corporation, USA	Air cellular cushioning material
Coke	Coca-Cola	Cola
Frisbee	Wham-O, USA	Flying disc
Hoover	The Hoover Company	Vacuum cleaner
Hula hoop	Wham-O, USA	Toy hoop
iPod	Apple Inc.	Portable media player
Jacuzzi	Roy Jacuzzi invented the bath with built-in water jets	Whirlpool bathtub
Kleenex	Kimberley-Clark	Tissue paper
Rollerblade	Tecnica	Inline skates
Tipp-Ex	BIC Corporation, France	Correction fluid
Wyteboard Marker	Pilot	Board marker pen

In reality, businesses will tend to use a range of branding strategies. For example, Microsoft uses family branding alongside individual product brand names, e.g. Microsoft Word, Microsoft Vista and Microsoft Encarta (Word, Vista and Encarta are all registered trademarks of Microsoft Corporation). The purpose is to allow customers to associate the product with a familiar family brand name but giving the product an element of individuality. Toyota, for example, has used its highly successful slogan "The car in front is a Toyota" on a global scale to promote the family brand of motor vehicles. However, it also uses company branding for its range of motor vehicles, such as the Toyota Corolla and Toyota Camry. It has also used the Lexus brand name for its strategic business unit of up-market luxury cars.

HIGHER LEVEL

HIGHER LEVEL

HIGHER LEVEL EXTENSION: BRANDING IN A GLOBAL MARKET

Branding can have a positive influence on the competitive strength of a business. Relative brand strength will mean that the firm has a higher chance of survival and success in overseas markets. Such firms are then able to benefit from global marketing economies of scale (see Unit 1.7). This gives the business a competitive cost advantage, thereby meaning that its market share is likely to increase.

Some brands have become so popular on an international scale that they are called **global brands**. Theorists differ slightly on the exact meaning of this term. It generally means that the same product is sold with exactly the same (or very similar) marketing strategies in overseas markets. Examples of global brands include: Coca-Cola, Microsoft, Disney, Dell and Mercedes-Benz. Their image, physical make-up and appearance are almost identical wherever they are marketed in the world, i.e. there is consistency in the marketing of these products. The key driving forces for global branding are brand loyalty and the cost savings gained from using a single marketing approach.

More recently, global brands have focused more on the local needs of overseas consumers. Thus, these brands have been '**glocalized**' to cater for local preferences whilst retaining the core elements of the global brand. For example, the core food menu at McDonald's is exactly the same throughout the world, but additional products are included to cater for local tastes and preferences.

Branding does, however, become a more complicated issue when operating in overseas markets. Language and cultural considerations become important to the success of an international brand. Box 4.3c outlines some brands that would probably not excel on a global scale. Unit 4.7 looks at the role of international marketing in more detail.

Box 4.3c International branding mishaps

- Swedish confectionery: Plopp and Skum
- Japanese sports drink: Pocari Sweat
- Swedish toilet tissue: Edet Krapp
- Chinese chocolate candy: Swine
- American clothing company: BUM Equipment
- Asian-based multinational clothes retailer: Wanko
- South Korean Bank: Woori Bank
- Taiwanese private airline company: FAT
- Bangkok restaurant chain: Cabbages and Condoms
- British air conditioning services: Stiff Nipples

Question 4.3.7

Ford Motor Company

Ford Motor Company launched the Pinto model in 1971. This was a compact-sized family car that came in several different engine sizes with slight variations such as 2-door and 4-door versions. The Pinto name didn't work well in Brazil as 'pinto' is slang for 'small male genitals'. Ford eventually became aware of this and renamed the car Corcel, which means horse. In America, the Pinto was named Mercury Bobcat. By 1981, the Pinto name had been replaced by Escort (and known as Mercury Lynx and Mercury Tracer in other parts of the world). In 1998, the Escort brand was finally replaced by a single global name: the Ford Focus.

a Explain the benefits to Ford Motor Company in using 'Focus' as a single brand name on an international level. *[4 marks]*

b Examine whether there are any justifications for Ford Motor Company using different brand names in different parts of the world. *[6 marks]*

PRODUCT AND BUSINESS STRATEGY

The products of a business are vital to its success. Microsoft, Apple, McDonald's, Boeing and Nike are all examples of market leaders that have managed to successfully market their products. Technology, fashion, tastes and trends are constantly subject to change and it is the businesses that are able to adapt their product portfolios that stand a chance of doing well. For example, Nokia started as a wood manufacturing business in 1865; Nintendo made playing cards back in 1889; Wrigley produced soap powder in 1891 before specializing in chewing gum, and Motorola initially produced car radios in 1928. The dynamic nature of business activity means that complacency is potentially disastrous. Theodore Levitt (1960) pointed this out when he wrote about **marketing myopia**. Marketing myopia exists when businesses become complacent about their product strategy or focus, thereby failing to keep up with market changes.

By increasing the product mix, a business is able to generate more revenue and to spread its risks. Starbucks, for example, market and distribute music and film (soundtracks, movies and DVDs) in addition to its coffee business. In the USA, Starbucks even managed to secure exclusive deals for the release of new albums by Alanis Morissette, Bob Dylan and Sir Paul McCartney. Virgin Group, headed by Sir Richard Branson, owns over 200 companies. The diverse range of products has made Branson one of Britain's richest people.

However, producing the 'right' products for the right people is far easier said than done, due to the costs and other complexities involved. For example, different products will require a different set of marketing mix. Fiat Group, Italy's largest car manufacturer, does not market Fiat cars in the same way it does for its Alfa Romeo, Maserati and Ferrari marques (brands). If a business is to remain competitive, it will have to carefully plan its product strategy, such as new product development whilst managing a diverse portfolio of products.

Product differentiation is also an important product strategy. A product can be made distinctive from rival products through various means, such as the use of branding, packaging and design. These all have cost implications for the marketing department and will affect the operations of the business as a whole. For example, branding strategy is more than just naming or designing. Successful branding is the result of a carefully planned and executed business strategy. Customer perceptions of quality and reputation are largely based on branding. Take the most globally recognized brand as an example – Coca-Cola. The soft drinks giant spends $2 billion each year to ensure that its brands continue to succeed. For example, the launch of Coke Zero in 2006–2007 managed to boost the company's worldwide sales. Brand management has become an increasingly important management task, especially as technology continues to shorten product life cycles of many types of products. Scientists and business analysts have shown that brand marketing can be so remarkable that it affects the workings of the human brain. For example, the *South China Morning Post* reported in October 2004 that scientists had discovered that the Coca-Cola brand stimulated parts of the human brain associated with cultural knowledge, memory and self-image.

Product and brand management can be aided by management tools such as SWOT analysis (see Unit 1.6). Managers can then analyse the strengths that can be developed, such as using brand extension strategies to launch new products. The SWOT analysis will also point out any weaknesses that need to be corrected. In addition, managers can identify market opportunities and decide on how to react to potential threats.

Many larger firms have benefited from developing a **multi-brand strategy**. This involves a business developing two or more brands in the same product category. Toyota, for example, use the Lexus company brand to market its more prestigious lines of motor cars. Professor David Jobber suggests seven components of an effective brand strategy: quality, positioning, repositioning, communications, internal marketing, long-term perspectives (brand management) and first-mover advantage.

Product portfolio analysis can also help managers to determine strategy. The Boston matrix, for example, suggests four different strategies for dealing with stars, dogs, problem children and cash cows (see Figure 4.3f).

Market Growth	Market share: High	Market share: Low
High (growing)	Harvest	Build Share
Low (mature)	Hold	Divest

Figure 4.3f The Boston matrix and business strategy

- The **Build Share** strategy is used to turn question marks into stars by investing necessary resources to gain market share. If nothing is done to increase the market share of dogs, they will simply drain cash from the business.
- The **Harvest** strategy involves reaping the benefits (profits) of a product. The purpose is to turn stars into cash cows. For example, this might mean huge amounts of advertising expenditure in order to turn the product into a cash cow.
- The **Hold** strategy involves the firm investing enough resources to keep the product in its current position in the Boston matrix. Investment is likely to be minimal since market growth for these products will be low.
- The **Divest** strategy involves phasing out or selling off dogs. This will release resources to be used elsewhere, such as for certain problem children. Some problem children might also face divestment, especially those that are unlikely to turn into stars.

Within the BCG matrix, the problem children are the main users of cash whilst the cash cows are the main generators of cash. The optimal **business portfolio** for a business is one that takes advantage of the firm's strengths (stars and cash cows) to develop other attractive opportunities (problem children and rising stars).

Finally, although product is often argued as the most important part of the marketing mix, it cannot succeed profitably without integration of the other elements of marketing. Price, promotion and placement of the product must be considered as they are key determinants of whether a product will succeed. Marketing planning is also of importance. For example, to fully understand and cater for different consumer needs, *market segmentation* (see Unit 4.2) may be necessary. Therefore, an understanding of different consumer profiles can enhance the chances of achieving product success. The use of *position mapping* (also covered in Unit 4.2) can give managers insightful information regarding consumers perceptions of a product. An understanding of customer perceptions of a brand can help managers to devise and implement appropriate product strategies.

REVIEW QUESTIONS 4.3

1. In business, what does the term 'product' mean?
2. Outline the differences between the 'emotional' and 'functional' values of a product.
3. What are the different methods of classifying a product?
4. Outline four ways in which product differentiation can take place.
5. Explain the various ways in which value can be added to a product.
6. State the four sources of new product development.
7. What are the stages in a typical product life cycle?
8. Use examples to explain the meaning of 'extension strategies'.
9. What is a 'strategic business unit' (SBU)?
10. Distinguish between the four quadrants in the Boston Consultancy Group matrix.
11. What is a 'brand' and why is it important for a business?
12. What is 'brand loyalty'?

Higher Level extension

13. What are the five main types of branding?
14. Explain one advantage and one disadvantage of generic brands.
15. Why might branding be an important part of business strategy for firms operating in overseas markets?
16. What is 'marketing myopia' and why might it cause problems for a business?
17. What is a 'multi-brand strategy'?

Boston matrix (the Boston Consultancy Group matrix) is a tool for analysing the product portfolio of a business. It measures whether products have a high or low *market share* and operate in high or low *market growth* industries.

Brand development is a long-term product strategy that involves strengthening the name and image of a brand in order to boost its sale.

Brand extension refers to the use of an existing brand name that is successful to launch a new or modified product.

Branding refers to the use of an exclusive name, symbol or design to identify a specific product or business. It is used to differentiate itself from similar products offered by rival firms.

Cash cow is a term used by the Boston Consultancy Group to refer to any product that generates significant sales revenue due to its large market share in a slowly expanding or mature market.

Consumer goods, or **consumer products**, are items bought by the final user for their own personal consumption. Examples include ***consumer durables*** (such as furniture, computers and cars) and ***perishables*** (such as flowers and food).

Differentiation, also known as **product differentiation**, refers to any strategy used to make a product appear to be dissimilar from others. Examples include quality, branding and packaging.

Extension strategy is an attempt by marketers to lengthen the product life cycle of a particular product. Such strategies are typically used during the maturity or early decline stages of the product's life cycle.

Generic brands are trademarks that have become synonymous with the name of the product itself. Examples include Coke, Rollerblade, Tipp-Ex and Frisbee.

New product development (NPD) is the process of getting the latest products onto the market. The easiest way is by making small improvements to existing products. Alternatively, a business could develop and launch entirely new products.

Marketing myopia refers to the short-sightedness and complacency of marketers in adapting to changes in the marketplace. Theodore Levitt suggested that marketing myopia exists in businesses that are heavily product orientated.

Product is a broad term that refers to any physical or non-physical item that is purchased by either commercial or private customers.

Product line is the term used to describe the varieties of a particular product that serves the same purpose in a particular market. For instance, there are many varieties of the BMW Mini, ranging from the basic model to the top of the range Mini Cooper S.

Product mix, also known as the **product assortment**, describes the variety of the different product lines that a business produces.

Product life cycle (PLC) is the typical process that products go through from their initial design and launch to their decline, and often their death (i.e. withdrawal from the market). Different products undergo each of the six stages (research, launch, growth, maturity, saturation and decline) at varying speeds.

Product portfolio refers to the range of products or strategic business units owned and developed by an organization.

Product range refers to all product lines of a firm's product mix, i.e. all the products sold by the business.

Rising stars (or **stars**) are products in the Boston matrix that have high or rising market share in a high growth market.

Strategic business unit (SBU) are businesses or divisions owned by a firm that operate as independent profit centres. Each SBU is in charge of a certain product or product portfolio.

Price

UNIT 4.4

What is a cynic? A man who knows the price of everything and the value of nothing.

Oscar Wilde (1854–1900), Irish author

Key topics

- The pricing decision
- Pricing policies: cost-based, competition-based and market-led

Higher Level extension

- Supply and demand

  Note: Diagrams are *not* required. (© IBO 2007)
- Price, income, cross and advertising elasticities of demand

  Note: Elasticity formulae will be provided in the examination. (© IBO 2007)
- Relationship between elasticities and the product life cycle
- Relationship between price elasticity and sales revenue

INTRODUCTION

The price decision is a crucial part of any marketing campaign. Deciding on the 'right' price for a product is not an easy task. In fact, research has shown that many products fail due to poor pricing decisions. The dilemma facing managers is to set a price that is competitive yet also profitable. Setting too high a price will put off customers. This will lead to lower levels of demand and potential financial problems for the firm. However, setting too low a price could lead to an undesirable image for the product which could prove difficult to put right.

This then means that prices affect the image of a business or its products. Producers and suppliers of luxury brands, such as Versace or Gucci, might benefit from some price cuts in the short term but sustaining lower prices in the long term will damage their reputation, perhaps irrevocably.

The price decision will also have a direct impact on the level of sales revenues. Marketers therefore need to have a clear understanding of the link between the price and the demand for their products.

This Unit examines the various forms of pricing that are used in businesses and how different pricing decisions affect the revenue and profitability of firms.

THE PRICING DECISION: PRICE MAKERS AND PRICE TAKERS

Some firms are in a better position than others to set prices. A **monopolist** (single supplier of a product) will have a high degree of market power and therefore has the ability to set its own prices (within reason). Monopolists are therefore said to be **price makers** or **price setters**. Box 4.4a outlines the various types of monopolists. At the other extreme are the firms that operate in highly competitive markets, where barriers to entry are low. They do not have much, if any, power over the setting of prices. Such firms are therefore referred to as **price takers**. They 'take' the price given by others in the market.

Irrespective of its degree of market power, a firm needs to formulate an effective pricing strategy in order to meet its marketing objectives. Within its chosen pricing strategy, different pricing methods (or tactics) are used. It is common for different pricing tactics to be used for different products of the organization.

Box 4.4a Types of monopolies

Pure monopolies – A pure monopolist is a firm that has 100% market share, i.e. it is the sole supplier of a product. Perhaps the nearest example to a pure monopoly might be Microsoft, which has over 95% of the market share in the personal computer operating system market.

Natural monopolies – These exist when the market can only sustain one supplier. For example, it is regarded as wasteful to have more than one supplier of telephone cables, gas pipes or rail tracks since a monopolist could provide these at huge savings in comparison to many smaller firms who would not benefit from economies of scale to the same extent.

Legal monopolies – These are firms that are protected from competition by law in order to prevent wasteful competition or in order for an essential service to be provided to the general public, e.g. postal services or public transport.

(cont.)

Regional monopolies – These are firms that hold monopoly power in a specific area or location. Any firm that is a sole supplier of a certain service or good in a remote town would be an example.

If monopolies, whatever their form, are seen to be acting against the interests of the general public (perhaps by deliberately restricting competition or by price fixing), the government may step in to break up the powers of the monopolists.

COST-BASED PRICING STRATEGIES

Cost-based pricing strategies are based on using *costs of production* to determine an appropriate price.

Cost-plus pricing (mark-up pricing)

This pricing strategy involves adding a *percentage* or *predetermined amount* of profit to the average cost of production to determine the selling price. Both fixed and variable costs are included in this calculation. The percentage or specified amount is known as the **mark-up** or **profit margin**. For example, if a product is estimated to have an average cost of $6 per unit and the producer wishes to have a 50% profit margin, the price will be set at $9. Alternatively, if the firm wanted to make $4 profit on each item sold, the selling price would be $10. Boeing uses this pricing method to sell its 747 Jumbo Jets to clients such as Japan Airlines and British Airways. The price charged is approximately $230 million which helps to cover its huge production costs of the 747 aircraft.

The advantage in using this method is that it is simplistic and easy to calculate. However, cost-plus pricing often relies too much on intuitive decision-making rather than focusing on the needs of customers.

A similar strategy is **floor pricing** which is used for *economy brands* (see Unit 4.3). A very low price is set to appeal to the price-sensitive customer. It is a suitable strategy for businesses that can survive on very low profit margins by selling in huge volumes.

Marginal cost pricing (contribution pricing) (Higher Level extension)

Marginal cost refers to the additional costs of producing an extra unit of output. In other words, it considers the direct or variable costs of any extra output. After all, fixed or indirect costs do not change as output levels change (see Unit 5.2). Marginal cost pricing is similar to cost-plus pricing except that this pricing method involves looking at the contribution made from the sale of each product, i.e. the amount left from the selling price after all direct costs of production have been accounted for. The surplus is then used as a contribution towards paying the fixed or indirect costs of production (see Unit 5.2).

For example, suppose a firm had a selling price of $8 and direct costs are $3 per unit. This means that the contribution per unit is $5 (selling price minus unit variable costs). Hence, each item sold enables the firm to contribute $5 towards paying its fixed costs of production. If the total fixed costs amount to $500 per time period, then this means the firm will make a profit once it has sold more than 100 units ($5 × 100 units).

This method allows a business to set different prices for different products based on its level of contribution. Hence there is more flexibility than using the cost-plus approach. One limitation in using this method is that it is not always easy to classify some costs as either direct or indirect.

HIGHER LEVEL

Exam Tip!
Worked example

The costs incurred by a firm that produces handmade leather shoes are as follows:

Cost (per pair of shoes)	$
Materials	15
Direct labour	20
Indirect costs	10
Total cost (per pair)	45

Question: Calculate the marginal cost of producing an extra pair of shoes.

Answer: The marginal cost refers the extra costs incurred by producing an extra pair of shoes. Indirect and fixed costs are excluded since they do not relate directly to the actual output of the shoes. Hence, the marginal cost would be $15 + $20 = $35. This means that the shoes must be sold for at least this price for the firm to make any contribution towards paying its indirect and fixed costs.

Full cost pricing (Higher Level extension)

Full cost pricing requires the business to allocate the total fixed costs between all the products that are sold. This helps to ensure that the price covers all costs of production. The method is simplistic in that it uses a single criterion to allocate the indirect costs.

The method can be explained through an example. Suppose for instance that a toy factory produces three products: Alpha, Beta and Gamma. Its total indirect costs are $12,000 per month. Full cost pricing would require the firm to allocate the $12,000 using a single criterion. For instance, the criterion can be based on the sales level of each product or the number of employees in each department. Even simpler, the criterion could be to split the indirect costs equally between all three products.

In order to allocate the indirect costs, first consider the information below:

Product (Department)	Alpha	Beta	Gamma
Direct costs (per unit)	$8	$5	$6
Floor space (square metres)	600	550	350
Output per month	500	800	600

In this instance, there are several criteria that can be used to allocate the $12,000 fixed costs.

Criterion 1: Apportion indirect costs equally

This is the easiest method to use. Each of the three departments would be allocated indirect costs of $4,000 (i.e. $12,000 / 3 product lines).

Using this information, the (minimum) price for each item can then be determined:

Product (Department)	Alpha	Beta	Gamma
Direct costs (per unit)	$8	$5	$6
Output per month	500	800	600
Total direct costs	$4,000	$4,000	$3,600
Indirect cost allocation	$4,000	$4,000	$4,000
Total costs	$8,000	$8,000	$7,600
Cost per unit	$16.00	$10.00	$12.67

Hence, charging no less than the cost per unit should help the firm to at least break-even. If, for instance, the desired mark-up was something in the region of 100%, the prices might be $32 (Alpha), $20 (Beta) and $25 (Gamma).

Criterion 2: Apportion indirect costs according to floor space

In this case, bearing in mind that the total factory floor space is 1,500 square metres, the allocation of indirect costs to each product is calculated as follows:

Alpha: (600 / 1,500) × $12,000 = $4,800

Beta: (550 / 1,500) × $12,000 = $4,400

Gamma: (350 / 1,500) × $12,000 = $2,800

Taking this one step further, we can then determine the minimum price that needs to be charged for each product:

Product (Department)	Alpha	Beta	Gamma
Total direct costs	$4,000	$4,000	$3,600
Indirect cost allocation	$4,800	$4,400	$2,800
Total costs	$8,800	$8,400	$6,400
Output per month	500	800	600
Cost per unit	$17.60	$10.50	$10.67

By using this criterion, Alpha and Beta have higher costs per unit than before and therefore prices will need to be set at a relatively higher level. By contrast, this method means that the price of Gamma is relatively lower.

Advantages of full costing

- Full costing is the simplest method of allocating overheads (indirect costs). It is a simpler version of *absorption costing* (see 'Absorption cost pricing' on page 530).
- It is a relatively inexpensive exercise as it is simple to use, especially for single-product firms. Complex methods of costing (such as absorption pricing) can still be somewhat inaccurate yet are more time consuming to calculate.
- Managers have greater cost control by allocating all costs of production to determine an appropriate price. Departments are also held more accountability for their contribution towards a firm's indirect costs.

HIGHER LEVEL

Limitations of full costing

- Full cost pricing is the least accurate method of apportioning overheads or fixed costs.
- The criterion used to allocate indirect costs may give misleading or unrepresentative information. Change the criterion used to allocate costs and the results will also change, without any fundamental shift in the productivity or efficiency of a department.
- The allocation of indirect costs is rather arbitrary. Some departments will feel that indirect costs have been unfairly distributed. This can be a huge concern if the departments are run as profit centres (see Unit 5.2).

Absorption cost pricing (Higher Level extension)

Absorption cost pricing is an extension of full cost pricing. It involves allocating overheads by working out which department has incurred what proportion of each of the indirect costs. For example, the rental costs of a commercial building may be split up based on how much floor space is used by each product line or department. Similarly, indirect labour costs can be allocated according to the number of employees in each department. Hence, absorption costing does not apportion costs based on a single criterion. This makes cost allocation much fairer as departments accounting for a larger proportion of overheads are apportioned a greater share of the costs. Price is then determined from the total costs allocated to each department.

Continuing from the previous example, suppose that the toy factory's overheads consist of the following:

Rent	\$8,000
Marketing	\$2,000
Depreciation	\$2,000
Total	\$12,000

The criterion used to allocate the \$8,000 rent could be the floor area occupied by each department. For example, Alpha takes up 40% of the floor area of the factory ($600\ m^2 / 1{,}500\ m^2$), so it is allocated 40% of the rental costs, i.e. \$3,200. Marketing costs could be split according to the sales volume of each product. Finally, depreciation costs could be allocated based on the value of machinery used in each department. Using the following information, absorption cost pricing can then be calculated.

HIGHER LEVEL

Product (Department)	Alpha	Beta	Gamma	Total
Floor space (square metres)	600	550	350	1,500
Rent allocation	$3,200	$2,933	$1,867	$8,000
Output (units per month)	500	800	600	1,900
Marketing allocation	$526	$842	$632	$2,000
Machinery (% owned per Department)	30	40	30	100
Depreciation	$600	$800	$600	$2,000
Total indirect cost allocation	$4,326	$4,575	$3,099	$12,000
Total direct costs	$4,000	$4,000	$3,600	
Total costs	$8,326	$8,575	$6,699	
Output per month	500	800	600	
Cost per unit	$16.65	$10.72	$11.17	

Therefore, the price of each product must be set above its cost per unit in order for the business to make any profit.

Advantages of absorption costing

Absorption costing shares many of the benefits of full costing. In addition, there are other benefits of this method.

- The method acknowledges that using a single criterion to allocate all indirect costs might be too simplistic for multiproduct firms.
- It makes managers more aware of the total costs of a product. This helps to ensure that an appropriate price is set to cover all costs of production.
- It is seen as a fairer method of allocating costs to different departments since it takes into account different rates of contribution towards different indirect costs.
- The profitability of each product line or department can be examined.

Limitations of absorption costing

- Not all indirect costs can be divided accurately. For example, it might be difficult to apportion the costs of insurance or stationery. Any criterion used is likely to be rather subjective.
- This method is more complex to calculate than full cost pricing, and hence it is more time consuming.
- The relative benefits of absorption cost pricing may not be significant to justify its use. This is especially the case in smaller firms that may lack the time and resources to use this method.

Finally, it is important to remember that whatever criteria are used, it is impossible to accurately allocate all indirect costs due to the rather subjective nature of absorption costing. More importantly, the indirect costs must be paid irrespective of whether a particular product is manufactured or sold.

HIGHER LEVEL

Question 4.4.1

Dolls-R-Us

Dolls-R-Us is a manufacturer of toy dolls, with three product lines: Penny, James and Lori the cat. Its annual fixed costs of $85,000 consist of the following:

Rent	$36,000
Administration	$25,000
Depreciation	$12,000
Other	$12,000

Information on the three products is shown below:

	Penny	James	Lori
Selling price	$14	$10	$20
Direct costs (per unit)	$4	$3	$5
Direct labour costs (per unit)	$3	$2	$5
Sales volume (units)	15,000	15,000	15,000
Number of employees	3	2	3
Floor space (square metres)	3,000	3,000	4,000
Value of machinery and equipment	$30,000	$25,000	$35,000

a Outline the evidence that suggests Dolls-R-Us has used a cost-based pricing strategy. *[2 marks]*

b Calculate the unit contribution for each of the three products. *[3 marks]*

c Explain three criteria that would be appropriate in allocating the firm's fixed costs to each of the three products. *[6 marks]*

d Use your answer to Question **1c** to allocate the total fixed costs. Prepare an analysis of the total costs, total revenues and profit for each product. *[9 marks]*

COMPETITION-BASED PRICING STRATEGIES

Competition-based pricing (also known as **competition-orientated pricing**) refers to a firm's pricing strategies that are based on the prices being charged by its competitors. Prices can be set equal to, lower than or higher than those charged by other firms in the industry. This strategy does not primarily take into consideration the costs of production or the level of demand for the firm's products. There are several categories of competition-based pricing methods:

Price leadership

Price leadership is a strategy that is often used for best-selling products or brands. There are few substitutes, in the eye of the customer, for such products so the dominant firm can set its own prices. Competitors then 'follow the leader' by establishing their prices based on the price set by the market (or price) leader.

Predatory pricing (Higher Level extension)

Predatory pricing is a strategy that involves temporarily reducing price in an attempt to force rivals out of the industry since they cannot compete profitably. Due to the aggressive nature of this strategy, it is sometimes referred to as **destroyer pricing**. The strategy often stems from an extension of a **price war**, whereby firms compete by a series of intensive price cuts. This might even mean selling products at below cost price. If the strategy is successful, the firm will benefit from being in a more dominant position, and can therefore raise its prices to recoup any losses incurred whilst using predatory prices. This method is likely to be used when an existing firm is threatened with new competition which it believes would harm its market share and profitability. Although price wars can bring some benefits to customers in the short term, predatory pricing itself is illegal in some parts of the world (such as the USA and the UK) since it is regarded as an anti-competitive practice.

A similar pricing strategy is called **limit pricing** or **pre-emptive pricing**. This method involves setting prices just low enough to discourage potential rivals from entering the market. Limit pricing therefore acts as a barrier to entry and is especially suited to markets where entry barriers are low. However, both predatory pricing and limit pricing are anti-competitive and may draw the attention of the authorities overseeing restrictive trade practices.

Going rate pricing (Higher Level extension)

The 'going rate' refers to the average price being charged by competitors in the industry. Going rate pricing therefore is a pricing method whereby a firm charges a similar price to that of competitors for their goods or services.

HIGHER LEVEL

Question 4.4.2

The price of price wars

The world's largest supermarket chains (such as Wal-Mart, Carrefour and Tesco) have huge market power to reduce prices. Price reductions are a key technique used by supermarkets. For example, the UK consumer has grown accustomed to supermarket **price wars**, with over £1 billion ($2 billion) of price reductions each year. Price wars are also increasingly common in the airline and mobile phone industries.

- **a** Describe what is meant by a **price war**. *[2 marks]*
- **b** Examine the winners and losers of a price war in the short run and the long run. *[6 marks]*
- **c** Justify two forms of non-price competition that supermarkets might use to increase their competitiveness. *[8 marks]*

MARKET-LED PRICING STRATEGIES

Unlike competition-based pricing methods that rely on the actions of competitors, market-led strategies are based on the level of customer demand for a firm's products or the level of demand in the industry in which the firm operates.

Penetration pricing

Penetration pricing is a strategy used for a new product to help establish itself in the industry. This method involves setting a relatively low price in order to gain market share and brand awareness. Over time, as the product establishes itself, the price can be raised (see Figure 4.4a). This strategy is suitable for mass market products that sell in large enough volumes to sustain low profit margins, such as fast moving consumer goods (see Unit 4.3). It also applies to new firms trying to enter well-established markets. It is highly suitable for products that have a high *price elasticity of demand* (see 'Price elasticity of demand' on page 542) whereby lowering price will lead to proportionately higher sales volumes. For example, Brilliance Automobiles of China launched its cars in Europe in 2007 at around 15% lower than the prices of rival Korean manufacturers such as Hyundai. One potential danger with this method is that setting prices too low could mean that the market may perceive the product as inferior and of poor quality.

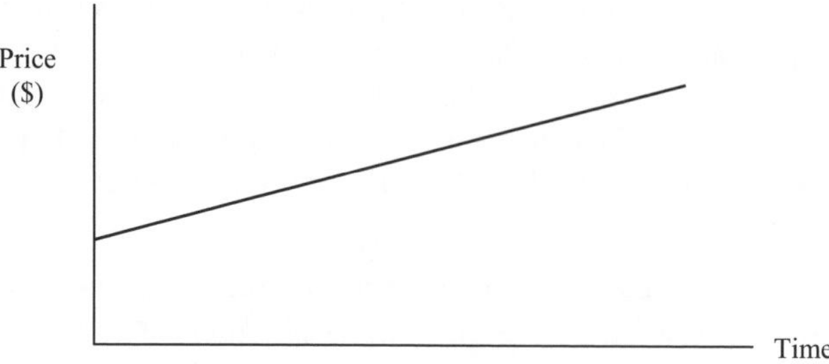

Figure 4.4a Penetration pricing

Skimming pricing

Price skimming (or **skimming price**) is a strategy that tends to be used for technologically advanced and innovative products. Since *new product development* can be very expensive (see Unit 4.3), a high selling price is initially set to recoup the costs of research and development. The strategy can also create a unique, high quality or prestigious image for the product. In addition, since there are unlikely to be many, if any, substitutes on the market, the firm can charge a high price to maximize profits before competitors are attracted to the industry. Games consoles, mobile phones and flat-screen televisions have all been priced using this strategy.

Due to the high potential profits that can be made, it is likely that other firms will be attracted to enter the industry. When this happens, the original firm will skim, or gradually reduce, its prices (see Figure 4.4b). It is important to remember, however, that marketing, by its very nature, is integrated. Skimming price can only be successful if it is supported by other elements of the marketing mix, especially promotion. Branding, for example, is vital to ensure that price skimming is profitable for a business.

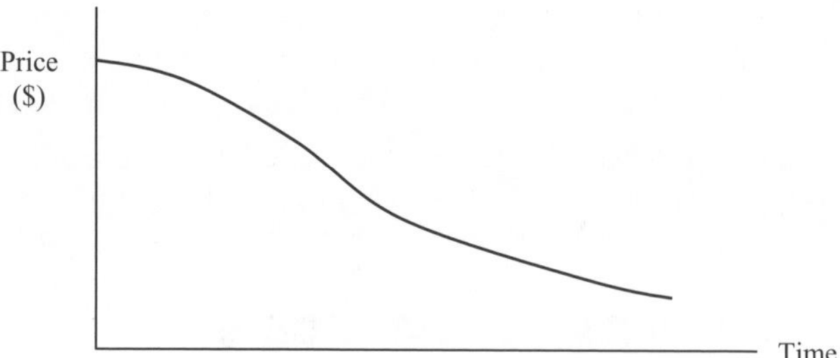

Figure 4.4b Skimming price

An alternative strategy to skimming is **prestige pricing**. Prestige pricing involves a firm permanently setting a high price because of the image, reputation or status associated with its product. The method would be appropriate for pricing products such as designer clothes, luxury cars and high-class jewellery. For customers of such products, the price itself would not be of major concern.

Price discrimination (Higher Level extension)

Price discrimination occurs when the same product, usually a service, is sold in different markets at different prices. This is a perfectly legal act. For example, children and adults pay different prices for entering the same cinema, theme park or hairdressers. The product they pay for is essentially the same but the prices being charged are different. Price discrimination is sometimes referred to as **variable pricing**.

Businesses are likely to raise prices during peak periods. For example, airline companies increase their prices during the Christmas and summer holiday periods. This is partly because there is increased demand and largely because firms know that the price elasticity of demand (the degree of responsiveness of demand to changes in price) during peak periods is lower, so customers are more willing to pay higher prices and are less sensitive to price variations.

Price discrimination is not only about setting higher prices to those customers that can afford to pay. Statistically, restaurants and cinemas throughout the world face their quietest trading day of the week on a Tuesday and that is why many of these businesses offer discounted prices to diners and cinema goers on Tuesdays.

There are three conditions that must be met in order to achieve successful price discrimination:

- The firm must have some degree of monopoly and price-setting powers. Hence, firms in highly competitive markets would be unwise to use this pricing strategy.
- Customers must have different price elasticities of demand (degrees of willingness to pay) otherwise the firm cannot set different prices to different customers.
- Markets must be kept separate to prevent resale. For example, a child cannot sell his or her cinema or bus ticket to an adult.

A similar strategy to price discrimination that is used by many large multinationals is **transfer pricing**. This refers to the use of internal prices being charged to other divisions of the same company. This helps to control the organization's costs. Multinationals also use transfer pricing to reduce tax liabilities by charging high internal prices to sections of the business located in countries with high tax rates. This, therefore, artificially but legally reduces profits, thereby cutting the company's tax bill.

Loss leader (Higher Level extension)

Loss leader pricing involves selling a product at or below its cost value. This is a short-term strategy that aims to entice customers to buy more profitable products at the same time as buying the loss leader. Retailers, such as supermarkets, often use this strategy by heavily marketing the loss leader in the hope of attracting customers. It is unlikely for customers to simply purchase only the loss leader when visiting a supermarket, but the existence of loss leaders can attract many customers to visit the supermarket. Loss leaders can also be used to increase brand loyalty, which in the long term can make up for any losses incurred whilst the product was priced at a loss.

Games console makers, such as Sony, Nintendo and Microsoft, often sell their hardware at a loss to attract buyers. For example, the Sony PlayStation 3 costs $800 per unit to make, but is sold for between $499 and $599 (see Question 4.4.3). The aim is to recoup the loss by sales of *complementary goods*, such as gaming software, and collecting royalty payments from games manufacturers.

Question 4.4.3

Sony PlayStation 3

Sony launched the PlayStation 3 in late 2006. It was quick to win positive reviews, although analysts questioned the price which was set at over $100 more than the Xbox-360 from Microsoft, its main rival. Sony said its state-of-the-art console with a built-in Blu-ray DVD player made the **premium price** value for money.

Despite the higher prices charged by Sony, the Japanese manufacturer loses money on each games console sold. It makes up for this when customers buy several games and other software products for the duration of the PS3's product life cycle.

a Define the term **premium price**. *[2 marks]*

b In the context of the case study, examine the relationship between a product's cash flow position and its life cycle. *[6 marks]*

HIGHER LEVEL

Psychological pricing (Higher Level extension)

Psychological pricing is a strategy that involves using numbers, such as $9.99 or $14,995, to make prices seem lower (than $10.00 or $15,000). Hence, customers psychologically feel that they are getting a bargain or better price for the product. This method is widely used and can work for almost any product, from groceries sold in a supermarket to expensive motor vehicles or residential property. Psychological pricing also works well when selling the same product in larger quantities. For example, supermarkets may sell a product at $4.99 for one or $14.97 for three (the price is exactly the same per unit but it can be deceiving to some customers). It does not work well for some businesses, such as taxi firms, since rounded or whole number figures are more suitable for the customer and the service provider.

Promotional pricing (Higher Level extension)

Promotional pricing is often used when marketing new products by charging a low price to entice customers to try the product and to build brand awareness. It is commonly used for products such as food items sold in supermarkets. Promotional pricing is also used to get rid of excess stocks or to renew interest in the business if sales have been falling. Promotional pricing has two key characteristics: it focuses on pricing being the most important part of the marketing mix and it is only used as a short-term measure to boost sales or market share. However, critics argue that promotional pricing is limited in effectiveness since rivals can simply copy the technique.

Promotional pricing is very similar to **discount pricing** in that both attempt to raise market share by lowering prices. However, promotional pricing tends to be used at the beginning of a product's life cycle whereas discount pricing is often used later in a product's life cycle, perhaps as an extension strategy (see Unit 4.3).

Pricing strategies are summarized in Table 4.4a.

Table 4.4a Summary table of pricing strategies

Cost-based	Competition-based	Market-led
Cost-plus	Price leadership	Penetration
Marginal cost	*Predatory pricing*	Skimming
Full cost	*Going rate*	*Price discrimination*
Absorption cost		*Loss leader*
		Psychological pricing
		Promotional pricing

Note: Pricing strategies in *italics* apply to Higher Level students only.

Question 4.4.4

Virgin Blue

Virgin Blue is the creation of Sir Richard Branson, founder and CEO of the Virgin Group. The airline carrier was launched in 2000 by Sir Richard Branson and Virgin Blue CEO Brett Godfrey, to enter the Australian market. Initially set up as a low fare carrier, the company only flew between Brisbane and Sydney. Since then, it has become Australia's second largest airline, catering for all major cities in Australia. Customers pay for their in-flight meals and drinks. To further cut costs, Virgin Blue uses a system of e-ticketing (a telephone and internet-based ticketing system).

a Describe three potential pricing strategies that airline companies can adopt when entering a new market. *[6 marks]*

b Evaluate two possible pricing strategies that airline carriers such as Virgin Blue could use to increase their sales revenue. *[8 marks]*

HIGHER LEVEL EXTENSION: SUPPLY AND DEMAND

Economists define **demand** as the level of *ability and willingness to pay* a particular price for a product, per period of time. The theory of demand states that the higher the price of a product, the lower the demand (ability and willingness to pay) tends to be, i.e. there is an inverse relationship between price and the quantity demanded (see Figure 4.4c). The vast majority of products conform to this rule, and are therefore known as **normal goods**.

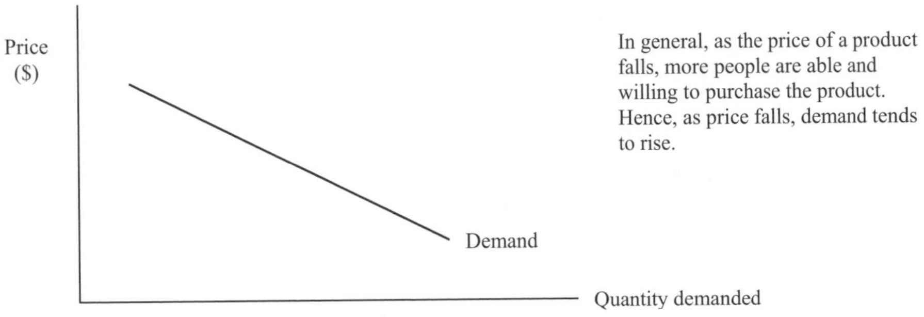

Figure 4.4c The negative relationship between price and demand

HIGHER LEVEL

Determinants of the level of demand

In reality, price is not the only factor that affects the level of demand for a product. Other factors include:

- **Consumer income** levels – The higher the level of income, the higher demand tends to be as people have greater purchasing power. This will generally increase the level of demand for most products.
- Price and availability of **substitutes** – Generally, the higher the number of substitutes that are available, the lower the price of a product tends to be. Fierce competition in the airline industry has, for example, reduced prices of airline travel throughout the world.
- Price and availability of **complements** – There is a negative relationship between the price of a product and the demand for its complement. For example, if there is an increase in the price of printers, the demand for ink cartridges is likely to fall.
- **Quality** – The quality of a product can refer to any combination of its design, build-quality, reliability, features and functions (see Unit 5.4). Sports cars and exclusive perfumes will attract certain clients, even at very high prices, due to their distinctive image and the feel-good factor generated by owning such products.
- **Marketing** – The successful use of persuasive and/or informative marketing, such as the use of advertising or celebrity endorsements can boost demand for certain products. Similarly, government advertisements to deter smoking and drinking can affect the demand for cigarettes and alcohol.
- **Fashions, habits and tastes** – Trends and changes in fashion will also affect demand. Media coverage or marketing activities can alter fashion and tastes for such popular products, irrespective of the price level. The hype of the Atkins low-carbohydrate diet has harmed many Irish potato farmers who have seen a huge drop in demand for their crop.
- **Utility** (or level of satisfaction) – Customers are more willing to pay for products that increase their level of satisfaction derived from the consumption or ownership of a product. Anyone who is fanatic about a particular sport or hobby will have high demand for such products.
- **Speculation** – Expectations and forecasts can also influence the level of demand. For instance, if share prices and property values are expected to rise steadily, that might raise the level of demand for these products today.
- **State of the economy** – Whether the economy is experiencing a boom or recession can affect not just individual income levels but also consumer and business confidence levels. When the level of confidence in the economy is low, it can trigger poor trading and a lack of consumer demand.
- Perceived level of **value for money** – Demand tends to rise if products are seen to be of greater value for money. All hotels, for example, offer buffet meals (breakfast, lunch and/or dinner) to boost demand for their catering services.
- Others – There are a host of other factors that can affect the demand for a product. The weather, different seasons, age of customers, peer influence or pressure, rivalry and cultural and religious beliefs are some examples.

There are, however, several exceptions to the general law of demand:

- **Ostentatious consumption** refers to the purchase of expensive products which impress and make the customers feel good about themselves. A large part of the satisfaction comes from knowing the high price paid for the product. Examples include Christian Dior perfumes, Rolex watches, Nike trainers, Armani suits and Vera Wang wedding dresses. Demand would fall if the price falls (an unusual situation) since the prestige and exclusivity associated with such products is reduced.

- **Conspicuous consumption** refers to the lavish spending of some (very rich) customers for the purpose of upholding their social status, rather than serving the real needs of the customer (see Question 4.4.5). There is often a grey area between the conspicuous consumption and ostentatious consumption, but the latter is also bought by people who are not necessarily on very high income levels. Conspicuous consumption is a term coined by the 19th century American economist Thorstein Veblen. Examples of **Veblen goods** include extremely expensive luxury cars (such as Rolls-Royce, Bentley and Maybach) and collector items (such as original paintings from Picasso and Van Gogh or unique and very expensive coins and stamps).
- **Expectations** of future prices have an important role in the demand for certain products, such as stocks, shares, property and foreign currencies. When prices rise but people believe that there will be further increases, demand may also rise. Stock and property booms are caused largely by speculation of higher demand for shares and property due to expectations that prices will rise in the future.
- **Giffen goods** are goods named after 19th century economist, Sir Robert Giffen, who discovered that when the price of bread rose, people (particularly poor families) spent *more* money on bread (an inferior good) because other substitute products such as meat and fruit were still relatively more expensive. The opposite would happen when prices fell, i.e. demand for Giffen goods would drop as prices fell (see Box 4.4b for a numerical example). Other examples of Giffen goods might include basic foods such as potatoes and rice. In reality, it is debatable whether there are any Giffen goods. However, their theoretical possibility has stood the test of time.

Box 4.4b Numerical example of Giffen goods

A consumer has $5.00 to spend.

Consumer buys 3 kilos of potatoes at $1.20 each plus 1 kilo of sausages at $1.40 ($3.60 + $1.40).

Assume the price of potatoes subsequently falls to $1.00.

The consumer now buys 2 kilos of potatoes ($2.00) plus 2 kilos of sausages ($2.80).

Hence, as price falls the demand for potatoes (the Giffen good) falls.

-

Question 4.4.5

Sony PSP

Fans of Sony's hand-held games console can personalize their machines by the various accessories available on the market. If they really want to stand out from the crowd, luxury department store Harrods, in London UK, sell the ultimate Sony PSP cover. The exclusive offering is from US fashion label Baby Phat, with a gold and jewel-encrusted case, priced at a staggering £20,000 ($39,200)!

- Explain why anyone would want to pay such a high price for a PSP accessory that is charged at over 130 times the price of the PSP games console. *[4 marks]*

HIGHER LEVEL

Supply

Economists define **supply** as the willingness and ability of firms to provide products at given price levels, per period of time. Usually, the higher the market price of a product, the more willing and able producers are to supply products to the market (see Figure 4.4d). There are two reasons for this positive relationship between price and the level of supply. First, existing firms can make more profit when prices are higher so will supply more. Second, new firms will be attracted to enter the market when prices are higher.

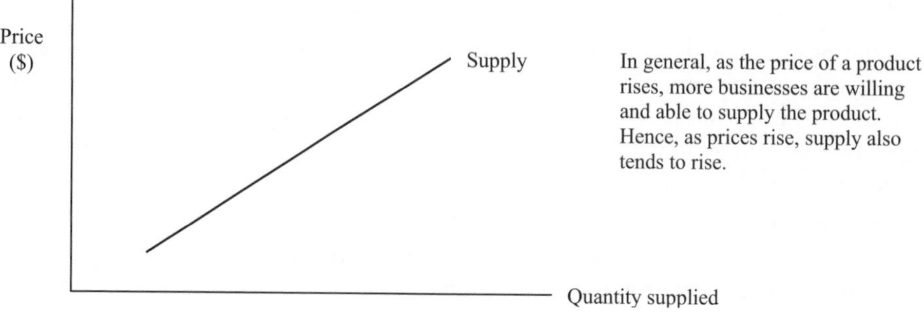

Figure 4.4d The positive relationship between price and supply

Determinants of the level of supply

- **Price of raw materials** – If the price of a raw material, such as oil, increases it will shift its supply curve to the left (all other things being equal). Since costs of production subsequently increase, this means that less will be supplied at each and every price level (vice versa).
- **Barriers to entry** – The nature of entry barriers to a market will determine the number of producers in the industry. The higher the entry barriers, the smaller the number of producers and hence the lower the level of supply tends to be. Due to the extremely high costs of airline manufacturing, Boeing and Airbus dominate the industry. At times, firms may deliberately erect barriers to entry to deter new firms from entering the market. This therefore limits the supply in the market.
- **Technology (production methods)** – Advances in technology will shift the supply curve to the right. If improved production techniques become available, a larger output can be supplied at each and every price level due to higher productivity and lower unit costs of production.
- **Taxes** – These compulsory charges by the government cause higher production costs, and therefore reduce the supply at each price level. Hence, a sales tax would shift the supply curve of a product to the left. Products that cause additional costs to society, such as tobacco and alcohol, tend to be taxed heavily.
- **Subsidies** – These have the opposite effect to taxes. Subsidies, such as business grants from the government, are a means of financial aid to reduce a producer's costs. This should then lead to higher levels of supply in the market. Products that yield additional benefits to society, such as education and health care, may well qualify for subsidies from the government.
- **Price of related goods** – There are two types of related goods: *substitutes* and *complements*. In terms of supply, some goods are in **competitive supply**, i.e. one good can be produced quite easily as an alternative to another good. An example would be Coca-Cola which produces Coke and other drinks such as Fanta and Sprite. The product with the higher relative profitability will be produced and supplied in larger volumes. In the case of **joint supply**, an increase in the production of one product necessarily increases the supply of another (joint) product, such as cows and milk or chickens and eggs.

- **Climate** (or weather conditions) – For agricultural products, such as fruits and vegetables, the climate can have a large impact on the quantity supplied. Favourable weather conditions will yield a good return, i.e. boost supply. Droughts, floods and other unfavourable types of weather will result in poor harvests and therefore reduce supply.
- **Time** – In the immediate or short term, it can be very difficult to alter the level of supply. For instance, agricultural products take time to harvest. Aircraft take a very long time to manufacture. Over time, producers can adjust their supply to suit market changes. Furthermore, new resources and supplies may be discovered in the future, thereby increasing the level of supply.

Question 4.4.6

Hurricane Katrina

In 2005 Hurricane Katrina caused a six-month halt to oil operations near America's Gulf Coast, affecting about a quarter of the USA's oil production. Shell, for example, announced a fall in production of 420,000 barrels of oil each day. Subsequently, oil prices soared.

a Identify two determinants of the demand for oil. *[2 marks]*

b Explain how natural disasters, such as Hurricane Katrina, can push up oil prices. *[4 marks]*

All markets require buyers (who have demand) and sellers (who create supply). The point at which the amount of a product demanded equals the amount supplied is known as the **equilibrium**. At the equilibrium price, the willingness and ability of customers to pay matches that of the suppliers – buyers are able to get all they demand at that price and firms are willing and able to sell that same amount at that exact price. Therefore, both parties are satisfied at the equilibrium. The interaction of the demand and supply curves (collectively known as **market forces**) in Figure 4.4e shows the equilibrium price and quantity traded.

The forces of demand and supply will, if left to their own devices, clear the market of any excess demand or excess supply. In the case of shortages (excess demand), prices will rise to deter excess demand or to encourage more supply. Either way, prices continue to rise until there is no more excess. In the case of surpluses (excess supply), businesses will offload the excess stock of products by reducing prices until there is no more excess. Hence, unless there is a change in the conditions of demand or supply, the equilibrium price will prevail in the market. Any change in demand or supply will, given time lags, result in a new equilibrium position.

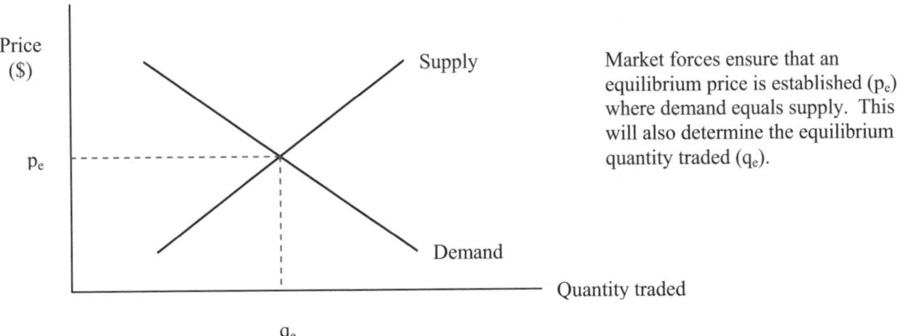

Figure 4.4e Equilibrium price and quantity

Question 4.4.7

The sports industry

The summer of 2008 saw major sporting events such as the Olympic Games in Beijing, the Wimbledon tennis finals held in the UK, the 2008 Rugby League World Cup in Australia and the Euro 2008 football championship held in Austria and Switzerland.

- Explain how the hype would affect the market for sports equipment and sportswear. *[4 marks]*

HIGHER LEVEL

HIGHER LEVEL EXTENSION: ELASTICITY

Elasticity of demand refers to the technique of measuring the degree of responsiveness of quantity demanded due to a change in a specific factor that affects demand. Examples would include changes in price, income advertising and the prices of other related products (complements or substitutes). There are four main measures of elasticity of demand:

- **Price elasticity of demand (PED)** measures the degree of responsiveness of changes in demand due to a (small) change in the product's own price. For this reason, PED is also known as *own price elasticity of demand.*
- **Income elasticity of demand (YED)** measures the degree of responsiveness of changes in demand due to a (small) change in consumer income levels.
- **Cross-price elasticity of demand (CED)** measures the degree of responsiveness of changes in demand for one product due to a (small) change in the price of another product (be that a substitute or a complement).
- **Advertising elasticity of demand (AED)** measures the degree of responsiveness of changes in demand due to a change in a firm's advertising expenditure.

Price elasticity of demand

Price elasticity of demand (PED) measures the extent to which demand for a product changes due to a change in its price. If there is a relatively small change in quantity demanded following a change in price, then demand is said to be **price inelastic**, i.e. customers are not very responsive to changes in price. Demand is said to be **price elastic** if there is a relatively large change in demand due to a price change, i.e. customers are highly responsive to changes in price. The formula for working out the PED is:

$$\frac{\text{Percentage change in quantity demanded}}{\text{Percentage change in price}}$$

or in annotation form, PED equals:

$$\frac{\%\Delta QD}{\%\Delta P}$$

Note that the value of PED will almost always be negative because of the inverse relationship between price and quantity demanded. The calculation of PED will give one of three possibilities:

- If the calculation of PED is between 0 and 1 (ignoring the minus sign), demand is **price inelastic**, i.e. unresponsive to changes in price as the percentage change in demand is relatively lower than the percentage change in price.
- If the calculation of PED is equal to 1 (ignoring the minus sign), demand is of **unitary price elasticity**, i.e. a change in price leads to a proportional change in the quantity demanded.
- If the calculation of PED is greater than 1 (ignoring the minus sign), demand is **price elastic**, i.e. demand for the product is relatively responsive to changes in its price.

Exam Tip!

Worked example of calculating PED

Suppose at $7 per ticket the demand for movies at a cinema is 4,000 per week. If the cinema raises its price to $8 per ticket and observes that demand falls to 3,000 per week, what is the value of PED?

- To calculate PED, first work out the *percentage change* in the level of demand, i.e. demand has fallen by 25% from 4,000 to 3,000 tickets per week.
- Then, calculate the percentage change in price (which caused demand to fall), i.e. prices rose by 14.28% from $7 per ticket to $8 per ticket.
- Finally, plug the percentage change figures into the PED formula: 25/14.28 = (–) 1.75

This means that since PED is greater than 1.0 (ignoring the minus sign), then demand for cinema tickets is said to be *price elastic*, i.e. customers are responsive to the increase in price. This will therefore mean a larger drop in the level of demand relative to the increase in price.

Implications and uses of price elasticity of demand

Knowledge of PED can give businesses and other stakeholders valuable information about how the sales revenue of a product is likely to change if its prices are adjusted. This information can be used in many ways, including:

- Helps firms to decide on their pricing policy. For example, a business with price inelastic demand for its product is likely to raise price.
- Determines which products are most affected by a downturn in the economy. Luxury products, for example, will have a high PED value and businesses will know that these tend to suffer the most during a recession.
- Helps predict the effects of a change in the exchange rate on the country's international trade balance. Exporters will generally benefit from lower exchange rates since their prices become more competitive, assuming the PED for exports is price elastic (i.e. PED > 1).
- Helps governments to determine the optimum level of taxes to place on certain products in order to maximize their tax revenues. Price inelastic products, such as petrol and cigarettes, tend to be heavily taxed as demand is price inelastic, therefore demand is not significantly affected by the tax but the government manages to raise large sums of revenues from taxing these products.

Question 4.4.8

Price elasticity of demand

a Explain whether the price elasticity of demand for the following products is relatively price elastic or inelastic. Remember to justify your answers.

i Petrol.

ii Mobile phones.

iii Bananas.

iv Tobacco. *[12 marks]*

b Analyse the reasons for governments raising the tax on tobacco, alcohol and petrol, often annually. *[6 marks]*

HIGHER LEVEL

HIGHER LEVEL EXTENSION: RELATIONSHIP BETWEEN PRICE ELASTICITY OF DEMAND AND TOTAL REVENUE

In Figure 4.4f, the demand curve is relatively price inelastic (rather unresponsive to changes in price). The firm should, therefore, raise prices. The percentage increase in price is far greater than the subsequent fall in demand. Hence, total revenue will increase. Conversely, a reduction in price for products with price inelastic demand will result in a net loss in total revenue.

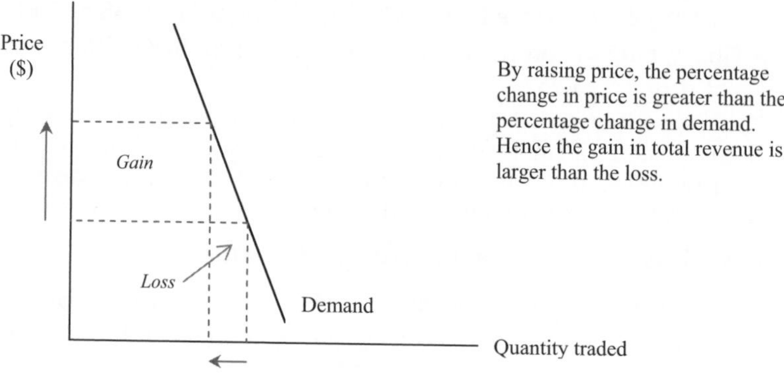

Figure 4.4f Relatively price inelastic demand curve

In Figure 4.4g, the demand curve is relatively price elastic (somewhat responsive to changes in price). The firm should therefore reduce prices since this would lead to a net gain in total revenue. However, if prices are increased, customers will simply switch to substitutes, thereby generating a net loss in total revenue.

The relationship between price elasticity of demand (PED) and total revenue (TR) is shown in Table 4.4b.

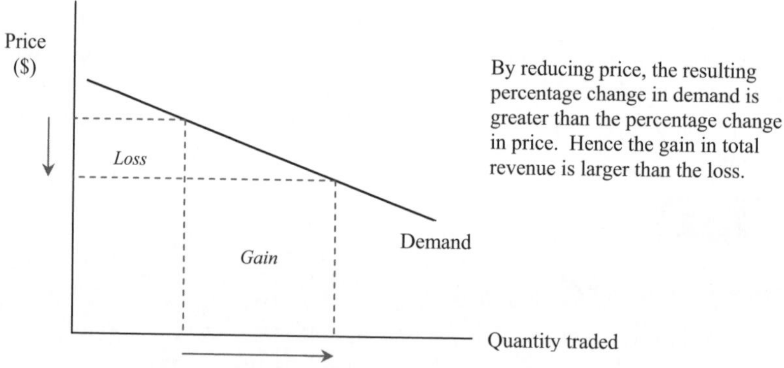

Figure 4.4g Relatively price elastic demand curve

Table 4.4b Relationship between PED and TR

	Inelastic	Unitary	Elastic
Value of PED	> 0 <1	1	>1
Increase price	TR ↑	no change in TR	TR ↓
Reduce price	TR ↓	no change in TR	TR ↑

HIGHER LEVEL

Question **4.4.9**

The business of music concerts

It is common knowledge that the price of a concert ticket keeps going up. Madonna fans in the UK paid between £80 to £160 ($160–$320), with an additional £13 booking fee for her 'Confessions on a Dance Floor' tour. The public opinion was split – some thought the prices were an outrage whilst others thought it represented good entertainment value.

Changes in **market forces** have meant that rock and pop stars can make huge amounts of money from each concert they do. Madonna's 2004 Re-Invention tour grossed $125 million worldwide – more than any other artist that year. Some analysts argue that music artists have been forced into doing concerts to combat the decline in their potential earnings caused by people illegally downloading music from the internet.

a Explain the term **market forces**. *[3 marks]*

b Outline two reasons why music fans might be prepared to pay such high prices for concert tickets. *[4 marks]*

c Justify whether you feel that concert tickets are relatively price elastic or price inelastic. *[8 marks]*

Factors affecting price elasticity of demand

- **Substitution** – This is by far the most important determinant of price elasticity. In general, the greater the number and availability of substitutes for a product, the greater its PED will be. It must be noted, however, that what is an appropriate or acceptable substitute for one person does not necessarily mean that it is equally suitable for other people. Examples of products with relatively price inelastic demand include oil, private education and medicines.
- **Income** – The proportion of income spent on a product will also affect the value of its PED. If the price of a box of household matches were to double, it would discourage very few buyers because the actual change in price is a minute proportion of their overall income. However, if the price of a motorcycle were to rise by 50% from $10,000 to $15,000, it would have a massive impact on quantity demanded; even though the percentage increase in the price of motorcycles is much lower than that of household matches. Therefore, the greater the proportion of income that the price represents, the higher the value of PED tends to be. On an individual level, people on high levels of income are less sensitive to changes in the price than those with low incomes.
- **Time** – The period of time affects the value of PED since people's habits and traditions, which have been established over a long period, may be slow to change. Over time, however, people will adjust to any permanent price changes and may seek alternatives if prices are increased. Parents with children in private education are unlikely to withdraw their offspring from school, partly because this could be very disruptive to their learning. Drivers of motor vehicles are unlikely, at least in the short to medium term, to get rid of their motor vehicles simply because of fuel price increases. Given time, however, both parents and drivers may well seek alternatives. Hence, in general, the shorter the time period in question, the less price elastic demand tends to be.
- **Durability** – Perishable products may need to be replaced, even if prices have risen. However, if the price of a consumer durable (see Unit 4.3) is on the rise, customers may try to make their existing possessions last a little longer. Items such as furniture, mobile phones and cars can all be upgraded at a later date. Hence, in general, the more durable a product is, the greater its price elasticity of demand tends to be.

HIGHER LEVEL

- **Fashion, addictions, habits and tastes** – Where a product is habit forming (such as tobacco) or highly fashionable, the price elasticity of demand will tend to be low, i.e. relatively price inelastic. Habits and tastes, which are largely affected by marketing strategies, will also reduce the degree of responsiveness of demand due to a rise in price. People who are seriously devoted to a hobby (be it sports, music or otherwise) are willing to spend a huge amount of money, so they are therefore less sensitive to changes in price.
- **Necessity** – The degree of necessity or urgency also affects PED. Products that are seen as 'essential' (such as fuel and food) tend to be relatively price inelastic. This is because people need these products so will continue to purchase them even if prices rise. On the other hand, luxury goods and services tend to be more price elastic. For instance, the demand for business-class air travel is less responsive to changes in price than the demand for economy-class air travel. Similarly, demand for fresh flowers during Valentine's Day and Mothers' Day is much less price sensitive than during off-peak periods.

Question 4.4.10

Toshiba

Toshiba is one of the world's largest manufacturers of flash memory chips used in mobile phones, digital cameras and digital music players. In April 2007, the Japanese electronics giant announced that its profits increased by almost 76% despite a fall in the price of memory chips by some 60%. Prices of memory chips are expected to fall even further as competition intensifies.

a Comment on the price elasticity of demand for Toshiba memory chips. *[3 marks]*

b To what extent does knowledge of price elasticity of demand prove useful for firms, such as Toshiba, that face intense competition? *[7 marks]*

Income elasticity of demand

Income elasticity of demand (YED) measures the degree of responsiveness of demand for a product following a change in the income level of consumers. Businesses are interested in the value of YED for their products so that they can make forecasts of the level of demand as the economy grows and prospers over time. When income rises, the demand for most products also increases. The formula for calculating YED is:

$$\frac{\text{Percentage change in quantity demanded}}{\text{Percentage change in income}}$$

or in annotation form:

$$\frac{\%\Delta QD}{\%\Delta Y}$$

There are three possible outcomes when calculating the income elasticity of demand for a product:

- YED is *positive* for **normal goods**, i.e. the demand for normal goods rises as incomes increase. One category of normal goods is **necessities**. In this case, the YED is greater than zero but less than 1. This means that demand for such products is not highly responsive to changes in price. People will not, for instance, purchase significantly more socks or consume that much more drinking water simply because prices have dropped. Indeed, the demand for baby foods and nappies (diapers) will increase as a result of an increase in consumer incomes, but not by a great amount.

- **Luxuries** are the second type of normal goods. In this case, the value of YED is greater than 1.0, i.e. demand is income elastic (or highly responsive to changes in income levels). This means that as income levels increase over time, the demand for luxuries such as designer clothing and sports cars rises by a proportionately greater amount.
- **Inferior Goods** are defined as those products that have a negative YED value, i.e. demand for these products *falls* as income levels rise (see Table 4.4c). If a product has a YED figure of –0.6, this means a 10% price increase causes the demand for the substandard product to fall by 6%. This happens because higher levels of income allow the customer to substitute inferior goods (such as sausages or supermarket economy brand cola) for **superior goods** (such as steak or Coca-Cola). The demand for public transport is often cited as an example of inferior goods.

Table 4.4c Relationship between YED and types of products

Value of YED	Type of Product
< 0	Inferior goods
> 0 < 1	Normal goods: necessities
> 1	Normal goods: Luxury / Superior goods

The value of YED is also affected by different segment groups. What is a necessity to one group of people (e.g. business air travel for senior executives) may be regarded as a luxury to others (such as holiday travellers). Equally, what is regarded as an essential product to one group (such as textbooks for high school students) is not necessarily applicable to other groups (such as younger children) (see Figure 4.4h).

Time can also change the value of YED for a product. Bus travel was, for example, once regarded as a normal good in many developed countries. However, with rising income levels, bus travel is now seen as an inferior good in countries such as Germany, USA and the UK where people choose to use trains, taxis and private transportation as alternatives. In addition, many products that are considered luxury items today will become the necessities of tomorrow. Examples include personal computers and mobile phones that have become an integral part of life in modern societies.

Knowledge and application of YED can be used by businesses to predict sales. The business cycle of booms and slumps (see Unit 1.5) means that the level of income and aggregate demand in the economy will fluctuate over time. Certain products (such as staple foods or education) are less income sensitive than others (such as expensive food products or private tuition) so are less prone to changes in demand during a recession. Luxury items on the other hand do well during an economic upturn but their sales are much more volatile during less prosperous times.

Businesses can use YED figures to plan their marketing strategies. For example, price discrimination can take place whereby higher prices are being charged to customers in more affluent areas or countries. With rising incomes in China and India, computer firms and car manufacturers have located or introduced distribution channels in these countries to make the most of the income elastic demand for such products.

i. Normal goods - including Luxury goods and Necessities

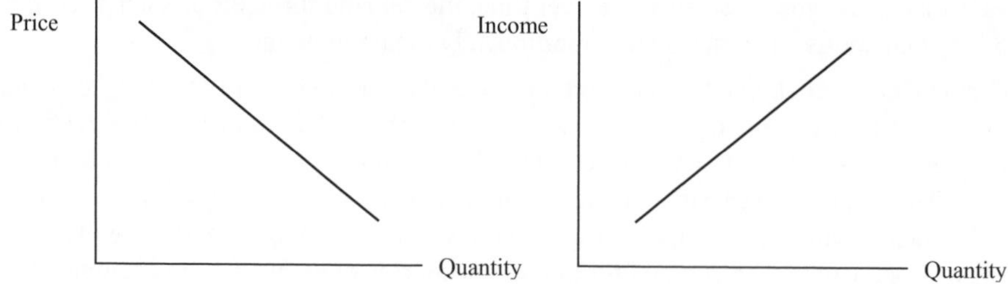

For normal goods, there is an inverse relationship between price and quantity demanded, i.e. a normal demand curve exists. There is a direct relationship between income and quantity demanded. This means that as income rises, so too does the quantity demanded for normal goods.

ii. Inferior Goods (excluding Giffen Goods)

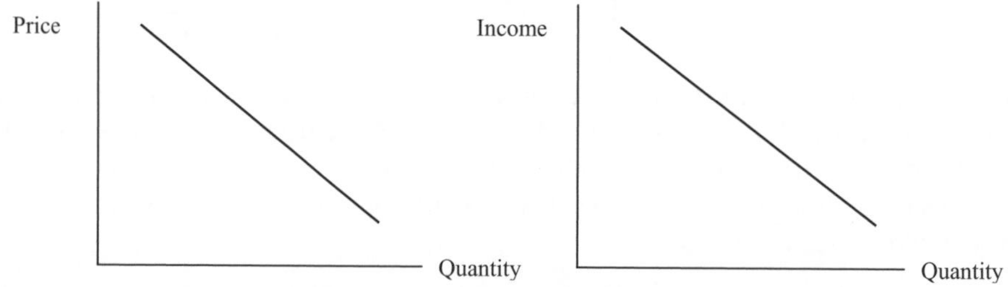

For inferior goods, there is an inverse relationship between price and quantity demanded, i.e. a normal demand curve exists. However, there is also an inverse relationship between income and quantity demanded. This means that as income levels rise, the demand for inferior goods will fall as consumers switch to more superior products.

iii. Giffen Goods - a special case of Inferior good

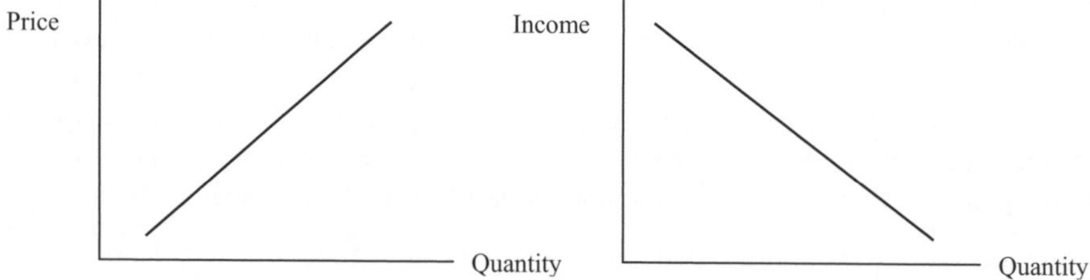

Since Giffen goods are a type of inferior good, there is a negative correlation between income levels and the level of demand. However, Giffen goods have an unusual demand curve, whereby there is a direct relationship between price and quantity demanded.

Figure 4.4h Diagrammatic representation of normal and inferior goods

Cross-price elasticity of demand

Cross-price elasticity of demand (CED) measures the degree of responsiveness of *demand* for one product due to a change in the *price* of another product, such as substitutes or complements. The formula for calculating cross-price elasticity of demand is:

$$\frac{\text{Percentage change in quantity demanded for Good A}}{\text{Percentage change in price of Good B}}$$

or in annotation form:

$$\frac{\%\Delta QD^{A}}{\%\Delta P^{B}}$$

Substitutes are products in competitive demand, i.e. they can be used in place of one another. Examples include tea and coffee, private education and state education or domestic and overseas holiday destinations. All things being equal, the demand for a product will tend to vary *directly* with the price of its substitute product. For example, if the price of a Samsung digital camera falls, the demand for Sony digital cameras is likely to fall, other things remaining equal. This relationship suggests that there is a positive CED value for substitutes, i.e. as the price of a product increases the demand for its substitute will also tend to rise.

Figure 4.4i illustrates this direct relationship for goods that are in competitive demand, such as strawberries and bananas.

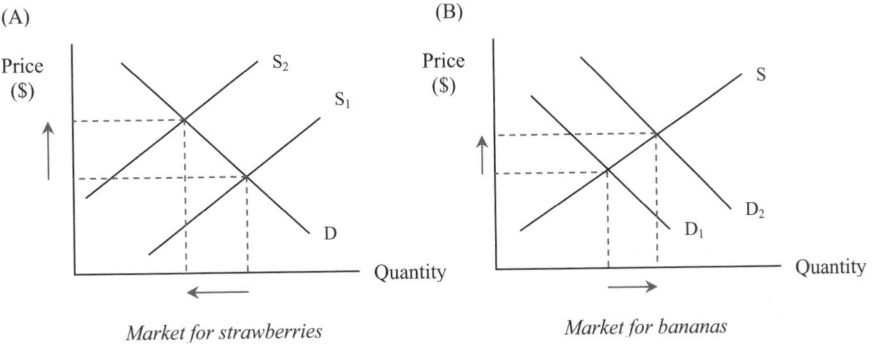

Market for strawberries *Market for bananas*

Figure 4.4i CED for goods in competitive demand

In Figure 4.4i(A), a fall in the supply of strawberries, perhaps due to a poor harvest, has caused an increase in its price and reduced the quantity demanded. The higher price of strawberries has subsequently caused an increase in the demand for bananas as shown in Figure 4.4i(B). In time, the increased demand for bananas will also cause its equilibrium price to rise although the quantity traded increases. The higher the value of CED for substitutes, the more customers see the products as being close substitutes.

Complements are products that are in joint demand, such as the demand for personal computers and computer software. A fall in the price of computers is likely to lead to an increase in the demand for computer software products. This means that there is a negative CED for goods that are in joint demand. For example, an increase in the price of tennis racquets is likely to cause a fall in demand for tennis balls.

Figure 4.4j shows the inverse relationship between complementary goods (those in joint demand). A fall in the price of contact lenses, perhaps due to advances in production technologies, has led to an expansion in their demand. This then leads to an increase in the demand for contact lens solutions.

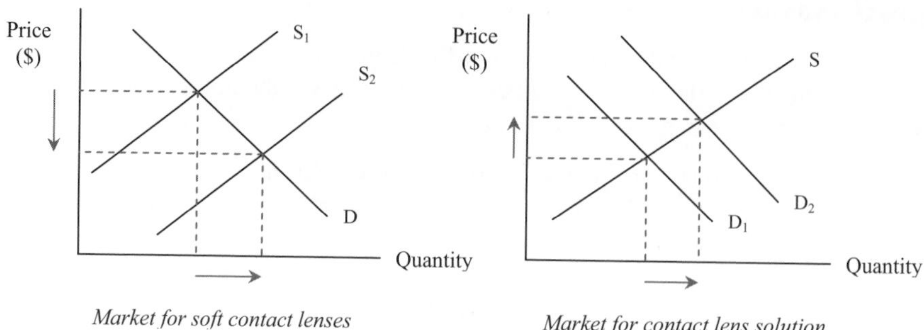

Figure 4.4j CED for goods in joint demand

In theory, CED can also equal zero. This suggests that there is no relationship between the price of one product (such as apples) and the demand for another (such as helicopters). Hence, the lower the value of CED, the weaker the relationship between complementary or substitute goods.

Knowledge and application of CED allows a business to devise appropriate pricing strategies. Firms can forecast the impact on their sales following a change in the price of a rival's products. For example, budget airline operators such as easyJet and Air Asia have catered well for relatively price-sensitive customers who now have an alternative to using the larger national airline carriers. Complementary goods that have a strong relationship, such as popcorn and soft drinks at the cinema, tend to have at least one of the products sold with a high mark-up. Games consoles, for instance, are often sold at a loss but there is a huge mark up on the games themselves. Sony claim to break-even on their PS3 console once a customer has bought two games. Popcorn and soft drinks are sold at a high (premium) price with the purchase of cinema tickets (their strong complementary good) at the cinema.

Firms will also aim to reduce the value of their CED in relation to substitute products. This can be done by branding strategies (see Unit 4.3) or any other approach that encourages customer loyalty. Not only does this mean that the business benefits from repeat purchases from its loyal customers, the falling value of CED in relation to substitute products also means that the business can charge a higher price to increase its total revenue and profit.

Question 4.4.11

Cross-price elasticity of demand

Explain how the demand for supermarket own-label cola would change in each of the following situations:

- **a** The price of Coca-Cola falls dramatically due to a special promotion. *[3 marks]*
- **b** The price of supermarket own-label cola is affected by an increase in its production costs. *[3 marks]*
- **c** A government advertising campaign warns of tooth decay caused by drinking fizzy drinks. *[3 marks]*

Advertising elasticity of demand

Advertising elasticity of demand (AED) measures the degree of responsiveness of demand for a product following a change in the advertising expenditure for that product. In other words, it acts as a measure of the degree of success of an advertising campaign on the demand for a particular good or service.

The formula for calculating AED is:

$$\frac{\text{Percentage change in quantity demanded}}{\text{Percentage change in advertising expenditure}}$$

Ideally, managers would want a highly elastic AED since this means that the change in advertising spending has led to a more than proportionate change in the level of demand for the product. An AED value that is above 1.0 suggests that customers are highly responsive to the changed spending on advertising. For example, if a business raised its advertising expenditure on a product from $1 million per year to $1.2 million per year, and subsequently the demand for the product also increased from 4 million units to 5 million units in the same time period, then the AED is 1.25 (i.e. 25% ÷ 20%). This means that demand is elastic to a change in advertising expenditure and that the extra spending would be more than compensated by the higher sales that would follow. Likewise, an AED figure below 1.0 suggests that demand is not so responsive to changes in advertising expenditure.

In reality, it is often difficult to determine whether changed advertising expenditure is the root cause of a change in demand. This is especially the case for firms that use family branding (see Unit 4.3) in their advertisements as opposed to advertising a single product. Furthermore, demand may have changed due to other reasons, such as a change in income levels. Marketers do, however, believe that there is a positive correlation between advertising expenditure and the level of demand. Big blockbuster movies that do well at the box office, for example, are backed by expensive advertising campaigns.

It is possible that the calculation of AED gives a negative number. This means that a rise in advertising expenditure would actually bring about a fall in demand. Hence the advertising campaign would be regarded as being ineffective (since higher advertising spending is supposed to lead to higher levels of demand). Alternatively, a negative AED figure can come about by spending less on advertising which leads to more demand. This suggests that it is possible to increase sales without always having to spend more money on advertising.

Question 4.4.12

Disney Pixar

Disney Pixar's huge movie hits such as *Toy Story*, *Monsters Inc.*, *The Incredibles*, *A Bug's Life*, *Finding Nemo*, *Ratatouille* and *Cars* owe much to their persuasive and successful advertising campaigns. Pixar's success has also been attributed to the sales of its movie-related merchandise, such as toys and clothing.

- **a** Outline why movies and merchandise might be classed as complementary goods. *[2 marks]*
- **b** With reference to price elasticity of demand, explain what is likely to happen to the demand curve for movies that have been effectively marketed. *[4 marks]*

HIGHER LEVEL EXTENSION: RELATIONSHIP BETWEEN ELASTICITY AND PRODUCT LIFE CYCLES

The price for a product is not simply set and then attention turns away to other matters. In many businesses, prices for existing products are constantly being monitored and compared with those offered by competitors. As a product passes through its *product life cycle* (see Unit 4.3) its price may need to be changed and adapted to each distinct stage. For example, end-of-season stock, such as Christmas cards or calendars in January, are heavily discounted (using discount pricing)

HIGHER LEVEL

HIGHER LEVEL

and sold at very low prices. The role of marketing managers is to continuously plan and oversee pricing strategy over a product's life cycle.

The value of PED for a product will tend to increase as it moves along its life cycle:

- **Launch** – Since the product is new, production levels are low and, hence, economies of scale are not possible. This means that costs and prices will be relatively high. A small number of innovators form the most likely group of customers to buy a product at this stage. Everett Rogers found that around 2.5% of the market for a new product comes from the initial group of innovators (see Unit 5.6). They are risk takers and are willing to pay high prices for exclusivity. Hence, the value of PED for a product at this stage is likely to be very low, i.e. price inelastic.
- **Growth** – As the demand for a product grows, production levels can increase so this will allow the firm to benefit from some economies of scale. Prices are therefore likely to be reduced slightly to foster growth. Skimming price or promotional pricing may be suitable at this stage. By now, competitors may have launched rival products (known as 'me too' products) so prices are also likely to fall in order for the firm to be competitive. Hence, the value of PED will tend to rise slightly during the growth stage.
- **Maturity** – By this stage in a product's life cycle, substitutes will have become available. This will increase the value of PED, i.e. customers become more sensitive to price differentials. The firm will maximize economies of scale as output is at its highest, thus prices can be reduced. Firms will use marketing strategies such as advertising and branding in order to minimize the increase in the value of PED for the product.
- **Saturation** – Customers at this stage in a product's life cycle are very sensitive to price differentials. There may be a degree of customer or brand loyalty, although late adopters and laggards (see Unit 5.6) will only be prepared to pay lower prices. The value of PED is therefore likely to be high especially as substitute products will be available on the market.
- **Decline** – As a product goes into decline, prices will continually fall. Bargain hunters will snap up the products which have been highly discounted in price in order to reduce stock levels. Customers will be extremely sensitive to the product's price. In fact, price will probably be the most important element of the marketing mix during this final stage before the withdrawal (death) of a product.

PRICE AND BUSINESS STRATEGY

In reality, a firm's pricing strategy will consist of a combination of the various pricing methods explained in this Unit. It is vital that the pricing strategy adopted by a business provides adequate profit for all products in its portfolio. It is also important that the pricing of a new product does not destroy profit margins on more established products. However, the pricing decision is not made without reference to other elements of the marketing mix. Essentially, the pricing decision must be consistent with all other aspects of marketing:

- *Marketing planning* – Pricing decisions need to consider the nature of the targeted market. Segmentation data such as income levels and demographics can prove useful in setting suitable prices.
- *Place* – The distribution methods used (see Unit 4.6) will also affect prices. For example, cosmetics sold through mail order catalogues will be priced differently from those sold at exclusive cosmetic boutiques (outlets). In addition, the more intermediaries used, the greater the costs and hence the higher the price tends to be.

- *Product* – Features of the product such as quality and design will affect the level of prices being charged. Innovative products will demand a high price whereas 'me too' products can only command lower prices.
- *Promotion* – The type of promotional methods used to market a product (see Unit 4.5) will affect its costs, which in turn will influence the price of the product.

In addition to marketing issues, there are other aspects of a business that will affect its pricing strategy:

- *Nature of the business* – Profit maximizing firms are likely to use high pricing methods such as price discrimination or destroyer pricing. By contrast, cost-based methods may be more appropriate for not-for-profit organizations.
- *Nature of barriers to entry* – This refers to the degree of competition within the industry (high entry barriers will limit competition in an industry). For example, firms operating in highly competitive markets will take more notice of the prices being charged by their rivals. By contrast, monopolists have much more power over the setting of prices due to the existence of high barriers to entry.
- *Business image* – Organizations with a reputable and prestigious image will charge relatively higher prices. By contrast, firms endeavouring to be cost leaders (see Unit 1.7) will charge much lower prices.

Exam Tip!

Questions often ask candidates to suggest and justify suitable pricing strategies that can be used by a business to enter new markets. Rather than simply explaining the various types of pricing methods that can be used, it is more important to put these into the context of the organization. For example, it may be appropriate to consider a few issues first, before advising suitable pricing strategies. These considerations may include the following issues:

- Even though the market is 'new' for the business in question, there might be well-established firms that already exist in the market. However, if the firm is the first entrant to a market, then price skimming may be appropriate.
- Unless the product is purely original and innovative, customers will already have perceptions about what the correct level of price ought to be.
- Which pricing method is most likely to attract the attention of customers? For some items, promotional pricing is highly suitable, whilst prestige pricing works better for other products.
- What sort of image does the business want to portray? Clearly, the pricing strategy used for high quality and exclusive products will be different from that used for mass market products that have plenty of substitutes.
- Finally, it is important to consider the likely reaction of competitors to the pricing strategies used by a firm. If low prices are used and this sparks a price war, most businesses will tend to lose.

Despite the huge importance placed on pricing decisions, businesses are also likely to employ **non-pricing strategies** to market their products. These may take the form of promotional strategies (see Unit 4.5) such as advertising, gift vouchers and packaging. Alternatively, non-price competition can take the form of differentiated products and branding (see Unit 4.3) or through innovative ideas (see Unit 5.6) and quality assurance (see Unit 5.4). It is evident that marketing is highly integrated and no amount of price discount can sell a product that does not meet the needs or wants of the consumer.

REVIEW QUESTIONS 4.4

1 Explain why the price decision (deciding on the 'right' price) is such a difficult task.

2 Explain the link between the price of a product and its perceived quality.

3 What is the difference between a 'price taker' and a 'price maker'?

4 What is 'cost-plus pricing'?

5 Explain the meaning of 'competition-based pricing'.

6 Differentiate between 'price skimming' and 'penetration pricing'.

Higher Level extension

7 What is 'marginal cost pricing'?

8 Differentiate between full cost pricing and absorption cost pricing.

9 Explain when each type of pricing would be suitable for a business:

  i going-rate pricing.

  ii predatory pricing.

10 What are the three conditions necessary for effective price discrimination?

11 What are 'loss leaders'?

12 What is 'promotional pricing'?

13 State four determinants of demand and four determinants of supply.

14 Explain the meaning of 'price elasticity of demand' and how it might be of value to a business.

15 Explain the relationship between the PED of a product and its sales revenue.

16 Distinguish between normal, superior and inferior goods.

17 How will changes in the price of each of these products affect the demand?

  i substitutes.

  ii complements.

18 How might the calculation of advertising elasticity of demand be of use to marketers?

19 Explain why the pricing strategy for a product will change as it moves through the product life cycle.

20 Outline three pricing strategies that businesses can use to enter new markets.

Absorption cost pricing is a type of cost-based pricing method that focuses on covering all costs of production (both direct and indirect costs). Indirect costs are apportioned to different departments based on a predetermined set of criteria.

Advertising elasticity of demand (AED) measures the impact on the demand for a firm's product following a change in its advertising expenditure.

Competition-based pricing refers to pricing strategies based on the prices charged by the rivals in the industry, rather than on the costs of production or the level of customer demand.

Complements are products that are jointly demanded as they go well together. Examples include tea and sugar, cars and petrol, or food and drink.

Cost-based pricing refers to setting prices based on the costs of production rather than on the level of demand or the prices set by competitors.

Cost-plus pricing, also known as **mark-up pricing**, takes place when a firm calculates its unit costs and then adds a percentage profit to determine the price.

Cross-price elasticity of demand (CED) measures the degree of responsiveness of the level of demand for one product due to a change in the price of a related good (either a complement or substitute).

Demand is the amount of products that customers are willing and able to buy at each price level. For the vast majority of products, as the price increases, demand will tend to fall.

Full cost pricing is a pricing method based on the apportionment of total indirect costs by using a single arbitrary criterion.

Income elasticity of demand (YED) measures the degree of responsiveness of changes in demand due to a change in consumer income levels. A positive YED figure means that the product is a *normal good. Inferior goods* have a negative YED figure.

Loss leader is a market-led pricing strategy that involves setting the price of a product that is below its costs of production to entice customers to buy other products with high profit margins.

Marginal cost pricing (also known as **contribution pricing**) calculates the cost of supplying an extra unit of output in order to determine a suitable price. Only direct costs are apportioned since fixed costs do not affect the marginal output.

Market-led pricing strategies are based on the level of customer demand for a firm's products, i.e. the level of demand in the industry rather than being based on costs of production or the prices charged by competitors.

Penetration pricing is a market-led pricing strategy that involves a firm setting low prices to gain entry into a new market. Once the product has established market share, prices can then be increased.

Predatory pricing is a competition-based pricing strategy that involves a firm setting prices so low that other competitors, especially smaller firms, cannot compete at a profitable level.

Price discrimination is a pricing strategy that involves charging different prices to different groups of customers for the same product, e.g. adult and child airline tickets.

Price elasticity of demand (PED) measures the degree of responsiveness of changes in demand due to a (small) change in the product's own price.

Price war is a less aggressive version of predatory pricing whereby firms compete by a series of intensive price cuts.

Skimming is a market-led pricing strategy that involves charging a high price for innovative or high-tech products for an initial period. As the novelty factor wears off, prices will be gradually reduced (or skimmed).

Substitutes are products in competitive demand, i.e. they can be used in place of one another.

Supply is the amount of product that firms are willing and able to provide at each price level. The law of supply states that as the price of a product increases, its supply will tend to rise.

Promotion

UNIT 4.5

> *Advertising is the art of convincing people to spend money they don't have for something they don't need.*
>
> Will Rogers (1879–1935), American comedian and actor

Key topics

- Objectives of promotion
- Types of promotion
- Above-the-line promotion
- Below-the-line promotion
- Promotional mix

INTRODUCTION

Promotion refers to methods of communicating messages to the market with the intention of selling a firm's products. Examples of promotion include sales promotion, branding, raising publicity (awareness) and advertising campaigns. Some types of promotion are paid for (such as with television and other mass media advertising) whilst some are not (such as word of mouth). Other types of promotion, such as magazine advertisements and public relations can also be targeted more specifically at certain market segments.

Although promotional activities are important, especially during the early stages of a *product's life cycle*, they can also be extremely expensive. For instance, the producers of the first Spider-Man movie spent $50 million on its marketing campaign in 2002. This spending has to be justified and the success (or otherwise) of the marketing activities measured. Determining the optimum promotional budget and forecasting its probable impact on sales is by no means an easy management task. This Unit looks at the different forms of promotion, their relative merits and weaknesses and the formation of an appropriate promotional mix for different businesses.

OBJECTIVES OF PROMOTION

The objectives of a firm's promotion will be set in line with the objectives of the marketing department's objectives (see Unit 4.2). These in turn will be based on the corporate objectives of the organization. Despite this, there are three key objectives to any promotional campaign: to *inform*, to *persuade* and to *remind* the market about the firm's product(s).

- **Inform** – Informative promotions aim to alert the market about a firm's products, especially new ones. It is also commonly used when promoting existing products that have been updated. The promotion may include information such as product functions and price. Informative promotion can equally be used to raise awareness of the business itself – its name, purpose and brand. It is often based on providing facts and figures about a business or its products. It is hoped that this will then give customers sufficient information to influence their purchasing decisions.
- **Persuade** – Persuasive promotions aim to encourage customers to make a purchase, to switch from rival brands and to create loyalty for the product or brand. It is therefore commonly used in highly competitive markets. In order to persuade customers, firms may adopt *product differentiation* techniques such as branding to create a unique identity or to enhance the product's image in order to entice customers to buy their products. Another strategy is to use *comparison advertising* which directly or indirectly compares a firm's product to that of its rivals. Successful persuasion can also generate **impulse buying**. This happens when customers make a purchase without intentionally planning to have done so, i.e. there is a subconscious urge to buy the product.
- **Remind** – Reminder promotion techniques are used to retain customer awareness and interest of an established product. Reminder promotion is suitable for products that are in the maturity or saturation stages of their product life cycle (see Unit 4.3). Leading brands such as McDonald's and Coca-Cola tend to use this form of promotion.

Most promotional campaigns contain an element of both persuasion and information. However, the vast majority of promotions, especially advertising, are of the persuasive kind. Governments and non-profit organizations tend to account for the majority of informative promotional campaigns.

TYPES OF PROMOTION

Promotional activities can be classified in four ways:

1. **Above-the-line** (ATL) promotion refers to the use of mass media sources (such as television, magazines and radio) to promote or to establish a favourable long-term image of a business, its brands or its products.
2. **Below-the-line** (BTL) promotion refers to the use of non mass-media promotional activities. Examples include the use of free samples (often used to promote toiletries, food and drinks), discount vouchers (to entice customers to buy the product) and added-value promotions (such as 'buy two, get one free' deals).
3. **Pull promotion** refers to promotional techniques used to stimulate demand for a product, i.e. to 'pull' (or attract) the customer into buying. Examples would include advertising and above-the-line promotional activities.
4. **Push promotion** refers to promotional methods that rely on intermediaries, such as wholesalers and retailers, to 'push' out (or get) products to the customer. Examples include sales promotions, price reductions and other means of below-the-line promotional activities.

Above-the-line promotion

Above-the-line (ATL) promotion refers to any form of paid-for promotional technique through independent consumer media. The main types of above-the-line promotion advertising on television, radio, billboard posters, magazines, newspapers, cinemas and the internet. These are considered in more detail below. A summary of the general advantages and disadvantages of ATL line promotion is shown in Box 4.5a.

Box 4.5a Merits and drawbacks of above-the-line promotion

General advantages of above-the-line promotion include:

- Due to potentially large audience figures, ATL promotion can reach a huge number of customers.
- Research has suggested that customers tend to take more notice of ATL promotion because they are more interesting and appealing.

General disadvantages of above-the-line promotion include:

- Promotion and advertising through the mass media may not appeal to the right segments or potential consumers. For example, many outdoor billboard advertisements go unnoticed because they do not specifically target a market segment and do not relate or appeal to a significant number of viewers.
- Many advertisements are simply ignored because people switch channels during television and radio commercial breaks; readers often take no notice of advertising placed in magazines and people complain about the number of pop-up advertisements appearing on the internet.
- They only cater for one-way communication and hence there is no easy way to determine the effectiveness of such promotional activities.

Television advertising

The first American television advertisement appeared in 1941. UK television advertisements first appeared in 1955 and had a profound impact on the marketing industry. According to Broadcasters Audience Research Board Ltd. (www.barb.co.uk) the UK television advertising industry is worth over £5 billion ($10 billion) per year. The fact that expenditure on TV advertising is such big business, and that it exceeds spending on all other forms of promotion, suggests that there are huge advantages in doing so. Advertising on television exploits the power of moving pictures – pictures speak for themselves. Combining sound and images can bring about very powerful messages to the viewer. TV advertisements can also be designed to meet specific needs, such as advertisements aimed at children being aired during children's television programmes. Rising income levels around the world have led to increasing ownership of television sets. Coupled with advances in technology, such as high-definition satellite television, this means it is possible to broadcast television advertisements to a global audience.

However, the key drawback is the huge cost of producing and broadcasting advertisements on television. Media specialist and author, Frank Dane explained this fact by stating, "Time is money, especially when you are talking to a lawyer or buying a commercial." Television companies sell 'advertising slots' to businesses based on the level of demand (peak-time slots will obviously sell for a higher price). This implies that marketers must try to get their message across in a very short time, usually within 30 seconds. In fact, the cost of a 30-second weekend advertising spot during peak time in Hong Kong and the UK starts from approximately $60,000. In the USA, the cost to advertise to the 93 million Americans watching the Super Bowl (American Football) is as high as $2.6 million per commercial!

Radio advertising

As with television advertising, radio time slots are sold to businesses, with peak listening times being during morning and evening rush hour periods. Commercial stations require a licence to broadcast. Their activities are monitored and regulated by a government agency. In the UK, for example, the content of radio advertisements must be *legal*, *decent*, *honest* and *truthful*.

Radio advertising can reach a very large audience yet it is significantly cheaper than television advertising. Unlike television advertising, radio commercials do not rely on moving images or people having to be immobile in front of a TV screen. Listeners are exposed to the promotions whilst they continue to do other things (such as driving, eating a meal or dressing). Advances in technology, such as broadband internet technology, mean that radio commercials can be broadcast to almost anyone in the world.

The main drawback of radio advertising is that it can only communicate audio messages, i.e. there is no visual impact. Research has shown that people can retain oral messages better when there is a visual stimulus. Another related disadvantage is that audiences have lower attention levels when compared to television advertisements which exploit the dynamics of moving images.

Cinema

The demand for visits to the cinema is *income elastic*, i.e. as the level of consumer income increases, the level of demand rises by a larger proportion (see Unit 4.4). Statistics show growing visitor numbers at cinemas and this has attracted more marketers to use the cinema as an advertising medium.

One key advantage of using cinema advertising is that the audiences can be directly targeted based on the movie. Promotion can be tailored to the specific market segments (such as genre of film and viewer age). The size of movie screens can exert more impact compared to other forms of promotion. Furthermore, unlike television or radio commercials, marketers have a captive audience since it is much harder for viewers to ignore or switch off the advertisements (especially as many viewers perceive the advertisements as part of the overall cinema experience). The main drawback of cinema advertising is its limited audience compared to those of radio and television.

Newspaper advertising

Newspaper advertising has the advantages of potentially reaching a wide audience and it is much cheaper than using television advertising. Furthermore, newspaper advertisements can be referred to at a later date meaning that important information can be detailed in the advertisement. Although TV advertisements can be targeted at specific market segments (at least to some extent), newspaper advertisements can better target different markets. For example, teaching jobs are advertised in *The Times Educational Supplement*, a specialist newspaper for teachers, and on its website (www.tes.co.uk). Different socio-economic classes can also be targeted based on the type or quality of the newspaper that they read. With the development of the internet, newspaper firms have their own dedicated websites. They therefore have a much wider reach and this makes newspaper advertising more attractive to businesses.

The main constraint of newspaper advertisements is the high costs, particularly for small businesses. Newspaper firms charge high prices for advertisements with colour, pictures or photos. Some newspaper firms base their charges on the size of an advertisement whilst others charge on the basis of the number of words, letters or characters used in the advertisement. In order for a newspaper advertisement to stand out from the many others that appear, businesses may need to spend a lot more money than their rivals to ensure that readers are drawn to the advertisement. Unlike other print media, such as magazines or outdoor posters, newspapers tend to have a very short shelf life; people will not usually read the previous day's 'news' and therefore many advertisements are simply left unseen.

Magazines

Promotion via magazines has the advantage of being able to use high photo-quality colour images to attract the attention of the reader. Targeting the right market segment is possible through the use of specialist magazines such as *Car*, *Brides*, *PC Gamer* and *Vogue*. Like newspapers, promotional advertisements in magazines can be referred back to at a later date. However, magazines benefit further in that they tend to have a longer shelf life than newspapers.

One downside to using magazine promotion is that it is static. Hence it is quite usual for a business to place several different advertisements in magazines (think of all the various advertisements used by fashion designers in clothing magazines, for example). In addition, readers are bombarded with advertisements (known as **advertising clutter**) in magazines so may accidentally miss, or deliberately ignore, the advertisements. A third disadvantage is that there is a long lead-time between submitting an advertisement and its actual publication in a magazine. This means that there is a period when sales are potentially lost unless other forms of promotion are used.

Outdoor advertising

Outdoor advertising refers to the use of commercial billboards, banners and posters to promote a business, its brands or its products. Examples of outdoor advertising can be seen at sporting events, in shopping malls, at the roadside and on vehicles (such as buses, trains and taxis). This method tends to be used by car manufacturers, food producers, clothing firms and businesses involved in leisure and tourism.

With advances in technology, the ordinary outdoor advertisement has been transformed to billboards that automatically rotate (thereby increasing the number of advertisements that can be shown on each billboard) and digital billboards that can combine moving images and sound. This opportunity has given outdoor advertising a dynamic dimension. Another advantage is that there is a high rate of exposure to the advertisements, especially as businesses will use the same advertisements in many different locations.

However, there are numerous disadvantages to outdoor advertising. It is difficult to monitor the effectiveness of outdoor advertising because targeting is very difficult (being only really suitable for promoting mass market products). Traditional billboards are also prone to damage caused by bad weather, vandalism and graffiti. Furthermore, there can be high levels of competition in terms of advertising clutter. Central business districts, such as New York, Hong Kong and London, are swamped with billboard advertisements. In Sao Paolo, Brazil, outdoor advertising has been outlawed because it had become so overused that critics argued it created 'advertising pollution', i.e. the billboards became such an eyesore and a distraction.

Question 4.5.1

The entertainment industry

The entertainment industry is a huge business. The movie and music industries are constantly using **above-the-line** promotional strategies to market their latest products. Trailers (previews) for the latest movies and music albums are constantly being aired on television commercials, whilst posters for these latest releases appear all over glossy magazines and newspapers. There are even dedicated internet websites, purely set up to promote the launch of a movie or music album. Most albums and movies tend to have a short life span, whilst a special few, such as The Beatles albums and the Star Wars movies, have entertained people since the 1960s and 1970s respectively.

a Describe the meaning of **above-the-line** promotional strategies. *[2 marks]*

b Analyse the reasons for using above-the-line methods to promote movies and music albums. *[6 marks]*

Below-the-line promotion

Below-the-line (BTL) promotion refers to all forms of non-media promotional activities. Unlike above-the-line promotion, this means that no commission has been paid to external media agencies. Instead, the business has direct control over the production of all its advertisements. These methods tend to be relatively cheap in relation to above-the-line methods. Examples of BTL promotion include: branding, slogans, logos, packaging, word of mouth, direct marketing, direct mail, sales promotion, point of sales promotion, publicity and sponsorship deals.

Branding

The idea of using brands to promote a business or its products is examined in Unit 4.3. A huge amount of money is spent each year on promoting brand awareness. Coca-Cola, the world's most recognized brand, has a promotional budget of $2 billion per year. Successful brands are instantly recognizable. Companies such as Virgin, Microsoft and Sony use branding to promote their company and their existing products. They also use brand extension strategies to launch new products under their company brand name.

Slogans

One way that businesses try to catch and retain the attention of customers is through the use of memorable catchphrases (known in the business world as **slogans**). A catchphrase is a concise message designed to represent the essence of a business or its products in a memorable set of words.

Sceptics of slogans argue that customers are not so simply fooled by the use of a few words that promise to deliver. The product itself, they argue, is of more importance to make firms stand out from their rivals. However, many slogans have become so well known that they are synonymous with the brand. Heinz, for example, launched their "Beanz Meanz Heinz" slogan in 1967 and although it was dropped for ten years, the slogan has been relaunched due to public demand. Box 4.5b shows examples of other highly successful corporate slogans.

Effective slogans can help to give a business a competitive advantage over its rivals. In order to judge the effectiveness of a slogan, marketers may look at the following criteria:

- It has simple catchphrases or statements so that the slogans are **memorable**. Techniques used to achieve this include the use of mnemonics, music and catchy tunes.
- It creates a sense of **desire** or need for the product.
- It creates an upbeat **image** for the business or its products.
- It outlines or hints at the **benefits** of the product or the brand.

Box 4.5b Popular business slogans

"Impossible is nothing" – Adidas

"The ultimate driving machine" – BMW

"Probably the best beer in the world" – Carlsberg

"The world's local bank" – HSBC

"Finger lickin' good" – KFC

"Because I'm worth it" – L'Oreal

"I'm Lovin' It" – McDonald's

"Just do it" – Nike

"Connecting People" – Nokia

"Always low prices" – Wal-Mart

Logos

Logos are essentially a form of branding that uses a visual symbol to represent a business, its brands or its products. The golden arches (the 'M') of McDonald's and the 'three stripes' of Adidas are two examples of globally recognized logos. Businesses can spend millions of dollars coming up with suitable logos which are distinctive and memorable. BMW, for instance, bought the Rolls-Royce 'RR' logo for £40 million ($80 million) in 1998. Many non-profit organizations, such as The International Red Cross and the World Wild Fund for Nature, also use logos as part of their marketing strategy.

Packaging

Packaging can be a powerful component of the marketing mix. Almost every manufacturer and retailer provides carrier bags or protective packaging for their product that displays the name of the business. Customers who reuse carrier bags are in effect helping to promote a business after a purchase has been made. The art of using carrier bags to promote a firm, its products or its brand has been jargonized as 'bag-vertising' by marketers.

Word-of-mouth promotion

Word of mouth (WOM) refers to the spreading of information from one person to another through oral communication. It is possibly the most effective form of promotion since messages about a product are passed onto friends and family without any direct costs to the firm. Likewise, it can also be potentially damaging if the word spreads that a business or its products are substandard. American artist Ray Johnson pointed out that ordinary people can spread news faster than marketers. Similarly, A. Milligan and S. Smith (2002) argue in their book *Uncommon Practice* that the fastest way to build a brand is through word of mouth marketing. Their research suggests that conventional advertising expenditure can therefore be very wasteful.

A similar method of promotion is known as **peer-to-peer (P2P)** marketing. This method of promotion relies on the electronic transfer of messages (known to some as 'word of mouse') to promote a product or brand. This is usually done through the internet via emails and online chat rooms. Viral marketing is a method that combines both P2P and WOM promotional techniques. Perhaps the most successful case of **viral marketing** is that of YouTube (see Question 4.5.2).

Question **4.5.2**

YouTube

YouTube, the internet video sharing website, was launched at the start of 2006 by Steve Chen and Chad Hurley, both in their late twenties at the time. By October 2006, YouTube had grown so immensely throughout the world due to **viral marketing** that Google bought the business for a staggering $1.65 billion. In the same year, *TIME* magazine had named YouTube as winner of its 'Invention of the Year' award. According to YouTube, there are over 100 million video clips accessed every day on its website. Google's goal is to use YouTube to earn money, mainly through advertising. It also strives to convince television, movie and music executives that YouTube is a huge revenue opportunity.

a Define **viral marketing**. *[2 marks]*

b Examine the benefits to businesses that choose to advertise on internet video sharing websites, such as YouTube. *[6 marks]*

Direct marketing

Direct marketing refers to promotional activities that aim to sell a product straight to a customer rather than using an intermediary. Property developers, for example, may use their database containing information of previous clients who may be interested in purchasing new property from the firm, rather than paying estate agents to help the business to find customers. Direct marketing techniques include making telephone calls (known as **telemarketing**), sending email advertisements, and distributing direct mail to clients. Some businesses, such as insurance and financial planning companies, use brokers (agents) who visit their clients in person.

The advantages of using direct marketing are that the business can take a larger share of any profits, since there are no intermediaries to pay. In addition, the business is free to market its products in a way that it sees fit (within the law, of course) rather than passing on control of marketing to an external agency. Direct marketing can also allow a business to contact clients that would otherwise be out of reach.

A major drawback of direct marketing is the cost of producing and distributing promotional material such as leaflets, menus, brochures and catalogues. In addition, research has shown that most people disregard and dispose of most 'junk' or unsolicited mail and that they do not welcome unwarranted telephone calls from telesales personnel.

Direct mail

Direct mail is an example of direct marketing that involves mailing promotional material to the home addresses of customers in an attempt to persuade them to buy a firm's products. Mail order businesses tend to rely heavily on this method of promotion. Locally run restaurants and fast-food outlets also tend to send out menus to local residents and offer a delivery service to entice customers. Due to the large volume of direct mail, a major drawback of this method is that people tend to regard most promotional material sent through the post as junk mail. Furthermore, direct mail does not always target the right audience, and hence represents a waste of resources. An example would be people who do not have young children but still receive mailed materials promoting schools, toys, children's books and other related products.

Sales promotions

Sales promotions are temporary ways of boosting sales and attracting new buyers. BOGOF (Buy one get one free) deals are an example of sales promotion that is often used to get rid of excess stock or sometimes as a *loss leader* (see Unit 4.4). Other examples of sales promotions used to entice people to try out a particular product or brand include:

- Money-off coupons (or discount vouchers) offering customers a discounted price on a product. These often appear as cut-out coupons in magazines and newspapers.
- Free samples of products, such as shampoo sachets or food and wine taster sessions.
- 'Free' gifts to customers making a purchase, such as a free spare battery when buying a mobile phone or digital camera.
- Customer loyalty schemes where repeat purchasers are rewarded with free gifts or discounts. Points collected on loyalty schemes can be swapped for gifts or special discounts. Some of these schemes have been so successful, such as the airline frequent flyer schemes, that they have become a long-term strategy to promote a firm's brands or products.
- Competitions that give purchasers the chance to win a prize, such as a holiday or a car.

Sales promotions can be beneficial to a business because they boost sales (at least in the short run). They can also sway customers away from other firms and brands. More importantly, sales promotion encourages 'action' (the desire to make a purchase), rather than informing or reminding customers about a product.

However, there are drawbacks in using sales promotion. Free samples, gifts, price discounts, competitions and so forth all add to the marketing costs of a business. Therefore, sales promotion reduces the profit margin on each product – the greater the value of the promotion, the lower the profit margin tends to be. In addition, these tactics are only short term and may not be sustainable in the long term, so other strategies still need to be devised for the future.

Point-of-sales promotion

The term **point of sales** refers to the promotion of a product at the place or location where the customer buys the product. Supermarkets use this method extensively. Whilst customers are waiting in line at the checkouts, they are exposed to the promotion and sales of batteries, confectionary items and magazines. Large in-store displays, stands and posters can attract customers to purchase products they had not intended to buy.

Publicity

Publicity is the process of promoting a business and its products by getting media coverage without directly paying for it. Famous celebrities are often photographed wearing designer labels and this gives those brands free publicity in the media. Ferrari, for instance, found that it was cheaper to give away a car to football celebrity David Beckham than to advertise their vehicles on television. The subsequent media publicity that was generated was much more favourable than Ferrari could have hoped for from any commercial advertisement.

Sponsorship

Sponsorship involves a business providing financial funds and resources to support an event or an organization in return for publicity and prime advertising space. London's Arsenal Football Club, for instance, received a €132 million ($178 million) 15-year sponsorship deal in 2006 with Emirates Airline. In return, Arsenal FC has named its new football stadium The Emirates Stadium. Emirates Airline also agreed to sponsor the football shirts of Arsenal FC until 2014.

Question 4.5.3

Sponsoring the Football World Cup

Deutsche Bank claimed that the 2006 FIFA World Cup held in Germany added €5 billion ($6.75 billion) extra spending in the economy. The world's largest sporting event, as measured by global viewers and **revenue**, attracts a phenomenal amount of **sponsorship** money. Fifteen companies paid an average of £19 million ($37 million) each to sponsor the event. Multinationals including Gillette, Yahoo! and Philips can benefit enormously from sponsoring the World Cup because their products are sold all around the world. The cumulative television audience for the tournament was forecast by *Forbes* magazine to be in excess of 40 billion viewers in more than 200 countries. The benefits were so encouraging that some of the larger sponsors (such as Adidas, Sony, Coca-Cola, Hyundai and Emirates Airlines) had already secured sponsorship deals for the 2010 and 2014 events before the start of the 2006 World Cup.

a Define the meaning of **revenue** and **sponsorship**. *[4 marks]*

b Examine *two* benefits to multinationals that sponsor events such as the World Cup. *[6 marks]*

PROMOTIONAL MIX

The UK Chartered Institute of Marketing defines the promotional mix as "the set of tools that a business can use to communicate effectively the benefits of its products or services to its customers". In essence, the promotional mix refers to the range of above- and below-the-line methods used to market a product as part of the larger marketing mix. In deciding on a promotional mix, marketers often consider the marketing acronym AIDA:

- Attention – The promotional mix should raise existing and potential customers' awareness of the product by engaging their attention.
- Interest – It should also stimulate and keep customers interested, perhaps by using memorable and interesting advertisements.
- Desire – The promotional mix should generate a desire or feeling of 'need' for the product, perhaps through the use of free samples to lure customers.
- Action – It is vital that the promotional mix encourages customers to take action, i.e. to purchase the product, perhaps through the use of discount vouchers or other sales promotion methods.

Exam Tip!
The AIDA acronym can be used as a set of criteria for judging the success of a promotional campaign. You can use this to judge the extent to which the promotional strategy draws the **attention** of the public, how it engages their **interest**, the intensity of **desire** from customers, and ultimately the level of **action** taken to make a purchase.

An alternative approach to AIDA is to use the abbreviation **FAB** (Features, Advantages and Benefits) when devising a promotional mix. FAB promotional campaigns focus not on what a product is, but what the product will actually do for the customer. In this case, trade fairs, exhibitions and demonstrations are likely to be used as part of the promotional mix.

Each method of promotion has its advantages and limitations. The important thing is to select the mixture of promotional activities that best suits the business's particular needs.

In devising a promotional strategy, marketers will consider a combination of factors, such as:

- *Cost of promotional medium.* Although television advertising has the highest potential reach, it is also the most expensive. Advertising on the internet is relatively cheap and this is one key reason why it has grown in popularity amongst businesses. Businesses may instead consider the cost per head when selecting the most appropriate methods of promotion to use.
- *The nature of the product.* Certain products are suited to a particular type of promotion. For instance, insurance services and financial planning are highly suited to personal selling whereas beauty and cosmetic products are suited to women's magazines. A recruitment advertisement would be placed in a newspaper or a trade magazine whereas an advertisement for new cars could be advertised on television or in specialist magazines.
- *The product's position in its life cycle* (see Unit 4.3). During the launch stage of a product's life cycle, there will be extensive promotion to get the product noticed and established in the market. During the decline stage, promotion may be withdrawn as the business focuses on marketing new products instead.
- *Legislation.* Laws may prevent certain products (tobacco products, for example) from being advertised in certain media such as on television. This means that other forms of promotion are required.

For most products, a combination of both above- and below-the-line methods will be used as part of the firm's promotional mix. Using a single promotional technique in isolation is unlikely to be effective. Different methods can be used to deliver a slightly different but reinforcing message about the product. When promoting a new movie, for example, the promotional mix may include the use of:

- Television – to show trailers of the movie
- Radio – to raise awareness and excitement and to inform residents about release dates
- Outdoor advertising – using large outdoor posters (billboards) to promote the movie
- Newspapers – to support the above methods and to show screening times of the movie
- Website – to provide detailed interactive information about the movie, the cast, the director and the producer
- Cinema – trailers of the movie are shown at the cinema (point of sale) and prior to the screening of other movies.

The Chartered Institute of Marketing puts forward four key elements to make up a promotional mix. These consist of advertising, personal selling, public relations and sales promotion.

Question 4.5.4

The Paris Motor Show

The Paris Motor Show is one of the top auto shows in the world. Established as the world's first motor show back in 1898, the show is a public exhibition of current, debut and concept automobile models. The biannual event attracts all the major motor manufacturers who see the show as a vital **publicity** exercise for promoting its cars. Television and press coverage of the event ensures that the major exhibitors get maximum publicity.

a Define the term **publicity** in the context of the case study. *[2 marks]*

b Explain why trade shows are so important for businesses such as car manufacturers. *[4 marks]*

c Comment on the reasons for car manufacturers using motor shows to exhibit debut (new) products rather than through the use of direct marketing. *[4 marks]*

Advertising

Stephen Butler Leacock (1869–1944), a Canadian economist, defined advertising as "the science of arresting the human intelligence long enough to get money from it". In other words, advertising as a form of communication can be used to shape and develop awareness, perceptions, knowledge and attitudes. It is a form of promotion that refers to any kind of paid-for communication. Examples include promotional advertisements on television, radio, billboards, in-store displays, mobile phone messages and email. Advertising is usually classified as being informative, persuasive or a combination of both.

The general public is bombarded with advertisements on a daily basis. There are advertisements on the radio, on buses and trains, on the street, on shopping bags, in shops and even in schools and offices. A successful advertising campaign must therefore be distinctive, rather than being relegated to advertising clutter, i.e. advertisements that are simply ignored by the average person. Quite often in marketing, *what* is said and *how* it is said are of equal importance when trying to stand out from the competition. Marketing experts therefore focus their creativity skills on devising original and outstanding advertising messages. Some frequently used advertising techniques are outlined in Box 4.5c.

Box 4.5c Common advertising techniques

Bargain appeals – good deals and give-away schemes that attract customers to buy a product on preferential terms, such as interest-free credit or a reduced price for a limited time only

Celebrity endorsement – using famous celebrities (such as movie stars or sports personalities) to advertise a product or brand. This method is also known as **hero endorsement**

Comparative advertising – Comparing a product or brand with substitutes on the market (should be used with caution as claims may be legally disputed by competitors)

Direct response advertising – using contact details (such as providing a phone number, email address, mailing address, fax number or enquiry form) to encourage customers to directly respond to an advertisement

Feel good factor – advertisements that focus on the morale and image boosting benefits of buying a particular product, such as health-care products or luxury sports cars

Guarantees – using promises, such as 'guaranteed to work or your money back' schemes, to entice and reassure customers

Numerical or scientific claims – advertisements that use alleged statistics to promote their product or brands, such as 'nine out of ten drivers prefer X', 'three in four doctors recommend Y' or 'research shows that Z can help with weight loss'

Sex appeal – methods that portray the sexual attraction of certain products, such as perfumes, aftershaves, lingerie and clothing

Slogans – using catchphrases, tunes and music that stick in the minds of customers.

Most businesses will employ an advertising agency to design and produce advertisements on their behalf. Advertising agencies are organizations that specialize in the planning, organization and production of advertising campaigns for their clients (other businesses). They produce television advertisements, radio commercials, billboard posters and so forth based on the requests and demands of their customers. The advantage to a business in using an advertising agency is that they are experts in their field so have the experience, know-how and resources to produce a relatively successful campaign. Agencies will also be more aware of legislation affecting advertising, such as legal considerations and copyright laws.

Personal selling

Personal selling refers to promotional techniques that rely on sales representatives directly helping and persuading potential and existing customers to make a purchase. The sales people promote a firm's product through their knowledge, assistance, presence and enthusiasm. Methods of personal selling include sales presentations, face-to-face meetings with clients, telemarketing (telephone sales) and door-to-door sales. It is a common technique used in the provision of financial services such as health insurance, life assurance and investment funds. Personal selling is also used by real estate agencies in the sale and letting (rental) of commercial and residential property. Customers may have many questions to ask about different schemes or products so specialist sales people are used to address these questions and concerns.

One benefit of using personal selling is that it can be tailored to the individual needs of the customer. The sales person and the customer engage in dialogue to establish the customer's views and preferences, to answer any questions and to promote the firm's products to suit the needs of the customer. Personal selling can also help the business to build a positive, trusting and long-term relationship with the customer.

A disadvantage to a business of using personal selling is that sales agents can be very expensive to hire. For example, sales representatives at perfume counters in large department stores are skilled in their product knowledge and application and are therefore rewarded accordingly. They also often earn good rates of commission on the sale of each item.

Public relations (PR)

Public relations refers to business activities aimed at establishing and protecting the desired image of an organization. PR is concerned with getting good press coverage, usually without directly paying for it (otherwise it would be considered as corporate advertising), to create the desired image of a business. PR experts will get the media to report events in a positive way and from the business's point of view.

Having a presence at trade shows and exhibitions can also help a business to promote its image to a selected target audience. Other examples include having a launch party for a new product, organizing press conferences and radio or television interviews, donating conspicuously to charities and distributing company literature (such as brochures, company annual reports and newsletters). PR is, however, a long-term and ongoing strategy. PR experts are relied upon heavily when a business faces a crisis (see Unit 2.8). They will try to get the press to cover the story in a sympathetic and reassuring manner.

Sales promotion

Sales promotions are short-term incentives designed to stimulate sales of a product. Examples include the use of discount coupons, prize draws, trade fairs and free product samples. Research has shown that people are more likely to take notice of paper-based advertisements if they feature discounts or special offers. Sales promotions can help firms to gain a short-term competitive head start, get rid of excess or old stock and encourage customer loyalty. They can also be a good way of attracting new customers. However, sales promotions can be very expensive, so marketing managers will carefully monitor the progress of the campaigns (such as free installation and a period of complementary viewing when customers subscribe to satellite television) to ensure that costs are kept under control.

Question 4.5.5

Kim Do Yi Limited

Kim Do Yi Ltd. (KDY) established in 1995 by President and Master Instructor Rickie Chan Ka Ching is a martial arts firm based in Hong Kong.

The organization specializes in the Korean martial arts of Taekwondo and Hapkido. It is affiliated to the World Taekwondo Federation (the governing body for Olympic-style Taekwondo). KDY's core target market is children of primary and secondary school age. KDY does not have its own kwans (training studios), preferring instead to hire venues in numerous locations throughout Hong Kong. KDY believes this approach makes access easier and cheaper for its customers.

Source: www.kimdoyikwan.com

a Outline why promotion is important to an organization such as KDY. *[2 marks]*

b Advise on a suitable promotional mix for KDY. *[8 marks]*

PROMOTION AND BUSINESS STRATEGY

Since it often takes several attempts for a promotional message to be noticed or understood, promotion can be a highly expensive business activity. In addition, some forms of promotion are considered to be socially irresponsible. Critics argue that much of the expenditure on promotion is wasteful and could have been better spent elsewhere, such as on researching better products. They question whether it is justifiable that a company spends millions of dollars on a logo or slogan rather than using the money to benefit their customers (lower prices) or employees (higher wages and benefits).

However, supporters of promotion state that it does benefit workers in the form of creating jobs; the advertising industry is a huge employer. Marketing executives argue that promotion leads to substantial increases in sales. One example of a highly successful promotional campaign is Levi Strauss. Levi's 'launderette' television commercial featured a 1980s pop idol taking off his Levi's 501 jeans and putting them into the washing along with a bag of stones (to symbolize the stone-washed jeans). The commercial helped to revive the Levi brand in the UK jeans market as sales rose by some 800% in just a year.

In assessing the effectiveness of a promotional campaign, managers are likely to look at quantitative indicators. In particular, they will examine whether the promotional campaign generates a high *advertising elasticity of demand*, i.e. more money is created through sales revenue than the business spends on the promotional campaign.

Promotion relies on the creativity of marketers. **Guerrilla marketing** is a promotional strategy used to raise maximum exposure of a brand, product or business by using minimum input and highly unconventional methods. It aims to ambush or catch the attention of customers through unusual and/or shocking techniques. Advances in technology such as the internet has made guerrilla marketing more accessible to many more small businesses. Supporters of guerrilla marketing believe that it is far cheaper and more effective than using traditional above-the-line promotional methods. Some examples are shown in Box 4.5d.

Box 4.5d Guerrilla marketing techniques – some examples

Bag-vertising – art of using carrier bags and luggage to advertise

Bra-vertising – using models (usually females) dressed only in their underwear to promote a brand

Fancy dress – dressing up in extravagant outfits to catch the attention of passers-by

Stickers – covering large areas of a city with stickers displaying the firm's logo or brand

Graffiti – painting or spraying the name of the brand in public areas, such as railway stations and bridges

Buzz marketing – using word-of-mouth to create a buzz or craze for a firm's products

Lavatories – advertising found in public washrooms

Whilst marketers need to be creative, they still have to obey the law. Legal constraints exist, such as cigarette advertising being banned from television or radio broadcasts in many countries. If promotional activities are considered to be socially unacceptable, authorities may withdraw the campaign. For example, with obesity being a growing problem in the European Union, television commercials featuring fast food are carefully monitored and there are time restrictions to prevent children from being exposed to such advertisements. Box 4.5e outlines other examples of promotional techniques that may be considered to be socially irresponsible.

Box 4.5e Unethical and socially irresponsible promotional techniques

Pester power refers to the controversial influence (which stems from advertising) that children have over purchases made by adults. Children have always nagged parents to buy them the latest toys, music, movies and computer games. Marketers have exploited parental weakness by targeting 'must have' purchases at children. More recently, marketers have extended this technique to marketing products that adults purchase, such as the type of car. For example, manufacturers such as Honda and Lexus have advertised on children's television programmes such as Disney's *ABC Kids* and *Nickelodeon*. The ethical issue is whether children should be exposed and influenced by mass marketing at a tender age.

Confusion marketing refers to the use of tactics that deliberately confuse the customer so that it is easier to guide (or mislead) them into making a purchase. This controversial method is often used by providers of financial services and mobile telephone network companies, where pricing options can be extremely varied with complicated choices thereby making price comparisons literally baffling, if not impossible.

Ambush marketing is the planned attempt by a business to associate itself with an event without incurring the costs of being an official sponsor. Nike, for example, deliberately chose advertising slots during television coverage of the Football World Cup (Adidas being the official sponsors for the 2006, 2010 and 2014 FIFA World Cup events). The idea is to gain maximum exposure at the cost of the official sponsors. Viewers are often confused about who the official sponsors are because of the large volume of advertisements from different companies.

Infiltration marketing involves marketers contributing to blogs and online chat rooms by acting as ordinary users or customers. For example, they may write about receiving excellent customer service or being highly satisfied with the purchase of a company's products, when in fact they are actually marketing their firm's products as personal endorsements.

Pop-up advertisements are internet advertisements that are randomly and automatically launched in a small window on top of another web page. Market research has suggested that these advertisements are highly annoying but not easy to ignore. Marketers have extended this strategy to children's websites and computer games where advertisements appear before users are able to access the website or progress to the next stage of the computer game.

Unethical promotional and other controversial marketing activities have prompted governments and pressure groups to introduce legislation and codes of practice. For example, a pressure group against offensive advertising has been established in the UK by SCAMP (Stop Crude Advertising Material in Public). Consumer protection legislation exists to ensure that consumers are not deceived by misleading or dishonest advertising. In some countries, advertising activities are monitored and regulated by government agencies, such as Britain's Advertising Standards Authority. The ASA deals with complaints about the nature of advertising of businesses. Fines and other sanctions can be imposed on businesses that break the law or do not abide with codes of practice.

Public relations campaigns and a devotion to *corporate social responsibility* (such as donating money to charity or through sponsoring local community projects) can be costly. However, there may be major benefits for the business: it helps to gain good media publicity since PR can promote the brand and corporate image and improve community relations.

The methods of promotion, be they above- or below-the-line techniques, will vary for different products and be dependent on the creativity of marketers. The promotional mix for a single product will also change over its product life cycle. Promotion then is a complex but vital component of any marketing strategy. It is important for managers to remember that promotion must be used in relation to other aspects of the marketing mix; no amount of money spent on promotional activities will generate sustainable sales growth if the other elements of the marketing mix are ignored.

REVIEW QUESTIONS 4.5

1 What are the objectives of promotion?

2 Differentiate between 'above-the-line' and 'below-the-line' promotion.

3 Give five examples of ATL promotion and seven examples of BTL promotion.

4 What is meant by a 'promotional mix'?

5 What are the advantages and disadvantages of sales promotion?

6 What does AIDA stand for?

7 Explain the difference between advertising and promotion.

8 Briefly explain how marketers would judge the effectiveness of a promotional campaign.

> **Note:** Guerrilla marketing is a marketing strategy increasingly being used by businesses (hence its inclusion in the section 'Promotion and business strategy'). The topic is not explicitly on the IBO syllabus.

9 What is meant by 'guerrilla marketing'?

10 State five examples of socially irresponsible promotional techniques.

Above-the-line promotion refers to any form of paid-for advertising through the mass media (such as television and radio) in order to reach a wide audience.

Advertising is a method of informative and/or persuasive promotion that has to be paid for. The ultimate aim of advertising is to raise the level of demand for a firm's products.

Below-the-line promotion refers to promotional methods that do not directly use the mass media as a form of promotion. Examples include branding, sponsorship, direct mailing, sales promotions and trade fairs.

Personal selling is a form of promotional technique that relies on keen and knowledgeable sales staff directly helping and persuading customers to make a purchase.

Promotion is a component of the marketing mix. It refers to the methods used to inform, persuade or remind people about its products, brands or business. It is a key element of any marketing strategy.

Promotional mix refers to the combination of individual promotional methods used by a business, such as advertising, direct marketing, packaging and sales promotion.

Publicity is the process of promoting a business and its products by getting media coverage without directly paying for it.

Pull promotion refers to promotional methods, such as pester-power marketing or television advertising, that lure customers into buying a product.

Push promotion means using intermediaries, such as real estate agencies or financial consultants, to help sell products.

Sales promotions are short-term incentives designed to stimulate sales of a product, e.g. discount coupons, prize draws, trade fairs and free product samples.

Sponsorship is a promotional technique which involves a business funding, supporting or donating resources for an event or business venture in return for prominent publicity.

Word of mouth (WOM) is the spreading of good or bad messages about a firm, its products or its customer service. Many people argue that WOM is the most cost-effective form of promotion.

Place

UNIT 4.6

When you have completed 95 per cent of your journey, you are only halfway there.

Japanese proverb

Key topics

- Channels of distribution

Higher Level extension

- Supply chain management

INTRODUCTION

Place is the final component of the Four P's of the marketing mix. Place (or **placement**) refers to the distribution of a product, i.e. how products get to the consumer. A common definition of distribution, from the Chartered Institute of Management, is "getting the right products to the right customers at the right price in the right place and at the right time". For instance, products may be available at large warehouses, through agents, at retail outlets or on the internet.

The placement decision requires management skill in persuading retailers to stock a firm's products. Retailers have limited shelf and floor space and will only want to hold stocks of products that they know will sell well. Cinemas have a limited number of screens so will only purchase and show movies that will generate high sales. Window display space in estate agencies are very limited and the advertisements they choose to place need to get quick sales, yet must also support the image of the agency. In essence, marketing managers need to convince distributors and other intermediaries to sell their products over those of their rivals.

This Unit looks at the different ways of distribution (known as **distribution channels**), such as retailing or online placement of a firm's products. For example, consumers can use banking services via the internet (online banking) or they can purchase clothes at a retail outlet. The placement decision also addresses the geographical distribution (local, national or international) of products and the market segments (such as age, gender and socio-economic class) for different products.

TRADITIONAL CHANNELS OF DISTRIBUTION

Distribution, or **placement**, is one of the four key components of any marketing mix. Most products are not sold directly from the manufacturer to the final consumer (the end-user of the product). Coca-Cola, for instance, does not sell their mass produced products to the general public. This is partly because individual consumers would never purchase enough cans of Coke directly from the manufacturer to make it worthwhile for the producer. Instead, Coca-Cola's customers are the supermarkets and other retail businesses that buy from the manufacturer and then split the bulk to sell to consumers in much smaller units.

The **chain of distribution** refers to the means of getting a product to the customer. **Intermediation** is used in to facilitate this. Intermediaries are agents or firms that act as a middle person in the chain of distribution between the manufacturers and consumers of a product. The traditional chain of distribution consists of manufacturers, wholesalers and retailers. A long chain of distribution will tend to raise prices for the consumer since each intermediary adds a profit margin to their price (see Unit 4.4). In addition, the distribution process is lengthened, meaning that long distribution chains are not appropriate for perishable products. Figures 4.6a–c show the various methods of distributing products to the end-user. Marketing guru Dr. Philip Kotler defined distributional channels as 'levels':

- A **zero-level channel** does not have any intermediaries, i.e. the producer sells directly to the consumer. Examples include direct mail, e-commerce, telesales and mail order. Direct distribution can also take place in the service industry. Customers at the hotel, for instance, can book their own rooms or make restaurant reservations at the hotel.

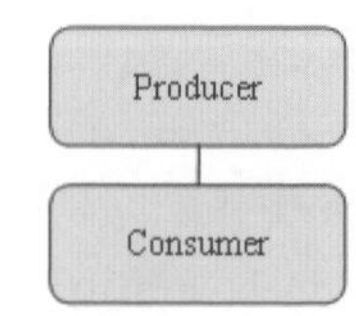

Figure 4.6a Zero-level channel chain

- A **one-level channel** has one intermediary, such as retailers or distributors being used to sell products to consumers. For instance, estate agents are used to sell residential and commercial property on behalf of their clients.

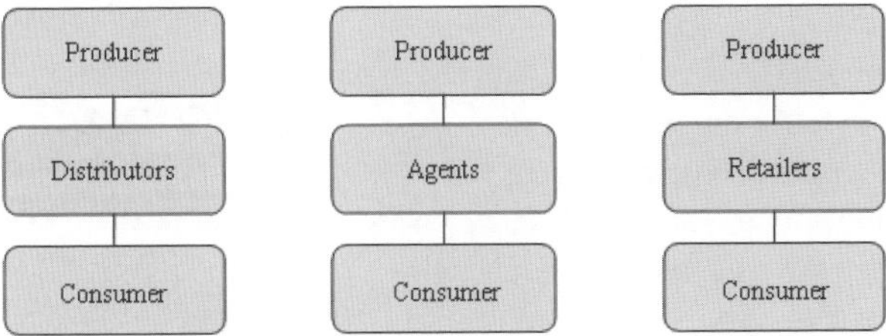

Figure 4.6b One-level channel chain

- A **two-level channel** has two intermediaries, such as the use of wholesalers and retailers to get products to consumers.

The main types of intermediaries are considered below.

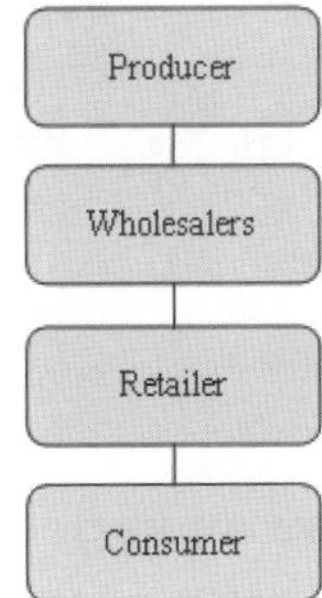

Figure 4.6c Two-level channel chain

Wholesalers

Wholesalers are businesses that purchase large quantities of products from a manufacturer and then separate or 'break' the bulk purchases into smaller units for resale to retailers. They act as the intermediary between producers and retailers. Examples of wholesalers that act on an international scale include Costco, Sam's Club (owned by Wal-Mart) and Makro. Using wholesalers has many benefits for producers and retailers:

- Wholesalers bear the costs of the storage, thereby freeing up space for retailers and manufacturers.
- By breaking bulk, wholesalers sell smaller batches of products to retailers thereby eliminating the need for retailers to purchase in huge quantities directly from a producer.
- The producer incurs lower transactions costs (such as invoicing and transportation) since the large wholesalers, rather than many smaller individual retailers, are the customers.
- Wholesalers deal with distribution issues and problems thus freeing up time for manufacturers to focus on production.

A key limitation of using wholesalers, however, is that the producer takes a risk in passing on the responsibility of marketing the firm's products. Wholesalers may not promote the manufacturer's products in a way that the producer might want, thereby ruining the firm's marketing efforts. In addition, some retailers (such as hypermarkets) do not use wholesalers as their suppliers, choosing instead to order directly from manufacturers. This will cut out the costs of using an intermediary to the detriment of the wholesaler.

Question 4.6.1

Costco Wholesale

Costco Wholesale Corporation is the world's largest wholesale chain. Its product range is huge, including items such as: electronics, appliances, beauty products, books, music and DVDs, CDs, clothing, flowers, fresh fruits and vegetables, groceries, beverages, wine, home and office furniture, fine jewellery, sporting goods, toys, tools, photo processing, automotive, home furnishings, optical, pharmacy and hearing aids – all under one roof!

The company was founded in 1983 and has grown to more than 510 locations throughout North and South America, Europe and the Pacific Rim. Costco boasts sales revenues in excess of $60 billion a year. Its clients are mainly small businesses and families. Costco usually does not carry multiple brands of the same product, thereby resulting in high volume sales for a single producer or supplier.

Source: adapted from www.costco.com

a Describe what is meant by a 'wholesaler'. *[2 marks]*

b Examine the benefits to both businesses and consumers of using wholesalers. *[6 marks]*

Distributors and agents

Distributors are independent and specialist businesses that trade in the products of only a few manufacturers. For example, car distributors will typically sell the products of one manufacturer, such as Honda or Ford, to the consumer.

Agents or **brokers** are negotiators who act on behalf of buyers and vendors (sellers) of a product. They are not usually employed by the producer but are used as an intermediary to help sell the vendor's products. They are experts in their particular markets and charge commission (a fee based on the level or percentage of the sales made) for their services. For instance, real estate agents earn commission on the sale of property made on behalf of their clients, whilst travel agents earn commission on the holidays and other leisure packages that they sell.

Agents will usually offer a range of products, perhaps from several different suppliers, for the consumer to choose from. Insurance brokers will often try to find the 'best deal' for their clients from the various insurance companies that they have access to. Financial advisors will also have a range of products, from savings accounts to high-risk stock market investments, that their clients can apply for.

Agents tend to rely on personal selling techniques, such as door-to-door selling, telesales, trade fairs and exhibitions. Personal selling methods allow the sales agent to demonstrate how the product they are selling actually works and to enable the consumers to ask questions relating to the product.

Retailers

Retailers are the sellers of products to the final consumer. They are often referred to as 'shops' in everyday language. They are an important role in the distribution of most products since retailers have the ability to reach large numbers of consumers, especially large multiple retailers that have a global reach. There are several types of retailers:

- **Independent retailers** are the small local vendors (sellers), often operating as a sole proprietorship. They usually sell a small range of products or are specialist outlets such as a hair salon.

- **Multiple retailers**, also known as **chain stores**, are retailers that have several or many outlets, such as McDonald's, The Body Shop and Mothercare. They have the advantage of being able to establish customer familiarity and brand loyalty.
- **Supermarkets** are retailers that mainly sell foodstuffs. They tend to buy their produce and other products directly from manufacturers, thereby missing out the wholesalers.
- **Hypermarkets**, also known as **superstores** are huge outlets that stock not just foodstuffs but other products such as consumer durables. Due to their enormous size, hypermarkets tend to be located in out of town areas where the space is available and where land costs are relatively low.
- **Department stores** are retail outlets that sell a large range of products, such as furniture, jewellery, kitchen equipment, clothing, toys and cosmetics. It is quite common that franchisors run different parts of the department store. Unlike hypermarkets that are built on one floor (storey), department stores are built over several floors and are located in busy retail districts.

Most retailers rely on stocking well-known brands to attract customers. They decide on the stock range based on sales (or profits) per square metre. For example, if Coca-Cola products generate more sales or profits than rival brands, then retailers will devote more shelf space to Coca-Cola goods.

Prime space, such as the entrance to a store or other busier areas of an outlet, will have higher demand (and hence a higher price). These areas tend to be reserved for the better selling products or for the client that can offer the highest rental price.

Most businesses will use a range of channels to distribute their products. This is known as a **multichannel distribution** strategy. An airline company, for example, will use travel agencies, the internet and airport outlets to sell their tickets. This will enable the business to reach a wider range of customers, located in different areas and in different market segments.

Question 4.6.2

7-Eleven

In November 2005, Japanese conglomerate Seven & I Holdings Co. completed the purchase of 7-Eleven Inc. (originally an American company). 7-Eleven is the world's largest chain of convenience stores, with over 35,000 stores throughout North and South America, Europe and SE Asia. Most of their stores are run as international franchises.

Source: www.7-eleven.com

a Outline the type of business that 7-Eleven might be described as. *[2 marks]*

b Examine the reasons for global conglomerates operating international franchises. *[6 marks]*

DIRECT MARKETING AS A CHANNEL OF DISTRIBUTION

Direct marketing refers to the direct selling of products to the consumer, i.e. marketing without the use of any intermediaries. Examples include: telesales, e-commerce, vending machines and direct mail. There are several generic advantages of direct marketing:

- Since there are no intermediaries, the business does not have to share so much of its profits.
- Firms can have direct control over their marketing, rather than relying on brokers, agents or retailers.

- Developments in e-commerce mean that this channel of distribution is growing in popularity among customers. They are also more willing to use the internet as a distribution channel due to improved online payment security.
- Direct marketing can also reach those potential customers who do not have easy access to retail outlets.
- Such methods are also usually cheaper than *above-the-line* techniques that use mass-marketing methods such as television and newspapers advertising (see Unit 4.6).

Telesales

Telesales, also known as **telemarketing**, refers to the use of telephone systems to sell products directly to potential customers. This can be done through automated voice or text messages that promote a firm's goods and services or by using sales people to call existing and potential customers. Telesales is commonly used by firms that have a database of existing clients, such as a satellite television company that calls their customers about a new special package. Insurance companies also call clients to remind them about renewing their insurance premiums.

One disadvantage of using telesales is that mass telephone calls can be very costly. In addition, a lot of customers do not like 'cold calls' where they are bombarded with telephone text and voice messages from marketers trying to make a sale.

E-commerce

E-commerce is the term used to describe trading via the internet (see Unit 4.8). The internet has had a profound impact on marketing for many businesses and is an increasingly suitable distribution channel for many products. More and more businesses now use dedicated websites to provide product information and payment facilities to entice customers from around the world to buy their products, from the convenience of their home or office. E-commerce is also an effective way to reduce the costs and risks of international marketing (see Unit 4.7).

Not all products, however, are suitable for online trading. Customers buying cars or jewellery will probably want to have direct contact with sales people who can deliver a more personalized service. For most retailers, such as supermarkets or motor vehicle dealers, the internet is not a replacement for traditional distribution activities but complements and supports the marketing strategies of the firms.

Online trading will become an increasingly important channel of distribution as more and more people have access to the internet. The growth in the number of credit cards issued around the world will only aid distributors and businesses that have an online presence.

Question 4.6.3

Sacha Cosmetics

The Barbados Investment and Development Corporation, the government's industrial development agency, sent out a message to the private sector to seize the full potential of the internet. The agency cited the power of the internet as the driving force for Sacha Cosmetics. The company has enjoyed the status of being the official cosmetics sponsor of events such as the Miss Universe and Miss USA Pageants and this has helped it to become a **global brand**. In addition, due to the company's **online presence**, American retail giant Wal-Mart now carries full displays of the Trinidadian make-up line in many of its stores.

a Define the terms **global brand** and **online presence**. *[4 marks]*

b Discuss the statement that the internet is an effective distribution channel for propelling businesses forward. *[8 marks]*

Direct mail

Direct mail involves a business sending promotional material via the mail system to entice customers to buy a firm's products. Businesses that have a database of customers, such as banks, tend to use this channel of distribution. Locally run restaurants and fast-food outlets also distribute their menus to nearby residents and offer a home delivery service to entice customers.

One benefit of using direct mail is that it can provide a personalized communication service since correspondence is directly addressed to the potential customer. This can help to improve sales since people are more likely to take notice of mail that is individualized. Furthermore, when a firm's customer base is widely distributed around the world it can still be targeted at relatively low costs. Finally, detailed information aimed at different market segments can also be used in an attempt to boost sales.

However, a major limitation of direct mail is that people tend to regard much of the correspondence as junk mail and therefore there is a low response rate, i.e. people do not bother reading the mail. In addition, the information in a database used to contact customers often goes out of date. For example, when people move, they do not necessarily inform the business of this, resulting in a large amount of mail getting sent to the wrong (old) address.

Vending machines

Vending machines are specialist machines that stock products such as cigarettes, drinks and snacks. Due to their compact size, they can be placed almost anywhere (such as an office, recreation centre, school or airport). Modern vending machines allow customers to pay by a range of methods such as cash, credit cards and debit cards, thereby enhancing their convenience. One key advantage of vending machines is that running and maintenance costs are minimal. For example, sales people are not needed to sell the products.

However, vending machines can be prone to vandalism. In addition, any mechanical failure will halt sales. Finally, due to the low capacity of any single vending machine, only a small range of products can be sold via this channel.

CHOOSING AN APPROPRIATE DISTRIBUTION STRATEGY

An efficient and cost-effective distribution strategy enables a business to make products conveniently available to potential consumers. This will therefore raise the likelihood of customers purchasing the products. There are several factors that can affect the distribution decision of a business. These issues include:

- *Cost and benefits* – Direct selling, without the use of intermediaries, will help to reduce the costs of distribution. However, retailers and distributors may have better access to customers. Hence, businesses will need to weigh up the costs and benefits of using intermediaries. In addition, firms will need to consider the relative costs and benefits of different transportation methods (road, rail, air or sea).
- *Product* – Some products, such as perishables, cannot be distributed through long chains of distribution, e.g. fresh flowers and fresh meat. Hence, shorter distribution channels will be necessary. By contrast, *fast-moving consumer goods* (see Unit 4.3) need to be sold in large volumes, so the use of wholesalers and retailers would be appropriate. Many products can now be sold directly through the internet, such as books, music CDs, DVD movies, clothes, toys and overseas holidays.

- *Market* – Small local niche markets can be catered for by the supplier without the use of intermediaries. By contrast, large and dispersed markets will usually require the services offered by intermediaries.
- *Time* – Whilst e-commerce can be a convenient channel of distribution, there is a time lag between paying for the product and receiving it. Hence, this method may not be desirable for purchasing items that require urgent delivery. In such instances, the most direct channel of distribution would be more suitable.
- *Legal constraints* – Government rules and regulations can prohibit the use of certain distribution channels. For example, many countries impose anti-gambling laws (including online gaming). Macau, renowned for its gambling business, is a casino magnet since many neighbouring countries such as Hong Kong, Singapore and Malaysia have strict gambling laws. Similarly, retailers and restaurants need special licences in order to sell alcohol on their premises. Hence, legal dimensions will affect the distribution decision.

In reality, there is a need for an integrated distribution strategy. For example, large supermarkets can no longer rely on customers visiting their outlets in order to maintain market share. The internet has meant that supermarkets now offer customers the added choice of online shopping.

Exam Tip!

Candidates often define the term *channels of distribution* as various methods of transport. This is wrong. The channels of distribution refer to the *intermediaries* that are used to get the product to the consumer, such as through wholesalers or distributors. It does not mean how products are transported (road, rail, sea or air) to consumers.

Question 4.6.4

Dell and Wal-Mart

Dell Inc. was founded in 1984 by Michael Dell, the company's Chief Executive Officer. In 2007, the computer giant announced plans to start selling its personal computers through Wal-Mart, another huge American company. Wal-Mart, renowned for its low prices, started selling Dell computers in its Wal-Mart and Sam's Club stores in the USA, Canada and Puerto Rico.

The move was a major shift for Dell, which had traditionally sold its products directly to the consumer, cutting out the need for **intermediaries**. The company hoped the strategy would boost Dell's competitiveness and market share against its main rivals Hewlett–Packard and Lenovo.

a Define the term **intermediaries**. *[2 marks]*

b Explain two advantages to Wal-Mart in establishing a deal with Dell Inc. *[4 marks]*

c Evaluate Dell's decision to use intermediation to broaden its channel of distribution. *[8 marks]*

HIGHER LEVEL EXTENSION: SUPPLY CHAIN MANAGEMENT

Supply chain management (SCM), also known as **logistics**, is the art of managing and controlling the sequence of activities from the production of a good or service to it being delivered to the end customer. Businesses are increasingly outsourcing distribution and transportation to other organizations that can provide such services more cost effectively. This allows the business to benefit from greater flexibility. Supply chains must be efficient and cost effective in order for the business to be profitable.

SCM will usually involve several key functions:

- Stock control – Managers must plan, implement and monitor the movement and storage of all stocks (raw materials, work-in-progress and finished goods) from its source to the point of consumption.
- Quality control – All suppliers in the supply chain need to ensure there is quality and value added in order for the product to be bought by the end customer. This will then generate profit for all firms in the supply chain.
- Supplier networks – There is a need for coordination and collaboration with suppliers from the primary stage of production to the product being distributed to the consumer. The decision will need to be made regarding which suppliers or intermediaries to use. Collaboration between the partners in the supply chain can facilitate improvements in logistics, thereby helping to reduce costs without compromising overall quality.
- Transportation (distribution) networks – The most cost-effective methods of distributing products to customers must be investigated. This will depend on issues such as the frequency, speed and reliability of different transportation systems. Large businesses are able to provide their own distribution networks, whereas smaller organizations may need to use subcontractors and couriers.

Reasons for using supply chain management

- Long supply chains provide opportunities for things to go wrong. Hence, effective SCM can prevent mistakes that would otherwise adversely affect the business.
- SCM helps to ensure that the appropriate supply of stocks is produced to meet the level of demand. Too much supply will generate stock accumulation and its associated costs, whilst a lack of stock will cause delays to the rest of the supply chain. SCM should help to identify and hence prevent such bottlenecks.
- SCM is a tool for achieving *lean production* (a system based on minimal input for maximum output). Effective SCM will help an organization to identify areas of wastage and inefficiencies. Hence, there should be both time and cost savings.

All suppliers in the supply chain are *interdependent*. For example, the retailer is dependent on the manufacturer, who in turn depends on its suppliers of components and raw materials. However, suppliers of raw materials rely on consumer demand in the tertiary sector. So, for example, there is very little need to harvest cocoa if there is no need to produce chocolates because of a lack of consumer demand for them. Hence, it is in the best interest of all firms in the supply chain to work collaboratively for their mutual benefits.

However, SCM has its potential problems and limitations:

- With increased globalization, international sourcing becomes more complex. There are more partners, perhaps from various parts of the world, in the supply chain to deal with. Time lags and potential conflicts can delay getting the right products to the right customers in a cost-effective way.
- Greater interdependence also means that a single problem in the supply chain can cause major disruptions. The greater need for partners to share information and to collaborate also requires building trust among the partners. This will necessitate sufficient time and resources.

HIGHER LEVEL

Question 4.6.5

Carrefour

Carrefour is a French hypermarket chain that operates on a global scale. It is the second largest retailer in the world, after America's Wal-Mart, with annual sales in the region of €75 billion ($100 billion). The vast amount of products sold in its stores (over 15,000 of them) means that the company must have effective management of its supply chain. Carrefour's brand strategy is simple: it places emphasis on price, complemented by its constant pursuit of improvement in services for the consumer.

Source: adapted from Carrefour website (www.carrefour.com)

a Define what is meant by 'supply chain management'. *[2 marks]*

b Examine how Carrefour can increase the efficiency of its supply chain. *[6 marks]*

PLACE AND BUSINESS STRATEGY

Place is concerned with how businesses can ensure that their products reach both current and potential consumers. Marketing managers must deal with two key placement issues: the best channels of distribution to use in order to get the firm's products to the consumer and how it will ensure that intermediaries will want to stock the firm's products.

In choosing a channel of distribution (the intermediaries), a firm will have to decide on the type of distribution that is most suitable:

- *Intensive distribution* – Used when the firm wishes to distribute mass-produced products, such as fast moving consumer goods (FMCGs) through as many channels as possible
- *Selective distribution* – The usual practice whereby the firm will deliberately choose suitable intermediaries to resell and stock the firm's products
- *Exclusive distribution* – The least commonly used method whereby only specially chosen intermediaries are given the exclusive right to sell the firm's products

Some businesses, such as Heinz and Coca-Cola, will aim to maximize the number of outlets that sell their products. This will help to increase their sales and profits. However, the marketing people at other businesses, such as Tiffany & Co and Rolls-Royce, do not aim to have their products distributed to a maximum number of outlets throughout the country; to do so would remove the exclusivity of their brands.

One obvious but relatively expensive method to ensure that outlets stock a firm's products is for the firm to open its own store. Nike and Adidas are two examples of businesses that use this approach. Alternatively, the firm can use *franchise agreements* (see Unit 1.7) which allow other certified people to run the stores under the name of the business. Most car manufacturers, such as Honda and BMW, use franchised dealerships to help sell their cars. The manufacturers grant permission to the franchisor to use their name in order to gain brand recognition and to reassure customers (since they are more familiar with the manufacturer's brands).

Alternatively, **vertical integration** (see Unit 1.7) can be used. This is a growth strategy that unifies the supplier, producer, wholesalers and retailers. This may arise because a manufacturer owns its own retail outlets (forward vertical integration) and/or owns its suppliers (backward vertical integration). Being vertically integrated allows a business to have more direct control over its supply chain and distribution channels. Hence, the business is able to retain control of all its marketing activities.

Vertical integration is not a realistic possibility for most businesses. This means that the majority of firms will need to compete for floor or shelf space in retail outlets. The producer needs to convince the retailer to stock its products rather than give preference to its rivals. This is usually decided on a predetermined criterion, such as sales or profits per square metre of retail space. Hence, placement can be a major barrier to entry for new and smaller firms. Retailers need an incentive to stock less established products, such as a unique selling point or a truly innovative product.

Branding (see Unit 4.3) is another strategy that businesses use to gain access to different markets. If a manufacturer has a highly regarded brand or is the market leader, they are more likely to benefit from having preferential distribution channels. This is because distributors and other outlets are more likely to stock and sell the manufacturer's products in order to maximize their own sales and profits.

Placement has a new dimension when it comes to international trade. Globalization of markets (see Unit 1.9) has been fuelled by the increasing number of businesses that sell their products in overseas markets (known as **exporting**). However, exporting presents further complications in the placement decision because of various external constraints, such as:

- Fluctuating exchanges rates – The changing nature of exchange rates can make products cheaper (in which case export sales are likely to rise) but can also lead to higher export prices (in which case, demand will most probably fall).
- Government intervention – Overseas governments may place trade barriers and legal constraints on exported products (see Unit 1.5). Such intervention aims to make it more difficult and/or more costly to distribute the product.
- Language barriers – Such constraints may cause communication problems with overseas buyers.
- Cultural differences – Diversity in cultural norms might mean that some products are not suited to certain regions or countries, such as pork products being sold in Muslim countries.

Finally, many businesses have been able to benefit from e-commerce as a channel of distribution. Firms that have been able to exploit internet technologies as a method of distribution have seen their costs fall significantly. Unit 4.8 covers the role of e-commerce in the marketing mix in more detail.

REVIEW QUESTIONS 4.6

1. What is meant by 'placement' in the marketing mix?
2. What are 'distribution channels'?
3. What are the three traditional channels of distribution according to Dr. Philip Kotler?
4. Explain the difference between wholesalers and retailers.
5. What are the benefits of using distributors and agents?
6. What is a 'multichannel distribution strategy'?
7. Explain the meaning of 'telemarketing'.
8. How has e-commerce benefited some businesses in terms of their placement decision?
9. State two advantages and two disadvantages of using direct mail.
10. What are the factors that affect the overall choice of distribution channels?

Higher Level extension

11 What is meant by 'supply chain management' and what does it involve?

12 Outline two benefits and two limitations of supply chain management.

Agents, or **brokers**, are negotiators who help to sell the vendor's products, such as real estate agents selling residential property on behalf of their clients.

Channels of distribution are the ways that a product gets from the manufacturer to the consumer. Examples include wholesalers, agents, retailers, e-commerce and vending machines.

Direct mail refers to promotional material sent directly to people's homes or place of work.

Direct marketing refers to any promotional activity that involves making direct contact with existing and potential customers, such as door-to-door selling, personal selling and direct mail.

Distribution is the fourth 'P' in the marketing mix, also known as **placement**, and refers to the process of getting products to customers at the right time and place in the most cost-effective way.

Distributors are independent businesses that act as intermediaries by specializing in the trade of products made by certain manufacturers.

Intermediaries are agents or firms that act as a middle person in the chain of distribution between the producer and consumers of a product. Examples include retailers, distributors and agents.

Supply chain management (SCM) is the art of managing and controlling the sequence of activities from the production of a good or service to its delivery to the end customer, in a cost-effective way.

Telesales, also known as **telemarketing**, refers to the use of telephone systems (audio and text messaging) to sell products directly to potential customers.

Retailers are the sellers of products to the general public (i.e. consumers) that operate in outlets.

Wholesalers are businesses that purchase large quantities of products from a manufacturer and then separate or 'break' the bulk purchases into smaller units for resale to retailers.

International Marketing

UNIT 4.7

Advertising is the mother of trade.

Japanese proverb

Key topics

- International marketing and global marketing
- Benefits of international marketing
- Entry into international markets
- Issues relating to international marketing

INTRODUCTION

Nokia, the world's largest mobile phone producer, generates around 99% of its sales revenues from outside Finland, its home country. **International marketing** refers to the marketing of a firm's products in foreign countries. International marketing is more difficult for businesses because they need to deal with external factors and constraints such as differences in political systems, legislation and cultures. In addition, international markets will probably need an amended marketing mix to suit the local market. A lack of comprehension of different cultures can prove troublesome for even large businesses. In 2006, Wal-Mart, the world's largest retailer, had to sell its stores in Germany to local rival Metro when it discovered that its American practices (such as helping customers to pack their bags at the supermarket) were unsuccessful and did not suit the German culture.

Global marketing, an extension of international marketing, refers to selling the same product using the same marketing approach throughout the world. Global brands such as McDonald's, Nike and Coca-Cola use this method. By contrast, international marketing refers to marketing strategies across national boundaries, i.e. marketing that is tailored to suit different countries.

Globalization and the aggressive growth strategies of large multinationals have promoted the increased use of international marketing strategies. Due to the growing presence of foreign competitors, businesses are finding it increasingly important to consider the opportunities and threats of international marketing.

ENTRY INTO INTERNATIONAL MARKETS

Once a business has decided to market its products overseas, there are various strategies that it can use. These strategies include internal methods (such as exporting, direct investment and e-commerce) and external methods (such as joint ventures, strategic alliances, franchising, mergers and acquisitions – all of which are covered in Unit 1.7).

- **Exporting** – Here, the business operating in the domestic country sells its products directly to an overseas buyer. The main advantage of this method is that it eliminates the need to set up a business (with its associated costs and risks).
- **Direct investment** – This refers to a business setting up production and/or distribution facilities in foreign countries. Having a wider distribution channel gets over the problem of exporting (which limits the potential number of foreign buyers). Honda, Toyota and Nissan all have manufacturing plants in the UK, for example. This allows the Japanese car producers to gain access to the huge market in the European Union. BMW's manufacturing plant in Chennai (India's fourth largest city) helps the German firm to avoid a 60% import tax on its cars. However, the main drawback of direct investment is the high cost of the investment.
- **E-commerce** – This is trading via the internet (see Unit 4.8). E-commerce is an effective way of reducing the costs and risks of international marketing. Many online retailers, such as Amazon.com and eBay, have gained access to foreign markets without having to physically set up retail stores.
- **Joint ventures** – This occurs when two or more companies invest in a shared business project, pooling their resources to form a separate business. The companies retain their separate legal identities but share the risks and returns from the joint venture. Many foreign firms have formed joint ventures with Chinese and Indian companies to gain access to these growing markets. For example, in 2007 Exxon formed a joint venture with China's Sinopec and Saudi Aramco (the largest supplier of oil to China) in a $5 billion deal. The project means the three firms being involved in oil supply, refinery and retail in China.

- **Strategic alliances** – These are similar to joint ventures in that several businesses pool their human, capital and financial resources in a shared project. However, they do not form a new business with a separate legal identity. Again, strategic alliances with foreign firms can allow a business to gain access to overseas markets. For example, Nissan (Japan's second largest car manufacturer) and Renault (a leading French vehicles producer) formed an alliance in 1999, giving both firms access to each others markets. The alliance places the companies fourth in global sales (after Toyota, GM and Ford) with approximately 10% of the world market share.
- **Franchising** – This involves a business allowing others to trade under its name in return for a fee and a share of the profits (see Unit 1.7). McDonald's, KFC, Pizza Hut and Burger King have all used this growth strategy to market their products overseas. Alternatively, businesses may use **licensing** to enter overseas markets whereby another firm buys the right to produce the goods of the business. Nike licenses the production of their sports shoes and sportswear to businesses in Indonesia; Disney licenses the production of their soft toys and other merchandise to businesses in Vietnam.
- **Mergers** – These take place when two businesses agree to integrate as a single organization. Merging with a foreign company can help businesses to gain access to overseas markets. For example, Mittal Steel Company (owned by the UK's richest man, Lakshmi Mittal) and Luxembourg's Arcelor merged in 2006 to form Arcelor-Mittal, the world's largest steel company.
- **Acquisitions** – Acquisitions, also known as **takeovers**, occur when one business buys out another by purchasing a majority stake in the target company. British mobile phone giant Vodafone's acquisition of India's mobile operator Essar in 2007 meant that it gained access to the huge potential market in the world's second most populous country.

Question 4.7.1

Colgate–Palmolive

Colgate–Palmolive is an American multinational that produces personal hygiene products (such as toothpaste and soaps) and cleaning products (such as detergents). The company has a **global marketing presence** across the globe, with operations in countries as varied as the USA and Vietnam. The company's growth has been driven by strong sales of its internationally recognized brands of toothpaste and other household products.

a Describe what it means if a firm has a **global marketing presence**. *[2 marks]*

b Explain, in marketing terms, what type of product Colgate toothpaste might be described as. *[2 marks]*

c To what extent do you feel that the name of a product, such as Colgate, is important for successful international marketing? *[6 marks]*

OPPORTUNITIES AND BENEFITS OF INTERNATIONAL MARKETING

Businesses may aim to market their products to an international audience for several reasons:

- **Capture a wider customer base** – The size of the market can be enlarged by marketing products to overseas buyers. This should, other things being equal, lead to greater market share for the business.
- **Economies of scale** – By operating on a larger scale, a business is likely to benefit from cost savings known as economies of scale (see Unit 1.7). These cost-reducing benefits can enable growing firms to reduce their prices, thereby giving them a price advantage.

- **Increase brand recognition** – Having a standardized marketing strategy across the world (such as using identical packaging and advertising in many different countries) not only reduces average costs of production, but can also lead to international recognition of a brand. This may lead to improved brand loyalty and sales.
- **Spread risks** – By operating in various countries, a business is less exposed to the risks in one particular country (such as a recession or changes in fashion).
- **Extend the product life cycle** – A firm may find that the domestic market for its product is saturated or in decline. By marketing the product overseas, the firm can expand its life cycle to generate higher revenues. Mobile phone companies use this strategy when selling older models of their phones in less affluent countries.
- **Gain more profit** – Ultimately, all the reasons above for international marketing act to generate more profits for the business. Overseas markets provide an extra source of customers and in some cases can be quite lucrative.

ISSUES AND PROBLEMS IN ENTERING INTERNATIONAL MARKETS

The cultural, legal, political, social and economic issues surrounding international marketing can pose both opportunities and threats to businesses.

Cultural issues

Successful marketing overseas can generate larger profits for an organization. **Cultural exports** refer to the commercial transfer of ideas and values from one country to another. Both cultural goods and services can be exported, such as American fast food or Hollywood movies. Other examples of cultural exports include drive-through outlets (first introduced in the USA in 1975), pop music, satellite television and sports apparel. Even the sales of Harry Potter books, for example, have proven to be one of Britain's most successful exports helping to make J.K. Rowling the world's first author to earn US$1 billion. Western traditions of celebrating events such as St. Valentine's Day and Halloween have also spread throughout the world, bringing huge commercial opportunities for businesses. Due to freer international trade and the growth in globalization (see Unit 1.9), trade in cultural exports has grown exponentially.

However, in their pursuit of selling more cultural exports or mainstream exports, a business must consider the cultural differences between different countries and regions of the world. For instance, marketers need to consider **local preferences** when formulating their international marketing strategies. In China, the menus in McDonald's restaurants rely more heavily on chicken than in other international markets. This reflects the local preference for poultry over typical menus based on the hamburger. The cultural difference has also meant that KFC, which specializes in chicken fast food products, has many more branches than McDonald's in China.

Language is embedded in culture. Although English is the official language of business in many parts of the world, ignorance of culture and language can have detrimental effects on a business. Many marketing mistakes, for example, have been made due to ignorance of cultural and language issues (see Box 4.7a).

Question 4.7.2

Viya Crab Products Company

Viya Crab Products Company is a Thai producer of several varieties of canned crab meat. Viya has a well-established local market, with healthy export earnings from various countries in SE Asia. However, the business has bigger plans to establish its products in the markets of Europe and the USA.

a Why might ready-to-eat canned crab meat be classed as a 'cultural export'? *[2 marks]*

b Discuss the role of international marketing to a business such as Viya Crab Products Co. *[6 marks]*

Box 4.7a Language, culture and marketing misjudgements

- Charlottetown Sewer and Water Department (Nova Scotia, Canada) repositioned their brand as 'AquaPoo'...
- In Sydney, Australia, a clothes retailer goes by the name of 'Shagwell Clothing'...
- In Sweden, two popular candy bar brands are 'Plopp' and 'Skum'... In China, a well-known brand of chocolate is named 'Swine'...
- Car manufacturers are renowned for getting names wrong. Roll–Royce produced a model that they named 'Silver Mist'. The word 'mist' is 'dung' in German. Ford had a similar problem in selling their 'Pinto' in Brazil, where pinto is slang for 'small male genitals'. Vauxhall (Opel) was yet another motor company that faced cultural problems with its small car, the 'Nova' – Spanish for 'does not go'. Toyota's MR2 in French means 'dung'. Shanghai Automotive came up with the name 'Roewe' for its range of cars to symbolize power, honour and the lion; but the English pronunciation is 'rong wei' or 'wrong way'...
- In SE Asia, a top-selling consumer electronics brand is Japan's 'Top Con'...
- Would you try these drinks: 'Pipi' (Yugoslavian orangeade), 'Pocari Sweat' (Japanese sports drink) or 'Zit' (Greek soft drink)?
- KFC's slogan 'We do chicken right' is literally translated as 'It is correct to be a prostitute' in Chinese...

Ethics is another culture-related issue that can present problems for international marketing. What is acceptable in one country may not be acceptable in another. In modern societies, the employment of children is likely to be illegal. In other countries, the use of child labour is seen as vital to their economic development. For religious reasons, Muslim women must be dressed in a conservative way, even whilst on holiday, but the men are free to dress as casually as they see fit. Smoking is allowed to be heavily advertised in some parts of the world whilst it is banned in other parts. Pester power marketing techniques (see Unit 4.5) aimed at young children are banned in the European Union but not in many other parts of the world.

A final cultural issue that businesses must consider when marketing overseas is the differences in **business etiquette**. Business etiquette is the mannerisms and customs by which business is conducted in different countries. An awareness and understanding of international business etiquette and cultural factors have become critical elements required for all global traders. A lack of awareness of the different ways in which business is conducted throughout different parts of the world is the same as a lack of table manners when attending a social gathering. The ignorant person will be frowned upon as their actions can be offensive (see Box 4.7b for examples). In business, this could mean firms fail to secure deals or contracts.

The three stage approach to dealing with international business etiquette is:

1 Research the country, its people and culture.
2 Consider the impact of the above findings on the businesses in question.
3 Implement a strategy to optimize the relationship with overseas clients.

Box 4.7b International business etiquette

Numbers – In most cultures, there is some association of luck (or bad luck) with numbers. In some western societies, for example, the number 13 is an unlucky number. In many Asian countries, such as China, Taiwan and Japan, the number 4 is the unlucky number (as the pronunciation of '4' sounds like the word for 'death'). Many multinational hotels are aware of this and do not have a 13th floor or a 4th floor (although they physically exist, of course).

Spoken language – Although English is the most widely spoken business language in the world, there are still subtle differences which can lead to communication problems. For example, Australians use the term 'runners' whereas the British use 'trainers'; they use 'thongs' whereas British use 'flip flops'. The British certainly wouldn't expect to walk out on the beach with thongs on their feet! The Japanese also prefer not to use the word 'no'. Confusingly for many, they may simply respond with a 'yes' but in fact clearly mean 'no'! Understanding this fact can be critical in a business negotiation.

Greetings – First impressions count. This does not just refer to physical appearance but also *how* you greet your employees, suppliers, clients and other key stakeholders. In the UK and USA it is the norm to offer a firm handshake upon greeting and leaving a business meeting. The Chinese language does not have an actual word for 'Hello', so it may seem odd that you are not greeted in the same way as expected in other cultures.

Physical contact – It is not generally accepted that a man should shake the hand of an Orthodox Jewish woman. This is a religious observation that should be respected. Many Europeans like to kiss each other on the cheek – once in some countries, twice in others or three times or more for others still! In Japan and Korea, open displays of affection are frown upon and physical contact with the opposite sex in public is regarded as highly inappropriate.

Dress code – In countries such as Hong Kong, Singapore and Malaysia, the weather can be incredibly hot and with humidity levels above 90%. Hence, business dress in these countries is often relatively casual. Suit jackets are not required. In Portugal, long-sleeved shirts and blouses are important; only expatriates in Portugal wear short-sleeved shirts. Women in Japan should not wear trousers in a business situation as the locals generally find this to be offensive.

Body language – What you *do* is often more important than what you *say*. Research has shown that words account for only 7% of the messages communicated by a person whereas the remaining 93% is non-verbal. In India, for example, placing your hands on your hips is seen as an angry and aggressive posture; whistling is rude; and winking may be taken as either an insult or a sexual proposition. In Japan, talking using your hands is not done and is regarded as distracting. Pointing at people is also unacceptable.

Legal issues

Entry into international markets can also be a problem due to different **legal systems**. Some countries will have very strict laws on what can and cannot be advertised. For example, it is not acceptable to advertise cigarettes on television in many parts of the world, such as in China and the UK. Advertising is largely prohibited in Cuba, so even for large multinationals this would present a major barrier to entering the country.

Copyright and patent legislation must be adhered to. This will cover issues such as brand names, slogans, trademarks, inventions and processes already assigned to other businesses. Marketers will obviously need to take this factor into consideration when devising their overseas marketing campaigns.

Pricing decisions must take account of any regulation on market power. In the UK any firm with at least 25% market share is classed as a **monopoly**. Anti-competitive legislation in the EU can prevent monopolies from raising prices to exploit customers. In fact, anti-competitive practices (also known as **restrictive trade practices**) can mean that the government breaks up the monopoly to protect the interest of consumers.

Differences in **consumer protection laws** must also be observed. Many countries have their own code of conduct on advertising and packaging information and these must be respected. The British Advertising Standards Authority, for example, states that all advertisements must be decent, truthful and accurate. In most European Union countries, there are legally binding controls over the use of advertisements aimed directly at children. In Sweden it is illegal to advertise products to children under the age of twelve.

Political issues

Businesses that market their products overseas need to take into consideration the political system abroad. Countries that have a stable political climate tend to be less risky and more receptive of foreign businesses selling products in their territory. There are few political barriers to a marketer wishing to sell in countries like Singapore or Hong Kong; but there are huge political hurdles to deal with if companies wish to market their products in countries such as Afghanistan or North Korea.

In addition, governments can have a huge impact on the economics of international trade. In order to protect domestic industries from foreign competition, governments may set up **international trade barriers**. Examples of such protectionist measures include:

- **Quotas** – Quantitative restrictions on imported goods (limits the number of foreign products entering the country)
- **Tariffs** – Import taxes (increases the price of foreign products and raises government tax revenues)
- **Embargoes** – Bans on certain products entering a country (due to health and safety reasons or political conflict)
- **Administrative barriers** – Barriers such as safety regulations, licences and employment visas (thereby making entry much more difficult)
- **Subsidies** – Financial assistance given to local firms to lower their costs of production (hence giving them a comparative cost advantage over foreign rivals)

Question **4.7.3**

Pakistan International Airlines

Pakistan International Airlines Corporation (PIAC) is the national air carrier of Pakistan. In 2007, the 27 member states of the European Union raised concerns over the age and poor maintenance of PIAC's 48-plane fleet flying into Europe. Subsequently, the EU imposed a ban on 41 of the 48 planes due to health and safety concerns. PIAC contested the ban, claiming that the EU's actions were discriminatory and unjustified.

a The European Union is a regional trading bloc. Explain what this means. *[2 marks]*

b Examine the role of corporate image for the success of PIAC in international markets. *[7 marks]*

Social and demographic issues

Different **socio-economic** and **demographic conditions** in overseas markets mean that marketers must reconsider their marketing mix. When exporting to less affluent countries, the product and price may differ from those in more prosperous areas. Japan does not cater well for the overseas customer in Japan (expatriates and tourists) as only 1% of its population are foreigners. By contrast, in highly multicultural societies such as Malaysia, marketing caters for a much wider audience, with the same advertisements in Malay, Chinese and Indian languages. With growing prosperity and income, marketers and businesses can target different customers with different products. China's phenomenal growth meant that supercar manufacturer Lamborghini opened its first showroom in China in 2006. Japan and Italy have the world's oldest average age of population so marketers will take a different approach to pricing, product, place and promotion when targeting these people than if they were marketing to countries with younger populations.

Pressure groups (see Unit 1.4) concerned about the impacts of business activity on society can also present problems for marketers hoping to gain a foothold in foreign markets. Hong Kong Disneyland faced many problems from animal activist groups when it first opened in September 2005, such as protests over its menus which included sharks fin soup. People for the Ethical Treatment of Animals (PETA) is the world's largest animal rights group and has presented many problems for companies such as McDonald's, KFC and Procter & Gamble.

Economic issues

A key economic argument for more and freer **international trade** is that it enables people to have a greater choice of products at more competitive prices. Another argument is that international trade allows citizens to have access to products that would otherwise be unavailable in their own country. This is because domestic producers cannot supply these products in a cost-effective manner, such as growing tropical fruits in cold countries. These arguments can present a major opportunity for large multinationals in their international marketing.

However, international marketing of products also increases the degree of competition in the marketplace. Transportation costs, exchange rate fluctuations, interest rates and communication costs are further economic issues that need to be considered when marketing products overseas.

Question 4.7.4

Tesco

Tesco is the UK's largest retailer, with annual sales in excess of £46 billion ($90 billion). Although the company has entered several international markets, such as France and South Korea, the vast majority of its sales still come from within the UK. Tesco finally arrived in the USA in 2007, but the American market remains almost untouched.

- **a** Explain how American customers might benefit from the arrival of Tesco in the USA. *[4 marks]*
- **b** Evaluate the opportunities and threats to Tesco of their overseas expansion plans. *[8 marks]*

INTERNATIONAL MARKETING AND BUSINESS STRATEGY

Businesses that are able to adopt global marketing strategies benefit from being able to market a single product in exactly the same way throughout the world. After all, having to adapt products to suit local preferences or cultures can be a costly exercise. The dilemma facing managers is that of trying to gain economies of scale by using a single global strategy yet still cater for local or regional likings and tastes. While it is possible for large multinationals such as Coca-Cola and McDonald's to make the odd costly mistake, smaller companies cannot afford to do so. Smaller firms therefore need to ensure that their international marketing strategy is very carefully researched and planned since failure overseas can be fatal to the business.

Branding (see Unit 4.3) can be a very powerful tool in marketing a product overseas. Scientists, psychologists and economists have all produced evidence to show that branding can have a huge impact on the buying decisions made by consumers. It is very common for consumers to make their purchasing decisions based on the perception of a brand rather than the qualities of the actual product. To extend the success overseas requires careful market research and planning. A successful brand in one part of the world does not mean that the same formula will work in other parts of the globe. Matt Haig, author of *Brand Failures*, found that highly successful brands can lose their value overnight because customer perception of products and brands can be fragile.

It is also important that managers remember not to assume that people overseas behave in the same way that they are personally accustomed to. David Ogilvy, a world renowned advertising executive, argues that firms trying to market their products to different people should use local language, i.e. the language in which these people think. International business etiquette is particularly important when doing business in other people's territory. The key point is that an awareness and understanding of the business context, the people involved and ethics of different cultures should facilitate a more successful business deal.

It is clear that today's business environment is much more global than ever before. Communication, whether via video-conferencing, telephones, emails or face to face meetings, can take place from anywhere on the planet. With developments in ICT there are huge opportunities to interact with clients on an international level. However, awareness and understanding of international etiquette and culture become increasingly important. Not doing your research can be very costly as it only takes one small slip-up, such as using first names inappropriately or dressing unsuitably, to lose a business contract (see Box 4.7b on page 592). Like much of business, there is no single rule that applies to all situations, so managers need to do their homework before meeting or communicating with their international clients.

As the world continues to become globalized at an increasing pace, perhaps the most important element of success for marketers with an international outlook may be the appreciation and respect for cultural differences and cultural diversity. It is useful to remember the saying "When in Rome, do as the Romans do" which is used to advise people to adapt to different cultures and etiquette when visiting other countries. Hence, the use of joint ventures and strategic alliances may prove highly practical. An understanding and awareness of international business etiquette can ultimately give an organization a competitive advantage in an ever-competitive business world.

REVIEW QUESTIONS 4.7

1. What is the difference between 'international' and 'global' marketing?
2. Explain why international marketing can be an important issue to businesses.
3. How can international marketing help a business to spread its risks?
4. Outline the various internal and external growth methods that can be used to market products overseas.
5. What is meant by 'international business etiquette' and why is the concept important to global businesses?

Business etiquette refers to the manner, social and cultural context in which business is conducted. International etiquette differs from one country to another so it is important for marketers to be aware of the different protocols that exist.

Direct investment refers to a business setting up production and/or distribution facilities in foreign countries.

Exporting is the practice of selling domestically produced goods and/or services to overseas buyers to gain access to larger international markets.

Global marketing refers to the marketing of a product by using the same marketing strategy in various countries. Businesses that are able to do this can gain from marketing economies of scale.

International marketing is the marketing of a firm's products in foreign countries.

E-commerce

UNIT 4.8

Unless in communicating with it one says exactly what one means, trouble is bound to result.

Alan Turing (1912–1954),
British mathematician and computer scientist

Key topics

- Business-to-business (B2B)
- Business-to-consumer (B2C)
- Costs and benefits of e-commerce to firms and consumers
- E-commerce and the marketing mix

INTRODUCTION

This Unit looks at the growing importance of e-commerce for businesses. E-commerce (electronic commerce) is the trading of goods and services via the internet. It has come a very long way since its humble beginnings in August 1991. Since then, the internet has become an increasingly important method of business activity as e-commerce allows businesses to operate 24 hours a day, with an international reach. E-commerce mainly takes place via the use of a computer linked to the internet. Mobile telephones and electronic personal organizers present further opportunities for online trading.

Some examples of e-markets include:

- Financial services such as banking, foreign exchange and share trading can all be transacted online.
- Utility services (gas, electricity and water companies) are sending bills and statements online to save costs and the environment.
- In the motor vehicle industry, anything from car registration plates to brand new vehicles can be traded online. This channel of distribution has intensified competition in the sale of cars throughout many parts of the world, especially in Europe.
- Retailing such as the trade in groceries, clothing, books, DVDs and toys – the list is growing – can be conducted online.

However, e-commerce is not simply about selling. For example, many organizations use e-commerce for passing on information (such as educational websites). E-commerce can be classified in two ways: Business to Business (B2B) or Business to Consumer (B2C). These are examined in next section below.

BUSINESS TO BUSINESS (B2B)

Business to business (B2B) refers to e-commerce catered for the needs of other businesses. Examples of B2B include: corporate banking services, suppliers of equipment and spare parts, insurance, general maintenance and advertising agency services. Note that B2B technically exists both online and off-line, although the term is now usually used in the context of e-commerce.

Specialists in the B2B field often argue that consumer marketing strategies (used by B2C businesses) are not suitable or sufficient for marketing B2B products and services. This is because B2B concerns professional buyers, who have a totally different agenda when it comes to marketing. For instance, look at how the telecom operators approach their marketing – aiming at teenagers, who cannot really afford the services, perhaps at the expense of the business community. It is the latter segment of the market that would really need mobile telephones with internet access and who could afford to pay for it. Hence, the focus of mobile phone operators in their marketing campaigns becomes questionable.

BUSINESS TO CONSUMER (B2C)

Business to consumer (B2C) refers to e-commerce directly catered for the end-user, i.e. the consumer. Some of the most well-known B2C businesses are listed in Box 4.8a.

It is important to note that many businesses are engaged in both B2B and B2C. Search engines such as Google and Yahoo! not only allow customers to carry out searches on their websites but also sell advertising slots to other businesses. They operate a 'Pay-Per-Click' scheme, where the advertisers will pay Google and Yahoo! each time a person clicks on the advertised banner.

Box 4.8a Ten highly visited English-language websites

1. Yahoo! – search engine which makes money primarily by selling advertising space
2. Google – another very popular search engine, now worth more than General Motors and Ford
3. MSN/Microsoft – popular Hotmail email service and other internet-related services
4. MySpace – social networking website
5. eBay – online auction site that sells literally anything and everything
6. YouTube – video sharing site
7. Amazon – probably the most well-known online retailer
8. Wal-Mart – world's largest 'brick' retailer expanding into e-commerce
9. Wikipedia – online encyclopaedia
10. BBC Online – website of the world's largest news broadcaster

Source: adapted from http://www.alexa.com/site/ds/top_500

Question 4.8.1

HMV

In 2006, HMV Group plc announced that sales at its HMV music stores and Waterstone's bookshops fell due to customers switching to Amazon.com and supermarkets. Not surprisingly then, HMV declared that it would end its partnership with Amazon.com. Instead, HMV chose to set up its own website. The performance of HMV has not been helped by the increasing number of people who download music or buy CDs, DVDs and books online and/or in supermarkets. In response to these threats, HMV has reduced prices.

The HMV logo is a registered ® Trade Mark of HMV Group plc through HMV (IP) Limited and reproduced here by the kind permission and authorization of HMV Group plc.

a Outline why HMV may be classed as a 'B2C' business. *[2 marks]*

b Explain why there has been an increasing trend in buying music and books online. *[4 marks]*

c Suggest one other strategy, apart from reduced prices, that HMV could use to prevent its sales from declining further. *[4 marks]*

THE ADVANTAGES OF E-COMMERCE

E-commerce can bring benefits to both businesses and for their customers. These advantages include:

- E-commerce provides another source of revenue for many organizations. In addition to traditional 'walk-in' stores, customers can now shop online from the comfort of their own home or office. In the UK, for example, most people have internet access at home whilst others have internet access from public libraries and internet cafés. It is no wonder then that sales via the internet rose from £39.3 billion ($75 billion) in 2003 to £103.3 billion ($198 billion) by the end of 2005 (source: Office for National Statistics). Other organizations, such as Google, have earned revenue from selling advertising space ('sponsored links') on their regularly visited web pages.

- The internet gives businesses another channel of distribution. It allows organizations to sell to anyone in any part of the world at any time of the day. E-commerce will therefore help a firm to increase its customer base. More importantly for e-commerce businesses, over one billion users of the internet are able to buy goods and services online. This trend is set to continue as more people and businesses are able to access broadband and because of improved confidence in internet security.
- E-commerce also represents an opportunity for organizations to respond to competitors more quickly. For example, a company can publicize revisions to its services and products, such as price changes, much faster via its website than through printing updated hardcopy material.
- Excessive packaging can be reduced. Many companies, such as Apple, now require their customers to use the internet to download or view manuals (technical guides), rather than the traditional way of businesses having to print these in several different languages. This not only reduces waste and excess packaging, but also cuts costs of production for businesses. In addition, information for innovative products such as Apple's iPod can be updated easily online. Ikea, the home furnishing giant, prints and distributes a colossal 160 million copies of its catalogue each year; without their huge product range being available on the internet, this figure could be even higher.
- Retail outlets tend to have higher **overheads** due to costs such as rent, storage, insurance payments and staffing costs. These can be reduced somewhat by operating online. Hence, the business is able to pass on some of these savings to customers. In addition, customers can also save on associated transactions costs (such as travel time and transportation costs) as there is no need for face-to-face trading. **Operating costs** are also reduced by e-commerce. For example, subscription newspaper websites such as Singapore's *Straits Times* or the USA's *Wall Street Journal* run their online editions for a tiny fraction of the costs of their paper-based publications. *The New York Times* sells single articles as well as offering bundle packages for those wishing to purchase a number of archived articles. For these businesses, the *marginal cost* of supplying extra online editions to new customers is close to zero. The use of the internet means that there is no significant difference to its total costs if it sells 100 or 10,000 online subscriptions.
- Customers have more **choice** and **convenience**. This is because e-commerce has reduced many barriers to entry, thereby allowing unknown firms to establish new businesses swiftly in order to compete with the better known firms. For example, Amazon.com has revolutionized the way that books are sold today. Customers can choose not only from their local bookstore but also from a vast number of online book retailers from the comfort of their own homes. E-commerce has effectively cut costs and intensified competition. Subsequently, businesses can reduce their prices yet offer a wider choice to customers.
- Speedy completion of transactions is possible. Search facilities on company websites can allow customers to find products quickly and place an order with relative ease. In addition, e-commerce can make trading more efficient and suitable for the customer. For instance, customers can now book tickets for the cinema, theatre, concert, theme park or overseas holiday at any time of the day from the comfort of their home or office.

Question 4.8.2

Christmas shopping online

Retailers looking forward to a bumper Christmas have turned to online sales. With so much competition during the festive season, a greater number of online retailers have lured customers with promises of free postage and delivery to take the hassle out of Christmas shopping (especially as more women start to shop online). Popular items bought on the internet for the holiday season include consumer electronics, toys and clothing.

a Use the case study to describe two opportunities that e-commerce presents for businesses. *[4 marks]*

b Explain the benefits to consumers using the internet as a channel of distribution. *[4 marks]*

THE DISADVANTAGES OF E-COMMERCE

E-commerce can also cause problems for both businesses and their customers. Such limitations include:

- **Set-up costs** can be high. Businesses are likely to hire specialists to set up and to market their website. Setting up electronic payment systems can also be very costly. There will also be additional **running costs**, such as postage and packaging costs, which the business will need to consider.
- Credit card companies will impose **finance charges** for using their services (for online payments). These charges may be passed onto the customers in the form of higher prices or absorbed by the business by accepting lower profit margins.
- **Fraudulent trade** takes place. For example, there is no way that a buyer can authenticate items being sold on eBay (a very popular auction website). *The Times* newspaper reported that banks lost £14.5 million ($28 million) to online fraud in the first half of 2005, representing a 260% increase in online fraud year on year. The UK Home Office reported in early 2006 that *identity fraud* was costing the UK economy an estimated £1.7 billion every year. 'Identity fraud' occurs when criminals use other people's personal details to gain access to bank accounts and credit cards.
- **Spam** and unethical marketing opportunities are rife. For example, there have been email claims that Nokia and Sony Ericsson mobile phones were being given away for free to recipients who forwarded the message onto 20 other people. The emails were a hoax and used as a way to obtain personal email accounts for sending on advertising spam (inappropriate and unsolicited online publicity and internet marketing messages). One business strategy to avoid spam is to use 'opt-in email', such as subscriptions to company newsletters, where email communication is explicitly asked for by the recipient. 'Pop-up ads' on websites can also be annoying and a waste of the customer's time. According to InsideSpam.com, around 40% of daily emails are considered to be spam.
- E-commerce may not be highly suitable for some businesses. Although e-commerce can be cost-effective, customers may find browsing online quite time consuming and onerous. The consumer may use the internet to search for more information about a motor vehicle before making a purchase, but will still want to visit a showroom to see the physical product and take a test drive. Moreover, customers cannot simply take the online-purchased products home as there is a time lag between purchase and delivery of the products. Many supermarkets will

now deliver frozen produce and fresh fruits and vegetables; but most customers still prefer to choose their own from a retail outlet. In addition, it may prove difficult or inconvenient for customers to return faulty products that were purchased online. Hence, a lack of effective after-sales care can harm the image and prospects of an online business.

- There are more internet web pages than there are people in the world. To deal with this, effective search engines such as Google, Lycos and Yahoo! have become very popular. Nevertheless, many websites and web pages have too much information or too many high resolution graphics and pictures, so loading time is very slow. Information overload can also mean that people prefer to visit a physical retail outlet to purchase their goods and services.
- E-commerce is reliant on advanced technology that is not necessarily available to all businesses or in all countries. In addition, websites and web pages need to be regularly updated, yet remain easy for viewers to browse and follow. Such maintenance costs must therefore be considered by the online retailer.
- The internet is volatile as is prone to hackers and breakdowns. Maintenance and upgrades will further add to the costs of e-commerce. For example, an earthquake on Boxing Day 2006 in South East Asia severely disrupted internet services for over 2 weeks in Taiwan, Singapore, Hong Kong, Vietnam, South Korea and Japan.
- A shift to e-commerce trading from traditional methods used in retail outlets may result in job losses. Businesses will need to devise strategies to deal with any redundancies (see Unit 2.1). Moreover, job losses may harm industrial relations at work and give the organization a poor image.

Question 4.8.3

Online banking fraud

The UK's finance watchdog, the Financial Services Authority (FSA), has revealed that half the internet users are either 'extremely' or 'very concerned' about the risks of online fraud, especially as the number of cases is on the rise. In Hong Kong, bogus online banking websites have been set up to capture people's personal banking details.

In response, banks such as HSBC have tightened up security. They claim to never ask for personal details and passwords in an email. Their customers have also been issued with a keychain security gadget that generates a random six-digit password based on a highly complex mathematical logarithm. The security code is used in addition to online usernames and passwords.

a Use the case study to outline two limitations of e-commerce to organizations such as banks. *[4 marks]*

b To what extent does e-commerce benefit customers of banking and other financial services? *[6 marks]*

E-COMMERCE AND THE MARKETING MIX

The emergence and importance of e-commerce for businesses have major influences on a firm's marketing mix. These are examined in more detail below.

Price

The internet increases **price transparency** to the advantage of the customer who is able to gain a better knowledge of price comparisons in an instant. They can use price comparison websites, for example, to instantaneously compare the prices of books, DVDs, toys, clothes or airline travel. This forces organizations to be ever more competitive in terms of pricing strategies in order to maintain their market share.

The internet also allows businesses to cut out intermediaries such as wholesalers and main-street retailers. Instead, they can sell directly to the consumer. Thus, prices may be reduced as there are reduced costs; with each intermediary there is a percentage *mark-up* in order to make a profit. Nevertheless, e-commerce firms (increasingly known as **e-tailers**) will usually add shipping costs to the price of their products, which may then make its prices less competitive. Furthermore, e-tailers need to be aware of international trading standards and regulation that may raise their costs, such as import taxes that may by imposed on products entering a foreign country.

Auctioning services such as eBay have exploited the benefits of the internet. Prices can be adjusted and updated instantaneously according to the level of demand. News media reported that a Picasso painting was sold on eBay in mid 2006 for a staggering sum of $95 million!

Many businesses offer benefits to their regular customers or registered customers, such as discounts or a wider range of services. This strategy aims to encourage and improve brand loyalty. The online iTunes store from Apple, for example, has different sections for people looking to purchase different types of music. It is quite common for people to now legally download individual music tracks, which they have purchased, without having to pay the price of a whole CD album.

Traditionally, businesses selling *price inelastic products* (see Unit 4.4), such as premium brands, are less vulnerable to price competition. In addition, a business may enjoy being a regional monopoly (the only supplier of a product in a particular geographical area). Both types of businesses – those selling premium products for a high price and those that enjoy being a *regional monopoly* – are presented with a new threat from the emergence of e-commerce. There is no longer the same degree of privilege or autonomy for these businesses in being able to set higher prices.

It is important to remember, as with all aspects of the marketing mix, that price should not be looked at in isolation. Consumers may not necessarily base their purchasing decisions on price; they will tend to buy the product that offers the best value for money in terms of reliability and the brand image.

Question **4.8.4**

Aggregators: Price-comparison websites

Knowledgeable shoppers know that the best deals can usually be found online. They also know better than to surf from one e-tailer to the next in search of the lowest prices. Instead, these savvy shoppers turn to price-comparison websites, known as aggregators, which show the prices from any number of online vendors. This saves the customer a huge amount of time and helps to secure the best deal – all within a few seconds of inputting the search.

Aggregators were originally devised for comparing the prices of computers and electronics, such as iPods, DVD players and high-definition televisions. However, there are plenty of other products catered for by aggregators, such as motor vehicles, golf clubs and kitchen utensils. More sophisticated aggregators will allow consumers to narrow their searches based on various criteria, such as price, brand and functions. However, it is difficult for aggregators to link to every single online merchant. Hence, the lowest price found on one site might not be the lowest price available elsewhere. So it may still pay to shop around.

a Explain two benefits of aggregators (price comparison websites) to customers. *[4 marks]*

b Evaluate the view that aggregators pose a threat for e-commerce businesses. *[6 marks]*

Place

Distribution is an integral part of any corporate strategy. Due to the emergence of e-commerce, firms are able to reach a global audience at a fraction of the cost. E-commerce also gives the opportunity of reaching a wider customer base. Nevertheless, there is still the logistics of ensuring that the products sold online can reach the customer. The growing trend of e-commerce has therefore provided many opportunities for delivery and courier companies such as DHL and FedEx. In addition, the internet has led to increased competition, as countless other firms start to realize the potential of e-commerce and introduce their own websites to reach the potentially enormous customer base.

Due to the reduction in intermediaries, e-commerce can shorten *channels of distribution*. This means that businesses can benefit from enormous savings on their operating costs, such as the rent for large premises in many different countries. Amazon.com is an example of a business that has benefited from being able to use the internet as a means of distribution. Starting out in July 1995, Amazon.com had become the world's largest book retailer in just six years, partly due to its relatively low costs resulting from not having to use intermediaries to sell its products.

The internet as an alternative channel of distribution is also often more convenient for customers. There is no need to travel to retail outlets as purchases can be made online. Many supermarkets around the world now have a dedicated website as an alternative distribution channel, offering online purchasing, in addition to its traditional retail stores. This gives customers the added convenience of being able to shop at any time, irrespective of whether the actual supermarket is open or closed for business. Not-for-profit organizations, such as universities, have also used the internet to enhance place in their marketing mix. For instance, the University of Hong Kong announced in late 2006 that it had uploaded its one millionth e-book.

Websites offer a further advantage as a distribution channel in that different languages can be used to capture an even larger audience. Language translation is a relative small operational cost, especially when compared to the potential benefits of being able to able to draw the attention of different customers from around the world. Websites that have options in Chinese, English, Hindi and Spanish will pretty much cover the languages understood by most of the people in the world.

However, as mentioned earlier in this Unit, customers may not be willing to purchase certain products online, perhaps because they cannot examine or test the product. Cautious or more reticent customers may feel that online descriptions may not be very accurate and that it is too much of a gamble to purchase products online. Instead, customers may feel a sense of security in dealing with people directly in a physical retail outlet. They can ask the sales people questions and get feedback. Online retailers offer a relatively impersonal service and there is always the potential that non-established e-tailers may simply disappear after taking money from the customer but without having delivered the products. Even in more economically developed countries such as the UK, customers generally still prefer to use the traditional cheque book than to carry out online banking transactions.

Product

The products being sold by a business (its **product range**) can be displayed online. This can make it more convenient for customers who can access this information at any time from home. It also benefits the business as there is no need to stock all items in its range; which would add to storage costs. Physical retail outlets face the problem of having to tell customers that they are 'out of stock' as space is limited so they will only tend to stock the best selling products. Jeff Bezos, the founder and chief executive of Amazon.com, started his business by storing books in his own home. Having a book shop would have meant the need to buy or rent premises to store all the books. Amazon.com is a *footloose company* which means it does not need to locate its huge warehouses in busy (expensive rental) districts.

Businesses need a sufficient level of demand to offer variety to their products. For example, the market for Ferrari cars limits production levels and the variations; original colours only come in red, black or yellow. With the introduction of the internet, the enlarged customer base for businesses means that they are able to sell their products internationally. For example, BMW uses an interactive website for its range of motor cars where customers can customize design features, such as changing the colour of the car and the styling of the alloy wheels. This not only gives customers a more interactive online shopping experience, but allows customers to visualize the product in a way that may not be possible in a physical car showroom. BMW stores the information on a database to determine the most popular customer designs. This information can then be used for developing their marketing strategy, such as which cars to display in their showrooms. Dell is an example of a successful e-tailer in promoting and selling its products online. Dell sells personal computers direct to customers who have placed a personalized order online. Customers can select their own specifications and add-on features, such as a DVD-RW drive, surround sound speakers or a webcam. The sophisticated tools of the internet allow businesses, such as Dell, to sell an increasingly wide range of products.

Packaging may also be less of an issue with e-tailers because these businesses do not have to rely so much on packaging, which tends to be less of an appeal to online shoppers. Therefore e-tailers may be able to reduce their expenditure on the packaging, thereby reducing their costs. This can then transform into higher profit margins for the business or reduced prices for its customers. For society, e-commerce may also mean less wastage as there is less of a need for excess packaging. If such trends continue, this will mean that the businesses that focus on their product designs around packaging will have to rethink their marketing strategies.

A further benefit of using e-commerce as a marketing strategy is that additional detailed information and regular updates about the product can be placed on the firm's website. It may not be possible to display all necessary information about a product on the physical object or on its packaging. Specifications for products can be very detailed without causing environmental damage by printing lots of colourful and expensive brochures. Manuals for electronic gadgets, for example, are often translated into many different languages and placed inside the packaging of products such as mobile telephones, digital cameras, MP3 players and plasma screen televisions.

With the internet, customers can instead download the manual in the language of their choice and receive regular updates from the business.

Nevertheless, it still remains that certain products seem to remain largely unaffected by the growth in e-commerce. These might include *perishable products* such as fresh seafood, *specialist products* such as medicine, and highly expensive *luxury products* such as diamonds or sports cars.

Question 4.8.5

Amazon.com

Amazon.com is probably the most widely recognized e-commerce business in the world today. It serves over 40 million customers in 220 countries, with annual **sales turnover** in excess of $10 billion. Founded in 1994, it was not until 2003 that the company started to make profit. From starting out as an online book store, Amazon.com has gone on to extend its product mix to include CDs, videos, DVDs, computer software, toys and games, food, jewellery, clothing, furniture, auctioneering and much more.

Amazon's success is a combination of maximizing market share and creating customer loyalty. This has been created by offering an unparalleled online shopping experience, with great choice, value for money and **after-sales service**. This has led to customers having trust and assurance in the brand.

a Define the terms **sales turnover** and **after-sales service**. *[4 marks]*

b Explain the strategies used by Amazon.com to ensure they achieved success in e-commerce. *[4 marks]*

c Evaluate the view that Amazon.com can be equally successful in selling its much broader product range as it has been with selling books online. *[7 marks]*

Promotion

Marketers must determine how best to create an online sales channel that will support the needs of the international community. Many businesses have tackled this by allowing browsers to select their preferred language option from the company's web page. Many organizations have also set up a 'frequently asked questions' (FAQs) section on their website to pass on important information to potential clients. Information can be easily updated and at a relatively low cost. This would not be possible with other promotional media such as posters or television advertisements.

Businesses spend a huge amount of money every year in developing and promoting their products to each of their target markets. With the growing importance of globalization, fuelled by the internet, successful business organizations have cut costs by using global marketing strategies that appeal throughout the world.

The internet provides new opportunities for promotional strategies. For example, more detailed information can be communicated via internet advertisements; customers can take their time when browsing information about products which may not be possible with above-the-line promotional techniques. Marketers can also use online video clips, audio and photos to promote their goods or services. Estate agents, for example, use the internet to showcase their properties for sale and rental. Many of these firms use 360 degree cameras so that clients can view the inside of properties by using their mouse to navigate around the rooms, thereby having a 'virtual tour' of the properties. Digital photos also allow clients to view the properties; and all this without having to leave their own home or office.

E-commerce has also enabled firms to implement **viral marketing** as a promotional technique. Viral marketing is similar to *word-of-mouth marketing* in that both 'spread the message' about the existence of a particular product. Viral marketing, however, focuses on emails and banner advertisements on the internet to spread the word. The internet allows such advertisements to be seen by potential customers around the world and it is a relatively cheap method of promotion. Mass emails can be sent to potential or existing clients, especially as email tends to be a very cheap form of promotion. However, unsolicited email may be described as spam.

Unlike word-of-mouth advertising, the use of viral marketing on the internet has been questioned. Email spam has been criticized as an unethical and undesirable method of promotion. In addition, people have become accustomed to online banner and pop-up advertisements and hence they tend to ignore these advertisements. Nevertheless, online advertisements if used in conjunction with other forms of promotion can be effective. Car manufacturers, for example, use their websites to promote the corporate mission as well as promote their product range.

Many businesses also try to lure customers by using competitions and prizes on their website. One purpose is to encourage users to visit and explore the various sections of the website to learn more about the organization. This is often done through an 'FAQ section' or an 'educational section' on the business's website.

Essentially, then, the internet provides an additional medium of promotion for businesses to reach their potential customers. As more and more people go online and as e-commerce continues to grow, increasing opportunities present themselves for marketers using the internet as a promotional tool.

Finally, e-commerce is likely to reduce the influence and importance of the other P's in the marketing mix: people, physical evidence, packaging and processes. These cannot, of course, be ignored but their relative importance for many e-tailers is likely to decline.

Question 4.8.6

Apple's iTunes

Data released by research consultants, Nielsen Media Research, have shown that the popularity of iTunes has never been greater. Online traffic to Apple's music service soared from 6.1 million unique visitors in December 2004 to 20.7 million in December 2005 (a 240% increase in just one year). Teenagers are reported to be twice as likely to visit the iTunes site compared to other age groups. Like many other websites that have followed, iTunes allows customers to purchase their hand-picked songs for legal downloading. This saves the customer money too as they do not need to purchase a whole music album. Since its beginnings in 2001, iTunes has added other products to its online store, including music videos, television shows, iPod games, audio books and movies. By early 2008, iTunes had overtaken Wal-Mart as the USA's largest music retailer.

a Describe two possible reasons for the huge increase in demand for Apple's iTunes. *[4 marks]*

b To what extent do you feel that e-commerce has saved the music and movie industries from copyright violation and piracy? *[8 marks]*

E-COMMERCE AND BUSINESS STRATEGY

E-commerce is having a huge impact on the way in which business is conducted today. It has accelerated the growth in world trade, with wider market opportunities and improved efficiency. E-commerce presents an opportunity for businesses to grow, whatever their size. The benefits also mean that businesses can provide much more information on their products and services than would otherwise be the case.

There is evidence to show that investment in ICT, with effective organizational change, can be critical for improved productivity. Businesses are selling more products and services online, in more markets and in more languages than ever before. With such a trend, e-commerce is becoming much more of a priority for managers. Having an **online presence** has subsequently become a vital part of business strategy. In her book *e.Volve!* Rosabeth Moss Kanter suggests that the internet could connect everyone throughout the world; a clear opportunity for businesses with a global stance. Having conducted thousands of interviews with businesses throughout the world, she suggests that the best business managers in the digital era will be those with curiosity, imagination and good communication skills in an international context.

E-commerce has also promoted consumer sovereignty through price cuts, price transparency, more convenience and choice for the customer. Consumer dedicated websites such as tripadvisor.com, allow customers to type in the name of hotels that they are planning to stay at and to read comments by customers that claim to have actually stayed at those hotels. Businesses will therefore have to place an even greater emphasis on their marketing mix because customers from any part of the world may want to access information.

However, having an online presence does not guarantee success. Almost all large companies will have a dedicated website and the resources to maintain it, so this creates another form of competition. Customers are also able to access important information, such as price comparisons, at an instance. Furthermore, businesses that trade online internationally still need to consider the **external environment** such as of fluctuating exchange rates and different legal and tax systems overseas.

Managers will also need to be aware of the legal and social obligations of e-commerce. Generic responsibilities include the careful treatment of personal data (Data Protection Acts place limits on how businesses can use their clients' personal details), compliance with copyright legislation and consideration for the online security of their customers. Furthermore, with the escalating reliance on e-commerce there is a threat that the traditional form of retailing will diminish and lead to job losses. Businesses may therefore be expected to manage such operations in a socially responsible manner.

One of the biggest mistakes made by many businesses with a website is to over-complicate their message on their homepage. According to consultancy firm Business Bricks Ltd., the average attention span of people browsing the internet is just 9 seconds. Another study reported by the BBC in November 2006 showed that most online shoppers spend up to only 4 seconds for a web page to load before abandoning the website. These issues then mean that businesses need to consider:

- prioritizing information that goes on the homepage of a company's website
- using only the most unique or interesting benefits of the business, its products or services on offer.

Given that there are so many web pages on the internet, businesses only have, perhaps, up to 30 seconds at best to captivate the minds of customers who are simply browsing the internet. In business, this idea is known as the **elevator pitch** which refers to the short time span available to a firm to hold the interest of customers. This concept doesn't just apply to e-commerce; think about why television advertisements rarely go beyond 30 seconds. There is no point, or enough time, in telling customers all the reasons why they should buy your products – it is more effective to keep the message simple and to focus on the key benefit offered by the business. For B2B and B2C businesses, they have to ask what they want their potential customers (on the internet) to do when they visit their websites.

So how do managers judge the effectiveness of their e-commerce strategies? There are several methods that can be used to measure whether an organization's e-commerce approach is successful. Some of these include:

- Increase in sales following the launch or relaunch of a business organization's website and e-commerce operations
- Increase in the proportion of sales revenue coming from the e-commerce section of the business.
- Increase in the business's overall market share following the implementation of an e-commerce strategy
- Increase in brand exposure and awareness (although this may be quite difficult to measure).

Some businesses use 'clicks-per-page' as an indicator of success. They buy advertising space on popular websites, such as Lycos and Google, and use 'pay-per-click' as a measure of the effectiveness of their advertisements, i.e. the business only has to pay for advertisements each time a customer clicks on the advertisement. Although this measures the number of visitors to the website, it does not necessarily mean that these visitors actually buy anything online.

One further method that can be used to judge the 'success' of an organization's website is 'website ranking'. Website rankings appear on popular web search engines, generally with more popular websites being placed at the top of the list. The drawback in this approach is the huge volume of websites and hence the reliability of such rankings. For example, a search on Google for 'book shops' reveals over 50 million links; although Amazon, Blackwell, Ottakar and WH Smith all appear on the first page.

Despite the potential benefits of e-commerce, most business analysts would argue that companies have yet to exploit the internet's true potential to reach a global audience and to reduce costs of production. PayPal Europe, the online payments and money transfers business owned by eBay, claims that 6% of the UK's annual sales will come from online sales by 2010. While this does represent a huge jump in e-commerce, there is still a long way to go yet. Businesses that can successfully integrate e-commerce into their operations can benefit from a boost in their efficiency and productivity, thereby giving them a competitive advantage in today's dynamic business environment. There is huge scope for e-commerce and the benefits it may bring to a business. However, it must be used in conjunction with other corporate strategies as the effects of e-commerce on a business depend largely on the extent to which the organization uses and relies on e-commerce. Nevertheless, most commentators believe that the rapid growth in e-commerce since the late 1990s is set to continue and significantly change the way in which business is conducted.

REVIEW QUESTIONS 4.8

1. What is meant by 'e-commerce'?
2. Distinguish between B2B and B2C.
3. Outline five advantages of e-commerce to businesses and customers.
4. Outline four drawbacks of e-commerce for businesses and customers.
5. How has price, place, product and promotion been affected by e-commerce?
6. What is meant by having an 'online presence'?
7. How can managers measure the success, or otherwise, of an organization's e-commerce strategy?

B2B stands for business-to-business and refers to online trade conducted directly for the *business customer* rather than the end-user, such as Amazon.com supplying books to other book retailers.

B2C stands for business-to-consumer and refers to online business conducted directly for the *end-user* (the consumer), such as Amazon.com selling books directly to private individuals.

Clicks and mortar (also known as 'brick and click') refers to businesses that combine the traditional main-street existence with an online presence. By contrast, other businesses, such as eBay and Amazon.com, have only an online presence.

E-commerce (electronic commerce) is the trading of goods and services via the internet.

E-tailers are businesses that operate predominantly online, such as Amazon.com, eBay, Yahoo! and Google. They are different to retailers that operate physical stores in shopping malls and other physical outlets.

Online presence means that a business has a dedicated website for e-commerce. In its simplest form, this is just to provide information about the business and its products or services. Having a large online presence means that a business is featured on major search engines and customers can browse and purchase online without the need to visit a retail outlet.

Spam refers to unsolicited and superfluous marketing messages via email. The common purpose of 'spamming' is to advertise a firm's products (such as credit cards or computer software) although this method of promotion is largely seen as being unethical.

OPERATIONS MANAGEMENT

UNIT 5

UNIT

Production Methods

UNIT 5.1

You can have any colour you want… as long as it's black.

Henry Ford (1863–1947), founder of the Ford Motor Company

Key topics

- Production methods: job, batch, line, flow and mass production

Higher Level extension

- Combining methods of production
- Implications of a change in production systems
- Cell production and teamworking

INTRODUCTION

Production, often referred to as **operations management**, is concerned with producing the right goods and services in the right quantities and at the right quality level, all in a cost-effective and timely manner. The term does not only apply to manufacturing since production is concerned with all three sectors of the economy:

- **Primary sector** – extracting raw materials, harvesting natural crops and rearing animals, e.g. mining, agriculture and fishing
- **Secondary sector** – turning natural resources into processed or finished goods, e.g. steel production and car manufacturing
- **Tertiary sector** – providing services, e.g. finance, insurance, travel and tourism, education and health care.

Essentially, the role of production is to turn factor inputs into outputs at a minimal cost. Figure 5.1a shows a simplistic model of the production (or transformation) process:

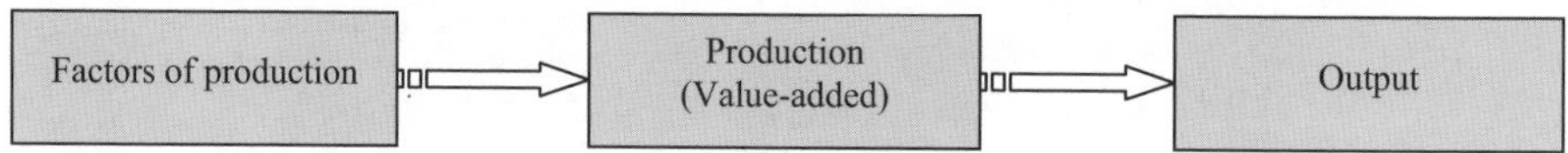

Figure 5.1a The production process

The four factors of production (land, labour, capital and enterprise) are known to many marketing and production managers as the **Five M's** – Materials, Manpower, Machines, Money and Management. These are the available resources to a business and the five M's can be a useful tool in devising both marketing and production plans. They are combined in a cost-effective way to ensure that there is **value-added** during the 'production' phase of the transformation process. This ensures that the value of outputs is greater than the cost of the factor inputs (hence earning the business a profit).

To ensure that products can be sold for more than their input costs, production managers need to deal with several key aspects of operations management:

- Size, scope and timing of production (see Units 1.7 and 5.8)
- Production planning, e.g. stock control and quality control systems (see Unit 5.4)
- Location of business (see Unit 5.5)
- New products and innovation (see Unit 5.6)
- Methods of production (the focus of this Unit).

This Unit looks at the need for businesses to decide *how* production should take place. The best method of production for one type of business is not necessarily the best method for others. For example, the type of product being produced (such as a haircut or a commercial building) will affect the production method chosen. Even the same kind of product can be produced using different methods, for example, Casio watches and Rolex watches.

PRODUCTION METHODS

There are four main methods of production – job, batch, mass and cell production. Note: The cell production method is only covered by Higher Level candidates.

Job production

This method of production involves a business creating an individual product from start to finish to the meet specific requirements of the customer. Typically, these products are one-off, unique items such as an office building, a wedding dress, a Hollywood movie, music composition, private dance lessons or a haircut. These items are tailored made to the specifications set by the respective customer.

Small firms are likely to use this method of production as there are few opportunities for economies of scale in job production. However, large firms can also use this method of production. The production of Boeing's 747 (the jumbo jet), for example, uses this method of production. These are *not* one-off items; each and every 747 aircraft has a fuel tank capacity of 57,000 gallons of petrol (enough petrol to last the average UK car driver for 100 years) and weighs 380 tonnes, yet can travel at 600 miles per hour. Most orders are placed by the large airline carriers but the production process is time consuming because usually only one aeroplane is worked on by a team of workers, so there is a long waiting list.

A single worker (such as a tailor) or a group of workers (such as a team of painters and decorators) handles the complete job. Job production covers a whole range of jobs from those that are small scale involving little or no technology (such as a private tutor or a hairdresser) to complex jobs that cannot be completed without high technology (such as the construction of a hotel or Disneyland theme park).

Whether job production is used by small or large firms using low or high technology, the general advantages of job production include:

- **Quality** of production (and service) because highly skilled labour is used. Customers may be willing to pay a premium to buy a prestigious sports car that is tailored made to their needs because of the high quality of the finished product. Quality also applies to customer service. A wedding planner is certainly more likely to give the customer personal attention than a cashier would to individual customers at a supermarket.
- **Motivation** of workers is also likely to be very high. Workers can feel proud of the finished project. Team spirit can also be a motivating factor (see Unit 2.5).
- **Uniqueness** of the product not only helps to maintain motivation amongst the staff, but adds much value to the production process. The exclusivity can also act as a unique selling point (USP) for the business. Therefore job production may help to guarantee a premium price for the finished product.
- **Flexibility** in the design and specifications are possible during the planning stages of job production. Each product can be altered to the customer's requests such as the type of car and flowers for a wedding. This means that job production creates a variety of **choice** for the customer that cannot be met by other methods of production. It is often possible to change the specifications of the job even when the work has already begun. This flexibility can provide major marketing benefits for a business.

There are also several disadvantages of job production:

- Job production tends to be **labour intensive** and is therefore a relatively **expensive** method of production. Since labour accounts for the largest share of costs in most firms, the final price charged to customers reflects the high costs of production.
- Quite often, due to the varying and specific requirements of customers, the production process is relatively **time consuming**. It is usually difficult and impractical to speed up production as quality standards may fall.
- Due to the length of time involved in producing a product (via job production) and then selling it, there is likely to be a relatively **long working-capital cycle**. Ferrari has a 9–12 months waiting list for their cars. This means that customers do not fully pay for their purchases until the final product is delivered. However, during this time, Ferrari still needs cash to pay for their ongoing costs such as labour, materials and utility bills. Hence, a long working-capital cycle can harm the *cash flow position* (see Unit 3.3) of a business.
- **Few economies of scale** can be enjoyed. Since each good or service is likely to be unique, there is little scope to produce these items on a relatively large enough scale to enjoy economies of scale. A tailor may enjoy limited purchasing economies of scale from buying materials in bulk. However, the cost of storing the materials, the irregularity of orders and the long working-capital cycle would mean that production is at too small a scale to really reap the true benefits of these economies.

Question 5.1.1

Bristol Cars Ltd.

Bristol Cars Ltd. is a producer of luxury cars, located in Bristol, UK. Each year, only around 100 cars are produced. Each car is uniquely made allowing the firm to claim that the Bristol car is "Great Britain's most exclusive luxury car". The firm has no distributors or dealerships. Every part of a car is given the necessary time and attention to detail to satisfy both the client and the company. Only when each task is performed to perfection can the highly skilled workers move on to the next task. The cost of perfection means it can take a long time to produce each car, but Bristol Cars claims that "the car is produced for those who can afford and appreciate the best".

Source: www.bristolcars.co.uk

a Define what is meant by 'Ltd.' as in Bristol Cars Ltd. *[2 marks]*

b Describe the method of production used by Bristol cars. *[4 marks]*

c Examine the consequences of this production method for:

i Bristol Cars Ltd.

ii Employees of Bristol Cars.

iii Customers of Bristol Cars. *[9 marks]*

Batch production

This method of production involves producing a limited number of identical products (known as a **batch**). Work on each batch is fully completed before production switches to another batch. Batch production is highly suited to businesses that make a range of products, unlike with job production. For example, a small bakery may produce 12 loafs of bread before changing production systems to bake 24 blueberry muffins. Hotels that offer buffet dinners prepare and cook their food in batches. Clothing outlets such as H&M and Gap have their garments produced in batches of different sizes and colours. Burgers at McDonald's restaurants are cooked in batches. Their 'Happy Meals', whist offering some variety, are also prepared in batches.

The key advantages of using batch production are:

- **Economies of scale** can be enjoyed since machines can be used to produce larger quantities (*technical economies*). In addition, raw materials and components can be bought in bulk (*purchasing economies*). This means that the unit costs of production are reduced.
- **Specialization** in the various production processes is likely to lead to increased *productivity* (output per worker) and better quality products.
- There is still some **variety** of products. For example, birthday cakes are produced in batches, but these can be tailored to the requirements of individual customers at a relatively low cost to the business.

Limitations of batch production include:

- A degree of **inflexibility** is likely because once the production run for a batch has started, it is difficult to switch to or work on another batch. This can therefore delay the overall production process.
- Since batch production results in a high amount of *work-in-progress* (semi-finished goods), **storage** is important. This will, however, increase costs of production (such as storage costs and insurance against damage or loss of stock).
- As with all systems of division of labour, jobs get repetitive and this may lead to **boredom**. The result may be a lack of motivation and lower productive efficiency.

Batch production also tends to be used when the level of demand for a product is not clear. Instead, estimates of sales volumes are made and carefully monitored. Output can then be adjusted accordingly. Production of one product line can be stopped if necessary, perhaps to work on another more urgent batch.

Flow, line and mass production

Flow, line and mass production are terms that tend to be used interchangeably. They focus on producing **standardized** (or homogenous) products, i.e. producing an identical product in large quantities. Printing one million standardized copies of a particular newspaper means that each and every copy of the newspaper appears to be exactly the same. Hence, it makes sense to produce such a large amount of output by using mass production.

- **Flow production** is a form of mass production whereby different operations are continuously and progressively carried out in sequence. When one task is completed, the next stage of production must start immediately. For example, producers of bottled spring water, beer or even an oil refinery will follow a system similar to the one shown in Figure 5.1b. Printers of daily newspapers also use this method of production.
- **Line production**, also known as *assembly-line production*, is a form of flow production whereby the product is assembled in various stages along a conveyor belt (or assembly line) until a finished product is made. Ford and other mass-market motor vehicle manufacturers use this method of production.
- **Mass production** is the manufacturing of large amounts of a standardized product. It tends to be highly *capital intensive* with high levels of productivity. Therefore unit costs of production are relatively low. An essential part of mass production is **specialization**. Specialized capital equipment and people are used at each workstation to carry out a different function essential to the overall production process. Unlike batch production, the standardized products (such as cars, mobile phones and DVD players) are produced or assembled individually on a large scale.

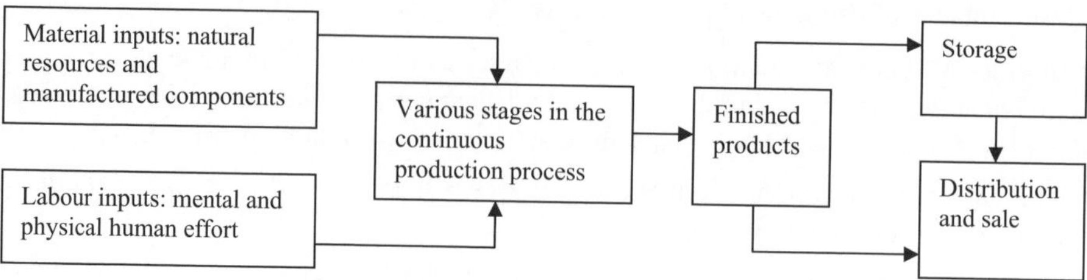

Figure 5.1b Basic mass/flow production process

Mass production was first commercialized in the USA by Henry Ford. Ford, who was heavily influenced by the work of F.W. Taylor (see Unit 2.5), introduced the world's first automated production line in the 1920s for the production of his Model T cars. Instead of the workers moving from one workstation to another (which is rather inefficient), he used an automated production line to boost the firm's productivity.

Advantages of mass/flow/line production

- Since these production methods are capital intensive, production is on a mass scale, so a high volume of output is produced and at a relatively low cost. Manufacturers of consumer electronic products, such as Samsung and Phillips, are able to produce individual DVD players within a minute when operating at full capacity! Since they produce for the mass market, they are also able to benefit from huge *purchasing economies of scale*.
- Despite the high initial costs of flow production, the costs can be spread over the high volume of output thereby reducing the *average fixed costs* (see Unit 5.2) through *technical economies of scale*. Machines can work 24 hours a day if necessary. Machines may break down from time to time, but they do not require wages, rest periods or motivating. This should help to reduce costs for the business in the long run.
- The use of dedicated machinery and equipment means that products are of a standardized quality. Workers also specialize so become experts in their area of the production process. This should enable the business to achieve a low *defect rate* (see Unit 5.4) and to maintain quality standards.
- Labour costs are low as relatively unskilled workers are required to operate much of the machinery. For example, workers in the Black and Decker factory in Shenzhen, China earn $1 per day for a 10-hour shift. They can be recruited very easily and trained to work on the assembly line within a couple of hours. Again, this helps to limit the costs of the business yet it benefits from the huge scale of output.

Disadvantages of mass/flow/line production

- The work is likely to be monotonous and therefore boring. Workers in Coca-Cola's bottling plants, for example, have to check every bottle to ensure that there are no cracks or defects before any beverage is poured into the glass bottles. There is little, if any, opportunity for workers to have any say in how work is done. Motivation levels are therefore likely to be low.
- Since there is such a reliance on the functioning of the assembly line, any breakdowns will cause major problems for the business. Similarly, any delays in the delivery of raw materials and components will also cause problems for mass production.
- There is very little flexibility with this production method, i.e. once the production process has begun there is very little chance of altering the design or specifications. A further inflexibility of the system is that products must be very similar or standardized so cannot be tailored made to the customer's individual taste. There can be some variety in the finishing touches towards the end of the assembly line, such as colour or decoration, although these will also be on a relatively large scale.

- Unlike batch or job production, it is not possible to rework products that are substandard because production is continuous. Any reworking of a particular part of the production process will bring other operations to a halt.
- Mass production is capital intensive and therefore involves huge *set-up costs* (e.g. purchase and installation), *running costs* (e.g. servicing and maintenance) and *replacement costs* (e.g. when the equipment and machinery become obsolete). This may act as a barrier to entry for many firms who are unable to raise the finance to enter the market. The high cost of capital may also negatively affect a firm's cash flow position, especially in the short run.
- Mass production also means the need for an effective storage system since there will be a large volume of stock. This may increase overall costs of production.

Question 5.1.2

Explain the most appropriate method of production for each product below:

a iPod MP3 media players.

b Wedding cakes.

c Cookies (biscuits).

d Navy battleships.

e Plasma televisions. *[10 marks]*

LABOUR AND CAPITAL INTENSITY

Some methods of production are **labour intensive**, whilst others are **capital intensive**. Production methods that use a greater proportion of labour (in terms of their cost) than any other factor input are known as being *labour intensive*. Examples range from rural farming in developing countries to management consultancy services in advanced economies. Job production and the service sector tend to be labour intensive. By contrast, *capital intensive* industries are those that have a relatively high proportion of capital costs in comparison to labour costs. Capital intensity is typically found in batch and mass production.

Many businesses have found that increasing their spending on capital investment (i.e. becoming more **capital intensive**) often leads to improved levels of output and productivity. This is certainly the case for firms that can mass produce their products. Machinery can be made to work efficiently 24 hours a day, 7 days a week without any rest breaks or financial compensation. This should then reduce average costs of production in the medium to long term since the firm's costs are spread over a larger volume of output (see Unit 5.2). However, for this to happen there must be sufficient demand for the product to justify its mass production.

A limitation for a business that is capital intensive is that products tend to be highly homogeneous. This is the opposite of having a *unique selling point* (USP). Standardization will result in a lower selling price for the product, with lower profit margins being made. In addition, capital-intensive businesses tend to have high fixed costs of production. This is because the cost of machinery, equipment and automation can be extremely high.

By contrast, **labour-intensive** industries have a higher proportion of costs attributed to its workforce rather than its capital structure. In teaching, for example, most of the costs go towards the payment of wages and salaries. This typically makes up around 80% of a school's budget. This means only around 20% is available for other sources of expenditure, such as the purchase of textbooks, stationery and electronic equipment. Unlike capital intensity, labour intensity can be seen in highly skilled professions, such as lawyers and financial consultants.

A key benefit of being labour intensive is that it is possible to offer a personalized service to the customer. Labour-intensive car manufacturers that hand-build their vehicles, such as Bristol Cars (see Question 5.1.1 on page 616), can benefit from having a USP. Customers can design their own specifications for their car order. A designated salesperson ensures that the customer receives a very personalized service even after the sale of the car. Teaching and health-care providers also offer a human touch, which would not be as effective if the services were more capital intensive – imagine being taught exclusively by computers!

Whether a business chooses to be more capital or labour intensive will depend on several factors, including:

- Relative cost of labour and capital. Assuming that substitution of resources is feasible, relatively higher labour costs will mean that the firm will choose to use more capital-intensive methods.
- Size of the market. Larger markets tend to use capital-intensive technology whereas small firms are likely to be more labour intensive.
- Aims and objectives of the organization. If profit is the main objective, businesses are more likely to want to provide for customers in a mass market, thereby choosing to use more capital intensive technologies. If firms are risk averse and worried about survival during a recession, then they may prefer to be more labour intensive since cost reduction and control are relatively easier.

HIGHER LEVEL

HIGHER LEVEL EXTENSION: COMBINING METHODS OF PRODUCTION

In reality, businesses are likely to combine different methods of production. For example, Burger King generally uses batch production. However, they also use job production to a lesser extent. Their corporate slogan "Have it your way" is based on the notion that customers can customize their burgers so long as the ingredients are available. So if a customer so desired, they could opt for a double Whopper with bacon, cheese and mushrooms added! Likewise, soft drinks manufacturers will often produce several batches of one kind of product and then send these to a flow production line for bottling or canning.

Combining different methods of production allows a business to gain from the benefits of each method used. The highly successful BMW Mini, for example, is only produced according to the number of orders that exist. Customers can even customize their cars from the manufacturer's predetermined options list. This is possible due to BMW's use of advanced automation technologies. The result is that Mini customers get a personalized product with the added benefit of lower costs of production from the use of line production.

Question 5.1.3

Explain why it may not be easy to categorize the production method used to provide the following products:

a Dell personal computers that are 'made to order', i.e. customers set their own specifications.

b Birthday cakes sold at large supermarkets, such as Carrefour, Tesco and Wal-Mart.

[6 marks]

HIGHER LEVEL EXTENSION: IMPLICATIONS OF CHANGES IN PRODUCTION SYSTEMS

A change in production systems may be caused by numerous reasons, such as new management thinking, a merger or takeover, or simply because of the growth of the firm. Whatever the reasons for a change in production methods used by a business, there will be direct impacts on the other functional areas of the organization.

- **Marketing implications**. The production method used will affect both the quality and the individuality of the product. Job production will generate an exclusive item that can be marketed for a very high price due to its exclusivity and high quality. Packaging, physical evidence and people will also play an important part of the overall marketing mix of different products. For example, customers of Maybach cars are invited for a three-course meal with the sales manager to discuss their personal requirements for the vehicle. By contrast, mass produced products will be standardized. There are likely to be plenty of substitutes available on the market and so prices will be much more competitive. Promotional strategies will also be more impersonal and aggressive in order to win market share from rival firms. Such businesses will rely on heavy volume to gain high profits, so they will aim to maximize the number of distribution channels to ensure that customers have easy access to purchase their products.
- **HRM implications**. A change in production methods can either reduce or increase the size of the workforce. Many multinationals have managed to enter China (prior to its membership of the World Trade Organization) by setting up labour-intensive operations. For instance, Black & Decker (the power tools manufacturer) hires a huge number of workers in its plant in Shenzhen, China even though many of the operations could easily be automated. Alternatively, a move towards mass production using capital-intensive technologies will tend to de-skill the workforce. Motivation of the workforce is also affected. Whilst flow production suffers from a lack of teamwork and group dynamics, *cell production* (see section below) benefits from using the individual skills of people working within a team. There are also training implications. Job production techniques will require much more training whereas mass production workers require minimal instructional training only. It will be relatively easy to hire workers for mass production whereas highly attractive remuneration packages may be needed to entice specialist workers for job production.
- **Finance implications**. Capital intensity requires heavy investment in machinery and equipment. This is very expensive, although the fixed investment costs can be spread out over time with mass production. Capital-intensive firms are likely to use *investment appraisal* techniques to assess whether the risk of investment will be worthwhile (see Unit 3.2). They are also likely to need external sources of finance (see Unit 3.1) to fund their investment projects. A *contingency fund* (finance kept for emergency use) may also be reserved in case of machinery breakdown or late deliveries from a supplier which would delay production. By contrast, job production and labour-intensive methods of production mean that a much greater proportion of a firm's costs go into remunerating labour with wages, salaries and other benefits.

HIGHER LEVEL EXTENSION: CELL PRODUCTION AND TEAMWORKING

One of the key drawbacks of traditional mass production methods is that people working in isolation become very bored and this reduces their levels of motivation and productivity. **Cell production** is a modern adaptation of assembly line production whereby sets of tasks are completed by teams (or 'cells'). Each cell is given responsibility for completing a part of the overall production process. Work is arranged so that each person can do all the tasks within their

HIGHER LEVEL

assigned group, even though each worker within a team may have different skills, i.e. the team is multiskilled. Cells are independent of one another but rely on each other to ensure that final production targets are met. Cell production is usually combined with *just-in-time production* (see Unit 5.7).

The advantages of using cell production include:

- There is some autonomy in decision-making. For example, the team selects its own team leader and arranges rest breaks for each member. In effect, each team operates as a small industrial unit.
- Teams hold some responsibility in the production process. They have responsibility for the team, individuals within the team and their production targets. They are also accountable for the quality of the items that they pass to the next group in the production process. *Accountability* can therefore lead to an improvement in quality standards.
- As teams have some degree of autonomy and responsibility, they are likely to gain some motivation. For example, the team decides how and when to rotate tasks to avoid boredom. In addition, cell production means that each team is likely to see a finished product (which is passed on the production line) so this has more meaning and creates a sense of achievement. By contrast, workers engaged in mass production processes tend to suffer from the boredom of repetitive work. This is not apparent with cell production as workers feel more empowered. Even for those who are reluctant to take on responsibility, working in teams can also be a form of motivation (see Unit 2.5).
- Although employees hold more responsibility in the production process, cell production workers still specialize in what they do. Teamworking, team dynamics and team spirit can therefore lead to higher levels of productivity.

The disadvantages of cell production include:

- The output is relatively lower when compared to traditional mass production methods.
- Tension and conflict may arise within teams, especially if the team leader is ineffective.
- Conflict can exist between different cells, especially when they work at different speeds (no one likes to be left waiting).
- Cell production is still rather capital intensive so the business has to spend a lot of money on buying, installing and servicing new machinery and equipment. Therefore, replacement costs will also be high.

PRODUCTION METHODS AND BUSINESS STRATEGY

In an ever-competitive business environment, organizations are constantly trying to improve their **efficiency**. In its simplest sense, efficiency occurs when a business is operating at its maximum output with minimum costs per unit of output. Efficiency is, therefore, a measure of how well a business uses its resources in the production process. An inefficient firm can have high unit costs due to its *idle resources* (human and capital resources that are not being used effectively but contribute towards the firm's costs). Hence such firms become uncompetitive and are unlikely to survive in the long term. Many firms have collapsed or been taken over due to their inefficiencies in production. Concorde, for example, proved highly unprofitable despite its unique selling point (supersonic air travel) and ceased operation in 2003.

Businesses will strive to stay competitive by looking at the various aspects of their operation and how they can raise **productivity** levels. Productivity is the rate at which inputs are transformed into outputs and are a good measure of a firm's efficiency level. For example, the productivity of post office staff could be measured by the number of customers that are served per period of time. Technological progress has meant that productivity can often be improved by using modern equipment and machinery. Alternatively, managers can also use methods of financial and non-financial motivation (see Unit 2.5) to raise labour productivity. However, achieving higher levels of productivity and efficiency is not straightforward. In theory, the increased capital intensity can increase both productivity and efficiency. However, in reality firms may not be able to afford such technologies. Furthermore, there is likely to be resistance to change from the workforce due to the uncertainty of new working practices and the threat of redundancies.

Management guru Michael Porter argues that firms cannot simultaneously and continuously offer high-quality products at very low prices. Instead, he argues that businesses must decide whether they wish to go for high profit margins by selling unique products of outstanding quality *or* aim for selling mass market products that earn low profit margins but sell in huge volumes. Porter also pointed out that there is a potential trade-off between quality and productivity; you cannot simply speed up the production of products that are of outstanding quality without sacrificing the standard of output. The decision will therefore have an implication of the type of production method used by an organization.

Different methods of production have varying implications on the other functional areas of a business. It is important for managers to consider the implications on the firm's human resources, finances and marketing. In addition, the choice of production method will affect other aspects of operations management (such as stock control systems and quality control). For example, in flow production it is important that firms use suppliers that deliver standardized raw materials and components in a timely fashion in order to prevent bottlenecks in the production process. Modern management thinking has led to a system of *just-in-time* stock control (see Unit 5.7) and *total quality culture* in the workplace (see Unit 5.4).

REVIEW QUESTIONS 5.1

1 What is meant by 'operations management'?

2 What is the 'production process'?

3 State the 5 M's necessary for the production process.

4 Distinguish between 'job', 'batch' and 'mass' production.

5 What are the advantages and disadvantages of 'job', 'batch' and 'mass' production?

6 Using examples, distinguish between 'capital-intensive' and 'labour-intensive' industries.

Higher Level extension

7 State the implications of a change in production methods on a firm's finances, human resource management and marketing.

8 What is meant by 'cell production/teamworking'?

9 What are the benefits and limitations of cell production?

10 Explain how productivity and efficiency in the production process are important to the survival of an organization.

Batch production involves producing a collection of identical products (known as a **batch**). Work on each batch is fully completed before production switches to another batch. It is used where the level of demand for a product is frequent and steady.

Capital intensive means that the manufacturing or provision of a product relies heavily on machinery and equipment, such as automated production systems. Hence, the cost of capital accounts for a higher proportion of a firm's overall production costs.

Cell production is a production method that organizes workers into independent 'cells' (teams). Each cell comprises of multiskilled employees who have responsibility and autonomy in completing a whole unit of work in the production process.

Flow production is a form of mass production whereby different operations are continuously and progressively carried out in sequence.

Line production is a form of flow production whereby a product is assembled in various stages along a conveyor belt (or assembly line) until a finished product is made.

Mass production is the manufacturing of large amounts of a homogeneous (standardized) product. Unit costs of production are relatively low when using mass production methods.

Job production is a method of production that involves the production of a unique or one-off job. The job is entirely completed by one person (such a tailor) or by a team of people (such as architects).

Productivity measures the level of labour and/or capital efficiency of a business by comparing its level of inputs with the level of its output.

Production process, also known as the **transformation process**, refers to the method of turning inputs into outputs by adding value in a cost-effective way.

Purchasing is the buying of raw materials, components and/or equipment needed for the production process. Large firms will often centralize this function to allow the business to negotiate better prices with suppliers in order to gain purchasing economies of scale.

Specialization means the division of a large task or project into smaller tasks that allow individuals to concentrate on one or two areas of expertise. Specialization is an essential part of mass production.

Standardization means producing an identical or homogenous product in large quantities, such as printing a particular magazine, book or newspaper.

Costs and Revenues

UNIT 5.2

He that wants money, means, and content is without three good friends.

William Shakespeare (1564–1616), English playwright

Key topics

- Types of costs: fixed, variable, semi-variable, direct and indirect
- Revenue and sources of revenue
- The role of contribution

Higher Level extension

- Contribution and multiproduct firms
- Cost and profit centres

INTRODUCTION

In everyday language, a consumer might say that a t-shirt 'costs $15'. In business language, the correct terminology is 'the **price** was $15'. **Cost** refers to the expenditure in producing the t-shirt, not the amount paid by the customer to buy it. Box 5.2a outlines some of the main business costs. **Revenue** is the money a business receives from the sale of products to customers. A positive difference between revenues and costs will then leave the business with a **profit**. This Unit looks at the various types of business costs and revenues. In addition, there is an examination of the various methods of cost control in a business.

Box 5.2a Examples of business costs for a clothes retailer

Set-up costs

- Buildings, e.g. physical alterations to the building as required
- Connection and installation of utilities and power, e.g. telephone lines, electricity and internet connection
- Equipment, e.g. cash register, computer, phone and office equipment (such as desks, tables and chairs)
- Fixtures and fittings, e.g. shop front, signage, counter, shelving and changing rooms for customers
- Initial stock of supplies
- Legal and professional fees, e.g. for licences
- Premises, e.g. down payment on a mortgage or a rent deposit
- Recruitment costs for the hiring of staff

Running costs

- Clothing or uniforms for the staff
- Corporation tax on business profits
- Depreciation on capital equipment
- Marketing costs
- Miscellaneous expenses, e.g. window cleaning, postage, stationery and internet connection
- Packaging materials, e.g. wrapping paper, gift tags and carrier bags
- Regular mortgage, rent and/or lease payments
- Repairs and maintenance
- Staff wages and salaries
- Stocks from suppliers
- Utility bill payments, e.g. electricity and telephone lines

TYPES OF COSTS

Fixed costs

Fixed costs are the costs of production that a business has to pay regardless of how much it produces or sells. Note that this means fixed costs have to be met even if there is no output. For example, rent on leased premises and interest on existing bank loans will have to be paid no matter how much a firm sells or produces. Other examples of fixed costs include advertising, market research, management salaries, stationery, security and professional accountancy fees. These costs remain unchanged in the short run. Figure 5.2a is a diagrammatic representation of fixed costs. The graph shows that the business in question has total fixed costs (TFC) of $5,000, i.e. this sum of money has to be paid regardless of the level of output.

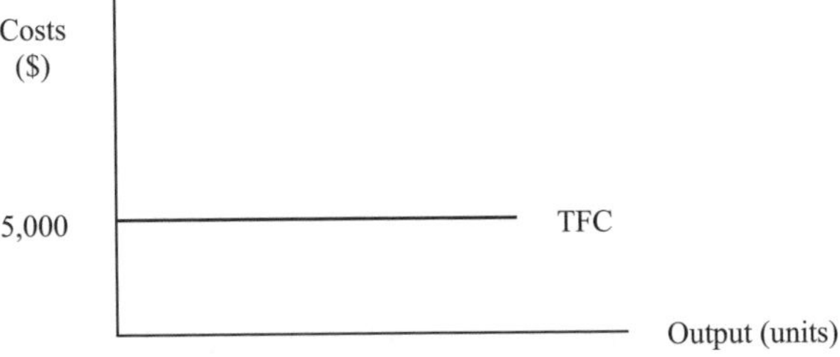

Figure 5.2a Fixed costs of a business

Note that fixed costs can change, but these changes happen *independently* of the level of output. For example, a property owner decides to raise rents due to higher property prices in the economy. Another example would be directors and managers being paid higher salaries due to rising costs of living. In both cases, fixed costs increase but are not directly linked to the firm's output level.

Variable costs

Variable costs are the costs of production that change in direct proportion to the level of output or sales. This means that if the level of output or sales doubles, the variable costs would also double. For example, raw material costs will increase if a textiles firm makes more curtains. Other examples of variable costs include commission earned by sales staff and the packaging costs directly associated with output or sales. In theory, if there is no production, the variable costs are equal to zero. As the product output increases, so too do the variable costs of production (as shown in Figure 5.2b).

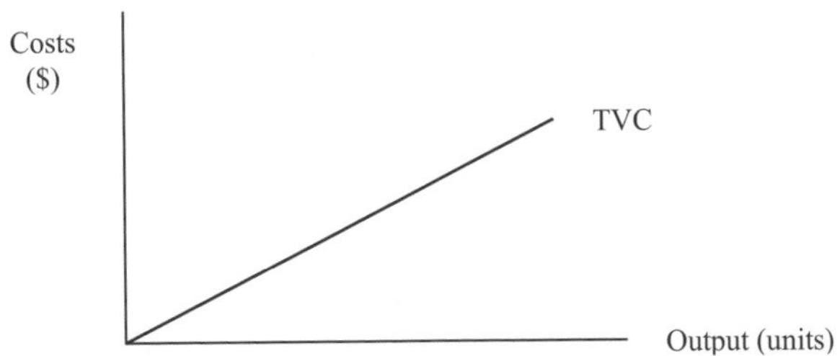

Figure 5.2b Variable costs of a business

Adding the total variable costs (TVC) of production to the fixed costs (TFC) gives the value for **total cost** (TC), i.e. TC = TVC + TFC. It can be seen in Figure 5.2c that the TC line starts at the same value of fixed costs because these have to be paid even if there is no output. Notice that the numerical difference between the TC and TVC lines at each level of output is equal to the value of the fixed costs.

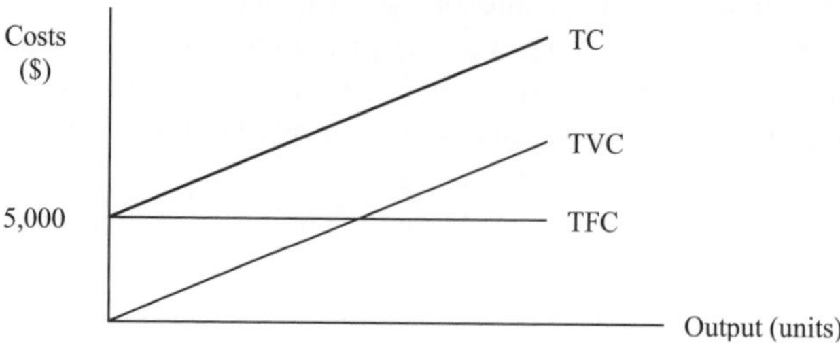

Figure 5.2c Total costs of a business

Semi-variable costs

Semi-variable costs are those that contain an element of both fixed and variable costs. They only tend to change when production or sales exceed a certain level of output. Mobile telephone bills, for example, may allow a user to have a predetermined number of 'free minutes'. However, there is also a 'standing charge' which means no matter how much (or how little) the person uses the phone, there is a fixed minimum monthly charge. If the user exceeds the quota of free minutes, then the telephone bill becomes variable.

In reality, many costs could be classified as semi-variable costs. The payment to labour is not necessarily as straightforward as either a wage (variable cost) or salary (fixed cost). For example, overtime payment could be a variable element for those earning salaries. Sales people tend to earn a fixed basic pay in addition to their commission (a variable element). Machinery and vehicles are usually classed as a fixed cost, but their maintenance and depreciation costs will increase as they are used more (due to higher levels of output or sales).

Direct costs

Direct costs are similar to variable costs in that they change with the level of output. However, a direct cost is specifically related to a particular project or the output of a single product; without that particular project or product, the costs would not be incurred by the business. By contrast, variable costs relate to the level of output in general. Since direct costs rely directly on output levels they are a type of variable costs but are more suitable to look at when dealing with businesses that produce more than one product (as measured by various *cost centres*). Examples of direct costs involved in the purchase of a commercial building include: consultancy fees, solicitor's fees, telephone bills, postage, photocopying costs, mortgage fees and bank charges.

Note that what is a variable cost for one firm is not necessarily so for another. For instance, catering costs for a flight on a mainstream airline carrier, such as Singapore Airlines, would be classed as *variable costs*. This is because the more passengers on the aeroplane, the more food and drinks will be required since they are included in the ticket price (hence raising the overall costs in proportion to the number of passengers). However, for a flight on a 'no-frills' airline carrier, such as Air Asia or Ryan Air, the catering costs are considered to be *direct costs*. The food and drinks are directly related to the flight, but passengers do not all demand meals and drinks since these are paid for on an individual basis.

Indirect costs (overheads)

Indirect costs, also known as **facilities and administrative costs** (F&A) or **overheads**, are those that cannot be clearly related to the level of output of any single product, i.e. they are not directly linked with the level of production or sale of a product. For example, the costs of fuel and power can be associated with the level of production, but may not be directly linked to a particular product but apply to several or all different areas of the business. Other examples of overheads might include: rent, advertising, legal expenses, administrative staff salaries, insurance, security, stationery, shipping and postage costs, utility bills and accounting fees. Unlike fixed costs, indirect costs are not readily identified with a particular business activity. However, most indirect costs could also be considered as being fixed costs since they do not directly relate to the level of output.

Exam Tip!
In general, the terms *indirect costs* and *direct costs* are used when referring to businesses that produce or sell a range of products and therefore operate cost centres and profit centres (covered later in this Unit). The terms *fixed costs* and *variable costs*, as used in break-even analysis (see Unit 5.3), tend to be used when referring to the sale or production of a single type of product.

Question 5.2.1

Airline costs

a Classify the following costs for a mainstream airline company as fixed or variable costs:

i Advertising and promotions.

ii Airport charges.

iii Fuel.

iv Meals and drinks onboard.

v Remuneration of administrative staff.

vi Remuneration of flight attendants. *[3 marks]*

b With reference to the airline industry, distinguish between direct and indirect costs. *[4 marks]*

Average costs

Unit 1.7 looked at how the cost per unit (average cost) could be reduced by engaging in larger scale production. The average cost of production is calculated by dividing total costs by the level of output. For instance, if total costs of producing 1,000 t-shirts amounts to $8,000, the cost of each t-shirt averages out at $8.

Average costs consist of two components: **Average fixed costs** (AFC) and **Average variable costs** (AVC). AFC is calculated by dividing the total fixed costs by the level of output, i.e. AFC = TFC / Q. Similarly, AVC is calculated by dividing the total variable costs by the level of output, i.e. AVC = TVC / Q (see Box 5.2b).

The average fixed costs of a firm will decline continuously with larger levels of output (see Figure 5.2d). This is because the total fixed costs remain constant but are spread over an increasing amount of output, i.e. the same (fixed) costs are being divided by a larger and larger number (level of output).

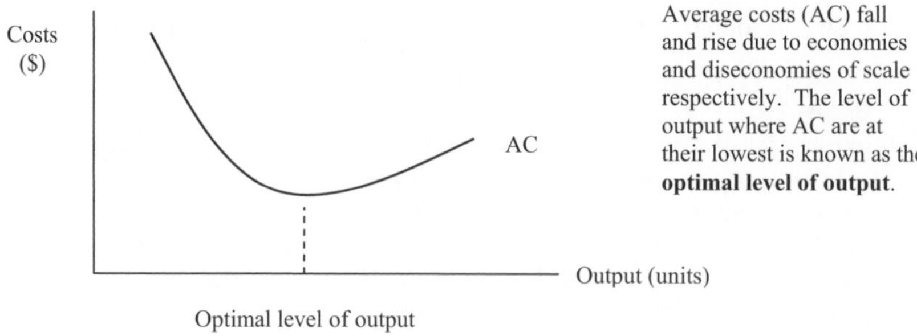

Figure 5.2d Average costs of a business

Box 5.2b Costs formulae

Key: Q = Quantity (or level of output)

- Total Cost (TC) — TC = TFC + TVC
- Average Cost (AC) — AC = TC ÷ Q
  or
  AC = AFC + AVC
- Average Fixed Costs (AFC) — AFC = TFC ÷ Q
- Average Variable Costs (AVC) — AVC = TVC ÷ Q
- Total Variable Costs — TVC = AVC x Q
- Total Fixed Costs — TFC = AFC x Q
- Marginal Cost (MC) — $MC = \frac{\delta TC}{\delta Q}$

Marginal cost refers to the extra costs incurred when increasing output by one unit.

Note: The above cost and revenue formulae are not given to candidates in the examination.

Question 5.2.2

Calculating business costs

a Complete the table for the costs of producing wooden toy trains. *[5 marks]*

Output (Units)	TFC ($)	TVC ($)	TC ($)	AC ($)
0	2,000			
100		500		
200		1,000		
300			3,450	
400			3,800	
500				9.00
600				9.70

(cont.)

b Use graph paper to construct two separate sets of graphs:

- **i** TFC, TVC and TC curves *[5 marks]*
- **ii** AC curve and mark the *optimum level of output* on the diagram. *[3 marks]*

c Explain the reason for the shape of the average cost curve. *[3 marks]*

d Explain why a business might not be able to produce at the optimum level of output. *[4 marks]*

REVENUE

Revenue refers to the proceeds coming into a business, usually from the sale of goods and/or services. Revenue that comes from the sale of a firm's products is called **sales revenue** or **sales turnover**. The formula for calculating sales revenue is:

Price x Quantity sold

For example, if a business charges $60 on average for each pair of its shoes and sells 100 pairs in a week, its total sales revenue for shoes will be $6,000 (i.e. $60 × 100) for that period.

Box 5.2c Revenue formulae

- Total Revenue (TR) $TR = P \times Q$
- Average Revenue (AR) $AR = \frac{TR}{Q}$

since: $P = \frac{TR}{Q}$

then: $AR \equiv P$

- Marginal Revenue (MR) $MR = \frac{\delta TR}{\delta Q}$

Marginal revenue refers to the extra revenue earned from selling an extra unit of output.

Revenue does not only come from the sale of goods and services. Money can come into a firm from other means, depending on the type of firm. Other sources of non-sales revenue for a business include:

- *Subventions* – These are subsidies offered to certain firms to help reduce their costs of production. They are usually given to organizations that generate benefits to society, such as schools and hospitals.
- *Grants* – Similar to subventions, these are also a form of government assistance. However, grants are a lump sum payment offered to both private and public sector organizations. Self-employed people, for example, may qualify for grants to help them set up their own business.
- *Donations* – These are financial gifts from individuals or other organizations. Charities and non-profit organizations (see Unit 1.2) tend to rely on this source of revenue.
- *Fund-raising* – Organizations can run special fund-raising events to help generate extra revenue. Schools, for example, often run annual carnivals to raise extra money to improve their school environment.

- *Sponsorship* – This is a form of below-the-line promotion (see Unit 4.5) whereby the sponsor financially supports an organization in return for a prominent display of the donor's brand or trademark.
- *Interest* – Businesses can earn interest from its cash holdings at the bank. For some cash-rich businesses, this can be a useful source of revenue.
- *Dividends* – Most companies will hold shares in other businesses. This means that they are shareholders of other companies and are therefore entitled to payments of any declared dividends.
- *Sale of assets* – Firms can sell off their underused or idle assets for cash.

In addition, firms can raise different sources of finance (see Unit 3.1) to fund their operations.

Question 5.2.3

Amechi's Fruit & Veg

Matthew Amechi owns and manages a fresh fruits and vegetables store (Amechi's Fruit & Veg) in a small village. Each morning, he drives his delivery vehicle to an out-of-town **wholesale market** to buy fresh fruits and vegetables. During peak seasons, Matthew employs two people to help him at the store. Matthew does not own the store but pays rent each month to his landlady. In addition, Matthew has to pay for the loan on his one-year-old vehicle plus other running costs such as lighting.

a Define the meaning of **wholesale market**. *[2 marks]*

b Outline two other indirect costs that Matthew Amechi might have to pay. *[4 marks]*

c Matthew buys his tomatoes at $0.80 per kilo. Calculate Matthew's monthly cost, revenue and profit on tomatoes if he buys 50 kg of tomatoes and sells them at $1.20 per kg. *[4 marks]*

d Matthew has bought 100 kg of apples this month. He manages to sell 80 kg of apples at the usual price of $2.00 per kg. In order to get rid of the excess supply, he reduces the price of the remaining stock to $1.50 per kg.

i State the marginal revenue generated from sale of the 81st kilogram of apples. *[1 mark]*

ii If he manages to sell all his apples, calculate the total revenue from the sale of apples. *[3 marks]*

CONTRIBUTION

Contribution refers to the amount of money that remains after all *direct* and *variable costs* have been taken away from the sales revenue of a business. The formula for contribution is therefore:

$$\text{Contribution per unit} = P - AVC$$

where P is the price (or average revenue) and AVC represents the average variable costs.

For example, if a firm sells its chairs at $100 each whilst the direct and variable costs are $45 per chair, the business makes a contribution of $55 per chair. Note that this is not the actual profit made because *fixed* and *indirect costs* have not yet been accounted for. However, each chair sold 'contributes' $55 towards the payment of the firm's overheads and fixed costs. Once these have been covered, further sales will contribute towards the profit of the business. In other words:

$$\text{Profit} = \text{Total contribution} - TFC$$

Hence, it is possible to see that profits can be increased in the following cases:

- Increasing sales of the product to help to raise the total contribution
- Decreasing variable costs, perhaps through negotiating better deals from current suppliers or seeking new suppliers that are more competitive
- Reducing fixed costs and overheads, perhaps through better financial control methods or the use of cost and profit centres (covered later in this Unit)

Contribution analysis can be useful in helping a business to identify areas that are relatively profitable and areas that may need a little more attention. Consider the data in Table 5.2a which shows how contribution analysis might be used.

Table 5.2a Contribution analysis – Café Cuppa

Product	Cappuccino	Latte	Mocha	English tea	Orange Juice	Spring Water
Average unit price ($)	5.50	5.75	6.55	3.20	2.55	1.80
Average variable cost ($)	2.25	2.75	3.15	0.95	1.05	0.80
Unit Contribution ($)	3.25	3.00	3.40	2.25	1.50	1.00

Examination of the above data suggests that all products are profitable and contribute positively towards the fixed costs of Café Cuppa. The strongest product is the Mocha; despite its relatively high unit cost of production, it earns the firm $3.40 contribution per unit sold. The most vulnerable product is the Spring Water which only earns the firm $1.00 per unit sold. It is important to also have access to the number of units sold before we can conclude which product is the most profitable. However, it is clear that twice the number of units of Orange Juice needs to be sold in order to earn the same contribution as one unit of Latte.

HIGHER LEVEL EXTENSION: CONTRIBUTION ANALYSIS FOR MULTIPRODUCT FIRMS

In a multiproduct firm, each product is likely to contribute something towards the payment of fixed and indirect costs. Even if a particular product is loss-making but has a positive contribution, managers will be unlikely to remove it. This is because the product contributes towards covering the fixed and direct costs of a business; profits of the firm would actually be lower if the positive contribution from the loss-making product ceased. The formula for calculating profits in a multiproduct firm is:

$$\text{Profit} = \text{Total contribution} - (\text{TFC} + \text{Overheads})$$

In general, any product that makes a positive contribution is worth producing since it will help towards the payment of the firm's fixed costs and hence profits. This can be seen in Table 5.2b which continues the analysis shown in the previous example (see Table 5.2a above). Assume that the firm's overheads are $8,600 per month.

HIGHER LEVEL

Table 5.2b Advanced contribution analysis – Café Cuppa

Product	Cappuccino	Latte	Mocha	English tea	Orange Juice	Spring Water
Average unit price ($)	5.50	5.75	6.55	3.20	2.55	1.80
Average variable cost ($)	2.25	2.75	3.15	0.95	1.05	0.80
Unit Contribution	3.25	3.00	3.40	2.25	1.50	1.00
Sales (units per month)	1,440	1,215	980	1,264	766	800
Contribution ($)	4,680	3,645	3,332	2,844	1,149	800
Total contribution ($)						16,450
Overheads ($ per month)						8,600
Profit / Loss ($ per month)						**7,850**

Whilst the Mocha was the largest earner (in terms of contribution per unit), things change around after the sales figures are analysed. The largest earner is now the Cappuccino. Notice that Spring Water outsells Orange Juice but the latter contributes more towards overall profits (because of its larger unit contribution). The same applies when comparing the figures for English Tea and Latte.

Contribution analysis has several uses for a business:

- **Contribution cost pricing** – Contribution analysis allows a business to identify the amount of profit it makes on an individual sale. This can help the firm in setting prices to ensure that contribution is made towards payment of fixed and indirect costs.
- **Product portfolio management** – The analysis can help firms decide which products should be given investment priority. In general, products with a higher total contribution per time period tend to be given priority. Products earning lower levels of unit contribution will rely on high sales volumes in order to avoid being withdrawn or replaced by other products.
- **Allocation of overheads to cost and profit centres** – Contribution analysis can ensure that costs are allocated fairly (see next section in this Unit).
- **Make-or-buy decisions** – Contribution analysis can help managers decide whether it should produce (make) the products or purchase them (buy) from suppliers. The relative difference between the unit contribution of making or buying is likely to determine the outcome. Make-or-buy decisions are covered in Unit 5.7.
- **Special order decisions** – These occur when a customer places an order at a price that differs from the normal price charged by the firm. The price could be higher (although the customer will request added benefits from offering a higher price, such as shorter delivery times) or lower (probably because the customer is buying a significant amount of the product). Whether the business takes on this special order will largely depend on the total contribution made from such a deal. Special order decisions are covered in more detail in Unit 5.3.

HIGHER LEVEL EXTENSION: COST AND PROFIT CENTRES

As a business grows in size, it becomes more difficult to manage its finances. Costs and revenues from different areas of the business become harder to account for. Hence, different sections of the business are divided up into either *cost centres* or *profit centres* with a manager being held responsible for the costs and/or revenues incurred for each department or centre. The various ways of allocating costs across different centres are explained in Unit 4.4.

Cost centres

A cost centre is a department or unit of a business that incurs costs but is not involved in making any profit. These costs are clearly attributed to the activities of that department, such as wages, salaries, lighting, components and capital expenditure. Making these different sections of a business aware and accountable for their contribution towards the firm's costs may help managers to have better cost control, i.e. to operate within their allocated budgets. Hence, a manager will be assigned to monitor and manage the expenditure of the cost centre. This will allow the business to identify which departments are costing the firm the most money.

Profit centres

A profit centre is a department or unit of a business that incurs both costs and revenues. They tend to be used by large businesses that are diversified or have a broad product mix. The costs and revenues are clearly attributed to the activities of that department or unit. Again, a manager is appointed to be responsible for the profit centre, including having to produce an independent profit and loss account. Each profit centre is responsible for contributing to the overall profits of the business. For example, a bank may split its profit centres based on geographical locations, i.e. branch by branch. Alternatively, it may be based on the source of revenue, such as private banking, commercial banking, foreign exchange, mortgages, loans, insurance and financial planning (such as stock exchange or pension services). Both Starbucks and McDonald's operate profit centres on a branch-by-branch basis. Having profit centres allows an organization to identify the areas that generate the most (and least) revenue.

Advantages of operating cost and profit centres are:

- It forces managers to be more accountable for their department's contribution towards the firm's costs, especially since the direct costs of production can easily be allocated to cost and profit centres.
- The business can identify areas of financial weakness. In large firms, it is not always clear whether a certain area of the business is making a loss, especially if the organization as a whole is profitable. Using cost and profit centres allows a business to identify sections or products of the organization that are loss-making.
- There is no need to fuss about whether a cost is fixed, variable, indirect or direct. All costs can be allocated or spread across the various cost and profit centres of a business.
- Departments and smaller teams tend to work much better than larger ones which may suffer from disorganization and a lack of effective communication. This promotes better team spirit within the different areas of an organization.
- Benchmarking with the most efficient cost and profit centres within the organization can take place to improve its overall efficiency.
- Delegating power to those in charge of cost and profit centres can be a form of motivating these people. They will develop important management skills in the process. In addition, delegation also helps to speed up decision-making in the organization.

- The performance of cost and profit centres can be used as a form of rewarding teams. Those that achieve their targets and/or operate effectively within their budget may be rewarded. This therefore acts as a form of motivation for a wider range of people.
- Ultimately, improved financial accountability and efficiency leads to improved cost control and therefore higher profits for the business.

Drawbacks of using cost and profit centres include:

- Allocating indirect costs such as rent, interest, insurance and administrative costs is a subjective task (see Unit 4.4). This means that it can be difficult to accurately calculate the overheads attributable to each cost centre.
- The profits of a profit centre can change simply because of the apportionment of fixed costs. Allocating a greater proportion of costs to a particular centre will reduce its profits, although this does not represent its underlying trading position.
- The performance of a cost or profit centre can be changed by external factors beyond its control, such as higher raw material prices. This therefore bears no resemblance to the productivity and efficiency of the individual departments.
- Data collection in order to accurately account for costs and revenues of each centre is likely to be expensive and time consuming.
- May promote unnecessary internal competition to cut costs and/or raise revenues. This can create tension and conflict between the various sections of an organization.
- Managing cost and profit centres can add to the pressure and stress on staff. This may therefore lead to motivational problems.
- Centres are less likely to consider social responsibilities and ethical objectives (see Unit 1.3) if they are run as profit centres. This is because the compliance costs of being ethical and socially responsible will raise the profit centre's costs, thereby lowering its profit level.

Question 5.2.4

Cathay Pacific Airways

Cathay Pacific Airways, Hong Kong's national carrier, is one of the largest Asian airline companies. It operates over 100 routes worldwide. Its operations are varied and include divisions that are responsible for cargo, in-flight entertainment, food catering, The Marco Polo Club (frequent flyer programme) and Codeshare Agreements (a strategic alliance with Oneworld member airlines).

a Explain why many businesses such as Cathay Pacific assign cost and profit centres to departmental managers. *[4 marks]*

b Comment on the difficulties likely to be involved in allocating Cathay Pacific's overheads. *[4 marks]*

Apportioning overheads to cost and profit centres

Unit 4.4 explains the different pricing strategies used by a firm. Prices have to cover the costs of production in order for the business to make any profit. Hence the method of allocating (or apportioning) costs to different profit centres will affect the prices that are charged. There are two main ways of apportioning costs:

- **Full costing** (see page 528) allocates the total indirect costs to each centre based on a single predetermined criterion, such as:
  - How much *output* a cost or profit centre produces as a proportion of the organization's total output

- Each profit centre's *sales revenues* as a percentage of the total sales of the business
- Percentage of *floor space area* used by each division (a useful criterion for allocating rents)
- *Number of employees* within each cost or profit centre as a percentage of the workforce (useful for allocating personnel overheads)
- *Value of capital equipment* for each centre (practical criterion for allocating depreciation costs).

Since most firms produce more than a single product, it is slightly difficult to allocate fixed costs to the various products. However, the use of contribution analysis makes this task a little easier (see 'Contribution analysis for multiproduct firms' on page 633). Dividing the overall profits of a business into different profit centres takes into account the different contributions made by each division.

- **Absorption costing** (see page 530) allocates both the direct and indirect production costs to appropriate cost and profit centres. The direct costs are easy to allocate since they are generated by and specific to each cost centre. Overheads are more difficult to allocate since they are not unique to a particular cost or profit centre. Unlike full costing which uses a single criterion to allocate all overheads to cost and profit centres, absorption costing divides indirect costs based on several or all of the above criteria. This may be a more representative account of their contribution to the costs of the business, although it is not as simple to calculate as using full costing.

Question 5.2.5

Allocating costs

Level 7 is an independent tuition college that runs IB revision courses in Art, Business, Chemistry and Design. Its indirect costs are $3,000 per month. Details of its costs and revenues are as follows:

Department	Art	Business	Chemistry	Design
Tuition fee ($ per hour)	$35	$40	$38	$32
Customers (hours per month)	225	125	320	185

a Calculate the monthly sales revenue for each profit centre. *[2 marks]*

b Apportion the overheads according to sales revenue for each profit centre. *[6 marks]*

c From your answer to Question **5b**, calculate the contribution made by each profit centre. *[4 marks]*

d Explain one other criterion that *Level 7* could use to allocate its indirect costs. *[3 marks]*

HIGHER LEVEL

COSTS AND REVENUES AND BUSINESS STRATEGY

Being aware of costs allows managers to be in control of their finances. Cost control is crucial if a business is to maintain and/or improve its profitability. Large firms in particular benefit from being able to measure the financial performance of each division of their organization. Many American firms use the acronym FORCE (Focus On Reducing Costs Everywhere) as a tool for staying competitive. For example, in 2007, Citigroup announced it would cut 17,000 jobs worldwide in a bid to keep its costs under control. The largest US financial company and owners of Citibank claimed that the job losses, which represent about 5% of its workforce, would save it billions of dollars each year. This does not mean that cost-cutting will raise the profitability of a firm, but it can help to keep costs under control. Cost-cutting can be justified if it leads to improved efficiency and profitability for the organization.

In order to control costs, managers must understand the different classifications of costs and how they arise. This can then allow a business to accurately allocate costs to different products in its portfolio and to set prices that generate profits for the firm. How the system of cost allocation is used will depend on the organizational culture of the business, such as its management style. After all, cost allocation is largely based on the subjectivity of managers.

Whilst costs are vitally important, revenues are just as important, if not more. The UK Institute of Management suggests that good businesses focus 80% of their energies on ways to raise revenues and only 20% of resources on cost-cutting. Indeed, forward-looking businesses can afford to spend more money provided that the revenues and profits allow it to do so. For example, PPR (the French owners of luxury brands such as Gucci and Yves Saint Laurent) bought out sports brand Puma in order to make more revenue – not to save on its costs.

In monitoring and managing a firm's costs and revenues, managers will use a variety of tools in addition to using cost and profit centres. For instance, budgeting and variance analysis are vitally important (see Unit 3.4) in controlling business activity. Human resources also have a key role in helping the business to control costs and to raise revenues. Managers must have the means to measure and assess the performance of staff, and to reward them appropriately. Again, these issues highlight the interrelated nature of business and management.

REVIEW QUESTIONS 5.2

1 Explain the difference between 'price' and 'costs'.

2 Give five examples of start-up costs and five examples of running costs for a new business.

3 Distinguish between 'fixed', 'variable', 'direct' and 'indirect' costs of production.

4 State five sources of revenue for a business.

5 What is 'contribution' and how is it calculated?

Higher Level extension

6 Why is contribution analysis useful for businesses that produce a range of products?

7 What are 'profit centres' and how do they differ from cost centres?

8 What is meant by 'apportioning costs'?

9 Distinguish between 'full costing' and 'absorption costing' as methods of apportioning costs.

Average cost refers to the amount a firm spends on producing one unit of output. It is calculated by dividing the total costs of production by the quantity produced, or by adding up the average fixed costs and the average variable costs.

Average revenue is found by dividing a firm's total revenue by its level of output. It is the same as the price charged since average revenue is the amount of money received for each unit sold.

Contribution is the difference between sales revenues and total variable costs. The difference is then used to contribute towards payment of fixed costs. Once all costs, fixed and variable, are covered then the firm has made profit.

Contribution per unit is found by dividing the contribution of a firm by its sales level (or using the formula Price minus Average Variable Cost). It works out the contribution made by selling a single unit of a product.

Cost centres are clearly identifiable autonomous parts of an organization for which costs can be attributed.

Direct costs are those that are directly linked to the production of a specific product.

Fixed costs are the costs that do not vary with the level of output. They exist even if there is no output, such as the cost of rent, management salaries and interest repayments on bank loans.

Indirect costs, also known as **overheads**, are costs which do not directly link to the production or sale of a specific product. Examples include rent, management salaries, cleaning staff wages and lighting.

Profit centres are clearly identifiable autonomous divisions of an organization for which both costs and revenues can be worked out.

Revenue refers to the money that a business collects from the sale of its goods and services. It is calculated by multiplying the unit price of each product by the quantity sold.

Semi-variable costs are those that have an element of both fixed costs and variable costs, such as power and electricity.

Variable costs are those that change in proportion to the level of output, such as raw materials and piece-rate earnings of production workers.

Break-even Analysis

UNIT 5.3

He who has no thirst has no business at the fountain.

Dutch proverb

Key topics

- Contribution
- Break-even
- Margin of safety

Higher Level extension

- Effects of changes in price and/or cost on the break-even quantity, profit and margin of safety
- Assumptions and limitations of break-even analysis
- Target profit and revenues

INTRODUCTION

Break-even exists when a business makes neither a profit nor a loss. This occurs at the level of output where *total costs* equal *total revenue*, i.e. TC = TR. Break-even is often a key objective of new and unestablished firms. This suggests that managers need to pay careful attention to their cash-flow situation (see Unit 3.3) by monitoring and controlling the money coming into the business (revenues) with the money leaving the business (costs).

This Unit looks at the quantitative and graphical methods used to calculate a firm's break-even level of output. The advantages and drawbacks of the model are also examined.

CONTRIBUTION

The concept of contribution (see Unit 5.2) is crucial to the understanding of break-even analysis. Recall that *unit contribution* is the difference between a product's price and its variable costs of production, i.e. contribution = price *less* average variable costs. Any product that makes a positive contribution will help towards paying some of the fixed costs of the business.

Therefore, contribution analysis suggests three broad ways in which profits can be improved:

- Increase sales revenue, e.g. by using appropriate marketing strategies to attract more customers.
- Reduce variable costs, e.g. by seeking cheaper production methods. This would help to raise the contribution made from selling each unit of output.
- Reduce fixed costs, e.g. negotiating cheaper rents or limiting extravagant company expenses. This will also help to reduce the break-even level of output.

BREAK-EVEN ANALYSIS

All business managers are concerned with the difference between revenue and costs. A business can only survive in the long run if revenues are greater than costs, i.e. if it is profitable. New firms, in particular, will want to determine the level of sales that must be generated for the business to earn a profit. Break-even analysis is a management tool that can be used to serve this purpose.

A business can be in any one of the following financial situations:

- **Loss** – when costs of production exceed the revenues of the business
- **Break-even** – when the revenues of the business equal the costs of production
- **Profit** – when revenues exceed costs of production.

Carrying out a break-even analysis can inform managers of two things:

- Whether it is financially worthwhile to produce a particular good or service, such as introducing a new product
- The level of profits that the business is likely to earn if things go according to plan.

Take the following as a numerical example. Suppose that a jeans retailer has fixed costs of $2,500 per month and that each pair of jeans sells for an average of $30. Variable costs are known to be $10 per pair of jeans. There are three ways to calculate or determine the **break-even point** (see Box 5.3a for break-even formulae).

1. Interpretation from a break-even chart by identifying the point where TC = TR.

In Figure 5.3a, the break-even level of output occurs at 125 pairs of jeans.

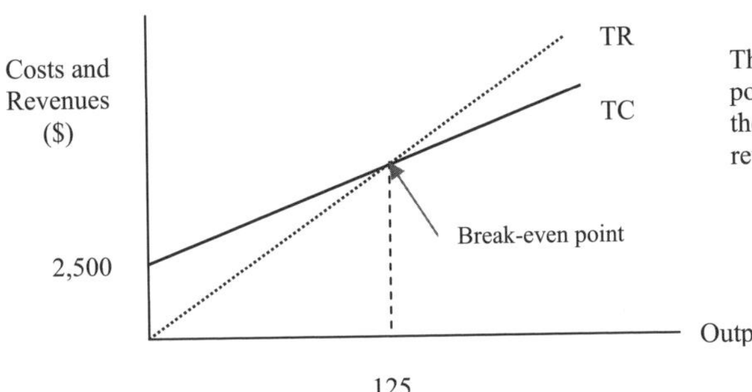

The break-even point refers to the position on a break-even chart where the total cost line intersects the total revenue line, i.e. where TC = TR.

Figure 5.3a Break-even chart

2. Using the TC = TR rule

Using this method, the break-even point can be calculated by comparing the total sales revenues with total costs. Recall from Unit 5.2 that total revenue is calculated as Price × Quantity sold and that Total Costs consist of both fixed and variable costs. Break-even can then be calculated as:

$P \times Q = TFC + TVC$

$30Q = 2{,}500 + 10Q$

$20Q = 2{,}500$

$Q = 125$ units (or pairs of jeans)

3. Using the Unit Contribution rule: Break-even = Fixed Costs ÷ Unit Contribution

This is the quicker of the two quantitative methods of calculating the break-even point. Putting in the figures gives us the following:

Unit Contribution = Price *minus* average variable costs = $30 *minus* $10 = $20

Therefore, the break-even is $2,500 ÷ $20 = 125 pairs of jeans.

Box 5.3a Break-even formulae

- Unit Contribution: P – AVC
- Break-even: TC = TR or $\frac{\text{Fixed costs}}{\text{Unit contribution}}$
- Profit (or loss): TR – TC

All three methods give the same answer, although it is usually quicker to use either methods 1 or 3. This shows that the business needs to sell 125 pairs of jeans each month in order for it to break-even. The break-even chart also reveals the sales levels needed to generate a profit. Any sales beyond the break-even level of output will generate a surplus (or profits) whereas levels of sales below the break-even point mean that the firm will make a **loss** for that month. The **break-even quantity** (BEQ) refers to the level of output where total costs equal total revenues. This can be shown in a break-even chart (see Figure 5.3b).

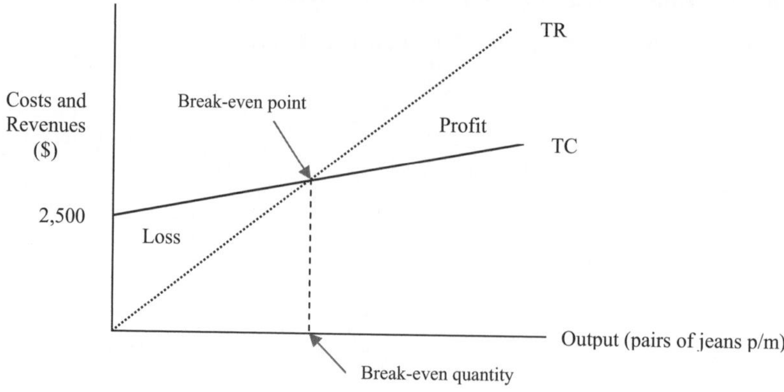

Figure 5.3b Break-even chart – profit or loss

Exam Tip!
Break-even is a popular examination topic. Therefore it is important to be able to accurately construct *and* interpret information shown in a break-even chart. For example, candidates often label the axes on a break-even graph inaccurately. Perhaps more importantly, candidates must be able to modify a break-even chart and analyse its implications for a business.

Question 5.3.1

a Use the *unit contribution* method to calculate the break-even quantity for a firm that has:

- TFC = $200,000
- AVC = $5
- Price = $30 *[2 marks]*

b Calculate the value of sales at the break-even quantity. *[2 marks]*

THE MARGIN OF SAFETY

The margin of safety measures the difference between a firm's current sales quantity and the quantity needed to break-even, i.e. it shows how much demand (for a product) exceeds the break-even quantity. The larger the positive difference between a firm's sales output and its BEQ, the safer the firm will be in terms of earning profits, especially if there are adverse changes in the marketplace. A positive margin of safety means that the firm makes a profit, whereas a negative margin of safety means the firm makes a loss. The margin of safety is also known as the **safety margin**. The formula for calculating the safety margin is:

Safety margin = Level of demand – Break-even quantity

For example, if the level of demand for the jeans retailer in the above example is 200 pairs per week, then the safety margin is 75 units (i.e. 200 – 125). This means that the business can sell 75 pairs of jeans less than its current level and still not make a loss, as shown in Figure 5.3c. Hence, the smaller the margin of safety, the more vulnerable a business becomes to changes in the market. Many businesses prefer to express the margin of safety as a percentage of the BEQ as this puts the figure into context and allows better comparisons to be made. In this case then, the safety margin is expressed as being 60% higher than the break-even level of output. Therefore, the margin of safety is included in a break-even analysis as it reveals the degree of risk involved in a business decision.

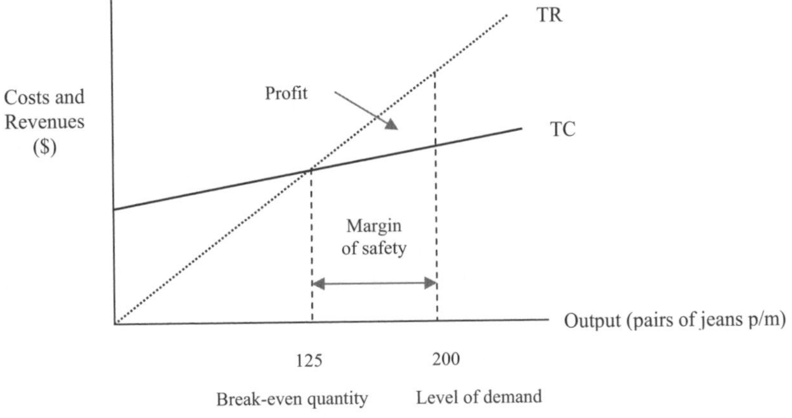

Figure 5.3c Margin of safety

Exam Tip!
Far too often, candidates will express the margin of safety as a monetary value. This clearly shows a lack of understanding and application of the concept. The margin of safety is calculated and shown on the x-axis of a break-even chart, i.e. the unit of measurement is the *volume* of output and not the *value* of that output.

Question 5.3.2

Tread-it and Play-it

Tread-it is a manufacturer of hiking shoes. Play-it produces wooden toys for children. Cost and revenue data for both businesses are shown in the table below.

	Tread-it	Play-it
Break-even quantity	250	500
Output	500	**i**
Margin of safety (units)	**ii**	300
Margin of safety (%)	100	**iii**

a Calculate the missing figures for **i**, **ii** and **iii** in the table above. *[3 marks]*

b Comment on which firm has the better margin of safety. *[4 marks]*

CONSTRUCTING A BREAK-EVEN CHART

When constructing an accurate break-even chart, the following rules must be adhered to:

- Although not necessarily required to show break-even, it is conventional to draw and label the Total Fixed Costs (TFC) line.
- The Total Costs (TC) line is drawn and labelled. Recall that even when there is no output, fixed costs still have to be paid, therefore the TC line starts at the same level as total fixed costs.
- The Total Revenue (TR) line, or total sales revenue, is drawn and labelled. When there is no output, the revenue is zero, so the TR line starts at the origin.
- The *x*-axis is labelled as 'Output' and measured in the appropriate units, per time period. It is important to put the *x*-axis into context.
- The *y*-axis is labelled as 'Costs, Revenues and Profits' and all are expressed in terms of a currency.
- A title, put into the context of the business, should also be added.

Before drawing a break-even chart, it is important to first work out the value of the costs and revenues at the break-even quantity. This will help to determine the scale needed to plot the figures on the *y*-axis. By working out the BEQ beforehand, it is also easier to determine the scale needed for the *x*-axis.

Consider the following worked example as a point of illustration. Suppose that Katia Jewellery Ltd. sells handmade jewellery at an average price of $20 with variable costs averaging $8 per unit. The fixed costs are $4,500. In order to plot the break-even chart, it is necessary to first calculate:

- The BEQ – Using the unit contribution method, the BEQ is calculated as (4,500 / (20 – 8) = **375 units**.
- The value of costs and revenue at the BEQ – Since the value of TC and TR are the same at the BEQ, it does not matter which component is worked out.
  For example, TC = 4,500 + (8 × 375) = **$7,500**. Equally, if we calculate the TR, the figure would be $20 × 375 = **$7,500**.

Using this information, it is now possible to plot the break-even chart (see Figure 5.3d). We know that the *x*-axis must go to beyond 375 units and that the *y*-axis must go beyond $7,500.

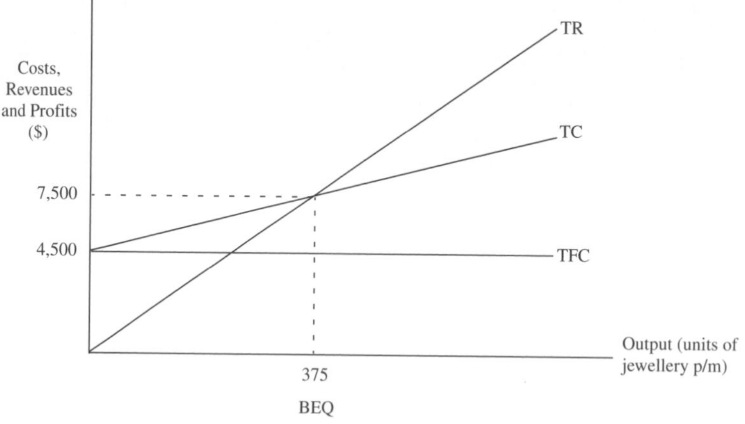

Figure 5.3d Break-even chart for Katia Jewellery Ltd.

Question 5.3.3

Lisa Chan's Day-Care Centre

Lisa Chan runs a children's day-care centre. The main clients are working parents who pay a fixed $20 per child for the whole day. Children at the centre learn through play and are engaged in activities such as art, music, dance and physical education. The business is open for an average of 22 days each month. The firm's expected costs and revenue for the next year are as follows:

Capacity	25 children per day
Demand	80% of capacity
Price	$20 per child per day
Materials	$4 per child
Rent	$600 per month
Salaries	$1,000 per month
Administration	$100 per month
Power	$140 per month

a Calculate the sum of the fixed costs. *[2 marks]*

b Calculate the break-even quantity per month. *[2 marks]*

c Construct a fully labelled break-even chart for Lisa Chan's Day-Care Centre. *[5 marks]*

d Identify both the break-even point and the break-even output on your chart. *[2 marks]*

e Calculate the margin of safety, per month, assuming that the business continues to work at 80% of its capacity. Show this on your break-even chart. *[3 marks]*

f Examine the strengths and weaknesses of using break-even analysis for a business such as Lisa Chan's Day-Care Centre. *[6 marks]*

HIGHER LEVEL EXTENSION: CHANGES IN BREAK-EVEN

One criticism of break-even analysis is that the model is static, i.e. it represents only a snapshot position of the business. However, computer software packages can show managers the effects of changes in costs and revenues on the BEQ. This makes the model a little more flexible. Manual calculations of changes in break-even can, of course, also be made. Note that if the BEQ is a decimal number, such as 333.33, the value has to be rounded *up* (since you cannot sell a third of a product to a customer).

HIGHER LEVEL

Question 5.3.4

Phoebe's Art Studio Ltd.

Phoebe's Art Studio Ltd. has overhead costs of $3,000 per month, variable costs of $5 per unit and an average selling price of $20. There are typically 500 customers each month but the firm's maximum capacity is 600 clients.

- **a** Calculate the break-even quantity for Phoebe's Art Studio Ltd. *[2 marks]*
- **b** Calculate the margin of safety for the business. *[2 marks]*
- **c** Construct the break-even chart for Phoebe's Art Studio Ltd. *[5 marks]*

Suppose in the subsequent period that rents increase, thereby raising the firm's overhead costs to $4,000. In addition, average selling price has been reduced to $17 and this has increased demand to 520 clients per month.

- **d** Calculate the new break-even quantity and comment on your findings. *[3 marks]*
- **e** Illustrate the new break-even level of output on your original chart. *[3 marks]*
- **f** Explain whether the change in price was a sensible decision. *[4 marks]*

HIGHER LEVEL EXTENSION: LIMITATIONS OF BREAK-EVEN ANALYSIS

Although break-even analysis can be a very useful tool for decision-making, it does have several limitations. One of the main drawbacks is the **assumptions** placed on the model which will hardly ever be met by any real business:

- Break-even analysis assumes that all cost functions are linear. In reality, the cost and revenue lines are unlikely to be linear because *economies of scale* could be enjoyed by operating on a larger scale, thereby changing the average costs of production over different units of output. Fixed costs may change, perhaps due to an increase in rent. This would lead to a 'stepped' fixed cost line, rather than a horizontal line.
- It also assumes that the sales revenue function is linear. In reality, customers would demand discounts for larger orders, thereby distorting the sales revenue line. Indeed, demand theory tells us that in order to sell more, a business may need to reduce its prices. Furthermore, a linear sales revenue function totally ignores the *price discrimination* policy used by some businesses (when a firm charges different prices to different groups of customers). Price discrimination is covered in more detail in Unit 4.4.
- It assumes that only one product is produced by the business. Despite this, break-even analysis can be used to make predictions that are much more realistic rather than relying on simple guesswork. For example, a restaurant owner can use past data and experience to estimate the average cost of a meal, the average number of customers and the average price paid for each meal. This data can therefore help a multiproduct firm to work out, albeit inaccurately perhaps, its break-even level of sales.
- It assumes that the business will sell all its output. However, in reality sales are not necessarily equal to output and most businesses will have some unsold stock. Unsold stock does not generate cash but costs the firm money (in terms of storage and insurance costs, for example). Furthermore, unsold stock may need to be sold at a discount to make space for new incoming stocks. Hence, this will inevitably affect the profits of the business.

Other limitations of break-even analysis include:

- Break-even analysis is a **static** model which may not be very useful in a dynamic business environment. For example, break-even calculations ignore the possibility that costs of production can and do change without warning. Exporting firms, for example, face the daily issue of fluctuating exchange rates which will alter their cost and revenue functions. The use of dedicated computer software, such as spreadsheets, can help to update data more easily, but each set of break-even calculations will only be valid for one point in time.
- As with all financial and numerical predictions, the principle of **garbage in, garbage out** (GIGO) applies. In this context, it means that the result of a break-even analysis is only as accurate as the original data used to generate the calculation. Unrealistic data will therefore generate dubious results. Data that is out of date, for example, will only be of very limited use. Hence, the validity of any break-even analysis largely depends on the skill and experience of the managers in estimating costs, output and revenues.
- Other quantitative and qualitative factors are ignored, such as the availability of human resources, spare capacity and finance. Break-even analysis ignores the impact on employees working under increased pressure to maximize output, for example. Not only might staff demand overtime payment to reach their production targets, there may also be a decline in productivity levels if staff are demoralized due to the added pressure. The reaction of competitors is also ignored in a break-even analysis. These factors will then alter the costs, revenues and profits of the business.
- Break-even analysis is really only suitable to single-product firms. For firms with more than one type of product, the overhead costs of production have to be split between the products in a subjective way (see Unit 5.2). Although it is possible to calculate multiproduct break-even, and there are software programmes that can help managers to do this, it does not truly represent the break-even for each product.

HIGHER LEVEL

Question 5.3.5

Airbus A380

© AIRBUS S.A.S. 2007

Production delays and soaring costs have plagued European aircraft giant Airbus since the A380 programme was unveiled in 2005. The Airbus A380, the world's largest commercial aircraft, was estimated to break-even on 270 aircraft orders. However, in October 2006, the company announced that the break-even quantity had been revised to 420 aircraft. At that time, Airbus had only sold 159 A380s, with the first plane scheduled for October 2007 – two years behind schedule. Airbus expects to sell more than 750 A380 planes over the life of the project.

a Calculate the revised margin of safety for the production of the A380. *[2 marks]*

b Comment on how the change in the margin of safety will affect the business. *[4 marks]*

c Explain how the delays and soaring production costs might affect the profits of Airbus. *[4 marks]*

d Discuss the value of break-even analysis as a management tool for businesses such as Airbus. *[7 marks]*

HIGHER LEVEL EXTENSION: TARGET PROFIT AND REVENUE

Continuing from the earlier example of Katia Jewellery Ltd., it is possible to use a break-even chart to work out the level of sales needed to earn a certain amount of profit. For example, in order for the firm to earn a target profit of $3,000, it can be seen from the graph that the firm needs to sell 625 units of jewellery, per time period.

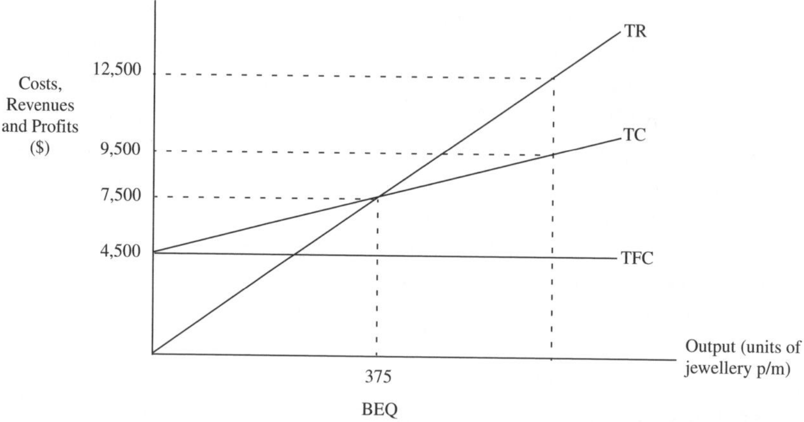

Figure 5.3e Break-even chart for Katia Jewellery Ltd.

Target profit can also be worked out manually, without the use of a break-even graph. Instead, the following steps are taken to work out the level of output needed for Katia Jewellery Ltd. to make $3,000 profit:

Profit = TR – TC

3,000 = 20Q – 4,500 – 8Q

7,500 = 12Q

Hence, Q = **625 units**

The target revenue can then be worked out as TR = $20 × 625 = $12,500

The total costs at 625 units of output = $4,500 + ($8 × 625) = $9,500

Therefore the target profit is $12,500 – $9,500 = **$3,000**

Whilst profit can be seen from a break-even chart, it is typically calculated by working out the difference between total revenues and total costs. For example, suppose that Katia Jewellery Ltd. has sales of 700 units per month. Profit can be worked out using the TR – TC rule:

TR = 20 × 700 = $14,000

TC = 4,500 + (8 × 700) = $10,100

Profit = **$3,900**

However, contribution can also be used to work out profits at each level of output.

Profit = Total Contribution – TFC

Total contribution = (20 – 8) × 700 = $8,400

TFC = $4,500

Profit = **$3,900**

In reality, actual profits (or losses) are likely to be different from those predicted in a break-even analysis. This is because there are so many factors that can affect the profit (or loss) that a business earns. These factors include:

- The difference between short-run and long-run profits. It may be necessary to lower prices (and hence break-even occurs at a higher level of output) in order to attract customers to a firm's products. In the long term, prices can be increased once a loyal customer base has been established.
- The level of demand is subject to change. Factors that change the level of demand, such as a change in income or fashion, will alter the break-even quantity and hence the amount of profits.
- Profit also depends of the level of risk involved. Whilst less risky projects will generally lead to a quicker BEQ, the monetary value of profits is unlikely to be very high. High risk projects, such as the Airbus A380 (see Question 5.3.5 on page 649) have the potential of returning huge amounts of profits.
- Innovation and the introduction of new ideas. For example, Dell computers, Dyson vacuum cleaners and Apple iPods have generated sales and profits far in excess of their original forecasts.
- Luck! Every business needs a little bit of luck to succeed. External factors such as changes in exchange rates, unemployment, national income and interest rates can have a direct impact (positive or negative) on the profitability of a business.

Question 5.3.6

Nicki's Hotdogs

Nicole Harvey runs a hotdog stall outside a busy shopping mall. Her expected costs and revenues for the next few months are shown below:

Capacity	200 hotdogs per day
Sales volume	110 hotdogs per day
Unit price	$2.50
Ingredients and materials	$0.80 per hotdog
Rent	$200 per month
Salary	$500 per month
Other overhead costs	$320 per month

a Construct a break-even chart for Nicole Harvey, showing the monthly break-even quantity. *[5 marks]*

b Assume that the average daily sales volume increases to 70% of capacity and that rents rise by 50%. Show the effect of these changes on the break-even chart and comment on your findings. *[5 marks]*

HIGHER LEVEL

BREAK-EVEN ANALYSIS AND BUSINESS STRATEGY

Although break-even analysis has its limitations, it is a useful tool for presenting data on cost and revenue in a visual form, making the data easier to understand. In particular, break-even analysis can help firms in making certain decisions, such as:

- *Product portfolio management* – Assessing the expected BEQ prior to the launch of a new product. This can help businesses to manage a profitable product portfolio. However, it is important to remember that the analysis is really only useful for single-product firms. Allocating overhead costs (see Unit 5.2) can help a little in getting around this problem.
- *Risk assessment* – Being able to accurately calculate a margin of safety can help a business gauge the level of risk involved in a particular project. A safety margin of 250% might justify the go-ahead for a project, whereas a forecast negative margin of safety can help prevent the firm from making a loss had it invested in the venture.
- *Make-or-buy decisions* – As their name suggests, make-or-buy decisions refer to the firm's choice of whether to produce the product itself or to buy it from a supplier. Break-even analysis can show the relative benefits of either decision.
- *Special order decisions* – Special orders are atypical and/or one-off orders for which a business will charge a price that differs from the norm. For example, the demands placed on the firm by the customer (such as speedier delivery times or amendments to the product specification) are likely to raise their costs of production. Break-even analysis can help to assess whether the change in profits (by accepting the special order) justifies taking on the offer. Box 5.3b gives a numerical example of a special order decision.

Box 5.3b Special order decisions – a numerical example

Suppose a charity wishes to buy 10 computers at a price of \$500 each instead of the usual \$800 price tag. Average variable costs of the computers are \$200 and fixed costs are allocated at \$3,000. Should the business take on this special order?

Break-even analysis shows that the BEQ is 10 computers, i.e. \$3,000 ÷ (\$500 – \$200).

There are three possible outcomes to the decision:

- Based on financial grounds, the firm only breaks even. For some managers, this will not be worth the risk, especially if production costs turn out to be higher than expected, for all sorts of reasons.
- Based on qualitative factors such as *corporate social responsibility*, the business may take on the order since they feel that the charity is supporting a worthwhile cause.
- Based on contribution analysis, the fixed costs exist with or without this special order, i.e. they have already been allocated within the firm. Therefore, by taking on the special order, there is a contribution of \$300 per computer. Hence, managers that take this view would accept the special order on financial grounds. This, of course, assumes that the firm has the capacity to take on the special order and that variable costs are not adversely affected.

As with all quantitative tools, it is important to consider the analysis in the context of the business. It is also essential to remember that break-even analysis should be used with caution, bearing in mind the assumptions made in the model. Finally, the analysis should be used alongside other tools such as SWOT analysis (see Unit 1.6) and Investment Appraisal (see Unit 3.2) in order to perform more comprehensive and coherent decision-making.

1 Explain the meaning of 'break-even'.

2 What is 'contribution' and why is it important to understanding break-even analysis?

3 What are the three ways that profits can be increased?

4 State the two formulae for calculating break-even.

5 Outline the difference between the 'break-even point' and the 'break-even quantity'.

6 What is the 'margin of safety' and how is it calculated?

Higher Level extension

7 State three assumptions made when carrying out a break-even analysis.

8 Outline three limitations of using break-even analysis.

9 What is a 'make-or-buy decision'?

10 What are 'special order decisions'?

Break-even chart is the name given to the graph that shows a firm's costs, revenues and profits (or losses) at various levels of output.

Break-even point refers to the position on a break-even chart where the total cost line intersects the total revenue line, i.e. where TC = TR.

Break-even quantity (BEQ) refers to the level of output that generates neither any profit nor loss. It is shown on the x-axis on a break-even chart.

Contribution per unit, also known as **unit contribution**, is used to work out the break-even quantity. Unit contribution is the difference between the selling price of a product and its variable costs of production. The surplus then goes towards paying the fixed costs of production.

Margin of safety, or **safety margin**, refers to the difference between a firm's level of demand and its break-even quantity. A positive safety margin means the firm can decrease output (sales) by that amount without making a loss. A negative safety margin means that the firm is making a loss.

Profit is the positive difference between a product's revenue and its costs at each level of output. On a break-even chart, profit can be seen to the right of the break-even quantity.

Special order decisions are unique and/or unusual orders for which a customer will pay a price that differs from the norm.

Quality Assurance

UNIT 5.4

I'm a slow walker, but I never walk back.

Abraham Lincoln (1809–1865), 16th president of the USA

Key topics

- The importance of quality
- Quality control and quality assurance
- Lean production
- Total quality culture (TQC)

Higher Level extension

- Kaizen (continuous improvement)
- Quality circles
- Benchmarking
- National and international quality standards

INTRODUCTION

Customers, producers and the government have slightly different but complementary views on the term **quality**. For the customer, quality means that a good or service must fulfil its purpose and meet or exceed the expectations of the user. This means that quality does not apply to only expensive products. Hence, a Honda or Ford motor car can be of good quality (and not just expensive BMWs or Ferraris) so long as the vehicles meet the standards desired by the customer. Likewise, the quality of teaching and learning in a government funded school is not necessarily inferior to that offered at an expensive fee-paying private school.

Customers perceive the quality of a product by observing and comparing several interrelated factors, such as:

- Physical appearance and design – Are the look and design appealing to customers? Are there any special features?
- Image and reputation of manufacturer or seller – A widely known and reputable brand or retailer will tend to be associated with high quality.
- Reliability – For example, Lexus cars are renowned for building the world's most reliable cars and hence are of good quality.
- Durability – Similarly, durability looks at the extent to which a product will last. Products that keep breaking down or are in regular need of maintenance are perceived as being of poor quality.
- Fit for purpose – How well does the product fulfil its purpose? For example, how accurate are watches; how reliable and safe are motor vehicles; how tasty is the meal, and how waterproof and wind resistant is the raincoat?
- Safety features – Are products safe to use? Do products need to be recalled due to safety problems?
- Customer service – High quality firms provide outstanding customer relations management, e.g. first class air travel, 5-star hotel services and designer jewellers.
- After-sales services – For example, are guarantees and warranties offered? Is there a technical support or customer service hotline? How long do customers have to wait for delivery of the product? Are spare parts easily available and at reasonable prices?

In essence, this means that quality is determined by the perceived value for money. Customers assess what they get for their money by comparing the benefits of purchase with the price of the product.

THE IMPORTANCE OF QUALITY

In operations management, quality can have a slightly different meaning to the producer. To manufacturers, quality means that a product matches the design specifications.

Many governments, such as those in the European Union, intervene in business activity to promote and monitor minimum quality standards for certain products (see 'National and international quality standards' on page 666). Meeting these government standards symbolizes that a firm has met safety and quality standards, thereby helping to reassure customers about the quality of a firm's products. This is an example of *quality assurance*, whereby firms give their customers greater confidence about the quality of their products.

Products that do not meet the needs or expectations of customers, producers or governments are said to be **substandard** and such products can be very costly to a business (see Box 5.4a). For example, in 1997, Mercedes-Benz launched their first small car – the A-Class. They had spent close to $2 billion on the research and development of the product but found very shortly after the launch that there were major safety problems and had to recall all the cars sold. To the credit (or the cost) of Mercedes-Benz, they spent another $280 million in fixing the problems and the car has been a huge success for the company ever since. The words of American poet Henry Wadsworth Longfellow (1807–1882) can be used to explain the problem of substandard quality: "It takes less time to do a thing right than to explain why you did it wrong."

Exam Tip!
Quality does not mean that a product has to be expensive, prestigious or exclusive. Many students incorrectly define quality as products that are the 'best' in their industry, such as a Rolex watches. There are plenty of good quality watches that are relatively inexpensive.

Four driving forces have led to quality being a paramount priority for many businesses:

- *Increasing consumer awareness* – Today's consumers have easier access to information through consumer protection organizations, the media and the internet. Any mistake made by large multinationals is likely to be reported in many sources very quickly all over the world.
- *Increasing competition* – Rivalry has meant that firms which provide higher quality products may be able to establish a larger customer base and brand loyalty. Quality, as a form of product differentiation, can give a firm a competitive advantage.
- *Government legislation* – Changes and developments to competition laws have forced many businesses to improve their overall quality standards.
- *Increasing consumer incomes* – With more disposable income, consumers are more able and willing to buy higher quality products, such as high-end plasma televisions and motor vehicles.

Box 5.4a The costs of poor quality

- Substandard quality will adversely affect the reputation of a business, perhaps irrevocably.
- Poor product design may lead to problems with the finished product, thereby affecting its demand. The number of customer complaints will rise and therefore customers are unlikely to purchase such products again.
- It costs time and money to rework the substandard products.
- Unsafe products may cause physical harm to customers.
- Equipment and machinery that regularly break down will need to be repaired hence adding to the costs of the business.
- Poor labour productivity will increase average costs of production.
- Late deliveries can result in compensation claims being made and/or harm the firm's reputation.

Ultimately, poor quality harms the competitiveness of an organization by affecting its reputation and costs in an unfavourable manner.

Question 5.4.1

Toyota

In August 2006, Toyota had to delay the distribution of 20,000 of its new model cars due to quality control issues resulting in poorly fitted windscreens. Car manufacturers are continually striving to reduce their costs by using the same components across a range of models. This can help firms such as Toyota to gain from **economies of scope**, but this has also led to an increase in the number of product recalls (defects). Despite the hiccup, Toyota has established a global reputation for reliability, which has been a key contributor to its success as the world's biggest car maker.

a Define the meaning of **economies of scope**. *[2 marks]*

b Analyse how a high product recall rate can be costly to businesses such as Toyota. *[6 marks]*

QUALITY CONTROL AND QUALITY ASSURANCE

The quality of an organization's products is important for two main reasons: its reputation and its ability to control costs. **Quality management** is the function concerned with controlling business activities to ensure that products meet quality standards, i.e. that products are fit for their purpose. Advocates of quality management argue that the quality of a product should be seen as an overall package, from the production and purchase of the product to its use and beyond. There are two main categories of quality management: quality control and quality assurance.

Quality control is the traditional way of quality management that involves checking and reviewing work processes, such as inspecting, testing and sampling the quality of manufactured items. Products must be made to the required specification. This approach to managing quality is mainly based on *detecting* defective output or poor quality, from the delivery of raw materials to the output of finished products. It helps to identify substandard quality or a problem before the product is sold to consumers. Quality control does not prevent mistakes being made and therefore can be very expensive. Hence, there has been a shift towards the use of quality assurance.

Quality assurance is the management process of guaranteeing (assuring) the consumer of a product's quality. It informs customers that products have been made to the required specification and that certain quality standards have been met. This can be an important source of competitive advantage for a business. Quality assurance is more concerned about *preventing* poor quality output than rectifying the problems. It also differs from quality control in that it takes into account the views of customers. Therefore, a key focus of quality assurance is product design and development.

Quality assurance programmes involve employee participation, such as through suggestion schemes and quality circles (see 'Quality circles' on page 663). Worker participation in quality management has two benefits:

- Involvement helps to improve the level of staff motivation as they feel more valued by management.
- Participation can generate new ideas for improving the quality of certain products, operations and processes.

In today's business environment, quality assurance is seen as being superior to traditional quality control methods. It is argued that prevention of poor quality is far better than conventional methods of detecting faults and imperfections. In other words, the prevention of a problem is better than the cure. Professor W. Edwards Deming (1900–1993), considered by many as the father of quality management, argued that quality control methods that aim to find and discard bad quality are ineffective and costly. He suggested that quality comes from a system that improves, rather than inspects, the production process. Deming's philosophy for quality improvement is based around four key phases:

- *Plan* – Improve quality by designing or revising operations and processes.
- *Do* – Execute the plan.
- *Check* – Monitor and measure the performance, and assess the results.
- *Act* – Decide on any necessary changes that are needed to further improve the process.

Quality assurance, as a major feature of a **total quality culture** (see 'Total quality culture' on page 660), is an ongoing process. Once a business has achieved a certain quality standard, its processes are regularly inspected by the respective awarding body to ensure that the standards are being maintained. If quality standards are subsequently found to have dropped below the expected standards, the organization will be stripped of its quality assurance award. For example, only schools that have been fully authorized by the International Baccalaureate Organization (IBO) can offer the IB programmes as an 'IB World School'. This status is in recognition of the school having met the quality standards set by the IBO.

Finally, whilst quality management can be costly to implement, it is important to recognize that it can be profitable in the long run. In other words, there are no shortcuts to quality assurance and businesses must spend money (on quality management) in order to earn money.

Question 5.4.2

McDonald's "100% quality food"

As part of its **quality assurance**, McDonald's inform their customers that they believe in great-tasting food, based on only the best quality ingredients. In-store displays and literature support this claim by stating that:

- Only 100% beef is used without additives.
- Only prime white fish is used.
- Only chicken approved by the national authority responsible for ensuring food safety is used.
- Only the freshest eggs are used. These are washed and sanitized to remove dirt from the shells.
- Only Russet Burbank potatoes are used to generate French fries (chips) that are fluffy inside and crispy outside.

Source: McDonald's in-store literature

a Outline the meaning of **quality assurance**. *[2 marks]*

b Examine the importance of quality management for multinationals such as McDonald's. *[6 marks]*

LEAN PRODUCTION

Lean production is the process of streamlining operations and processes in order to reduce all forms of waste. In turn, lean production should lead to reduced costs and improved quality. It was first used in Japan during the 1950s. Businesses are increasingly trying to reduce wastage (or **muda**, the Japanese term for 'waste') in the production process. Different forms of muda exist, such as:

- Materials and resources – There can be wastage of materials and resources that have not been used efficiently, such as raw materials or floor space.
- Time – Delays have a large negative effect on productivity and quality levels and hence lead to wastage.
- Energy – Leaving on lights, heating or air conditioning when not needed is a huge and unnecessary drain on the financial resources of a business.
- Human effort – Tasks may need to be reworked due to waste from substandard and defective (poor quality) output.

In adopting lean production, several principles are followed:

- Waste minimization – This requires that the business remove any operation or process that does not add value to the product. It will also involve making more efficient use of a firm's scarce resources (its land, labour and capital).
- Right first time – This means that businesses aim for zero defects by identifying and resolving all problems at the source. It is better to use resources to prevent mistakes than trying to spot them. This will eliminate the need for quality controllers to spend time checking and re-checking the quality of output.
- Flexibility – Capital and human resources must be adaptable to the changing needs of the business. They may, for example, use multiskilled workers who can work on several projects simultaneously.
- Continuous improvement – This refers to the continual strive to reduce costs and improve quality.
- Supply chain management – This means that the business must develop and maintain good professional working relationships with its suppliers and intermediaries to facilitate streamlining its operations. Unit 4.6 covers supply chain management in more detail.

The pursuit of lean production has led to the development of several important management techniques: Cell production (see Unit 5.1), Just-in-time production (see Unit 5.7), Kaizen (see 'Kaizen – continuous improvement' on page 662) and Quality circles (see 'Quality circles' on page 663).

TOTAL QUALITY CULTURE

A **total quality culture (TQC)** is a philosophy that occurs in organizations that embed quality in every business operation and process. It places quality as the core focus in all functional areas, i.e. every employee is responsible for quality assurance, rather than it being the traditional role of the quality control department.

TQC empowers every employee to take corrective measures if quality is unacceptable (substandard). The purpose is to achieve **zero defects** in the organization. This means that all products, operations and processes are monitored and managed to ensure that they meet the required quality standards without any faults. If achieved, this will eliminate waste and the need to rectify mistakes. Furthermore, it will lead to improved customer satisfaction. TQC is synonymous with **total quality management (TQM)**.

TQM is a process that requires the dedication of everyone in the organization to commit to achieving quality standards. Quality is seen from the perspective of the consumer rather than the producer. In addition, TQM will remove wastage and inefficiencies in all forms of business activity (production, marketing, finance and personnel). This will, however, mean that all employees are properly trained to check and correct their own work.

Advantages of TQM

- Motivation is likely to improve since workers are empowered and involved in decision-making.
- Wastage is reduced or eliminated thus preventing firms from having to dispose of defective goods. This can therefore lead to lower costs of production.
- TQM can improve the image and reputation of an organization.
- Customer needs (quality management and assurance) are a central focus of the production process. Hence, TQM can help to give a business a competitive edge over its rivals.

Limitations of TQM

In trying to achieve TQM, businesses will face potentially high costs of maintaining or improving the quality of their products.

- There are costs in establishing and maintaining a quality management system. For example, market research into customer satisfaction levels will be an ongoing cost of developing a TQC in an organization. CAD-CAM systems used to achieve zero defects can also be very expensive (see Box 5.4b).
- Trying to improve quality will also require sufficient finance for the costs of training and developing staff or the cost of investing in new technologies.
- TQM only works if every member of the organization, irrespective of their position or role, is fully committed to quality assurance. This also means that managers must set an example for others in the organization.
- TQM can become quite bureaucratic as procedures and processes must be properly audited and administered.
- There is a time lag (often lasting several years) before the benefits of TQM actually surface. A further complication is that there is no guarantee that TQM can be successfully implemented.

Box 5.4b CAD and CAM

Firms such as Ikea have used CAD and CAM technology to help achieve zero defects. **Computer-aided design** (CAD) is the process of using dedicated computer hardware and software in the design process, such as in three-dimensional designs of a product. CAD software enables a much wider range of designs to be completed and in a much quicker time. **Computer-aided manufacturing** (CAM) uses sophisticated automation and machinery in the production process. CAM is far more superior to human speed and accuracy of output.

Question 5.4.3

Durex

Durex is the most popular brand of condoms in many parts of the world. SLL International, the British multinational that produces the product, has around 25% of the world market share, with output of 1 billion units each year. According to its website (www.durex.com), each Durex condom can hold up to 40 litres of air or 9 gallons of water before bursting. Samples, including condoms that have been artificially aged, are tested to destruction for physical strength. The Durex factory in Bangkok, Thailand reports a greater than 97% pass rate. Thailand is the world's leading exporter of condoms, with an annual output of over 300 million units from the Durex factory alone.

a Calculate the approximate quantity of defective Durex condoms produced each year at the Bangkok factory. *[2 marks]*

b Explain why quality assurance is crucial to firms such as Durex. *[4 marks]*

c Comment on how total quality management might help Durex to reduce its defect rate. *[4 marks]*

HIGHER LEVEL EXTENSION: KAIZEN – CONTINUOUS IMPROVEMENT

Dutch artist Vincent Van Gogh (1853–1890) once said, "Great things are not done by impulse, but by a series of small things brought together." Kaizen is the Japanese word for a philosophy of **continuous improvement**. Kaizen is made up of two words, 'Kai' meaning *change* and 'Zen' meaning *better*. Hence, the continuous improvement in an organization comes about by changing for the better. Kaizen has become a widespread approach in the workplace where people are constantly trying to find ways to improve work processes and tasks.

The concept of Kaizen is therefore a process of productivity and efficiency gains within a firm that comes from *small* and *continuous* improvements being made by the workforce, rather than a large one-off improvement. Turkish people have a saying that "Stairs are climbed step by step." Confucius, the Chinese philosopher, once said, "It does not matter how slowly you go, so long as you do not stop." This philosophy is similar to the famous children's fable about the hare and the tortoise (see Box 5.4c).

The process involves forming small groups of employees (known as **Kaizen groups**) whose role it is to identify changes and improvements to the organization's products, processes and procedures. The aim is establish a steady flow of small improvements rather than a one-off or a few radical changes. This is partly because people tend to be resistant to change, especially those changes that are large scale and disruptive to the organization. This is often much easier to do when there are (continuous) improvements in the organization since job losses or pay cuts are unlikely to surface in such situations. Kaizen groups do not tend to directly look at cost cutting; the focus remains on continual improvements in quality. However, by doing so, Kaizen often brings about cost savings.

Kaizen also aims to eliminate waste by looking at ways to improve the productivity and efficiency of the firm's processes and operations. For instance, if a worker is late to work for just one minute each day, it equates to 5 minutes per week or over 4 hours per year. If this was the norm for a workforce of 50 people, then the lost production time would be over 200 hours each year (or around 25 days of lost output). Kaizen is therefore an integral part of quality assurance and used in line with other quality issues such as TQM, quality control, quality circles, lean production and new product development.

Kaizen groups differ from quality circles in that the latter are better empowered to put their ideas for improvements into action, i.e. they have decision-making power. In addition, the philosophy behind Kaizen is that the system encourages small-scale suggestions that can come from *anyone* in the organization, irrespective of their position, whether as an individual or as part of a group (be it large or small). Many of the best suggestions for improvement often come from shop floor employees who have direct contact with customers. They are the ones best positioned to understand the benefits of changes to certain operations or processes. This has the added benefit of motivating staff since they are able to use their initiative and to have some input into the decision-making of the organization.

Box 5.4c The hare and the tortoise – a case of continuous improvement

A hare and a tortoise were in a race together. The hare thought that its natural superiority would mean winning the race would be simple. The hare leapt ahead of its rival and after a short while the tortoise was nowhere in sight. Complacent, the hare decided to take a rest and fell asleep. This allowed the tortoise, with its small but continuous steps, to eventually overtake the hare and win the race.

HIGHER LEVEL EXTENSION: QUALITY CIRCLES

Quality circles refer to small groups of people who are organized together to examine issues relating to the quality of output and to make recommendations for improvement to management. The term was coined by Professor Kaoru Ishikawa in 1962. Members of the quality circle, sometimes referred to as a **steering group**, consist of volunteers from various departments. Communication within the quality circle is often based on a *circle network* or an *all channel network* (see Unit 2.2), although it is usual for a senior manager to chair the meetings. It is believed that such networks encourage communication and team work in order to solve problems that have a negative effect on quality. Like Kaizen groups, quality circles are a vital part of total quality management that emphasize improvement through the involvement of staff. However, unlike Kaizen, members of the quality circle are also directly involved in the execution and management of the solution.

Advocates of quality circles emphasize the importance of team cohesiveness in managing and improving quality. It is argued that businesses that fail to acknowledge the contribution of their staff often find a drop in the level of motivation and standards of work. Furthermore, such business cultures result in employees being only motivated by self-interest rather than feeling a sense of responsibility towards the success of the organization.

Businesses that adopt quality circles and Kaizen believe that there is always room for improvement, in all aspects of their operation, and not just the production process. This includes investigating ways to improve marketing, human resource management and financial control. The ultimate benefits to the organization are increased efficiency, productivity and profitability.

However, a huge limitation to Kaizen and quality circles is that many individuals remain unmotivated by teamworking, extra responsibility or empowerment. They prefer to be told what to do and only see work as a means to an end.

HIGHER LEVEL

Question 5.4.4

Subway

Subway is a private limited company, founded in 1965, that operates on a global scale. It has become the world's fastest growing franchise. The secret to its success is its focus on promoting an image of being a health-conscious restaurant chain. With operations in over 28,000 restaurants in around 100 countries, quality assurance is a critical aspect of Subway's operations. Its homepage (www.subway.com) has a dedicated section for customers to comment on their experiences at Subway, which helps the firm to gain customer feedback to further improve its quality standards.

a Define the term 'franchising'. *[2 marks]*

b Explain why quality assurance is important to a global franchise business such as Subway. *[4 marks]*

c Examine the potential problems for quality assurance as Subway continues its rapid expansion plans. *[6 marks]*

HIGHER LEVEL EXTENSION: BENCHMARKING

Benchmarking, or **best practice benchmarking (BPB)**, refers to a business comparing its products, operations and processes to those used by others in the same industry, especially market leaders. BPB then becomes a point of reference or exemplar for the business to follow. The purpose is to allow the business to emulate **best practice** (excellent performance) in order to improve its operational efficiency. Luxury car manufacturers, for instance, might benchmark their products and processes against market leaders such as Mercedes-Benz and BMW. Box 5.4d outlines the various types of BPB.

Box 5.4d Types of benchmarking

- *Strategic benchmarking* – used for benchmarking the overall performance of an organization
- *Performance benchmarking* – used to benchmark the key products (goods and services) of businesses
- *Process benchmarking* – used to benchmark the processes and operations of businesses
- *Internal benchmarking* – involves benchmarking different operations or functions within the same business, such as the productivity of staff in different departments
- *External benchmarking* – involves benchmarking against other organizations that are classed as the best in the industry
- *International benchmarking* – benchmarking against the performance of organizations that operate overseas

There are several stages in the benchmarking process:

1 Identify the area of the business to be benchmarked.

2 Measure the internal performance in the chosen area against a set of criteria.

3 Identify the most appropriate competitors in the industry to measure against (usually those with best practice).

4 Measure the external performance (of rivals).
5 Use the comparative data to ascertain the main areas of weakness in the firm.
6 Establish the standards for quality improvements.
7 Implement changes to achieve the required standards.
8 Evaluate outcome of implementation to check for measured improvements.

There are two methods of benchmarking:

- *Historical benchmarking* – Involves comparing the same performance data over time. This is used for internal benchmarking whereby the performance of the organization can be measured in due course. Sales turnover, market share, profits and staff turnover can all be benchmarked this way.
- *Inter-firm benchmarking* – Involves comparing the same performance data of different businesses. For example, Citibank might compare its staff turnover rate to other financial institutions such as HSBC or Bank of America.

Benefits of benchmarking

- It allows a business to close the performance gap if BPB is successfully implemented.
- Dealing with problems of quality by using external benchmarking can be quite fast and is more effective than simple guesswork.
- It looks at comparisons from the perception of customers and therefore this should help the firm to take appropriate action to meet their customers' needs and wants.
- The successful implementation can help to lower production costs and to improve a firm's overall competitiveness.

Limitations of benchmarking

- The cost and time implications of collecting relevant and up-to-date information from other firms in the industry can be a major constraint to effective benchmarking.
- Relying on replicating the ideas and practices of other firms may be seen as second best. Products might be seen as 'me too' products (see Unit 4.3) with no distinctive selling point. Relying on BPB can therefore discourage initiative and innovative ideas.
- Sufficient time and finance must be made available to implement the findings from the benchmarking exercise.

Like the concept of Kaizen, benchmarking cannot be a one-off exercise if the organization is to achieve quality assurance. To be effective, benchmarking has to be a continuous process that involves the commitment and involvement of every employee. This allows the firm to gain lasting improvements in both quality and productivity.

Question 5.4.5

Mercedes-Benz

Mercedes-Benz is one of the most recognized brand names in the world. Rivals such as Lexus, BMW and Audi often **benchmark** against the quality standards set by Mercedes-Benz. All new Mercedes-Benz cars have a 1 to 3 year warranty, with the manufacturer undertaking any necessary work arising from a defect in the product, free of charge. Its top of the range sports engines carry the 'AMG' badge as a sign of its superior build quality.

a Define the term **benchmark**. *[2 marks]*

b Discuss the extent to which benchmarking can help businesses, such as Mercedes-Benz and Audi, to achieve quality assurance. *[8 marks]*

HIGHER LEVEL EXTENSION: NATIONAL AND INTERNATIONAL QUALITY STANDARDS

HIGHER LEVEL

National and international quality awards are used to show that certain quality standards have been met. Businesses that meet or exceed these standards are permitted to include the quality award symbols or logos on their products. This helps to assure customers that the product is of high quality. Quality awards help to:

- Promote quality awareness within the organization
- Improve organizational performance
- Recognize quality achievements (which can have motivational effects on the workforce)
- Help attract high calibre employees to the organization
- Strengthen the competitiveness of an organization.

There are numerous organizations that promote product and service quality. They usually operate as autonomous bodies, i.e. they function independently of any government. Such organizations exist to promote and recognize the quality performance of businesses. Examples of national and international quality awards include:

- *The CE Marking* – This is the European Union's award for products that meet mandatory health and safety standards. 'CE' stands for *Conformité Européenne*, French for European Conformity.
- *The ASQ Award* – The American Society for Quality (ASQ) is an organization dedicated to the promotion and advancement of quality in the USA. It administers the prestigious Malcolm Baldrige National Quality Award which recognizes businesses that have achieved performance excellence. It is one of only two US Presidential awards given to businesses.
- *The BSI 'Kitemark'* – The British Standards Institution (BSI) is the official organization responsible for setting quality standards in the UK. Products that carry the BSI Kitemark help to inform customers that they have been manufactured to a high level of quality, and are fit for their advertised purpose.
- *The Lion Mark* – This is awarded by the British Toy and Hobby Association (BTHA) for products that meet a strict code of practice on toy safety. It also assures the customer that the product is genuine and not a counterfeit.

For a business to achieve a quality standard award, its product must undergo stringent and regular testing by independent agents. Only if and when a business has proved that its products meet or exceed these standards is it given the quality award in recognition of its achievements. Displaying the quality award without having met the quality standards is not only deceptive but can also get the business into trouble.

The most prominent global organization for quality assurance is the **International Standards Organization (ISO)**, founded in 1947 and based in Geneva in Switzerland. It is made up of representatives from approximately 160 national quality standards bodies, such as the ASQ and the BSI. The ISO's goal is to facilitate international trade by providing a single set of quality standards that consumers and businesses throughout the world would recognize and respect. The ISO is one of the most powerful non-governmental organizations (NGO) in the world because it is influential in affecting government legislation surrounding quality assurance.

Perhaps the most widely recognized ISO Standard for quality management is the ISO 9000. It is awarded by independent auditors who certify that the ISO Standards have been met. The ISO then endorses that the business has:

- Proper recordkeeping
- Monitored operations and processes to ensure that quality products are being produced
- Checked products for defects before they are distributed and has carried out corrective measures where necessary
- Regularly reviewed its operations and processes to sustain or improve its efficiency.

Businesses that meet the ISO Standards can publicize their achievement by stating 'ISO 9000 certified' or 'ISO 9000 registered'. The ISO Standards do not only apply to manufacturing of goods but also the provision of services.

HIGHER LEVEL

Question 5.4.6

The BSI Kitemark

The British Standards Institution (BSI) is the organization responsible for setting quality standards in the UK. Products that carry the BSI Kitemark help to inform customers that they have been manufactured to a high level of quality and are fit for their advertised purpose. According to the BSI, around 82% of the British population recognize the Kitemark as a sign of high quality. It also claims that around 69% of the public would be prepared to pay higher prices for products that carry the Kitemark.

Source: www.bsi.org.uk

a Examine the role of a regulatory body, such as the BSI, in ensuring quality standards of businesses. *[4 marks]*

b Analyse the advantages to organizations that hold an external quality assurance certificate such as the BSI Kitemark. *[6 marks]*

QUALITY ASSURANCE AND BUSINESS STRATEGY

Traditionally, consumers had to make a choice between the price and the quality of a product. Quality used to come at a high price. Today, advances in technology and growing national and international competitive pressures have meant that quality is an integral part of business activity. Quality assurance is crucial for retaining customer loyalty. It also affects the reputation of an organization. Hence, quality plays a vital role in determining the profitability and success of a business. Quality management must be considered at all stages in the production process, from the initial design of a product to its sale and beyond (after-sales services).

However, to achieve an organizational culture that is committed to quality, all managers and employees must constantly strive to improve their working practices. Businesses can do this through motivational methods (see Unit 2.5), developing multiskilled workers, and using flexible working structures (see Unit 2.1). A business with a highly trained, flexible and motivated workforce is much more likely to achieve total quality management. Lean production and TQM may also require flatter and/or more flexible organizational structures (see Unit 2.2). This should enable the organization to be more effective in responding to market changes.

Modern business strategy focuses on quality assurance being an ongoing process that involves the continual updating and improvement of an organization's products, functions and processes. Every single aspect of business activity can be improved, which will then lead to zero defects. Today's competitive environment leaves no room for error. Hence, quality assurance requires all internal stakeholders to be dedicated to this total quality culture and philosophy.

In an attempt to exceed the expectations of customers, many businesses have adopted the **Six Sigma** approach to quality assurance. Six Sigma is a system devised by Bill Smith (1986) who was working at Motorola. The purpose was to increase quality by reducing defects to no more than 3.4 defects per million units of output (this is the statistical value of six sigma), i.e. a success rate of 99.73%. In essence, it is a systematic approach to achieving near perfection or zero defects. A Six Sigma defect is defined as anything outside of the customer's specification. In addition to Motorola, other companies that have used the Six Sigma approach include Boeing, General Electric, Ford, Apple and Bank of America. Motorola announced a saving of over $17 billion during the first 20 years of using Six Sigma. Similarly, General Electric estimated a saving of $10 billion during its first five years of implementing the Six Sigma approach.

Finally, although the costs of meeting quality assurance standards may be very high, the costs of *not* meeting these standards may be even greater to a business, particularly in the long run.

REVIEW QUESTIONS 5.4

1 What is meant by 'quality'?

2 What are 'substandard products'?

3 Why is quality important to both consumers and producers?

4 What is 'quality management'?

5 Distinguish between quality control and quality assurance.

6 Define 'lean production'.

7 How might a business encourage a 'total quality culture'?

8 What are the advantages and disadvantages of total quality management (TQM)?

9 What are CAD and CAM?

Higher Level extension

10 What is meant by 'Kaizen' and why is it important for quality assurance?

11 What are 'quality circles'?

12 Explain the costs and benefits of best practice benchmarking (BPB).

13 What is the purpose of national and international quality standards?

14 Outline two benefits to an organization that holds an internationally recognized quality standard.

15 What is meant by the 'six sigma' approach to quality assurance?

Benchmarking is the process of identifying best practice in an industry, in relation to products, processes and operations. It sets the standards laid down by the best businesses in the industry for the organization to emulate.

Computer-aided design (CAD) is the process of using dedicated computer hardware and software in the design process, such as three-dimensional designs of a product.

Computer-aided manufacturing (CAM) is the process of using sophisticated machinery and equipment in the production process.

International Standards Organization (ISO) is the most prominent global organization for quality assurance. Founded in 1947, the ISO is made up of representatives from around 160 countries.

Kaizen is the Japanese term for 'continuous improvement'. It is a philosophy followed by those who strive for a total quality culture.

Lean production refers to the approach used to eliminate waste (muda) in an organization. As a result, lean organizations benefit from lower costs and higher productivity.

Muda is the Japanese term for 'wastage'. Businesses that strive to achieve lean production try to eliminate the causes of muda, such as time wasting, overproduction, defected products and excess stockpiling.

Quality means that a good or service must be fit for its purpose by meeting or exceeding the expectations of the consumer.

Quality assurance refers to the methods used by a business to reassure customers about the quality of their products in meeting certain quality standards, such as the ISO 9000.

Quality circles are groups of workers that meet on a regular basis to identify problems related to quality assurance. They then give consideration to alternative solutions to the identified problems, before finally making recommendations to management.

Quality control is the traditional way of quality management that involves checking and reviewing work processes. This is usually carried out by quality controllers and inspectors.

Total quality culture (TQC) is a philosophy which occurs in organizations that embed quality in all aspects of business activity, with every employee accustomed to being responsible for quality control and quality assurance.

Total quality management (TQM) is the process that attempts to encourage all employees to make quality assurance paramount to the various functions (production, finance, marketing and personnel) of the organization.

Zero defects refers to the objective of producing each and every product without any defects (mistakes or imperfections). The benefits of such an approach are eliminating waste and reworking time (the time taken to correct faults). Achieving zero defects can also lead to a better reputation for a business.

Location

UNIT 5.5

Man cannot discover new oceans unless he has the courage to lose sight of the shore.

Andre Gide (1869–1951), Nobel Prize for Literature

Key topics

- National and international location of production

Higher Level extension

- Effects of globalization on location
- Impact of location on business activity (marketing, production, finance and human resources)

INTRODUCTION

All businesses need to be located somewhere. Sole traders might operate from a room in their own home. Amazon.com operates from huge warehouses in out-of-town areas. Giant multinationals are located throughout the world. Managers have a crucial role in weighing up the costs and benefits of a specific location. In the real estate industry, managers play by the same three rules to business success: 'location, location and location'! This is somewhat of a generalization, but there is a large element of truth in this thinking, as will be examined later in this Unit.

Location refers to the geographical position of a business, i.e. where it is sited. The location decision will depend on many factors such as the nature of the business (e.g. retail outlet or oil extraction), the nature of the product (e.g. agricultural products or tourism) and the nature of human resources (e.g. skilled or unskilled). Location decisions need to be made in different situations. When firms are new, they need to think about the location of their first premises. Firms planning to expand, domestically and internationally, also have to consider alternative new locations. The **relocation** decision occurs when managers need to consider moving to alternative premises, perhaps because of uncompetitive or unaffordable rents.

The location decision is one of the most important decisions that any manager has to take, especially as many see it as an irreversible decision. This means that for most businesses, they cannot simply afford to relocate if things do not work according to plan. For many new businesses, the location decision incurs a highly significant proportion of the costs. It is unlikely that most of these costs can be recovered (known as **sunk costs**) if the firm were to be unsuccessful. Hence, the location of business can have profound implications on the profitability and survival of the firm. The decision is so important that it is classed as a long-term strategic goal and the decision is only made by senior management. Relocation is, of course, possible but the costs of doing so can be extremely high. However, for firms that are new or have poor cash flow, the location decision may not be reversible.

QUANTITATIVE FACTORS AFFECTING LOCATION DECISIONS

Quantitative factors are those that can be numerically calculated, such as the cost of purchasing or renting premises. The finance department and the management team will be keen to look at the financial costs and benefits of locating or relocating the organization. Such quantitative factors include the following.

Availability, suitability and cost of land

The quantity, quality and cost of land are all important factors when choosing a location. Managers face a trade-off. They have to balance the cost of land with earning potential; the busier the area, the higher the earning potential, but the higher the cost of land. Since rents form a large proportion of fixed costs for most businesses, the high cost of land may reduce the profits of a firm. However, choosing the cheapest location is not necessarily ideal as it will be 'cheap' for a reason – perhaps the location has very little passing trade or the premises are in need of attention.

There are two main reasons why the value of land in city centres is more expensive than land elsewhere. First, there is more *demand* for land in city centres, largely due to the convenience it provides for customers, suppliers and employees. Second, the *supply* of land is very limited in these areas. The combination of high demand and low supply means that property prices and rents are higher in cities than elsewhere.

For some businesses, the suitability of land must also be considered. Those in agriculture will need to locate in areas with arable land and suitable climate. Firms engaged in the production of dangerous products or harmful by-products will need to locate away from highly populated areas.

Some organizations, such as hypermarkets or vehicle manufacturers will need to buy cheap land simply because they need so much of it. Hence, they will tend to locate away from central business districts where land is both scarce and expensive. Provided that there is adequate infrastructure, such as road and communication networks, this should not be a problem for such businesses as they do not need to locate near their customers. Motor vehicles are distributed to showrooms and franchises that sell the vehicles and hypermarket customers tend to drive out of town to do their shopping.

These issues also apply on a global scale (see Question 5.5.1). The opportunities found in lower-cost locations abroad have led many businesses to move their operations overseas. Nike, Phillips and Coca-Cola are just some examples of manufacturers that have relocated to less affluent countries, largely due to the lower cost of land in these places. The cost of land is a highly important consideration for such businesses that require a large amount of space.

Question 5.5.1

Location, location, location!

Growing demand from financial companies and other businesses has raised land and property prices in central business districts throughout the world. The world's most expensive places to rent office space include London, Tokyo and Hong Kong. Prime office rents have also been surging in Moscow, Paris, Dublin and Abu Dhabi.

Figure 5.5a Costly office rent in London's Canary Wharf

a Outline how rising demand for a product, such as land, can push up its price. *[2 marks]*

b Using a PEST framework, analyse the advantages and disadvantages to a firm deciding whether to relocate overseas. *[8 marks]*

Availability, quality and cost of labour

Another crucial quantitative factor affecting location is the availability and quality of labour. Both will essentially affect the level of wages paid to workers and will therefore be critical in any location decision. Some businesses, such as BMW or Boeing, may need highly skilled labour. Others, such as Wal-Mart and Coca-Cola, require a large supply of lower cost and relatively unskilled labour. Tenneco, an American manufacturer of exhaust pipes for General Motors, Volkswagen and Peugeot chose to locate in Shanghai, China in 1998 largely due to the high supply and low cost of labour. A study of the Tenneco plant in China carried out by *Fortune* magazine in October 2006 found that labour accounts for just 1% of its production costs.

The supply and quality of labour will vary even within a country, affected by factors such as the quality of local schools, socio-economic dynamics and local unemployment rates. The inequality is much greater on an international scale. Businesses requiring highly skilled engineers may locate in Germany, where there is a readily available supply of skilled labour. Likewise, businesses that wish to locate in Norway, Japan, Iceland, France, Denmark and Finland need to consider the high cost of living when remunerating their workforce in these countries. On the other hand, manufacturers of mass market products, such as Nike, may locate in Indonesia (the fourth most populous country in the world) where there is an abundance of labour at a relatively low cost.

Proximity and access to raw materials

The nearness to and availability of raw materials is a major factor in determining the location of many firms that operate in the primary and manufacturing industries. **Bulk-reducing businesses**, also known as **weight-losing industries**, locate near the source of raw materials that are more heavy and costly to transport than the final product, i.e. the weight or size of the finished product is less than that of the raw materials used to produce the product. For example, it is cheaper to extract steel, iron, sugar and oil at source rather than transport these resources to other manufacturing sites because of the sheer weight and large amount of waste products from the raw materials.

Proximity to the market (customers)

On the other hand, certain products such as bottled water or alcohol, will increase in weight during the production process. These are known as **bulk-increasing** or **weight-gaining industries** and are commonly found in businesses that assemble components. If they were to locate near the source of raw materials, such as lakes and hob farms (for alcohol), it would increase their transportation costs when the final heavier and bulkier product needs to be delivered to the market. Hence, it makes more sense for these firms to locate nearer to their markets instead.

In the manufacturing sector, firms that rely on *just-in-time production* (see Unit 5.7) need to locate near their customers. This will reduce transportation costs and time thereby minimizing delays in the delivery of products to customers. However, it is not always possible to move the final product. In the tertiary sector, proximity to the market is also vital. In retailing and service industries, customers demand convenience, so it is important for businesses such as hotels, restaurants and hair salons to be suitably located near their markets.

A final point is that the cost of land (see 'Availability, suitability and cost of land' on page 672) is largely determined by the size of the market (or population) in the area. A highly populated city will tend to be attractive to businesses due to the large potential market. It is no wonder then that the 35 million people who reside in Tokyo (the most populous city in the world) make it one of the world's most expensive cities for businesses to locate.

Government incentives and policies

Whilst it is true that a multinational can pose a threat to domestic firms, it is more likely that the multinational will create more jobs. For this reason, governments may offer incentives to attract businesses to locate in, or relocate to, a certain region. This could be due to the relatively high unemployment that exists in those areas.

Such incentives are likely to be financial. A government could try to attract businesses to locate or relocate in a certain area by offering grants and subsidies to help reduce their cost of equipment and machinery. Low or interest-free loans may also be offered by the government to encourage businesses to invest in a particular location. Such financial incentives are more likely to be approved if the business locates in areas suffering from high unemployment, low incomes or in areas undergoing economic regeneration. Such areas are known as **assisted areas** or **enterprise zones**.

Although the government may offer incentives, it can also impose limitations that affect business location. For example, a business may not necessarily be able to obtain a licence to trade overseas as easily as within the domestic country. Planning permission for extensions or modifications to a site might also be a problem and therefore affects the choice of business location. Corporation tax rates can also have a large implication on the international location decision. In late 2006, for example, Audi halted investments of over €1 billion ($1.3 billion) in Hungary where it makes the Audi TT sports car. This decision was made because the Hungarian government had decided to increase taxes to reduce its huge budget deficit (which occurs when the government's spending exceeds its revenues).

Feasibility of using e-commerce

Unit 4.8 outlined the role of e-commerce and place in the marketing mix. E-commerce can have a huge impact on reducing the financial cost of location. Many businesses are now able to sell products via the internet. This gives those businesses more options over the location decision as they no longer need to be located near their customers. Insurance companies, book retailers and music distributors can be located anywhere in the world yet still sell to a global audience.

However, e-commerce is still relatively new and having a virtual business (e-business) rather than a physical presence (retailer) is not feasible for all businesses. Boeing's aircraft would not, for example, be purchased online. Boeing can use its website to market its company and products, but the actual purchase is done through other means.

Choosing a location

In reality, it is a combination of all the above factors that makes a certain location, be it domestic or overseas, attractive to businesses. It is important to consider these factors in the context of the business. Many firms have been attracted to India and China because they want to be located near their markets. Deregulation and the introduction of capitalism have stimulated a better political and economic climate for trading in these countries. Different stakeholders will have different views about the best choice of location. Managers will also need to consider the **qualitative factors** that affect the location decision (see 'Qualitative factors affecting location decisions' on page 676).

Question 5.5.2

Singapore

Singapore has for a very long time been highly rated in the World Bank's annual "Ease of Doing Business" report. The report ranks 178 economies in terms of regulations that either enhance or constrain business activity. Such regulations include: starting a business, obtaining licences, employing workers, registering property and protecting investors.

Singapore is often ranked the top country in the world in which to do business due to its streamlined business procedures. For example, it only takes six days to start a business in Singapore, whereas it takes 97 days in Indonesia, 141 days in Venezuela and 694 days in Suriname! Singapore is also a global manufacturing hub and a regional financial centre.

Source: adapted from The World Bank (www.doingbusiness.org)

a Explain how government rules and regulations can constrain or enhance business activity. *[4 marks]*

b Examine the quantitative factors that a business may need to consider before deciding whether to locate in a highly rated country such as Singapore. *[6 marks]*

QUALITATIVE FACTORS AFFECTING LOCATION DECISIONS

Qualitative factors are those that deal with the psychological and emotional aspects of location or relocation, such as familiarity with an area or consideration for the welfare of workers in the local community. Qualitative factors are not easy to measure, if measurable at all, but they can be just as important as quantitative factors when deciding where to locate a business.

Management preferences

The headquarters of The Body Shop is in Littlehampton (UK) simply because its founder, Dame Anita Roddick, was born and grew up there. For Roddick, there is an emotional attachment to the area rather than basing her location decision on financial reasoning. Managers may prefer a certain location due to personal preference, familiarity, and gut feeling (instinct) or because they feel that the location will serve workers and the local community better, thereby increasing their 'quality of work life'. They may also prefer a certain location because of its history. When Hollywood movie director Oliver Stone filmed *The World Trade Centre* which recalled the tragic events of the September 11th 2001 attacks in the USA he had little to think about when choosing New York as the location for filming.

Local knowledge

A similar reason for the above is that managers may locate in a certain area because they know the locations and its culture well, thereby giving it a potential competitive advantage. This inside information makes it easier and less risky for a business to establish itself. HSBC's highly successful global slogan "HSBC – the world's local bank" suggests that multinationals must consider the cultural differences that exist throughout the world. A lack of local knowledge can prove disastrous. For example, the USA launch of *OK!* magazine was, at that time, the world's largest magazine launch as measured by advertising and publishing expenditure, but sales of the magazine proved a disaster because the UK firm did not realize that the size of US supermarket shelves was too small to hold the oversized magazine! Similarly, the multinational Sock Shop went for a huge-scale launch in Florida (nicknamed the Sunshine State) and found sales were disappointing because it is not so customary to wear socks in Florida due to the hotter climate there.

Infrastructure

The availability of infrastructure is perhaps the most common qualitative factor affecting the location decision. Infrastructure is the term used to describe transportation, communication and support networks.

- **Transportation networks** include links to roads, rail, sea and air. The most appropriate means of transportation network for a business will depend on the size of the business and the products that it sells. For example, courier firms such as DHL and Fed Ex will want to be located in areas with good road and air networks.
- **Communication networks** refers to access to telephone lines for telephone and broadband internet services, and mobile phone coverage.
- **Support networks** refers to the support and complementary services that are essential for running a business, such utility firms that provide fuel and power or other maintenance and back-up services.

The government of a country is responsible for the economy's infrastructure. Not only does the infrastructure affect the locations of businesses, it also affects a country's international competitiveness. For example, many large multinationals have been reluctant to move into India due to its lack of sufficient infrastructure.

Businesses will want to be located in areas with good infrastructure so that expenses such as transportation costs are minimized. Good infrastructure can help businesses supply goods and services more efficiently and cost effectively. It will help to increase national output and reduce costs of production so can therefore improve a country's international competitiveness. Manufacturers and distributors need easy access to rail, port and road networks. Although Amazon.com and eBay can be located almost wherever they choose, they still need easy access to transportation networks to ensure that deliveries are swift.

Infrastructure is also important in ensuring that employees can get to and from work without too much difficulty. Location can therefore have an impact on recruitment, retention and motivation of staff. For example, people who work at out-of-town theme parks or at the airport often have their travel expenses subsidized. This helps to compensate for the cost and time involved in travelling to work. However, this also means an increase in the organization's costs.

Political and economic factors

For businesses with a global outlook, quantitative factors such as government incentives and the cost of labour will need to be considered. However, even if these monetary-related factors are favourable, managers need to consider the economic and political stability of the country in which they wish to locate. A stable economic and political environment will help a business to trade effectively in the future, thereby reducing the risks in operating overseas.

Countries that can offer political harmony free from corruption, a good law and order system, a stable exchange rate and low rates of taxation will tend to be more attractive to businesses. Reports by the World Bank show that Congo is one of the world's worst places to conduct business. This is largely attributed to corrupt government activities, huge rates of taxes and poor infrastructure.

Government restrictions and regulations

Businesses will also consider government policies and regulations that constrain business activity. Administrative and bureaucratic processes vary from country to country. For example, it takes just two days to register a company in Canada and Australia, whereas it takes an average of 8 days in France, 152 days in Brazil and a tedious 203 days in Haiti (source: *The Economist*). The difficulty in obtaining licences, permits and copyright or planning permission may lead to businesses looking to locate in alternative countries.

The Heritage Foundation, a research organization based in the USA, publishes an annual 'Economic Freedom Index' which ranks the attractiveness of countries based on how government intervention can restrict or aid economic relations and business activity. The annual survey ranks the freedom (or ease) of doing business in 161 countries, based on criteria such as economic freedom, political freedom, measures of anti-corruption and fiscal freedom (tax rates). Hong Kong, Singapore, Ireland, Luxembourg and Iceland tend to rank very well in the Heritage Foundation's 'league tables'.

Ethical issues

Decisions regarding the international location or relocation of a business often include an ethical element. For example, a business that produces lots of waste, noise or pollution may choose to locate in out-of-town and remote areas to avoid complaints from the local community. It may also be seen as unethical for a business to relocate if this will cause major job losses in a certain area. Consequently, the firm's reputation may be spoilt, leading to negative effects on its level of sales and profits.

Comparative shopping (clustering)

Clustering means that businesses locate near other organizations that provide for similar or complementary markets. For example, customers of computer hardware stores and mobile phone stores tend to locate near one another to make the most of the passing trade. Fast-food chains locate in busy shopping malls to take advantage of people who will need to eat and drink whilst at the mall. Shoes and clothes shops also locate near one another. Similarly, accountancy and law firms locate close to one another.

For example, London's Savile Row is renowned worldwide for its bespoke (custom made-to-measure) suits for men and women. The main clientele of businesses located on Savile Row are the rich and famous, such as highly successful business people and famous celebrities. Suits prices start from around $1,500 and range to $6,000 and more from any of the various tailors on the street.

Question 5.5.3

Fifth Avenue, New York

Retail space in New York's Fifth Avenue has one of the highest rental values in the world. The high price of leasing land has been accelerated by the world's top brands competing to secure a key spot in this prime location. Other highly sought after retail locations include Causeway Bay in Hong Kong, Oxford Street in London and Avenue des Champs-Élysées in Paris.

a Explain why location is an important management decision for retail businesses. *[4 marks]*

b Examine why retail businesses might be prepared to pay exceptionally high rents in prime areas such as Fifth Avenue. *[6 marks]*

LOCATION VERSUS RELOCATION

From time to time, businesses may need to consider relocation. This might be due to higher rents being demanded or more attractive locations becoming available, especially in overseas areas where production costs are lower.

However, there are problems with relocation (see Box 5.5a) and hence there is a reluctance to relocate. This concept is known as **industrial inertia**. The term was coined by Allan Rogers (1952) who found that American steel producers tended to continue to invest and reinvest in an existing location, even when the competitive advantages for such location no longer existed. The reluctance to relocate may come from the existence of external economies of scale caused by businesses being highly concentrated in a particular region. This can generate a regular pool of customers and other cost-reducing benefits. In addition, decision-makers will need to assess the acquired advantages from being located in its current position. The **acquired advantages** are the benefits that have been established over time by the firm's presence in a certain location.

Box 5.5a Potential limitations of relocation

- Relocation costs, e.g. transportation and insurance fees
- Lower morale and higher anxiety caused to the workforce
- Loss of skilled and loyal (but geographically immobile) workers
- The potential need to find new customers and suppliers
- Strong links with the existing local community will be lost
- Potential damage to corporate image (since the business is seen to value profits over its people)
- Redundancy payments to retrenched employees
- Problems encountered during the transition phase whilst adjusting to the new location

In deciding whether to relocate, managers are likely to conduct quantitative analysis of how profits will be affected. This is achieved through forecasting the effects of the relocation on the costs and revenues of the organization:

- Fixed costs, e.g. the cost of land (rental or purchase) in different locations
- Variable costs, e.g. the costs of labour, raw materials and distribution in different locations
- Revenue, e.g. the income of customers and forecasts of the *price elasticity of demand* in different locations.

Two recent developments in the relocation decision concern the development of the internet and globalization. Internet technology has meant that e-commerce businesses (see Unit 4.8) are not so restricted to certain locations. Such businesses are known as **footloose organizations** because there are no cost advantages from being tied down in any particular location. Amazon.com started with the founder selling books from his own home. Dell computers are mainly ordered online and there is no need to visit a conveniently located retail store. Banks offer online financial services, such as electronic bill payments, funds transfer, stock exchange dealings, foreign exchange transactions and travel insurance – all through the internet. Again, there is no need for customers to physically visit a bank to enjoy these services. Hence, even banks have become more mobile with the introduction of e-banking.

Globalization (see Unit 1.9) has meant that an increasing number of organizations must consider both domestic and international location decisions. This undoubtedly makes decision-making more difficult since there are external factors to consider (such as language and cultural issues, fluctuating exchange rates and the political stability of the country).

Question 5.5.4

Volkswagen

Volkswagen, the German car manufacturer and owner of **brands** such as Audi, Bentley and Beetle were given permission in 2006 to build a car plant in Punjab, India. Volkswagen announced that it was to invest about 15 billion rupees ($340 million) in the plant and create 5,000 jobs. In addition, there would be around 50,000 jobs created indirectly. Other car manufacturers also have a presence in India, such as Mercedes-Benz (since 1983) and BMW (since 2007). Analysts expect car sales in India to carry on booming as the country continues to enjoy high rates of economic growth.

a Define the meaning of **brands**. *[2 marks]*

b Evaluate the decision by Volkswagen to locate its business in India. *[8 marks]*

HIGHER LEVEL

HIGHER LEVEL EXTENSION: IMPACT OF GLOBALIZATION ON LOCATION

Globalization has been fuelled by the removal of trade restrictions (see Unit 1.9). The drive for global dominance has meant that many businesses need to consider both national and international location decisions. In addition to the factors mentioned earlier in this Unit, multinational businesses will need to examine several other factors when deciding on their international location. Some of these issues present opportunities, such as:

- **Production costs** – The costs of labour and materials can be significantly cheaper in overseas markets. However, these benefits will need to be considered in relation to potentially higher distribution costs from the new location.
- **Government rules and regulation** – Direct investment in overseas locations can help a business to by-pass government bureaucracy, such as import restrictions and duties (taxes). However, this would need to be weighed up against the costs of relocation.
- **Economies of scale** – Large international firms can gain huge cost savings by operating on a global scale. These economies of scale (see Unit 1.7) can therefore help the business to be more competitive.

However, the international location decision can also bring about its potential limitations, such as:

- **Language** – Verbal and written communications can become a problem if there are insufficient resources to deal with the problem. The costs of hiring linguists and translators can be quite considerable.
- **Culture** – Societal norms and business etiquette will vary from country to country and region to region (see Unit 4.7). A lack of cultural awareness can get a business into all sorts of trouble!
- **Regulations and legalities** – Different countries have different laws surrounding issues such as consumer protection, employee rights, and health and safety regulations. It can be costly to get correct legal advice.

- **Communications** – There could be issues surrounding communications within the organization. For instance, time zone differences and longer chains of command (see Unit 2.2) may be barriers to effective communication.
- **Social responsibilities** – There are ethical and moral issues that may need to be considered. Coca-Cola, a company that is symbolic of American culture, opened a bottling plant in Afghanistan during the USA's 'war against terrorism' under the presidency of George W. Bush. This decision was seen as very controversial by most analysts.
- **Political environment and stability** – The political stability of a country will affect the profitability of businesses. For example, corrupt governments will hinder economic and business growth. By contrast, government incentives and tax concessions can ease financial burdens associated with international location and relocation decisions.
- **Economic environment** – The economic prosperity of a country will also determine the profitability of businesses. Controlled inflation, unemployment, interest rates and exchange rates (see Unit 1.5) will all help a country to attract foreign direct investment.

The spread of technology and development in e-commerce have made international location decisions somewhat easier for many businesses. For example, teleworking is very common in India and many companies have relocated their call centres to India where there is readily available and suitably skilled labour. The spread of e-commerce means that retailers have an extra channel of distribution and do not need to worry as much about location. For example, banks such as HSBC provide the convenience of e-banking facilities that reduce the need for many customers to physically visit a bank.

Question 5.5.5

KFC, Vietnam

American fast-food giant KFC opened its first store in Hanoi, Vietnam in 2006. KFC was the first high-profile fast-food chain to locate in the former communist country. Economic and political reforms have transformed the country with its relatively untapped retail potential. Vietnam has a large and youthful population and a fast-growing economy. Its entry into the **World Trade Organization** (WTO) in 2007 has undoubtedly led to a significant increase in foreign direct investment. It has been earmarked to become a developed country by 2020. It is no surprise then, that KFC announced plans to open its 100th store by 2010. McDonald's, Pizza Hut and 7-Eleven have followed KFC's move by opening their first outlets in Hanoi, the country's capital city.

a Describe what is meant by the **World Trade Organization**. *[2 marks]*

b Outline one benefit to KFC in being the first well-known fast food chain to locate in Vietnam. *[2 marks]*

c Examine the factors that make Vietnam such an attractive location for global giants such as KFC, McDonald's, Pizza Hut and 7-Eleven. *[6 marks]*

HIGHER LEVEL

HIGHER LEVEL

HIGHER LEVEL EXTENSION: LOCATION AND BUSINESS ACTIVITY

Location decisions will have varying effects on the functional areas (personnel, marketing, production and finance) of a business. Questions that may need to be addressed include the following.

Personnel

- Is there a sufficient pool of suitable workers in the area?
- Are there skilled people available in the location?
- What skills and training needs will there be?
- What is the cost of local labour?
- What remuneration packages are being offered by rival firms in the area?

When relocating a business, managers will need to consider addition issues such as:

- How many managers and employees are willing to relocate?
- Will replacement labour be readily available?
- How many redundancies are there likely to be and what are the expected costs?
- Will there be strong opposition from trade unions?

Marketing

- Will the business be able to identify and exploit market opportunities in the area?
- What is the customer profile in the area? What is the average income? Retail outlets that supply luxury brands, for example, should be located in high-income areas.
- Is the product readily available in the area or is this a potential niche market?
- How will the location decision affect costs of production? This can have a direct impact on the prices charged by a business. The attractiveness of low-waged countries has meant that many multinationals have relocated to gain a price competitive advantage.
- How do exchange rate fluctuations affect prices? International location decisions will also need to take account of the role of exchange rates in determining prices.
- What promotional strategies are most appropriate in the area? Are moral and ethical issues related to marketing a concern for people in the locality?
- Are there sufficient distribution networks in the area?

Unit 4.7 covers the issue of international marketing in more detail.

Production (operations)

- What resources are needed to run the business? Will these be available in the chosen location?
- Are there suppliers nearby? How will they be found and how will contact be established?
- How many competitors are there? How much of a threat do they pose?
- How might quality be affected by a change in location?
- What complementary services exist in the region? For instance, access to distributors and utility services may be of importance in the location decision.

Finance

- What is the cost of land and premises?
- What available sources of finance are there to fund the location or relocation?
- What are the costs of obtaining licences, permits and registrations?
- Are there any tax concessions in the new location?
- What are the tax rates and insurance costs?
- When is the firm expected to break-even on its investment?
- What are the costs of leasing or purchasing equipment, machinery and vehicles in different locations?

Ultimately, the location decision is likely to affect all functions and aspects of business activity. The scope of the impact will depend on the type and size of business, the products it sells and the features of the location itself. Putting the factors into the context of the organization can allow better judgements to be made.

LOCATION AND BUSINESS STRATEGY

The location decision is one of the most important strategic decisions of all businesses. However, it is also possibly one of the most difficult decisions that managers have to make. Good location decisions require significant planning and quantitative analysis of the costs and benefits of alternative options. Some managers may also wish to use qualitative factors in their assessment of the location decision.

Two commonly used quantitative methods are *investment appraisal* (see Unit 3.2) and *break-even analysis* (see Unit 5.3). Investment appraisal methods are used to calculate the site with the quickest and/or highest financial return. However, these methods must be used with caution since the figures are based on forecasts. International location decisions are further complicated by differences in the exchange rate, so this makes comparisons rather more difficult. Break-even analysis can help a business to identify which location is most likely to break-even first. Thereafter, the firm will start to earn profit for the organization. Break-even is a key business objective, especially for those with large start-up costs and high fixed costs of production.

International locations are undoubtedly more complicated. Globalization has meant that businesses have to increasingly consider qualitative factors when locating overseas. For example, McDonald's, KFC and Wal-Mart have all been heavily criticized in the past for allegedly paying staff low wages. Hence, international location decisions have increasingly been influenced by ethical factors. Other issues also need some consideration, such as differences in language, culture, etiquette and the political environment.

Changes in *workforce planning* (see Unit 2.1) have meant a larger pool of flexible staff that work from their own home. This has help in the relocation decision of many firms since they no longer need such large premises. It may also be possible to relocate to less expensive areas if staff do not have an issue with transportation and access to the new site.

Finally, with developments in internet technology, the location decision becomes less of an issue for many businesses. Indeed, many e-commerce businesses can be described as operating in footloose industries. Nevertheless, for the vast majority of businesses, the location decision is crucial to their long-term prosperity and survival.

REVIEW QUESTIONS 5.5

1 What is meant by the 'location decision'?

2 Why might a location decision be said to be 'irreversible'?

3 Outline four quantitative factors that affect the location decision.

4 How might government incentives help to boost assisted areas (enterprise zones)?

5 What are 'qualitative factors' and how do they affect the location decision?

6 Why is the relocation decision a difficult one?

7 What is meant by 'industrial inertia'?

8 What are 'footloose' companies?

Higher Level extension

9 How has globalization affected the location decision?

10 How is business activity affected by location decisions?

Assisted areas, or **enterprise zones**, are those regions identified by governments to be suffering from relatively high unemployment and low incomes. Hence, government assistance (through use of financial incentives) is used to regenerate these areas.

Bulk-increasing businesses, or **weight-gaining industries**, are those that need to locate near their customers in order to reduce costs. This is because the products increase in weight during the production process.

Bulk-reducing businesses, also known as **weight-losing industries**, are those that need to locate near the source of raw materials because they are heavier (and hence more costly) to transport than the final product.

Clustering means that a business locates near other organizations that operate in similar or complementary markets.

Footloose organization refers to a business that does not acquire any cost-reducing advantages from locating in a particular location. Therefore, the firm can locate in almost any area.

Industrial inertia describes the reluctance to relocate due to the inconvenience of moving. Managers who hold this perception believe that the potential inconveniences and costs of relocation cancel out any of the benefits.

Infrastructure is the term used to describe the transportation, communication and support networks in a certain area.

Location refers to the geographical position of a business. The location is a crucial one, and will depend on both quantitative and qualitative factors.

Sunk costs are those that cannot be recovered if the business collapses, such as purchasing the lease and licence fees for a commercial property.

Innovation

UNIT 5.6

Anyone who has never made a mistake has never tried anything new.

Albert Einstein (1879–1955), Nobel Prize for Physics

HIGHER LEVEL

Key topics

Higher Level only

- Types of innovation
- Costs, benefits and goals of innovation
- Research and development
- Intellectual property rights: patents, copyrights and trademarks
- Factors affecting innovation
- Diffusion of Innovation theory

INTRODUCTION

Innovation can be described as the process of pioneering new and creative ideas in the production process. In business, the term is regarded as the commercial exploitation of new ideas and inventions. It can refer to both radical and incremental changes. Although there are technical differences between innovation and inventions, the terms are often used interchangeably. Examples of innovation include:

- Discovery of new production processes – Henry Ford, for example, discovered and applied the benefits of mass production and mechanization to the automobile industry. Likewise, online banking in the early 21st century transformed the finance industry.
- Successful implementation of creative ideas – James Dyson is renowned for inventing the bagless vacuum cleaner. This helped turn Dyson into a multimillion dollar business. Sabeer Bhatia, inventor of Hotmail, sold his email idea to Microsoft for $400 million (see Question 5.6.1).
- Introduction of new products – Coco Chanel popularized the 'little black dress' (simple but stylish black evening dress) in 1928 which is still as popular today. Apple's iPod revolutionized the way in which music is delivered to customers. Many observers argue that Apple's iTunes led to the global decline in music CD sales as customers switch to buying music online. Its launch of the multimedia iPhone also modernized the mobile phone market.
- Entering new markets – Ferrari has, for a long time, faced the dilemma of wanting to sell more cars without damaging its image of exclusivity. In recent years, it has expanded into China, thereby allowing it to exceed its quota of 5,000 cars produced each year since the Chinese market will not affect the elitism enjoyed by Ferrari customers in Europe and North America.

Innovation is at the heart of problem solving and is a major force of change. Stelios Haji-Loannou, founder of easyJet and the easy Group, made his millions by being innovative. He suggested that entrepreneurs ought to be pioneering, rather copying the ideas of others, so that customers would choose their products over those of their rivals. Some industries, such as pharmaceuticals, rely more on innovation than others. Nevertheless, innovation can give any business a large competitive advantage over its rivals and hence most businesses will tend to devote time and resources to research and development. This Unit looks at the nature and importance of innovation and the factors affecting the degree of innovation in a business.

TYPES OF INNOVATION

There are several classifications of innovation, which include:

- **Process innovation** refers to changes in the way production takes place. The aim of process innovation is to improve the method of production. For instance, toothpaste was originally produced and sold in jars until Colgate introduced toothpaste in tubes in 1908. Using online transactions, introducing credit to customers, or restructuring the hierarchy of a business are further examples of process innovations. Such changes to the traditional way in which things are done may well contribute to a changing corporate culture (see Unit 2.6).
- **Product innovation** refers to new creations or the radical development of existing products. Examples include the introduction of new products, improved functionality, improved ease of use and better reliability or performance. Product innovation is especially common in the industries that devote a huge amount of money into research and development, such as pharmaceuticals, consumer electronics, telecommunications and movies. The term also applies to innovations in the service sector. For example, HSBC first opened its doors to business on Sundays in September 2006 in Hong Kong.

HIGHER LEVEL

- **Cost reducing innovation** refers to improved processes that reduce the costs of production for a business or industry. This has two effects on businesses: the ability to increase supply and the scope to enjoy higher profit margins. The microchip revolution, for example, helped to reduce costs across all industries. The internet has also enabled many businesses to cut their operating costs.

Consumers can also gain from innovation since they are able to access new goods and services (product innovation), better product functions (process innovation) and/or lower prices (cost reducing innovation). For example, the introduction of low-cost 'no-frills' airlines such as Air Asia and Ryanair has led to lower prices being charged by airline carriers. Another example is the way in which the internet has revolutionized buying and selling (see Unit 4.8), bringing about greater choice and convenience for consumers.

Question 5.6.1

Hotmail

Hotmail, the free email service, was established in 1996 by Sabeer Bhatia and Jack Smith, both ex-employees of Apple Corporation. Their vision was to give people access to email from any computer in the world. Bhatia and Smith had attracted its one millionth subscriber within the first six months of Hotmail's launch. By its 18th month, the company had been bought by Microsoft, for a sum of $400 million.

Hotmail has moved on since its early days. MSN Messenger, for example, was launched in 1999 which allowed Hotmail subscribers to use instant messaging services. Webcam technology also allowed MSN Messenger customers to use audio and visual features. This has since been replaced by the upgraded Windows Live Messenger. In May 2007, Hotmail was finally revamped and rebranded as Windows Live Hotmail.

a Explain why Hotmail was seen as an innovative product. *[4 marks]*

a Analyse the importance of innovation to high-tech firms such as Microsoft. *[6 marks]*

Innovation can also be classed as either radical or incremental innovation:

- **Incremental innovation** refers to minor improvements to products or work processes. For example, car manufacturers might work on developing safer and more energy efficient vehicles.
- **Radical innovation** is much more disruptive and involves larger risks. For example, vinyl and cassette tapes were replaced by CD technology (which has been threatened by the growing use of internet downloads); VHS videos were replaced by DVD technology, and digital photography replaced film photography.

COSTS, BENEFITS AND GOALS OF INNOVATION

American management guru Peter Drucker once said that all successful businesses at some point required a manager to make courageous decisions. He argued that businesses cannot grow through cost cutting alone, but required innovation to sustain or increase their profitability. For instance, Apple's revolutionary iPod was introduced in October 2001 and in just 5 years had sold over 60 million units worldwide. By early 2007, Apple had sold its 100 millionth iPod, thereby helping the company to boost its earnings.

Benefits and goals of innovation

- Growth opportunities – Innovation can be a source of business growth and evolution. Nintendo, the producer of games consoles, started off as a Japanese business that sold playing cards. Nokia, the world's largest manufacturer of mobile phones, started business in the pulp mill industry.
- Productivity gains – Process innovation can help to increase productivity. This can give a business an advantage over its competitors.
- International competitiveness – Innovation can also give a business or country a competitive edge over its international rivals.
- Brand switching – This refers to the act of consumers turning away from rival products for the more appealing or innovative product (see Unit 4.3). Games console and mobile phone manufacturers are constantly trying to get customers to switch to their products.
- Job creation – Product innovation can create plenty of employment opportunities.
- Social benefits – Innovation can often improve the quality of life for many people in society. Developments in laser technology for correcting people's eyesight, for example, has meant that many people no longer need to rely on glasses or contact lenses.

Limitations of innovation

- High costs – Investment in innovation and research and development is highly expensive and requires sufficient labour and financial resources.
- High failure rate – Most new ideas fail to materialize, often due to internal and external constraints (see Box 5.6a). Even for the few ideas that might work, most will not be commercialized. Failure not only leads to a loss of investment funds, it can also demoralize the workforce.
- Budgetary constraints – Innovation is often held back by funding problems. Innovative ideas may be generated and may be realistically achievable, but budget constraints can prevent the project from being undertaken.

Box 5.6a Common causes of innovation failure

The acronym ARTICLE can be used to outline why the innovation process often fails, namely due to the firm's poor:

- Administration (organization)
- Resources (finance and human)
- Team collaboration and participation
- Information (access and interpretation)
- Communication
- Leadership
- Empowerment and delegation

RESEARCH AND DEVELOPMENT (R&D)

Unit 4.3 looked at the importance of *new product development* to an organization's long-term survival and success. Kodak, for example, almost went bankrupt after falling behind the times as customers switched to digital camera technology. *Research* refers to investigating the unknown, such as new products or processes. *Development* refers to using research finding to create products that might be commercialized. Development can also mean improving existing processes or products, i.e. improvements in *process innovation* and *cost reducing innovation*. The purpose of **research and development (R&D)** is to provide continual advancement (including modifications or improvements to existing products) and to launch new products that will satisfy customer needs.

R&D involves carrying out extensive research into new products, their designs, testing, and development of prototypes (trial or test products). The most successful prototype (based on the research findings) is the most likely one to be commercialized. However, the R&D process can be extremely lengthy and drain the financial resources of a business. Large multinationals spend hundreds of millions of dollars each year on R&D.

Benefits of R&D

- R&D can lead to the improved performance of an organization.
- It can lead to higher sales growth.
- Value added is likely to improve.
- There is the possibility of increased market value.
- It can give a business a first mover advantage.

R&D tends to pay off for businesses that operate in **sunrise industries**. These are industries that have rapid growth potential, such as high-tech industries. Furthermore, R&D can help a firm to generate a *first-mover advantage*. This refers to the benefits of being the first company to launch a new and innovative product, such as Apple's iPod in October 2001 or Pfizer's Viagra (impotence drug) back in March 1998. Such benefits could include the ability to charge a high price, to build up a favourable corporate image and to establish strong market share. Hence, having a first mover advantage can better prepare a business to contend with the competition that is likely to follow.

By contrast, R&D expenditure in **sunset industries** (where there is negative or deteriorating growth potential) is likely to accelerate their decline. In addition, studies have consistently shown that only one product reaches commercialization for every ten products that are developed and test-marketed. Hence, the successful product that is launched must recoup the high costs of R&D, even if this takes several years.

R&D is a continual process. Some people suggest that innovative firms will continue to invest in R&D, even if everyone else is cutting back (perhaps due to an economic recession). Firms that continue to conduct R&D are the ones most likely to thrive by having a competitive advantage when there is an upswing in the economy. As American inventor Thomas Edison (1847–1931) once said, "I have not failed. I've just found 10,000 ways that won't work."

Most of the spending on R&D comes from large firms operating in **oligopolistic markets**, i.e. industries where market share is dominated by a few large businesses. For example, the production of mobile phones is dominated by four key manufacturers. Successful R&D can give oligopolistic firms a competitive advantage in the form of cost advantages and/or quality improvements in the long term.

HIGHER LEVEL

Question 5.6.2

Johnson & Johnson

Johnson & Johnson is one of the world's largest health care and pharmaceutical companies. According to its website, the company sells its products in over 175 countries around the world. Its brands include Johnson's Baby products, Acuvue contact lenses, Neutrogena skin and beauty products and Band-Aid bandages.

Johnson and Johnson's website has a section dedicated to innovation, which invites the general public to submit their ideas for the firm's consideration.

Source: Company website (www.jnj.com/student_resources)

a Explain the importance of research and development (R&D) to Johnson & Johnson. *[4 marks]*

b Given the high failure rate of new products on the market, to what extent can R&D expenditure be justified? *[8 marks]*

INTELLECTUAL PROPERTY RIGHTS

Intellectual property rights (IPR) refers to the legal rights to make exclusive ownership claims to certain inventions or pieces of work. They act to protect the inventor or creator from others replicating their ideas. Hence, IPR act as an incentive to the innovator but also as a barrier to entry from a competitor. For example, IPR allow the owner to benefit from having a first-mover advantage since there is scope to make the most of the monopoly situation. The main types of IPR are patents, copyrights and trademarks.

Patents

A **patent** is the legal right to be the exclusive producer or user of a newly invented process or product, for a finite period of time. History books record the beginnings of patents as far back as 1449, when a patent was granted in the UK for the process of making stained glass windows. The patent is granted after the inventor has registered and satisfied the conditions stipulated by the government. Not all applications for a patent are granted as they are not 'inventive' or new, but are minor improvements on existing technologies or processes.

Like all assets, a patent can be held by an individual or by a business. Patents are not free, so patents applications are only made for inventions that are likely to be commercially profitable in the long term. Ownership of the patent can then act as a barrier to entry for other competitors as the patent prevents other firms copying the invention, without the prior consent of the patent holder. The patent holder is also entitled to sell the technology or invention to larger businesses.

A famous patent is that of the Tetra Pak, a registered trademark, used for packaging drinks such as milk, soup and fruit juice (see Figure 5.6a). Ruben Rausing, a Swedish inventor, came up with a tetrahedral container idea in 1943 and successfully patented it the following year. Today, Tetra Pak is the world's largest supplier of drinks cartons.

Figure 5.6a The Tetra Pak

Another famous example of a patent is Dyson Appliances. James Dyson pioneered the bagless vacuum cleaner in 1978 and patented the technology five years later through licensing his invention in Japan. The invention made Dyson one of Britain's best known and richest people. His company now sells products throughout the world and has annual sales of over £3 billion ($6 billion).

The main drawback of using patents is that the whole process is time consuming and bureaucratic. It can easily take three years from applying for a patent to having it being granted. In addition, most applications are rejected. For instance, Microsoft applied for almost 3,500 patents in 2006 and less than half of these were authorized. Those businesses that are granted a patent will have to pay for their renewal, often on an annual basis. Nevertheless, the advantages of owning a patent can be quite significant, as shown by the above examples of Dyson Appliances and Tetra Pak. Box 5.6b outlines some further examples.

Without patents, there could be very little incentive for innovation as other rival firms simply copy the invention without having to invest in the initial research and development costs. Alternatively, a business might buy a patent from the inventor. This can be cost effective in relation to having to spend an uncertain amount of money on R&D. This is especially true for patents that are nearing their expiry date, so the value or cost of the patent is lower.

Box 5.6b Some famous inventors and inventions

Levi Strauss and partner Jacob Davis (1873) successfully applied for a patent for trousers strengthened with metal rivets to make work wear more durable and later modified this to become the world famous blue denim jeans.

Coca-Cola (1886) was invented by John Pemberton, an American pharmacist. He sold the product, which originally contained traces of cocaine, as a remedy for depression, hysteria and anxiety.

Band-Aid (1920), the adhesive bandage, was invented by Earle Dickson, an employee of Johnson & Johnson. Dickson went on to become vice president of the company.

Laszlo Biro (1938) was a Hungarian journalist who invented the ballpoint pen.

Bubble wrap (1957) was accidentally invented by Alfred Fielding and Marc Chavasnnes, the founders of the Sealed Air Corporation. Bubble Wrap is a registered trademark of the company which specializes in the production of packaging material.

Roy Jacuzzi (1968) invented the first autonomous bath with fitted water jets.

Post-it notes (1968) which were originally used as bookmarkers were invented by Spencer Silver, an employee of 3M. The company's slogan is simply "Innovation".

Microsoft (1983) announced the introduction of its new operating system – which was originally called Interface Manager – named 'Windows'.

Copyrights

Copyrights provide legal protection for artists and authors by preventing others from using or copying their published work without permission. Governments grant the permission to hold copyrights for a finite period of time. Works that has been protected by copyright often carry the © symbol. Copyrights are popular in the music, film, drama, art, photography, software and publishing industries.

Authors such as J. K. Rowling have become multimillionaires from selling their copyrighted works to large Hollywood movie studios. J. K. Rowling's highly successful Harry Potter books has earned her international fame and she goes into the record books for being the first person to earn over $1 billion from writing.

Trademarks

A trademark is a sign or logo that represents a business or a product belonging to that business. If the trademark is registered at a patent office, it acts as a barrier to rivals wanting to imitate the product name or symbol. Trademarks that have been registered can, but do not necessarily, carry the ® symbol next to the mark. However, it is illegal to use this symbol if a trademark has not been registered.

Trademarks are often used as a form of branding (see Unit 4.3). For example, **suggestive trademarks** are used to give customers a suggestion about the nature or characteristic of a product, such as Nike's *swoosh* (tick) or Apple's *Nano* (small). A **descriptive trademark** is used to show a direct link between the mark and the product, such as the *Pictionary* and *Monopoly* board games. Finally, **arbitrary trademarks** are pure random and meaningless names, such as Kodak cameras and Apple computers.

Question 5.6.3

BMW

In 1998, BMW paid £40 million ($80 million) for the Rolls-Royce logo and name, which it has been able to use since 2003. This was considered as a major bargain by most analysts, given the high status and reputation of the **trademark**. This allowed BMW to set up Rolls-Royce Motor Cars Ltd.

a Define the term **trademark**. *[2 marks]*

b Examine the role *and* importance of intellectual property rights for BMW. *[6 marks]*

Today, the issue of intellectual property rights has become of greater concern for businesses because of developments in internet technology. Many countries do not have laws governing the use of IPR on the internet. The practice of music and video downloads, for example, is still very hard for governments to police. Hence, the complexity of enforcing IPR over the internet has led to many commentators doubting its efficiency and effectiveness.

FACTORS AFFECTING INNOVATION

There are two main sources of innovation.

- *Manufacturer innovation* occurs when a person or a business commercialises their invention or discovery.
- *End-user innovation* occurs when a person or a business innovates for their personal use because there are no existing products that meet their needs or wants.

Breakthrough innovations or radical innovations, such as the internet, tend to come from R&D. By contrast, incremental innovation will tend to come from daily practice which leads to identification of improved processes and procedures.

Management guru Peter Drucker (1985) found seven sources of new opportunities or ideas for innovation (see Table 5.6a). His findings provide a framework to help managers to consider the innovation opportunities in their organization. By monitoring the seven sources of innovation, it is then possible to identify opportunities for innovation.

Table 5.6a Drucker's seven sources of innovation

Source of innovation	Description	Example (Opportunities)
The Unexpected	Are there any surprising successes or failures?	Coca-Cola's highly successful global sales of Coke Light (Diet Coke) led to the launch of other products such as Coke Zero.
The Incongruities (strangeness)	Are there any differences between what people believe and reality?	Selling low-calorie food and drink because customers think 'no sugar added' means there are no calories.
Process need	Are there any weaknesses in the current production process that provides an opportunity for improvement?	Overly complex airline ticketing procedures led to the creation of e-ticketing which has reduced queues at the airport.
Industry and market structure	Are there any changes to the underlying conditions of demand and supply in an industry or a market?	Pressure group action and health-conscious consumers have led to healthier menus being introduced in fast-food restaurants.
Demographics	What are the current and forecast demographic trends/changes?	Changes in population size, age structure, gender structure, educational attainment, and income levels can all provide wide opportunities for many businesses.
Changes in perception	What are people's general attitudes, assumptions and beliefs? What do customers perceive as 'value'?	Socially responsible business behaviour is increasingly expected. Hence there are opportunities for implementing environmentally friendly innovations.
New knowledge	What opportunities can new knowledge provide?	Technological knowledge has led to the development of the internet and e-commerce.

Innovation can also come from competitive market pressures; such as the increased competition brought about by globalization (see Unit 1.9). In rapidly changing markets, such as the movie industry or the computer games market, innovation is the key to business success. Product life cycles in these markets are very short and the demand of consumers is constantly changing (demanding 'better' and more exciting films and computer games). In addition, production costs tend to be very high, thereby making the risk of failure a real threat. Therefore, innovation is paramount in these businesses. Seeking new market opportunities through the creative skills of employees is a crucial source of innovation. For example, movies and computer games can now be downloaded onto mobile telephones and portable media players.

Question 5.6.4

Nintendo Company

The Nintendo Company (Nintendo) is a Japanese multinational that specializes in the games console market. Established in 1889, the company originally produced playing cards. Nintendo introduced its first video games in the late 1970s. Since then, games such as *Donkey Kong* and *Mario Bros* and products such as *Game Boy, Super Nintendo* and *Nintendo GameCube* have made the company a household name throughout the world. In December 2006, the company launched its seventh generation games console, the *Nintendo Wii* which uses wireless and Bluetooth technology. According to media reports, Nintendo allocated over $200 million for the launch of the *Wii* to ensure its success.

a Comment on the importance of innovation in a rapidly changing industry, such as the games console market. *[4 marks]*

b Analyse the factors that affect the degree of innovation in a business such as Nintendo. *[6 marks]*

DIFFUSION OF INNOVATION THEORY

Everett M. Rogers (1931–2004) came up with the **diffusion of innovation theory**, also known as the **new product cycle**, to show the various points at which individual groups of consumers will become involved with a technological innovation. It allows managers to see the timeframe of adoption of the new innovation and the size of the market at each stage of adoption. The tool is often used when introducing a new product, process or project.

Rogers found that people have different adoption rates, i.e. some people like to be the first to purchase a new technological innovation whilst others are more conservative or sceptical and therefore prefer to wait a while before adopting the innovation. For managers, this means that it is important to consider the market when launching something innovative and the speed at which it goes from being new to commonplace.

Rogers came up with five different groups of consumers (see Figure 5.6b), each with different adoption rates. Geoffrey Moore (1999) developed the work of Rogers and found that in the high-tech industry, the consumer groups consisted of 2% innovators, 15% early adopters, 34% early majority, 34% late majority and the laggards make up the remaining 15% of the market.

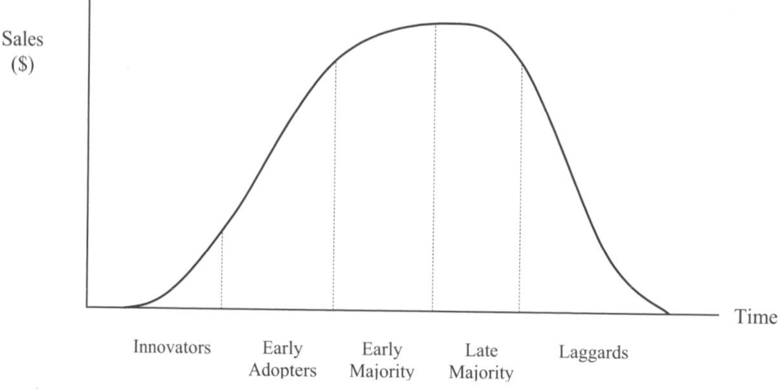

Figure 5.6b Roger's diffusion of innovation (innovation adoption) model

- *Innovators* – These are the technology enthusiasts who like to buy new things, simply because they are new. These consumers are prepared to pay a high price for such exclusivity. Such customers tend to have high socio-economic standing. Marketing will focus on the newness of the product.
- *Early adopters* – This group consists of visionaries who buy a little later than the innovators who have already tried and tested the product. Marketers may allow tasters (trials, previews or samples) to encourage purchase.
- *Early majority* – This group consists of the pragmatists who buy the product after the initial hype. Marketers will have removed the emphasis on the novelty (newness) of the product by this time. The business may benefit from economies of scale by operating on a larger scale and therefore prices may have fallen to entice more adopters.
- *Late majority* – These are the rather conservative consumers who purchase the product only when they are confident that there are enough people who have already bought the product, which by this stage is considered as a 'best seller'. Economic necessity or social pressures means that the late majority adopt the innovation. Prices will have fallen (at least slightly) by this stage.
- *Laggards* – These are the sceptics or technophobes (those who doubt or fear technology) who only buy when almost everyone else has already bought the product, i.e. they are typically the last group of consumers to adopt the innovation.

The speed of the various adoption rates are affected by several factors, which include:

- *Relative advantages* – This measures the extent to which the new product is believed to be better than existing products, such as plasma televisions compared to LCD televisions, or Bluetooth technology versus wi-fi technology.
- *Observable features* – This factor refers to whether the results of the innovation can actually be seen to work. Whist the relative advantages may be explicit, consumers are more likely to adopt the innovation if the results can be observed. For example, health-related products are marketed to show their relative benefits (such as weight loss or better looking skin); but do they really work? Hence, marketers are likely to target the innovators and early adopters to get the evidence that the other groups of consumers need in order for them to adopt the innovation.
- *Compatibility* – This refers to the extent to which the new technology will fit existing systems. Incompatibility may mean that major changes are likely to take place. For example, the major digital camera producers have their own dedicated format of memory cards in order to make it more difficult for customers to switch brands (since it could require throwing out all the previous memory cards, batteries and chargers from a different manufacturer).
- *Complexity* – This refers to the level of difficult in understanding the innovation and how to use it. Mobile phones, for example, are increasingly more complex with evermore sophisticated functions. The core benefits must also be clearly expressed and understood in order to encourage adoption.
- *Testability* – Customers are more likely to adopt a new innovation if they are able to test it. For example, test driving the latest car or having a demonstration on the latest home entertainment system is quite straightforward. This can then help consumers to make a decision. However, it is not possible for a consumer to 'test' the latest heart transplant technology or laser eye technology, so adoption rates are likely to be much lower and slower for such products.

HIGHER LEVEL

Question 5.6.5

Oasis Hong Kong Airlines

Oasis Hong Kong Airlines (Oasis) is a low-budget airline. It is the first airline to adopt the budget airline model for long-haul flights since the collapse of Laker Airways in 1982. Oasis's maiden flight from Hong Kong to London, UK in October 2006 attracted negative media coverage as the flight was delayed by 24 hours due to airspace clearance problems from Russia. The return flight was also delayed by over two hours due to a damaged emergency exit door. Faced with intense competition from stronger and more established rivals, such as Cathay Pacific and Singapore Airlines, and with only two aircraft in its fleet, customers were not keen to jump at Oasis's low prices. Nevertheless, by June 2007 Oasis had launched its second flight route from Hong Kong to Vancouver, Canada, even though the airline was not making any profit.

a Outline why Oasis's business approach may be classed as innovative. *[2 marks]*

b Comment on why customers may not have been overly keen to fly with Oasis, despite the airline's low prices. *[2 marks]*

c Analyse the key differences in the marketing strategies that Oasis could have used to attract *innovators* and the *late majority.* *[6 marks]*

INNOVATION AND BUSINESS STRATEGY

Charles H. Duell, Commissioner of the US Office of Patents in 1899 claimed, "Everything that can be invented has been invented." How wrong he was! Innovation is an ongoing phenomenon in today's business environment. Bill Gates, the world's richest man and the co-founder of Microsoft, famously underestimated this fact when he claimed in 1981 that 640 kilobytes of computer memory was enough for people. However, Bill Gates has since clearly recognized that change and innovation are vital to the long-term survival of a business. Businesses, he argues, should not become complacent with their successes but continue to innovate.

R&D is expensive and there is no guarantee that it will generate profits for a business. Mistakes will be made and most products will fail to ever be commercialized. However, firms need new products and ideas to survive and grow. This is especially the case in markets where rapid and constant changes are commonplace, such as the high technology and fashion industries. Yet as experts such as Peter Drucker and Tom Peters argue, most improvements in the innovation process come in small steps and from the simplification of design, manufacturing and processes.

In his book *Innovation and Entrepreneurship: Practice and Principles* Peter Drucker (1985) suggested five principles that can help businesses to take advantage of a new innovation:

- Identify the opportunity from one of the seven sources of innovation, as identified by Drucker.
- Analyse the opportunity in order to assess whether people are likely to be interested in adopting the innovation.
- The innovation must be simple, by being clearly focused on a specific consumer need.

- It must initially appeal to a small, limited market (since R&D costs are potentially so high). As the market grows for the innovation, the firm has time and resources to fine-tune its innovation. This will allow the firm to stay ahead of the mounting competition.
- The innovation should aim at market leadership; otherwise, it is unlikely to be seen as leading edge or revolutionary enough to establish itself profitably.

Innovation is also affected by government policies that may either hinder or encourage innovation. For example, some governments offer tax incentives for investment and R&D expenditure. Countries with lower corporation tax rates also tend to attract more foreign direct investment. Governments might also offer financial support to small businesses to encourage innovation and entrepreneurship. Finally, governments may increase their funding to universities to promote research and development.

Governments can also provide incentives for innovation by effective administration and management of intellectual property rights. Patents, copyrights and trademarks are all forms of *intangible assets* (see Unit 3.5). They can be invaluable in helping a business to gain a competitive advantage by having monopoly power in the production process of an invention for the duration of the patent, for example. By holding the patent, the business can set high prices to recoup the costs of R&D and to establish customer loyalty and high market share before rivals can enter the market.

The changing nature of the business environment has meant that innovation has become a continuous process. Shorter product life cycles and the use of innovation as a source of competitive advantage have led to businesses placing a greater emphasis on being innovative.

Whilst innovation provides potentially huge benefits to an organization, the cost implications and the high failure rate often prove too large a barrier. R&D expenditure cannot and does not guarantee success. As Coco Chanel once said, "One cannot be forever innovating. I want to create classics." On the other hand, 'classics' can only be achieved if businesses are prepared to take risks. After all, it is not possible for firms to grow without taking calculated risks. As Charles Darwin (1809–1882) famously said, "It is not the strongest of the species that survive, not the most intelligent, but the one most responsive to change." The challenge for managers is to strike the right balance.

HIGHER LEVEL

REVIEW QUESTIONS 5.6

1. What is meant by 'innovation'?
2. State the three types of innovation.
3. State three examples of innovation.
4. Distinguish between incremental and radical innovation.
5. State three advantages and two drawbacks of innovation.
6. What is 'research and development'?
7. What are the benefits of research and development?
8. What are intellectual property rights?
9. Distinguish between patents, copyrights and trademarks.
10. According to Peter Drucker, what are the seven sources of innovation?
11. What is the 'diffusion of innovation theory'?
12. What are the factors that affect the speed at which consumers adopt new innovations?

Copyrights provide legal protection, for a finite period of time, to artists and authors by preventing others from using or plagiarizing their published works without permission.

Cost-reducing innovation refers to improved processes that reduce the costs of production for a business or industry.

Diffusion of innovation is Everett Roger's theory that shows the various points at which individual groups of consumers will become involved with a technological innovation.

Incremental innovation refers to minor improvements to products or work processes.

Intellectual property rights (IPR) are the legal rights to exclusive ownership of certain inventions or pieces of work. Examples include patents, copyrights and registered trademarks.

Innovation means the commercial development, use and exploitation of an invention or creative idea that appeals to customers.

Patents provide legal protection, for a finite period of time, to the registered producer or user of a newly invented product or process.

Process innovation refers to changes to the way production takes place.

Product innovation refers to new creations or the development and improvement of existing products.

Radical innovation refers to rather major and disruptive innovations that tend to involve high risks.

Research and development (R&D) is the technological and scientific research that helps to generate a flow of new ideas and processes.

Trademarks are a form of intellectual property right that uses signs or logos to represent a business or its brands and products.

Production Planning

UNIT 5.7

It's a bad plan that cannot be changed.

Italian proverb

Key topics

- Stock control methods: Just-in-case and Just-in-time

Higher Level extension

- Traditional stock control: lead times, buffer stocks, reorder levels and usage rate
- Optimum stock levels
- Capacity utilization
- Outsourcing and subcontracting
- Make-or-buy decisions

INTRODUCTION

One of the key aims of production planning is to minimize the costs of holding stocks whilst ensuring that there are sufficient resources for production to be able to meet customer demand in a timely manner. This issue is further complicated by seasonal fluctuations in demand, such as high demand for fresh flowers for Valentine's Day and Mothers' Day whilst there may be little demand for flowers at other times of the year.

This Unit looks at the different types of stock control methods and their relative merits. It also examines the need for businesses to recognize and establish their optimum stock levels in order to remain competitive. This requires careful production planning to enable flexible processes to be designed, such as spare capacity being available during peak trading periods. It also requires multiskilled staff who are able to perform different jobs at short notice.

Domestic and international competitive pressures have led firms to focus on cost competitiveness. Outsourcing and offshoring are strategies used by businesses to remain internationally competitive. These concepts are examined towards the end of this Unit. The final part of this Unit looks at 'make-or-buy' decisions, whereby firms need to decide whether to produce products themselves or to purchase these from a lower cost supplier.

STOCK CONTROL

Stocks, also known as **inventories**, are the materials, components and products used in the production process. There are three categories of stocks:

- *Raw materials* – natural resources used for production, such as crude oil, metal ores, soil and timber
- *Work-in-progress* – semi-finished or unfinished products, i.e. output that is not yet complete, e.g. parts and components to be used in the production process
- *Finished goods* – complete units of output that are ready for sale.

Managing stock levels is an important task for any business. Without sufficient stock, production and sales will be interrupted. Stock control involves careful planning and monitoring to ensure that sufficient stocks are available and at the right time. Businesses have to decide on the optimal level of stock because there are costs and drawbacks in holding too much or too little stock.

Costs of holding stock

The costs of holding stock include:

- Storage costs such as rent, insurance and security costs. This can be expensive for firms that produce large, bulky and valuable products such as motor vehicles or aircraft.
- Stock may be prone to fire, theft or damage.
- Some types of stock, such as fresh flowers or food products, may perish or deteriorate. Hence, holding large volumes of stock can be wasteful and expensive.
- Stock can be illiquid (see Unit 3.3) so it ties up working capital which could have been used elsewhere.
- Stock may become obsolete if demand suddenly changes.
- Changing fashions and tastes will mean that excess stocks will need to be heavily discounted in order to offload the products.

Stockpiling occurs when a business builds up excessive stock. This may have been caused by overproduction or falling demand. Alternatively, stockpiling can be deliberate as a business prepares for seasonal peaks in demand, such as during the Christmas trading period. Whatever the cause or purpose, by holding too much stock, a firm incurs even higher costs which can lead to liquidity problems.

Costs of holding insufficient stock

When a business does not hold enough stock to meet orders, the result is known as a **stock-out**. The consequences of a stock-out include:

- Lost sales since stocks are not available to meet customer orders. Worse still, customers may choose to buy from a rival business.
- Halted production due to insufficient stocks. This leads to inefficiency as machinery and other resources are left idle.
- Damaged corporate image and reputation due to disgruntled customers (caused by late deliveries or loss of sales). This will also damage customer loyalty and goodwill.
- Higher costs since staffing costs still need to be paid, even though production may have been brought to a standstill.
- Higher administration costs will be incurred as the firm places more orders more often. This may also mean that these smaller orders do not attract discounts for bulk purchases.

Question 5.7.1

Ford

At the turn of the millennium, Ford Motor Company had struggled to remain profitable with huge **stockpiles** of its cars. Its continued efforts to cut costs saw the company cutting production by 21% in North America in 2006. A year later, Ford had sold off its luxury brand Aston Martin (which it acquired in 1995).

Ford claimed that the cuts were necessary to remove excess and unprofitable production, despite the negative effects on employees and suppliers. The company said that the reductions would better align its stocks and output with actual customer demand.

a Define the term **stockpiles**. *[2 marks]*

b Analyse the costs of poor stock control to a firm such as Ford Motor Company. *[6 marks]*

JUST-IN-CASE VERSUS JUST-IN-TIME STOCK CONTROL

Just-in-case (JIC)

Just-in-case (JIC) is the traditional stock management system that recognizes the need to maintain large amounts of stock in case there are supply or demand fluctuations. A reserve stock (known as the **buffer stock**) of raw materials, semi-finished goods and finished goods is used just in case there are any contingencies, such as late delivery of stocks from a supplier or a sudden increase in demand for output. JIC systems are used to ensure that there is always sufficient stock available to meet customer demands.

However, JIC may mean that a business holds too much stock or overestimates the level of demand for its products. This can lead to major problems for the business. In the 1980s and 1990s, Rover tried desperately to compete with BMW but the lack of demand for their cars led to huge stockpiling of Rover cars and its eventual financial crisis. This led to BMW buying out the Mini brand from Rover, which it has used successfully since 2000, having rebranded it as the BMW Mini.

Advantages of JIC include:

- JIC allows a business to meet sudden changes in demand.
- There is increased flexibility because having sufficient stocks enables the firm to speed up production if necessary.
- JIC allows a business to take advantage of purchasing economies of scale (bulk buying raw materials and components for production).
- JIC reduces downtime caused by a stock-out (lack of stock) since there is no need to wait for delivery of stocks from suppliers.

The drawbacks of a JIC system are outlined above (see 'Costs of holding stock' on page 700). Perhaps the key limitation with JIC is the high costs of storage. There is also an opportunity cost of money being tied up in stocks, i.e. the money could have been used more profitably elsewhere in the business.

Just-in-time (JIT)

Just-in-time (JIT) is a stock management method based on having stocks delivered as and when they are needed in the production process. Since stocks are delivered just before they are used, there is no need for the business to use traditional just-in-case stock control systems. Instead, only the absolute minimum level of stock is held. Finished goods are dispatched as soon as they have been produced, i.e. there is minimal or no storage of finished goods. JIT is a Japanese philosophy first advocated by former Toyota Executive Taiichi Ohno and is seen as a prerequisite to lean production (see Unit 5.4). It is a useful management tool when flexibility is important.

JIT is widely used by car manufacturers. For example, the BMW Mini is assembled using a JIT system. A customer places a specific order before the vehicle is made. Each component on the assembly line is ordered to be available when needed for production. The use of barcodes for each component helps to ensure the right parts are supplied at the right time. Unlike traditional assembly lines that are used in mass production (see Unit 5.1), JIT allows a series of Minis, all of different colours and engine sizes, to be produced on the same production line. The JIT system relies on automation, barcodes and the use of highly skilled and motivated workers.

Advantages of JIT include:

- JIT reduces the costs of holding stock, such as: rent (of storage space), insurance, stockpiling and the opportunity cost of theft or spoilage of stock.
- Since there is minimal money tied up in stock; working capital can be better used elsewhere.
- JIT improves cash flow and the working capital cycle (see Unit 3.3) as there is no need to hold large volumes of stock (raw materials, work-in-progress and finished goods).
- JIT has helped many firms to reduce their break-even point (see Unit 5.3). For example, Rolls-Royce claimed that its annual break-even level of output had halved following its implementation of JIT.
- JIT allows firms to be more flexible and responsive to the needs of their customers, such as seasonal changes in demand.
- JIT system can improve motivation in the workplace by promoting employee participation and teamworking (both important elements of any JIT scheme).
- JIT implies that its implementation can reduce waste. Stocks do not perish or go out of date (since there is no buffer stock). In addition, the need for accuracy or zero defects means that there is no time used on reworking substandard output, i.e. JIT promotes a 'right first time' approach to production.
- JIT can help strengthen a firm's relationship with its suppliers, thereby helping reduce lead times in the production process.

Limitations of JIT include:

- There is a huge reliance on external suppliers. There will be major problems if stocks are not delivered on time. Hence, there is a need to establish good relationships with efficient and dependable suppliers. Choosing suppliers with ISO certification (see Unit 5.4) may help.
- Minimal stock levels mean that there is little room for mistakes. The need for 'right first time' production means that there is no room for error and can add pressure to staff.
- JIT systems often prove inflexible in trying to cope with a sudden increase in demand.
- Since stock levels and stock orders are minimal, there are fewer opportunities to exploit purchasing economies of scale (see Unit 1.7) such as price discounts for bulk purchases.
- Administration costs will be higher as the frequency of stock ordering increases under a JIT system.
- Stocks must be of good quality in order to prevent bottlenecks in the production process. Hence, there is no time for quality control (see Unit 5.4).
- JIT relies on sophisticated computer technologies to ensure that the correct stocks are ordered and delivered at the right time and place. Any error or malfunction could bring production to a standstill.
- Since JIT is a philosophy, it must be embedded into the culture of the organization. JIT requires management to truly believe in the system. It also requires the agreement and commitment of the workforce. However, this will not happen overnight.

Question **5.7.2**

Karoo's Cafe

Karoo's Café is run by Ned Baloo as a **sole proprietorship** in Auckland, New Zealand. Sales have been falling and the high level of stock held at the business is causing cash flow problems. Ned feels that he is too busy to place orders based on sales forecasts produced by his deputy manager. A further complication is that Ned's main supplier has suddenly gone out of business and he will now need to search for a new supplier.

a Define the term **sole proprietorship**. *[2 marks]*

b Explain how introducing just-in-time might be suitable for Karoo's Café. *[4 marks]*

c Comment on why it might be advisable to place inventory orders based on sales forecasts. *[4 marks]*

HIGHER LEVEL EXTENSION: TRADITIONAL STOCK CONTROL

The traditional stock control system (JIC) uses a purchasing department to take charge of stock control. The roles of the purchasing department are:

- Purchase good quality raw materials, components and other supplies at competitive prices.
- Ensure that the right quantity and quality of products are available for production.
- Arrange for timely delivery of stocks to ensure that they are available for production.
- Develop good professional relationships with suppliers.

HIGHER LEVEL

Stock control charts

Stock control charts (see Figures 5.7a and 5.7b) are used to graphically illustrate a simplistic system of stock control. The diagram is usually drawn on the assumption that sales are constant (for ease of illustration), although the chart can be easily adjusted to suit the needs of most businesses.

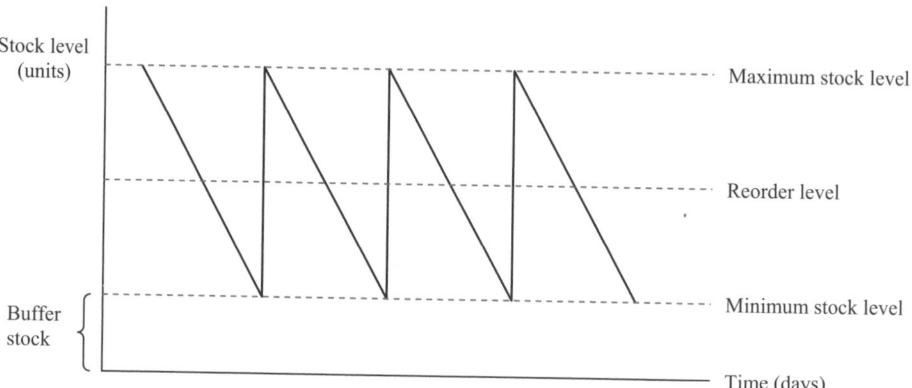

Figure 5.7a Traditional stock control

There are several key concepts used to construct and explain stock control charts. With reference to Figure 5.7a, we can see several important features of the stock control chart:

- **Maximum stock level** – This refers to the upper limit of stock that a business wishes to hold. The maximum limit is determined partly by the physical storage space that is available and the level of demand for its output, per period of time.
- **Reorder level** – There is a time lag between a firm placing an order for stocks and it being delivered. Hence, when stocks fall to the reorder level, the next order is placed. This should help to ensure that the new order arrives just before stocks fall below the predetermined minimum level.
- **Minimum stock level** – This refers to the smallest amount of stock that a business wishes to hold. For most businesses, this minimum is above zero, as a precautionary measure. If this minimum is greater than zero, the minimum stock level is also known as the buffer stock. Buffer stock refers to the minimum stock level held by a business in case there are any unexpected occurrences, such as delays in the delivery of raw materials or a sudden increase in demand for the firm's product. Generally speaking, the more efficient the firm, the lower the buffer stock tends to be.

Stock control charts can also help businesses with their management of stocks. With reference to Figure 5.7b, several other features can be seen.

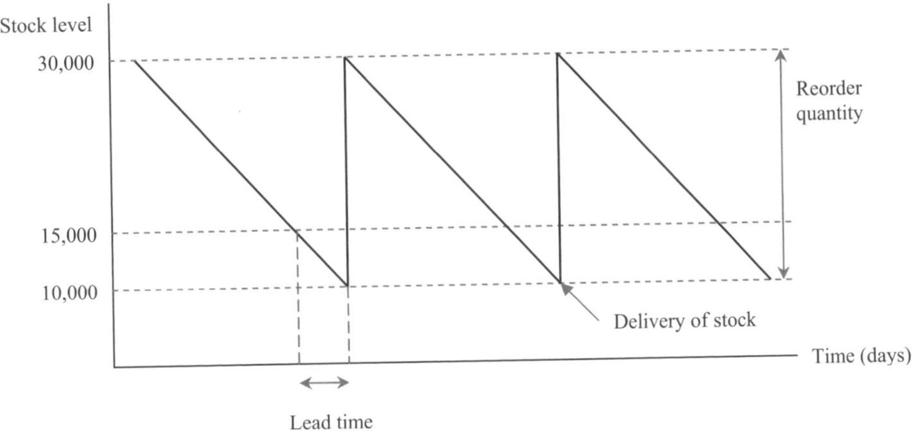

Figure 5.7b Reorder quantity and lead times

- **Reorder quantity** – This refers to the amount of new stock ordered. In this case, the reorder quantity is equal to 20,000 units (i.e. 30,000 minus 10,000). This order is placed whenever stock levels reach the *reorder level* (in this case, it is 15,000 units).
- **Lead time** – This measures the amount of time between placing an order and receiving the stock. The greater the lead time, the higher the buffer stock tends to be. By contrast, just-in-time stock control systems have minimal buffer stock, if any at all. In reality, delays can prolong lead times so it may be important to have some stock to deal with contingency situations. This will mean that stock levels go below their desired minimum level (but are above zero).
- Also, notice from the graph that the level of stock increases vertically whenever there is a delivery of stock. Assuming that the correct amount of stock is delivered on the right day, the increase should bring stock levels back to their maximum.
- In reality, the graph may not be so predictable due to miscalculations, such as late deliveries or the incorrect amount of stocks being delivered. Further, the **usage rate** (the speed at which stocks are depleted) may be higher or lower than originally predicted. The consequences of miscalculating the usage rate are shown in Box 5.7a.

Box 5.7a Consequences of miscalculating inventory usage rates

Consequences of faster usage

- Faster depletion of stocks mean that more orders will need to be made or the business has to do without stocks, i.e. halt production.
- Stocks will fall below the minimum stock level line. This highlights the importance of having a buffer stock.
- The stock control line will be steeper, leading to more frequent reordering of stock.
- There will be a knock-on effect so stock will only return to its normal levels once the reorder quantity is increased.

The opposite effects occur in the case of usage rates that are lower than originally forecast.

Optimum level of stock

The best level of stock for a business will vary from one business or industry to another. For example, the optimal stock level for a supermarket will be quite different from that of a florist or restaurant. Businesses face a dilemma when they order stocks: a large order will generate cost savings through economies of scale, but will also involve higher storage costs to hold the additional stocks. Striking a balance relies on the expertise of managers. This balance is known as the **economic order quantity**, i.e. the optimum level of stocks which ensures that there are sufficient stocks for production to take place without any interruptions, but also allows a firm to incur only minimal costs.

There is a number of factors which influence the amount of stock that a business holds and orders. These factors include:

- Type of product – *Fast-moving consumer goods* (FMCGs), such as soft drinks and personal hygiene products sold in supermarkets, will need to be reordered in large quantities. This is because by the time that new stocks are delivered, the firm would have sold many more units of the FMCGs. Conversely, *consumer durables* such motor vehicles, furniture or consumer electronics, will be reordered in much smaller quantities since there is a slower stock turnover for such products. Unlike FMCGs, stockpiling *perishable products*, such as fresh flowers and seafood would be disastrous for a business.
- Forecast level of demand – The higher the level of demand, the greater the amount of stock will be held. A supermarket will stock more of the better selling brands on its shelves. Car showrooms will stock more of its relatively cheaper, better selling models. Stock levels will rise during peak trading periods, such as barbecue products during the summer, and decline again during off-peak seasons.
- Lead times – Suppliers that can guarantee short lead times allow a business to have minimal buffer stocks. Conversely, larger volumes of stock will need to be reordered if there are long lead times, such as shipment of heavy and bulky products from an overseas supplier.
- Costs of stockholding – The higher the opportunity cost of holding stock, the lower the optimal stock level tends to be. It may be costly for a luxury car producer or jeweller to stock its most expensive brands and products (due to the lack to demand for these and the high costs of theft or damage). By contrast, the pace at which low-cost FMCGs are sold allows retailers to hold large volumes of stock.

Today, most large businesses use computerized stock control systems, such as the use of electronic barcode readers. Computerized systems enable businesses, such as large supermarkets, to manage stocks from thousands of product lines. For example, each time a barcode on a product is scanned at the checkouts, the computerized system updates the level of stocks. When the stock level reaches the reorder level, the computer system automatically reorder stocks. It is quite common for the more popular product lines in a supermarket to be replenished two or three times a day.

It is possible with the more sophisticated systems to input data such as public holidays and festivals in order to determine the optimal level of stocks at different times of the year. Supermarkets again use this for stocking different products at various times of the year for events and holidays such as Christmas, New Year, Valentine's Day, Mothers' Day, Easter, Fathers' Day, summer holidays, 'back to school' season, Halloween and so forth. Being able to stock the right products at the time when consumers want them can certainly help to give the business a competitive advantage. It is also possible for the firm to decide which of the less popular products should be discontinued (since they take up shelf space without the expected sales revenues).

Computerized stock control systems have led to huge efficiency gains. For example, there is no longer a need for workers to manually count stocks (which would be a horrendous task for large retailers such as Costco, Tesco, Wal-Mart and Carrefour). Computerized systems known as **Electronic Point of Sale (EPOS)** automatically keep a running balance of stock levels and reorder them when necessary. However, EPOS does not completely eliminate the need for manual stock control by staff (known as **spot checks**) since computerized systems do not account for damaged or stolen stock.

Question 5.7.3

QE Bakery

QE Bakery is a profitable firm that produces bread and cakes for several large supermarket chains in the local area. Despite this, the production manager, Andy Blair, has a number of concerns regarding the manufacturer's high level of stocks. Andy believes that QE Bakery holds too much stock and this has limited its growth and profits. He has produced the following stock control chart to present at a board meeting alongside his proposals for introducing a just-in-time stock system.

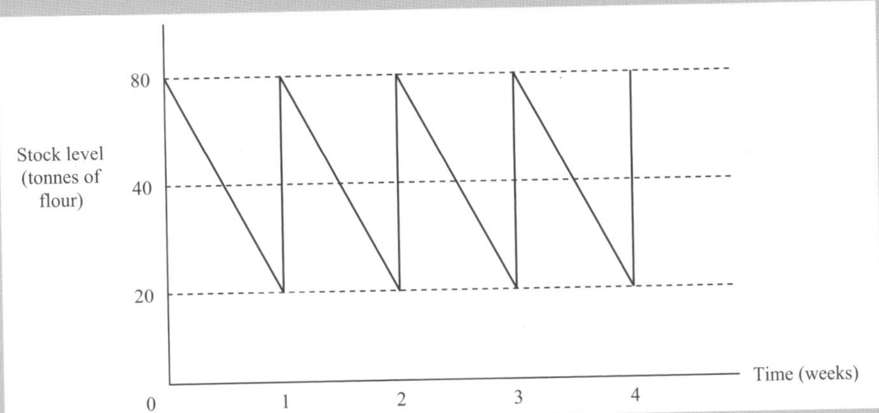

a Use the stock control chart to identify QE Bakery's:

i Reorder level.

ii Reorder quantity.

iii Buffer stock.

iv Lead time. *[4 marks]*

b Explain why a supermarket is likely to have a higher reorder level than QE Bakery. *[4 marks]*

c Examine the advantages and disadvantages for QE Bakery of using just-in-time production rather than the traditional just-in-case system. *[6 marks]*

HIGHER LEVEL

HIGHER LEVEL EXTENSION: CAPACITY UTILIZATION

Capacity utilization measures the existing level of output of a firm as a proportion of its total potential output. A high level of capacity utilization means that output levels are close to their maximum level (known as the **productive capacity**), per period of time. For instance, 80% capacity utilization means that there is 20% spare capacity in the organization. Hence, the capacity utilization is a measure of a firm's efficiency level as it looks at the extent to which there are idle (unused) resources in the organization. High capacity utilization is financially important as it helps to spread out fixed and indirect costs of production (see Unit 5.2) over a large level of output.

Capacity utilization is calculated by using the following formula:

$$\text{Capacity utilization} = \frac{\text{Actual output}}{\text{Productive capacity}} \times 100$$

For example, if a firm's maximum possible output is 10,000 units per month but it actually produces 8,500 units per month, its capacity utilization is 85%.

High capacity utilization is likely to be relatively more important to firms that have:

- High fixed costs – Higher capacity utilization will help to reduce the *average fixed costs* (AFC) of production. The higher the firm's capacity utilization, the lower the fixed costs per unit will be. For example, suppose a firm has fixed costs of $10,000 and a productive capacity of 2,000 units per month. It would have AFC equal to $10 if output was 1,000 units. However, if it operates at full capacity, the AFC would fall to $5 ($10,000 / 2,000 units).
- Low profit margins – Products with low profit margins contribute little to the profits of a business. Hence, they will need to be sold in large quantities to be profitable. Mass market products such as *fast-moving consumer goods* (see Unit 4.3) have low profit margins, but the high level of output and sales justifies their existence.
- High levels of break-even – Similarly, high capacity utilization is needed if a firm has a high break-even level of output (see Unit 5.3). This might be because of exceptionally high production costs (such as in the case of commercial aircraft manufacturing) or because profits have low profit margins (thereby reducing the unit contribution and raising the break-even level of output).
- Low marginal costs – If the extra cost of providing a particular good or service is close to zero, high capacity utilization will be important. Airlines, schools, theme parks and hotels are examples of businesses that fall into this category.

Business costs are incurred 24 hours a day. For example, a restaurateur will need to pay rent, insurance and salaries, no matter how busy the restaurant is. Hence, it is rational to want the firm to earn as much revenue as possible. Empty tables represent spare capacity and a burden on costs. Schools, for instance, often rent out their facilities in the evening, at weekends and over the school holidays in order to generate higher revenues. Idle resources not only represent wastage and inefficiency, but are also a drain on finances. Box 5.7b outlines various ways that a firm can increase its capacity utilization.

Box 5.7b Methods to increase capacity utilization

The method used to increase capacity utilization will depend on the reasons for the current rate of utilization.

- The use of marketing strategies can help to increase sales. This will automatically lead to higher capacity utilization. Of course, it is not necessarily as simple as spending more on marketing to generate more sales. There are many other factors besides marketing that influence the level of demand for a product (see Unit 4.4).
- A relatively quick way to increase productive capacity is to subcontract work (covered later in this Unit). This involves using external firms to help supply the firm's products. The main drawback in using this approach is that profit margins are likely to be lower (if prices are kept constant) or prices need to be raised (in order to maintain profit margins). Higher prices can dampen the demand for a firm's products.

(cont.)

- Spare capacity might exist because of excess capacity, i.e. there is no need to have such a large productive capacity. Many firms, such as General Motors, Ford and Dell, have closed down operations to reduce excess capacity. This approach is likely to cause job losses, although will often be necessary for the firm to return to profitability.
- If the cause of low capacity utilization is an economic recession, there is little that the firm can do (see Unit 1.5). When the economy recovers, capacity utilization should automatically increase to meet the increasing level of consumer demand.

Drawbacks of high capacity utilization

Although there are significant benefits to working near or at full capacity, there are also potential drawbacks. As the English proverb says, "A full cup must be carried steadily." In other words, operating at full capacity will bring its own burdens and potential drawbacks:

- High capacity utilization will mean that equipment and machinery are being used constantly without any time for routine servicing and maintenance. This is likely to lead to breakdowns which will delay output.
- Operating at full capacity can lead to stress being placed on workers. This can be counter-productive, especially if staff are constantly required to work overtime. Quality is also likely to fall if there is continual pressure on running at full capacity.
- For services such as theme parks, restaurants or hair salons, operating at or near full capacity can lead to all sorts of problems, such as longer waiting times and lower standards of customer service. There may also be health and safety concerns, such as overcrowding.
- The firm may experience *diminishing marginal returns* as it operates near full capacity. This means that each additional unit of output costs increasingly more because resources are overstretched. This might be caused by people getting in each other's way, which makes work become less efficient. Alternatively, there may be declining returns because working at full capacity may necessitate spending more money on overtime pay, thereby increasing labour costs.
- High capacity utilization is not a substitute for organizational growth. In order for a business to take on more orders to meet rising levels of demand, it will need to expand its scale of production, i.e. raise its productive capacity.

Finally, it is important to remember that whether higher or lower capacity utilization is a good thing depends on the context of the business. For example, a business with a product in the launch phase of its life cycle is likely to have low capacity utilization. Only if demand for the product surges will the business need to operate at a higher level of capacity utilization.

Exam Tip!
Do not confuse the drawbacks of higher capacity utilization with diseconomies of scale. The above disadvantages can apply when a business operates near or at its productive capacity. Diseconomies of scale can only happen if the business is operating on a larger scale, i.e. if its productive capacity has increased.

HIGHER LEVEL

HIGHER LEVEL

Question 5.7.4

AMC Theatres

AMC Theatres (or AMC Cinemas as the company is known in some parts of the world) is the USA's second largest chain of cinemas. AMC Theatres holds the record for the first American cinema chain to expand operations into foreign countries. When movies are being screened, the marginal cost of an extra customer is close to zero. Hence, cinemas rely heavily on high **capacity utilization**. However, overcapacity might bring even greater problems for AMC if it has to refuse some customers.

a Define the term **capacity utilization**. *[2 marks]*

b Explain why the 'marginal cost of an extra customer [at the cinema] is close to zero'. *[3 marks]*

c Examine the importance of high capacity utilization for a cinema such as AMC. *[6 marks]*

HIGHER LEVEL EXTENSION: OUTSOURCING AND SUBCONTRACTING

Globalization has led to ever more competitive markets. In order to compete internationally, firms need to have some sort of competitive advantage. Cost advantages, for example, mean that the firm can reduce prices to gain greater market share. Alternatively, prices can be left unchanged but the cost advantage gives the firm greater profit margins.

One way in which businesses have strived to gain a cost advantage is by **outsourcing**. Outsourcing, also known as **subcontracting**, refers to the practice of transferring internal business activities to an external firm as a method of reducing costs. Subcontractors should be able to carry out the outsourced work for less than the business would be able to, without compromising quality. For instance, both Dell and Apple outsource the production of their laptop batteries to Sony. Other examples of work that are often outsourced are shown in Box 5.7c.

Outsourcing, or **contracting out**, tends to be used for three interrelated reasons:

- When activities are not core to the functions of the business. For example, many firms will outsource marketing and security functions to subcontractors. A school may subcontract its catering services. This allows the organization to concentrate its efforts on its core activities, i.e. teaching and learning.
- When the business lacks the specific skills. Subcontractors are often used to maintain the ICT functions of a business, such as networking and systems upgrades. The services of lawyers and accountants are further examples.
- To cut costs of production. Outsourcing is used if it leads to productivity gains and cost advantages. Many international firms, both manufacturers and service providers, have outsourced operations overseas in order to benefit from significantly lower labour costs.

Box 5.7c Typical business activities that are outsourced

- Catering
- Cleaning
- Customer service call centres
- Maintenance of information technology systems
- Manufacturing components
- Property maintenance
- Public relations
- Recruitment and selection (recruitment agencies)
- Security systems
- Training and development (continuous professional development)

Advantages of outsourcing

- Specialists are hired to carry out the work to high quality standards. This is especially important if the firm does not have the necessary skills and expertise available internally. Outsourcing also allows the firm to access the latest technologies and developments in industries in which it does not have expertise.
- Different subcontractors will bid (or tender) to carry out the outsourced work. The firm with the most attractive overall package will be awarded the contract. This means that the subcontracted work is provided at competitive prices, enabling the business to control its own costs of production without jeopardizing quality assurance.
- Contracting out also helps to reduce labour costs. Subcontractors are not, by definition, employees of the organization and therefore costs of labour are reduced. For example, there is no need to remunerate subcontractors with holiday pay, bonuses, sick leave or pension contributions.
- Outsourcing allows the business to concentrate on its core activities, i.e. what it is best at doing. This can therefore help to improve the overall efficiency of the organization.
- Outsourcing has become popular as it improves workforce flexibility (see Unit 2.1). For example, during busier trading periods, there is no need to recruit workers since subcontractors can be hired to increase output. Conversely, during less busy periods, there is no need to reduce (internal) staffing.
- Contracting out production facilities to overseas organizations (known as **offshoring**) can help a business to get around protectionist measures used by the government (see Unit 1.5). For example, Nike and Adidas outsource the manufacturing of their sports apparel to firms in China and Indonesia. This helps them circumvent the problem of import taxes being placed on the sale of their products in these countries.

Disadvantages of outsourcing

- Outsourcing will initially cause redundancies in the organization and will therefore need to be managed carefully as it will affect the level of morale and motivation within the firm.
- Subcontractors need to be monitored to ensure that deadlines and quality standards are observed. This will increase the costs of administering outsourced activities.
- Outsourcing and offshoring have often been associated with ethical concerns and problems. For example, offshoring may involve the exploitation of labour in less economically developed countries. This may include low pay, poor working conditions, an absence of health and safety policies and the use of child labour.

- Quality management becomes more difficult. The quality of the outsourced work is put in the hands of the subcontractors, placing huge responsibility and trust on the subcontractor. Things can go wrong, such as conflicting views on the quality of the output. Critics argue that allowing external parties to have such a large influence on the reputation of a firm can be potentially disastrous.
- Similarly, in their strive to cut costs, subcontractors have been known to 'cut corners' by hiring under-age, illegal and unqualified workers in order to optimize their own profits. This has often led to substandard quality and conflict between the contractor and subcontractor. As the saying goes, "If you pay peanuts, you get monkeys", i.e. there is no shortcut to achieving high quality.
- The benefits of offshoring are subject to changes in the external environment. For example, the cost savings from using an overseas subcontractor may be wiped out simply because of adverse fluctuations in the exchange rate (see Unit 1.5). The overseas country may suffer from an economic recession or uncontrollable rates of inflation. If these problems are prolonged, the business may need to reconsider the use of outsourcing in such countries.

Offshoring

Offshoring is an extension of outsourcing that involves relocating business activities and processes abroad. It tends to take place in less economically developed countries where labour costs are relatively low. For example, Nike and Reebok outsource the production of their footwear to China's Yue Yuen Industrial, the world's largest manufacturer of sports shoes. The Philippines has also proved to be a highly attractive place for outsourcing. Global companies see the location as ideal due to the country's western-orientated education system and English-speaking population. Activities commonly outsourced to the Philippines include call centres, financial management, computer software development and legal transcriptions.

American and British firms dominate the practice of offshoring. This has made countries such as India and the Philippines highly attractive locations due to their large pool of educated English-speaking workers who earn significantly less than their western counterparts. However, critics of offshoring have complained about quality standards. For example, can someone in India really address 'local' banking issues of clients in London, Paris or New York?

Question 5.7.5

Norfolk and Norwich University Hospital

The Norfolk and Norwich University Hospital (UK) wants to save money and reduce the burden on overworked staff by **outsourcing** non-core activities to India. Doctors' notes and letters will be typed by English-speaking graduates employed in India. Around 80% of India's 2 million graduates each year speak fluent English. The hospital said it was hoping for 98.5% accuracy.

a Define the term **outsourcing**. *[2 marks]*

b Explain two drawbacks of health care providers operating near their productive capacity. *[4 marks]*

c Discuss the arguments for and against The Norfolk and Norwich University Hospital outsourcing some of its operations to India. *[9 marks]*

HIGHER LEVEL EXTENSION: MAKE-OR-BUY DECISIONS

Make-or-buy decisions refer to a firm's choice of whether to produce a product itself or to purchase the product from a supplier and then resell it. There are several quantitative methods that can be used to help in this decision. Examples include break-even analysis (see Unit 5.3), investment appraisal (see Unit 3.2) and cost–benefit analysis. Quantitative methods can show a business the relative benefits of either decision.

The make-or-buy decision involves an assessment of both quantitative (financial) factors and qualitative factors. As with outsourcing, the 'buy' decision requires a business to consider whether it has the expertise and equipment to manufacture a quality product and at a competitive cost. If the firm does not, then the 'buy' decision should go ahead. Hence, non-core functions and products are contracted to outside suppliers. If the firm is financially better off by producing the product, then the 'make' decision is pursued. These activities would constitute the organization's core competencies.

The most straightforward method for deciding whether to make or buy is **cost–benefit analysis**. If the cost of producing the product (make) is lower than the supplier's price (buy), then it makes financial sense to manufacture the product rather than use outsourcing. Of course, this decision assumes the business has the necessary skills and resources to do so (such as equipment, machinery and personnel). When using cost–benefit analysis to approach the make-or-buy decision, four key variables must be known:

- Expected sales volume or quantity (Q)
- Fixed costs (FC) associated with making the product, e.g. tools, equipment and machinery costs
- Average variable costs (AVC) of making the product, e.g. wages and material costs
- Price per unit (P) charged by the supplier.

In deciding whether to make or to buy, a firm needs to work out the values of both:

- Cost to buy: $CTB = P \times Q$
- Cost to make: $CTM = FC + (AVC \times Q)$.

If CTM is greater than CTB, it is more financially desirable to 'buy'. Likewise, if CTB is greater than CTM, it makes financial sense to 'make'.

Exam Tip!
Worked example

Question: Suppose a firm was deciding between buying and making 1,000 garden benches. Suppliers could offer the product at a price of \$20 per unit. However, there is sufficient capacity for the firm to produce these extra tables with direct costs estimated to be \$13 per bench and allocated fixed costs of \$5,000. On financial grounds, should the firm make or buy the garden benches?

Answer:

CTB = \$20 × 1,000 = \$20,000
CTM = \$5,000 + (1,000 × \$13) = \$18,000

Therefore, based on the limited information, it makes financial sense for the firm to make the products (thereby saving itself \$2,000).

HIGHER LEVEL

HIGHER LEVEL

Qualitative factors are also usually taken into account when considering make-or-buy decisions. These factors include issues such as:

- An assessment of the firm's core competencies and its non-core activities and functions
- The relative product quality
- The reliability of subcontractors, e.g. their track record and reputation of delivering products on time
- Whether the manufacturer has spare capacity to meet extra orders
- Whether the decision is irreversible, i.e. the terms and conditions of the contract.

Question **5.7.6**

To make or to buy?

Brothers Luke and Jake are about to celebrate their 3rd and 5th birthdays next month. They have asked for a train table for their collection of wooden trains. Their father, Eddy, has found just one retailer in the town that stocks the product, made out of high quality solid wood at a price of $155. However, the design is very bland and rather simplistic and Eddy feels that the boys may not like the design. If he were to make a similar product, he could personalize the train table for his sons. Eddy has estimated that if he chooses to make the train table, the cost would be approximately $80 for all the materials plus about fifteen hours of his time.

1 Describe what is meant by a 'make-or-buy decision'. *[2 marks]*

2 Advise Eddy on whether he should make or buy the train table. Use both quantitative and qualitative considerations in your answer. *[8 marks]*

PRODUCTION PLANNING AND BUSINESS STRATEGY

Production planning and stock management are vital to a firm in order to improve its operational efficiency and cost control and can give the firm a competitive advantage, especially if it is able to pass on some of the cost savings to consumers in the form of lower prices. Effective stock control can help to ensure production can meet the demand of customers, thereby contributing towards customer satisfaction and winning their loyalty.

As has been explained in this Unit, there are advantages and disadvantages in increasing the level of stock. Insufficient stocks will lead to production problems for the business, which will disappoint customers. However, overstocking (stockpiling) can lead to cash flow problems due to storage and other related costs. Establishing the optimal level of stock is not an easy task and often relies on trial and error. More objectively, stock control will require the purchasing and marketing departments to work collaboratively to determine the optimal stock level. For example, the marketing department might be able to provide data from sales forecasts (see Unit 4.2) to inform the operations department about the right stock levels needed for production.

Since most firms find it difficult to know the exact amount of stock to hold at any one point in time, they will often hold a buffer stock. This acts as a safety net, just in case there are unforeseen issues or problems, such as a sudden surge in demand or late deliveries of stock. *How* firms decide on what its minimum stock level should be is another matter. The decision will depend on several factors such as the type and size of the business, the level of consumer demand, lead times with suppliers, and the costs of holding stock for the firm.

Outsourcing has provided many opportunities for businesses in terms of cost control, access to stocks and productive efficiency gains. However, outsourcing is not problem free, so the ultimate requirement for successful outsourcing is a 'win-win' outcome (see Unit 2.7) for the business and the subcontractor. For example, contracts should be fair and financially beneficial to both parties. There should also be some degree of flexibility, such as reasonable exit clauses, in recognition of the dynamic and changing nature of the business environment. Furthermore, outsourcing does not mean that the subcontractor takes over and holds all responsibilities for the project. Indeed, there must be proactive involvement from both parties in any outsourcing contract.

Effective stock control and production planning are based on the notion that higher levels of productivity lead to improved competitiveness. However, stock control is one of the many ways in which a firm can achieve greater productivity and lean production (see Unit 5.4). Other methods to achieve productivity gains include: staff training and development (see Unit 2.1), improved staff motivation (see Unit 2.5), enhanced quality management and reduced wastage (see Unit 5.4). These points highlight the integrated nature of business and management. Nevertheless, this Unit has shown that there is little doubt that careful production planning and control are vital to the competitiveness of a business. As US Army General George S. Patton (1885–1945) once said, "A good plan today is better that a perfect plan tomorrow." In today's fast-paced and highly competitive business world, a so-called 'perfect' plan that is poorly timed will often prove too little too late.

REVIEW QUESTIONS 5.7

1 What is the purpose of production planning?

2 Outline the three categories of inventories.

3 State four costs of holding stock.

4 What is meant by 'stockpiling'?

5 What is a 'stock-out' and why is it costly to a business?

6 Outline the meaning of 'just-in-case' and state three advantages of using JIC stock control systems.

7 What is 'just-in-time'?

8 State three advantages and three limitations of using JIT stock control systems.

Higher Level extension

9 Outline the roles of the purchasing department.

10 Why do businesses hold a maximum and a minimum stock level?

11 What is a 'buffer stock'?

12 Distinguish between the 'reorder level' and the 'reorder quantity'.

13 Explain whether businesses prefer to have short or long lead times.

14 What is meant by an 'optimal stock level'?

15 Define the term 'economic order quantity'.

16 What is 'Electronic Point of Sale' (EPOS)?

17 Distinguish between a firm's 'productive capacity' and its 'capacity utilization'.

18 Outline three methods that businesses can use to increase their capacity utilization.

19 State three advantages and three disadvantages of outsourcing.

20 Explain how cost-benefit analysis might be used in 'make-or-buy' decisions.

Buffer stock refers to the minimum stock level held by a business in case there are any unexpected occurrences, such as late deliveries of raw materials or a sudden increase in demand for the firm's product.

Capacity utilization measures the existing level of output of a firm as a proportion of its total potential output. High capacity utilization means that the output level is close to the firm's maximum limit (productive capacity).

Cost–benefit analysis is a financial decision-making tool. It compares the financial costs of a decision with the quantitative benefits of that a decision.

Electronic Point of Sale (EPOS) is a computerized system that automatically keeps a running balance of stock levels and reorders them as and when necessary.

Just-in-case (JIC) is the traditional stock management system that recognizes the need to maintain large amounts of stock in case there any emergencies (such as delayed delivery of stocks) or supply and demand fluctuations.

Just-in-time (JIT) is a stock control system that originated in Japan. Under a JIT system, materials and components are scheduled to arrive precisely when they are needed in the production process.

Lead time measures the amount of time between placing an order and receiving the stock. The longer the lead time, the higher buffer stocks tend to be.

Make-or-buy decision refers to a situation where a firm has to decide between manufacturing a product and purchasing it from a supplier.

Maximum stock level refers to the upper limit of inventories that a business wishes to hold at any point in time.

Minimum stock level refers to the least amount of inventories that a business wishes to hold. For most businesses, this minimum is above zero, as a precautionary measure.

Offshoring is an extension of outsourcing by using an overseas firm in another country as the subcontractor.

Optimum stock level, or the **economic order quantity**, refers to the best inventory level for a firm, which ensures that there are sufficient stocks for production to take place without any interruptions, yet also allows the firm to incur only minimal costs.

Outsourcing, also known as **subcontracting**, refers to the practice of using external firms to provide goods or services as a method of reducing costs. Subcontractors should be able to carry out the outsourced work for less than the business would be able to, without compromising quality.

Productive capacity refers to the maximum output of a firm if all its resources were fully and efficiently employed.

Reorder level refers to the desired level of stock when a new order must be placed. Since there is a time lag between a firm placing an inventory order and it being delivered, the reorder level helps to prevent production problems arising from a lack of stock.

Reorder quantity refers to the amount of new stock ordered. It can be seen from a stock control chart and is calculated by the difference between the maximum and minimum stock levels.

Project Management

UNIT 5.8

The people may be made to follow a path of action, but they may not be made to understand it.

Confucius (551 BC–479 BC), Chinese philosopher

HIGHER LEVEL

Key topics

Higher Level only

- Network analysis: critical path analysis
- The value and limitations of network analysis

INTRODUCTION

Project management is an important role for firms dealing with large assignments and developments, such as the construction of motorways (highways), bridges or residential property. Such projects can involve the planning and coordination of hundreds or thousands of different jobs and tasks. Some activities will take longer than others, whilst some jobs must be completed before another task begins and yet other activities can take place at the same time.

The most frequently used tool in project management is **network analysis**, which serves to improve the efficiency in the production process by systematically scheduling tasks and resources. Unit 5.7 explained that idle resources and stockpiling are costly to a business. There is little point in buying stocks and hiring labour in advance when they are not to be used for several days, weeks or even months. Network analysis will also set deadlines for all the different tasks to ensure the smooth operation and progress of the project. From the network analysis, which is presented as a diagrammatic interpretation of the various sequences of tasks in the project, managers can also attempt to minimize production costs.

The costs of a delay can be enormous. For example, Airbus initially claimed it would break-even on its 'super jumbo' Airbus A380 on the sale of 250 units. Due to major production problems and delays, the firm announced within a year of the initial statement that the revised break-even figure increased by 68% to 420 units. A large part of this increase was due to compensation being paid out to airlines, such as Singapore Airlines and Emirates, for late deliveries.

NETWORK ANALYSIS

The ultimate purpose of network analysis is to identify the minimum amount of time needed to complete a project. It requires the various tasks of a project to be planned in a logical and coherent way so that the different processes are completed with minimum delay and maximum efficiency.

The process of network analysis, which is also commonly known as **critical path analysis (CPA)** involves:

- Identifying all the operations required for the completion of a project
- Breaking down the project into separate jobs and tasks
- Determining how long each task will take
- Identifying all dependencies, i.e. activities that cannot start until the completion of other jobs
- Determining which tasks can take place concurrently to minimize production time
- Placing all operations in the right sequence and placing these on a network diagram
- Showing the earliest start time and the latest finishing time of each activity
- Identifying the *critical path* from the network diagram (i.e. the route which generates the minimum time needed to complete the whole project).

Activities that cannot be delayed are known as **critical activities**. Any hold-ups to the operations on the critical path of a network diagram will delay completion of the project.

CONSTRUCTING NETWORKS

There are several key features shown in a network analysis diagram:

- **Nodes** – These show the start and finish times of each activity within the project (see Figure 5.8a). Each node is numbered to identify the sequence of activities.
- **Arrows** – These are used in a network diagram to show the duration of each activity or task.
- **EST** – The Earliest Start Time (EST) of each activity is shown in the top right-hand part of the node (see Figure 5.8a). The EST will depend on the duration of all previous activities.
- **LFT** – The Latest Finishing Time (LFT) of each activity is shown in the bottom right-hand part of the node. The LFT is the deadline for a particular activity to be completed so that the entire project can finish in minimal time.
- **Float** – This shows the difference between the EST and LFT for each activity to identify any spare time that might exist.

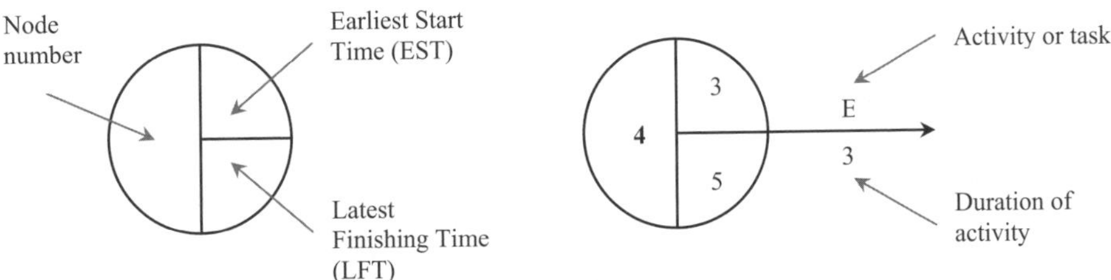

Figure 5.8a Network nodes

Putting the network together will help to identify the sequence of tasks in the project, as shown in Figure 5.8b.

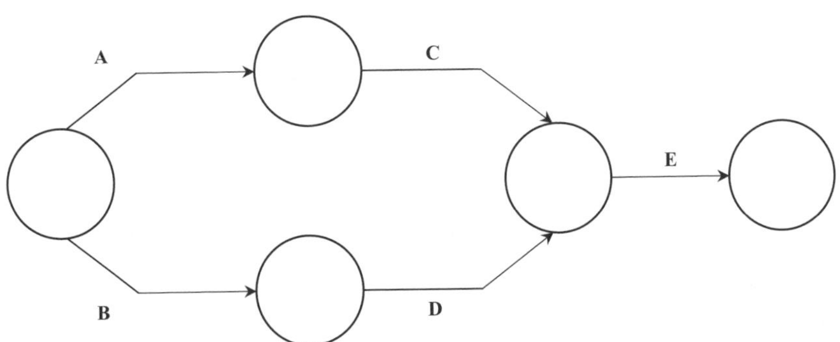

Figure 5.8b Simplified network

In this particular project, we can see the following:

- Activities A and B can be started at the same time.
- Activity C cannot start until activity A is completed.
- Activity D cannot start until activity B is completed.
- Once both activities C and D are completed (not necessarily at the same time), then activity E can start.

HIGHER LEVEL

To construct a network diagram, consider the following simplified example which involves planning an end-of-year office party. Assume that the date has already been set. In order to construct the network diagram, follow the steps below:

1 Identify all the tasks involved in the project.
2 Order these in the correct sequence.
3 Identify tasks that can take place at the same time.
4 Design the network.
5 Identify the critical path.

The first three steps can be shown in the table below. Steps 4 and 5 are shown in Figure 5.8c.

Activity	Description	Preceded by	Duration (days)
A	Send out invitations and wait for replies	–	7
B	Research and book suitable venue based on numbers	A	2
C	Book entertainment (music and awards ceremony)	B	5
D	Order wines and cake for delivery	B	7
E	Set up hall and stage for the party	C, D	3

Without network analysis, the individual tasks require 24 days. However, through working out the critical path, the project is reduced to 19 days, as shown in Figure 5.8d. First though, it is necessary to design the network as shown in Figure 5.8c.

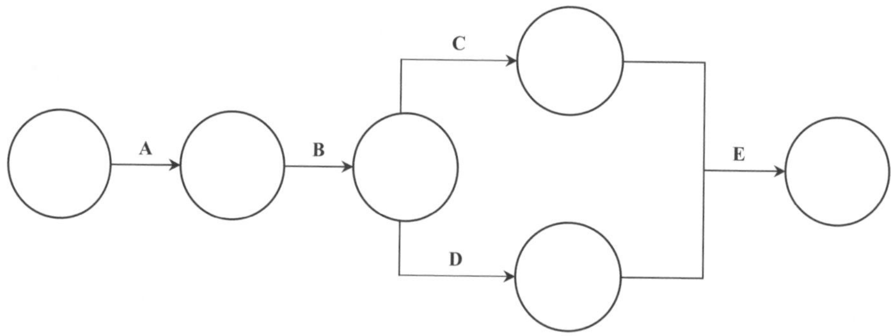

Figure 5.8c Critical path analysis

The next step is to put in the figures for the earliest start time for each activity, as shown in Figure 5.8d.

HIGHER LEVEL

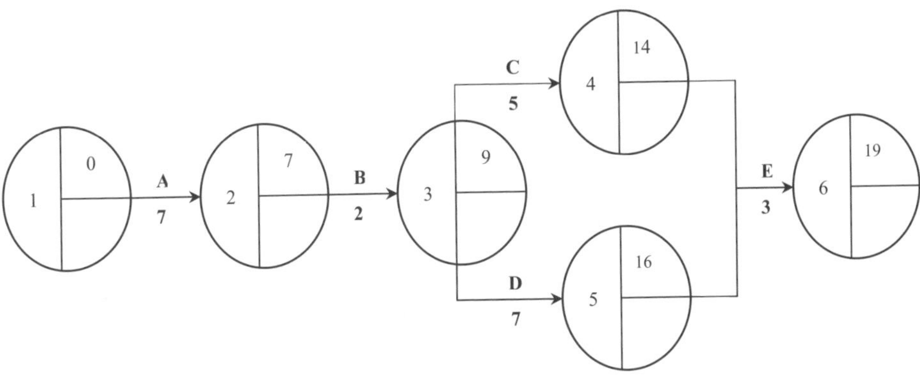

Figure 5.8d Critical path analysis (with EST)

The following can be seen from Figure 5.8d:

- Task A takes 7 days to complete. Therefore, the EST for activity B is in 7 days time.
- Task B takes 2 days to complete. This means that activities C and D cannot start until the 9th day.
- Task C, which starts on day 9, has a duration of 5 days. Hence, task C is completed by the 14th day at the earliest.
- Task D can take place at the same time as Task C. It takes 7 days to complete activity D.
- Although task C can be finished by the 14th day, task E cannot start until activity D is completed. Hence, there can be a slight delay to the completion of activity C without there being a delay to the overall project.
- Task E can only start when both tasks C and D are completed. Since task D starts on the 9th day and lasts 7 days, it will be on the 16th day that task E can be started.
- Task E takes a further 3 days, thereby meaning that the shortest time in which the project can be completed is 19 days.

The next step is to calculate the latest finishing time for each activity and to place this value into the bottom right-hand section of the node. This will show the LFT of each task without extending (or delaying) the whole project. To calculate the EST, we work from left to right. Conversely, to work out the LFT, we must work back from right to left, i.e. we start at Node 6, as shown in Figure 5.8e. Since the shortest time needed to complete this project is 19 days, then the LFT must also be 19 days if there is to be a critical path. The LFT for all previous nodes is calculated by using the formula:

LFT = LFT (current node) – Duration

HIGHER LEVEL

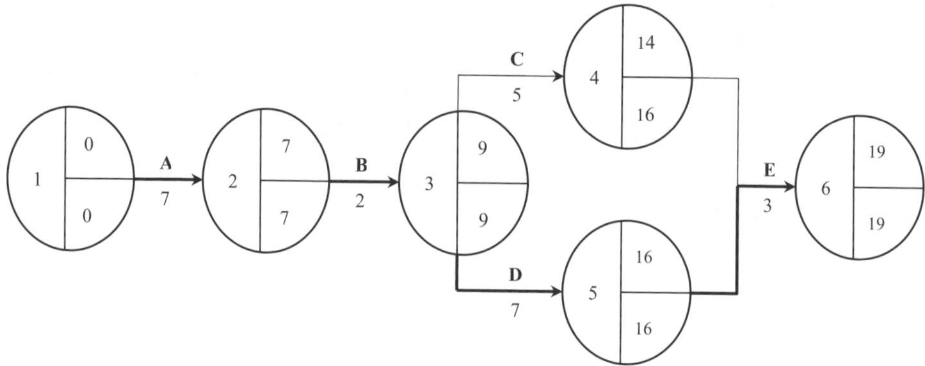

Figure 5.8e Critical path analysis (with EST and LFT)

- The LFT for task D is therefore 16 days. This is because the LFT at Node 6 is 19 and the duration of task E is 3 days (19 – 3). This figure is then placed in the bottom right section of Node 5.
- The LFT for task C is also 16 days for the same reason as above.
- For Node 3, the LFT is 9 since Node 5 gives 16 – 7 = 9 days. Similarly, Node 4 gives 16 – 5 = 11 days. When choosing between two different latest finishing times, use the path that gives the *lowest* LFT to prevent any delays to project.
- The critical path is shown by the lines in bold in the diagram. Alternatively, this can be shown by marking '//' on all activities on the critical path.
- Node 4 has a float period of 2 days (16 – 14 = 2 days). This means that activity C can be delayed by up to 2 days without affecting the completion date of the project.
- Notice that the EST and LFT are exactly the same for all nodes on the critical path. This simply means that the next activity is started as soon as the preceding task has been completed. This helps to prevent any delays in the project.

HIGHER LEVEL

Question 5.8.1

Calculating the EST and LFT

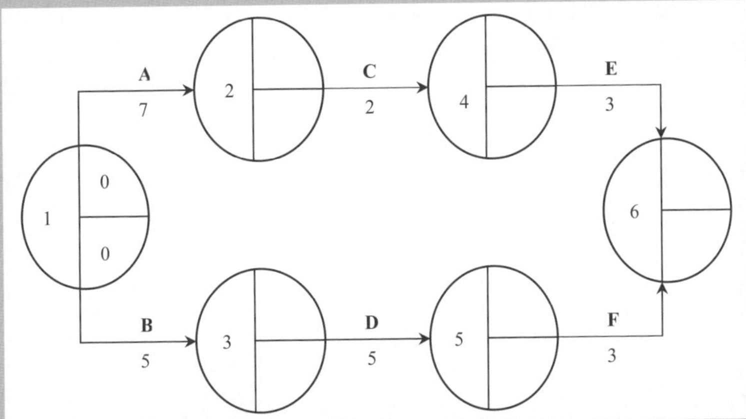

a Distinguish between the terms 'earliest start time' (EST) and the 'latest finishing time' (LFT). *[3 marks]*

b Calculate the missing figures for the EST and LFT in the network diagram above. *[6 marks]*

c Identify the critical path from the above network. *[1 mark]*

Exam Tip!
Worked example

Question: Construct a network diagram from the information below and mark the critical path. *[5 marks]*

Task	Preceded by	Duration (days)
A	–	2
B	A	2
C	A	3
D	B, C	2

Answer:

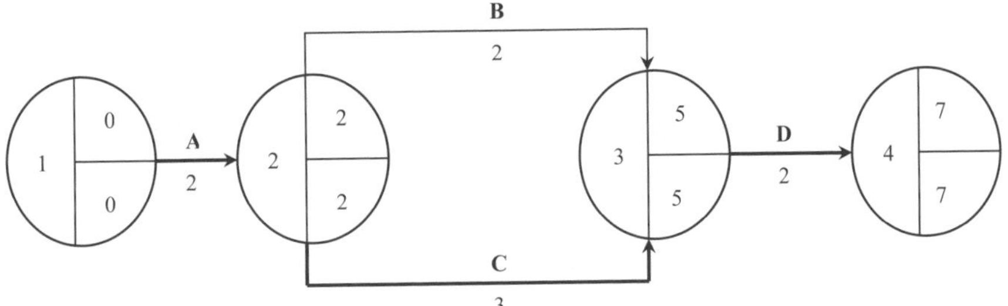

The critical path is A–C–D. Any delays in the critical path will prevent the project from being completed in 7 days. Note that although activity B can be completed by day 4, the project cannot proceed until completion of activity C on day 5.

HIGHER LEVEL

Question 5.8.2

St. John Contractors

St. John Contractors (SJC) specialize in the planning and construction of houses in Nîmes, southern France. The operations director, Tracy St. John, has recently taken on a project to build a four-bedroom home with an outdoor pool. The project's tasks are outlined below.

- A: Lay foundation to house: 1 week.
- B: Construction of house: 6 weeks. B is preceded by A.
- C: Excavation and foundation for pool: 2 weeks. C is preceded by A.
- D: Tiling and sealing of pool: 2 weeks. D is preceded by C.
- E: Internal décor and fixtures for the house: 3 weeks. E is preceded by B.
- F: Final testing and handing over keys to the new owner: 1 week. F is preceded by activities D and E.

a Construct a network diagram for St. John Contractors using the information from above. Clearly mark the critical path on your diagram. *[6 marks]*

b Explain why critical path analysis is important for a business such as St. John Contractors. *[4 marks]*

Exam Tip!
CPA is a regularly tested concept in the examination. Quite often, students are required to construct a network diagram from given information. Experience shows that this topic is very challenging for a lot of students, so the only way to improve is by practising your technique. Even if the diagram is slightly wrong, you can still earn marks by correctly interpreting and explaining your diagram.

CALCULATING THE FREE AND TOTAL FLOAT

As mentioned earlier, the **float** in a network analysis identifies any activities that can be delayed without affecting the deadline. Calculating the float allows managers to know by how long an activity can be delayed. This can be done by calculating the *free float* and the *total float*.

First, consider the following sequence of events for Project X:

Task	Preceded by	Estimated time (weeks)
A	–	1
B	–	3
C	B	2
D	C, A	3
E	D	2
F	D	3
G	E, F	2

The order of the above events is represented in Figure 5.8f.

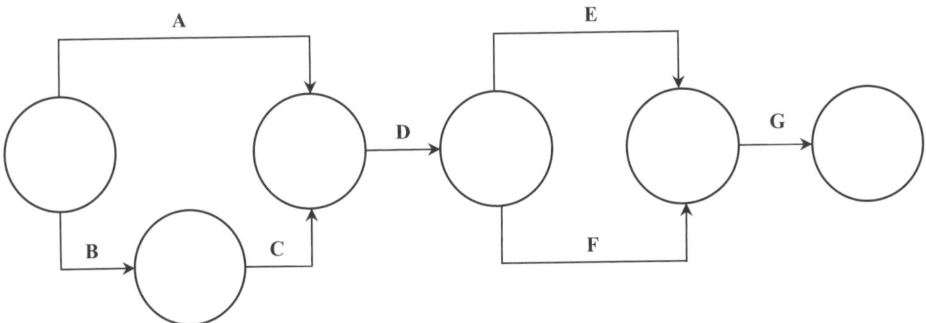

Figure 5.8f Network diagram for Project X

The next stage is to put in the figures for each node, as shown in Figure 5.8g.

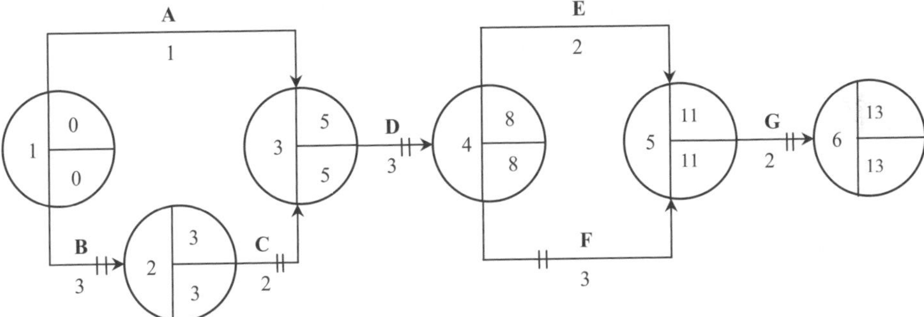

Figure 5.8g Network analysis for Project X (with EST and LFT)

Hence, the critical path for Project X is B, C, D, F and G. This is shown in the network diagram by 'double-striking' the activities on the critical path.

The activities that are not on the critical path, i.e. tasks A and E in this case, have some spare or float time. This means that they can be delayed without affecting the estimated eleven weeks completion time. In other words, trying to speed up these activities will not mean the project gets completed any sooner. It can be important to calculate the float since managers will become aware of the maximum time that the activity can be delayed; hold-ups that are longer than the float time will cause a delay to the overall project. Recall that there are two main ways to calculate the float: the free float and the total float.

The free float

The free float refers to the amount of time that an activity can be delayed without affecting the EST of the next activity in the project, i.e. it represents the maximum spare time for an activity. Of course, all activities on the critical path do not have any float time. The formula for calculating the free float is:

Free Float = EST (of next activity) – Duration – EST (of this activity)

For Project X, only two activities do not lie on the critical path, namely activities A and E. Using the formula, the free float for activity A is $3 - 1 - 0 = 2$, as shown in Figure 5.8h. The free float for activity E is $11 - 2 - 8 = 1$ week.

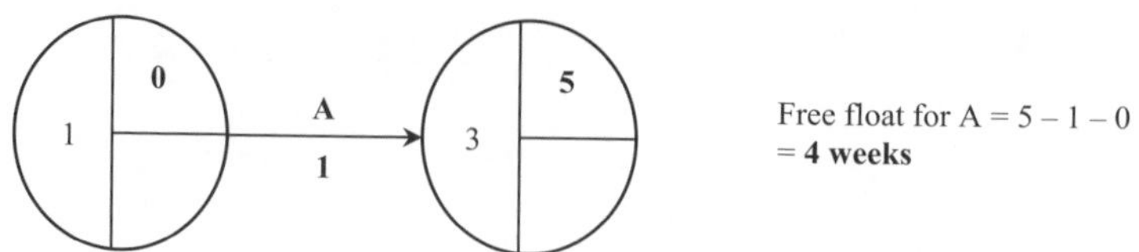

Figure 5.8h Calculating the free float (Activity A)

The total float

The alternative approach to calculating the float is to use the total float. This refers to the amount of spare time available without causing

a delay to the overall project.

The calculation of total float for each individual activity is found by the formula:

Total Float = LFT – Duration – EST

So, for activity A the total float is 3 – 1 – 0 = 2 weeks. For activity E, the total float is 11 – 2 – 8 = 1 week, as shown in Figure 5.8i.

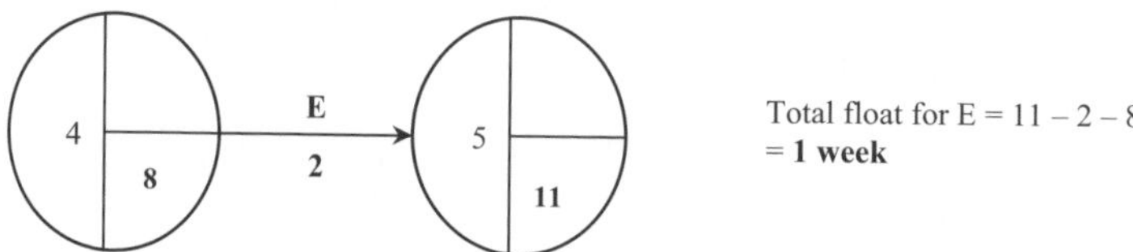

Figure 5.8i Calculating the total float (Activity E)

The float for all activities for Project X is shown in Table 5.8a.

Table 5.8a Free float and Total float for Project X

Task	Duration (weeks)	EST	LFT	Free float	Total float
A	1	0	5	4	4
B	3	0	3	0	0*
C	2	3	5	0	0*
D	3	5	8	0	0*
E	2	8	11	1	1
F	3	8	11	0	0*
G	2	11	13	0	0*

* Activities that have no total float lie on the critical path.

HIGHER LEVEL

Question 5.8.3

Tonin Decorators Ltd.

Tonin Decorators Ltd. is a home improvement firm that operates in the suburbs of Toronto, Canada. The firm has recently taken on a project which involves eight key phases, as shown in the network diagram below.

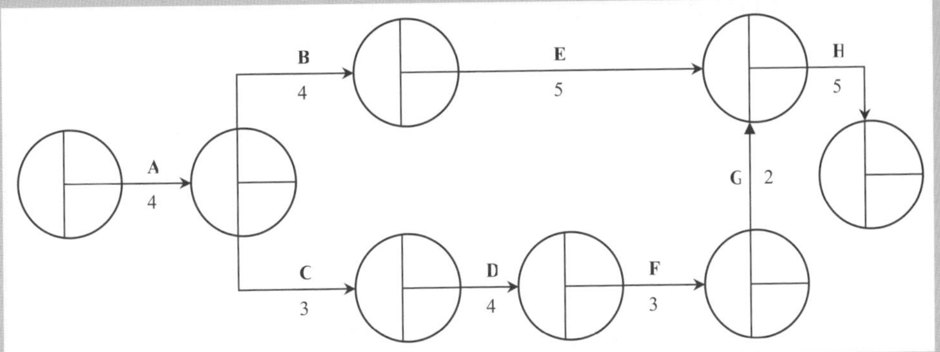

a Calculate the minimum time needed (in days) to complete the project. *[6 marks]*

b Define and identify the critical path for Tonin Decorators Ltd. *[3 marks]*

c Define and calculate the total and free float for the above project. *[6 marks]*

DUMMY ACTIVITIES

A **dummy activity**, or **dummy variable**, is a logical dependency between two indirectly linked tasks in a project. It is used in a CPA to prevent an illogical path from being followed, and is shown by a dotted arrow line in a network diagram (see Figure 5.8k).

As an example, consider the following plan of events for Project Y:

Activity	Duration (days)	Preceding activity
A	2	–
B	3	–
C	2	A
D	3	A, B

Without using a dummy variable, the network diagram might look like the one shown in Figure 5.8j, where figures cannot be completed for Node 3, making the project illogical (which defeats the purpose of network analysis).

HIGHER LEVEL

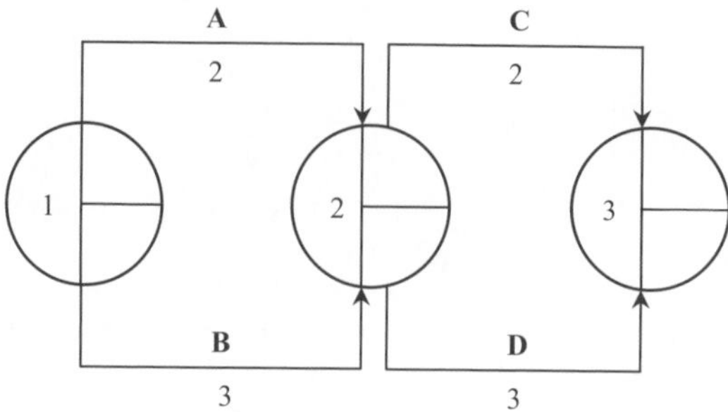

Figure 5.8j Incorrect network for Project Y

In the above case, it is not possible to complete the EST and LFT for Node 3 as there is conflict between tasks C and D, which are not directly related. The network diagram suggests that task C is dependent on both A and B being completed (the same applies to task D); but this is clearly not supposed to be the case. Hence, the project requires the use of a dummy activity, as shown in Figure 5.8k. Technically, dummy activities are not activities (since they do not consume any time in the project) but act as a visual aid in a network diagram to clarify logical dependencies. Hence, they are often referred to by their other name, dummy variables.

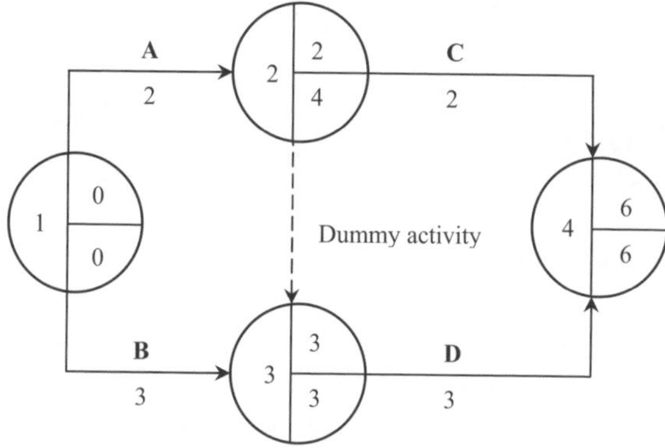

Figure 5.8k Correct network chart (with dummy) for Project Y

The dummy variable shows that activities C and D are not linked, i.e. C follows A only and D happens on the completion of activity B.

Question 5.8.4

Task	Order (preceded by)	Estimated time (weeks)
A	-	4
B	-	4
C	A	6
D	B	5
E	B, C	2
F	D	4
G	E, F	3

a Construct a full network diagram using the information above and identify the critical path. (*Hint*: there is a dummy activity in this project.) *[6 marks]*

Question 5.8.5

The network diagram below is for a planned outdoor rock concert. Task E cannot start until both C and D (which are independent of each other) are completed. The duration periods are in weeks.

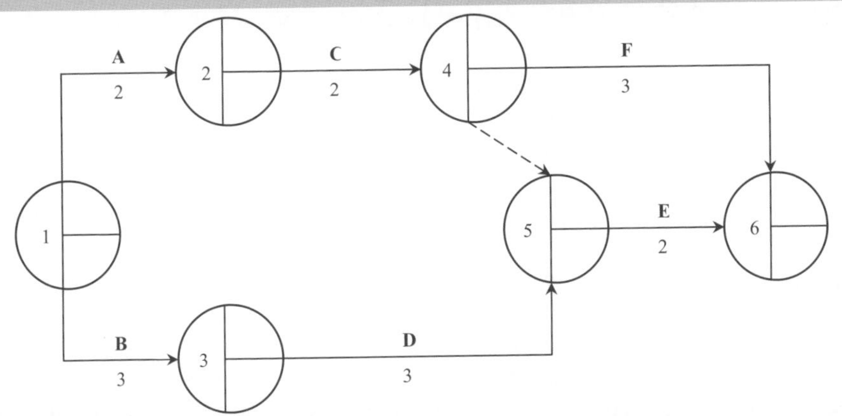

a Complete the network diagram by calculating the EST and LFT for each activity. *[5 marks]*

b Comment on what the dotted arrow line indicates. *[3 marks]*

c Evaluate the use of CPA as a decision-making tool for the concert organizers. *[7 marks]*

VALUE AND LIMITATIONS OF NETWORK ANALYSIS

Critical path analysis can provide several benefits for project management. These advantages include:

- CPA provides a visual representation of a problem which can therefore make it easier for some people to interpret. The plan can help a project to run more smoothly.
- As a decision-making tool, CPA encourages forward planning. It also encourages managers to consider different aspects of a particular project, such as the management of different resources at different stages of the project.
- It promotes operational efficiency by identifying the critical path, i.e. the shortest time in which a project can be completed. By calculating the float time and tasks that can be carried out simultaneously, managers are able to reduce any lost time between different activities, thereby ensuring the project runs smoothly. Operational efficiency also means that the customer will get timely delivery of their order.
- CPA can help a firm to have better cash flow management (see Unit 3.3). By identifying when certain activities can start and how long certain tasks should last, managers can control costs more effectively.
- Network analysis can also prove useful for stock management (see Unit 5.7). Stocks of raw materials and components only need to be ordered in time for the EST of each activity and no sooner. This helps to reduce storage costs and other expenses linked with holding stocks.
- CPA can be used for a range of business issues and problems, as has been outlined in this Unit. It can be used for small-scale projects to huge undertakings that involve thousands of processes. It works particularly well with just-in-time production systems (see Unit 5.7).

However, CPA also has drawbacks and limitations:

- Construction of a CPA, no matter how impressive or well planned, does not guarantee that everything will go according to plan. Internal and external factors can cause delays to the completion of a project. For example, the critical path is unlikely to materialize if the workforce is demotivated. Poor weather is an example of an external factor than can prolong construction projects.
- As with most methods of quantitative forecasts, CPA is only useful if the data used to construct the network is accurate and reliable.
- Similarly, if necessary steps are missed in the network analysis, the critical path as identified in a CPA will be void since the time will need to be increased.
- Constructing a CPA for huge-scale projects can be very complex, highly challenging and time consuming. This might make the process unmanageable (although there are dedicated software packages that can help deal with such problems).

PROJECT MANAGEMENT AND BUSINESS STRATEGY

Network analysis (critical path analysis) is a management tool for planning and decision-making. It stresses the importance of placing activities into a coherent sequence. This is particularly important for complicated and large projects that need to be managed and controlled carefully. Since many real life projects are likely to be much more complex than the examples used in this Unit, businesses will tend to use dedicated software packages to construct their network diagrams. For example, Microsoft's project management software package, MS Project, has been used by businesses since 1987.

Critical path analysis has wide ranging applications for business strategy and links directly with other aspects of business and management. Some examples include the following issues:

- As with all business plans, CPA will only work if the staff is motivated to achieve the organization's objectives (see Unit 2.5).
- As a planning tool, CPA can help managers in considering the implications of various decisions and can therefore help in devising appropriate contingency plans (see Unit 2.8) in case there are delays to activities on the critical path.
- Network analysis promotes lean production by minimizing lead times and the elimination of waste (see Unit 5.7).
- Since CPA focuses on operational efficiency, it can aid financial control and budgeting (see Unit 3.4) and cash flow management (see Unit 3.3).

The consequences of poor project planning and management can lead to major problems for a business. Production hold-ups are not only wasteful and costly, but are likely to lead to customer dissatisfaction. These problems can damage the organization's reputation, perhaps irrevocably, and can lead to a loss of future sales.

However, CPA must be used with some caution. In theory, network analysis can help projects to run smoothly and efficiently. However, in reality, it is highly likely that most projects will encounter some unexpected problems which will cause delays, that is, when things do not go according to plan. External factors that are beyond the firm's control can render the CPA invalid. For example, storms and floods can cause major delays to construction projects such as the construction of roads, bridges and buildings.

Nevertheless, in today's fast-paced and ever-competitive business environment, the need for rapid product development and launch means that CPA can provide firms with a competitive edge. Coupled with effective production planning (see Unit 5.7), CPA can reduce the total time used in the production process. As the example of Airbus has shown (see page 374), delays in output can severely harm the financial position of a business.

HIGHER LEVEL

REVIEW QUESTIONS 5.8

1 Why is project management important to business organizations?

2 What is 'network analysis'?

3 What does the process of critical path analysis involve?

4 What do nodes in a CPA show?

5 What do arrows in a CPA show?

6 What does the EST show and how is it calculated?

7 What is meant by the 'LFT' and how is it calculated? How does it help to identify the critical path?

8 Distinguish between the 'free float' and the 'total float'.

9 What is the purpose of a dummy activity?

10 State three advantages and two disadvantages of CPA.

Critical path refers to the most efficient sequence of activities in a project which minimizes the time needed to complete a project. It is usually shown in a network diagram by double-striking ('//') the critical activities.

Critical path analysis (CPA) is a project management tool, also known as **network analysis**, which serves to improve the efficiency in the production process by systematically scheduling tasks and resources. The ultimate purpose of CPA is to identify the minimum amount of time needed to complete a project.

Dummy activity, also known as a **dummy variable**, refers to a logical dependency between two indirectly linked tasks in a project. It is used to prevent an illogical path from being followed and is shown by a dotted line on a network diagram.

Earliest start time (EST) shows when a particular activity can begin. It is shown in the top right-hand part of a node. The EST will depend on the duration of all previous activities.

Float refers to the spare time (if any) that is available. It can be inferred by looking at the difference between the EST and LFT for each activity.

Latest finishing time (LFT) is the deadline for a particular activity so that the entire project can be completed in the minimum time. It is shown in the bottom right-hand part of a network node.

Nodes appear on a network diagram and show the start and finish times of each activity within a project. Each node is numbered to identify the sequence of activities in the project.

Project management involves the planning and coordination of a variety of different jobs and tasks in a particular project. It is especially important when dealing with large assignments and developments.

HIGHER LEVEL

BUSINESS STRATEGY

UNIT 6

UNIT

Business Strategy

UNIT 6

If you don't drive your business you will be driven out of business.

B.C. Forbes (1880–1954) founder of *Forbes* magazine

Key topics

- Business strategy resources
- Summary table of key business strategy concepts

WHAT IS BUSINESS STRATEGY?

There is no new content in Unit 6. All preceding Units have ended with a section on business strategy. In short, Unit 6 is about synthesizing the different business theories, concepts and techniques covered in this book. It is about devising a plan to achieve the long-term goals of an organization. The idea behind each section on Business Strategy is to allow students to apply the different techniques that will help to make more informed decisions. Business Strategy is explicitly assessed in Section C of Paper 1 for Higher Level students.

There are three stages to business strategy:

Stage 1: Strategic analysis – determining the current position of an organization.

Stage 2: Strategic choices – determining where the organization is headed.

Stage 3: Strategic implementation – determining how the organization should get there.

The case studies in this textbook have questions directly related to business strategy; there are further examples in the IB Business and Management syllabus guide (pages 40–43).

Formulating strategy

Business strategy should focus on, among other issues:

- Organizational aims and objectives
- Stakeholder interests
- Resources (human, capital and financial)
- Strengths (and weaknesses) to be developed
- The long term
- The external business environment (e.g. state of the economy)
- Customers and customer service
- Quality management
- Motivation of the workforce
- Cost control.

Resources

Two useful websites on business strategy:

http://www.strategy-business.com

http://www.12manage.com

Three very student-friendly books that are useful in covering Business Strategy:

Strategy Express, J. Middleton and B. Gorzynski, Capstone Publishing (2002), ISBN: 1-84112-218-1

Business Strategy: A Guide to Effective Decision-Making (The Economist Series), J. Kourdi, Bloomberg Press (2003), ISBN: 1-86197-459-0

Guide to Management Ideas (The Economist Series), Tim Hindle, Bloomberg Press (2003), ISBN: 1-86197-423-X

TOOLS FOR DEVISING BUSINESS STRATEGY

The table below summarizes some of the key business strategy concepts covered in this book and the Unit where you can read more information about the concepts. However, the list is by no means exhaustive.

Key business strategy concepts covered in this book

Concept	Unit	Concept	Unit
Above-the-line promotion	4.4	Ethical marketing	4.1
Added value	1.1	Extension strategies	4.3
Ansoff matrix	1.7	Fishbone (Ishikawa) model	1.6
Asset-led marketing	4.1	Five Forces analysis	4.2
Below-the-line promotion	4.4	Flexible organizational structures	2.2
Benchmarking	5.4	Flexible working	2.1
Best practice benchmarking	5.4	Focus	1.7
Boston Matrix	4.3	Force field analysis	1.8
Branding	4.3	Franchising	1.7
Break-even analysis	5.3	Initiative decision-making	1.6
Budgeting	3.4	Innovation	5.6
Business plans	1.6	Intellectual property rights	5.6
Capacity utilization	5.7	Investment appraisal	3.2
Cash flow management	3.3	Joint ventures and strategic alliances	1.7
Competitive advantage	1.7	Just-in-time production	5.7
Competitor analysis	4.2	Kaizen	5.4
Conflict resolution	1.4	Market research	4.2
Contingency planning	2.8	Market mix	4.2
Core competencies	4.1	Marketing orientation	4.1
Corporate social responsibility	1.3	Marketing planning and strategy	4.2
Cost benefit analysis	1.6	Matrix and project teams	2.2
Cost leadership	1.7	Mergers and acquisitions	1.7
Crisis management	2.8	Mission and vision statements	1.3
Critical path analysis	5.8	Motivational theory and practice	2.5
Customer relations management	4.2	New product design and development	4.3
Decision-making tools	1.5	Niche marketing	4.2
Decision trees	1.6	Offshoring	5.7
Differentiation	1.7	Organic growth	1.7
Disintermediation	4.7	Organizational objectives	1.3
E-commerce	4.8	Outsourcing	5.7

Key business strategy concepts covered in this book (cont.)

Concept	Unit	Concept	Unit
Perception mapping	4.2	Segmentation, Targeting, Positioning	4.2
PEST analysis	1.5	Shamrock organization	2.1
Porter's generic strategies	1.7	Social marketing	4.1
Portfolio analysis	4.3	Supply chain management	4.6
Product life cycle	4.3	SWOT analysis	1.6
Production planning	5.7	Synergy	1.7
Productive efficiency	5.7	Team building / Team working	2.1
Profit and cost centres	5.2	Total quality management	5.7
Promotional mix	4.4	Training and development	2.1
Quality management	5.4	Unique selling point	4.2
Ratio analysis	3.6	Variance analysis	3.4
Repositioning	4.2	Viral marketing	4.5
Research and development	5.6	Window dressing	3.5
Sales forecasting	4.2	Workforce planning	2.1
Scientific decision-making	1.6	Working capital management	3.3

The challenge facing leaders and managers in the modern business environment today is much greater than has been in the past. With the trends such as e-commerce, flexible working practices and intense competition from China and India, leaders and managers have less control than ever. Strategies that worked in the past may not necessarily work today and new problems may demand new strategies and solutions. This is the beauty of Business & Management as a subject.

Index

D

E

F

G

H

M